In memory of Philip Barker (1920–2001)

Urban Growth and the Medieval Church

Gloucester and Worcester

Nigel Baker and Richard Holt

ASHGATE

Published by
Ashgate Publishing Limited
Gower House
Croft Road
Aldershot
Hants GU11 3HR
England

Ashgate Publishing Company
Suite 420
101 Cherry Street
Burlington, VT 05401-4405
USA

Ashgate website: http://www.ashgate.com

British Library Cataloguing in Publication Data

Baker, Nigel
  Urban growth and the medieval church : Gloucester and
  Worcester
  1.Urbanization – England – Gloucester – History – To 1500 2.Urbanization – England –
  Worcester – History – To 1500 3.Religious institutions – England – Gloucester – History –
  To 1500 4.Religious institutions – England – Worcester – History – To 1500 5.Gloucester
  (England) – Church history 6.Worcester (England) – Church history
  I.Title II.Holt, Richard
  307.1′416′0942414′0902

Library of Congress Cataloging-in-Publication Data

Baker, Nigel.
  Urban growth and the medieval church : Gloucester and Worcester / Nigel Baker and
  Richard Holt.
    p. cm.
  Includes bibliographical references and index.
  ISBN 0-7546-0266-4 (alk. paper)
    1. Gloucester (England) – Church history. 2. Worcester (England) – Church history. 3.
  Cities and towns – England – Growth. 4. Cities and towns – Religious
  aspects – Christianity – History. I. Holt, Richard. II. Title.

BR765.G58H65 2003
274.24′1403–dc21

2002027783

ISBN 0 7546 0266 4

Printed on acid-free paper

Typeset in Times New Roman by Bournemouth Colour Press, UK and printed in Great Britain by MPG Books Limited, Bodmin.

Contents

The *burhs*: extramural and post-mural growth
Conclusions: the Church and town-planning in Gloucester and Worcester

List of illustrations

Tables

List of Plates

Preface and acknowledgements

The research for this study was undertaken largely during the period 1988 to 1994, when the authors were working on the Leverhulme Trust-sponsored project 'English medieval towns and the Church', at the University of Birmingham. The authors wish to express their deep gratitude to the Trust for its generous financial support and its interest in the project.

The interdisciplinary and collaborative nature of this project was based on the wide expertise in the history, archaeology and geography of medieval towns that was to be found in the University of Birmingham. Professor Nicholas Brooks, Dr Gervase Rosser and Dr Terry Slater, the project directors, and our other colleagues in the Schools of History and Geography who together formed the consultative group to whom we presented our findings, gave us necessary support and encouragement. We are greatly indebted to them all. The directors, Steven Bassett, Robert Swanson, Jens Roehrkasten, Keith Lilley and Christopher Dyer have all read draft chapters and given valuable advice; we should also like to thank the members of the Urban Morphology Research Group, and particularly Professor Jeremy Whitehand, for their support and comments. Additional drafting work on the figures has been done by Harry Buglass of the Department of Archaeology, and photographic work for the volume by Graham Norrie.

Only we know how great a debt we owe to the historians and archaeologists working on our two cities. We particularly wish to thank, in Gloucester: Carolyn Heighway, Malcolm Atkin (now head of the Worcestershire county archaeological unit), Michael Hare, John Rhodes, and the members of the Gloucester and District Archaeological Research Group – especially Nigel Spry and Phil Moss. In Worcester: Charles Mundy and James Dinn (former and present city archaeological officers), Hal Dalwood, Victoria Bryant, Rachel Edwards and Robin Jackson (all of the county archaeological unit), Chris Guy and the late Philip Barker (Worcester cathedral). Patricia Hughes kindly shared with us her great knowledge of Worcester and its buildings, particularly from the early-modern period. Our volunteer plot-measurers generously gave their time to help with metrological analysis of building frontages. Especially we wish to acknowledge the advice and encouragement given by the late Professor M.R.G. Conzen and the pleasure we had in exploring Worcester with him.

In our research and our writing we worked very closely together and every part of this book is the product of a long process of discussion and joint revision. We therefore share joint responsibility for every statement. However, Richard Holt was primarily responsible for Chapters 2, 5, 10, 11 and 13; Nigel Baker for Chapters 3, 6, 12 and 14. Nigel Baker composed and drew the figures.

Nigel Baker
Shrewsbury

Richard Holt
Tromsø

List of abbreviations

ASC: Anglo-Saxon Chronicle

B: Birch, W. de G. (1883-99), *Cartularium Saxonicum*, 3 vols and index, London

BL: British Library, London

Cal. Recs Corpn Glouc.:   Stevenson, W.H. (ed.) (1893), *Calendar of the Records of the Corporation of Gloucester*, Gloucester

DB: Farley, A. (ed.) (1783), Domesday Book, 2 vols, London

GBR: Gloucester Borough Records, in GCRO

GCL: Gloucester Cathedral Library, Gloucester

GCRO: Gloucestershire County Record Office, Gloucester

H: Hearne, T. (ed.) (1723), *Hemingi Chartularium Ecclesiae Wigorniensis*, Oxford

HE: *Historia ecclesiastica gentis anglorum* (Bede's *Ecclesiastical History of the English People*)

Hist. et Cart.:   Hart, W.H. (ed.) (1863–7), *Historia et Cartularium Monasterii Sancti Petri Gloucestriae*, 3 vols, Rolls Series, 33, London

HWRO: Hereford and Worcester Record Office (now Worcestershire County Record Office

PRO: Public Record Office, London

1455 Rental: Stevenson, W.H. (ed.) (1890), *Rental of all the Houses in Gloucester AD 1455*, Gloucester

S: Sawyer, P.H. (1968), *Anglo-Saxon Charters: An Annotated List and Bibliography*, Royal Historical Society, London

SMR: Sites and Monuments Record

VCH: Victoria County History

WCL: Worcester Cathedral Library, Worcester

WCM: Worcester City Museums

WCRO: Worcestershire County Record Office, Worcester

The registers and cartularies of Lanthony Priory in the Public Record Office are referred to in the text by the pressmarks they carry:

A3:   PRO C115/K2/6682
A5:   C115/L1/6687
A7:   C115/K2/6684
A11:   C115/K2/6685
A12:   C115/L1/6688
A13:   C115/K1/6678

Chapter 1

Introduction

This interdisciplinary study of early town development was designed to examine the role of the Church in the origins and the evolution of the larger English towns; that is, to assess the extent to which church institutions might have played a part in the processes of urban development, and to investigate what impact they had on the physical shape of the growing towns. The study combined the approaches of the historian, the archaeologist and the geographer.

Despite important work by both archaeologists and historians, many aspects of the early stages of urbanization in England are still poorly understood. Not least, there are many unanswered questions concerning the processes by which the larger towns emerged as planned settlements during the pre-Conquest centuries. The commitment of the Wessex kings is recognized, but to what extent did other powerful elements in society affect or participate in the process? Specifically, how much did early town growth owe to the major churches which – where these sites had been occupied at all – had been the major occupants? Had the great churches presided over a 'proto-urban' phase of development, and was there a significant ecclesiastical element in the state-sponsored programme of planning and development?

Further to that: how, if at all, did the Church influence the later development of the towns? How and when were the parish churches founded, and what specific factors determined and influenced the parish boundaries that had been established by about 1200? And lastly, to what extent did the different churches, as the major landowners in the towns, shape the continually evolving identity of the towns and their growing suburbs?

As this was to be a study in depth, our original intention was to concentrate on just one town. In selecting a suitable subject for intensive study, consideration had to be given to several factors.

The chosen town had to be a prominent Anglo-Saxon city, probably a *burh* of the Alfredian period with, preferably, some previous recorded history as a central place. The town needed to be the location of an old and important church: either that of a bishop, or a major minster subsequently reformed to become a great religious house. There needed to be a range of available documentation, including early material, and it was essential that there should have been recent archaeological work. A final requirement was that the town should not have been so affected by nineteenth-century industrialization and rebuilding that its historic plan failed to survive in a reasonably intact form to be surveyed for the first-edition large scale ordnance survey maps of the 1880s; and that there should be earlier nineteenth-century and eighteenth-century maps to provide additional information on the older form of the town.

The city of Worcester was at once identified as meeting these requirements; but it soon became apparent that a study of two neighbouring towns sharing a similar historical development would offer greater opportunities. It held out the prospect that what was inexplicable or even invisible in one town might be documented or otherwise detectable in the other; moreover, there would be advantages in drawing comparisons between the ways in which specific developments and phases of development were achieved in each town. Gloucester, a neighbouring shire capital only some 25 miles (40 kilometres) distant, was only a little larger than Worcester in the medieval period and had many close similarities in its chronological development – and also some marked dissimilarities. It offered, moreover, topographical evidence of the highest order, and the results of varied archaeological work over a large number of years. Accordingly, a parallel study of Gloucester was undertaken, to set beside that of Worcester.

Gloucester: sources

In addition to the valuable work of earlier antiquarian writers (Rudder 1779; Rudge 1815; Fosbrooke 1819), there has been more recent historical writing of a general nature on medieval Gloucester. L.E.W.O. Fullbrook-Leggatt's *Anglo-Saxon and Medieval Gloucester* (1952) is, despite its limitations, a useful digest of published documentation; Carolyn Heighway's *Gloucester: A History and Guide* (1985) provides a welcome account of the medieval period, and brings the results of much of the important archaeological work of recent years to a wider public. In 1988, the fourth volume of the *Victoria County History of Gloucestershire*, dealing with the city of Gloucester, was published. In addition, there have been over the years numerous shorter treatments of particular aspects of the history of Gloucester that have a close bearing upon the development of the medieval town and the ecclesiastical institutions, of which the best by far have been those by Langton (1977), Langston (1941), Thompson (1929), Ellis (1929) and Heighway (1984a; 1984b).

For more than a century, historians of Gloucester have been able to use the published work of W.H. Stevenson. Stevenson visited the city in 1889, to prepare his report on the contents of the corporation's archives for the Royal Commission on Historical Manuscripts (1891). His transcript of a rental of the whole town, made in 1455 (see below), was published in 1890, and in 1893 he published the *Calendar of the Records of the Corporation of Gloucester*. These works are invaluable, although the Calendar in particular is not without its shortcomings: Stevenson followed a policy of omitting certain information from the deeds he transcribed, in particular the dimensions of properties, and was inconsistent in his treatment of other documents such as wills.

More thoroughly executed was Stevenson's edition of the town rental made in 1455 by Robert Cole, canon and rent collector of Lanthony Priory. This remarkable itinerary of the town, street by street and house by house, recording in many cases the names of both the owner and the occupier, and in its first part the rents that were paid, was evidently a response to the bailiffs' financial difficulties (Holt 1990, 156–8). It was commissioned in an attempt to restore to the level of previous centuries the revenue from the landgable or chief rents that were due to the Crown, and which the bailiffs collected as the farmers of the borough. Cole identified about half of the properties as owing landgable, and for each of them he provided not just the bare description of the tenement and its tenants but also the names of all the earlier tenants, which he had taken from the old landgable rolls at his disposal. This was obviously to establish in each case the ancient liability to pay – and for many properties landgable had not been paid since the early fourteenth century or before, judging by Cole's inability to name subsequent tenants. The rolls he had went back to the early years of the reign of Henry III, as the earliest tenants he could name were active in and around the 1220s (*Cal. Recs Corpn Glouc.*, *passim*). The notional value of the landgable was £10 15*s* 7½*d* – although, try as he might, Cole could not quite account for every penny of this total, presumably because that figure had ceased to be entirely realistic even by the time of the earliest surviving records (*1455 Rental*, 114 and *passim*).

But the rental was also designed to be a more effective aid to easing the revenue crisis. The care that Cole took to record both the effective owners and the tenants of all the properties facing onto the main streets stands in contrast with his failure to complete for each tenement the formula with which each entry ends: *et continet in fronte* – . Obviously he was never called upon

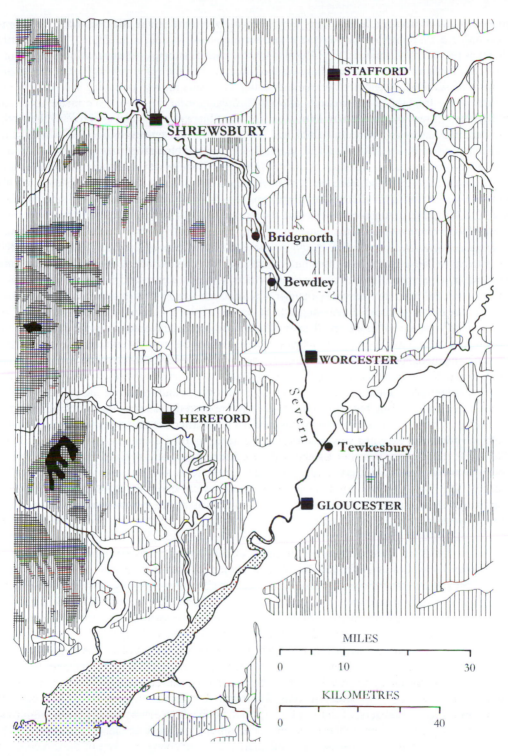

1.1 Regional location map: Gloucester, Worcester and the principal towns of the Severn valley

to measure each frontage, and to enter the information into the rental; the document we have is thus only the first phase of an exercise whose second phase was never attempted. There is little doubt as to what all this means, for 1455 also saw the bailiffs attempt – unsuccessfully – to secure an Act of Parliament which would have enabled them to pass the responsibility for repairs to the major streets on to householders, each either doing the repairs himself or paying according to the length of the frontage of his property (*Rotuli Parliamentorum*, vi, 49a). Cole made his rental before the bill was presented, therefore; after its failure there was no need to complete the work.

Once we understand why the rental was compiled, the idiosyncrasies in Cole's method of working cease to be a puzzle. For all his thoroughness in describing properties on the main streets, he can be very uninformative about the houses lining the back streets and lanes, and certain parts of Gloucester are excluded from the rental altogether. But this was entirely consistent with his purpose, which was to provide all the information that the bailiffs needed to know – and no more than that. Wherever landgable was charged, the property and its surroundings were described well enough for a future rent-collector to identify; the principal lanes – even if no landgable was owed – were adequately recorded and preparations made to enter details of frontages. But Cole showed no interest in house frontages in the minor lanes and the suburbs, where the road surfaces were evidently not maintained by the bailiffs; such districts, if there were no landgable-paying properties there, were dealt with in a desultory manner. The southern suburb was missed out, as were those parts of the northern suburb that belonged to St Oswald's Priory. The streets around the church of St Mary de Lode are not in the rental, evidently because no landgable was due to the bailiffs from that area, and there was no suggestion that the streets should be properly surfaced. Cole was not a careless and thoughtless worker, therefore. He was, on the contrary, conscientious in fulfilling his commission.

Interestingly, it is quite obvious that the document we possess was not the property of the fifteenth-century bailiffs, but was Cole's own copy. He used the dorse to construct an elaborate genealogical table of the kings of England, and 16 years after the rental was made he added a note recording the battle of Tewkesbury and the death of Prince Edward (*1455 Rental*, 125). Stevenson failed to see that this showed that the document was still in Cole's hands, or felt that the point was unimportant. Furthermore, the only marginal notes on the rental are in Elizabethan hands (ibid., 126–8), so that it is most likely that this copy came into the town archives only after Lanthony's dissolution – at the same time, presumably, that the original text of another brief Lanthony rental of 1535 was acquired, and of which the town preserved a copy (GCRO GBR 1314; *1455 Rental*, xii).

As he had spent years immersed in study of the documentation relating to Lanthony's Gloucester lands, Cole was the bailiffs' obvious choice for this difficult task of re-establishing their right to numerous small rents that had not been paid within living memory. It is in keeping with his task as *rentarius* that, having made such a rental, Cole should have taken care to preserve his own copy: it contained much information that he and his successors at Lanthony would find useful. The early to mid fifteenth century had seen a flurry of archival activity at Lanthony, as the priory's muniments had been put into order; the purpose was to facilitate the identification of its properties and to document their acquisition, not only to maintain the level of its rents but also as a response to the bailiffs' occupation of property that the priory regarded as its own (see below, pp. 302–4). From Lanthony, therefore, comes a rare series both of cartularies and of registers of some of the priors of the fourteenth and fifteenth centuries, together with a most comprehensive rental of Lanthony's Gloucester lands that was largely completed by Cole in the 1440s (A13). In all, there are 13 surviving volumes of these records of Lanthony Secunda, of which 12 are in the Public Record Office. One of the volumes is a cartulary concerned entirely with Lanthony's lands in Ireland, and has been published by the Irish Manuscripts Commission (Brooks 1953). The most important of the charters contained in the earlier cartularies were rearranged and entered into two new cartularies in 1449. The second of these, containing 139 folios, is concerned only with charters of land in Gloucester and its suburbs (A5). There are also the registers of five of the priors: that of Simon Brockworth (1362–77), William Cheryton (1377–1401), John Wyche (1408–36), John Hayward (1457–65) and Edmund Forrest (1501–25) – this last unfortunately having been unavailable for at least a decade for reasons of conservation. Consisting mainly of materials relating to ecclesiastical and political matters, these registers also contain details of many financial and legal transactions, such as agreements to lease property and disputes in which the priory was involved (Davis 1958, 60–61; Jack 1970–73).

The most important of the sources for St Peter's Abbey is the *Historia et Cartularium* of St Peter's Abbey, Gloucester, edited by W.H. Hart for the Rolls Series. The abbey's history reached its final form during the abbacy of Walter Froucester (1381–1412), although it is clearly the work of several different periods from the late eleventh century onwards (*Hist. et Cart.*, i, x–xii). The cartulary contains a variety of material, including a small number of documents relating or purporting to relate to the abbey's early centuries. In addition, there are other records of St Peter's Abbey which are preserved in Gloucester Cathedral Library. A cartulary of about 1400 contains numerous transcripts of deeds relating to properties in and around Gloucester, and there are three registers which cover the period 1500–28, and from which Hart published some extracts in the third volume of his edition (Davis 1958, 51–2; Kirby 1967, 1–2; *Hist. et Cart.*, iii, v–cxvi). A collection of deeds formerly belonging to the abbey is also kept in the cathedral library, mounted in the nineteenth century into ten bound volumes (Kirby 1967, 2–21).

While the early writers on Gloucester took note of casual discoveries, the first deliberate archaeological activity began only in the late nineteenth century. John Bellows, a printer, has been claimed as the city's first archaeologist. Having found, cleared, and preserved a section of the Roman fortress wall when building his new print works in 1871; he went on to trace the remainder of the wall around the city. In 1890, with a visit by the Royal Archaeological Institute pending, he excavated another section near the north transept of the cathedral, and produced the first reconstruction plan of Roman *Glevum*. The Corporation was beginning to take the remains of Gloucester's past seriously around the same time. The museum was built upon and incorporated a section of the wall south of the East Gate, and the surviving stretch to the south was, from 1888, protected, preserved, and made available for public inspection on application to the mayor (Fullbrook-Leggatt 1967, 5–7). The 1880s and 1890s were also distinguished by the work of Henry Medland, an architect, who was an active recorder of discoveries made on building sites. In 1931 W.H. Knowles, President of the Bristol and Gloucestershire Archaeological Society, formed the Gloucester Roman Research Committee, with the aim of studying the antiquities and artefacts of the Romano-British town and preparing a complete survey of it; their excavation reports appeared in the county transactions through the 1930s. There was a hiatus in the war years, followed by a resurgence in the 1950s and early 60s with further excavations published by Helen O'Neill; in 1967 the committee was reconstituted with a wider remit than the Roman period, and survives as GADARG (the Gloucester and District Archaeological Research Group), an active body responsible for the annual publication *Glevensis*.

The Gloucester City Museum was also active in the 1930s, excavating and publishing, and in 1966–7 organized major excavations on the new Market Hall and Longsmith Street sites, the first rescue excavations in the city funded by central government. In 1968 the museum set up a new permanent post, that of Gloucester Field Archaeologist, held first by Henry Hurst and later by

Carolyn Heighway. The early 1970s saw a number of major excavations by Hurst and Heighway, on such sites as 13–17 Berkeley Street, St Oswald's Priory, and 1 Westgate Street. Most of these were published first as interims in *The Antiquaries Journal* (1972, 1974 and 1975), the final reports appearing steadily thereafter, and it is this generation of excavations that has set the subsequent and continuing research agenda for the city's archaeology. The City Excavation Unit was also founded at this time, with the post of Field Officer, filled by Patrick Garrod, allowing what has in effect been an unbroken watching-brief ever since, monitoring all manner of intrusions into the city's buried deposits. Further major excavations took place in the 1980s and 90s, many under the direction of Malcolm Atkin as Head of the City Excavation Unit.

Worcester: sources

Like those of Gloucester, Worcester's antiquaries provided accounts of uneven reliability of the historic city and its ecclesiastical institutions (for instance Nash 1799; Green 1764 and 1796; Noake 1849, 1866). The early prominence of the Church of Worcester has commanded the attention of historians; by contrast, the almost complete loss of the city muniments has encouraged historians to neglect secular aspects of the medieval city. The evidence for the Anglo-Saxon city received excellent treatment at the hands of Howard Clarke and Christopher Dyer (1969), but between the period of their work and Alan Dyer's on Tudor Worcester (1963) there is a substantial gap in the secondary literature, which Sir Frank Stenton's contribution to the fourth volume of the *Victoria County History* – although useful – does not succeed in filling. Caroline Barron's paper on the social geography of late-fourteenth century Worcester (1989), however, comes as a welcome demonstration that important source materials still wait to be explored.

By contrast with Gloucester, both the churches and the city of Worcester are well documented for the Anglo-Saxon period. Post-Conquest Worcester is not so favoured: there is above all very little of the detailed topographical evidence that exists for Gloucester. There is no equivalent of the records of Lanthony Priory, and needless to say there is no equivalent of the 1455 rental. But the records of the cathedral priory, now of the Dean and Chapter and housed in the library of Worcester Cathedral, form a very useful collection. To add to the early records of the Church of Worcester contained in Hemming's Cartulary (Hearne 1723), two of the priory's volumes have been edited: the rental of 1240, designated as the priory register by its editor (Hale 1865), and the cartulary compiled at about the same date (Darlington 1968). A priory rental of 1458–98 (D&C A 6) survives, as do rentals of the priory's Worcester lands from the fourteenth and the sixteenth centuries. The several hundred medieval charters and other records of land transactions were calendared by J. Harvey Bloom (1909), although with so many errors that his edition is quite unreliable and should not be used. Fortunately it has now been superseded by the authoritative work of Susan Brock (1981), whose catalogue of the 2000 'B' class documents from the medieval and modern periods is accurate in every respect. The only shortcoming of this calendar is its failure to include the dimensions of properties which are generally to be found in leases and occasionally in medieval charters. (It is very much to be regretted that this typescript work – like the equivalent calendar of the 'A' class documents by Ben Benedikz and Brock – is available only at the libraries of the cathedral and Birmingham University.) The Worcester properties of the bishops are less well recorded, although invaluable rentals from the twelfth and thirteenth centuries are entered into the Red Book of Worcester (Hollings 1934).

Little other medieval evidence for city tenements remains. A collection of charters and other documents in the Bodleian Library relating to St Wulfstan's Hospital was edited by F. T. Marsh

(1890), who confusingly described it as a cartulary; and the County Record Office at St Helen's church holds small collections of muniments for the lands held by the wardens of some of the city churches. The only one of these collections that contains a substantial amount of medieval material – and that mainly post-1450 – is that from St Swithun's church: this was partly calendared by Bloom (1912) in an edition that can only be described as consistently inaccurate.

The chronology of archaeological research in Worcester is quite different from that of Gloucester. The eighteenth-century county histories included observations on ancient monuments and reports of accidental discoveries, and antiquarian interest in the cathedral led to tomb openings and the recording of Roman artefacts found during building work. The levelling of the castle earthworks between 1823 and 1843, and excavations for new locks at Diglis in 1843–4, yielded substantial quantities of artefacts, reported in print by Jabez Allies between 1836 and 1856.

Despite the relatively early foundation of the Worcestershire Archaeological Society (1854), the second half of the nineteenth century – and a period of intensive redevelopment in the city in the years around 1900 – saw surprisingly little recorded archaeological activity. With the exception of F.T. Spackman, reporting in the period *c.* 1905–30, it was only in the 1950s that an active amateur archaeological community appeared, the geologist Linsdale Richardson and Hugh Russell in particular watching construction sites and reporting their observations in print. Small-scale excavations by Peter Gelling (1958) were followed by Philip Barker's crucial large-scale salvage excavations on the Broad Street-Blackfriars and Lich Street sites in the mid 1960s: the latter a development so savage in its impact on the archaeology that it was to have national repercussions. These sites were reported in the *Origins of Worcester* (Barker 1969) – a significant milestone in the publication of the city's archaeology that defined the form and character of the Roman town for the first time and set the agenda for the study of later periods, with a number of significant contributions from the other historical disciplines.

Excavations in Sidbury by Martin Carver and John Sawle in the late 1970s were the first large-scale excavations in the city to take place under completely controlled conditions. The medieval and Saxon sequences from the site were published by Carver in his *Medieval Worcester: an archaeological framework* (1980), a second publication of major significance for the study of the medieval city and its archaeology, a volume that again sought selective contributions from other disciplines. As with other West Midlands towns, not the least of Carver's many contributions to the archaeology of Worcester was his collection of earlier observations and data into a comprehensive catalogue.

The 1980s were marked by a series of major excavations by Charles Mundy and his team of archaeologists from the then Hereford & Worcester County Council. These – the Blackfriars and Deansway excavations – provide a substantial and soundly-collected sample of the intramural city and figure largely in the arguments rehearsed in the pages below. The 1980s also marked the first permanent archaeological post to be established by the City Council.

The urban landscape

To assess the contribution made by church institutions to the physical growth and the evolving form of the two towns, neither the documentary resources described above, nor the archaeological evidence (narrowly defined), would on their own be adequate. The documented ownership of property and its liability for tax may, or may not, reflect its origin; documents designed to record ownership of property may sometimes describe its physical form, but rarely in more than a schematic or formulaic way. Excavation has, at the end of the twentieth century, provided an investigated sample of something under two per cent of the respective intramural areas. But this sample is, of course, dependent upon activities that leave a trace in the ground, is reduced further in size and scope by later disturbances to such fragile traces, is a source that has little to say about the agencies responsible for development rather than the process of development, and is finally a sample that has not been collected in order to answer historical research questions but has been determined by modern commercial development.

Given the limitations of these traditional sources, the only hope of resolving the contribution of church organizations to the development of landscape, it may be argued, is the landscape itself. This, however, raises a number of fresh problems.

Urban landscape as an historical-archaeological source

A map or plan drawn solely from the 1455 rental of Gloucester would be schematic to say the least, and, as described, complete only for the areas that were liable to pay landgable. It is also the case that the 1455 rental was detailing an urban landscape that was already ancient: it was as distant from the foundation of the town as we are from it. But, to an extent, the medieval landscape of this shire town, like many others, still exists today, and landmarks described in 1455 can often be located with reference to features that survive, or features that are known from maps surveyed in the last century and a half, or known from other post-medieval documentation or illustration. This study makes use of modern, as well as contemporary, source materials to analyse the medieval topography of the two subject towns and their evolution. It draws in particular on maps published in the mid and late nineteenth century, as these – particularly the first Ordnance Survey plans – were based upon accurate survey information but pre-dated the destruction of acres of historic landscape during slum clearance, road building and commercial redevelopment after World War I. But to what extent can such an exercise be justified? How close is the relationship between landscapes surveyed in the 1880s and in the mid fifteenth century? And is it feasible to reconstruct processes in the initial urbanization of an area in, say, the late tenth century, from evidence recorded five hundred or a thousand years later? The answers to these questions are relevant to many more places than Gloucester and Worcester: can the early physical development of English towns be reconstructed where contemporary texts do not exist and archaeologically excavated samples are on a minute scale, and likely to remain so?

In the study that follows, Gloucester is examined first because it has the great advantage of the detailed town and priory rentals of the mid fifteenth century, drawing upon sources extending back into the early thirteenth. These allow a crude assessment to be made of the degree to which Gloucester, when first accurately surveyed in the mid nineteenth century, had changed physically since the late Middle Ages. The conclusions of this assessment vary from area to area within the town and are examined in detail in the course of the urban landscape analysis (Chapter 3): they are, however, broadly optimistic. In summary, the 1455 rental allows a comparison to be made between the number and type of properties in the main intramural street-blocks at that date, and the number of plots surveyed in the same areas in the late nineteenth century – at least in enough detail to establish whether there had been gross amalgamations or other large-scale disturbances in the local plot pattern. The information from the town rental can be supplemented with data from the Lanthony Priory rentals, including detailed measurements of properties. For most main-street intramural areas, the relationship between fifteenth-century and nineteenth-century landscapes was very close, the 1455 rental recording similar numbers of tenements to the number of plots surveyed in 1883. Some areas show a slight reduction in the number of plots, suggesting a degree of amalgamation; in several cases this can be traced to the amalgamation of a single group of properties in a block – a row building, for example – by a single landlord, other properties in the area remaining relatively unchanged, as far as it is possible to tell.

Relationships between plots or series of plots and their surroundings were often stable. Plots that backed onto, say, the River Severn or a particular lane in the fifteenth century generally still did so in the nineteenth. Where plot-series adjoined, back-to-back, or at a corner, there frequently appears to have been an exchange in the ownership of land parcels between the two series, though often within a stable system of physical boundaries. This is apparent in the medieval documentation and, in some areas (Berkeley Street, for example), in the excavated evidence. There are certainly parts of central Gloucester, mapped in the nineteenth century, where plots on adjacent streets interlocked in very complex arrangements, giving the appearance of having been subject to the repeated exchange of small parcels of land, with no hope of reconstructing an 'original' arrangement. The behaviour of corner plots, and plots in the smaller central-area street-blocks, was particularly unpredictable, as has been found in recent work elsewhere, like Wells, Somerset (Scrase, 1989).

The Gloucester material shows that the most serious limitations in the use of later cartography for topographical analysis lie in what could be termed the unsustainable extremes of the medieval urban environment. The central street-spaces were characterized in the High Middle Ages by dense clusters of very small encroaching properties, many only a few feet wide. These peaked in number *c.* 1300, and thereafter underwent a protracted process of amalgamation and, ultimately, clearance. As the latter had taken place well before all but the earliest and crudest maps were produced, these properties, though once a significant part of the townscape, are cartographically invisible to us (though in this particular instance some reconstruction has been possible from a combination of documentary sources and the archaeologists' ground-penetrating radar). The largest properties were similarly vulnerable. Of a number of 'great tenements', very large high-status plots in the central area of Gloucester in the fifteenth century, only one – occupied by the medieval New Inn – escaped dismemberment, immunized by the great building upon it and the continuity of its business. The most vulnerable of all the extremities of the medieval town-plan were, however, the suburbs. Late-medieval documentary sources clearly demonstrate not only the decay and desertion of plots away from the principal frontages, but also the disappearance, by encroachment from gardens, of some suburban lanes (see Chapter 13). Estimates of the extent of the medieval built-up area are, in consequence, bound to be problematic, and any conclusions as to the form of particular suburbs, and thus the possibility of their organized promotion at some point, must bear in mind the fact that we are unlikely to be able to see the whole picture.

In summary, the Gloucester evidence suggests that street-spaces, street-patterns and plot-patterns in most areas of the densely built-up city centre exhibit a mixture of long-term stability and recognizable, if not always reconstructable, mobility. In many areas the coarse physical characteristics of street- and plot-systems – local orientation, the shape of plots, their relationships to common boundaries and back lanes – can be demonstrated to have been relatively stable between the fifteenth century and the arrival of the Ordnance Survey, a physical framework maintained despite fluctuations in the property market and in individual property holdings. It is these coarse physical characteristics that will provide the raw material for subsequent analysis.

The problem is that Gloucester – though it lacks the exceptional documentation of Winchester, London or Oxford – is still atypic of English shire towns in the quantity of recorded evidence for its medieval form. Worcester is much more typical. It is not possible to demonstrate, with anything like the same degree of detail, that the town-plan surveyed accurately in (in this case) 1879 had a close relationship to that of the medieval town: such a relationship can be demonstrated only for scattered individual properties or clusters of properties (as in the work of Dr Pat Hughes). Yet it is almost certainly the case that there was a close relationship. Certainly the streets that emerge from the documentary record in the thirteenth century were those known and mapped in later centuries. At a more general level, Gloucester and Worcester were of comparable size, and their respective economic trajectories into the nineteenth century were broadly similar. It would be remarkable if there were not some general correspondence in the development of and influences upon their respective town-plans. And in Worcester, as in Gloucester, the survival of large numbers of late- and sub-medieval buildings, particularly prior to the 1930s, suggests a degree of stability in the framework of containing properties. Also, as elsewhere, where archaeological excavation has taken place in Worcester, persistence in urban boundaries – sometimes from the Roman period, more often from first medieval urbanization – has been recorded (see Chapter 6).

The explanation for such persistence and continuity in urban landscape has been expressed in both theoretical and empirical terms. The geographer M.R.G. Conzen saw urban landscape as being composed of three fundamental 'form categories': the town-plan (i.e. the physical framework), the building fabric, and the pattern of land and building utilization, all of which are genetically and functionally interrelated. Each form category, Conzen proposed, responds at different rates to the changing functional requirements of an urban community: land-use may change most rapidly of all in response to functional stimuli, building fabric, and most particularly, the town-plan being the most conservative 'as they tend to reflect the pattern of past landownership and capital investment more tenaciously … the town plan emerges as the form category of greatest value to the historian' (Conzen 1968, 116–7). The everyday practicalities of this process were summed up for Winchester by Derek Keene:

> It was probably in the most densely occupied areas that physical boundaries were most stable, at least near the street frontages. The reason for this seems to have been primarily mechanical, for once the frontages were fully built up the standing buildings, each in separate tenure, defined a framework which the holders of individual properties were obliged to respect when they rebuilt their houses. Only in areas of decline and decay, or as a result of royal intervention, or by the imposition of a twentieth-century redevelopment programme, has this ancient pattern been entirely swept away. (Keene 1985, 181)

This is not, of course, to suggest that the town-plan of Winchester (or, indeed, of Gloucester or Worcester) was unchanging in all its detail throughout and after the Middle Ages. Far from it.

> The tenement histories … demonstrate that many medieval boundaries have survived into modern times, although few of them can be traced with any certainty earlier than *c.* 1300. The histories also show, however, that many property boundaries changed during the later Middle Ages as a result not only of the depopulation of the city but also of the continuous operation of the property market. (Keene 1985, 180)

It is becoming clear that the operation of the property market in and after the Middle Ages probably has different implications for the relative stability and persistence of settlement pattern detail at various levels of the urban hierarchy, just as it might for different areas within a single town. This, of course, has consequences for topographical investigation. In the Cheapside area of central London, for example, documentary evidence has revealed an exceptionally complex pattern of land use and tenure that changed rapidly with the urban economy. Stone buildings provided fixed points in the landscape of the side streets, locally stabilizing street frontages and alleyways, but provide few clues to the form of the plots in which they were built. The rapidly changing cadastral geography within these street blocks is accessible only from the contemporary documentation. But the streets themselves are a different matter, and many remain in use since their creation in the late ninth or tenth centuries (Keene 1990b). Towards the lower end of the medieval urban hierarchy, the extensive surviving medieval documentation for Wells, Somerset, shows that a similar mixture of continuity and change to that identified in Winchester, and apparent in Gloucester, shaped the town plan in the Middle Ages and in later centuries. Within the relatively stable framework of the street pattern, house-plots typically were subject to a limited series of possible mutations and trends. 'Plot boundaries', Scrase wrote, 'are complicated … but the complexities can be mastered' (Scrase 1989, 363).

Approaches to the analysis of urban landscape: the composite town

The briefest study of the physical form of our two towns reveals that neither is likely to have been created by a single act of planning on the lines of one of the classic, grid-planned, medieval new towns – Salisbury for instance, an episcopal foundation of 1219. Both Gloucester and Worcester have town plans or settlement patterns that might once have been described (inappropriately) as 'organic'. Modern scholarship would reject this in favour of the more accurate and descriptive term 'composite' (Slater 1990): like the vast majority of medieval English towns, Gloucester and Worcester are composed, beyond any doubt, 'of a series of units of different periods' (Schofield and Vince 1994, 35).

The historical record prepares us for a pattern of development like this. In Lincoln, in the 1080s, Coleswein had '36 houses and two churches to which nothing belongs, which he has built on waste land that the king gave him, and that was never built on before' (DB, i, 336). It would be surprising if at least a proportion of the large numbers of proprietary church foundations in other early medieval towns were not associated with similar episodes, otherwise unrecorded. If such developments embraced streets and plots, as well as short-lived buildings, then there is at least the potential for them to have left an enduring and recognizable trace in the urban landscape. And when excavation is conducted on a large enough scale, such episodes can and have been detected through the common development chronology and common measurements of neighbouring plots, as at Coppergate, York, in the early years of the tenth century (Hall 1984, 49).

In the more recent historic past the concept of the incrementally developed composite town is completely familiar, and many very different examples may be cited. For instance, the process by which the squares west of the City of London were speculatively developed in the period from *c*. 1660 is well known: their individual extent is apparent despite rebuilding, and surviving discontinuities in the street-pattern of this part of the capital may be traced directly to this primary urbanization process. Or, by way of an extreme contrast, but effectively demonstrating a number of similar processes in action, one might turn to modern down-town San Francisco. This classic Amercian grid-plan city is diagonally bisected by the line of Market Street: grid orientations, block sizes and street widths are different either side of it, and these differences can be traced directly to the design of urban extensions developed respectively before and after the 1849 gold rush (Reps 1979).

Individual medieval urban extensions may be on an altogether different – smaller – scale, but may be no less distinct. Bristol, for instance, was marked by vigorous growth in the eleventh and twelfth centuries, and the principal twelfth-century extramural extensions were established on sites physically separated from each other by river channels. In the enormous Redcliff suburb, the plots lining the three principal streets terminated at long common boundary ditches mid-way between the streets. The Feria, the Old Market east of the castle, took the form of an axial cigar-shaped street-market bounded by long plots reaching to back lanes, within an oval enclosure. The

New Borough of the Meadow, to the north, was laid out to a loose rectilinear grid (Lobel 1975, 4–7). The point is that had these extensions taken place elsewhere – on a single broad site not interrupted by the Frome and the Avon – they would still have been individually distinguishable as separate components in the town-plan. Although founded within a few decades of each other, their street spaces, street-patterns, plot-patterns and common boundaries were in each case quite different, arranged in quite different relationships within each area. In M.R.G. Conzen's definition, these features 'enter into individualised combinations in different areas of the town. Each combination derives uniqueness from its site circumstances and establishes a measure of morphological homogeneity or unity in some or all respects over its area. It represents a plan-unit, distinct from its neighbours' (Conzen 1969, 5).

The recognition of the composite character of many English town-plans arguably began with Conzen's work in the 1960s. His complex analysis of the form of Alnwick, Northumberland, provided a model approach for a generation of historical geographers, though it was the demonstration of the multi-phase genesis of Ludlow, previously considered to be the result of a single act of town-planning, that was perhaps more widely influential, reaching a larger audience in the volume edited by Dyos, and in summary form in Platt's *The English Medieval Town* (Conzen 1969; Conzen, in Dyos 1968; Platt 1976). Conzen identified recurrent phenomena in town-plans that, he argued, were evidence of incremental growth:

> The recognition of plan-units is of great importance and can often illuminate the growth stages of a medieval town, especially earlier ones, when available written records fail to give any information. Such recognition depends on the careful scrutiny of plan detail such as the behaviour of street spaces and their bounding street lines, and the shape, size, orientation, and grouping of plots, all such evidence leading to the identification of the 'seams' along which the genetically significant plan units are knit together. (Conzen 1968, 120)

Conzen argued that, once an area was built up, differences in the design of particular urban extensions, and discontinuities where one extension adjoined another, would persist in the townscape, and could be recovered from large-scale town-plans surveyed centuries later.

The practicalities of this recovery process – plan-unit resolution, the disaggregation of a town-plan – are not always, however, quite straightforward. In the course of this study it was found that areas exhibiting 'a measure of morphological unity' could be defined at a variety of scales, potentially from a whole intramural area down to a minor plot series. Additionally, in some cases, characteristics distinguishing an area from its neighbours were not uniformly present throughout that area: a core might exhibit the full range of defining characteristics (for example, streets and plots each with particular features), but have marginal areas around it in which only some characteristics were present. In this study, the term 'plan-unit' has been adopted for areas recognized as distinct and morphologically homogeneous at the level of the individual street with its associated plot-series, or the street-block; these correspond approximately to Conzen's second- and third-order plan-units in his analysis of Alnwick (1969). Local variations distinguished at a smaller scale are described as sub-units, following Slater's (1989) town-plan analysis of Doncaster. Larger-scale units, representing whole intramural areas and major suburban developments of composite character, have been termed plan-regions.

It is also recognized that the extent and boundaries, or seams, of distinguishable town-plan components may be subject to change through time. If it is accepted that the plot pattern recorded in the nineteenth century represents a snapshot in time of a continuously, slowly, evolving system, it follows that any boundaries of a plan component that follow property boundaries will themselves be subject to this process, and liable to shift with the workings of the property market (Baker and Slater 1992).

The interpretation of town-plan components

It is also true, and has certainly become clear in the course of this study, that the genesis of some town-plan components – even those giving the impression of a single-phase planned development – may be much more complex and long drawn-out than might at first be apparent. A planned urban extension may be provided with an infrastructure of streets and plot boundaries that are established as a single act, but the actual take-up of plots by new tenants may take place over a greatly extended period, and as the plots within that area become subject to the workings of the property market, many of their original distinguishing characteristics may be lost or altered. But it is also the case that elements of what appears to be a contemporaneous framework for settlement may, on investigation, prove to have origins in more than one period. A classic instance of this may be the northern part of the High Street in Worcester. Forming, with its associated plots, a very distinct and highly visible unit within the town-plan, it was identified early on in the course of this work as a plan-unit with a single-period origin, subject to a continuous process of minor change thereafter (Baker and Slater 1992; Baker, Dalwood, Holt, Mundy and Taylor 1992). Subsequent excavation within it has, however, raised the possibility that its genesis was more complex, its individual components created over an extended period of time (see pp. 172–3).

The fundamental point that arises from these questions is that of the interdependence of sources. The towns that form the subject of this volume are larger, more complex, and have longer histories than most towns previously subjected to this kind of analysis. In such contexts the probability of establishing the absolute chronology, relative chronology, or internal chronology of town-plan components from landscape evidence alone is negligible. Archaeological evidence in particular is essential as a means of establishing chronologies, and as the only means of recovery of past major town-plan components that have been erased by redevelopment in the pre-modern period.

The medieval Church and the composite town

In order, therefore, to assess any direct role that Church institutions may have played in urban growth, it is necessary first of all to identify whether there is evidence of incremental growth, and to isolate what appear to be the principal plan components – to disaggregate the town-plan. The plan components then have to be interpreted: what do they represent? Do they display features consonant with an organized origin – 'planning' or higher-order decision making? What is their chronology? And finally, if they do appear to represent the outcome of higher-order decision making, were church institutions or other agencies responsible? This study is but a preliminary exploration of hitherto unexplored and undescribed geographies – unique, complex, urban settlement patterns – with the aim of answering a specific historical question. Further analysis of all the source materials, and the extension of the excavated sample in particular, is essential, not just to test any models of urban development proposed here, but to widen the field of enquiry and produce a broader understanding of the evolution of each town.

Chapter 2

Gloucester and the Church before 1100

Organized urban life in Roman Britain came to an end in the chaos of the opening years of the fifth century (Cleary 1989, 144–57), but this did not entail Gloucester's complete abandonment. Perhaps for some considerable time it continued to be occupied as a central place, as a base for those who exercised authority over the surrounding countryside. The early fifth-century burial of a young man in an impressive mausoleum within the extramural cemetery at Kingsholm (Hurst 1975, 290–94; Hurst 1985, 35) certainly suggests as much; both the style of his tomb and the wealth of his personal accoutrements – his fine silver buckles (one of them brand new), silver strap-ends, and silver-decorated knife – are testimony to the undiminished wealth and influence of the post-Roman aristocracy of the locality. Whether or not the details of the account of the West Saxon victory in 577 at the battle of Dyrham are to be accepted (ASC *sub anno* 577), it is quite feasible that it was only during the later sixth century – and perhaps indeed in the 570s – that British kingdoms centred on Gloucester, Cirencester and Bath succumbed to a campaign of conquest from Wessex. Even then, English settlement may not have closely followed military defeat. Certainly there is no evidence of Anglo-Saxon settlement in the Severn valley in the pagan period: no pagan Saxon burial has been found west of the Severn, whilst east of the river, in the Cotswolds region, pagan burials come to an end as the flood-plain is approached (Pretty 1989, 175). H.P.R. Finberg, observing that the names of several places close to Gloucester contained Celtic elements, inferred that 'Welsh continued to be spoken in the old Roman-British capital and its vicinity well into the Anglo-Saxon period' (Finberg 1957, 1–2). However unsatisfactory such evidence may be regarding the identity of those exerting political control in the region during the period, nevertheless it does serve to reinforce the perception that Gloucester's prominence as a British centre extended into the sixth century.

The foundation of the Old Minster

According to the Anglo-Saxon Chronicle, it was in 628 that all of the region around Gloucester fell under Mercian overlordship, when Penda fought the West Saxons at Cirencester and apparently defeated them. By the late seventh century it was part of the kingdom of the Hwicce, whose rulers were often subject to the Mercian kings; by the ninth century the region was indisputably part of Mercia (Stenton 1971, 46; Sims-Williams 1990, 39).

St Peter's Abbey preserved a story of its own foundation by Osric, the sub-king of the Hwicce, in around 679 (*Hist. et Cart.*, i, lxxi–lxxiv, 3–4). The date, and indeed the course of events, is questionable: firstly we have what is said to be a charter of King Æthelred of Mercia, granting 300 *tributarii* at Gloucester to Osric, his man; subsequently, it is stated, Osric purchased from Æthelred permission to build a minster there, and to establish a community of monks. To this end, and so that he might freely possess the city of Gloucester *cum agro suo* – with its *ager* or agricultural hinterland – Osric paid apparently some 30,000 coins. In a statement that is a masterpiece of contradiction, this latter transaction was said to have taken place in 671 – in the fifth year of Æthelred's reign (that is, in 679) – whilst Deusdedit was Archbishop of Canterbury (655–64) and whilst Seaxwulf was Bishop of Mercia (675–c. 691). Through the haze of inconsistency, Finberg perceived that the use of years of Incarnation was not in use in the seventh century, and that it was the regnal year that was likely to be more accurate than anything else (Finberg 1961, 160). 679 is therefore the most reliable of the given dates – and is certainly preferable to 681, which was what the medieval monks of St Peter's settled on (*Hist. et Cart.*, i, 3, 5; Finberg 1961, 163, n. 4).

How much faith should be placed in this account? It is, at least, not inconsistent with other charter material. In 676 Osric had provided land for a new minster dedicated to St Peter at Bath, his overlord Æthelred confirming the grant according to the charter (B 43; S 51; Finberg 1961, 163), and the foundation of a church at Gloucester fits into a series of reported events which included the virtually contemporary foundation of the see of Worcester in Hwiccian territory, and there too the construction of a church of St Peter (see below, p. 127). Whether indeed a seventh-century Hwiccian king would have needed to pay his Mercian overlord for the privilege of founding a church and enjoying undisputed possession of a city well within his own territory may seem a doubtful detail, at best inserted at a later date; Æthelred's confirmation, on the other hand, would have been needed if his rights of overkingship extended even to the Hwiccian dynasty's own lands. Finberg proposed that both the Gloucester foundation charter and the list of early benefactions that followed were a composition of the ninth century (Finberg 1961, 162). They provided a fitting prologue for what was said to be King Burgred's confirmatory charter of 862 in favour of the minster (*Hist. et Cart.*, i, lxxiii–iv; S 209), and demonstrate what the minster clergy of that time believed about their community's origins, as pieced together from oral traditions, obits, tombs and their inscriptions, with perhaps some authentic early records. But the possibility must be admitted that much or even all of the text could have been composed at St Peter's Abbey after the Conquest – a time when, arguably, there would have been a greater need for a fitting foundation myth. Whether, in that case, any genuinely early material relating to the minster could have found its way into the text is questionable: there may indeed be very little truth at all in this early history of St Peter's.

What can be inferred regarding the religious affinities of the local population in 679? Like the people of the Worcester region they were Christians, according to Bede (HE, iv, 13; and p.183 below), who tells us that Eafe, a princess of the Hwicce who married Æthelwalh of Sussex, had been baptized in her own land where her father and uncle, and all their people, were Christians. She is likely to have been born no later than the middle of the century, and by implication the conversion of the Hwicce had been early and is otherwise unrecorded. If the Anglian settlers of the northern part of the kingdom were converted by the native British population, as Steven Bassett has argued, then in the south of the Hwiccian lands the lack of any noticeable English settlement following on the West Saxon conquest of the late sixth century points strongly to the population there never having ceased to be predominantly Christian in belief (Bassett 1989a, 230–31; 1992). The foundation of a minster at Gloucester – like those at Worcester and, by inference, at Bath – is therefore not to be seen as a missionary act, bringing Christianity to a heathen people; rather it would have been the imposition of a new institution to oversee existing pastoral work. It is unthinkable that Gloucester, the central place of a largely Christian region, did not already have a church or churches, with a resident priesthood. If the 300 *tributarii* ostensibly granted to Osric for his new church was not a later invention but was indeed an established administrative and political unit, then an equivalent ecclesiastical organization for that territory might be presumed to have already existed.

Steven Bassett has been able to demonstrate that the church of St Helen in Worcester originated as the main church of its region before the establishment of the Anglo-Saxon see (1989a, 225–56; 1992, 20–26). Can the principal church of the earlier ecclesiastical organization of the Gloucester district be identified in the same way? An examination of the parochial structure of the region around Gloucester in the later Middle Ages reveals obvious parallels between the status then of the church of St Mary de Lode and that of St Helen's, and Bassett has put forward a persuasive argument for identifying St Mary's as the principal British church of the region (1992, 26–9). And in the case of St Mary's – unlike that of St Helen's – there is archaeological evidence to reinforce the impression of its early importance. Excavation has shown the church of the twelfth century to have been preceded not only by earlier church building of the tenth century but also by a mausoleum of the fifth–eighth centuries, which contained oriented burials. This had been constructed upon the foundations of a demolished Roman house. Whilst St Mary's cannot be shown conclusively to have been a British church, nevertheless the succession of buildings on the site points to a continuity of purpose and use. (For a fuller discussion of the church of St Mary de Lode and its parish, see below, pp. 97–9.)

Early grants to the Church of Gloucester

The record of donations from successive kings during the minster's early years confirms its importance. If the charter evidence is to be relied on, by 800 it had benefited from at least six such grants (*Hist. et Cart.*, i, 3–5, 9–10, 58, 64, 67, 72; Finberg 1961, 35, 36, 40, 41) – four from the Mercian kings Cenred, Æthelbald and Offa, and two from Aldred, the last, apparently, of the Hwiccian dynasty to rule as king. Thus St Peter's began to acquire lands scattered over the northern part of what was to become Gloucestershire, as well as closer to Gloucester. There were grants of estates at Badgeworth, Arle and Hartpury, all within a few miles of the minster; and before the death of Abbess Eafe, in 767 or so, Aldred the sub-king was said to have granted 100 or possibly 120 hides 'where now the Abbot's Barton is', as the fourteenth-century monk believed (*Hist. et Cart.*, i, 64; Finberg 1961, 41). This great demesne manor, which took in much of the agricultural land around the city of Gloucester, was retained by the abbey until the Dissolution (*VCH Glos.*, iv, 392–3). A number of estates were presumably detached from Abbot's Barton during the Anglo-Saxon period, for in 1086 – when it still included sub-manors at Barnwood, Tuffley and Morwents End – it was assessed at no more than 22 hides (DB, i, 165c).

Abbesses and clergy

According to the abbey's *Historia*, the minster was at first under the rule of abbesses. Cyneburh – described as Osric's sister – was the first abbess of what would seem to have been a double monastery of nuns and clerics (*Hist. et Cart.*, i, 4; Finberg 1961, 164–6). At Lanthony Priory in the fifteenth century it was believed that the Cyneburh in question was not Osric's sister but the daughter of Penda (A11, fo.14v), an understandable error – as presumably it was – given the relative prominence of that St Cyneburh who, after her marriage to Alhfrith, son of King Oswiu of Northumbria, founded the convent of Castor in Northamptonshire and died as its abbess in *c.* 680 (Farmer 1978, 97–8). Despite Farmer's scepticism of the existence of the Gloucester abbess, Osric's choice of his sister to rule his foundation seems unremarkable enough. After what the *Historia* said was a rule of 29 years, Cyneburh died in 710, and her successor at St Peter's was Eadburh, a kinswoman described as the queen of Wulfhere of Mercia (*Hist. et Cart.*, i, 4, 6). As Wulfhere had ruled from 658 until his death in 675, and at his death had left a queen, Eormenhilde, the daughter of Erconbert of Kent, who died as Abbess of Ely in about 700 (Farmer

1978, 135), little credence need be given to what was quite clearly a clumsy attempt to inflate the minster's royal – and Mercian – connections. Eadburh in turn died in 735 and was succeeded by Eafe, of whose origins nothing sensible is said (*Hist. et Cart.*, i, 4, 7), although we have seen that her name had been borne by a Hwiccian princess of a previous generation. Is this to be taken as a sign of authenticity in the *Historia*, or might it simply show that the author – as we should expect – had read Bede? As the *Historia* absurdly makes Abbess Eafe, too, a widow of Wulfhere (who had undoubtedly died long before she was born, as her reputed death came some 94 years after his), it is easy to conclude that this account of the early years of St Peter's is an unintelligent concoction based on inadequate and inappropriate sources. Yet there may be some independent support for the *Historia*, if – as Sims-Williams has suggested – the nun Eafe, to whom Æthelbald of Mercia (716–57) granted part of a building at Droitwich with two salt-furnaces, was the Abbess of Gloucester (Sims-Williams 1990, 123 n. 45; H 565–6; S 1824). Eafe remained abbess until her death in 767 or more likely 769 – the date was also given as the twelfth year of Offa's reign (*Hist. et Cart.*, i, 7). She was the last recorded abbess, and thereafter, the *Historia* claimed, regular life at St Peter's ceased.

There is at least one other detectable, crude embellishment to the *Historia*. For we read that Osric did not die by *c.* 680 as other evidence would suggest (Sims-Williams 1990, 35), but went on to succeed to the throne of Northumbria where he died in 729 (*Hist. et Cart.*, i, 5) – a preposterous story that erroneously identifies the Hwiccian Osric with the Osric, son of Aldfrith, who must have been at least a generation his junior. As it is Bede who provides the precise date of the Northumbrian Osric's death (*Hist. et Cart.*, i, xiii; HE, v 23), there is confirmation, therefore, that the author of the *Historia* had indeed used this source in his attempts to expand the barest of biographical details – which was evidently all that the Gloucester sources (at best) could provide. The information that Osric and Cyneburh lay side by side before the altar of St Petronilla, and that when Eafe came to die she was buried near her predecessors (*Hist. et Cart.*, i, 6, 7), suggests that for some centuries, and perhaps until the major rebuildings of the eleventh century, a group of early tombs with their inscriptions may have been prominent features of the minster church – although the altar itself must have been a later addition. The cult of Petronilla became prominent in Rome only in the eighth century, and was promoted by the French monarchy (Farmer 1978, 352); at Gloucester, it could have been a post-Conquest innovation. It is quite possible that tomb inscriptions were the principal record of the individuals active in the early years of the minster, and alone were the main source for the early part of the *Historia*.

The Minster and the city of Gloucester 679–*c.* 880

According to the later record of its history, therefore, the Minster of St Peter was a foundation of the Hwiccian royal dynasty, and through successive female members of the family remained under Hwiccian control for nearly a century and perhaps longer. The evidence of substantial Mercian royal gifts as early as 704x709 indicates how far that control was limited by the subordination of Osric's successors to their overlords; alternatively, it may be that attribution of these gifts to Mercian rather than to Hwiccian kings was a later rationalization – particularly if the language of any original charters had associated these kings with the Hwiccian donors, just as Æthelred was said to have been associated with Osric's foundation. The ending of the line of royal abbesses during the eighth century is likely to reflect the disappearance by 800 of the Hwiccian kings (Sims-Williams 1990, 38), rather than any decline in the Minster itself, as the author of the *Historia* thought; but a withdrawal of local patronage might nevertheless have had adverse consequences. Burgred's charter – if at all genuine – may imply what was in effect a re-foundation of the church under Mercian royal tutelage, and a restoration of its fortunes.

There is no evidence that the abbesses and clergy of the Minster had any secular authority in the region – unlike the Anglo-Saxon bishops of Worcester, who were lords of their city (see below, p. 128). Royal influence in and around Gloucester remained strong throughout the Anglo-Saxon period, and not just during the tenth and eleventh centuries when it is known that there was a royal palace there: although the manor of King's Barton that lay outside Gloucester was valued at only nine hides in 1086 (DB, i , 62d), this was but the remnant of what had once been an important royal estate which before the tenth century had included the lands given to the New Minster, later St Oswald's (see below). The existence of the palace by the 890s (see below), and the already established need for an administrative centre for the estate, together suggest that earlier kings – Burgred and his predecessors – had also maintained a local residence, dominating the city and its hinterland. Osric's reputed choice of Gloucester for his burial place suggests that here – rather than Worcester or Winchcombe – was the chief palace of his kingdom. The location of the Kingsholm palace in the tenth century, emphatically outside the walls while St Peter's was prominently within them, may have been of long standing. But the impression gained from recent archaeological work that the south-west corner of the Roman city may have remained in use through the early Anglo-Saxon centuries as a stronghold or fortress (M. Atkin, pers. comm.) would go to confirm the importance of the city of Gloucester as a primary focus of secular authority under both the Hwiccian and Mercian kings.

During the early Anglo-Saxon centuries, Gloucester also fulfilled certain central-place functions in the regional economy. Within the Roman walls, the relative sparsity of occupational debris among thick deposits of animal manure and other organic matter dated to the seventh century onwards (Heighway 1984a, 364–5) suggest a regular pattern of major cattle markets and fairs rather than the day-to-day activities of a settled population of any size. Probably most of the intramural area remained open ground during the ninth century, judging by the Danish army's choice of Gloucester as a suitable refuge in which to pass the winter of 877–8. It is true that the contemporary chronicler did not describe Gloucester in the same terms as he did Chester in the entry for 893, as 'a deserted city' (ASC s.a. 893); even so, the attractiveness of Gloucester must have lain not only in its Roman walls but also in the availability within of enough open space to accommodate a bivouacking army. As well as the need to erect the temporary shelters or booths reported by Æthelweard (Campbell 1962, 42; Whitelock 1979, 195 n. 7), there would have been winter stores and booty – including inevitably large numbers of animals – for which room had to be found.

With the Danish occupation, the population of the district must have fled, leaving their churches and houses to be looted. It may be no coincidence that the timber church of St Mary de Lode was rebuilt in the late ninth or early tenth century (see below, p. 98), whilst the incorporation of at least two broken cross shafts from the ninth-century into the early tenth-century fabric of St Oswald's, with two others found nearby (see below, p. 100), also strongly suggests a recent episode of despoliation. Above all, as a substantial and wealthy complex of buildings, St Peter's was an obvious target for looting, which – incidentally – would have provided a context for the subsequent rewriting of early charters in favour of the Minster, up to and including Burgred's charter of only some 15 years previously. Thus the clumsy composition purporting to be the record of Æthelred's grants to Osric – and which, as we have seen, Finberg suggested did indeed date from the late ninth century (1961, 162) – could have been prompted not just by Burgred's confirmation of the Minster's lands, but more urgently by the destruction of the Minster's archives. Under such circumstances, it would have been natural for the returning clergy to have attempted to place on record what they could remember of their lost charters and traditions, a process perhaps guaranteed to distort through simplification and rationalization the account of the Minster's foundation, yet nevertheless capable of preserving genuine information about the events of the seventh century.

The foundation of the *burh*

Archaeological evidence points to a marked increase in activity within the walls by the early years of the tenth century (Heighway 1984a, 377–9), and there are further signs that by 900 the city was a newly renovated centre of royal authority with at least a small resident population. The refurbishment of Gloucester as a *burh* had taken place most probably during the 880s and – unlike the works at Worcester where the fortified district needed to be extended by new defences – could have been achieved by repairs to the Roman walls and gates which already defended a large area. There is no contemporary notice of when this happened, although the establishment of a mint during the reign of Alfred (Grinsell, Blunt and Dolley 1973, 96) points to Gloucester's burghal status (Loyn 1961), and the single Gloucester coin yet found can be dated with considerable confidence to the mid 880s (Dolley and Blunt 1961, 83–4). Thus the context of the decision to found the *burh* was the reconstruction following the defeat of the Danes in 878 (Stenton 1971, 264–5). Without direct evidence for the chronology of the laying-out of streets and houseplots within the refurbished walls, it is not possible to be certain that it had been an inherent feature of the foundation; it is, however, clear that by the end of the century the city was a favoured political and military base. The implication of ealdorman Æthelred's choice of Gloucester as the meeting-place for the Mercian *witan* recorded in 896 (B 574; S 1441; Anon. 1880–1) is that he had a palace either within the walls or nearby; whilst the part played by the men of Gloucester in 914 in combining with the men of Hereford to defeat a Danish incursion up the Severn estuary (ASC s.a. 917) is a measure of the military role the city could be expected to play in the region. Stenton suggested that it was during the reign of Edward the Elder that the shires of western Mercia were formed (1971, 337), although it was only in the eleventh century that Gloucestershire attained its full medieval extent when it incorporated the neighbouring shire of Winchcombeshire (Taylor 1957, 17–51; Whybra 1990)

The New Minster

As if to emphasize Gloucester's renewed importance, Æthelred and Æthelflæd founded a new church there – during the reign of Alfred, according to William of Malmesbury (Hamilton 1870, 293) – thus lending some support to the 880s being the period of the city's refurbishment. It was only later, in 909, that the relics of St Oswald were brought into Mercia from Bardney in Lincolnshire (ASC s.a. 909), and laid to rest at Gloucester in the new church (Hamilton 1870, 293). Archaeological evidence perhaps supports that sequence of events, for after the first phase of construction of the New Minster it was during a distinct second phase that a mausoleum-like building was added at the church's east end (Heighway 1986). This has every appearance of being the chapel and crypt that would have been considered the appropriate setting for such prestigious relics. So it is reasonable to suppose that by 909 the church had been in existence for some years.

In the post-Conquest period the New Minster fell under the control of the archbishops of

York, and was reformed as a house of Augustinian canons in 1153 (Thompson 1921, 98; *VCH Glos.*, ii, 85). As a minor religious house it was to remain poor and unimportant, its income from lands and other sources amounting to no more than £90 10*s* 2½*d* at the time of its dissolution in 1536 (Caley 1810–34, ii, 487). But its later history detracts from the fact of its foundation as a prestigious and wealthy secular minster, richly decorated (Heighway 1984b, 46), and in its early years 'it was enthusiastically extolled and carefully cherished by the people [of Gloucester] as if it were the mother and lady of their city', as Reginald's life of St Oswald recorded in the middle years of the twelfth century (Arnold 1882–5, i, 326n, 369). Without question, from its foundation until, presumably, its decline which accompanied the post-Conquest loss of the greater part of its temporal income, the New Minster was Gloucester's principal church.

Given its position and its status, the new church was not founded primarily for the convenience of the population of the *burh*. It lay outside the defended area, and well away from the new street-grid centred on Northgate Street and Southgate Street. Its special status later in the medieval period as a royal free chapel (*Cal. Close Rolls 1313–18*, 596; Denton 1970, 51–7) would seem to have originated with its foundation specifically as a suitable and convenient place for the devotions of visitors to the royal palace. Not that the matter of the New Minster's location is entirely straightforward, however. The Kingsholm palace, in use from at least the late Anglo-Saxon period until the thirteenth century (Hurst 1975), was almost half a mile away from the minster and latterly, at least, had its own chapel of St Nicholas (*Cal. Patent Rolls 1258–66*, 622). Whilst it cannot be ruled out that earlier palaces of the tenth century and before occupied a different site, much closer to Gloucester or to the New Minster, there is no evidence at all to support that. Quite possibly this particular site was chosen for a new principal church because it was already an important cult area: the broken cross-shafts from the site and from the earliest fabric of the church suggest that there had been a cemetery there during the ninth century and perhaps before, and, moreover, one containing high-status burials. Heighway has suggested that this may have been either a Hwiccian or a Mercian royal cemetery (1984a, 372; 1984b, 45); whether or not there had already been an associated chapel on the site, the location would clearly have suggested itself as an appropriate one for a major royal church.

As a prominent royal martyr, Oswald was a major saint, and his bones were potent relics. Alan Thacker has proposed that Æthelflæd's placing of royal relics at Gloucester, Shrewsbury and Chester had a political dimension: the fact that at both Shrewsbury and Gloucester the relics were of Northumbrian saints might have further served to reconcile the Mercians to rule by what could have been seen as an alien dynasty – albeit one with Wessex connections (Thacker 1982, 210–11). But in singling out the New Minster at Gloucester to be the repository for the relics of so prestigious a saint, Æthelred and Æthelflæd were favouring it above all other Mercian churches; in so doing, they surely intended this to be their own burial-place, to serve their own royal line as Repton and Winchcombe had served earlier dynasties of Mercian rulers (Taylor 1971, 351–89; Thacker 1985, 1–20; Bassett 1985, 82–100).

Both Æthelred and Æthelflæd were indeed buried at Gloucester (Campbell 1962, 53; ASC s.a. 918), but at first sight the evidence is against their burial at the New Minster: the Anglo-Saxon Chronicle was quite specific that Æthelflæd's burial place at Gloucester was in the east chapel of St Peter's, whilst William of Malmesbury's apparently confused account – which places her burial within St Peter's but defines it as the church Æthelflæd founded and hallowed with the relics of St Oswald – would seem to carry less authority (Stubbs 1887–9, i, 136). Yet, under the circumstances, it seems improbable that either of them should have preferred the Old Minster to their own foundation, and an alternative interpretation of these accounts of Æthelflæd's burial is called for.

It is significant that William of Malmesbury elsewhere wrote that the burial places of Æthelflæd and Æthelred at St Oswald's had recently been discovered (Hamilton 1870, 293), so there was really no confusion in his mind as to precisely which church had contained their tombs. Furthermore, it has already been remarked that the New Minster was evidently not built specifically as a resting place for St Oswald's bones, which were acquired subsequently as spoils of war in the joint West Saxon and Mercian campaign deep into the Danelaw of 909. Before then the church would have been dedicated to another saint, and is likely to have kept that earlier dedication for some time thereafter. When William of Malmesbury wrote, apparently in 1125 (Hamilton 1870, 442), the church's dedication to St Oswald was well established, but his account may have preserved an earlier form of words: taken literally, they imply that the minster founded by Æthelflæd and housing St Oswald's relics had originally been dedicated to St Peter. This is perfectly feasible, despite the existing dedication of the Old Minster to the same saint: St Peter was for long the most common dedication, and at Worcester the dedication of the cathedral church to St Peter did not prevent the same dedication being chosen for the nearby St Peter's church at some date before 969 (see below, p. 211). The Mercian Register's account of Æthelflæd's death, incorporated into the Anglo-Saxon Chronicle, was written presumably little more than a decade after St Oswald's bones arrived at Gloucester: an earlier dedication of the New Minster to St Peter would in all probability not yet have been superseded. The first reference to it as St Oswald's minster dates only from 1022 (*Hist. et Cart.*, i, 9).

In confirmation of this earlier dedication, Bishop Giso of Wells (1060–88) wrote in the 1070s or 1080s that his predecessor, Duduc (1033–60), had endowed his bishopric with the monastery of St Peter, Gloucester, which Cnut had given him before he became bishop. This, together with other valuable possessions of the bishopric, were subsequently seized by Harold as Earl of Wessex, and given to Archbishop Stigand. Giso went on to record his own success in recovering some of these lost lands from the newly crowned William, who further promised that as soon as he was able he would add to his gifts 'the monastery of Oswald' (Hunter 1840, 15–8). Now, the text does not unequivocally equate this monastery of Oswald of the 1060s with the Gloucester St Peter's that Duduc had brought to the bishopric, and which had been subsequently lost to Stigand, although the identification is implicitly made. But the story of Stigand's possession for a time of St Oswald's can be corroborated from other sources (see below), while what is known of the history of the Old Minster during this period shows that this cannot have been the St Peter's that Duduc gave to Wells. Emphasizing the last point, Barlow realized that it must in fact have been St Oswald's that Cnut had given to Duduc, and which Duduc had given to Wells; but he concluded that in calling it St Peter's Giso was simply mistaken (1963, 75n).

The Old Minster has not been excavated, and it is impossible to know whether it had an east chapel or not; but we have already seen that the New Minster did, in the shape of the mausoleum-like structure that was added to its east end and which we have suggested was built to house St Oswald's bones. It may indeed have been there that Æthelred and Æthelflæd were buried, as the Chronicle said. However, it was within the southern *porticus* of the church that William of Malmesbury said the tombs had been found during building work ordered by Thurstan, Archbishop of York, at some time between his accession in 1114 and William's stated date of writing of 1125 (Hamilton 1870, 293, 442). Perhaps William was misinformed on this occasion; but it is also possible that as the reputation of the royal couple waned with time – or as one or other of the tenth-century kings acted to minimize the prestige of his Mercian predecessors – their remains had been removed from their place of honour with St Oswald.

The tenth and eleventh centuries

St Oswald's continued to enjoy royal favour after Æthelflæd's death. In 1304, when the priory's status as a royal free chapel was disputed by the Archbishop of Canterbury, a transcript was produced in the court of King's Bench of what was said to be a charter of Æthelstan, given in the first year of his reign, in 925–6. According to the transcript, Æthelstan had confirmed to God 'the *monasterium* called New' where the remains of Oswald rested, and had freed it of all secular obligations. He went on to say that the minster had been founded by Ealdorman Æthelred, and that it had been built outside the old wall of the city of Gloucester (Sayles 1936–9, iii, 141).

Æthelstan and his court may have habitually visited Gloucester: certainly it was there, in 939, that he died (ASC, ms. D, s.a. 940). Otherwise, with the end of Mercian independence and the imposition of rule from Wessex after 919, Gloucester's importance as a centre of government inevitably diminished. The court must have visited Gloucester less frequently than the Mercian court had done under Æthelred and Æthelflæd. It is not possible to measure the effect that royal visits would have had on the development of the new *burh*, although the frequent presence in Gloucester of large numbers of nobles and their retinues would have been a stimulus to economic activity. But it is possible to exaggerate the extent to which Gloucester might have depended on such patronage, as there are clear indications that the city by now contained an urban population living by catering to the needs of the settled community of the district. Not only did the people of Gloucester make objects of wood and leather, perhaps as much for their own use as to sell; more importantly they were producing pottery to be traded to Worcester and Hereford, and manufacturing luxury items of silver and glass (Heighway 1984a, 377). The local market in these latter commodities was as likely to have been dominated by the ritual and individual needs of the ecclesiastical personnel of the two minsters as by the secular aristocracy who followed the court.

Already Gloucester had entered upon a period of sustained growth, judging by its evident size and wealth by the middle of the following century. According to Domesday Book, before 1066 it had paid £36 in farm as well as substantial amounts of iron – a reflection, together with the customary due of 12 sesters of honey, of its mercantile domination of a region which included the Forest of Dean (DB i, 162a). By 1086, its farm had increased to £60, its mint alone being worth £20 to the Crown. Domesday Book itself fails to reveal the full extent of Gloucester's population, but the survey made at most some fifteen years later and entered into the Evesham Abbey cartulary (BL Cotton MS. Vespasian B xxiv, fol. 57r; edited by Howard Clarke in Moore 1982, EvK) records that before 1066 there had been 300 burgesses dwelling in the city and paying landgable to the king, but that through houses becoming waste the number had fallen to 194 in 1100; in addition the lords of a further 312 tenants in 1100 were listed, bringing the reported total of burgesses dwelling in late eleventh-century Gloucester to 506. Even by the most cautious of population estimates this number of households would have contained at least 2000 people; it is most unlikely, moreover, that the head of every family held a tenancy directly from a great lord, so that Gloucester must have had a population considerably in excess of that figure.

The total of 10 churches reported in the *c.* 1100 survey is in keeping with such a population. As the city continued to grow, so Gloucester found itself by 1200 – and probably well before that date – with 14 or more churches, including the two monasteries and at least two of the four non-parochial chapels that are recorded (see Chapter 4 below).

The Gloucester minsters in the eleventh century

In 1070 St Oswald's minster suffered a severe – and as it turned out an irreversible – decline in status, when it lost the better part of its lands to the archbishopric of York. Domesday Book recorded that in 1086 Archbishop Thomas held a group of manors around Gloucester: Churchdown, Hucclecote, Norton, Swindon and Compton Abdale (DB i, 164c), and while only Swindon was specifically said to be of the land of St Oswald, there is little doubt that formerly the other manors had been as well, as the churches serving them were to remain chapelries of St Oswald's Priory until the Reformation (Astle, Ayscough and Caley 1802, 224; Caley 1810–34, ii, 487). In 1066 all these lands had been held by Stigand, who must subsequently have lost them on being deprived of the Archbishopric of Canterbury in 1070. Lassington, too, the church of which continued to pay a pension to St Oswald's (Caley 1810–34, ii, 487), was held by the Archbishop of York in 1086, as were Shipton and Hampen which it has been suggested were also originally lands of St Oswald's (DB i, 164c, 164d; Thompson 1921, 92). These three manors had been held by tenants in 1066. Two other manors which St Oswald's still held in 1086, Widford and North Cerney, were held now from the Archbishop of York as tenant in chief (DB i, 164d). In late eleventh-century Gloucester, the Archbishop of York held the largest number of houses after the King – 60 – while St Peter's Abbey held 52, and St Oswald's was listed as holding none (Moore 1982, EvK). Here, too, the minster had clearly lost its lands to the archbishopric. In recorded instances from later centuries, landgable was paid to the archbishops from tenements to the north of the precinct of St Peter's Abbey, close to St Oswald's and within its parish (see below, p. 284).

In fact, this loss of lands to the archbishopric was only the culmination of a series of reverses suffered by St Oswald's, which had begun half a century before. For as we have seen, it was evidently St Oswald's that Cnut gave to Duduc, before he became bishop in 1033, to be his by hereditary right, and which Duduc was to give to his own bishopric of Wells (Hunter 1840, 15–8). In 1061 the minster came into Stigand's possession (Barlow 1963, 75n). And why St Oswald's, with all its lands, was then given to the archbishopric of York after Stigand's disgrace, and not returned to Wells as Bishop Giso was promised, is really no mystery. For St Oswald's had not been alone in having suffered a loss of lands to York: St Peter's, too, by 1086 had similarly lost to the Archbishop of York its manors of Standish, Oddington – with its outlier Condicote – and Northleach – with its outliers in Stowell, Upper Coberley and Farmington (DB i, 164c, 164d).

It had been through their Worcester episcopacy that the archbishops had secured these lands of St Peter's. The arrangement following on Bishop Oswald's appointment to York in 972, that he should retain the wealthy see of Worcester in plurality, continued under his successors until 1016, and was revived briefly in 1040–41. When Bishop Ealdred of Worcester was appointed to York in 1061 he attempted to restore the link, and retain his Worcester see, until the intervention of Pope Nicholas II forced the appointment of a separate bishop for Worcester (Thompson 1921, 86–7; Stenton 1971, 436, 468). In 1062, therefore, Ealdred consecrated Wulfstan to be his successor at Worcester, but also perhaps in effect to be his suffragan, as Thompson suggested (1921, 86–7). As Bishop of Worcester Ealdred had, we are told, rebuilt St Peter's Abbey before 1058, when a kinsman of his was abbot, and in recompense had retained the manors of Northleach, Standish and Oddington (*Hist. et Cart.*, ii, 115). Domesday Book puts a different gloss upon events when it says that in 1066 St Peter's had held Northleach, and that 'Ealdred the archbishop held it with the abbey' (DB i, 164c): by implication St Peter's had remained firmly under his control even after his move to York in 1061. And it was surely the possession of these valuable estates in Gloucestershire after 1058 that made it logical for the archdiocese to seek to increase its holdings in the same locality.

One reason for the long association of Worcester with York was doubtless the relative impoverishment of the northern archdiocese (Stenton 1971, 436) during the tenth and eleventh centuries. This can only have been accentuated by William's devastation of wide areas of Northumbria in the winter of 1069–70, with its inevitable consequences for the archbishopric's revenues. Ealdred had died in September 1069, so the crisis came at a time when York was without an archbishop; at the same time, the excommunicated Stigand was now the only metropolitan in England, a situation that required swift resolution. The council necessary for his deposition met in April 1070; Stigand's removal from Canterbury, therefore, and the confiscation of most of his property – including evidently St Oswald's and its lands – coincided with the urgent need to provide new revenues for the northern archdiocese. During the last week of May, at Whitsun, William appointed Thomas, a canon of Bayeux, to the vacant archbishopric of York (Stenton 1971, 659, 664), and in view of the valuable estates York already held in Gloucestershire, Thomas might be expected to have asked to be given St Oswald's and its lands. Perhaps even before he had been installed at York at Christmas 1070 these lands had been relinquished by the King – although the church of St Oswald's itself, with its immediately adjacent property, remained for the time being in the hands of the Crown (Thompson 1921, 94).

By the end of the century, St Oswald's had become entirely subject to the archbishopric. It was still a possession to be coveted, for although it had lost most of its temporal revenues, it retained its substantial spiritual revenues from its former lands which continued to constitute its extensive parish. In the 1090s William II gave it to Archbishop Thomas, in part compensation for York's relinquishing to the new bishopric of Lincoln its claims to the ancient province of Lindsey. Thus St Oswald's and its dependent parishes became part of the diocese of York, and after the minster's reform as a house of Augustinian canons in 1153, the archbishops exercised their right to appoint successive priors (Thompson 1921, 97, 98, 131). The eclipse of St Oswald's was final, and it remained a minor religious house until the Dissolution.

By contrast, the revival of St Peter's during the post-Conquest period was spectacular. Its recovery began obviously with the appointment of the vigorous and forceful Serlo as abbot in 1072, although firm foundations on which he could build already existed. The minster had been reformed as a house of Benedictine monks, reportedly by Bishop Wulfstan I in 1022, and in 1058 a new church was consecrated (*Hist. et Cart.*, i, 8, 9). St Peter's had been the recipient of generous gifts of land during the Anglo-Saxon period, and despite the recent losses of land to York it must still, in 1072, have been a wealthy institution. But a measure of the prevailing neglect of recent years was Serlo's discovery, on his arrival, of only two adult monks and eight novices. When he died in 1104 there were reportedly 60 monks at Gloucester, and a new church – on which building had begun in 1089 – had been consecrated in 1100 (*Hist. et Cart.*, i, 10; *VCH Glos.*, ii, 54). In effect he had refounded the abbey, and on an ambitious scale. He recovered the abbey's manors of Standish, Oddington and Northleach, Archbishop Thomas having been forced to restore them to the abbey in 1095 (Thompson 1921, 95; *Hist. et Cart.*, i, 11–12); meanwhile, St Peter's had begun to be the recipient of numerous gifts of land from the new aristocracy of the region and beyond (*Hist. et Cart.*, i, 58–125; *VCH Glos.*, ii, 53–4), eager to associate themselves with this expression of the new religious and political order.

Chapter 3

The landscape of medieval Gloucester

Introduction

The physical setting

The siting of pre-Conquest and medieval Gloucester, as of Roman Glevum before it, was determined by the River Severn, the town – until recently – marking the lowest bridgeable point. The first Roman fort was built in the late 40s or 50s AD at Kingsholm, on the eastern edge of the floodplain (Heighway 1985, 1). A new fortress, which was to become the *colonia*, was established on a higher gravel terrace to the south, on a slight knoll lying west-east, the ground falling off towards stream-beds to the north and the south (Atkin 1991a, 6). The fortress was built about 250 metres from the riverbank opposite a small inlet (Atkin 1991c, 16) (fig. 3.1).

The course of the Severn through the Gloucester area is distinctive in that it divides into a number of separate channels of roughly equal width (there are at present two); additionally, the

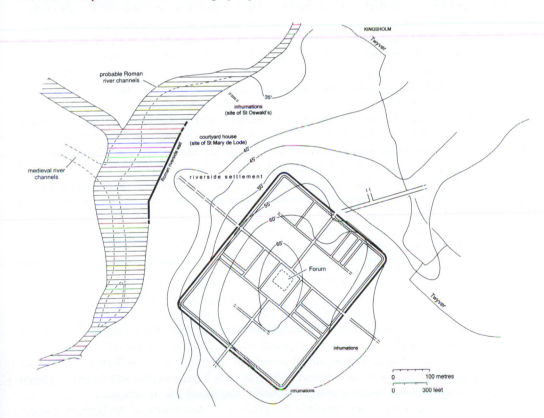

3.1　Roman Gloucester: the site (modern contours and Roman and medieval river channels) with the fortress and its street-plan

Severn is joined here by the River Leadon feeding in from the west. The Severn channels appear to have changed in course and in number between the late prehistoric and modern periods as a result of both natural processes and human intervention; an evolutionary sequence has been worked out by Rowbotham (1978). A single primary river channel running along the eastern side of the floodplain had bifurcated by the Roman period, developing a secondary westward loop (the west or Maisemore channel). This parted company from the primary channel about 2 kilometres north of the site of Gloucester, rejoining the main channel directly opposite the town site. The return leg of this western channel effectively formed a tidal watercourse crossing the floodplain diagonally from shore to shore, a distance of about 1.5 kilometres. Rowbotham suggests that this channel was used in the Roman period by ferries making use of the tides, but also able to be towed from a towpath along the south bank; this towpath was later used as the basis for the causeway known as Over Causeway.

Rowbotham also argues that, with the tidal flows in this configuration of river channels, there would have been no need for a major bridge here in the Roman period (1978, 4, 6). This is a contentious point. While there is certainly a lack of evidence for a Roman bridge at Gloucester (see Hurst 1986, 116), much the same may also be said of both Worcester and Wroxeter, and of early medieval Shrewsbury upstream (Carver 1980, 19–21; Pannett 1989). It is difficult to believe that the Severn was bridged at none of these points and was therefore uncrossable for several weeks in each year. It seems more likely that the same conditions that would have made permanent bridges essential in any period – strong currents, rapid winter flooding and shifting channels – have resulted in the destruction or concealment of the relevant archaeological evidence.

During the post-Roman centuries a third watercourse was formed by natural action, bisecting the island between the primary channel and secondary western channel. Rowbotham suggests that this occurred in the sixth or early seventh century, but gives no supporting evidence (1978, 8–9). The new channel joined the return leg of the western channel just short of its confluence with the primary eastern channel. Two changes took place thereafter that were either wholly artificial or were at least promoted or enlarged by human interference; these will be discussed in greater detail later. First, the final stretch of the latest, central, channel was diverted or broke out of its previous course, breaking through the line of the suggested Roman towpath and rejoining the primary channel to the south of it; its old bed to the north of the towpath or causeway silted up rapidly but remained a minor watercourse until much later; the area thus defined by the primary east channel and the new and old legs of the central channel formed the area known as Westgate Island. Secondly, the return leg of the western channel was diverted southwards to rejoin the primary channel well south of the town site: this may have been an action taken to reduce silting at the town quays (Rowbotham 1978, 8–9).

So, by perhaps the end of the twelfth century, a traveller leaving Gloucester for the west bank would have had to cross two or even three arms of the River Severn. The Foreign Bridge carried traffic from the built-up area on the east bank over the primary eastern channel and on to Westgate Island. Next, the Westgate Bridge led over the recently established course of the middle channel to Alney Island, lying between the middle and the western or Maisemore channel. Alney Island was crossed on Over Causeway, suggested by Rowbotham to represent a development based on the line of the Roman towpath. Whether the western channel still flowed along the northern side of the causeway, or whether it had already been diverted southwards, making necessary a third and final bridge-crossing just before the west bank, is uncertain.

The final episode in the story concerns the gradual disappearance of the primary eastern channel. This was possibly due in part to the deposition of silt as the current was slowed by the piers of the Foreign Bridge. But urban reclamation processes and dumping certainly contributed, excavation having shown that the process of urban extension westwards at the expense of this channel began as early as the second century (Atkin 1991c). By 1370 the eastern channel was known as the 'Little Severn', the middle or Westgate Channel as the 'Great Severn' (Hurst 1974, 36); Speed drew the eastern channel in the early seventeenth century as a minor watercourse or ditch, as did Kip a century later; by the 1880s it was culverted, and invisible above ground.

In addition to the natural line of communication provided by the Severn, medieval Gloucester inherited its Roman predecessor's road system. Five main roads left the town: from the north gate heading north, past the site of the Kingsholm fort, up the Severn valley to Worcester; north-east, to join the Ermin Way running from the Kingsholm site to Cirencester and London; south-east from the east gate along the Port Way into the densely populated agricultural countryside below the Cotswold Escarpment; south from the south gate, into the Vale of Berkeley; and west over the Severn towards Ariconium, Caerwent and Stretton Grandison.

Roman Gloucester

In the late 60s AD the Kingsholm fort was dismantled. The new fortress that was built to the south occupied an area of some 43 acres (17.4 hectares) and was defended by a turf-faced clay rampart with timber towers and gates. After AD 87, possibly in AD 96–8 following the foundation of the *Colonia Nerviana Glevensium*, the military barrack blocks within were demolished and replaced by civilian buildings, built to more or less the same plan but equipped with stone footings for a longer life. The military street-system was retained, and the defences were probably improved at this date by the addition of a stone wall to the front of the legionary ramparts (Heighway 1985; Hurst 1976; 1986).

By the second century the town had acquired a monumental civic centre. A forum had been built in the centre of the fortress on the site of the military *principia* – placed, unusually, across the line of the principal north-south axial street. The forum basilica stood to the south of a paved courtyard flanked by colonnaded ranges. The *insulae* to the north and west also contained large colonnaded public buildings of some description; one may possibly have been a public baths. Finds of wooden water pipes and stone drains suggest that public services as well as public buildings were provided (Hurst 1976; Heighway and Garrod 1980).

Outside the forum, some of the first-generation colonial terrace buildings remained in use, and were to do so until the end of the Roman period. Others were replaced, and there was a general trend towards the construction of smaller numbers of larger houses: wealth, it seems, was gradually concentrated in fewer hands within the *colonia*. Evidence of buildings with mosaic floors has been found throughout the fortress area and also in the western and northern suburbs (Hurst 1976, 78).

By the end of the second century suburban occupation had developed to the north, south and west of the fortress. Of these areas, the most densely occupied and most prosperous may have been that by the river to the west of the fortress. Buildings with mosaics are known from sites either side of the *via principalis* (the predecessor of Westgate Street), most notably the substantial and richly appointed building discovered in 1825 underlying the church of St Mary de Lode (Bryant 1980). The waterfront itself was the subject of substantial investment over a long period of time. A number of excavations have been able to document the process of westward reclamation, and the construction along the new shoreline of a substantial masonry wall in the second or third century (Hurst 1974, 46–9; Hurst 1986, 115–16; Atkin 1991c). There has been extensive discussion of the possibility that the riverside wall had a defensive function, linked to the fortress walls to form a secondary defensive enclosure, not unlike the *Lower Colonia* at Lincoln (e.g. Heighway 1984a,

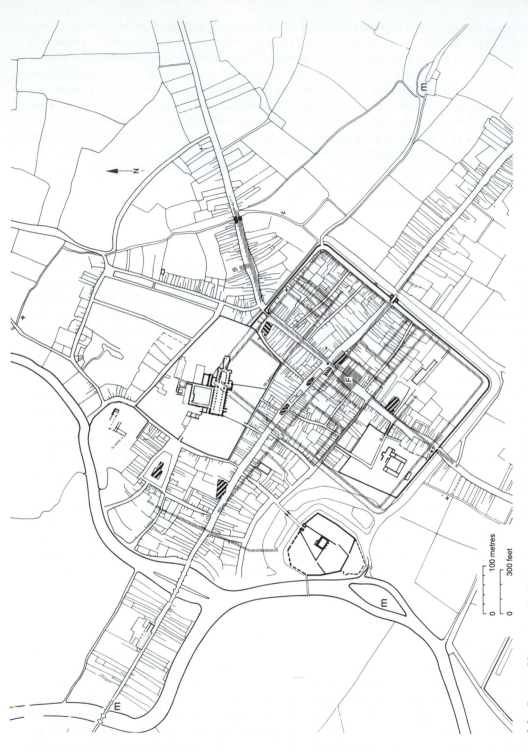

3.2　Roman Gloucester: the Roman street-plan and its relationship to the medieval and later city

359). However, evidence for return walls linking the riverside wall to the main defences has not been forthcoming, and the most recent contribution to the debate suggests that the riverside wall was constructed for revetment and mooring only and was unlikely to have been defensive in origin (Hurst 1986).

Suburban settlement also developed outside the south gate, though its extent was limited (Atkin 1990). Far more extensive were the suburbs extending from the north gate northwards towards Kingsholm and north-eastwards along London Road. A boundary – possibly the River Twyver – just north of the later St Catherine's Street may have defined the northern extent of suburban settlement north of the fortress; occupation beyond this, extending into the Kingsholm area, was based on a different, local, alignment (Hurst 1986, 115). Cemeteries were established at the limits of the occupied area; a municipal tilery excavated by the river on the St Oswald's site in the western suburb represents another extramural land use (Heighway and Parker 1982).

The end of Roman Gloucester

Late Roman Gloucester witnessed a number of changes that were widely paralleled in contemporary towns. The evidence for the transition from Roman *Glevum* to early medieval Gloucester is sparse: it illuminates processes of change in the landscape of some areas, but not yet in others; what it does show is that different parts of the Roman built-up area could be subject to very various fortunes – from clearance and vigorous re-use, to abandonment and slow decay. The evidence for the strength and direction of the local economy is, likewise, too incomplete for the formulation of general models to explain the processes of change, but it is certain that the late- and post-Roman periods cannot be characterized simply in terms of either swift collapse or lingering economic decline.

At the end of the third century or in the early fourth, the town's defences were strengthened. The walls themselves were rebuilt in concrete over the re-used oolite blocks of the earlier wall, external bastions were added, a new wider inner ditch dug and the outer ditch recut, and the town gates were modified (Hurst 1986; Heighway 1983a). There is also some evidence for the fate of the monumental public buildings in the centre of town. The excavations at No.1 Westgate Street, within the confines of a narrow, cellared property, exposed a thin slice across the Roman east–west *via principalis* with the buildings on its north frontage and the colonnaded edge of the forum forecourt on its south frontage. Excavation at 11–17 Southgate Street straddled the east range of the forum and the corner of the forum basilica. The building on the north side of the *via principalis* underwent a process of sub-division and possibly conversion to industrial or domestic functions in the late third or early fourth century. Later in the fourth century (*c.* 370–90) it was demolished and a small wooden building – possibly used by a butcher – was built on its site (Heighway, Garrod and Vince 1979; Heighway and Garrod 1980). The forum buildings themselves, where excavated, appear to have been dismantled well before the end of the fourth century; the surface of the forum courtyard, denuded of its flagstones, acquired a deposit of soil and contemporary rubbish (Hurst 1972, 58). After *c.* 390 an extensive metalled surface composed of re-used Roman building materials was laid over the site of the forum and its building-ranges, extending northwards over the *via principalis* and over the site of the buildings that had lain on its north frontage.

The re-organization of the forum area was accompanied by the realignment of the access from the west gate. In the middle of the insula to the north of the forum and the *via principalis*, a row of columns about 32 metres north of the old frontage was left standing, as was an adjacent row on roughly the same line in the insula to the west. These appear to have been used to define the north side of a new route to the central area. The line of the *via principalis* can be shown to have gone out of use – at least in the area of the forum – immediately before the new central area metalling was laid, as a number of pits had been dug through it (Heighway, Garrod and Vince 1979; Heighway and Garrod 1980). The new approach – which eventually became Westgate Street – appears to have taken a pragmatic course across open ground south of the line of columns through an area that had been used for iron-smelting, perhaps in the third and fourth centuries (Atkin 1992b, 45; Garrod, in Heighway and Garrod 1980, 81). The details of the evolution of Westgate Street as a successor to the *via principalis* are, however, still less than clear. While the Roman street was eliminated at the forum end as the fourth century drew to a close (Heighway, Garrod and Vince 1979, 163), the line of medieval Westgate Street in the area of the western fortress wall was only established in the 'Saxo-Norman period' following the demolition of surviving Roman buildings on the *intervallum* road just inside it; the Roman west gate must, by implication, have survived in use long after the diversion of the *via principalis* close to the centre (Atkin 1992b, 46). The earliest metalling on the line of Westgate Street at a point roughly half-way between the forum site and the west wall, excavated in a trench at No. 30 Westgate Street, contained eleventh-century pottery; it overlay an undated hearth built on top of green silty soil containing bone and late Roman pottery (Garrod, in Heighway and Garrod 1980, 83).

To interpret these sequences simply as evidence of decay and impoverishment would be wrong. Buildings were demolished – a deliberate and even costly process – so that their sites or their materials could be put to new uses. These events demonstrate beyond any doubt that, just as at the beginning of the fourth century, so too at the end of the century some kind of civic authority was being exercised in the town, though where this authority was exercised from remains unknown. There is, so far, little hard evidence of the functions that the successor-forum was expected to house, but by far the most likely is that of an inherited role as a central market place (Heighway et al. 1979, 163–5); it may have remained in use for as long as five hundred years, until the postulated replanning at the end of the ninth century. As Darvill has noted, it is just as difficult to detect mercantile activity in Gloucester in the Roman period as it is in the post-Roman period; this, and the presence of fourth- to sixth-century imported amphorae from various sites suggest that it would be dangerous to dismiss the possibility of continuing economic activity as well as other central-place functions at the heart of late- and post-Roman Gloucester (Vince, in Heighway et al. 1979, 171; Darvill 1988, 45). The events noted here bear some resemblance to those in the civic centre of Wroxeter, though the large-scale reorganization of the baths basilica site there may have taken place over a century later than the reorganization of the Gloucester forum (White and Barker 1998).

The retention of the line of columns along what was to become Westgate Street raises an interesting question. It is difficult to believe that, despite their large size (one metre or so in diameter), they were left because their removal presented insoluble technical problems; as far as we know no such problems were encountered in the removal of the forum basilica. Rather, we must accept the possibility that the colonnades were retained for their architectural value. Wroxeter again provides a parallel, in the form of the symmetrically planned, winged and colonnaded but timber-framed building constructed on the site of the baths basilica, probably in the mid sixth century (White and Barker 1998, 121–4). Roman monumental building forms may have been impossibly expensive to maintain and difficult to adapt, but their symbolic significance was still important to the town – or to whatever authority governed it.

In the intramural areas away from the forum there is, so far, no sign of the kind of radical reorganization of the late-Roman landscape that took place at the centre. Instead, the evidence from excavations over the last twenty years suggests that much of the former fortress was gradually abandoned by any permanent population and given back to agriculture. So, in the absence of any comprehensive redevelopment, elements of the late-Roman landscape survived. Apart from the diversion of the *via principalis* west of the forum, the line of the Roman through-streets was maintained into the medieval period; doubtless this was in part due to the stabilizing influence of the surviving gates, but continuity of traffic may also have been a factor. Not just the through-streets survived: in the south-west quarter a minor north–south street on the Blackfriars site was found to have been maintained into the late pre-Conquest period when it was re-metalled (Atkin 1992a, 35–7); the medieval Smith Street (Longsmith Street) also reflects the line of a minor east–west Roman street, which must have been fossilized as a boundary if it was not maintained as a thoroughfare. Roman streets (or boundaries based on them) may also have defined the block of land in the north-west quarter which formed the first precinct of the Old Minster in the late seventh century (see below, p. 44).

The town's domestic buildings show signs of continuing, if dwindling, occupation through the fourth century and probably into the fifth. Some underwent a slow process of adaptation and gradual abandonment; elsewhere there is evidence of a return to timber construction, and disused buildings could be subject to sporadic re-occupation. The character of the final use of a building on the south side of a minor Roman street on the New Market Hall site varied from room to room: in some, original floors were kept and patched; in others, new crude flooring was introduced; one room had a hearth installed, posts and a gully were cut into the floor of another. In one room a collapsed roof sealed a collection of the latest Roman pottery types and some metal-working debris; a hoard of late Roman coins concealed in the roof collapsed with it. This building came to an abrupt end, destroyed by fire; a human jaw bone in a deposit overlying the floor in one room and a spearhead lying on the surviving mosaic in another suggested troubled times for the last occupants (Hassall and Rhodes 1974, 27–30).

On a site excavated at 28–32 Commercial Road, in the town's south-west quarter and within the confines of the first motte-and-bailey castle, a large, well-appointed, possibly official, courtyard house remained in use in the late fourth or early fifth century, though not in the way its builders had intended. Silts accumulated on floors, and hearths were built inside and on the verandah. In the phase of activity that followed, occupation debris, with large quantities of animal bone and several pieces of human bone, was thrown into the yard outside to form a midden whose composition was very similar to that of the 'dark earth' deposits found covering Roman levels over much of the town. The midden contained late Roman pottery and pieces of imported north African amphorae. There was also a quantity of hand-made pottery probably from the fifth to seventh centuries, not previously seen in Gloucester but similar to types previously found in the upper Thames Valley (Vince 1988, 21). Pottery of this type was also found in residual contexts in a later excavation about 70 metres to the north, also within the confines of the first castle (site 20/90: Atkin 1991a, 7). Taken together, these discoveries may suggest that there was a nucleus of activity before the end of the seventh century in this corner of the fortress enclosure, though it would be stretching the evidence too far at present to suggest that the siting of the eleventh-century castle was in any way associated with this (pers. comm., Malcolm Atkin). The Commercial Road building was re-occupied by a farrier's workshop in the late pre-Conquest period and remained standing until the first castle earthworks were constructed (Darvill 1988).

A courtyard house excavated at 13–17 Berkeley Street was demolished within the Roman period and replaced by a timber building with walls founded on sill beams; its occupation and destruction were associated with late Roman coinage. Other buildings remained occupied until the last quarter of the fourth century; in the ruins of one a wall was built on a timber sill, while a sequence of ovens associated with rubble layers appeared in its former courtyard (Hurst 1972, 43; 1974, 23). Another courtyard house excavated in the Blackfriars area (the Ladybellegate

Street Car Park) showed possible signs of late pre-Conquest re-use: at the same time as a surviving Roman road outside was re-metalled, a new dividing wall was inserted into the building (Atkin 1992a, 37).

The late-Roman levels on the Berkeley Street site were covered by a thick layer of grey loam which, analysis suggested, had been formed by cultivation. It contained late Roman pottery, coins and bone, and Roman building materials mixed in at the bottom, but became progressively cleaner towards the top. Some Saxo-Norman pottery occurred in it, and it was sealed by Saxo-Norman clay floors and occupation layers (Hurst 1972, 43; 1974, 23–4). Similar 'dark earth' deposits have been found on widely scattered sites in Gloucester, as in many other towns. That on the Commercial Road site, formed by midden accumulation, has already been described. A deposit of this kind was also found covering a Roman metalled surface in a suburban context, at the Tanners' Hall site on Hare Lane. Analysis of this suggested that it had been deliberately dumped and organic matter added to provide a cultivable soil (Heighway 1983b, 90).

Post-Roman deposits significantly different in character have however been seen on a number of sites at the centre: these are the manure-like organic deposits dated to the eighth to the tenth centuries that accumulated over the successor-forum, probably representing intensive occupation by humans and animals (Heighway et al. 1979; Heighway 1984a, 364–5). A similar deposit between the west gate and the river on the Shire Hall site may possibly be indicative of another concentration of activity at a similar date or may simply reflect ground conditions in the area of a former stream or inlet (Abbott 1967).

The decline in the permanent population evident within the walls is reflected by the contraction of the suburbs. The maximum extent of the earlier Roman occupied area can be reconstructed from the location of a ring of cremation cemeteries; inhumation cemeteries likely to belong to the final years of the Roman period occur well within this zone, notably in the Kingsholm area and on the site of St Oswald's Priory in the western suburb (Hurst 1985, 131–2). But the rapidity of this contraction should not be exaggerated. A building with monumental features outside the North Gate 'continued in use well into the fourth century or later' (63–71 Northgate Street: Hurst 1972, 43 n.1 and 63–5).

Late-Roman suburban cemeteries have a special place in European archaeology as sources of evidence for exotic elements in urban populations and as potential settings for long-lived cult activities. Heighway has drawn attention to coincidences between Roman cemeteries and places of significance in the late pre-Conquest period, as at the Wotton Pitch cemetery on the Ermin Way – a hundredal meeting-place in the tenth century, marked by a cross-shaft – while noting that such instances may indeed just be coincidental (1984b, 36). By far the most spectacular example in Gloucester of a persistent focus of activity developing from a late-Roman suburban context is that of the church of St Mary de Lode. Here, a lavish Roman building close to the waterfront became the site of a fifth to eighth century mausoleum and, ultimately, a church (Bryant 1980; Bassett 1992; see below p. 98). And, to the north of the city, a cemetery on the former Kingsholm fort included late-Roman burials of high status; this was eventually to become the site of a late-Saxon royal palace.

An introduction to the medieval town-plan (figs. 3.3, 3.4 and 3.5)

The town-plan of late-medieval Gloucester – the principal features of which are reconstructed in fig. 3.3 – was dominated by three major enclosures. Of these, the largest and most striking was the incomplete form of the Roman fortress, its distinctive rounded corners visible to the north-east and south-east. The invisibility of the fortress's west wall is perhaps as striking as the survival of

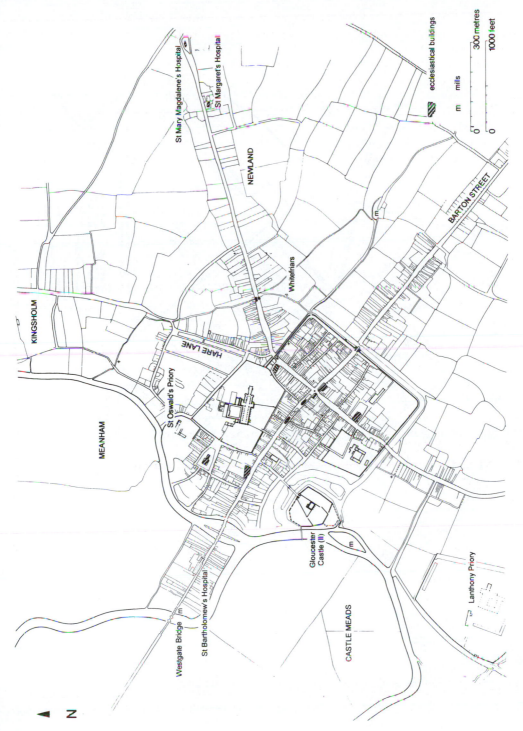

3.3   Gloucester: the principal features of the medieval city and suburbs

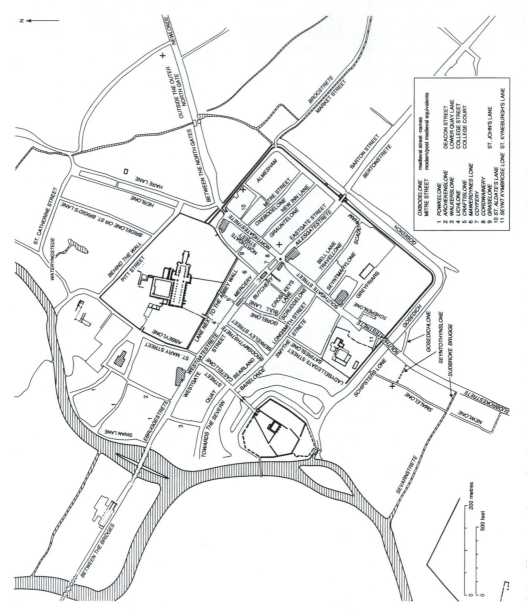

3.4   Gloucester: the medieval and modern street-names (medieval names are *italicised*)

the remainder and immediately, inevitably, provokes the question: what happened to it? When, and how, did it disappear? The town-plan itself seems to offer at least a partial answer through the apparently superimpositionary character of the two remaining major enclosures: on the north side, the rectilinear precinct of St Peter's Abbey, the Old Minster; and on the south, the massive ditches and curtain walls of the twelfth-century royal castle. Within the old fortress area the main streets leading from the central crossroads (the Cross) to the surviving gates give the illusion of an intact Roman street-system, one strengthened by the replication of the Roman alignment by most of the minor intramural streets and property boundaries. Nevertheless, the west wall of the fortress remains invisible in the plan even in the narrow gap between the military and ecclesiastical precincts, the built-up area extending westwards to the river with no obvious sign of discontinuity.

Suburbs extended from the gates in the intact walls – simple linear growths from the south and east sides, and on Westgate Island across the first river channel, with more complex forms outside the north gate. There, the main approach road forked immediately, the more northerly branch – the elongated rectangle of Hare Lane – forming one side of a roughly rectilinear arrangement of subsidiary streets, the other branch (London Road, the link from the north gate to the earlier Roman alignment of the Ermin Way) accompanied by another linear suburb whose plots decreased in density with distance from the gate.

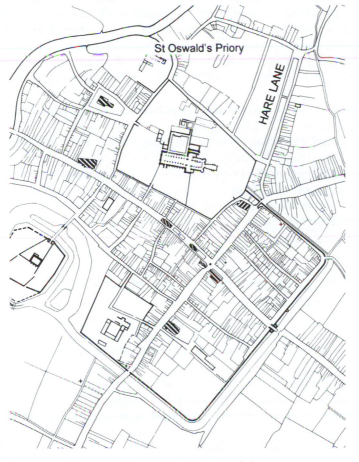

3.5   Gloucester, the principal features of the medieval intramural city

The built-up area to the west of the fortress and north of the castle extended down to the river around the two distinct foci of Lower Westgate Street, the axis of what was in effect a further linear suburb, and St Mary's Square. The latter, symmetrically disposed about the church of St Mary de Lode, appears as a separate nucleus of settlement clustering outside the west gate of the abbey precinct. Adjoining it to the north was the precinct of St Oswald's Priory, its curved eastern boundary reflecting its origin as a ditched enclosure with one side adjoining the river. From its plan alone, it is fairly readily apparent that late-medieval Gloucester was an amorphous entity that had outgrown its Roman enceinte in a number of directions, without the formative constraint of a single later outer defence. The plan alone shows that late-medieval Gloucester must have been defended – if at all – by a series of separate, linked, defences.

Dismantling the town-plan (figs. 3.6 and 3.7)

A brief examination of Gloucester's town-plan shows that analysis is unlikely to be a simple process. The initial stage of disaggregation – the definition of individual components within the plan – immediately presents difficulties. To begin with, there is a marked difference in the visibility of components between the centre and the periphery, a phenomenon also noted by Lilley (1991) in Coventry. The suburbs to the east, south and west (Barton Street, Southgate Street and Westgate Island) were physically separated from neighbouring built-up areas by fields, watercourses or defences; each arguably displayed a degree of internal morphological homogeneity in their respective landscapes and may thus be claimed to satisfy Conzen's original definition of a 'plan-unit'; they correspond approximately in scale to the second-order plan-units defined in his study of Alnwick (Conzen 1969, 108–18). They present a marked contrast to the intramural area.

   Within the walls the picture is much more complicated but, nevertheless, a number of localized variations in the character of the plan may be defined. Leaving aside for the moment the abbey precinct, a fundamental distinction existed between the western and eastern (more correctly, the north-west and south-east) halves, based on the different characteristics of the street-systems in each area. At the beginning of the 1970s Henry Hurst drew attention to what appeared to be a planned rectilinear grid of streets lying to the east of the Northgate–Southgate Street axis; it bore a marked resemblance to the street-plan of Winchester and was on this basis interpreted as an example of late-Saxon town-planning (Hurst 1972; Biddle and Hill 1971). Within the western half of the intramural area, although nearly all the streets reflected the controlling alignment of the containing Roman walls, no such grid-system was evident: the hypothesized pre-Conquest replanning appears to have been restricted to the eastern half of the fortress. But within the western half, a further fundamental distinction may also be drawn between the areas either side of the east–west axis of Westgate Street. To the north lay the abbey precinct, fringed by distinctive street-blocks containing series of plots facing outwards to the main streets and backing onto the minor lanes following the precinct walls. To the south of Westgate Street a more random, if still rectilinear arrangement of streets and lanes, framed series of plots that varied in character at a very small scale – from street to street and lane to lane.

   But the intense local variations in the character of plots visible in the western half of Gloucester is equally apparent in the eastern half, within but unregulated by the much more uniform arrangement of streets. In short, 'morphological unity' is apparent at a number of quite different scales, within the various form complexes that made up the town-plan as a whole. At the largest scale, the built-up area of medieval (or indeed modern) Gloucester may be defined as a single entity separable from the surrounding countryside. Insights into the development of the town may, however, only begin to be found at the next level of definition, what may be termed a 'plan-region'.

Six such regions may arguably be discerned within Gloucester's medieval landscape; each contained a number of quite disparate, large-scale components but nevertheless had some factor – generally a street-system – that imparted a degree of overall unity to that area. So, as outlined above, within the walls a distinction may be drawn; first, between the north-west quadrant containing the abbey precinct and the blocks of property surrounding it (characterized here as plan-region I); second, the south-west quadrant, containing an irregular street network framing a diverse collection of individual plot-series (plan-region II); and third, the eastern half of the town, containing a similarly eclectic cadastral landscape but set within a regular framework of streets (plan-region III). Within these plan-regions, smaller-scale plan divisions may be defined. The great majority of these are plot-series particular to individual streets or street-blocks, generally covering an area of less than two acres (0.8 hectare), and many less than one. They correspond approximately to Conzen's fourth-order sub-types in Alnwick (Conzen 1969, 108–18) and Slater's plan sub-units in Doncaster (Slater 1989); Slater's terminology is adopted here. Somewhat larger-scale components, comparable with some of the suburbs, are also apparent within the north-west and eastern plan-regions: the street-blocks fringing the abbey precinct and those lying either side of Eastgate Street. These have been treated as plan-units (I.2, I.3 and III.1), approximating to the second-order plan-units in the Alnwick study (Conzen 1969, 108–18).

The built-up area between the fortress and the river has been defined as a fourth plan-region – albeit a very loosely structured one. It contained four areas, treated as plan-units, utterly distinct from each other in terms of both their morphology and their known land-use, though their common relationship to the eastern channel of the Severn and – consequent upon this – some parallels in their development, provide a degree of unity. These components were Lower Westgate Street (plan-region IV, plan-unit 1); St Mary's Square (IV. 2); the precinct of St Oswald's Priory (IV. 3); and the second castle (IV. 4). Each of these plan-units contained smaller-scale plan-divisions (sub-units). The integrity of Lower Westgate Street as a plan-unit is arguable on the grounds that the area was obviously distinct in form and in function from the castle to the south, and was separated by a long, continuous, common boundary from the plots around St Mary's Square to the north. The plots on either side of the road were also of approximately equal depth. Yet within this distinct plan-unit lay subtle but nevertheless equally distinct variations in the character of the plots in each of the four component street-blocks; these have been treated as sub-units (IV. 1. i–iv).

To the north lay the Hare Lane–Wateringtead area (plan-region V). A discrete part of the town, it was enclosed by the course of the River Twyver and a degree of unity imparted to its very diverse components by its street system. Analysis of this area is hampered by loss of information through late- and post-medieval desertion. The remaining parts of the medieval built-up area were linear suburbs. The Northgate Street/London Road suburb was the most extensive and had the most complex structure, and warrants treatment as a plan-region (VI). It was a distinct area of ribbon development, separated by undeveloped land or by a clear boundary from neighbouring areas. Within the suburb were a number of distinct areas containing plots of different character; these have been treated as plan-units (VI.1–3) and have, in turn, been further broken down into sub-units where there appear to be significant morphological differences between adjacent plot-series. Finally, Barton Street, Lower Southgate Street and Westgate Island – each less extensive and more unified in structure than Northgate Street – have been treated as three independent suburban plan-units (1–3), though they too exhibit some degree of internal variation in their morphology notably, in Barton Street and Lower Southgate Street, between the character of the plot-series on either side of the respective streets.

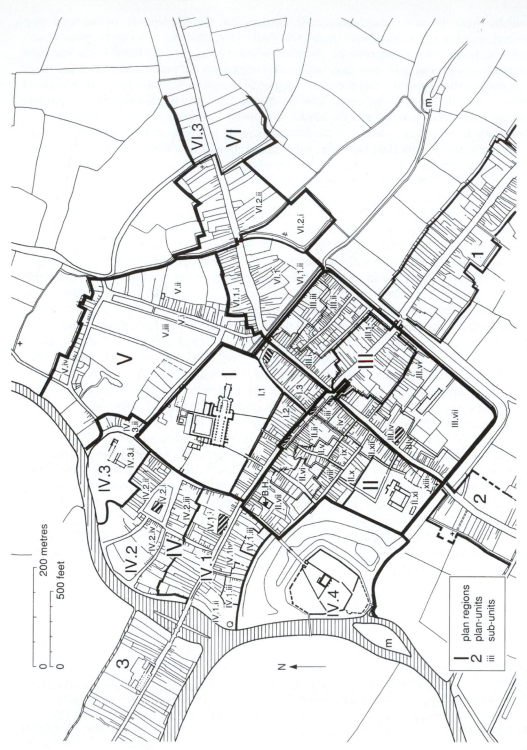

3.6 Gloucester: town-plan analysis. The plan components of the city and suburbs

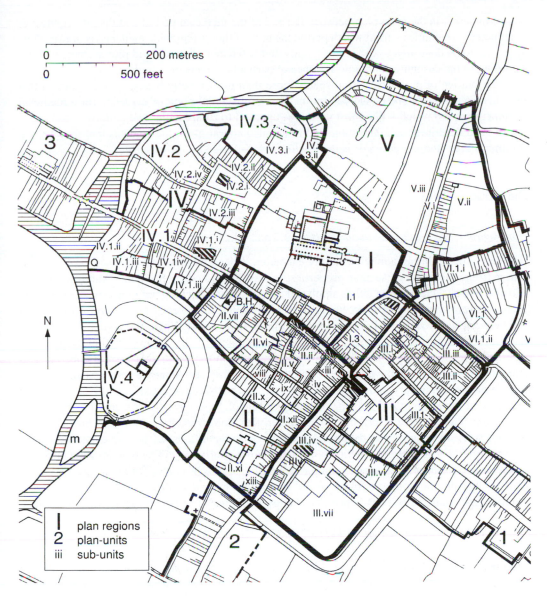

3.7 Gloucester: town-plan analysis. The plan components of the intramural city

This disaggregation process is a necessary first step towards an understanding of the sequence of and processes behind the growth of the medieval town, and the agencies responsible for it; it is a means to a historical end, not an end in itself. The historical significance of the plan-divisions defined here may be expected to vary greatly, and their chronology, formation, and administrative or jurisdictional relationships (or our ignorance of them) will be explored in the following section and in subsequent chapters. But it is equally necessary to make some assessment of the degree of change apparent in the town plan between the end of the medieval period and the late eighteenth and nineteenth centuries – from which period the bulk of the cartographic evidence is drawn. This, again, has to be done area by area, the stability and behaviour of street- and plot-systems varying according to the changing economic fortunes of particular streets or suburbs.

If the burden of pure description seems more than occasionally heavy, it is because in this town (as we shall also see in Worcester) there is a substantial body of evidence for a medieval settlement pattern which – like most urban (as opposed to rural) settlement patterns – has never before been described, let alone subjected to detailed appraisal. In the analysis that follows, the intramural area (loosely defined) is dealt with first, followed by the suburbs.

The intramural city

Plan-region I: the north-west quadrant (figs 3.7 and 12.2)

The landscape of this area may be simply characterized as that of a large ecclesiastical precinct with a fringe or screen of secular properties. It was dominated by St Peter's Abbey – the Old Minster; narrow lanes ran around its south and east walls, and backing onto these were tenements facing outwards onto the main streets. There is no evidence of any early tenurial or jurisdictional link between the precinct and the properties forming this secular fringe: the component parts of this plan-region were tenurially and functionally quite distinct. They were, nevertheless, morpho-genetically related, though in different ways. The plots on the south side form a coherent and distinct series whose extent was clearly related to that of the precinct at the rear; it is argued later that the precinct boundary and the plot-series were laid out simultaneously. On the east side, the boundary of the precinct and the lane following it (St John's or Grass Lane), and thus the extent of the plots outside, were determined by an underlying Roman road. The way in which the plots on both sides were subsequently developed was certainly influenced by the existence of the precinct behind. Commercial functions (and therefore the formation of new plots) were inhibited on the single-frontage back lanes running around the walls. In contrast, the two narrow lanes leading through the southern block from Westgate Street to gates into the precinct were commercially valuable and developed dense clusters of small intensively subdivided properties.

PLAN-UNIT I.1: THE PRECINCT OF ST PETER'S ABBEY (fig 12.2)

The precinct, in the form seen in fig. 12.2, represents the end result of a process of expansion that was completed in 1218 (*VCH Glos.*, iv, 275). The late-medieval internal geography of the fully developed precinct will be described and the evidence for the stages in its expansion discussed subsequently. It will not be appropriate here to stray far into the architectural history of the conventual or domestic buildings, which has received attention elsewhere (Hope 1897; *VCH Glos.*, iv. 275–88; Welander 1991).

The later-medieval monastic precincts were divided into six principal zones. The abbey church, the present cathedral, lies centrally placed within the precinct, orientated approximately east–west, in contrast to the north-west–south-east alignment of the Roman and later town. The planning of the church and the claustral ranges conforms broadly to the familiar Benedictine tradition. The church is substantially that built by Abbot Serlo between 1089 and 1100, the main modification to its external plan being the addition of the lady chapel of 1224–8. The cloisters lay to the north, this arrangement allowing the removal of the monastic offices from the principal public approach to the church, and the use of the water supply of the Fullbrook that may previously have flowed outside the Roman north wall. The claustral ranges appear to have been built and completed in the twelfth century, though they were largely reconstructed in the fourteenth. The refectory, raised over a vaulted undercroft, lay opposite and parallel to the church, forming the north range. In the east range was the dormitory, probably linked to a reredorter over a channel of the Fullbrook, and the three-bay chapter house which survives. The west range included a tower at the south end that may originally have accommodated the abbot (St John Hope 1897, 87–102; *VCH Glos.*, iv, 277–9).

To the north of the claustral area lay further detached ranges, built at a later date on ground acquired from St Oswald's Priory. To the north-east lay the thirteenth-century infirmary, a six-bay aisled hall incorporating the earlier chapel of St Brigid in its east end; this had formerly been free-standing on St Oswald's property (see below p. 125). To the north-west of the cloisters stood the abbot's lodgings, built after 1329. A hall with chambers stood at the west end, a chapel at the east; the ranges were extended in the fifteenth century and again in the early sixteenth (Hope 1897, 103–6, 109–10; *VCH Glos.*, iv, 282–3).

To the west of the refectory lay Miller's Green – the monastic inner court – containing a mill over one of the culverted watercourses, kitchens and other service buildings. The area was divided by an east–west range, penetrated by a gateway, from the Outer or Great Court occupying the south-west quarter of the precinct. This, the most public space, was and still is dominated by the west front of the abbey church. Buildings were ranged around the precinct walls to the west and south and are likely to have included lower-status guest accommodation. The original abbot's lodgings on the west of the cloisters, taken over by the prior in the early fourteenth century, consisted of two blocks facing into a courtyard. A square tower-like block on the south, adjoining the church and the principal external entrance to the cloisters, contained the abbot's/prior's lodgings on the first floor, with the highest-status guest accommodation above. The adjoining buildings, at the north-east corner of the Great Court, were also devoted to the reception of the abbey's guests and included what may have been the guest hall, in which the Commons sat in 1378, and what was probably the abbot's hall (Hope 1897, 107–9; *VCH Glos.*, iv, 282; Welander 1991, 306–7).

To the south of the abbey church was the Lay Cemetery, accessible from Westgate Street through two gates: St Edward's Gate on the west, reached via the medieval Lich Lane, and the smaller St Michael's Gate to the east, standing at the end of Crafts Lane. Further east still, separated by a wall from the Lay Cemetery and extending around the east end of the church, lay the Monks' Cemetery.

All of the features so far described originated – as far as we know – in Serlo's late-eleventh-century rebuilding or in subsequent modifications and additions: no pre-Conquest features are known to survive above ground. In 1980–81 a small-scale excavation took place immediately west of the west cloister range. This revealed a number of burials sharing the alignment of Serlo's church, cut into a soil containing disarticulated bones. The burials were carbon-dated to AD 970 (uncorrected), and were cut by the foundations of structures that underlay the walls of Serlo's cloister and were on a slightly different alignment – one shared by the Abbot's Lodging ranges abutting the Great Court (Garrod and Heighway 1984, site 11/80, 53–5). Garrod and Heighway interpreted this sequence as commencing with a late pre-Conquest cemetery of at least two generations' use, replaced by a claustral layout more or less on the site of the later one but following a different alignment; possibly, they suggested, it belonged to the known rebuilding of the church under Ealdred (1047–62: see below). The sequence showed that the precinct had indeed broken through the west fortress wall before the Norman Conquest and that the latest pre-Conquest church lay under Serlo's.

This interpretation was rejected by Hurst (1986, 130–31) who argued that the entire sequence was Norman and later, as the earliest burials shared the orientation of Serlo's buildings. While the coincidence of orientation between the early burials and the Norman conventual buildings requires an explanation that is not at present forthcoming, it is difficult to share Hurst's confidence in dismissing the excavators' original interpretation, if only on account of the number of events to be fitted into the sequence prior to the late eleventh–early twelfth centuries. The early burials appear to represent part of a cemetery, and this must surely have been unassociated with the known claustral arrangement – they appear to belong to an otherwise unknown ecclesiastical geography. None of the burials is reported to have had any characteristics of high status and they may be taken as only the very vaguest guide to the whereabouts of the Old Minster church. They could even have belonged to an extramural cemetery beyond the intact Roman west wall, though if the succeeding buildings were indeed part of a claustral arrangement the west wall must by then have gone. The evidence of building ranges on an alignment different from that of Serlo's buildings seems clear enough, and the preservation of this alignment only by the buildings of Church House (the abbot's/prior's lodgings) could be explicable if, for instance, the 1089 rebuilding commenced with the church and cloisters while leaving continuously occupied domestic accommodation untouched, to be rebuilt piecemeal at a later stage. Different orientations were forced upon the ranges further north and west by the constraining influence of the precinct walls.

The perimeter, and the expansion of the precincts   The construction of a precinct wall is recorded between 1104 and 1113; this has been tentatively identified as the precinct wall that survives in part around the west, south and east sides of the precinct. Archaeological evidence provides corroborative dating on both the south and east sides (Heighway 1983a, site 27/73, 17–18; Garrod and Heighway 1984, site 12/77, 39–41). The great gate – St Mary's Gateway – stood in the centre of the west wall. This was first recorded in 1190 (*Hist. et Cart.* i, 22), roughly the date of the surviving vault over the passageway. The north side of the precinct represents the result of a slightly later phase of expansion.

There is little doubt that between the foundation of the abbey in *c.* 679 and the mid thirteenth century, the precincts of the Old Minster more than quadrupled in size, though only the latest stages of the process are documented and considerable uncertainty surrounds the date of the earlier episodes. A reference to the re-siting of the Old Minster in 1058 under Bishop Ealdred 'nearer the side of the town' is, moreover, utterly ambiguous (ASC s.a. 1058; Hope 1897). However, there is slender archaeological evidence to suggest that, when it was first founded St Peter's was allocated an area based on a surviving, recognizable or tenurially-fossilized Roman insula in the north-west corner of the fortress. St John's Lane, marking the eastern side of the medieval precinct, originated as a north–south minor Roman road whose north end eventually diverged eastwards away from the original line, over the remains of levelled and robbed buildings, to form a short cut to the north gate (Heighway, Garrod, and Rhodes in Heighway 1983a, 13; see below). The position of the southern precinct boundary seems also to have been initially determined by a Roman street and later modified. Excavation at the south-east corner of the precinct showed that it marked the junction of the north-south Roman street with another at right-angles (site 50/64: Heighway 1983a, 13, 15). What determined the eventual, unique and eccentric, alignment of the southern boundary remains a mystery to be solved, perhaps when the internal geography of the pre-Conquest minster is better known.

The most crucial stage in the development of the precinct is also the least securely dated, and therefore the most controversial. When did the precinct break through the fortress walls? Serlo's church, whose north transept and slype straddle the north-west corner and ditch, provides a *terminus ante quem* of 1089–1100 but it is uncertain whether this great rebuilding was also the occasion for the destruction of the Roman walls, or whether these had already been removed. If Garrod and Heighway's interpretation of the excavated sequence from the west cloister range is correct (see above), the Roman west wall must have been removed during or before the rebuilding and re-siting of the minster church in 1058. This is probably the most attractive historical context, but there is an obvious danger in attributing a particular physical process to one of only a tiny number of recorded events. While a final and definitive answer is not yet possible, further excavated evidence from just outside the southern precinct boundary lends support to the contention that the expansion across the west fortress wall took place before the Conquest – possibly well before (see below).

The last two stages in the growth of the precinct took place in the early twelfth and early thirteenth centuries. The construction of the precinct wall in the early twelfth century necessitated the acquisition of land from St Oswald's, presumably on the north side if – as the evidence seems to suggest – the precinct had already attained its maximum westward extent (*Hist et Cart.* i, 13; ii, 65). The acquisition of further land from St Oswald's, north of the abbey's refectory and including the site of St Brigid's chapel, took place in 1218 (see p. 125, below; see also Heighway and Bryant 1999, fig. 1.7).

Plan-unit I.2: Westgate Street north

This area comprised the plots that lay between Westgate Street and the south side of the abbey precinct. The plots backed onto the narrow lane running along the precinct wall, shown as King Edward Street by the nineteenth-century Ordnance Survey (and named as Little Abbey Lane by Heighway in her discussion of it: Garrod and Heighway 1984, 41). The lane was not separately built up at the time of the 1455 rental and does not appear to have been used as a means of access to develop derivative or secondary independent plots on the tails of the plots fronting onto Westgate Street; secondary plot development was confined to the narrow lanes giving access to the abbey gates. The lane had virtually disappeared beneath encroaching buildings by 1780 (Hall and Pinnell's map).

While no definitive account of the behaviour of the plot-pattern here is possible without extensive and detailed research into a large number of individual property descents, a schematic impression of the stability (or otherwise) of the plot-pattern since the fifteenth century may be acquired by comparison of the 1455 rental and other medieval documentation with the large-scale Ordnance Survey plans of 1884. The plots on the north side of Westgate Street were divided into three principal blocks by the two lanes that gave access from the main street to the abbey precinct: College Street/Lich Lane to the west; College Court/Crafts Lane to the east. An alleyway known as Mawerdin's Lane, now a cul-de-sac but probably originally giving access to the lane around the precinct walls, further split the easternmost block into two. As already noted, the blocks of property backed onto this lane and, because of the eccentric alignment of the south side of the precinct, the plots at the east end were substantially longer than those at the west. The plots shown in these blocks in 1884 were all densely built up; some plots took the form of strips running the full depth of the block, while in some areas boundaries had become obscured away from the frontage by the lateral exchange of parcels of ground between adjoining properties.

Fronting the westernmost block in 1455 were between 15 and 18 properties; by the late nineteenth century these had been reduced by amalgamation to 11 (*1455 Rental*, 40–44b). Much of this may, however, have been achieved by the clearance of a densely packed block of abbey property at the western end, the remainder of the plots being relatively stable through the post-medieval period. East of this, a Lanthony property recorded in 1338 can be located from its position in the 1455 rental and from the survival unchanged of its boundary measurements (though the plot was subdivided) in 1884. It had a frontage of about 31 feet (9.45 metres) and ran through to the lane at the rear (A5, fos 60–60v). But another much smaller Lanthony property recorded in 1372, a seld with a 12-foot (3.66 metre) frontage near the corner of Lich Lane (College Street), left no trace in the nineteenth-century landscape (A12, fo. 75). Lich Lane (College Street) was densely built up in 1455, the plots on either side probably formed by the lateral sub-division of pre-existing Westgate Street plots (for analogues, see Spearman 1988, 48; and Scrase 1989, 360). The central block was, again, subject to a limited degree of property amalgamation in the post-medieval period. The same applies to Crafts Lane (College Court), though the outline of a property recorded in 1372 and rebuilt as a row building of four tenements in 1413 can still be recognized in three post-medieval properties now occupying the site (A7, fo. 70; A3, fos 61v–62). The same process is apparent in the eastern block extending to St John's Lane: 15–16 properties in 1455 had been reduced to 12 by the 1880s (*1455 Rental*, 30–34b).

Early development and relationship to the abbey precinct   A strong case can be made for the development of this area well before the Norman Conquest. It can be argued, first, that the tenth-century occupation revealed on the southern frontage of Westgate Street in the excavated sequence at No.1 (Heighway, Garrod and Vince 1979; see p. 54–5) is likely to have extended to both sides of the street, at least in the area of the central cross-roads. The case is further advanced by the discovery of a probable late tenth-century building on the northern frontage of Lower Westgate Street, well beyond the Roman west wall (Hurst 1974, 48).

A case can also be made for this plan-unit originating in an episode of town-planning, an episode that was probably associated with a phase in the expansion of the Old Minster precinct. King Edward Street is a feature that has no role as part of the planning of the ecclesiastical precinct. There is no question but that it was a thoroughfare from the start; it did not, for instance, reflect the line of an infilled ditch used as a convenient footpath around the precinct boundary (see below). It is most convincingly interpretable in relation to, and as part of, the domestic plots bordering it: as a rear service lane, a feature common to planned urban layouts from Alfredian times onwards (Biddle and Hill 1971). This is also the only area other than the abbey precinct itself in which Heighway's point, that the line of the Roman west fortress wall is not represented in the historic plot-pattern, is really valid (Heighway 1984a, 366–7). Across the road, south of Westgate Street, the line of the Roman wall is represented by Berkeley Street which replaced it; the recorded plot-pattern developed later, in relation to Berkeley Street. But north of Westgate Street, in the area under discussion, the wall-line is indeed unreflected in the plot-pattern; the total invisibility of the wall here suggests, even if only very tentatively, that the area was comprehensively levelled and replanned.

Excavated evidence from just outside King Edward's Gate, in College Street (Lich Lane) is relevant, though the scale of the investigation was very small and in several respects the evidence is ambiguous. Two small trenches were excavated (Garrod and Heighway 1984, 40–42). One, some 15 metres south of the gate in College Street, found a pit containing late-eleventh- or twelfth-century pottery sealed by the second in a sequence of metalled surfaces belonging to the medieval lane; the earliest, also containing late-eleventh- or twelfth-century pottery (TF41B: see Vince in Heighway *et al.* 1979), appears to have been cut by the pit. The first abbey precinct wall was found to have cut levels containing further late-eleventh- and possibly early twelfth-century pottery, and the earliest gate was contemporary with this wall. The excavators therefore concluded that the wall and gate were probably built as part of the known building campaign of 1104–13, and that the lane was also new at that date, driven through an area of domestic occupation. The only ambiguity in the evidence so far is the status of the first metalled surface, apparently cut by the pit. However, the second trench, dug immediately in front of the gate on the line of both College Street (Lich Lane) and King Edward Street encountered five street-surfaces pre-dating the gate (and therefore the wall), at a level below the surfaces that definitely belonged to College Street. The lowest of the five contained pottery type TF41A, of tenth- or early-eleventh-century date (Vince in Heighway *et al.* 1979). It appears that – unless the trench in College Street was completely misleading – King Edward Street (and by implication the line of the precinct boundary) pre-dates College Street/Lich Lane and was considerably earlier than the documented construction of the first precinct wall in the early twelfth century. Given the imprecision of the dating of the pottery types and the potential problems of residuality, the presence of TF41A in the lowest surface outside the gate need not in itself be significant, but the presence of a sequence of five surfaces earlier than *c.* 1100 suggests – as the excavators concluded – that King Edward Street and the line of the precinct boundary here are probably pre-Conquest, and therefore that the abbey precinct had expanded and broken through the west fortress wall before the Norman Conquest, and probably before the resiting of the Minster in 1058 (Garrod and Heighway 1984, 40–42). Hurst (1986, 130–31) appears to doubt the validity of this interpretation and the dating evidence upon which it is based, but neglects to say why.

If the suggestion that King Edward Street was laid out as a service lane for a series of contemporaneously developed plots is accepted, the balance of probability is that this plan-unit came into being as a result of an episode of pre-Conquest town-planning. But its relationship to the precinct is still ambiguous, chronologically and tenurially. The possibility cannot be ruled out that the block of plots was laid out first and the precinct subsequently expanded out of its original insula to fill the gap; similarly, the Roman west wall could have been broken through in two distinct phases, one for the plots, another for the precinct. But a simpler and more likely explanation is that these events were simultaneous, part of a comprehensive replanning exercise. The demolition of the Roman west wall alone would have been a significant and perhaps costly project that would probably have required royal approval and even assistance. There is no evidence from post-Conquest documentary sources that St Peter's Abbey had ever had a significant stake in the Westgate Street properties: they appear to have been held from the King and paid landgable to the Crown. Arguably, the town-planning exercise that seems to have taken place here was a co-operative venture between the Old Minster and the pre-Conquest Crown; the former acquiring an enlarged precinct, the latter, new rents. As we shall see, there are also signs in Worcester of a major town-planning episode arising from the levelling of former defences and embracing the replanning of the Minster precinct as well as secular plots outside it.

College Street (Lich Lane) was a later feature, inserted through the Westgate Street plot-series when the precinct boundary was first defined by a stone wall. Garrod and Heighway's contention (1984, 41) that the abbey would not previously have been accessible from Westgate Street is doubtful. The Old Minster must have had some means of access into the intramural area, particularly as it claimed burial rights there; it also seems likely that this access would have led to one of the principal streets – for processional and political as much as for purely functional reasons. Possibly the postern gate at the end of Crafts Lane (College Court) represents a down-grading of an original principal gateway between town and precinct, centrally placed between the Cross and the end of the newly developed, but antiquely colonnaded, Westgate Street frontage. It may have led directly towards the minster church, perhaps lying just south of the east end of Serlo's abbey church.

PLAN-UNIT I.3: NORTHGATE STREET WEST (fig. 3.13)

This comprised the block of properties on the west side of Northgate Street, bounded by St John's Lane (Grass Lane) to the west and north. The plot-pattern within it was not unlike that on the north side of Westgate Street, most property boundaries passing without deviation from the Northgate Street frontage through to the lane behind. St John's Lane was substantially wider than King Edward Street and had an additional function as a by-pass for through-traffic heading for the north gate and wishing to avoid the Cross. In consequence, some separate properties were developed along it. In 1455 its east side was occupied by tenements generally held separately from those on the Northgate Street frontage (*1455 Rental*, 66b–78b), but the number of property boundaries extending through the block suggests strongly that the Northgate Street plots originally backed onto the lane, and that their tails were subsequently developed to provide derivative west-facing plots. The lane appears to have retained a definite service function, a number of stables being amongst the tenements on the east side in 1455 (*1455 Rental*, ibid).

By 1884 the west side of Northgate Street was divided between 20 properties. Some were small shops as little as 11–12 feet (3.35 to 3.66 metres) wide, confined to the frontage; others were more substantial properties extending back into the street block. In the mid fifteenth century the same frontage would have presented an even greater contrast between large and small properties, though the picture was changing and the greatest differences were in the process of being ironed out.

The Northgate Street selds   At the southern end of the block was a row of *selds*, as such premises are called in the Gloucester sources. In the 1455 Rental, Robert Cole provided details from the earlier rentals he possessed to show that they had existed in the time of Henry III (66b–68b). Originally there had been 12 selds but now he described the first 5, belonging to the abbey, as 'divers tenements'; the rest of the row remained largely intact, although the 7th and 8th selds had been amalgamated, as had the 11th and 12th. Cole called this part of the street the Cordwainery (not necessarily a name that was current in the fifteenth century, given his use of earlier rentals), and presumably these selds were – or had once been – the traditional working and living places of the better-quality shoemakers and workers in fine leather.

Judging by the names of previous tenants he provided for other properties in 1455 (and by comparison with the earlier deeds in the Gloucester borough records: *Cal. Recs Corpn Glouc.*), Cole's rental from the reign of Henry III dated from early in the reign, probably from the 1220s; this row of selds had therefore been built already at the beginning of the thirteenth century. Landgable was paid for the whole row, but traditionally in 7 separate payments rather than in 12: for the first 5 selds the abbey made a single payment of 3½d; for the 6th 2½d was paid; 4d and 3d for the 7th and the 8th; 1d for the 9th; 3d for the 10th; and 6d – perhaps a combined rent – for the 11th and the 12th. When these landgable payments were established, the row was held by seven separate individuals or institutions, therefore; the fact that five and perhaps originally seven of the payments were for individual selds implies that the row – whether in whole or in part – existed already at that date. But at what date had these rent charges been imposed? It is not clear at what point new landgable rents ceased to be charged, although roughly speaking it was during the twelfth century. There were Gloucester properties that were laid out, it seems, in the early years of the twelfth century, and which paid landgable; we have only that earliest of rentals that Cole used, from the 1220s, to supply a date by which time the total of landgable payments was evidently stable. So the evidence of landgable payments cannot as yet be used to show that this row had been built appreciably before the 1220s, although the suspicion must be that these selds existed either as structures or at least as separate properties well before 1200.

The demolition of Southern's Stores at 3 Northgate Street in about 1970 revealed it to have been a late-fifteenth-century building, and therefore the successor of one of these selds; it had occupied a plot 13 feet (4 metres) wide, and 22 feet (6.75 metres) deep (Moss and Spry 1972). Doubtless these had been the dimensions of the former seld on the site, and possibly the depth of 22 feet had been common to the whole row: the neighbouring plot was still 22 feet in depth when this area was surveyed for the 1 : 500 plan, and 22 feet was given as the depth of the tenement that replaced selds 11 and 12 when it was leased out by Lanthony Priory in 1417 (A3, fo. 121v). As this was recorded as being 12 feet 4 inches (3.8 metres) wide, each of the selds it replaced must have been far narrower than 3 Northgate Street: there was apparently, therefore, no regularity of plot-widths in this row. That is a further sign that it had not been built by a single developer, following on the evidence for the variable and separate landgable rents originally charged upon these selds.

The Lanthony tenement was described in 1417 as consisting of a shop, a solar and a cellar; it was, therefore, a two-storey building, by contrast with the later 3 Northgate Street, which had been a three-storey, jettied building. Perhaps, too, this had possessed only two stories before it was rebuilt. As it clearly came well within that part of the row that belonged to the abbey in 1455, it must have been the abbey that rebuilt it, and perhaps, too, those around it. A replacement of ageing tenements by larger and better premises would have been consistent with what the abbey was doing elsewhere: in 1498 it rebuilt the block of selds it owned nearby in Westgate Street, an indication of its commitment to improving the commercial properties it owned in the town centre (see below, p. 283).

Immediately to the north of the Northgate Street selds was a group of much more substantial tenements. In the thirteenth century these had contained houses set back behind shops on the frontage; one property had a frontage of 40 feet (12.2 metres) or more, occupied by five selds and an entry (A5, fos 83–83v); the property was rebuilt by St Peter's Abbey in *c.* 1400 with new shops and a great entrance (A13, fos 68v–69). Another substantial property abutted its south side; this was rebuilt by the abbey as an inn in the early fifteenth century (A13, fos 65v–66) at which time a lane running along its southern boundary was obstructed (see also p. 408). As well as revealing distinct concentrations of very contrasting properties that are but scarcely apparent in the cartography, the documentary evidence for this area also raises a related issue. A series of charters describes the conveyancing, in the early thirteenth century, of parts of one of these plots. It can be identified, with certainty, with one of two plots on the 1884 plans opposite the New Inn. These plots had well-defined boundaries passing all or most of the way through the street-block – they were quite coherent strip-plots of conventional urban type. The charters reveal, however, the degree of contemporary tenurial complexity that these simple, mapped, physical forms may conceal, dealing as they did with the conveyance of multiple portions of the tenement, one as small as a cellar window (A5, fos 76–77v).

The early-post-Roman development of this area is largely unknown. Northgate Street itself lies directly over its Roman predecessor, and continuity of use may not unreasonably be surmised, given that it gave access to long-distance routeways. An absence of finds of late pre-Conquest pottery from this street seems more likely to reflect an absence of excavation than an absence of occupation. St John's church, at the north end of the frontage, is argued elsewhere (p. 102, below) to have been a tenth-century foundation, but its siting is as likely to have been associated with extramural settlement as a nucleus of population around it within the walls.

The origins of St John's Lane (the medieval Grass Lane) are better known. A series of small excavations within the lane itself and on its west and north frontages suggested that the lane originated as a minor north–south Roman road. This probably formed the eastern boundary to an early precinct or enclosure around the Old Minster; excavations at the point where the later precinct wall runs westwards away from the lane suggested that the southern boundary too may have been determined initially by a Roman road (Heighway, Garrod and Rhodes in Heighway 1983a, 13). The distinctive curving north end of the lane has, on the basis of an excavation just west of St John's church (site 14/76), been suggested to represent a short cut towards the gate established over the ruined and robbed remains of a Roman building, but the period at which this was developing remains unclear (Heighway, Garrod and Rhodes, ibid., 19).

Plan-region II: the south-west quadrant

Bounded by Westgate Street to the north and Southgate Street to the east, this area is distinguishable from the surrounding plan-regions in that while, like them, it is composed of a number of morphologically diverse landscapes, it alone has no unifying features – no uniform framework provided by a regular street-system, no early precinct conditioning the form and development of properties on its periphery. This plan-region is a collection of minor, small-scale plot-series varying in character from lane to lane; even the plots facing Westgate Street vary considerably from one street-block to the next.

SUB-UNIT II.i: THE CROSS AND WESTGATE STREET ENCROACHMENTS (figs. 3.8 and 3.9)

The main street spaces in central Gloucester were subject to intensive encroachment by permanent or semi-permanent buildings. This took the form of an elongated island of encroachments down the centre of Westgate Street, stretching westwards from the Cross for a distance of about 150 metres, and clusters of small buildings encroaching outwards onto the street from the walls of All Saints' church and St Michael's church. The properties were distinguished by their very small size; all appear to have been buildings or parts of buildings without attached yards or open ground. They are further examples of or close relatives to the market encroachments discussed by Conzen in Alnwick, where 85–100 per cent of each plot was covered by buildings (Conzen 1969, 34–8).

While the area was a quite distinct part of the town, encroachments were not solely confined to this central zone but also occurred singly along the main streets in the form of buildings with projecting upper storeys supported on posts in the street. The 1455 Rental lists examples on Westgate (Ebrugge) Street near the corner of Walkers Lane, and on Northgate Street at the corner of Oxbode Lane (*1455 Rental*, 52a 82b); a Lanthony property documented in 1429 (A3, fo. 200) a short distance north of the latter provides a further example.

The ambiguous relationship of All Saints' and St Michael's churches to the frontages poses problems of definition. The term 'encroachment', when not applied to a discrete island of buildings in a public open space (whether a street or a marketplace), implies an advance from an established frontage. But how far the early medieval street frontages in this area were ever static is questionable. There are some grounds for believing that the early-medieval frontage of No. 1 Westgate Street may once have been further forward than it was in the late-medieval period (see p. 55). On the west side of Southgate Street, excavations in 1893–4 showed that the chancel of All Saints' projected some distance beyond the line of the frontage to the south (Medland 1894–5); similarly, the north wall of St Michael's projected into Northgate Street from the adjacent frontage. In each case the encroaching walls were of medieval date, the chancel of All Saints' being possibly late pre-Conquest (see pp. 109, 114, below), and so the churches themselves may be considered to have constituted a phase of encroachment onto the street, pre-dating that represented by the clusters of small buildings around their walls. But it is also noticeable that –

with the exception of Westgate Street – the main streets narrow as they approach the central crossroads. Southgate Street is the most extreme example: a maximum width of about 60 feet (18.3 metres) reducing to about 35 feet (10.66 metres) just south of the two churches. There is at present no way of knowing whether the churches actually represent a secondary stage of encroachment from frontages that had already moved forwards into the streets around the Cross or whether the churches were the primary encroachments, substantially forwards of primary

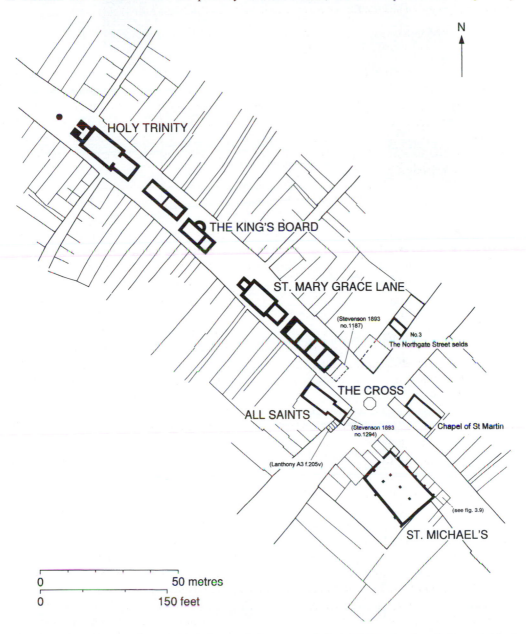

3.8 Gloucester: medieval encroachments around the Cross and the central streets, based on geophysical survey and excavation (after Atkin 1992b) and documentary sources

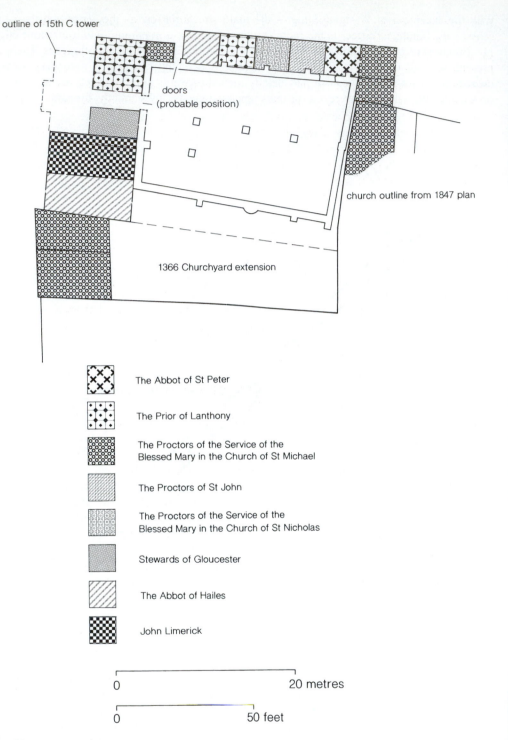

outline of 15th C tower

doors
(probable position)

church outline from 1847 plan

1366 Churchyard extension

The Abbot of St Peter

The Prior of Lanthony

The Proctors of the Service of the
Blessed Mary in the Church of St Michael

The Proctors of St John

The Proctors of the Service of the
Blessed Mary in the Church of St Nicholas

Stewards of Gloucester

The Abbot of Hailes

John Limerick

0   20 metres

0   50 feet

3.9   Gloucester, St Michael's church: medieval encroachments, based on documentary sources
and a plan of the church in 1847

frontages that subsequently followed them into the street. Whatever the answer it seems likely that the 'encroachments' described below, of probable twelfth-century origin, were but the final phase of an extended process. Another problem of definition arises from the evidence that the distinction between permanent and portable structures was not always clear (see below). Finally, as a distinct town-plan component, this area is unique within Gloucester in that its existence and character can only be demonstrated from documentary and archaeological sources, its features having been largely removed by the time detailed cartographic evidence becomes available.

Archaeological monitoring of excavations for a new sewer and a survey by ground-penetrating radar revealed the foundation-plans of a number of large stone buildings in the middle of Westgate Street (fig. 3.8). These are known from the historical evidence to have been, from west to east, Trinity Well and Holy Trinity Church; a two-cell building; the King's Board (see below); the church of St Mary Grass (or Grace) Lane; and a four-cell block of tenements and shops.

The infilling of the centre of Westgate Street was not the result of a spontaneous process of encroachment, a coalescence of stalls and other temporary structures as Conzen suggests happened at Alnwick (Conzen 1969, 38). It was, on the contrary, brought about through a deliberate policy of exploitation of this land by the public authorities acting in the name of the Crown. Both Holy Trinity and St Mary's belonged to the Crown until they were granted to St Peter's Abbey in 1391 (see p. 122, 123 below), and the mint, too, must have been seen as belonging to the Crown. The Lanthony Priory evidence shows that it occupied the same site as the building known in the fifteenth century as the King's Board: Ralph's property of the 1170s that was said to lie between Holy Trinity and the mint (Walker 1960, 202) was defined as lying between Holy Trinity and the King's Board in the 1440s (A13, fo. 54v). The 1455 rental, likewise, shows it as a block of properties along the middle of the street between the King's Board and the church (34b–36b). The Gloucester mint ceased to function after 1249 and the subsequent use of this building remains unexplained; its name, however, may point to its use – certainly before 1249 – as an official place of exchange (we are grateful to David Symons for suggesting this). As late as 1498 that part of Westgate Street along the south side of the King's Board was called *Myntes smyth* (*Cal. Recs Corpn Glouc.*, 1189).

The building of both churches as well, probably, as the mint, was authorized by one of the kings of the twelfth century, or – which is more plausible – by one of the constables, acting with the authority of the Crown. Ralph son of Pichard, too, had been given the land next to Holy Trinity church by Earl Miles, between 1141 and 1143 (Walker 1960, 197, 202). We do not know whether or not it was then built up, but the urgent need to provide for a political supporter in economic distress – Ralph being an adherent of the Angevin cause who had been forced to flee from Winchester (Walker 1960) – would have provided a suitable pretext for a decision to release hitherto undeveloped land in the market place for commercial development. It is not clear whether or not this implies that the public buildings in the street had already been built by 1143.

Nevertheless, this and other evidence points to the twelfth century as the period during which Westgate Street close to the Cross ceased to be an open street market as a succession of buildings began to encroach upon the public space. Land between Holy Trinity church and the mint was amongst the property that Ralph son of Pichard gave to Lanthony in 1174–5 (Walker 1960, 200–202); in the 1440s two tenements built upon at least part of it were described as lying to the east of the chancel of the church (A13, fos 54v–55). This land had already been built up in Ralph's time, apparently, as three shops next to Holy Trinity in the middle of the market – *in media foro* – were granted out by prior Roger, presumably soon after Ralph's gift in 1174–5 (A5, fo. 61v; A13, fo. 55).

The King's Board stood in the middle of the street until it was moved to the castle grounds in the eighteenth century (*VCH Glos.*, iv, 250). St Mary Grass Lane was demolished in 1654–5; Holy Trinity was demolished in 1699 though its tower and spire survived longer; the eastern block of tenements and shops also survived into the eighteenth century (*VCH Glos.*, iv, 295, 303; Kip's plan of 1712).

SUB-UNITS II.ii, II.iii, AND II.iv: WESTGATE STREET SOUTH (fig. 3.10)

Archaeological evidence   The early medieval settlement history of this part of the town depends very largely upon evidence from the Berkeley Street excavations of the early 1970s (Hurst 1972; 1974) and the smaller-scale excavations at No. 1 Westgate Street (Heighway, Garrod and Vince 1979). The earlier post-Roman phases of the sequence at No.1 Westgate Street have been summarized already in the context of evidence for the development of the forum area and the emergence of Westgate Street itself.

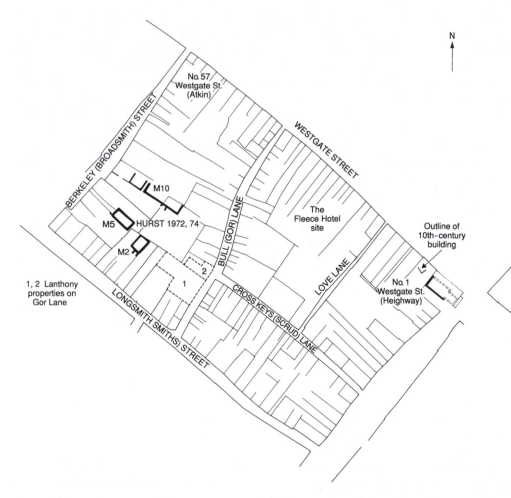

3.10   Gloucester: plan of the Westgate Street–Berkeley Street area, based on the first edition
Ordnance Survey and showing buildings excavated by Hurst (1972) and Heighway *et al.* (1979)

Commencing probably in the ninth century, the metalled surface of the successor-forum was buried by a rapid accumulation of organic occupation deposit around minor structural features of timber and wattle, with associated domestic and cobbling refuse. Animal manure and stable litter probably formed a substantial component of the organic deposit. This deposit had been seen before, on the opposite side of Southgate Street, in Hurst's excavations on Nos 11–17 and in the earlier excavations under St Michael's church (Heighway et al. 1979, 165–7; Hurst 1972; Cra'ster 1961). In the tenth century a timber-lined cellar was constructed on the No.1 Westgate Street site close to the modern street, but at an angle to it. Clearly it was not part of a continuously built-up frontage. It may in fact have been built behind a frontage range lying beyond the excavated area under the present street, urban sunken-featured buildings of this date and later being most frequently found behind contemporary frontages (e.g.Thetford: Davison 1967, 192; London: Horsman, Milne and Milne 1988, 109; York: Hall 1984, 67; see also Berkeley Street, below). Evidence for the later development of the Westgate Street frontage was truncated by nineteenth-century cellarage.

A problem remains in this sequence: the transition of this site from a public space to a private plot – by what process did the late- and post-Roman metalled area disappear? The most likely explanation is that, as is suggested below, and as Heighway suggested (Heighway *et al.* 1979, 167), the postulated replanning of the eastern half of Gloucester before *c.* 900 may have been responsible. However, while the evidence of a planned street-system is clear enough, the implications of this for the area west of Northgate Street/Southgate Street are uncertain. The scale of the No. 1 Westgate Street excavation was too limited to stand any chance of placing the excavated features within the context of a developing plot-pattern. Perhaps the two most likely processes to have transformed this area from a public to a private space are: first, encroachment onto the central open space from its margins, a process that, if unchecked by a central authority, would eventually confine the open space to linear movement zones contiguous with the streets feeding into it; secondly, deliberate replanning of the area. These need not be mutually exclusive: re-organization of this area in the late ninth century may have seen the replacement of *ad hoc* accretions by formal, bounded properties.

The excavations on the east side of Berkeley Street (the medieval Broadsmith Street) in 1969–71 suggested that, at least in this part of the town centre, areas away from the four major through-traffic streets began to be built up at a rather later date than those on the principal frontages. The development of the Berkeley Street area commenced with the demolition and levelling of the west wall of the fortress and the establishment of Berkeley Street over it – events variously interpreted as having taken place before the early eleventh century (Heighway in Garrod and Heighway 1984, 5) or in the late eleventh century (Hurst 1986, 130). Occupation of the east side of Berkeley Street began towards or soon after the end of the eleventh century with a post-built surface building and two lined-cellar buildings (both well behind the frontage); iron slag in levels of this period, though not associated with any structures, suggested that the industrial character of this area (evident later on) was already becoming established (Hurst 1972, 44; 1986, 130). The mid-twelfth century saw an increase in the density of buildings in the street block between Berkeley Street and Bull Lane (medieval Gor Lane); stone buildings were found at the front and rear of two plots facing Berkeley Street, and at the rear of one plot facing south onto Longsmith Street (Smith Street) (Hurst 1972, 46–50; 1974, 24–7).

The behaviour of the plot-pattern   The excavated evidence from the Berkeley Street site also allows, in conjunction with historical and cartographic sources, some check on the behaviour and relative stability of the local plot-pattern (though at the time of writing the excavations are published only in interim form and any conclusions drawn from them must be regarded as provisional).

With the intensification of settlement in the mid twelfth century, recognizable elements of the enduring plot-pattern in the Berkeley Street–Bull Lane block became established. Until the redevelopment of the area in the 1930s 'nearly all the buildings on the site were of eighteenth-century or earlier date with gardens to the rear and, where it has been possible to check the evidence, very largely the same boundaries as centuries before' (Hurst 1974, 26–7). This should not be taken to mean that the plot-pattern remained static within or after the medieval period. Some plots may have remained unchanged in extent: for example, the plot containing building M2, and its neighbours on Longsmith Street. But the plot containing buildings M10 and M12 on Berkeley Street appears to have remained laterally static between the thirteenth and nineteenth centuries while exchanging ground at the rear with properties facing Bull (Gor) Lane; the M4/5 plot facing Berkeley Street remained longitudinally static while there was some lateral exchange of ground with plots either side. Adjoining the corner plot on Bull Lane, a fourteenth-century Lanthony property consisting of a tenement and curtilage with two cottages adjacent can be located with the aid of its position in the 1455 rental; by the late nineteenth century it had undergone limited changes in its extent, having lost a parcel of land at the rear consisting of the back of an adjoining plot facing south onto Longsmith Street (1373: A12, fo. 77; 1384: A7, fo. 95; see fig. 3.10). The Longsmith Street plot on the corner of Berkeley Street had undergone fairly intensive sub-division for terraced properties by 1843 (Causton's map). In general it may be said that there is a marked correspondence between the medieval and nineteenth-century plot-patterns in this street block: some of the characteristics of individual plot-series associated with particular streets survived, plots mutating by the addition or subtraction of land parcels, or remaining unchanged; back boundaries common to a series of plots were evidently particularly stable features. The least reliable correlation appears to be in the relationship of plot-series lying back-to-back not separated by common continuous fence lines. Even so, the greater depth of the Berkeley Street plots compared to those on Bull Lane appears to be a true reflection of the medieval reality – and also, doubtless, of the continuing differential economic status of these two streets (see below, and Scrase 1989 and Keene 1985, 181, for analogous processes).

The behaviour of plots on the two principal frontages (Westgate Street and Southgate Street) is less certain. Some impression of the degree of correspondence between the late-medieval and modern plot-patterns can be derived from a comparison of the 1455 rental and the 1:500 Ordnance Survey plans. For example, on Southgate Street Cole listed ten properties between the rectory adjoining All Saints' church and Scrud (Cross Keys) Lane (*1455 Rental*, 4a–8a): the 1884 plan also shows ten plots on the same frontage, implying a degree of lateral stability on the frontage with no gross amalgamations or sub-divisions, but not necessarily that every plot was unchanged in extent since the fifteenth century. In 1455 seven properties occupied the principal frontage of the small street-block between Scrud Lane and Smith (Longsmith) Street (*1455 Rental*, 8a–10a); in 1884 there were six, and here the changing extent of one medieval plot can be documented (below).

Comparisons on Westgate Street are more difficult, partly because of the greater length of frontage between identifiable landmarks. The 1455 and 1884 totals for properties between All Saints' church and the corner of Bull Lane (Gor Lane) is comparable (*c.* 21 in 1455, 18 in 1884) and suggests a degree of lateral stability in the plot-pattern (*1455 Rental*, 34a). This conclusion also finds some support in the unchanged dimensions of Lanthony's Gor Lane east-corner property between 1415 (A3, fo. 10) and 1884.

The plots fronting Westgate Street within this area fell into two distinct groups, separated approximately by Love Lane. The plots to the west (sub-unit II.ii) were characterized in the 1880s by the absence of any clear or common rear boundary, and were intermingled with the plots at the rear fronting onto the lanes. East of Love Lane (plan-unit II.3), all but the first plot shared a common back boundary, the side boundary to the adjoining Southgate Street plot. The latter was enlarged southwards to accommodate a covered market in 1786 (*VCH Glos.*, iv, 260).

Love Lane itself is a feature of uncertain origin. Cole makes no obvious reference to it in the 1455 rental, and as a public thoroughfare it could be post-medieval in origin. It was in existence by 1714, when it was known as Love Alley (*VCH Glos.*, iv, 366). However, narrow lanes or alleyways with identical or related (but equally suggestive) names, and with precisely the relationship to the principal market street or market place seen here, are widely paralleled in other English medieval towns from the thirteenth century onwards (in London, York, Oxford and Shrewsbury, for example: Holt and Baker 2001). The combination of their names – often far more sexually explicit than here – and their position implies their use as places for casual sexual encounters. Whether this implies a medieval origin for the Gloucester example, or whether the phenomenon of such streets generally persisted later is not yet known. While the date of Love Lane as a thoroughfare is uncertain, it can be conjectured to have been inserted down the side boundary of a plot running from Westgate Street to Cross Keys (Scrud) Lane at the rear: the east side of the lane is straight, the west side irregular, suggesting that the east side of the lane followed a property boundary while the west side was formed by buildings facing it. Another long, narrow plot reaching from Westgate Street to Cross Keys Lane appears to have lain to the east of the alley, its east boundary – in part a parish boundary – forming a common rear boundary to the adjoining Southgate Street plots. This plot appears on Causton's map of 1843 though it had been largely erased by rearward expansion of the Southgate Street plots by 1884 (reconstructed in fig. 3.10).

Quite possibly these instances of very long plots fronting Westgate Street were fragments of a more extensive series. If, as the archaeological evidence suggests, the Westgate Street frontage was developed before the lanes and areas at the rear, it is possible that at some stage – perhaps in the earlier eleventh century – plots on Westgate Street had extended all the way back to Longsmith (Smiths) Street or a boundary pre-dating it, and that these plots were gradually reduced by the creation of secondary plots facing the lanes and Longsmith Street itself. Possibly the three blocks formed respectively by the hypothesized long Westgate Street plots, the Southgate Street plots to the east, and the very short Westgate Street plot-series opposite the Cross (plan-unit II.3) represent three primary – or at any rate early – land-parcels that were later subdivided.

SUB-UNIT II.v: BULL LANE (GOR LANE)

By analogy with the excavated evidence from Berkeley Street, occupation on Bull Lane (the medieval Gor Lane) may be expected to have begun long after the development of the Westgate Street frontage, probably towards the end of the eleventh century (see above). The plot-pattern recorded here in the nineteenth century resembled that on Berkeley Street, with longer plots away from the Westgate Street frontage and shorter plots nearer to it. Irregularities in the plot boundaries reflected the distinctive winding course of the street – for which, at present, there is no explanation, other than that the lane may have formed at an early date within a large land parcel that was not built up. Occupation in 1455 appears to have been more intensive on the west side of Gor Lane than on the east, the former built up with tenements and cottages, the latter with stables and cottages north of Scrud Lane, and cottages and tenements to the south that were not listed individually (*1455 Rental*, 20b–24b). Amongst the properties on the east side, north of Scrud Lane, was a 'gateway with a tiled wall' held by the Countess of Shrewsbury and her son; presumably this provided rear access to her tenement with its entrance and shops on Westgate Street (*1455 Rental*, 24b; 30–32a). The position of both the Gor Lane gateway and the Westgate Street frontage property correspond with the existing Fleece Hotel property, which retains this arrangement of front and rear/side entrances. This is likely to have been a secondary arrangement effected by the acquisition of contiguous blocks of property and has parallels elsewhere in the town.

SUB-UNIT II.vi: BERKELEY STREET (BROADSMITH STREET) (fig. 3.10)

The archaeological evidence from the plots on the east side of Berkeley Street has already been discussed. Rather less is known of the plots on the west side of the street, save that their development must have post-dated the mid or late eleventh century when the slow filling of the underlying ditch appears to have been nearing completion (Heighway, in Garrod and Heighway 1984, 5). Whether the ditch filling was completed and the plots laid out simultaneously as part of the general process of the levelling of the western defences is uncertain. As recorded in the nineteenth century the plots ended against a straight back fence line formed by the side boundary of the County Hall and Law Courts of 1815 (*VCH Glos.*, iv, 249), but this was a recent arrangement. The extent of the plots prior to this is not known in detail, though one Lanthony property towards the north end had extended westwards for a distance of over 92 feet (28.04 metres) in 1369 (A12, fo. 25v) so this at least had been truncated. Hall and Pinnell's map of 1780 also shows plot boundaries extending west about 100 feet (30.48 metres) from Berkeley Street to an alleyway (reconstructed in fig. 3.7); these boundaries may possibly have been schematically drawn but, again, suggest that the plot-series was truncated and the back boundary to these plots newly created in 1815. That this new boundary was in part followed by the parish boundary between St Nicholas and Holy Trinity suggests that the parochial boundary may have been rationalized when the County Hall was built, and the detailed course of the parish boundary here cannot be used to reconstruct topographical developments in the eleventh century (Heighway, in Garrod and Heighway 1984, 5).

SUB-UNIT II.vii: THE BERKELEY STREET–CASTLE STREET BLOCK

The pre-nineteenth-century layout of this area is more than usually difficult to determine because of the imposition of the County Hall and law courts. Long properties extended southwards from Westgate Street; those at the west end of the block interlocked at the rear with short west-facing properties facing Upper Quay Street (Castle Lane), but the impression given by Hall and Pinnell's plan of 1780 is that properties in the centre of the block may have passed through to the street at the rear – the arrangement that has been suggested further east. Within this block lay the medieval Boothall. Like its counterpart in Hereford, the hall itself lay at right-angles to the street occupying the full width of the rear of the plot, set back behind a subdivided commercial frontage. This area is also notable for the presence, under the Boothall and Shire Hall site, of a post-Roman, pre-thirteenth-century, dark organic deposit of the type otherwise seen only in the forum area. The deposit was excavated in a limited area only and it is not possible to be certain whether its presence here is indicative of waterlogged local site conditions or a particular settlement sequence (Abbott 1967).

The Boothall served as law courts and the meeting place for the burgesses as well as being, more prosaically, the market hall. It was called indifferently the Gild Hall or the Boothall (*Cal. Recs Corpn Glouc.*, 220, 11, 13; *Cal. Charter Rolls 1327–41*, 303–304; *1341–1417*, 371–2; *1455 Rental*, 46). The tenement to the west of the Boothall, which in the mid fifteenth century was an inn called Flete's Inn, had been given to Lanthony Priory in about 1170, but it was not then described as lying next to the Boothall, as it was in later documentation. It was said to lie next to the *magnam aulam domini regis* – next to the great hall of the lord king (A5, fo. 59; A13, fo. 53; *1455 Rental*, 46–8). Thus the origins of the Boothall or Gild Hall did not lie with the Gild Merchant, which was in effect recognized as the governing body of Gloucester in the charters of 1194 and 1200 (*Cal. Recs Corpn Glouc.*, 3, 5), but with the appointed reeves who previously had governed the town for the King. Doubtless the hall had been built by them as the multi-functional centre of town life that it was in later centuries, and as a matter of course the burgesses inherited the seat of town government when they acquired control of the day-to-day administration. A reminder of the Boothall's origins was the continued right (guaranteed in successive royal charters to Gloucester) of the county sheriff to use the hall for all court sessions under his jurisdiction (*Cal. Recs Corpn Glouc.*, 20, 33).

SUB-UNITS II.viii AND II.ix: LONGSMITH (SMITH) STREET – NORTH SIDE (fig. 3.10)

Occupation on this street has been explored archaeologically only on the Berkeley Street excavations where (as on the Berkeley Street plots) it appears not to have commenced until the late eleventh century. The origins of the street itself should probably be sought in the perpetuation of a minor Roman road underlying its southern frontage, either as a thoroughfare or as a persistent boundary. Following the removal of the western defences south of Westgate Street, Longsmith Street may have developed rapidly as a route between the city centre and the waterfront; this location doubtless encouraged the rapid establishment of the iron industry around it.

Like the rest of this quarter, the character of the plots varied from one street block to another. The north side of the street illustrates this contrast. West of Bull (Gor) Lane was the series of plots explored in part by Hurst's excavations (plan-unit II.8). Occupation was shown to have begun in the late eleventh century. The first excavated structure dated to the mid twelfth, and the short plots probably established at that time remained relatively stable thereafter, until the 1930s (Hurst 1972, 46; 1974, 23). Archaeological and historical sources have something to add on the subject of their internal organization. Occupation within the excavated plot (M2) on Longsmith (Smith) Street, and on one of the Berkeley (Broadsmith) Street plots (M3–M6) followed the same pattern over a considerable period of time. On Berkeley Street in the late eleventh century a timber-built cellared building (M3) occupied the back of a plot with a post-built surface building (M6) in front; the rear building was replaced in stone in the mid twelfth century (M4). On Longsmith Street a stone semi-subterranean building (M2) occupied the back of a plot from the mid twelfth century until its demolition in the fourteenth (Hurst 1972, 44–8). The description in 1455 of a 'tenement lying within the tenement … with a little entrance' (*1455 Rental*, 20a) on this or a neighbouring plot suggests that the same pattern of occupation may, as Hurst noted, have persisted (1974, 26). The property had a shop with a solar on the frontage in the 1440s (A13, fos 34v–35).

The block to the east of Bull (Gor) Lane (plan-unit II.9) was more complex, and there is no archaeological evidence available that can usefully contribute to a discussion of its chronology, or of changes in the pattern of plots or in their internal organization. This small street-block, bounded by Cross Keys (Scrud) Lane at the rear, contained a dense pattern of small plots of which only the eastern half survives. The rear of the plots facing Southgate Street was defined in 1884 by the side boundary of one of the Longsmith Street plots that ran almost all the way to Cross Keys Lane. There was no continuous back fence line separating the Longsmith Street plots from those on Cross Keys Lane, though some back boundaries were shared by groups of plots. One or two boundaries passed through the block from one frontage to the other, though it is not known whether these had any particular chronological significance. In 1455 the Smith Street frontage was built up with tenements listed individually except for a group of 'diverse tenements' at the west end (*1455 Rental*, 22–24a); the south side of Scrud Lane was occupied by tenements and cottages, the latter described only schematically.

None of the Lanthony properties in this block can be identified from their position in the 1455 rental and their recorded dimensions. The recorded depths of plots on Smith Street varied from about 63 to 65 feet (19.2–19.8 metres) and do not correspond to the mapped boundaries separating north- and south-facing plots; lateral and longitudinal changes in their extent evidently took place. One property only can be accurately placed without further detailed local research: a Lanthony property on the corner of Smith Street and Southgate Street. Complex changes are recorded in the middle ages – it was one tenement in the thirteenth century, then two, then one again, then two houses and three shops, then one tenement again in 1445 (A5, fos 32, 33v; A13, fos 29–29v; A13, fo. 28v) – and its fifteenth-century form bore no relation to the boundaries mapped in the nineteenth century. The street-block's complex plot-pattern may then be regarded as having been relatively fluid during and after the middle ages. Scrase (1989) has drawn attention to the potentially unstable character of small street-blocks and corner properties in Wells, Somerset, and this part of Gloucester appears to offer a splendid example.

Of the origins of the frame containing this plot-pattern – Bull Lane and Cross Keys Lane – it is possible only to speculate. Neither of these lanes appears to have any relevance to the underlying Roman street-pattern. They seem most likely to have been later features, though the winding course of Bull Lane stands out from the prevailing rectilinearity of the intramural town plan; it has been suggested (above) that the lane evolved in the earlier pre-Conquest period on open ground. Cross Keys Lane may well have been secondary to Bull Lane. The most plausible context for its creation would be to provide rear service access to a series of plots facing Longsmith Street – as part perhaps of a small-scale development of the later eleventh century. In such a case the Longsmith Street plots developed in this block could be expected to have originally run through to the lane at the rear, and any subsequent derivative plots created by building on the tails would develop individual back-fences, not one common or continuous line shared by the series as a whole. This is entirely consistent with the *ad hoc* separation of south-facing from north-facing plots here, and with the one or two apparent primary boundaries passing through the block, visible in the 1880s. But the fluidity of features evident in this area leaves a considerable degree of uncertainty.

SUB-UNIT II.x: LONGSMITH STREET (SMITH STREET) SOUTH SIDE AND LADYBELLEGATE STREET (SATIRES LANE) (fig. 3.11)

The character of the plots on the south side of Longsmith Street was different again. The plots facing Southgate Street were separated from the easternmost Longsmith Street plots by a common back-fence line. As shown by Causton (map of 1843) and the Ordnance Survey (1884), the south side of Longsmith Street was occupied by long rows of terraced houses occupying the frontages of short, sometimes very wide, plots backing onto plots facing Ladybellegate Street. In 1455 the south side of the street was built up with tenements, but the description of those west of Ladybellegate Street (Satires Lane) is schematic (*1455 Rental*, 18a–20a).

Between the Longsmith Street properties and the Blackfriars precinct wall at the rear lay a few plots facing Ladybellegate Street (Satires Lane). The plots on the west side of the lane had by 1884 been largely absorbed by properties on Longsmith Street, with only a narrow strip of gardenless houses now left facing the lane. Behind these lay a large rectangular parcel of land with access from the Longsmith Street houses, possibly originally a plot, or amalgamated plots, facing the lane. A similar parcel lay opposite, on the east side of the lane, still facing it. In the

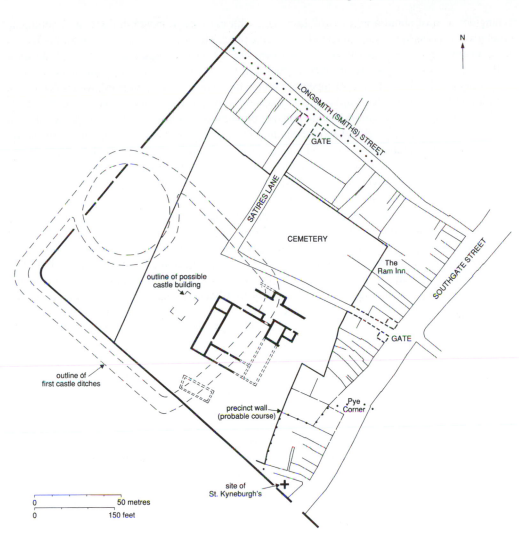

3.11   Gloucester: the Dominican Friary or Blackfriars (plan after Knowles 1932) and the site of the first royal castle, from archaeological evidence (after Atkin)

Lanthony rentals of 1445 and the town rental of 1455 three plots can be identified on each side of the lane. The measurements of the northernmost plot on the west side were recorded in 1240 but it cannot be identified from modern boundaries. This is not perhaps suprising. One man, John Rede, held adjoining properties on the main frontage and at the rear, on both sides of the lane in the mid-fifteenth century, giving ample opportunity for boundary changes (*1455 Rental*, 18a–20a, 112b; Lanthony A5, fos 45v, 46; A13, fos 33, 33v, 34).

SUB-UNIT II.xi: THE BLACKFRIARS PRECINCT AND THE FIRST CASTLE (fig. 3.11)

South of Longsmith Street, between the later royal castle and the back of the plots on Southgate Street, lay the Dominican friary. By the fifteenth century the precinct occupied a roughly rectangular area of about 4 acres (1.62 hectares), with gates on Longsmith Street and Southgate Street giving access to the site via lanes between the plots. The course of the precinct wall is known approximately, but rarely precisely, on all sides. On the west, Speed's map of 1610 shows a north–south boundary a short distance to the east of the twelfth-century castle ditch; Hurst's reconstruction (1984 and his fig. 4) appears to follow this. The course of the north wall is detectable on Hall and Pinnell's map of 1780 and later maps, west of Ladybellegate Street, about 40 metres (*c.* 130 feet) from the Longsmith Street frontage; this line was continued eastwards by an alley at the back of the Longsmith Street plots extending towards the rear courtyard of the Ram Inn on Southgate Street. Nothing survives of the precinct wall above ground in this area, but its course has been confirmed by geophysical survey, which showed a 'line of disturbance … consistent with that of a robbed-out wall, with very different zones of activity to each side' (Atkin 1992a, 37).

Southwards from there to the Blackfriars lane leading off Southgate Street, a building line is apparent on Causton's map crossing adjoining properties. It continued south of the lane, clearly marked on Causton's map but broken-through in part by 1884. A further group of plots to the south also shared a common north–south back boundary, but on a line slightly displaced to the west. The precinct wall may, as Hurst shows (1984, fig. 3), have had a westward dog-leg but there is no reliable information as to where exactly this was. A westward deflection in the line of the wall is implied by a Lanthony deed of a property that backed onto it: on the north side of the property the wall lay 74 feet (22.55 metres) from the frontage, on the south, 86 feet 4 inches (26.31 metres) (A7, fo. 71); but at present this property cannot be precisely located. The southern precinct boundary was defined either by the city wall – shown intact on Speed's map as far as the precinct's west boundary or, as Garrod states, slightly north of the line of the Roman wall (in Hurst 1984, 113).

While the precinct lay hidden behind the plots of the surrounding streets, both friary gates stood on the frontages at the ends of the lanes leading into the precinct (*1455 Rental*, 18a, 12a; both are shown on Speed's map of 1610). They did not mark the boundaries to the precinct but advertised its existence to the outside world (see p. 316).

The conventual buildings lay in the south-east quarter of the precinct. The church and claustral ranges were mainly built in a single extended campaign between the foundation in 1239 and *c.* 1270 (Rackham, Blair and Munby 1978, 105). The original church consisted of an undivided nave and choir, north and south aisles, a north transept, a short south transept characterized by Knowles (1932, 173) as a transeptal porch and a probable vestry opening off the choir. There appears to have been no tower – or at least no stone tower – over the crossing. The north transept was remodelled in the fourteenth century and the north aisle demolished (Knowles 1932, 173–7; Rackham, Munby and Blair 1978, 106). The claustral buildings lay to the south. The west range had the finest architectural detailing and housed the refectory and possibly guest accommodation. Serving hatches to the refectory suggest that the west end of the ground floor of the south range was used as a buttery or servery; an external door here with a roof scar over it may represent access via a pentice to a detached kitchen to the south. The east end of the south range was suggested by Knowles to have possibly served as a school (1932, 186). Over, at first floor level, was a single long chamber with rows of niches or carrels along the long walls – each individually lit – which may have been a purpose-built library (Knowles 1932, 188–200). The east range (which was the closest to the main street) was the least well-preserved. A chapter house with fifteenth-century detailing was centrally placed between a probable service room to the north and warming-room to the south; the dormitory occupied the first floor. The north cloister walk also appears to have been two-storied (Knowles 1932, 181–200; Saunders 1963). The earliest plan of the conventual buildings, made by J.G. Buckler in 1820 (published in Palmer 1882) before the insertion of Commercial Road across the corner of the precinct area in the mid-nineteenth century, also shows two further buildings parallel to and south of the main claustral ranges; one of these is also represented on the Ordnance Survey plans of the 1880s.

The first acquisition of land after the foundation, in 1246, suggests that there was a cemetery to the east of the church (see below). A recent trial excavation in conjunction with a survey by ground-penetrating radar has also revealed that much of the northern part of the precinct area was occupied by another extensive cemetery, almost certainly used by the lay population (Atkin 1992a, 37–40, and see below, p. 246).

The precinct was assembled over a period of about a century and a quarter following the foundation in 1239 (Palmer 1882, 296). The location of the friary within the city was determined by the availability of an area of royal property that had very recently become surplus to requirements. This was the site of the first castle, located in the south-west corner of the former fortress area (Hurst 1984; Darvill 1988; Atkin 1991b). Excavation, the recording of service trenches, and survey by ground-penetrating radar suggests that the first castle consisted of a rectangular bailey with a motte in the north-west corner built on a slight natural knoll just within the Roman west wall (Atkin 1991a). The castle first appears in the documentary record in Domesday Book (fo. 162a), when it was said to have occupied the site of 16 houses – or 24 according to the Evesham Abbey survey of *c*. 1100 (BL Cotton Vespasian B xxiv fo. 57r; text edited by Howard Clarke in Moore 1982, appendix). It was replaced by a new royal castle on a fresh site immediately to the west, outside the Roman walls, in the early years of the twelfth century (Hurst 1984, 76–9).

The location of the houses destroyed by the castle is uncertain. Excavations close to the south-west corner of the fortress, within the area of the castle bailey, found that the surviving shell of a Roman building had housed a farrier's workshop in the late tenth or early eleventh century before demolition for the castle (Darvill 1988, 45–6); this may, as the author suggests, just possibly have been amongst the 16 or 24 lost houses. But the survival of a ruined building housing semi-industrial functions is equally consistent with what one might expect to find in a peripheral zone beyond or behind the built-up area. The destruction of 16 houses, let alone 24, could perhaps be most convincingly accounted for by the clearance of a built-up street. Possibly the lane known to us as Satires Lane (Ladybellegate Street) represents a truncated late-Saxon street, or possibly the cleared houses were located along the north–south Roman street, found by excavation crossing the site, re-metalled in the late pre-Conquest period (Atkin 1992a, 37). However, the archaeological evidence for the late-eleventh-century development of the west end of Longsmith Street (above) may suggest that this corner of the fortress area is likely to have been only lightly developed away from the main through-street frontages. The 16 or 24 houses may well have lain beyond the castle defences on one of the main street frontages. The area by far the most likely to have been affected by such an event is the west side of Southgate Street south of the friary gate, where clearance of plots would have given the castle garrison an uninterrupted view of the main road and gate. Such an episode would parallel the clearance in the thirteenth century of plots on the north side of Bareland, between the later castle and Lower Westgate Street (see p. 80, below).

While the Dominicans appear to have been given the site of the first castle, a substantial portion of it may not have been immediately available for their use. Excavations and boreholes have shown that the friary buildings lie on the eastern edge of the site – the church, and by implication the claustral area, overlying the bailey's east ditch (Hurst 1984, 76–81; Atkin 1991a). There is at present no further evidence to explain the relationship between the friary and the castle, but there is little doubt that the initial unrecorded grant of land was inadequate. In 1246 the friars were granted the funds to acquire further land on which to build their church, extend their cemetery, and make a road through to the High Street of Gloucester (*Cal. Liberate Rolls 1245–51*, 65). The latter was doubtless Southgate Street, and the road the friars created was the lane known later simply as Blackfriars; the need for extra land for the church suggests that the newly acquired plot directly abutted the east side of the old castle defences. The precinct was further enlarged in 1292 when licence was granted for the acquisition of three plots of land and for the enclosure by the friars of 'a lane amongst the said lands leading from the street to their garden' (Palmer 1882, 298). The location of these properties was not specified, but the lane in this case was probably Satires Lane, leading from the friars' gate on Smiths (Longsmith) Street southwards towards the conventual buildings. The enclosure of the lane and the acquisition of land either side of it may have been associated with the construction of the gate itself. The last known stage in the enlargement of the precinct took place in 1365 when a plot of land 6 perches long by 1 perch wide 'for the enlargement of their manse' was acquired from William de Chiltenham (*Cal. Patent Rolls 1364–7*, 121; Palmer 1882, 299–300). This may have been on the south side of the precinct, where Lanthony property was concentrated (*1455 Rental*, 12a–16a).

The friary was dissolved in 1538. Thomas Bell – alderman, clothmaker, draper and capper – who was already leasing two gardens from the friars, bought the conventual buildings. The church was converted into a mansion, which became known as Bell's Place, having been reduced in length to make its north elevation symmetrical about the north transept gable (Knowles 1932, 177). The claustral ranges were used by Bell to accommodate his business. In 1538, when Bell was manœuvring to acquire the site, it was claimed that he was employing more than three hundred people and that his premises were 'confined' (Palmer 1882, 301). How many were actually employed thereafter working in the claustral ranges is not recorded. Excavation and survey at the north end of the east range revealed the conversion of that area to domestic use, with the insertion of a fireplace, oven and partitions (Saunders 1963).

Most of the Blackfriars precinct survived as open ground until the late nineteenth century, and its development after the Dissolution can be followed schematically from the cartographic sources. Speed's map of 1610 shows the conventual buildings standing within an enclosure on the south side of the lane leading to Southgate Street; the precinct area remained open, though a building symbol is shown to the west on the strip of ground between Ladybellegate Street and the western precinct boundary. Kip's plan of 1712 shows little evidence of change, but garden plots are shown on the east side of Ladybellegate Street, and only the west side of the friars' gate on Longsmith Street appears to survive (Kip's rendering of the conventual buildings is, unfortunately, difficult to reconcile with the known or surviving fabric). By 1780 little change had taken place, though if the course of the eastern side of the precinct wall has been correctly identified the plots on Southgate Street had by this date already expanded over it. Causton's map of 1843 marks the beginning of development on the lanes leading into the precinct. By 1884 this process was far advanced, with well built-up plots on the east side of Ladybellegate Street; at this date only the north-west quarter remained open.

SUB-UNITS II.xii AND II.xiii: THE SOUTHGATE STREET WEST FRONTAGE (fig. 3.11)

The west frontage of Southgate Street between Longsmith Street and the defences can be divided into two contrasting sections, divided by the lane and gate leading to the Dominican friary. To the north (plan-unit II.12), the plots resembled those nearer to the Cross. The group of plots on the Longsmith Street corner shared a common back boundary about 130 feet (*c.* 40 metres) from the frontage, but in 1884 the plots to the south, starting with the Ram Hotel property, were considerably longer, sharing a back boundary of about 188 feet (*c.* 57 metres) from Southgate

Street separating them from plots facing west onto Ladybellegate Street. This was probably a post-medieval feature, the plots extended rearwards over the course of the Blackfriars precinct wall (see above).

To the south of the Blackfriars gate, as far as St Kyneburgh's Lane, lay a contrasting area (plan-unit II.13), much of which was destroyed by the insertion of Commercial Road in the mid-nineteenth century. Its component plots were distinguished by their relatively small size and generally irregular layout. The area contained a significant topographical anomaly. This was Pye Corner, a dog-leg in the Southgate Street west frontage forming a corner projecting 10 metres eastwards into the street. The eastward deflection in the course of the street marked the point at which it turned away from the line of the underlying Roman street, towards the site of the medieval gate. The street had been diverted away from the old Roman gate to a new one to the east: when did this take place?

Causton's map of 1843 is the only useful cartographic source for this area: earlier maps lack detail, later ones post-date the insertion of Commercial Road. Causton's map shows that the line of the frontage north of Pye Corner was continued southwards by a building line within the Pye Corner plot, behind the contemporary frontage; the line also carried the parish boundary between St Kyneburgh's and St Mary de Crypt. The diversion of the street appears to have happened after the frontage was built up, and to have left an enduring imprint on the building pattern. While a settlement chronology for this end of Southgate Street has yet to be established, what is known of the central area might lead us to suspect that built-up frontages close to the gate would be unlikely before the tenth century at the earliest – though a possibly aceramic pit (seen in a watching brief) cutting Roman levels may indicate occupation in the tenth century, or earlier (Hurst 1974, 28). A watching brief on the opposite side of the street at No. 47 Southgate Street revealed a probable 'Saxon undercroft', though not closely dated (Garrod 1992, 50). The sites of the gates themselves have not been excavated and there is little direct evidence to show when the Roman gate was replaced. However, masonry recorded in a service trench suggested that the medieval south gate may have been a late-eleventh or early-twelfth-century building (Garrod and Heighway 1984, 55).

The site of the Roman gate was also that of the pre-Conquest and medieval church of St Kyneburgh. The original church may well have been located within the structure of the gate, as Heighway has suggested (*VCH Glos.*, iv, 11). In 1147 St Kyneburgh's was rebuilt on a new liturgical orientation; if the church had indeed been part of the Roman gate structure this event would provide a *terminus ante quem* for the relocation of the gate (see p. 107, below). The construction of the new gate and the diversion of Southgate Street may then have taken place in the earlier part of the twelfth century, by which time frontage buildings cleared when the castle was built (see above) could have been replaced.

Plan-region III: the eastern intramural city

INTRODUCTION: THE PLANNED STREET-SYSTEM (figs 3.12 and 3.13)

The urban landscape east of the Northgate Street–Southgate Street axis in some ways resembled that of the south-west quadrant. The morphology of the plots on the main-street frontages rarely remained constant from one street-block to another, and the morphology of the (generally smaller) plots on the lanes at the rear was similarly variable. But, unlike other parts of intramural Gloucester, a degree of unity was imparted to this area by a distinctively regular street-system.

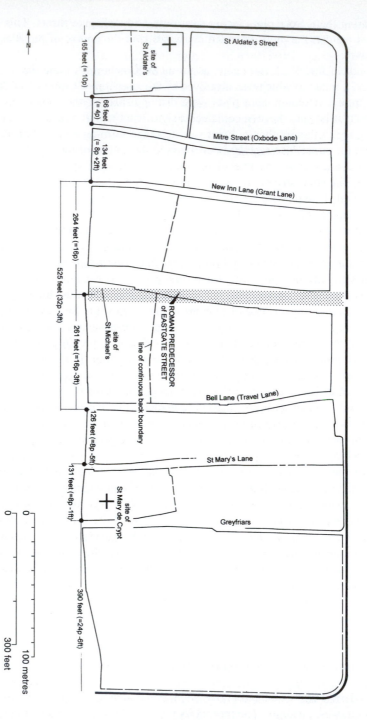

3.12   Gloucester: the pre-Conquest street-system. Plan based on the first edition Ordnance Survey, with excavated evidence for Roman Eastgate Street. (Measurements in feet, with statute perch equivalents)

This was first commented upon in print by Biddle and Hill (1971, 84, acknowledging information from Henry Hurst) who cited it as one of a number of probable examples of town-planning by the West Saxon kings. It was examined in more detail by Hurst who argued similarly that it was a militarily inspired planned layout of late pre-Conquest date, closely analogous to that at Winchester, with main streets linked to the defences by subsidiary streets, and evidence of metrological regularity in its design (Hurst 1972, 67–8). This hypothesis has since found general acceptance by writers on pre-Conquest Gloucester (e.g. Heighway 1984a, 366).

Nevertheless, archaeological evidence from some of the component streets has raised serious doubts about the date, or the integrity, of the street-system. Part of St Mary's Lane was excavated in the early 1970s and a sequence of six metalled surfaces was found. The earliest surface, of rubble and slag, was undated, but the second surface sealed twelfth- and thirteenth-century pottery (Hassall and Rhodes 1974, 30). At St Aldate's Street, the northern intramural street, excavation in the early 1970s found the first post-Roman metalling overlying a thick layer of dark loam with a turf-line on top. The metalled surface, composed of large stones with slag in the interstices, was *c.* 2.5 metres wide. It could not be dated, but appeared to be identical to a surface excavated nearby by Hunter in 1958–9 which had sealed a sherd of TF41A, the Gloucester late-Saxon ware, and a sherd of TF41B, probably from the early eleventh century (Hurst 1986, 91; Hunter 1963). 'Metallings containing abundant iron slag' had also been observed beneath the eastern intramural street (Hurst 1986, 93), all of which led Hurst to conclude that there was enough evidence for metalling of a consistent character to suggest that a large-scale road-building campaign had taken place around the walls, but that this post-dated the foundation of the *burh* and was most likely to have happened in the aftermath of the Norman Conquest (Hurst, 1986, 91). Some doubts might also be entertained regarding the origins of the Greyfriars lane, the southernmost of the east–west lanes. It now runs along the south wall of the friary church and thence to the site of the defences but must, before the Dissolution, have been completely blocked by the friary cloisters (see below). In its modern and cartographically recorded form it is therefore post-medieval. For it to have originated in the late-Saxon period, as suggested, we must assume that it was maintained as an entry from the main street during the lifetime of the friary and the remainder of its course re-established thereafter.

In short, the archaeological evidence alone does little to advance the claim that the street-system was a single-phase, pre-Conquest, creation. However, the case may still be strongly argued on other grounds. To begin with, the stylistic affinities of the street-pattern to that in Winchester remain – and it can be argued that these were closer than has hitherto been realized. One of the distinguishing characteristics of the Winchester street-system was a pair of back lanes running parallel to the axial High Street at the rear of the properties on the main frontages. In Gloucester, the plots on the west side of Northgate Street were serviced in this way by St John's (Grass) Lane, though this is known to have developed from a Roman street and there is no evidence that the area was ever subject to substantial replanning. But, at least by the later middle ages, a short stretch of lane ran parallel to Northgate Street on its east side as well, behind St Aldate's churchyard. Its line was continued southwards to Oxbode Lane by an alleyway; this is not recorded until it appears on Hall and Pinnell's map of 1780, but its absence from the 1455 rental may mean only that it was then a private entry. The same line was maintained by property boundaries between Oxbode Lane and New Inn Lane, and was then continued further south by primary (frontage-to-frontage) property boundaries to Eastgate Street, and thence still further south to Bell (Travel) Lane. Behind St Aldate's the lane lay about 227 feet (69.2 metres) from the Northgate Street frontage; at the south end, the property boundary continuing its line lay about 146 feet (44.5 metres) from Southgate Street. The New Inn property ended at it, as did the longer plots between St Michael's church and Bell Lane on Southgate Street. While it cannot at present be proved, it is possible that this line represents a former back lane that disappeared gradually through encroachment in the same way as did – for example – King Edward Street around the abbey precinct and Sheep Lane near the south gate (see p. 75, below). It survived into the nineteenth century as a thoroughfare only at the north end; elsewhere, its line was perpetuated as a property boundary, forming the rear of the deepest main-street plots.

However, the strongest evidence for the integrity of the street-system and the contemporaneity of the minor east–west lanes – as boundaries or thoroughfares if not as metalled surfaces – may be found in their metrology. Hurst identified a recurrent measurement of *c*. 130 feet (40 metres) in the main street frontage lengths between Oxbode Lane and New Inn Lane, Bell Lane and St Mary's Lane, and St Mary's Lane to the Greyfriars Lane (1972, 67). Further examination generally confirms, and in some important respects refines, this conclusion.

Measurements were taken from the first edition 1:500 plans. While measurement on the ground would have been preferable (see Slater 1981) there is regrettably, in this area, very little left to

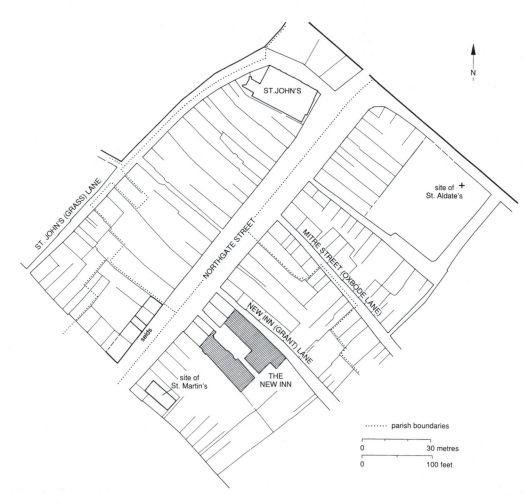

3.13   Gloucester: the Northgate Street area, based on the first edition Ordnance Survey

measure. Inaccuracies are inevitable in such a process and are likely to be compounded by the variation which is possible through taking measurements from one side or another, or from the centre, of any given street. With these caveats in mind, re-examination of the metrology nevertheless appears to suggest that the internal east–west lanes of this street-system (excluding the intramural street) were laid out at regular intervals along the north–south axial street. The measurements are set out in fig. 3.12. In general, they support Hurst's claim that a module of – approximately – 130 feet (40 metres) recurs in the spacing of the lanes. The most immediately important new observation to be made is that the distance between Bell Lane and New Inn Lane, either side of Eastgate Street, is also compatible with this suggested module: a distance of some 525 feet (160 metres) between the outermost lane frontages, it appears to represent four units of 131.25 feet (40 metres) and effectively unites the northern and southern halves of the street-system.

The recurrent *c.* 130 foot unit is very close to the equivalent of eight statute perches of 16½ feet (132 feet), and the Gloucester street-system may represent another example of the use of a four-pole module in early medieval town-planning, argued by Phillip Crummy (1979) to have been used in Winchester and elsewhere. Variations in the measurements are expressed in the figure; they may perhaps in part be accounted for by setting-out errors, the establishment or movement of lanes to one side or another of an original measured point, and possibly the need to adjust a perch-based modular system to the pre-existing framework of the Roman walls.

It is possible that the measurement system was extended to the laying-out of property boundaries. The frontage between Oxbode Lane and New Inn Lane was precisely bisected by a property boundary that may originally have separated two primary four-perch plots; the frontage length of the adjacent block to the north, as far as the return leg of St Aldate's Lane, may represent another. Anomalies remain. The distance northwards to the defences from the centre of the western leg of St Aldate's Lane (which is perhaps more likely to represent an original property boundary than a thoroughfare) was 165 feet (50.3 metres), the equivalent of 10 statute perches, but less obviously part of a system of whole four- or eight-perch modules.

The greatest and most interesting anomaly lies in the relationship of medieval Eastgate Street to the surrounding streets. While Northgate Street and Southgate Street together form the main focus of this street-system – the equivalent of the High Street in Winchester – Eastgate Street has an obvious importance as a secondary focus and axis. However, the street-blocks north and south of it were obviously of very different widths (184 and 282 feet/56 and 85.95 metres respectively) and medieval Eastgate Street is clearly not a part of the metrologically regular scheme defined so far. But the same cannot be said of its Roman predecessor. The course of this has been determined by the archaeological monitoring of excavations for a new sewer (Greatorex 1991). This confirmed that the Roman street lies slightly south of its successor at the central cross-roads, while the two coincide at the gate. A point measured half-way between the further corners of Bell Lane and New Inn Lane coincides with the centre line of the Roman street at its west end, with a margin of error of about 1½ feet (0.46 metres). The distance from the Roman street to the lanes to the north and south (264 and 261 feet/80.46 and 79.55 metres respectively) appear to represent 16 statute perches (264 feet).

There seems then to be a reasonable case for suggesting that it was the Roman predecessor to Eastgate Street that was used as the axis of the planned street-system, and this in turn strongly suggests that the layout was established at a date well before the Norman Conquest. The stratification cut through by the sewer trench suggested to the archaeologist monitoring it that the road alignment may have been 'drifting north to its present setting' at some date before the eleventh century (Greatorex 1991, 29). Dating evidence for the first metalling on the present, medieval course of Eastgate Street appears to have been inadequate, but it seems most unlikely that the street could have shifted, or been moved, once built-up frontages had formed.

A rationale for the drift or diversion of the street northwards is not difficult to find. Westgate Street had, it seems, long abandoned the route of its Roman antecessor and had moved northwards. It has already been suggested that its medieval course may finally have been formalized by a planning episode associated with the enlargement of the Minster precinct. If the replanning of the eastern half of Gloucester was, as suggested, based on Roman Eastgate Street, this would have left a staggered junction at the heart of the town as a replacement for the 'successor forum' – whatever condition that might by then have been in. Of Gloucester's four cardinal streets, Eastgate Street always carried the least long-distance traffic and is likely to have lagged behind the others in the development of its frontages, possibly allowing its diversion some years after the street-system was first laid out, though not in all probability as late as the Norman Conquest. Quite possibly the replanning of the north side of Westgate Street – which had distinct overtones of the monumental or ceremonial – provided the imperative for the creation of a central cross-roads. St Michael's church may have had its origins in this process, as an architectural cornerpost marking the diverted street and as a place of worship at the town's new central focus.

In these circumstances, the unsatisfactory nature of the archaeology recorded beneath the church in 1956 is all the more frustrating (Cra'ster 1961). Very little coherent stratification was recorded surviving beneath the Victorian structure, and what little there was raises a number of problems. These may be simply summarized. First, there was almost no depth of Roman deposit either within the church or in the churchyard to the south. 'Natural gravel' was found at a level corresponding closely with nearby observations of what Heighway identified as the late-Roman metalling of the successor-forum (Heighway *et al.* 1979, 165; Hurst 1969, 9). Earlier Roman deposits might well have been removed by levelling for the forum – a process identified by Hurst (1969, 6) – but what became of forum-period and later Roman deposits on this site? This introduces the second problem: the absence of the Roman road. Its course has been positively identified under Eastgate Street and correlates with the Roman predecessor to Westgate Street across the forum, but was not identified in the St Michael's excavation trenches. All might be explicable in terms of a drastic late- or sub-Roman levelling episode – perhaps on the lines seen at Wroxeter, where a length of road metalling was dug out and replaced by sifted materials (White and Barker 1998, 122) – but there was no apparent evidence of this either. A third problem is created by the excavated remains of two stone buildings, neither of which shared the orientation of the forum ranges or the later medieval topography. One of these (wall 1) pre-dated the thick organic deposit found in the churchyard excavations, the other (wall 2) appears to have post-dated it. Fourthly and finally, the organic deposit itself raises difficulties. Up to 7 feet (2.13 metres) thick and rich in plant remains, this has been convincingly identified as the equivalent of the peaty organic deposit accumulating in the ninth century on the No.1 Westgate Street site (Cra'ster 1961, 64 and Appendix 3; Heighway *et al.* 1979, 165–7). Unfortunately the St Michael's excavation report describes its sealing a rubble destruction layer associated with the Roman wall 1 containing 'some green-glazed mediaeval pot-sherds' (Cra'ster 1961, 66). There is simply no way of resolving these problems at present; the only possible answer lies in further excavation, or in the steady accumulation of data from the observation of commercial groundworks – a process which in Gloucester is (happily) very well established.

PLAN-UNIT III.1: EASTGATE STREET (fig. 3.7)

Of the four 'great streets' within the city walls, only on Eastgate Street was there any great degree of similarity in the form of the plots on the opposing frontages – and even here differences between the north and south frontages are clearly apparent. Eastgate Street is distinguished from the other main streets by the fact that most of the plots facing it appear to have passed, at some period, through their respective street-blocks and terminated at a lane to the rear. Those that did not were the ones at the west end of the street that are likely to have been carved out of long plots facing Northgate Street and Southgate Street. While by 1884 only one or two properties on either side of Eastgate Street extended all the way back to one of the lanes at the rear, it is clear that more had once done so. This is suggested by the number of primary boundaries running through each street-block from the principal frontage (or just behind it) to the rear, and by the limited development of common back-fence lines separating main-street from lane properties. Both rear lanes led from the main north–south streets only to the wall street; neither was an important thoroughfare, and plot development on each was consequently limited. Nevertheless, plots did develop on the lanes; the nineteenth-century cartographic evidence suggests that this took place to a much greater extent on Bell (Travel) Lane to the south than on New Inn (Grant) Lane to the north. But to what extent is this evidence relevant to the medieval period?

Comparison of the main frontages in 1455 and in the 1880s is made difficult by the listing in 1455 of 'diverse tenements' in two blocks on the south frontage and one on the north. Fifteen other properties were individually listed on the southern frontage, 17 on the north (*1455 Rental*, 86b–102b); this compares with 17–18 properties shown on the south frontage in 1884 and 25 on the north, suggesting a degree of lateral stability in the post-medieval plots – but more so on the south side than on the north. The only known major disturbance to the traditional plot-pattern in this area was the Eastgate Market of 1786 (*VCH Glos.*, iv, 260), occupying amalgamated properties on the southern frontage and extending through the block to Bell Lane. Adjoining plots leased by Lanthony Priory in this area in the late fourteenth and fifteenth centuries were roughly one-third and two-thirds the depth of the street block here (A12, fo. 16, fo. 77v; A3, fo. 86) and the back and side boundaries of these were partially preserved as fragmentary building-lines amongst the properties amalgamated for the market.

The 1455 rental also reveals that the more extensive development of tail-end plots visible in the nineteenth century to the south of the street correctly represents the late-medieval situation. In 1455 the north side of Travel Lane was built up mainly with cottages and stables in ten separate properties (*1455 Rental*, 14–16b). The depth of a property held by Lanthony Priory near the east end of the lane was recorded in 1371 as being nearly 73 feet (22.25 metres), extending just under half-way into the street block (A12, fo. 64v). In 1455 it was described as a 'vacant piece with a great gateway' and held by the heirs of R. Gilbert; John Gilbert, the son of Robert Gilbert, held extensive property on the Eastgate Street frontage to the north and it seems likely that the 'great gateway' provided rear access to it (*1455 Rental*, 16b; 94–96b). This arrangement is likely to have dated only from the end of the fourteenth century. In 1396 the Travel Lane plot was leased to John Bannebury and his wife as a vacant plot to be built upon, abutting a tenement already held by Bannebury at the rear (north); when the plot had been leased previously (in 1371) it and the Eastgate Street property behind were held by different individuals (A12, fo. 64v; A7, fo. 187v; A13, fo. 27). The process appears to parallel one already observed on Westgate Street: main-street plots, suspected as having originally run the full depth of a street-block to a lane at the rear, suffered truncation by the development of derivative plots on their tails. Rear or side access to a lane was, in some cases, later restored by wealthy owners of the main-street plots by the acquisition of contiguous land parcels.

Other documentary evidence relates to the conveyance of separate parcels of land between the two frontages. In 1417 a long, narrow strip of land was leased by Lanthony Priory behind and to the side of one of Robert Gilbert's tenements; it appears to have been a parcel formed by the multiple sub-division of a plot-tail, the south end of which was already held separately (A3, fo. 21). Behind the street's north frontage the development of separate properties facing New Inn (Grant) Lane was more limited; here in 1455 were 'those tenants who have their houses in the eastern street' and a number of curtilages (*1455 Rental*, 78a).

Of the four 'great streets', Eastgate Street carried the least long-distance traffic and may well have been the least highly regarded for its market and retail potential. Although the same width as Westgate Street, its space was encroached on only in the immediate area of the Cross around St Michael's church. The profusion of very small properties observable in the Mercery on the north side of Westgate Street was largely absent from Eastgate Street; the only comparable properties were two adjacent tenements or booths at the west end of the north frontage in 1455 (*1455 Rental*, 86b–88b). One of these was granted in fee by Lanthony Priory in the mid-thirteenth century, at which time the plot had a frontage of about 11 feet (3.35 metres) and a depth of about 26½ feet (*c.* 8 metres) (A5, fo. 74). Despite its probable commercial limitations, later medieval Eastgate Street had an ample share of wealthy inhabitants and property holders. The presence of the Jewish quarter in the street before 1275 may have been influential, just possibly in terms of a legacy of stone buildings that continued to attract high-status occupants. The amalgamation of holdings was not confined to the south side: the 1455 rental records two adjacent tenements held by the Countess of Shrewsbury 'joined … under one roof' (91b).

Eastgate Street and its immediate environs have not been sampled archaeologically to the same extent as other areas of the city. Finds of the pottery TF41a from various sites along the southern frontage suggest that it was occupied before the mid to late eleventh century (Garrod and Heighway 1984, fig. 3).

SUB-UNIT III.i: THE NORTHGATE STREET EAST FRONTAGE (fig. 3.13)

The plots on the east side of Northgate Street varied considerably in their shape and dimensions, much as the plots on the south side of Westgate Street did. It is not therefore possible to claim more than a very limited degree of internal morphological homogeneity here, though the plots were clearly different from those found in the neighbouring areas: the small, irregular plots of the Oxbode Lane and St Aldate's area, and the generally larger plots of the north Eastgate Street series. It is possible that the east Northgate Street plots originally terminated at a rear service lane parallel to the street (see above), in which case they would have resembled the series opposite, outside the postulated late pre-Conquest replanning.

A substantial degree of continuity can be demonstrated between the plots of the fifteenth century and those of the nineteenth. The northern block, between the two legs of St Aldate's Lane, contained eight properties in 1455 and nine (including one subdivided plot) in 1884. One of the properties in this block was granted in fee by Lanthony in *c.* 1217–45; its dimensions remained unchanged in 1884 (A5, fos 86–86v). The short block between St Aldate's Lane and Mitre Street (Oxbode) was more fluid, three plots on the frontage in the 1880s having replaced the fifteenth-century arrangement of four tenements, the southernmost of which extended behind the others (*1455 Rental*, 80–82b). Between Mitre Street (Oxbode) and New Inn (Grant) Lane, five tenements and a block of 'diverse tenements' were represented by six plots by 1884. One of these, recorded in 1379 (A7, fos 28–28v) had acquired an entry from the adjoining plot but otherwise retained its dimensions in 1884. In the southernmost block, the surviving structure of the New Inn has guaranteed the stability of that property, while five tenements and a block of 'diverse tenements' (probably four units) on the Eastgate Street corner in 1455 (*1455 Rental*, 84–86b) had become five frontage plots by 1884.

Many of the plots on this side of the street were of a fairly consistent size, with an average frontage width of about 21 feet (6.4 metres). The series of plots in the northernmost block backed onto the churchyard wall of St Aldate's, about 90 feet (27.43 metres) from the frontage; the plots further south lacked a common boundary and were instead interlocked with the plots at the rear facing the lanes, but they too terminated between *c.* 90 feet and 120 feet (36.6 metres) from the frontage. The plots nearest the Cross, as might be expected, were the shortest and the most closely interlocked with plots facing adjoining streets.

A single plot appears to have had nothing whatever in common with its neighbours: the New Inn, on the south corner of New Inn (Grant) Lane. The surviving early fifteenth-century building, built with galleried timber-framed ranges around a courtyard, spans the full width of the plot – about 71 feet at the frontage (*c.* 21.60 metres). The principal access is via an entry off Northgate Street, centrally placed between shops. A further passage through the east courtyard range gives access to a backyard containing ancillary buildings, with access to the lane; this area would certainly have contained extensive stabling for most of the inn's history (Pantin 1961, 173). With its backyard, the property extends to the well-defined rear boundary that is suggested to represent a section of a rear service lane, here about 200 feet (*c.* 60.9 metres) from the Northgate Street frontage. In the late nineteenth century the New Inn was still one of the largest properties in central Gloucester, approached in size only by its rivals in the hotel trade and exceeded only by public buildings on assembled properties. Although documentation is lacking, it seems certain that the New Inn plot must have been equally extensive in the fifteenth century – given the requirements for stabling that cannot have been met within the surviving ranges. The site had been acquired by the abbey as early as 1263, when it consisted of a tenement with six shops on the frontage and a mansion behind, reached through a centrally placed entry. The mansion had been the dwelling of the donor's father, Maurice Durant, a leading Gloucester merchant (*Hist et Cart.*, ii, 198). Being so close to the Cross, it was a quite exceptional piece of thirteenth-century mercantile real estate, and it is unfortunate that there are no sources with which to explore its earlier history. It may have been assembled by the amalgamation of smaller plots, possibly three plots within the size-range of the remaining plots on this side of the street; alternatively it was an ancient survival, similar to plots on the principal commercial street of thirteenth-century Shrewsbury – of similar dimensions, with four to six shops on the frontage, halls behind, and of possible pre-Conquest origin (Baker, Lawson, Maxwell and Smith 1993).

SUB-UNITS III.ii AND III.iii: OXBODE LANE AND ST ALDATE'S (fig. 3.13)

The north-east corner of the fortress area had a particularly distinctive plot-pattern: a concentration of extremely small, irregular, plots. Their form varied considerably. Small, narrow, strip-plots were evident on the north side of Oxbode Lane and around the corner facing east towards the city wall. Broader but extremely short rectangular plots occupied the block between Oxbode and New Inn (Grant) Lane (plan-unit III.2). Rather larger plots occupied the single frontage of St Aldate's Street east of the church (plan-unit III.3).

Only on Oxbode Lane is it possible to compare the characteristics of this pattern with some late-medieval data. The 1455 rental recorded ten tenements on the north side eastwards from Northgate Street, followed by a block of eleven cottages, a further tenement and then two tofts at the eastern end. On the south side, two blocks of 'diverse tenements' separated by three individually listed tenements occupied the western half of the frontage; the eastern half was mainly occupied by curtilages, with two cottages in use as stables (*1455 Rental*, 72a–78a). These descriptions, taken with the bald listing of 'diverse tenements' for the north frontage of Grant Lane, leave little doubt that most of this area was built up with poor-quality housing. The small size of the post-medieval plots – given that these frontages were not commercially prized for through-traffic – probably offers a not-too-misleading representation of the character of the late medieval settlement pattern in this area. The concentration of tiny strip-plots in the centre of the north frontage of Oxbode Lane may even represent the evolution of individual properties from the row of eleven cottages recorded in 1455. One Lanthony property at the east end of this row was leased in 1365 as a cottage and curtilage; it then had a frontage of just under 20 feet (6.09 metres) and extended nearly 120 feet (36.6 metres) back from the street (A12, fo. 7v). These dimensions correspond with either of two fragmentary plot-tails visible in 1884 amongst the densely packed courts that characterized these properties; the frontage had however been redivided on different lines. What appears to have been part of this property was first recorded in a charter of *c.* 1210–20; the dimensions then were, however, entirely different – a much wider frontage of over 32 feet (9.75 metres) and a shorter length (*c.* 63 feet/19.20 metres). If correctly identified, there appears to have been a considerable degree of fluidity in properties here between the thirteenth and fifteenth centuries. This evidence does, however, support the contention that the nineteenth-century plot-pattern did, to an extent, reflect the late-medieval version.

It has previously been suggested that this area also represented the extent of a middle-Saxon urban estate (Heighway 1984a, 364). This is discussed in full elsewhere (pp. 115–17, below). The distinctive character of the plot-pattern here should probably be interpreted as a manifestation of late-medieval economic and social pressures acting within the earlier morphological frame. Occupation can be demonstrated here only in the post-Conquest period – though this may to an extent reflect patterns of survival and recovery of evidence.

SUB-UNIT III.iv: THE SOUTHGATE STREET EAST FRONTAGE (fig. 3.7)

The disparate character of the form of the plots on the east side of the north–south axial street was maintained to the south of Eastgate Street. A series of plots of fairly consistent character occupied the Southgate Street frontage between St Michael's church and Bell Lane (Travel Lane), those towards the north ending on a common back-fence line about 115 feet (*c.* 35 metres) east of the frontage, those towards the south extending a few feet further to the common boundary that extended northwards on the line suspected to have been that of a former back service-lane parallel to Northgate Street and Southgate Street (see above). The plots further south, between Bell Lane and St Mary's Lane, were shorter, with the exception of the southernmost plot. This was substantially longer than all the others, extending back from the frontage the same distance as the churchyard of St Mary de Crypt – a hint that the churchyard too may have been a domestic plot in origin.

The cartographically recorded plot-pattern here appears to bear some resemblance to that in the late-medieval period. In 1455 a pair of Lanthony tenements lay two plots south of St Michael's churchyard. Their boundaries – specified in thirteenth-century grants (A5, fos 22–22v) – can be identified in the outlines of the northern part of the Bell Hotel site, as mapped by the Ordnance Survey. The short frontage between Bell Lane and St Mary's Lane underwent rather more drastic post-medieval change: in 1455 it was occupied by Thomas Deerhurst's 'great building' – a tenement in multiple occupancy – and two further tenements to the south (*1455 Rental*, 8b, 10b); by the late nineteenth century this frontage had become six densely built-up plots, and Deerhurst's tenement heavily subdivided.

The Bell Hotel site, between St Michael's church and Bell (Travel) Lane, was excavated in 1968–9 and found to overlie the east range of the Roman forum and its courtyard (Hurst 1972, 52–62). The first post-Roman structural remains overlying the forum area organic deposit took the form of two stake-and-wattle buildings, one near the street frontage, but (like that at No.1 Westgate Street) not aligned on it; carbon-14 determinations gave an eighth-century date (Hurst 1972, 61; Heighway *et al.* 1979, note 58). These buildings were succeeded by two plank-built structures aligned on the street but set back slightly from the frontage, probably built before the mid-eleventh century (Hurst 1972, 61).

Immediately south of St Mary de Crypt and Greyfriars Lane was a further group of hetero-geneous plots, most of which had backed onto the Greyfriars' precinct wall. In the centre of the group was a series of properties that had, in the late middle ages, been leased by Lanthony Priory; these backed onto a lane which branched off Southgate Street at its north end (A12, fo. 78v; A7, fos 28v–29; A7, fo. 111v; A13, fo. 20; A13, fo. 21v). The 1455 rental recorded, south of St Mary's, 'the little lane there entering to Schepen Lone' (13b). Sheep Lane is absent from Hall and Pinnell's map of 1780 and had probably disappeared by that date; a plan of 1826 (City Plan Book for 1826, 32) records what appears to have been the former lane as a strip of corporation property occupied by gardens and out-houses (we are grateful to John Rhodes for this reference). Archaeological observation of stratigraphy in this area identified a possible pre-Conquest sunken-featured building and undated metalling possibly belonging to Sheep Lane itself (site 10/91: Garrod 1992, 50).

SUB-UNIT III.vi: BELL LANE (TRAVEL LANE), SOUTH SIDE

The north side of this lane has been described already as part of the Eastgate Street plan-unit, it being argued that the plots there were created from the tails of Eastgate Street plots. The plots on the south side did, nevertheless, closely resemble those on the north and were of almost exactly the same depth, backing onto St Mary's Lane. It is likely that the mapped properties on the south side of Bell Lane bear little resemblance to their late-medieval forbears, other than in their southward extent. By the late nineteenth century the area was mainly occupied by a small number of large and obviously wealthy houses on wide plots, and a scattering of more pedestrian properties. In 1455 the same frontage housed a mixture of tenements (including a block of 'diverse tenements'), cottages, stables and curtilages; several groups of these were held in single ownership, but the impression is nevertheless one of a multiplicity of small properties or tenancies of low value, with a notable service element (*1455 Rental*, 16b–18b).

SUB-UNIT III.vii: GREYFRIARS

The Franciscan friary was founded in *c.* 1231 behind the built-up frontage of Southgate Street on land given by Thomas of Berkeley. This land, recorded as tenements of John le Boteler, had recently been conveyed by Lanthony Priory (Fosbrooke 1819, 296; *VCH Glos.*, ii, 111; *VCH Glos.*, ii, 291). It was soon to prove inadequate and in 1239 was enlarged by an additional gift, sanctioned on the grounds that 'it was better for the friars to have land to cultivate that they might provide sustenance instead of begging from others' (*VCH Glos.*, ii, 111). In 1285 the friars sought permission to acquire another plot of land near their church, and added a further half-acre in 1359. The precinct, with its cultivable land, now extended to the city walls to the east and south and covered an area of about four acres (*VCH Glos.*, ii, 111–12; Dallas 1932, 121).

Building must have been in progress by July 1236 when the friars received a grant of timber from the Forest of Dean (*Cal. Close Rolls 1234–7*, 283), an order repeated the following year, and was still in progress in 1241 when a further grant is recorded (*Cal. Close Rolls 1237–42*, 319). The surviving church is an early-sixteenth-century building, rebuilt at that time with money given by the Berkeley family; the nave and north aisle were spared demolition at the Dissolution when they were converted into a brewery (*VCH Glos.*, iv, 291). The claustral ranges lay south of the church. A lease of 1556 of the house and site of Greyfriars included a pasture bounded by the city wall on the east, St Mary's Lane to the north, the friars' church to the south and the 'walls of the late churchyard' to the west (*Cal. Recs Corpn Glouc.*, 1253). It was also said in 1888–9 that, forty years previously, 'fragments of the priors lodging and the conventual buildings were in existence on the south side of the church' (Dallas 1932, 124; *Trans. Bristol and Glos. Arch. Soc.* 13, 1888–9, 186); Causton's map of 1843 shows, however, virtually the same buildings south of the church as were there in 1884, so what this sighting was referring to is not clear.

The difficulties of the relationship between the claustral area and the Greyfriars Lane – which has been suggested to be a part of the planned pre-Conquest street-system – have already been outlined. The lane cuts directly through the claustral area, and in its recorded form should be a post-Dissolution feature. Possibly it reinstated an earlier lane that had been blocked by the construction of the friary buildings and survived only at the point of entry to the site from Southgate Street – but, if so, the evidence is lacking.

Plan-region IV: the riverside area

INTRODUCTION

This plan-region represents the area that lay between the western defences of the Roman fortress and the east channel of the River Severn. Though, in origin, settlement of this area may be characterized as 'suburban', the western defences had probably largely vanished by *c.* 1100 and there is little sign that by the later middle ages this area was regarded as being in any way different from or outside the city centre; in 1455 Cole treated that part of it with which he was concerned as a seamless extension of Westgate Street (*1455 Rental*, 46–8).

The way in which the riverside zone was developed in the post-Roman period and later varied greatly. The area is bisected by the line of the western approach road (Lower Westgate Street), the Roman road lying slightly south of its successor. By the time of the Conquest, Lower Westgate Street had become the focus for a ribbon of settlement extending from the western defences to the river-crossing. To the north of Lower Westgate Street and its plots lay St Mary's Square, a separate focus of activity with origins in the late-Roman period. Still further north lay, from *c.* 900, the precinct of the New Minster, possibly an earthwork enclosure with its back to the river. To the south of Lower Westgate Street lay the multiple stone and earthwork defences of the second royal castle, established in the early twelfth century. It has been suggested that this area was included within the pre-Conquest *burh*, and may even have formed an early pre-Conquest nucleus of commercial activity developing along the riverside. However, supporting evidence for this remains elusive, despite the undoubted significance of both St Mary de Lode and the New Minster (later St Oswald's). The Roman quayside wall also seems most likely to have been just that, without a defensive function or return walls to link it with the fortress and provide a secure riverside enceinte (Garrod and Heighway 1984, 4–6; Hurst 1986, 115–16; Heighway and Bryant 1999, 6 and note 13).

The riverside zone can be seen to have consisted of a number of quite separate component areas of very diverse character: essentially two defended precincts, one military, the other ecclesiastical, framing two quite separate built-up areas. These are the four constituent plan-units of the riverside zone, and each of the two central plan-units may be broken down into further distinct settlement components. The landscape of the area as a whole cannot be said to have exhibited any degree of morphological homogeneity other than that imposed by the containing framework of the river and the fortress wall. However, in archaeological terms, the relationship of these features to the component areas offers a strong unifying theme – that of reclamation.

A number of excavations and observations have shown that the east bank of the eastern river channel moved (or was moved) westwards over time, from the early-Roman period to the late-medieval (see above); in fact the process cannot be claimed to have been completed until what was left of the eastern channel was culverted in the nineteenth century. A significant stage in the river's retreat was marked by the construction of a masonry riverside retaining wall in the second–third centuries or later (Hurst 1986, 115–16; see above). This seems to have survived standing above ground into the twelfth century or later as a boundary between properties on Lower Westgate Street, though to the west of it dry inhabitable ground had arisen or been created – at least along the street – well before the Conquest (e.g. site 15/73: Hurst 1974, 48). The course of the Roman riverside wall has been established from Clare Street, north of Lower Westgate Street, southwards across the latter as far as Quay Street (Bareland). It may have extended northwards into the area of St Oswald's precinct and southwards under the castle, but in neither of these areas has the wall yet been seen nor the way in which the waterfront shifted been determined.

There is no doubt at all that, whatever the natural dynamics of the river channel, its westward movement and eventual disappearance were in part brought about through reclamation by landfill as a prelude to the extension of the settled area. Some of the details of this process are known through excavation around Lower Westgate Street (see below) but, while we may guess that reclamation also took place further to the north, and in the castle area to the south, this cannot yet be demonstrated.

Reclamation of a different, though related, kind may also be argued to have helped shape the eventual morphology of the eastern boundary of the riverside area, as the Roman western defences – the fortress wall and ditch – were removed by demolition and infilling. That process and its possible chronology have already been described but may have taken place in distinct episodes either side of Westgate Street. By 1100, if not before, the riverside zone was no longer suburban.

PLAN-UNIT IV.1: LOWER WESTGATE STREET (fig 3.14)

Between the line of the western fortress wall and the eastern channel of the Severn, Westgate Street and the plots fronting it constituted a distinct plan-unit, differing in character from the area further along Westgate Street within the walls, and separated from St Mary's Square and its plots to the north by an almost continuous boundary. A degree of internal homogeneity may be suggested on the basis of the approximately equal depth of the blocks each side of the street: that on the north side ranged from about 210 to 230 feet (*c*. 64–70 metres) deep, on the south from about 215 to 245 feet (*c*. 65–75 metres) deep; and on the similarity of at least some of the southern plots to those on the north. The area nevertheless contained a number of distinct character variations at a smaller scale. It can also be shown that the fairly straightforward recorded morphology of the area – one suggestive of a linearly built-up street – conceals a complex developmental process.

Comparison of the plots surveyed by the Ordnance Survey and properties recorded in the 1455 rental and other medieval sources shows most parts of the settlement pattern in this plan-unit to have been relatively stable from the end of the middle ages. In 1455 there were 19 properties on the Westgate Street frontage between Castle Lane and Walkers Lane (Lower Quay Street) (*1455 Rental*, 48a–54a); in 1884 there were between 15 and 17. From Walkers Lane to the Foreign Bridge were 12 individually listed properties and 'diverse tenements' in 1455 (54a–56a); in 1884 there were between 15 and 17. At the back of these were further plots facing Bareland to the south. The Lanthony rental shows there to have been 4 here in 1445 (A13, fo.

44v); there were 5 coherent plots here in the 1880s. From the boundaries mapped in the nineteenth century and the abuttals recorded in the fifteenth century it is possible to identify particular documented plots on both the Quay Street (Bareland) frontage and on the main Westgate Street frontage to the north.

Such a high degree of stability and continuity is not so apparent in the plots on the north side of Westgate Street. While they appear to have been longitudinally stable – mostly running back to the more or less continuous common rear boundary – there seems to have been a greater degree of lateral fluidity. In 1455, 5 tenements were recorded on the main frontage between Archdeacons Lane (later Archdeacon Street) and Dockam Lane (later Swan Lane) (*1455 Rental*, 46b–50b). The same block in 1884 was occupied by between 15 and 17 separate frontage properties, spread between about 10 identifiable plot tails visible to the rear – the sub-division evident in the plot series after the fifteenth century seems to have particularly affected the frontage. These changes also appear to have resulted in the disappearance of a minor lane – Powke Lane – that ran north from the Westgate Street frontage to the west side of St Oswald's precinct, where it was enclosed in 1290. Powke Lane has previously been identified with Swan Lane, but has recently been shown to have been a separate thoroughfare between Swan Lane and Archdeacons Lane; it has also been suggested that it may have marked a distinct stage in the westward advance of the pre-Conquest waterfront (Heighway and Bryant 1999, 6, 20 and note 14). To the east, three plots between Archdeacons Lane and St Nicholas's church in 1455 had

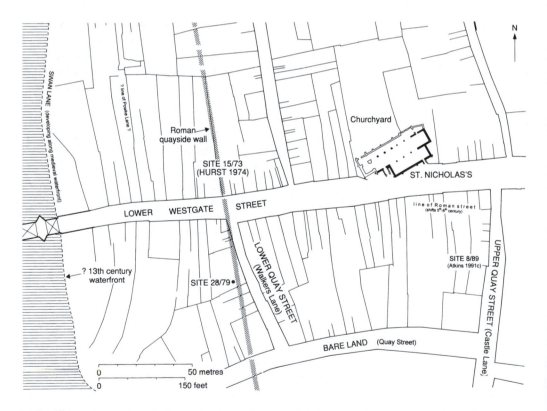

3.14   Gloucester: Lower Westgate Street, based on the first edition Ordnance Survey plans, showing excavation sites and the line of the Roman quayside wall

been divided into six by 1884 (*1455 Rental*, 46–48b). While there is good evidence for pressure on land here in the late-medieval period, there is at present no explanation for the apparent difference in plot behaviour either side of Lower Westgate Street.

One final process of change between the medieval period and the modern should be mentioned: the infilling of the river channel itself. The maps in this volume (e.g. figs 3.1 and 3.14) show the Foreign Bridge, river channel and the island in mid-channel, reconstructed as they may have appeared in the thirteenth century, based largely on archaeological evidence (e.g. Hurst 1974, 48–50; site 29/76: Garrod and Heighway 1984, 32–3). But a quite startling level of demand for new land here can be demonstrated within the late-medieval period. The bridge itself had tenements built on it even before the end of the thirteenth century (*1455 Rental*, 58a), and by 1455 there were ten individually listed properties and 'diverse adjoining tenements' occupying the northern Westgate Street frontage between Powke Lane and whatever remained of the channel (50–52b).

The homogeneity of the plot-series on the north side of the street was disturbed only where fairly intensive lateral sub-division of corner plots had taken place to form small plots facing into Archdeacons Lane, and the series as a whole may be treated as a single entity (sub-unit IV.1.i). Most of these plots terminated at a back-fence line running almost continuously from St Mary's Street (Abbey Lane) to Swan Lane (Dockams Lane) alongside the river. There is little dating evidence for this boundary, though given the number of plots it served and its apparent tenurial significance, it would be surprising if it were not a primary feature of the plot-pattern, and archaeological evidence does in fact imply a pre-twelfth century date for it (see below).

The south side of the street was more heterogeneous in character, and three distinct components or sub-units can be defined. Perhaps the most distinctive of these lay immediately east of the Foreign Bridge. Here, two or three plots curved strongly westwards towards the river (IV.1.ii). The detailed documentary record of these properties needs examination, but related plot-patterns are found in a number of other medieval towns where major traffic streets make a perpendicular approach to a waterfront (for these parallels see Baker, Lawson, Maxwell and Smith 1993). Their form suggests that the plots were laid out to accommodate a demand for properties with access to both street- and river-frontages, but by 1390 they ended at the common quay (*VCH Glos.*, iv, 251). In part, an explanation might be found in the gradual silting of the east channel of the Severn and the westward movement of the waterfront: an area of new dry ground might have become available for communal use. But this is not enough to explain why the usual rules of foreshore reclamation did not operate, and – as witnessed on countless excavated waterfronts – the plots extended *ad infinitum* as the waterfront moved. An explanation should possibly be sought in the clearance of land around the castle in the thirteenth century and its subsequent appropriation by the burgesses (see below). A demand for watered plots of this type is likely to have come from a number of different crafts. The abundant historical evidence for fullers in precisely this part of Westgate Street in the late twelfth century suggests this craft's early prevalence, and dyers were here in strength in the thirteenth century (*VCH Glos.*, iv, 26). A grant in *c.* 1220 of land reaching from the *vico fullonum* to the Severn lying next to land of Haulf the Schipsmit gives a further clue to the diversity of trades that would have found such premises useful (*Cal. Recs Corpn Glouc.*, 206).

Immediately east of these plots, within the same street-block, the adjacent Lower Westgate Street plots terminated against a common boundary with a series of plots facing south onto Quay Street (Bareland) (IV.1.iii). This pattern was maintained in the larger street-block to the east; here, a number of plots extended from the main frontage through to the Bareland at the rear but rather more were curtailed by the development of south-facing plots. These were separated from the Lower Westgate Street plots by a discontinuous arc of property boundaries about half-way between the two streets. Plots in what was to become the Bareland were built up by the beginning of the thirteenth century, when tenements here were being accumulated and rented out by Lanthony Priory. Most were then described as lying in Smiths Street, although others were said to be situated in Castle Street, near to the fullers' land, next to the castle ditch, or beside the Severn (A5, fos 38v–45; A13, fos 42v–44). All of these properties were subsequently cleared when the castle defences were extended in 1265 during the Barons' War (*Cal. Patent Rolls 1485–94*, 46; A13, fos 43v–44), and the land then lay open. The Bareland was reported in 1373 to be the customary place for the constables of the castle to hold musters of their soldiers, but domestic pressure on this open space had turned it into a dumping-ground for the people of Gloucester, who had filled it with dung and other refuse (*Cal. Patent Rolls 1370–74*, 293).

By the early fifteenth century, as the military necessity for this cleared zone had declined, the south-facing plots had once again been built on. The stewards of Gloucester claimed the land as part of their waste, and in 1440 they were drawing rent from 18 tenements and curtilages – much to Lanthony's disgust. Probably this was a recent development: several of the tenements were described in Lanthony's rental of *c.* 1445 – and perhaps in the lost 1440 rental of corporation lands that Steymur and Cole cited – as newly-built upon the vacant land (A13, fos 44–5). And not all that part of the Bareland was yet let to tenants, for in 1454 a vacant plot measuring 24 x 60 yards (22 x 55 metres), next to the Severn and to the north of the castle ditch, and which was anciently called *Myrivale*, was given to the Butchers' Gild as a place to dump their offal (A13, fos 45, 61; Stevenson 1891, 521–2). The existing identity of this plot, and the name *Oldehey* recorded as that of the vacant land on which the carpenter William Rede's newly built tenement stood (A13, fo. 44v), suggest that in at least some of the Bareland the identity of the ancient plots had survived.

It is difficult to say whether the arc of south-facing plots seen on the map accurately represents the extent of the pre-thirteenth century plots, or represents a tide-mark left by the 1265–6 clearance. Just possibly it represents both, the clearance itself having respected contemporary property boundaries on the margin of the affected area. On Lower Westgate Street, the third tenement east of the corner of Lower Quay Street (Walkers Lane) can be shown from its measurements to have extended back to this arc in 1278–82: it was granted to Lanthony by St Bartholomew's, at which time it abutted the 'land formerly of Gilbert Gobihc' at the rear (A5, fo. 57v).

The fairly simple morphology of this area is thus shown by the documentary evidence to conceal a more complicated developmental sequence involving the changing relationship of the built-up area to the castle: there is no doubt that the southern edge of this plan-unit was shaped by the second castle. The question that now arises is that of the likely morphology of this area before the castle was constructed in the early twelfth century. Quay Street (Bareland), the curving road behind the Westgate Street frontage, may reasonably be supposed to owe its form to the presence of the castle and the lip of the outer ditch – which it follows. Whether or not an east–west thoroughfare existed here before the castle was built is unknown. Possibly one existed for a very short time, after the breaking-through of the old west fortress wall and before the construction of the second castle; earlier, we might speculate that the plots on the south side of Westgate Street outside the fortress area more closely resembled those on the north, ending at a similar back-fence line, about the same distance from the street, on roughly the line later occupied by Bareland.

While the cartographic and documentary sources stress this north–south progression of events, the archaeological evidence reveals the morphological origins of this part of town to lie in the general east to west movement and eventual infilling of the eastern channel of the Severn. The Roman quayside wall was of particular importance in this process. Its line bisects the area, dividing it into an eastern half that was certainly dry and habitable in the Roman period and subsequently, and a western half, formerly open water, but in the early-medieval period subject to silting and reclamation processes that now – with their relationship to the mapped topography – have to be determined. Three excavated sites are particularly relevant. The wall itself was excavated on the north side of the street on the Westgate Street Flats site in the early 1970s, and dry ground found on its east side and alluvial deposits on its west (site 15/73: Hurst 1974, 46–8; Garrod and Heighway 1984, 48–51; Hurst 1986, 115–16). About 15 metres west of the wall, also on the north side of Westgate Street, excavations for a cellar revealed the presence of a late pre-Conquest building, the first in a structural sequence overlying the alluvial silts (Hurst 1974, 48). Hurst's original dating of this to the eleventh century was later revised (by Alan Vince) to the late tenth century, though not explained (Heighway 1984a, 368 and note 11). If – as Heighway's note suggests – it was on the basis of the presence of Stafford-type ware (*alias* Chester ware), the date range could be as wide as the early ninth to early eleventh centuries (Ford 1995). The riverside wall was found again, to the south, on the west side of Lower Quay Street (site 28/79: Garrod and Heighway 1984, 48–51). On this site, silts to the west of the wall were overlain by 'a series of metallings with rubble, indicating the reclamation of this area as dry land' (Garrod and Heighway 1984, 48); this material contained late-eleventh-century pottery, and the wall was interpreted to have remained in use as a quayside wall as late as the tenth century. It survived until the early twelfth century when it was robbed (possibly quarried for the construction of the castle). The line of the wall was then immediately overtaken by the development of housing on the lane, the ensuing sequence of timber buildings interrupted between the mid-thirteenth and the fifteenth centuries – perhaps as part of the Bareland clearance (Garrod and Heighway 1984, 49-51).

The Roman quayside wall had a subtle but definite and enduring impact on the town-plan in this area. Where it crosses it, Westgate Street bends slightly northwards; the same effect is more strongly apparent in the back-fence line to the northern plot series – it was deflected northwards at the point where it crossed the line of the Roman wall. Given the archaeological evidence outlined above, a case can be made for the establishment of this back-fence line to an initial plot-series on dry ground within (east of) the Roman quayside wall. When – by whatever process – land to the west became suitable for habitation, the series was extended westwards to the new waterfront. On the south side of the street, an initial plot-series matching that to the north was probably laid out on dry land to the east of the old quayside wall, quite possibly as part of a single operation – though no metrological regularity has been detected in the cartographically recorded boundaries. This 'dry land' series was subsequently extended westwards over the Roman wall following a reclamation episode or episodes, though the archaeological evidence suggests that this occurred perhaps a century after the extension of settlement on the north frontage. The apparent time-lag may, however, be accounted for in the relationship of the excavated sites to Westgate Street. The information from the north side was derived close to the frontage; the Lower Quay Street site lay about 30 metres away from it. If, as seems to be the case, Westgate Street west of the Roman quayside wall was raised on a causeway across wet or floodable ground, excavated sequences from other medieval towns suggest that settlement along it may well have proceeded both by linear accretion ('ribbon development') and by reclamation in stages back from the causeway-street frontage, as happened at, for example, Oxford and at Wigford in Lincoln (Durham 1984; Young and Vince 1992). It is possible that the late-eleventh century (or later) landfill beyond the Roman wall, encountered by the Lower Quay Street excavation, lay within the back of a Westgate Street plot whose frontage had been reclaimed and used for a century or more. The cartographically recorded settlement pattern within the wet, western half of the plan-unit – a probable extension of that in the eastern half – may at first have formed a framework for properties that were intensively exploited only at the frontages.

PLAN-UNIT IV.2: ST MARY'S SQUARE (fig. 3.15)

Most of the historic landscape of this area was destroyed without investigation in the 1960s. It consisted of four main components: the square itself (IV.2.i), two main plot-series to the north and the south (IV.2.ii and IV.2.iii); and a lesser plot-series to the west (IV.2.iv) facing the square, with limited plot development behind on the two curving lanes heading for the river. As no landgable rents were due to the Crown from this area, it was not covered by the 1455 rental, and there is almost no documentary evidence with which to examine the relationship between the landscape recorded in the nineteenth century and that of the medieval period. Before clearance in the late 1960s the square was surrounded by mixed housing of traditional character, including a proportion of timber-framed building; the chances of major post-medieval transformations in the local plot-pattern are probably slight.

The square and the church   The church of St Mary de Lode is discussed fully elsewhere (below, pp. 97–9). In summary, excavation determined that it lay on the site of a well-appointed Roman building that stood in an open metalled area and was demolished at the end of the Roman period. A timber-framed building was erected, possibly in the fifth or sixth century, with burials

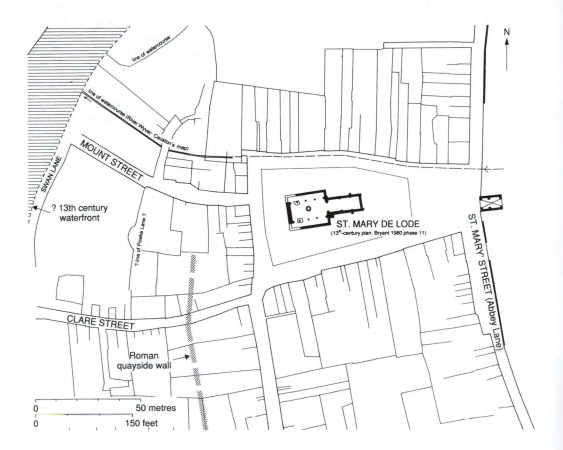

3.15   Gloucester: St Mary's Square, plan based on the first edition Ordnance Survey, with St Mary de Lode in its thirteenth-century form

sealed beneath its floor and further burials outside in a 'paved forecourt'. By the ninth century a structure that was without doubt a church occupied the site, still preserving the Roman alignment (Bryant 1980, 8–9). The archaeological evidence for a very early date for St Mary's church is reinforced and amplified by the extensive historical evidence for its early importance over a wide area of the surrounding countryside (Bassett 1992). This convergence of evidence is very fortunate as it establishes beyond all reasonable doubt the relationship between the church and the surrounding urban landscape: St Mary's Square in its known – nearly triangular – form was placed symmetrically about the church, and not vice versa. Possibly, the square may represent a continuation and reshaping of the open area that had surrounded the original Roman building.

As recorded in the nineteenth century, the south side of the square was lined by a series of large, wide, rectangular plots subject to a degree of sub-division at the frontage (iv.2.iii). These terminated at the nearly continuous back-fence line, discussed earlier. The plots on the north side (IV.2.ii) may be divided into two series, a longer one to the east with a narrow alley running part-way along the back-fence, and a shorter series to the west; it is difficult to know whether the difference between these two represented different phases of development, or whether one group of plots was truncated or another extended. Perhaps the most striking feature of the local plot-pattern was the differential development of plots between the north and south sides, and the west side of the square. Here (IV.2.iv), the plots were considerably smaller. An explanation may be found in the presence, about 30 metres to the west, of the former Roman riverside wall. Possibly this, with wet or floodable ground beyond, inhibited the rearward development of plots; just conceivably, the west end of the square was actually used for a time as a waterfront and left open when the plots on the long sides were developed. All depends on the relative chronology of settlement within and reclamation beyond the riverside wall; there is little enough evidence for the latter, and virtually none for the former.

Observation of a sewer-trench section along Clare Street, running westwards from the square, was able to locate the course of the Roman riverside wall and show that it was robbed before the twelfth century, when buildings were constructed over it (Garrod and Heighway 1984, site 59/74, 17). The northern lane led to a crossing-point over the east channel, spanned by a footbridge by 1518; this gave access to the abbey's meadows across the river (*VCH Glos.*, iv, 66). The area was still largely open in the nineteenth century. Slightly curved property boundaries running between the two lanes about 60 metres west of St Mary's Square, and a cul-de-sac lane running north from Mount Street (fig. 3.15) probably represent the course of the former Powke Lane, on its way from the Lower Westgate Street frontage to the west side of St Oswald's precinct (Heighway and Bryant 1999, 6 and note 14; and see above).

Archaeological investigations have been confined largely to the interior of the church and to the western area on and beyond the line of the Roman quayside wall. The only dating evidence for the establishment of St Mary's Square is circumstantial – inferred from historical sources and from relationships between this and other components of the town-plan. At present, what little evidence there is suggests that the square was a creation of the late pre-Conquest period. This is based, first and foremost, on the evidence that this area was almost exclusively abbey property, was populated by its tenants, and did not render landgable payments. The Evesham survey of *c.* 1100 records that the abbey had 52 burgesses in Gloucester (BL Cotton Vespasian B xxiv fo. 57r; text edited by Howard Clarke in Moore 1982, appendix). Just possibly this refers to a scattered population, but it is more likely to refer to the inhabitants of a coherent block of property (see pp. 278–9, below). If St Mary's Square was, as the Victoria County History and others have suggested 'the site of the abbey's ancient burgage property' (*VCH Glos.*, iv, 66), what was it doing here?

Its relationship to the abbey precinct is the critical factor. The square faces and tapers towards the abbey's west gate: it appears to be a classic instance of a market place and settlement developed at the gate of a substantial ecclesiastical house. Whether this was so or not depends very much on the date of this side of the abbey precinct and its extension westwards over the Roman fortress wall, and this, as discussed earlier, is a matter of some controversy. The evidence from King Edward Street and College Street suggests that the precinct had probably expanded westwards to achieve its final extent well before the Conquest. If this is accepted, it is possible that St Mary's Square too was of pre-Conquest origin and indeed the site of the 'abbey's ancient burgage property' in *c.* 1100.

PLAN-UNIT IV.3: ST MARY'S SQUARE AND ST OSWALD'S PRECINCT

What was the relationship of St Mary's Square to the New Minster precinct, St Oswald's? It seems very unlikely that the square, in its known form with its associated plots, could pre-date the first decade of the tenth century and the foundation of St Oswald's – unless the origins of St Mary's Square are really non-urban, to be sought instead in a primary monastic enclosure around the church. St Oswald's appears to lie within a ditched riverside enclosure. A ditch has been located on its north-east side (Spry, in Hurst 1974, 40–41), and may have returned to the river to the north of St Mary's. Speed's map of 1610 shows two watercourses flowing into the river between St Mary's and St Oswald's, either of which could have been a successor to or a substitute for a ditch defining the south side of St Oswald's precinct (see Heighway and Bryant 1999, 8–9). Or, just possibly, the New Minster was founded within a much larger, older enclosure that had previously been monopolized by St Mary's. Outside the precinct to the north-east, a curved series of short plots (IV.3.ii) occupied the east side of the street. Excavation found that housing built with earth-fast foundations developed here by the thirteenth century, replaced by timber-framed buildings in the fourteenth century (Spry, ibid).

PLAN-UNIT IV.4: THE SECOND CASTLE

Nothing now remains above ground of Gloucester's second royal castle, though the continuing presence on the site of the County Gaol provides a thread of institutional continuity. The castle's development and topography have been reconstructed from scattered and fragmentary archaeological, cartographic, and documentary sources by Hurst (1984) and it would not be appropriate to offer anything more than the briefest summary here.

The construction of the second castle commenced with the building of a stone keep, to the west of the old castle and whatever was left of the Roman walls there, in *c.* 1110–20. It was evidently a substantial building – in plan it has been compared to the keep at Rochester (Hurst 1984, 109–10). For a time it appears to have co-existed with the old castle; material from the old motte was used in the construction of an east-facing earthwork barbican (Atkin 1991a, 9). By the mid thirteenth century the new castle had acquired concentric defences of curtain walls and substantial ditches, covering an area of about 9 acres (3.6 hectares), very similar in scale to the royal castles in the neighbouring shire towns of Hereford, Worcester and Shrewsbury. In the thirteenth century further clearance of buildings beyond the outer ditch took place. The military importance of the site declined thereafter, and its exclusive use as a prison began in the reign of Richard III (Hurst 1984, 110–11).

Plan-region V: Hare Lane–Wateringstead (fig 3.16)

The area to the north of the Roman fortress and the abbey precinct constitutes perhaps the most singular element of Gloucester's medieval town-plan. It consisted of what appears to have been a long rectilinear marketplace or street, with associated streets and plot-series. Most of these were provided with access to the watercourses that surrounded, and may have defended, the whole area.

The outer boundary was (at least later) defined by the curving course of the River Twyver. Evidence that this watercourse had a defensive function, or at least that it was considered as a boundary across which the movement of traffic was controlled, may be found in the location of two medieval gates at the points at which it ran across major roads. The outer north gate on Lower

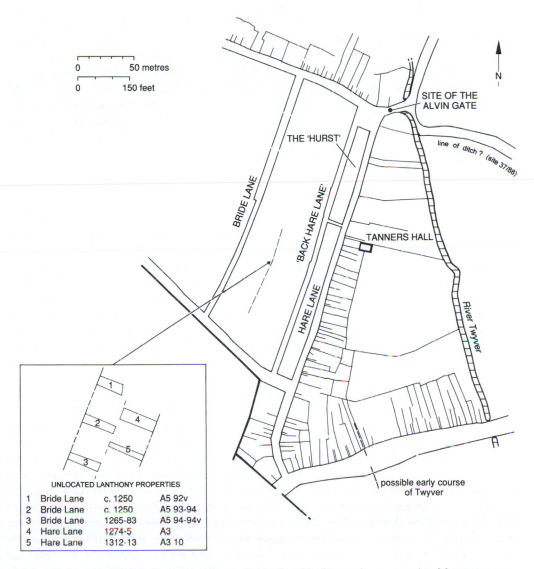

	UNLOCATED LANTHONY PROPERTIES		
1	Bride Lane	c. 1250	A5 92v
2	Bride Lane	c. 1250	A5 93-94
3	Bride Lane	1265-83	A5 94-94v
4	Hare Lane	1274-5	A3
5	Hare Lane	1312-13	A3 10

3.16   Gloucester: the Hare Lane–Wateringstead suburb, with plans to the same scale of former Lanthony Priory properties between Bride Lane and Hare Lane

Northgate Street is discussed later. The Alvin Gate (Ælfwine's gate) at the head of Hare Lane, giving access to this area from the north and the palace site at Kingsholm, was first recorded in *c.* 1190–1200 (Heighway 1983b, 7). The early appearance of the gate in the historical record, and the Old English personal name attached to it, suggest that it was a pre-Conquest feature.

The course of the Twyver revealed by cartography of the eighteenth century and later is probably oversimplified, there being evidence for a subsidiary channel west of the main channel, closer to Hare Lane (Heighway 1983b, 83; Garrod 1990, 14: site 5/89). On the northern side of the area the main channel ran 100–150 metres to the north of St Catherine's Street, passing close to the chapel of St Thomas on the road between the royal palace at Kingsholm and the New Minster (see p. 125, below). There is no doubt that this channel had some significance as a boundary, and it appears to have done so in the early-Roman period as the prevailing orientation of Roman roads and buildings differed either side of it (Hurst 1986, 115). There was additionally a post-Roman or early-medieval ditch or second watercourse on the line of St Catherine's Street (Wateringstead) itself, disused and levelled by the late eleventh or twelfth century when there is evidence for buildings facing the street (Hurst 1974, 40–41; 1986, 115). The Alvin Gate may possibly have been associated with this feature, as well as with the Twyver to the south. Finally, a third possible defensive barrier, also heading for the Alvin Gate, has been seen following the curving line of Alvin Street to the east. No dating evidence is yet forthcoming, but it raises the possibility that – at least at some stage – Hare Lane and the adjoining London Road suburb were both enclosed within a wider defensive scheme (see pp. 326, below).

Plan-units V.1–3: Hare Lane and Bride Lane

The elongated rectangle of Hare Lane was formed by a pair of parallel north–south roads: Hare Lane on the east, and Back Hare Lane (now Park Street) on the west. They were separated by a narrow block of land (V.1) known as the Hurst, which was built up at the time of the 1455 rental (82a). Trenches dug along the west side of Hare Lane revealed an undated but well-made primary metalled surface with a side ditch. The ditch, possibly recut, contained eleventh/twelfth to fourteenth-century pottery; the primary road metalling was 'cut from a post-Roman dark loam layer into Roman ground level', and was itself cut or worn away by a stretch of sunken lane with thirteenth–fourteenth-century pottery amongst its metalling and silting. Overlying the post-Roman dark soil within the Hurst was a sequence of metalled, trampled and soil layers. The earlier stratigraphy in this sequence could not be dated, though later stony surfaces were associated with some structural features and fourteenth-century and fifteenth-century pottery. (Garrod 1990, 15–16: site 5/89; 18: site 10/89).

The east side of Hare Lane was occupied by a distinctive series of plots (V.2). The very schematic coverage of this area by the 1455 rental does not allow any comparison of the density of plots then and in the 1880s but a number of surviving or recorded late-medieval and sub-medieval buildings suggest that the plot-pattern here was substantially stable between the late-medieval period and the late eighteenth century. Plots at the south end were interlocked with those on Lower Northgate Street. Most of the Hare Lane frontage was divided into short, narrow plots ending on one of two common back-fence lines parallel to the street; that at the south end may have coincided with the subsidiary channel of the Twyver referred to earlier. These back-fence lines were interrupted by long primary boundaries running from the frontage back to the more easterly channel of the Twyver; two of these at the south end curved northwards, so that their line was perpendicular to Hare Lane close to the frontage but parallel to Lower Northgate Street nearer to the watercourse (see also p. 90, below). The layout was such that the maximum number of plots had access to one or both watercourses. At the north end of the street the plots assumed a different form, a few much wider plots divided by boundaries extending to the eastern watercourse.

There is no doubt that access to running water was a concern for plot-holders here from as far back as historical evidence is available. The area was colonized by tanners from at least the early thirteenth century, Hare Lane being known as the tanners' street in the 1230s. Their company hall was here, a first-floor hall of the late thirteenth century, towards the back of the northernmost of the shorter plots. Excavation found only a single sherd of eleventh/twelfth-century pottery as definite evidence for earlier activity on this frontage, though a possible find of pottery type TF41a may suggest pre-Conquest activity (Heighway 1983b, 91). 'Successive medieval domestic and/or industrial floors' have been recorded in commercial excavations on the western side of Back Hare Lane (Park Street), the earliest seen contained pottery of the eleventh to thirteenth centuries (Garrod and Heighway 1984, 39: site 11/77).

Bride Lane (St Brigid's Lane) ran parallel to Hare Lane, about 60 metres to the west (V.3). Historical evidence clearly shows its late- and post-medieval decline and depopulation, with tenements amalgamated or waste (see pp. 328–9, below). An estate plan shows it to have survived, deserted, in the 1740s (GCL NQ 30/36), though it had disappeared by 1780 (Hall & Pinnell's map). Its parallel course suggests that Bride Lane may have been contemporary or nearly contemporary with Hare Lane. The latter has all the characteristics of a substantial act of town-planning (see below) and Bride Lane may have been created as part of the same scheme. It is less certain whether Bride Lane was intended to function as a rear service-lane to plots fronting Hare Lane, or as an independent street with its own plots. Some details of the medieval Bride Lane plots, and plots on the west side of Hare Lane, can be reconstructed with the help of the handful of Lanthony Priory leases that record dimensions. Although the individual plots cannot be located accurately on the ground, the leases show that the Hare Lane plots backed onto the Bride Lane plots fairly consistently slightly west of half-way between the two frontages. This may – tentatively – suggest that the Bride Lane plots were not created by the secondary development of the tails of former Hare Lane plots extending from lane to lane, but that each lane had its own, independent plot-series.

Bride Lane and domestic occupation along it has been glimpsed archaeologically in one trench during the observation of works for a new road. The lane itself was represented by a narrow band of three successive worn, rutted, and silted metalled surfaces, a piece of fourteenth-century pottery resting on the lowest. Very little in the way of domestic occupation was found on the east side of Bride Lane, though to the west there was a concentration of eleventh/twelfth to fifteenth-century pitting – presumably within former tenements (Garrod 1990, 17–19: site 10/89).

Discussion   Hare Lane is generally, and probably correctly, considered to have been a street-market, created and used as such for only a short period of time. Hard evidence for the development of this area before the Conquest is not abundant, resting primarily on the names attached to the Alvin (Ælfwine's) Gate, and Hare Lane itself (*here straet* – the military street) (Heighway 1984a, 369). Good ceramic evidence for pre-Conquest activity in this suburb is forthcoming from the area north of St Oswald's (see below) but not as yet from Hare Lane itself, and the substantial early metalling of the street cannot be closely dated. If, as it appears, this area was laid out before the Conquest, its non-appearance as a market in the documentary record would not be significant.

Hare Lane, and apparently Bride Lane, probably came into existence as the result of a significant town-planning exercise. Hare Lane – the military street – represents the principal road between Gloucester and the late-Saxon palace site of Kingsholm, and beyond that part of the long-distance route northwards along the east bank of the Severn. But some uncertainty surrounds the Roman background to this area. Hare Lane may have replaced (and been a diversion of) a Roman street lying a short distance to the east, roughly on the line of the eighteenth-century Worcester Street joining the Cirencester and London Road (Lower Northgate Street) about half-way between the inner and outer north gates (Garrod and Heighway 1984, 36–7). But another Roman street may partially underlie Hare Lane itself, as a Roman frontage has been spotted under the Back Hare Lane frontage (the west side of Hare Lane). This observation (by Patrick Garrod), together with the Roman metalling found under Tanners Hall, could suggest that the medieval streets in this area originated in the remnants of an earlier, Roman, layout (C. Heighway, pers. comm.).

If Hare Lane, in its recognizable form, and Bride Lane had originated or been improved in a planning or replanning exercise in the pre-Conquest period, it is probable that the New Minster (St Oswald's) and the Crown shared responsibility for it. The Crown's interest in new defensive works and the diversion of a strategic road are obvious, and the tenements on the east side of Hare Lane lay in St John's parish and rendered landgable to the Crown (see p. 104). The remainder of the area was the property of St Oswald's and lay within its parish.

External parallels for Hare Lane are discussed below. Here it is sufficient to note that it may well belong to the large family of rectilinear planned street-markets characteristic of both early-medieval intramural planning (e.g. Wallingford) and suburbs (e.g. St Giles', Oxford). The possibility of Hare Lane having been planned more specifically as a cattle market has been discussed before (e.g. Heighway 1984b, 44). The evidence for the provision of water-access to the plots on the eastern side offers some support for this interpretation, and a parallel may be found at Pride Hill in Shrewsbury, where what appears to have been an extramural or peripheral market street was established, with large, planned, watered plots on one side arguably dedicated to the watering of livestock, before eventual subdivision and colonization for industrial use (Baker, Lawson, Maxwell and Smith 1993).

If, as suggested, Bride Lane represented an independent component of the same planned layout, the scale of this enterprise becomes all the more striking, particularly so given that intramural development in Gloucester was largely confined to the main streets before *c.* 1100. The physical evidence of the Hare Lane area is dominated by the archaeological and cartographic evidence of infrastructure rather than occupation – particularly for the pre-Conquest period. One possibility is that, as an urban development, it was not a great success. Another that cannot be dismissed is that these features were not intended to be, or not expected to be, a framework for permanent settlement but were instead intended to accommodate seasonal events: perhaps, given the New Minster's interest, an annual fair on the feast day of St Oswald.

Plan-unit V.4: St Catherine's Street (Wateringstead)

The origins of this road have already been mentioned: it appears to reflect the line of a post-Roman or early-medieval ditch, infilled and replaced by housing from the late-eleventh or early-twelfth centuries onwards (Hurst 1974, 40–41). The medieval name reflects its use 'by townspeople for collecting water from the river' (*VCH Glos.*, iv, 66). One surviving Lanthony lease for a short (*c.* 58–63 feet/17.7–19.2 metre), wide (*c.* 40 feet/12.2 metre) plot in 1413 (A3, fos 65v–66) is compatible with the cartographically recorded plot-pattern on the north side – a series of short, squat, irregular plots with intensive sub-division on the frontage. Whether these plots at some stage had tails or associated crofts extending northwards to the Twyver is unknown, but it seems not unlikely given the character of the plots in the adjoining areas.

Excavation of a site on the west side of the western arm of the street, within a broad plot extending back to the eastern channel of the Severn, found a metalled surface extending from under St Catherine's Street into the site. The surface sealed a pit containing tenth-century flint-tempered pottery and had Saxo-Norman pottery scattered on the surface (Garrod 1987, site 21/85, 18). This is useful, firstly, as an indicator of activity here before the Conquest; secondly, it may possibly – as Garrod noted – be related to the use of these plots for access to a Severn waterfront, recalling traditions that the predecessor to the late-medieval public quay lay in the area of St Oswald's.

It remains to consider the question of the relationship of the Hare Lane suburb to the Roman and pre-Conquest walled town, and to the neighbouring London Road suburb. The precise relationship of Hare Lane to the Roman fortress is not clear. This is because the north-west corner of the old defences was obscured by the expansion of the St Peter's Abbey precinct, a process not completed until the early thirteenth century when it expanded northwards onto land that belonged to St Oswald's. How was the line of the new northern precinct boundary of 1218, the line of the modern Pitt Street, determined? There seems to be no way of knowing at present whether it was a completely new feature in 1218, post-dating and perhaps impinging on the Hare Lane suburb, or whether the abbey precinct acquired land up to a pre-existing road or boundary. This will only ever be decided finally by excavation or geophysical survey, but it is worth noting that the orientation of Pitt Street and thus the abbey precinct's north wall is quite different from the prevailing orientation of Hare Lane and the other streets of that area, and seems most likely to have been imposed upon them. Assuming then that Pitt Street and the north wall of the precinct were indeed secondary to Hare Lane, a brief speculation on the likely form of the pre-1218 and pre-Conquest landscape may be worthwhile. One particularly likely scenario is that Pitt Street replaced a pre-Conquest road that had also connected the base of the Hare Lane marketplace with the area around St Mary de Lode, but perpendicular to the line of Hare Lane, running just past the corner of the defences, and the watercourse outside. The abbey precinct needed to expand furthest in the area to the north of the claustral ranges and it was this requirement that determined the line taken by the new north wall of 1218.

The question of the relationship between the Hare Lane suburb and the adjacent but separate suburban development to its south-east, along London Road (plan-region VI), arises from the discovery of a large ditch, probably medieval, following and probably determining the line of Alvin Street, linking the two suburbs (Garrod 1989, 15: site 37/88, see fig. 3.16). This feature raises the possibility that the Alvin Gate may, perhaps at a later stage of its history, have been associated with a defensive or jurisdictional boundary that enclosed the inner part of the London Road suburb, possibly in succession to the Outer North Gate on the line of the Twyver channels flanking the east side of Hare Lane. Little more can be said until archaeological evidence for the date and function of this ditch is forthcoming – though it does underline the potential impermanence of suburban boundaries, and the potential spectrum of function that lies between serious defence and the demarcation of jurisdiction.

Plan-region VI: the London Road suburb

Although this suburb is given an identity, and a degree of morphological unity, by its dependence upon a single road (Lower Northgate Street/London Road), it is impossible to characterize it as a single indivisible entity because the street-space itself, and the character of the plots along it, changed at intervals in a fairly marked way. Three principal constituent areas have been identified and defined as plan-units; further differences have also been noted in the character of the plots north and south of the street.

PLAN-UNIT VI.1: LOWER NORTHGATE STREET (WEST), BETWEEN THE GATES

Immediately beyond the Roman and medieval North Gate lay an area of suburban settlement whose outer limit was marked by the eastern channel of the Twyver and by the Outer North Gate, the area expressed in the 1455 rental as 'betweeen the north gates' (88a). The street itself within these bounds is distinctive – irregular frontage lines still defining a swollen street-space. The street directly overlies its Roman predecessor (Garrod and Heighway 1984, 36 and fig. 9: site 33/76 VIII). The plot pattern differed somewhat either side of the street. The plots to the north (VI.1.i) were, at least in the nineteenth century, generally narrow, and interlocked at the west end of the street with plots fronting Hare Lane. Comparisons with plot-densities in 1455 are hindered in this area by streets inserted in the eighteenth and nineteenth centuries. The north side plots shared a common back-fence line, lying roughly parallel to the street, in the form of the first of several primary boundaries to plots fronting Hare Lane, extending eastwards to the main channel of the Twyver. These features tentatively suggest that the partitioning of the Northgate Street frontage in this area post-dated the establishment of plots on Hare Lane. Excavations behind Victorian cellars on the north frontage at 63–71 Northgate Street found medieval occupation commencing in the late twelfth century. A pit containing pottery of that date was sealed by the floor of one of two timber buildings; these were replaced by two further timber-framed buildings – one of them a forge – with stone ground-walls, in the late thirteenth or early fourteenth century (Hurst 1972, 65–6). From the outset, the buildings respected the property boundary between Nos 69 and 71 and, while the scale of investigation was limited, the evidence from this site suggests a degree of stability in the local plot-pattern. It also suggests initial urbanization in *c.* 1200; this may well be misleading, a product of a small archaeological sample, as other evidence points to settlement here at an earlier date (see below, pp. 326–7).

The plots on the southern frontage (sub-unit VI.1.ii) were of more irregular layout than those on the north; they were of varying depth, with no common back-fence line, ending instead against irregular parcels of land confined within the curving course of the River Twyver. With the exception of those immediately outside the city wall, the plots all curved eastwards, the longer tails accommodating the angle formed by the city wall and the street. A number of these plots had access to water; some, particularly those nearer the outer gate, may have had rearward access to the channel of the Twyver connecting the Outer North Gate with the east corner of the fortress. This may well have been an eastward diversion from the former western channel passing straight through the middle of the plot-series. This was found in building work in the mid nineteenth century (Fullbrook-Leggatt 1964, 81–2; Heighway 1983b, 6), and also noted in the 1455 rental, which recorded a St Peter's Abbey tenement about half-way along the northern frontage 'built and situated near and above the brook there' (93a). Two tanners held tenements in this part of the southern frontage in 1455, one practising his craft there (*1455 Rental*, 108a). His premises may perhaps have been at no. 84, where excavations in the early 1970s behind the cellared frontage found a late-medieval yard area cut by a pit containing cattle skulls and horn-cores. The site was rebuilt in the early sixteenth century with new timber-framed ranges running back from the frontage incorporating tanning pits (Hurst 1974, 34–8).

SUB-UNIT VI.2.i: THE WHITEFRIARS

The Carmelite friary was founded in *c.* 1268, and occupied a site just to the south of this part of Northgate Street, in the pear-shaped parcel of land between two channels of the River Twyver that converged on the outer north gate. The precinct was enlarged after its foundation by the gift of additional land in 1343. Most of its buildings were destroyed in the mid sixteenth century though two that survived played a part in the siege of 1643 (*VCH Glos.*, iv, 292). The monitoring of service trenches in 1974 located mortared limestone walls on an east–west alignment and a floor of medieval plain glazed tiles. These are suggested to have belonged to the friary church, which appears to have stood immediately east of the western channel of the Twyver (Garrod and Heighway 1984, 13 and fig. 9).

PLAN-UNIT VI.2: LOWER NORTHGATE STREET (EAST) – WITHOUT THE OUTER NORTH GATE

The character of the suburb changed again beyond the Outer North Gate and the Twyver. Larger plots occupied both sides of the street. In the eighteenth and nineteenth centuries those on the north side between the site of the gate and Alvin Street (the medieval Fete Lane) lay on two different alignments: those nearest the gate lying roughly perpendicular to the street, those to the east assuming a north-west/south-east axis that was roughly parallel to that of Alvin Street but, surprisingly, was echoed across the street by all of the south side plots in this area. The latter, at least by the late eighteenth century, ended at a common back-fence line – the north side of a large parcel of land, on a not-quite perpendicular north-east/south-west axis. The explanation for this clash in orientations may simply be due to a conflict between the north-east/south-west axis of the street and the prevailing 'grain' of the local field system. In this area the field boundaries and the ditched, canalized and diverted watercourses followed a general north-west / south-east orientation (that of Barton Street). While this may largely have been determined by the topographical constraints of the natural drainage pattern, at least in the immediate area of Barton Street the trend may have been regularized and reinforced by an element of planning.

The curving course of Alvin Street (Fete Lane) probably determined the orientation of the plots on the north side of the street. Superficially a simple short-cut across the angle of the Kingsholm Road and the London Road, it was lightly built up in 1455 with tenements, curtilages, land and 'diverse tenements'. By the late eighteenth century all trace of these had disappeared, leaving no obvious imprint in the succeeding field pattern. However, archaeological observations on the south side of the street near its junction with London Road disclosed the large and probably medieval ditch, following the line of the street, which may (as discussed earlier) have continued north to the Alvin Gate. But its precise date, and its course to the south of London Road (if it continued), are both unknown.

PLAN-UNIT VI.3: NEWLAND

Beyond Alvin Street and the ditch, the physical character of the suburb changed yet again. For most of its length eastwards to the two hospitals, the road was flanked by continuous parallel back-fence lines, though at the west end of the south side the back-fence line was deflected sharply southwards as it merged with the local field-pattern (see above). Historical evidence gives some clues to the changing extent and density of occupation in this area, as does the archaeology. Recent excavations near the eastern end, around the site of St Margaret's Hospital, located the remains of a timber building from the late eleventh century aligned on the street. Disused by the early twelfth century it was cut by a boundary ditch for the hospital (Walters and Atkin 1991, 11). What can the contemporary context for this building have been? Possibly it suggests continuous ribbon-development – even if only widely-spaced – along the south side of the street this far eastwards by *c.* 1100. Or it may represent one element of an intermittent and basically rural settlement-pattern substantially pre-dating the extension of a more densely settled suburb. The 'Newland' place-name is widely paralleled and certainly suggestive of a late urban extension; additionally, the foundation of St Margaret's as a leper hospital by 1158 should lead one to expect that settlement then was not that extensive.

The east, south and transpontine suburbs (figs 3.3 and 3.6)

In contrast to the complex landscapes of the mainly pre-Conquest west and north suburbs, the remainder were all relatively simple, relatively well-defined and discrete entities separated from the urban core by the known Roman and later defences and extending outwards into the country-side. Given their greater internal morphological coherence and simplicity, these suburbs have been characterized as plan-units (suburban plan-units 1–3). While internal variations in their landscapes are certainly apparent these, to an extent, appear to have been the product of post-medieval transformations, and the processes underlying their original development appear to have been more straightforward than the complex institutional and developmental histories underlying the growth of the west and north suburbs.

The historical development of all of these suburbs is more fully discussed in Chapter 13.

SUBURBAN PLAN-UNIT 1: BARTON STREET

The maximum eastward extent of the medieval built-up area along Barton Street – the least important of the four main approach-roads for long-distance traffic – is likely to have coincided approximately with the Bar, about 430 metres beyond the east gate, that appears on Hall and Pinnell's map of 1780. The map also shows that the street narrowed here, the buildings on the frontages changed abruptly from long blocks or terraces to isolated single structures, and the northern plot-series came to an end. This – the end of the suburb – lay well outside the city boundary, first recorded in a perambulation of 1370 (*Hist. et Cart.*, iii, 256–7). This crossed the north side of the street about half-way between the east gate and the Bar, turning west along the street and then south again, leaving about two-thirds of the southern plots outside the city.

The eighteenth- and nineteenth-century maps show differences in the arrangement of the plots on the north and south sides of the street. On the north side all the plots terminated at a continuous back-fence line approximately parallel to the street, the deepest plots in the centre of the frontage. Behind the plots lay four fields (shown on Hall and Pinnell's map) reached via an alleyway between the plots, and then the Fullbrook, running in a straight line parallel to Barton Street. The rectilinearity of this layout suggests, firstly, that the brook was artificially channelled in this area, and secondly, that the area as a whole – road, plot-series, field boundaries and brook – had been laid out at some time as a planned urban extension with associated fields, though how far this rectilinear arrangement reproduces antecedent Roman features is unknown.

This is not, however, the first impression given by the arrangement of the plots on the south side. These were more varied in character and, while back-fence lines were common to groups of plots, no single boundary was common to the whole series. But this may be misleading. A group of Lanthony properties (that cannot be precisely located) lay on the southern frontage across the road from and slightly east of the 'common path', described above. These had frontages of between 22 and 27 feet (6.7–8.23 metres) and extended back from the frontage for distances of 187 to 200 feet (56.99–60.96 metres), approximately the same depth-range as the northern plot series. Fourteenth-century leases for two of these properties record their abutting a field at the rear (A5, fos 105–105v; A7, fo. 60; A5, fos 106–106v; A13, fo. 84v); but a property in the same area granted in the early thirteenth century ended at 'the King's ditch', about 199 feet

(60.65 metres) from the frontage (A5, 108+–108+v). In 1273 there is a further reference to an unlocated property outside the east gate extending from the highway to the King's ditch (*Cal. Recs Corpn Glouc.*, 631). It cannot be proved that this ditch – most probably a jurisdictional boundary and not in any way defensive – maintained a course parallel to the street, but it is certain at least that there was a more formal definition to the rear of the southern plot-series than is apparent from the post-medieval cartography. The fourteenth-century abuttals suggest that the ditch was no longer significant even then. Most probably the chaotic pattern that characterized the rear of the southern plots, in contrast to those on the north, was exaggerated by, or resulted from, post-Dissolution multiple lay ownership of the land there – in contrast to the stable and conservative ownership of property on the north side by the Dean and Chapter (see pp. 330–31, 362, below).

In short, Barton Street possessed a number of characteristics that show it to have been subject to a degree of organization and planning in its layout. One feature of this process appears to have been a decision to replicate the existing characteristics of the street and its plots within the walls in the new urban extension beyond. The back-fence line to the north suburban plots aligns exactly with New Inn (Grant) Lane within the city wall, which formed the rear boundary to the northern Eastgate Street plots. Similarly, a ditch bounding the southern suburban plots about 200 feet (61 metres) from the frontage would have reproduced the original depth of the southern Eastgate Street plots, bounded by Bell (Travel) Lane. The rationale behind this can only be guessed at. Quite possibly there was some conception of an 'ideal' layout, of an extension of the city made in the image of the city, new suburban plots made more attractive by virtue of their apparent continuity with those inside. Possibly the motivation was solely practical, aimed at ensuring comparability of plot-sizes and rent-charges, but such motives may not have been mutually exclusive.

The alleyway passing through the north plot-series provides a useful landmark for comparing this frontage in 1455 with the cartographically recorded plot-pattern. The alleyway seems to be the 'common path' recorded in the 1455 rental (104b). In 1455, between it and the city ditch lay 17 individually listed tenements and a block of 'diverse tenements'. The 1884 plans show about 14 clear plot-tails (some subdivided) between the alley and an inserted road a short distance outside the line of the ditch, suggesting at least that the fifteenth-century plots may not have been dissimilar from the nineteenth-century plots. Dimensions recorded for a group of Lanthony properties in the area around the alleyway in the early thirteenth and late fourteenth centuries support this conclusion. The back-fence line was clearly a stable feature; the frontage widths (*c.* 23, 45, and 65 feet/7.01, 13.7, 19.8 metres) also fall within the range of frontage widths of the plots in the nineteenth century (A7, fo. 54; A13, fos 82v–83; A5, fos 103v–104; A12, fo. 88). The burning of the suburbs in the Civil War may have destroyed buildings, but the evidence suggests that here at least, property boundaries were maintained (*VCH Glos.*, iv, 93–4).

The greatest landscape discontinuity in this area may be found in the complete disappearance of the Brook Street suburb. Brook Street was the narrow lane following the watercourse, parallel to Barton Street, feeding into the city ditch at the north-east corner of the fortress. Housing developed along this, presumably after the insertion of the Almesham postern through the north-east corner in the 1250s (*Cal. Recs. Corpn Glouc.*, 492), and in the late thirteenth century the abbey had ten houses there (*Hist. et Cart.*, iii, 154–5). The street decayed in the late-medieval period, was still there when Speed's plan of 1610 was made, but had disappeared entirely by the time the earliest detailed cartographic evidence becomes available in the eighteenth century.

SUBURBAN PLAN-UNIT 2: LOWER SOUTHGATE STREET (fig. 3.6)

The medieval southern suburb had by the late nineteenth century suffered more destructive change than any other in Gloucester. The process began with late- and post-medieval depopulation (see below, p. 492). The Civil War brought about the demolition of properties around the south gate and the construction of new defences and siege-works, and the building of the Gloucester Infirmary in 1755 on the east side of the street, while the construction of the canal and docks from 1794 on the west side, completed its destruction (*VCH Glos.*, iv, 93–4, 253, 269). So, while this suburb is rather more comprehensively documented than the others, its physical layout is known only schematically. Some aspects of its physical character are recoverable from pre-Ordnance Survey cartography; fortunately many more – and a chronology of its earlier years – are forthcoming from archaeological evidence.

The maximum southward extent of the medieval built-up area cannot be determined with precision – it may, anyway, have fluctuated and may never have been sharply defined. Speed's map of 1610 shows that housing then extended along Southgate Street for a distance equivalent to about 300 metres from the south gate, to a point just beyond the junction with Severn Street. In this respect there may have been little change since the late fourteenth century, when Lanthony Priory leases refer to three tenements, followed by a block of eight, extending southward from the corner of Severn Street to the now-lost New Lane (A13, fo. 4v, A7, fos 111, 137v, 153, 192, 201v, 202).

The extent of medieval settlement on the east side of the street is more difficult to define. A boundary is shown here by Hall and Pinnell (1780) running parallel to the street and continuing the back-fence line of the built-up suburban plots far out into the countryside to the south. This may well have been a feature of the pre-existing local field pattern that, closer to the city, was adopted by suburban development, but there is no way – other than via historical evidence or by excavation – of telling how far settlement extended along it.

On the west side of Southgate Street most of the medieval tenements between the city wall and Severn Street backed onto Small Lane, a narrow lane running parallel to the main street. Cited frequently in the Lanthony documents as a rear boundary to the main-street properties, it had disappeared by the late eighteenth century, but was located by excavation lying just within the common back boundary to the plot-series, the plots having encroached across it. Excavation also found a curved metalled path leading from the Southgate Street frontage westwards towards the church of St Owen and its cemetery. This was probably the St Owen's Lane that features in the medieval documentation; it may have been inserted in the later thirteenth century to maintain access to the church after the approach from Shipsters Lane to the north was destroyed by the recutting of the city ditch. The church of St Owen stood on the west side of Small Lane, but excavation showed that at least part of its cemetery (perhaps an extension?) lay on the east side, at the rear of shortened Southgate Street plots (Atkin 1990, 1991b; and see below). The presence of Small Lane, serving as a boundary and as access to a series of plots, immediately suggests that there was a degree of organization in the settlement of this side of the street

The plots to the south of Severn Street had no lane at the rear but ended at a common rear boundary, parallel to the street, beyond which lay the garden of the Renter of Lanthony (A7, fos 111, 137v, 153, 201v); the back-fence line mapped in the nineteenth century was in approximately the same position as that revealed by the recorded dimensions of the Lanthony properties. These properties were of about the same depth as those to the north, and the block may represent a planned extension to the suburb, albeit one without the additional provision of back-lane access.

The form of the plots on the east side of the street is more difficult to reconstruct. Comparison of the dimensions of Lanthony properties with the boundaries mapped in the eighteenth and nineteenth centuries suggests that there had been a considerable degree of fluidity in the properties on this side of the street; nevertheless, the medieval plots here appear to have been more heterogeneous in character than those opposite. The east-side plots had a staggered back-fence line defining the rearward extent of groups of plots of varying depth, perhaps representing the partitioning of a number of larger land-parcels or fields.

The cartographic evidence for the area as a whole fails to do justice to the intensity of the medieval occupation. Small Lane, which did not survive long enough to be mapped, is shown by the documentation to have been at least partly built up by cottages, very probably by the familiar process of tail-end development of the main-street plots; Severn Street too was the site of a number of poorer tenements which have left no trace in the cartographic record (see Chapter 13, below).

Archaeological evidence shows that occupation began here in the pre-Conquest period. On the west side of Southgate Street, excavations (site 3/89) revealed three post-built buildings of the tenth or eleventh century, separated by metalled yards and set back a short distance from the frontage. Then, on the excavated site, there appears to have been a hiatus in the occupation. The buildings were demolished and their sites were cut by a ditch at least 60 metres long, roughly parallel to the street, and interpreted by the excavator as a boundary ditch to the Norman castle orchard. A series of stone-built houses was later constructed over the ditch. These will have been amongst the properties recorded in the Lanthony Priory records from the thirteenth century and later, and appear to have been built after the acquisition of the suburb by Lanthony Priory in 1136 (Atkin 1990, 3–4). The implication of the excavated evidence is clearly that the suburb – or at least this part of it, together with Small Lane at the rear of the plots – was created by Lanthony Priory in the twelfth century, after the castle orchard ditch had gone out of use. The question that remains is whether this chronology applies to the suburb as a whole, or just to this part of it. There is sound historical evidence for occupation of the Southgate Street suburb by the mid twelfth century, and there are hints that suburban development was taking place earlier, under the Norman constables (see p. 332–4, below). The problem remains, for the moment, unresolved.

St Owen's church was probably founded in the 1080s as a chapel serving the first castle, which lay opposite it, to the north, within the city wall. By 1095 the priests serving St Owen's, together with some other of the constable's servants, lived on Shipsters Lane, which ran along the outside of the city wall and was to be destroyed by the digging of a new city ditch in the 1260s (see p. 332, below). It seems that in general terms the church was part of the private estate of the constables, close to the castle but away from the English population, with its priests and the castle servants close at hand. Despite its close proximity to Small Lane, the church may not have been founded to serve a suburban population.

SUBURBAN PLAN-UNIT 3: WESTGATE ISLAND

Between the Foreign Bridge and Westgate Bridge lay the area known later as Westgate Island, or in the medieval period as *inter pontes* – 'Between the Bridges'. It was, indeed, surrounded by water. The central channel of the Severn lay at its west end and curved around its south side; its east side was defined by the dwindling eastern channel; the north side was bounded by a ditch that ran parallel to the street and connected the two river channels. The origins of this suburb (in the form in which it is known to us) appear to lie in actions taken by the hereditary constables of the castle, probably Walter of Gloucester, specifically to contrive or at least assist the diversion of the central channel of the Severn from a former line represented by the ditch along the north side of the island to a new or improved channel to the south of the street – approximately its present course (Rowbotham 1978; see above). The diversion may have taken place in or shortly before 1119 when, according to at least two sets of annals, a bridge – probably Westgate Bridge – began to be built at Gloucester (see p. 118).

There is very little archaeological evidence for the first settlement of this area. The earliest material found so far dates only to the late twelfth or thirteenth century (Heighway 1984b, 45). St Bartholomew's Hospital was certainly in existence by the 1220s and may have been founded well before, probably in the twelfth century (see p. 119). Its foundation legend (for what it is worth) and its topography suggest that it was established within an existing plot-series. The plot-pattern on the island appears inseparable from the overall rectilinear arrangement of the street and watercourses, and reinforces the impression that this area was an entirely artificial creation – a product of civil engineering and town planning. All of the plots, on both sides of the street, had access to running water; the plots on the south side were routinely described in contemporary documents as extending from the street to the Severn (e.g. A5, fos 53–53v of the mid thirteenth century).

The number of plots mapped here in the nineteenth century appears to have been quite closely comparable to the number present in the mid fifteenth century. For example, on the south side in 1455 were 24–28 properties; in 1884 between 22 and 24 substantial plot-tails may be defined behind a more intensively subdivided frontage (*1455 Rental*, 52–6, 60–64). Two recorded frontage widths in the thirteenth century (14 feet and 23 feet/4.26 and 7.01 metres) fall within the range suggested by the nineteenth-century plot-tails (A5, fos 52v–53v).

The precinct of St Bartholomew's is described in more detail elsewhere (pp. 322–3, below). The hospital buildings occupied the frontage of a large plot in the centre of the northern series, and the infirmary hall and church projected into the street. Parallels may be drawn between this relationship and that of St Bartholomew's functional predecessor, the church of St Nicholas: both probably had a financial interest in a prominent – even protruding – position on the street frontage (see p. 121, below).

Chapter 4

Gloucester: churches, chapels and parishes

According to the survey of Gloucester compiled between 1096 and 1101 – probably nearer the latter year – and preserved in the cartulary of Evesham Abbey (BL Cotton Vespasian B xxiv fo. 57r; text edited by Howard Clarke in Moore 1982, appendix), there were then ten churches within the city. Most of Gloucester's medieval churches, therefore, were founded in the eleventh century or before, and we can be certain that the medieval pattern of city churches dated in large part from before the Conquest. But what is not immediately clear is precisely which were the ten churches of the survey. They are certainly not to be identified with the ten parish churches of later medieval Gloucester, which were then quite distinct from the greater religious houses and the lesser places of worship: the survey's compiler is unlikely to have discriminated between parochial church and non-parochial chapel, at a time when such distinctions of status were still emerging, and we cannot even be sure that he would have drawn a distinction between the Benedictine abbey of St Peter and the lesser churches. St Oswald's, still in 1100 a minster church, would certainly have been counted as one of the ten. At the end of the medieval period Gloucester had two major religious houses – three if the outlying Lanthony Priory is included; ten parish churches; some six non-parochial chapels; three hospital chapels and three friaries. And of that total of 25 churches, only 7 – Lanthony Priory, the hospitals and the friaries, can be confidently identified as having been founded after 1100.

Churches with parishes

St Mary de Lode

In the medieval period this church was called St Mary before the Abbey Gate, or St Mary Broadgate (*VCH Glos.* iv, 303, and see for instance the will of Richard Baret dated 1401: PRO Prob II 2a Marche, fo. 4). It was undoubtedly much older than the earliest reference to it, from around 1150 (GCL D&C Register B, 56). Indeed, the evidence points to its having been the oldest of Gloucester's churches, with a history longer even than that of St Peter's Abbey, the Old Minster.

Already in the twelfth century St Mary's belonged to St Peter's Abbey; in 1200 Pope Innocent confirmed the abbey's possessions, including the church of St Mary before the abbey gate (*Hist. et Cart.*, iii, 2–4). Its largely rural and unusually extensive parish was discussed by Carolyn Heighway – who also pointed out that the later medieval parishes of Maisemore, Barnwood and Upton St Leonard's had earlier been dependent chapelries of St Mary's (1980, 219). She concluded that it had been founded by St Peter's at an early date to serve the abbey's estates, a view echoed by the Victoria County History (*VCH Glos.*, iv, 303). But as Steven Bassett has demonstrated, this oversimplifies the relationship between the two churches, and the relationship between St Mary's parish and the abbey's estates, as the parish also included lands held from the royal manor of King's Barton. Citing the archaeological evidence for early Christian use of the site (see below), Bassett went on to argue that the situation of St Mary's, outside the precinct of St Peter's rather than within it, was not consistent with its having originated as the abbey's parish church. Its situation was closely analogous with that of similarly early churches at Worcester and

Wroxeter (and see the case of St Helen's, Worcester, pp. 197–200, below). He suggested that in the immediate post-Roman period Gloucester became an important British political centre, controlling a large hinterland and accommodating an episcopal see; in St Mary's massive parish, originally embracing all of Gloucester's hinterland, should be seen an indication that this had originated as the principal church of the region, the seat of a bishop of the Celtic church (Bassett 1992, 26–9). It is to Thomas Fosbrooke's credit that, writing in 1819, he too deduced as much, citing the size of St Mary's parish as proof of the church's very great antiquity, and concluding that 'it is probable that this was the British Parochial Church' (Fosbrooke 1819, 343).

The archaeological evidence for the use of the site during the Roman and post-Roman periods leaves little doubt that St Mary's church predated the development of the square – actually a triangular open area – which lay symmetrically around it. St Mary's Square probably represents an extramural (at least in relation to the late pre-Conquest town) market-place created by the abbey, formalizing and redeveloping an existing, originally Roman, open space overlooking the retreating waterfront (see above, p. 83–4). From the second century, a substantial heated building with mosaic floors stood within this metalled open area; the building was damaged by fire in the late-Roman period and partially demolished. The remains of the building were then used as the site for a new structure, at least partly of timber construction on oolite footings, which maintained the alignment of the earlier building. Inside, sealed by the floor, were two east–west grave slots and an east–west 'headless burial'. Outside there may have been a paved forecourt and further burials. The excavator interpreted the building as 'a mausoleum, a church or an oratory … built in or after the fifth to sixth centuries' (Bryant 1980, 8). This was to become the site of the church of St Mary. By perhaps the ninth century, burials were taking place here immediately outside a new building with timber-framed walls on stone footings; fragmentary foundations suggest, however, that this had replaced an earlier stone-built structure. Across the interior of the building was the foundation for a screen or more substantial feature, possibly a gallery; this was later removed and a large and long-lived font installed. Thus St Mary's possessed baptismal rights by this date. Another pre-Conquest addition, contemporary with or later than the font, was a stone western annexe or tower, possibly containing a gallery at first-floor level (Bryant 1980, 8–9).

The first Norman rebuilding of the church saw the probable replacement of the chancel, the addition of a central tower, the replacement of the nave – left aisleless – and the insertion of a new west doorway in the surviving western annexe. In the mid twelfth century north and south aisles were added, and in the last quarter of the century the tower and chancel were rebuilt, possibly in response to the collapse of the first tower. The nave and aisles were probably extended westwards by the addition of a single bay in the thirteenth century; the chancel was also extended at the same time. Subsequent changes appear to have been on a very modest scale until the church was rebuilt in 1824 (Bryant 1980, 10–12).

Although the known sequence of structural events between the late- or sub-Roman building and the ninth-century church cannot be shown to be either continuous or complete, the historical evidence for the breadth of St Mary's influence in the area around the city suggests very strongly that the church's importance indeed pre-dates the ninth century, and lends support to the contention that the location of the Anglo-Saxon church on the site of the sub-Roman mausoleum was more than coincidental.

In addition, reconsideration of the Roman quayside wall and the probability of its non-defensive function has re-opened the question of the existence of a defended Roman western extension to the fortress area (Hurst 1986, 113–16; and see the topographical analysis of this district, p. 80–81 above). In this light it now seems very probable that the mausoleum or church, and its Anglo-Saxon successor, were both truly extramural; St Mary de Lode, indeed, deserves a place in the corpus of suburban sites where early ecclesiastical use can be shown to have had a sub-Roman funerary background (Morris 1989, 34–5). Exactly what, in this case, that background represents is a mystery – and will probably always remain so. We might expect, however, that the sub-Roman burials within and around the mausoleum or church would have been of individuals, whatever their status or beliefs, who had dwelt within the city walls. This may not have been the case later, when St Peter's Abbey had a virtual monopoly on burials within the city and St Mary's had become the parish church for an extensive extramural district. In this context it seems more likely that extramural burial was for an extramural population, at least until the development of the built-up area around the church and its eventual inclusion within the expanding defences.

The Gloucester part of St Mary's extensive parish, around the church itself, was almost exactly coterminous with the extent of the abbey's plots surrounding St Mary's Square, with a westward extension around Clare Street and Mount Street between the Square and the eastern channel of the Severn. This area was extramural in relation to the *burh*, and almost certainly represents the core of the formerly much larger extramural parish, reduced – and isolated from the remaining extramural portions – by the insertion of St Oswald's precinct and parish to the north and by St Nicholas's parish to the south. The southern boundary (also discussed under St Nicholas's, see below) follows – with minor variations – the property boundary separating the St Mary's Square and Clare Street plots from those facing Lower Westgate Street. As a property boundary, this line is likely to date from the late tenth century and the extension of settlement down Westgate Street outside the Roman fortress wall; as a parish boundary, it is datable to the foundation of St Nicholas's, probably in the early twelfth century, to serve the growing population in this area and service the new bridge or bridges. The northern boundary with St Oswald's parish and precinct followed the back-fence line of the plots on the north side of St Mary's Square; west of this plot-series, the boundary was carried by one of two watercourses draining into the eastern Severn channel. These watercourses (channels of the Fullbrook flowing west out of the abbey precinct in the area) may represent the original boundary between the two parishes before the development of the St Mary's Square plots.

There is no indication from later in the middle ages that St Mary's had parochial responsibility for any of the intramural area of Gloucester during the Anglo-Saxon period. Just as St Mary's had continued to serve the district around the city, even after the foundation of St Peter's, so St Peter's had been the church of Gloucester itself. Until the tenth century, it was intramural Gloucester's only church, and its claim still in the twelfth century to burial rights over all the city – however unrealistic in practice – is a sign of its early primacy (see below, pp. 244–7).

St Oswald's Priory, the New Minster (see fig. 12.3)

Like St Mary's, this would have been one of Gloucester's ten recorded churches in 1100. Having been founded as a minster church before 900 (see above, p. 20), it retained that status until its transformation into a house of Augustinian canons in 1153 (*VCH Glos.*, ii, 85; Thompson 1921, 130); even then, it retained its parochial functions until the Dissolution (Thompson 1921, 105–6).

Like that of St Mary de Lode, St Oswald's parish was principally rural, and contained in addition a number of dependent chapelries. The churches of what had been its estates previous to their transference to the archbishopric of York (see above, p. 24) remained dependent on St Oswald's until the Reformation: from Churchdown, Norton, Sandhurst and Compton Abdale the priory was drawing a total of £40 2s 6d annually in the 1530s (Caley 1810–34, ii, 487). As a further similarity with St Mary de Lode, St Oswald's Gloucester parish lay outside the area of the *burh* defences – indeed, it remained distinctly suburban throughout the middle ages, although the precinct and part of the parish were brought within the extended defences, probably in the late tenth or early eleventh century (see below, p. 326). Probably as early as the twelfth century, the precinct walls of St Oswald's were themselves considered to be part of the town's defences (Hurst 1986, 132); the view of a local jury in 1387 was that the town wall between the Blind Gate of Gloucester and the Old Severn ought to be repaired and maintained by the prior of St Oswald's (PRO KB9/32, m.18). The transcript of Æthelstan's confirmation of the New Minster's privileges that was produced in court in 1304 (see above, p. 23; Sayles 1936–9, iii, 141) referred to the church's having been built outside the old wall of the city of Gloucester – implying that the precinct wall was already part of a new defensive circuit as early as 925–6. It would be a mistake, however, to place much trust in such a locative detail that – even if the text of the charter were basically genuine – might well have been updated.

The suburban part of St Oswald's parish embraced most, but not all, of the Hare Lane–Wateringstead suburb. The southern boundary with the parish of St Mary de Lode, as we have seen, followed the backs of the St Mary's Square plots and a channel of the Fullbrook running into the Severn. Further east, the boundary followed the north side of the abbey precinct (the line of which was established in 1218) before returning northwards up Hare Lane, excluding the watered plots on its east side, which remained in St John's parish. St Oswald's included Wateringstead Street to the north, and extended further in the same direction, into the rural hinterland around and including Kingsholm, and its royal hall and chapel (see Heighway 1980, 217–20).

None of the properties that owed landgable to the bailiffs of Gloucester, acting as the proxies of the Crown, lay within St Oswald's parish (*1455 Rental, passim*). Several tenants of land within the parish are known to have paid chief rents to St Oswald's or to the archbishopric of York, indicating that the property here had originally belonged to St Oswald's (see below, p. 284). Thus the boundaries of the parish appear to follow those of the land that was given to the New Minster at its foundation.

St Oswald's precinct occupied a low-lying site next to the river, immediately north of St Mary de Lode and the housing around St Mary's Square. The shape of the precinct was that of a quarter- or half-circle formed by the curve of St Mary's Street (formerly Water Street) around the northern boundary. Archaeological evidence shows that the curve derives from a substantial, water-filled, early medieval ditch, beneath the medieval street and outside the line of the medieval precinct wall. The southern side of the precinct too was probably demarcated by one or more watercourses – channels of the Fullbrook, flowing westwards into the Severn from the precinct of St Peter's Abbey, through which they had been diverted by *c.* 1100, if not long before (Spry 1974; Heighway and Bryant 1999, 3–5, 8).

The site was occupied in the Roman period by a municipal tilery which may have made use of the Roman quay. The tilery went out of use within the Roman period and the site was then given over to a thin scatter of burials. When the first church of St Oswald was built (dated on archaeological grounds to the late ninth or early tenth century) it incorporated quantities of re-used masonry, including a number of cross-shaft fragments of the late eighth to ninth century. Their original setting was almost certainly a cemetery of some status, but as only one of the pre-church burials on the St Oswald's site was demonstrably of post-Roman date, it is uncertain whether the church was founded within an actively used or at least recognizable cemetery, or whether the cross-shaft fragments had been imported from elsewhere. The first church was also built with quantities of re-used Roman masonry, some of it probably derived from a temple, and this had certainly been imported – if only, perhaps, from the area south of St Mary de Lode. A small proportion of this masonry had actually been re-used before, suggesting that it was derived from a site that had experienced a phase of late- or sub-Roman adaptation of earlier buildings (Heighway and Bryant 1999, 10).

The first church was a modest rectangular building with a north, south and east *porticus* and a western apse – a feature of contemporary Carolingian design. Though small by comparison with contemporary foundations of importance (e.g. the New Minster at Winchester), it was richly decorated, painted within and rendered without. Soon after the initial construction, though not closely datable from archaeological evidence alone, a square free-standing building (building 'A') was added to the east end, with a floor level well below that of the rest of the church. This is interpreted by the excavators as a mausoleum, on the lines of the (somewhat earlier) building beneath the chancel at Repton, and almost certainly built to accommodate the newly translated relics of St Oswald, brought to the site in 909. It is probable that with the deaths of Æthelred (911) and Æthelflæd (918) the minster's founders were laid to rest alongside the saint; fragments of richly decorated grave covers of this period (broken up within a century) may have derived from their tombs. As the mausoleum was being built a screen-wall was added across the nave, suggestive perhaps of the introduction of a more complex and exclusive liturgy along with the relics of the saint (Heighway and Bryant 1999, 10–12).

The late tenth and early eleventh centuries were marked only by relatively minor changes to the fabric (a central tower was added) and it was not until the early twelfth that more substantial alterations took place, with all three of the original *porticus* demolished. A northern annexe was added alongside the nave, to be superseded by a north aisle built *c.* 1150–75. Royal gifts of timber mark further building campaigns in the first half of the thirteenth century, and a two-bay extension was added to the west end of the nave at this time, together with a cloister and associated ranges to the south of the church: the site and planning of pre-thirteenth-century claustral ranges are largely unknown. With the loss through gardening of the uppermost strata from the site of the church, its later medieval development remains obscure, though the eastern crypt-mausoleum appears to have remained accessible via a chamber containing an altar or monument, at the east end of the north aisle: the cult of St Oswald probably remained active in the church until the Dissolution. At the Dissolution, the north aisle continued in use as the parish church of St Catherine, perhaps maintaining the aisle's original use. All but one wall of the church was demolished by the end of the seventeenth century (Heighway and Bryant 1999, 17–20).

St John the Baptist

The earliest specific reference to any of Gloucester's parish churches is a grant, dated 1100, by Bishop Sampson of Worcester to St Peter's Abbey, of 20 shillings annually from the church of St John in Gloucester (*Hist. et Cart.* ii, 41). Presumably this pension had constituted the whole of the bishop's rights in St John's, as in 1138 the abbey was given the church itself by the Crown (*Hist. et Cart.* i, 224). Gloucester Abbey remained the patron of St John's until the Dissolution (*VCH Glos.*, iv, 298).

But St Oswald's, too, had an early interest in St John's. In a wider settlement reached with St Peter's in 1218, St John's at the north gate provided just one of the issues that required resolution – the abbey granting 20 shillings annual rent as compensation for all the priory's claims (*Hist. et Cart.*, i, 25, 83). The nature of the priory's grievance was not revealed, although it was unlikely to have been a major matter: the 20 shillings rent was to compensate also for the loss of St Brigid's chapel and the land it stood on, as well as grievances concerning the chapel of St

Thomas and a number of payments of tithe from named individuals. Yet the abbey's recognition that St Oswald's had a valid claim on St John's confirms the link, which surely points to St John's having been originally dependent upon the New Minster. Its parish – certainly the principal part that lay outside the walls of Gloucester – has the appearance of at one time having formed part of the minster parish of St Oswald's that surrounded it; not that the division was an arbitrary one, nor did it necessarily follow the natural boundaries of Fullbrook and Roman roads for convenience only. Evidence of the landgable paid in the fifteenth century indicates this also to have been a property division between the land that had been given to the New Minster and land retained by the Crown: no landgable was collected by the bailiffs of Gloucester from the parish of St Oswald, whereas properties paying landgable were thickly clustered along the originally extramural Lower Northgate Street within St John's parish (fig. 4.1; *1455 Rental, passim*). Thus this parochial division respected – and presumably followed or accompanied – the substantial gift of royal land to the New Minster at or after its foundation. Similarly, St John's intramural parish consisted entirely of a block of properties that paid landgable and which had thus remained Crown property (*1455 Rental*, 60b–64b; 66b–78b).

St John's, therefore, would have been one of the ten churches of 1100, and shows every sign of having been a royal foundation. The alternative – that it had been founded by St Oswald's, and had come into the hands of the Crown when most of Stigand's possessions were confiscated in 1070 (see above, p. 24) – is an unlikely one. There is no obvious reason why this one church should have been retained by the Crown in 1070 when all the rest of the New Minster's property was given to the see of York. Fosbrooke came across the legend – in Ralph Bigland's manuscript collection – that St John's had been founded by Æthelstan in 940 as a house of Augustinian canons, of which latter detail he was rightly dismissive (1819, 312) ; Æthelstan, too, died in 939. Bigland, he believed, had had the story from the historical collections of one Abel Wantner; given his subsequent judgment upon Wantner's works, that 'it is happy for his memory that they were never published' (ibid., 313), it is perhaps surprising that Fosbrooke gave the story any credence at all. But he argued that the tradition might have begun with Æthelstan's foundation of St John's as a secular college or minster, which is a plausible suggestion, given the virtual certainty that one or other of the kings of the tenth century had founded the church. Its foundation, plainly, had come after that of St Oswald's, while its prominent position by the north gate of the *burh* points to an origin before the eleventh century when such a prominent site might no longer have been still available.

The orientation of the church is eccentric, and is obviously different from that of the other churches in the central part of Gloucester which conform with the street-grid of the *burh*. This may be simply an adaptation to the curving post-Roman short-cut line of St John's Lane alongside its site (Heighway 1983a, 13–19).

The strongest indication that St John's was both an early and an important church is its possession of burial rights over its extramural parishioners – if perhaps not over those who lived intramurally – which was admitted in 1197x98 (see below, pp. 245–7). In practice, pressure on space may in time have led to the virtual cessation of burial at St John's, as in 1407 half an acre of ground near the church had to be purchased for use as a graveyard and to allow a parsonage house to be built (*Cal. Patent Rolls 1405–08*, 376); in the 1440s this 'new cemetery', as it was described, lay to the west of the tenement that occupied the plot between Grass Lane on the south, the town wall to the north, and Northgate Street to the east (A13, fo. 69v). The cemetery can thus be identified as the corner plot defined by the town wall, the precinct wall of the abbey and Grass Lane.

The parish of St John was divided between a large extramural portion and a much smaller

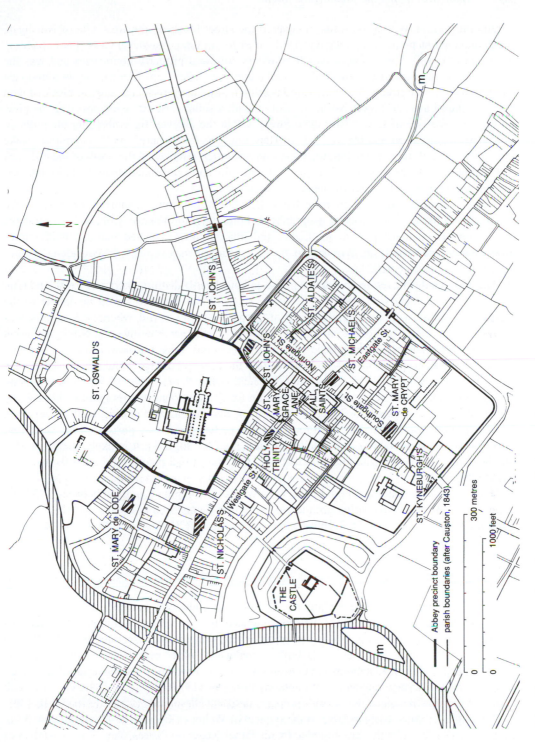

ST. OSWALD'S

ST. JOHN'S

ST. ALDATE'S

Northgate St.

ST. MICHAEL'S

Eastgate St.

ST. JOHN'S

ST. MARY GRACE LANE

ST. MARY de LODE

HOLY TRINITY

ALL SAINTS

Southgate St.

ST. MARY de CRYPT

ST. NICHOLAS

Westgate St.

ST. KYNEBURGH'S

THE CASTLE

N

—— Abbey precinct boundary

||||| parish boundaries (after Causton, 1843)

0   300 metres

0   1000 feet

4.1 Gloucester: intramural parishes and ecclesiastical geography

intramural portion. Within the walls, it covered the street block on the west side of Northgate Street and the few properties on the north side of St John's Lane (medieval Grass Lane) backing on to the city wall. The southern parish boundary followed property boundaries and was the subject of at least one agreement in the middle ages (see below, pp. 255–6); the west and east boundaries followed streets. The extramural portion mainly comprised a triangular block of land between Hare Lane and Lower Northgate Street, with a southward extension covering the plots on the opposite side of Lower Northgate Street within the Twyver. By embracing the plots on Lower Northgate Street and the east side of Hare Lane, St John's parish had an important stake in the commercial frontages within the pre-Conquest outer defences to the north of the old *burh* walls, although – to the east of the Kingsholm Road – the parish extended several hundred metres beyond this line, up to the later medieval city boundary.

These extramural interests were reflected in the siting of the church a short distance within the north gate. In terms of its parochial geography and proximity to the north gate, St John's mirrors St Kyneburgh's relationship to the south gate, and although it was situated near to (20–25 metres away), rather than actually on, in or next to, the gate, St John's may similarly be considered to have begun life as a gate-church.

The 1455 landgable return shows this parish to have been a distinct district of royal land (fig. 10.1; *1455 Rental, passim*). Outside the walls, most of the tenements paid landgable to the bailiffs, in contrast with the adjoining parts of the parish of St Oswald, where no landgable was paid. In the intramural part of the parish, every tenement, whether fronting on to Northgate Street or on to Grass Lane, paid landgable; the only exceptions were the new cemetery – which nevertheless had been said in 1407 to be held from the king in burgage – and the house between it and the gate, which in 1455 Katherine Gyse held (*1455 Rental*, 78b) in fee from Lanthony Priory (A13, fo. 69v). The earliest documentation for this plot concerns its grant in 1141/43 by Miles, as Earl of Hereford, to Roger de Tocheham, his chaplain: acquitting it of all services, including landgable, Miles also had it recorded that he had previously purchased the land from Peter the Writer, described as a counsellor of the King (A5, fo. 83v). It is likely, therefore, that this land, too, had been royal land, and that the landgable it had paid until the 1140s had been paid to the King.

The medieval church was rebuilt by the Woodwards of Chipping Campden between 1732 and 1734; little is known of its earlier architecture save that it consisted of a nave and chancel with a south aisle, north porch, and fifteenth-century west tower (*VCH Glos.*, iv, 299; Fosbrooke 1819, 313).

St Kyneburgh's and St Owen's

Although of minor status during the later middle ages, St Kyneburgh's had once been an important church. It is first referred to as one of the endowments of the new suburban church of St Audoenus or Ouen, and always known in Gloucester as St Owen, which was consecrated in 1095 (Walker 1964, 37–8). In effect, St Owen's was built to replace its older neighbour, which became its chapel. Together with St Kyneburgh's, St Owen's was granted by Miles of Gloucester, Walter's son and successor, to his new foundation of Lanthony Priory in 1137 (Caley *et al.* 1849, vi, 136). Both church and chapel remained the priory's property until the Dissolution (Caley 1810–34, ii, 430).

Although dedicated early in 1095 at the request of Walter of Gloucester (Walker 1964, 37 n. 2), St Owen's had evidently been founded by his father Roger de Pistres, sheriff and castellan of Gloucester from the early 1070s until his death before 1086 (Walker 1964, 4, 37 n. 1; Walker 1958, 66–9). When Miles of Gloucester, Walter's son, established Lanthony Priory in 1137, and gave it St Owen's with all its possessions, he described them as having been granted by his ancestors Roger and Walter; in listing them, however, he made no distinction between the gifts of Roger and Walter, and in fact the total of lands and tithes as recounted in 1137 was identical with those of Walter's dedication charter (Caley *et al.* 1849, vi, 136). So either Roger had given nothing to St Owen's or – which is more likely – Walter's charter of 1095 was essentially a confirmation of his father's gifts, placed on record with the account of the church's dedication. As a further indication of the earlier origin of St Owen's, the charter affirms that Walter's chaplains there were to hold as previously they and their predecessors had held from him and his predecessors (Walker 1964, 38).

Certainly at Lanthony Priory in the fourteenth century, Roger was regarded as the founder of St Owen's (A11, fo. 9), although this may have been based on nothing more than Miles's charter. Nevertheless, so well-informed were the canons about aspects of the history of their house that they evidently did possess other records – perhaps a chronicle – in addition to the early charters they preserved. No such original material now survives, but in 1378 the Bishop of Worcester appointed Robert More, the Archdeacon of Llandaff, to search the priory's early muniments and to present whatever evidence might have a bearing on the growing areas of disagreement between Lanthony and the burgesses of Gloucester (A11, fo. 10v) (For a fuller treatment of this series of disputes see Chapter 11 below.) The result was the short account of Lanthony's origins and privileges which was copied into Hayward's register during the late 1450s (A11, fos 9–16v). Given the care that evidently went into this work, it is all the more interesting that More's account recorded that Walter's grant of 1095 had actually been made to his chaplains serving God in the chapel of St Kyneburgh (A11, fo. 9). If we are to accept this statement – and there seems no reason why we should not – then we may conclude that Roger de Pistres had begun to build St Owen's, probably in the 1080s, as a grander and more fitting replacement for his church of St Kyneburgh; in 1095 the new church was ready to be dedicated, and so Walter installed his chaplains already celebrating at St Kyneburgh's, having confirmed to them all of their lands and possessions.

To accompany the refoundation, Roger and Walter contributed new endowments to augment those already owned by St Kyneburgh's. Tithes from the family's lands, from manors such as Haresfield and Barrington, held in 1086 either by Durand – Roger's brother and immediate successor as sheriff – or by Walter, and which before the Conquest had had English secular owners (DB, i, 168d, 169a), were recorded in 1095 as gifts to St Owen's (Walker 1964, 37–8). But the existing possessions of the priests of St Kyneburgh's seem to have constituted the core of the endowment: there was their own parish, within but chiefly outside the south gate of Gloucester; but there was also the large parochial block, adjoining to the south-west, of the chapelries of Quedgely, Hempstead and Elmore, with all their tithes. The later dependence of these chapelries on St Owen's (A2, fos 210–11, 215) presumably echoed their earlier relationship with St Kyneburgh's. In the same way the burial rights enjoyed by St Owen's by the 1130s and by implication from the time of its foundation had been acquired with St Kyneburgh's (see below, p. 244). Thus with its two priests, according to the account compiled by the Archdeacon of Llandaff, its early burial rights and its extensive extramural parish with dependent chapelries, St Kyneburgh's can be identified as a minster church by John Blair's generally accepted criteria (Blair 1985, 106).

The fact of Roger's possession of St Kyneburgh's throws a little light on to his family's lands within the immediate vicinity. We have no information as to how he came by the church: whether he had been given it as an individual, or whether it was his by virtue of his office as sheriff and constable of the castle. Nor is it clear how and when Roger or his successors acquired their land inside the gate, and the land outside the south gate – the manor of the Hide – which was Walter's by 1095 when the tithes from the Hide were confirmed to be part of the endowment of St Owen's. The tithes must previously have gone to St Kyneburgh's, and the Hide lay at the core of the gate church's parish, although it is not clear that ownership of land and church necessarily went together during the 1080s. As Roger had died by 1086, his acquisition of St Kyneburgh's pre-dated the compilation of Domesday Book; there is no certainty that his family held the Hide by that time. It was not obviously identified and described in Domesday Book, although Durand the sheriff, Roger's brother, may have held it as part of his five-hide manor of Whaddon which before the Conquest had been held as five manors by five brothers (DB, i, 168d). In 1137 Miles of Gloucester gave the Hide – calling it the Hide of Gloucester – to his new foundation of Lanthony Priory, along with St Owen's and all its endowments (Caley *et al.* 1849, vi, 136); under Lanthony the court of the Hide was held at St Owen's, and it was by virtue of this lordship that Lanthony claimed jurisdiction over all the land outside the south gate, and over the tenants of the suburb that had grown up on its land (A11, fo. 10; and see below, p. 302).

The Hide, therefore, included all the land adjacent to the south wall of Gloucester. Other land so close to the town seems to come under the manors of King's Barton and Abbot's Barton, or within manors once part of them (*VCH Glos.*, iv, 390–96); probably the Hide, too, had at some earlier date been detached from one of these ancient lordships. The small number of properties in the 1440s that lined Lower Southgate Street, and which were held not from the Hide but from King's Barton (A11, fo. 10; and see below, p. 331–2), may be an indication that the Hide had been separated from the royal rather than from the ecclesiastical estate.

St Kyneburgh's immediate parish was not just the Hide but also a small block of land inside the town wall. In the clause of his charter conveying St Owen's parish to Lanthony, Miles called it 'the parish of the constable's land within the south gate, and all the parish which is outside the same gate' – *parochia terrae constabularii infra portam de Sut' et tota parochia quae est extra eandem portam* (Caley *et al.* 1849, vi, 136). Not his own land, but the constable's; the formality of the terminology implying that the land within the gate did not belong to Miles by simple hereditary right but had come to him by virtue of his hereditary office. In later centuries Lanthony claimed that its rights of jurisdiction over the Hide had extended also to the lands of the constable within the south gate, until the bailiffs of Gloucester had unjustly deprived them of this right (A11, fo. 10): what they appear to have been claiming was that the 'constable's land' of 1137 had historically constituted a private jurisdiction, subject to the constable, over which the reeves of the town had had no authority. This could have been an arrangement devised for the eleventh-century constables and sheriffs, whose castle occupied the south-west corner of the town; but it is far from impossible that a block of intramural land over which St Kyneburgh's and its successors had parochial rights had belonged to the pre-Conquest sheriffs, who had also exercised personal authority over it.

The intramural part of St Kyneburgh's parish – and later of St Owen's – was a small enclave of just over an acre (0.4 hectare) within the south gate, covering plots on both sides of Southgate Street. On the west, it followed the Blackfriars precinct wall at the back of the Southgate Street plots and, for a few yards, the probable former line of the street frontage before the diversion of the street to the new medieval south gate (see below). On the other side of Southgate Street the parish boundary followed the backs of the plots there, on the probable line of the Greyfriars precinct boundary. Thus the medieval intramural parish is probably only visible to us in its partly post-thirteenth-century state, as a sandwich of secular property between two friaries.

This distinctive parochial geography – large extramural possessions and a tiny intramural parish around the church – can be seen elsewhere: in Gloucester at St John's, and in Worcester at

All Saints' (see below, pp. 206–7). In those cases the arrangement appears to have been characteristic of gate-churches, a function that St Kyneburgh's shared, judging by its location. The site of the church lay about 15 metres to the west of the medieval south gate, on the site of the Roman gate, within which – as Heighway has suggested (*VCH Glos.*, iv, 11) – it is likely to have been located. The site of St Kyneburgh's is revealed in the post-medieval cartography by the row of almshouses that succeeded it in the sixteenth century, the west end of the church having been retained as a chapel adjacent to the west end of the almshouses (*VCH Glos.*, iv, 316, 354–5). These buildings were arranged along the south side of St Kyneburgh's Lane but – as Heighway has also noted – their alignment was not that of the Roman defences, running nearly east–west, and in all likelihood represented the known reconstruction of the church by Lanthony before 1147, when the new St Kyneburgh's was dedicated (*VCH Glos.*, iv, 11, 316). In the topographical analysis of this area it was argued that the replacement of the Roman gate and the road diversion that followed were probably post-Conquest events: the western frontage of Southgate Street appears to have been built up before the diversion, and – in part – fossilized as a building-line within the plots fronting the newly moved street. This chronology is compatible with the date of the rebuilding of St Kyneburgh's, and with the probable late eleventh- or twelfth-century date of the medieval south gate proposed by Garrod and Heighway on the basis of masonry recorded in a service trench (Garrod and Heighway 1984, 55). The new church remained close to the town wall and was apparently built into it. In the mid fifteenth century people complained that the canons of Lanthony had cut a new door through the wall into the church, by which the town itself was imperilled as it provided illicit access from outside the wall (A11, fo. 14). In summary, then, it appears that the pre-Conquest church of St Kyneburgh continued to operate within the old Roman south gate until the first half of the twelfth century. A new gate was built to the east, the street diverted to it, and the old gate and its church demolished, to be replaced by a new structure on the same site, but (as elsewhere in the city by this date) on a more respectable liturgical alignment.

The transference of its parochial rights to St Owen's did not entail the abandonment of St Kyneburgh's as a place of worship, and indeed from the twelfth century onwards it can be seen to have been the centre of a considerable local cult. The saint to whom it was dedicated was presumably not the more famous St Cyneburh, the daughter of Penda, who was recorded as the founder of Castor and who died *c.* 680 (Farmer 1978, 107), but the reputed first Abbess of the Old Minster, the sister of Osric (see above, p. 17). A cult of this local saint is likely to have been current soon after her death, especially if her tomb remained a prominent feature at St Peter's. Interestingly, by the late middle ages her true identity had been quite forgotten, the legends that surrounded her cult now making her a virgin princess who had taken refuge with a baker, and who had been thrown down a well by his jealous wife. The church, it was said, had been built on the site of the well, which had become known as St Kyneburgh's fountain (*Hist. et Cart.*, i, lxv–lxvii; Farmer 1978, 107). Even at Lanthony Priory the identity of the saint had been forgotten by the 1450s, for in an obvious attempt to bolster the legend's credibility with details taken from other, reliable sources, Prior Hayward in his register identified her as the daughter of Penda (A11, fos 14, 14v). He knew the essential facts of Penda's life, including the date of his death in 655, but either failed to see the contradiction or had respect for an already extant tradition when he noted that St Kyneburgh's had been founded 600 years before Lanthony – that is, in 536. In itself the date is valueless, though it shows that in the fifteenth century there was a tradition of the church's antiquity.

Legend had it that the saint had been buried within the church, near the well in which she had died. Certainly there were relics of the saint, which Lanthony Priory removed in 1389 and was required to replace in the following year, when the Bishop of Worcester celebrated their translation, and when the saint's help for the sick and infirm was implored. Miracles of healing were recorded, and St Kyneburgh's attracted pious gifts from the people of Gloucester (*VCH Glos.*, iv, 316; *Hist. et Cart.*, i, lxvii–lxviii). These included the grant, around 1220, of a messuage in Oxebode Lane, given by Edith Poly to the church of St Kyneburgh for the maintenance of the lights there, for the soul of her late husband Silvester (A5, fo. 88). The cult seems to have retained some vitality into the sixteenth century: David Vaughan, a Gloucester merchant, was reported in 1500 to be engaged in the Severn trade with a ship called the *Kynburgh* (*Cal. Close Rolls 1500–1509*, 66).

The origin of the cult, however, presents something of a mystery. If the assumption is correct that this St Kyneburgh was in reality the abbess whose burial had surely taken place at the Old Minster, it is difficult to see why major relics of her should have come to another church. Could the cult have originated only with the dedication of the new church in 1147? It is possible that a tomb conveniently identified as hers came to light at the demolition of the old gate church, although that would leave unanswered the questions of why the specific identification should have been made then, and how it could have been that the old church was – apparently – already dedicated to the saint. How reliable, though, is the evidence for the church's dedication to St Kyneburgh before 1147? Walter's charter of 1095 to St Owen's provides the earliest reference (Walker 1964, 38); it exists only in later copies, and whilst there is no obvious reason to doubt its contents, quite possibly it is a later composition that recalls the details of an oral grant. The record of Earl Miles's grants to Lanthony, certainly, does not date from 1137 but only attained its final written form some time after the donor's death in 1143 – and that document, again, is known only from later copies (Caley *et al.* 1849, vi, 136; Walker 1964, 13). Thus the only pre-1147 references to St Kyneburgh's church by that title could in fact be subsequent amendments, substituting a new current dedication for an earlier, and now lost, saint's name. However, in favour of the authenticity of the dedication, and the existence of the cult before 1147, is the evident local importance of this church before the foundation of St Owen's; furthermore, the place in the cult of the well hints at an earlier origin than the twelfth century for this Kyneburgh story. It is unclear whether St Kyneburgh's well really was a feature of the medieval church, though presumably it had some existence outside the legend. The possibility that there was an ancient holy well by the south gate is not to be ruled out.

Nor did St Kyneburgh's replacement by St Owen's put an end to burials at the older church, although St Owen's quickly acquired its own burial ground (see below). In the fourteenth century St Kyneburgh's cemetery was evidently located on the other side of the town wall from the church, between the wall and the ditch, as trees in the cemetery were felled by the burgesses when they cleared and widened the town ditch in 1377 (A11, fo. 12v). Perhaps the use of this site represented a relatively recent and opportune colonizing of public land, earlier burials having taken place in an intramural cemetery more directly associated with the church. However, given the original situation of St Kyneburgh's – apparently within the structure of the gate – an extramural location for its cemetery may always have been logical. Ritual use of the area outside the south gate, therefore, could have pre-dated the foundation of St Owen's, and would undoubtedly have influenced the later church's siting only some 75 metres from its predecessor.

This was not the only factor determining the location of St Owen's, which also lay opposite the old castle within the town wall, and in the vicinity of the houses of a number of Walter's servants (A11, fo. 9). The description of the church in the period 1143–55 as 'St Owen's beneath the castle of Gloucester' – *sancti Audoeni sub castello Glouc'* (Walker 1964, 28) – emphasizes its proximity to its patrons, the constables. Whatever the balance of their motives in founding St Owen's, the provision of a new church to take on St Kyneburgh's pastoral functions was not their sole aim: the secular college, as a recent study has shown, was an institution still favoured by both English and Norman lords in the eleventh century (Franklin 1988, 97–104), and the purpose of the foundation as stated in 1095 was to maintain Walter's chaplains – who as well as praying for his soul would have occupied key administrative positions in his great household.

St Michael (plate 7)

The earliest reference to this church comes from around the middle of the twelfth century, although without question it was far older than that might suggest. In a charter of 1143x55 Earl Roger of Hereford granted a kinsman by marriage two selds beneath the north wall of St Michael's church (Walker 1964, 29; A5, fo. 73v). Later evidence for the size and position of these and neighbouring properties shows them to have been encroachments onto the street around the church (fig. 3.9; A3, fo. 6v; A13, fo. 61v) – encroachments which on the evidence of Earl Roger's grant would seem to have been originally authorized by the town's public officials, and in this case by the family who had effectively been the lords of Gloucester since the eleventh century (Walker 1964, 1–11). Yet whether or not such encroachment was new in the mid twelfth century, there is no clue here to the earlier history of this church which, given its prominent central location, must have been one of the ten churches already in existence in 1100.

In 1285, the advowson of St Michael's, together with that of its dependent chapel of St Martin, was granted to Gloucester Abbey by Bishop Peter of Exeter in return for £13 6*s* 8*d*. The formal agreement would seem to have followed on an arrangement in force at least a year earlier, for the first presentation to be made by an abbot of Gloucester was by Abbot Reginald (1263–84) (Walker 1976, 15–17). Whilst there is no firm evidence for the means by which the bishops of Exeter had acquired not only these churches but also those of St Mary de Crypt and All Saints, it is likely that some or all had been acquired with the lands and houses in Gloucester that Bishop Osbern of Exeter held in 1086, and which had formerly been held by Edmar (DB i, 162a). Described as a *thegn*, Edmer may have been an important man in Gloucester before the Conquest, for he had also held two hides locally in Haresfield, Down Hatherley and Sandhurst – land which in 1086 belonged to the King (DB i, 162d). But Edmer himself is an improbable candidate for the founder of St Michael's. Its position at the very centre of Gloucester, on the corner of Eastgate Street and Southgate Street, was so prominent that it was surely earmarked for a church when the street-system of the eastern half of the *burh* was laid out. St Michael's would then be the earliest of the group of churches in this area. And if it was in lay hands in the eleventh century, that may indicate it was founded by a layman. That, and the likely context of its foundation, together point to St Michael's having originated as a royal foundation.

Later in the middle ages, St Michael's was the Eastgate Street parish: with some significant local variations it covered the area occupied by plots fronting on to that street both within and without the city wall. The western boundary ran down Northgate Street and Southgate Street, though a westward extension brought in a single plot near All Saints on the opposite frontage. The southern boundary – with St Mary de Crypt – is discussed below and seems likely to have originally followed the line of Bell Lane and thus the rear of the Eastgate plots. The northern boundary – with St Aldate's – lay mid-way between New Inn Lane and Oxebode Lane, the parish including the northern Eastgate Street plots and the much smaller plots across the lane from them at the rear. This boundary (to be discussed further below) is of particular importance, as it has a direct bearing on the origins of St Aldate's parish and thus of the original extent of St Michael's. The alternative hypotheses are that St Aldate's parish represents a very early, pre-*burh*, estate, or that it represents a much later regular bisection of the north-east quadrant of the *burh* when St Aldate's was founded – at the expense of St Michael's parish (see below).

The close association between St Michael's parish and Eastgate Street was maintained outside the city wall. There the parish encompassed all but the south-eastern Barton Street plot-series, and the associated field-systems on both sides of the road within the city boundary. Detached portions of St Michael's parish were scattered still further eastwards against the background formed by St Mary de Lode.

According to the terms of the agreement made in 1197 between the abbey and Lanthony, St Michael's did not then possess the right to bury its parishioners (see below, p. 245). The gift in 1321 of the messuage adjacent to the church – which can only mean that on the south side – for the purpose of enlarging the building to accommodate a chapel of the Virgin Mary, implies that there was then no burial ground there (*Cal. Patent Rolls 1321–24*, 21). Land adjacent to the south was acquired subsequently to allow the provision of a graveyard soon after the middle of the century: in 1366 St Peter's Abbey agreed to waive its right to bury the parishioners of St Michael's in return for a payment of £1 a year, and in 1368 the Bishop of Worcester lifted his interdict on the new cemetery which he said had been consecrated without his authority (*VCH Glos.*, iv, 305). The graveyard was small, representing no more than the tail of the plot which had been acquired, for in 1455 the frontage of this plot was divided into two tenements, described as newly built, in the hands of the wardens of the service of St Mary in St Michael's church (*1455 Rental*, 4; see fig. 3.9).

The medieval church consisted of a nave with a single aisle on the south somewhat wider than the nave itself, a chancel with a south chapel, and a west tower with a two-storey porch. The irregular plan reflected the congested corner site and the constraints imposed on the growing building by tenement boundaries on varied alignments. Documentary evidence reveals building activity in the fourteenth century – not only was the chancel chapel built for the chantry of St Mary in 1321–4, as we have seen, but the chancel itself was rebuilt in 1392 (*VCH Glos.*, iv, 307). Illustrations pre-dating the demolition of most of the medieval building in 1849 show a north elevation in an ornate fourteenth-century Decorated style with large windows, and a door close to the east end. But the illustrations pose some problems, notably the position of the door to the street. The 1455 survey reveals a row of at least five small tenements between the east end of the church and the Eastgate Street door; some of these were two-storied and would undoubtedly have blocked most of the illustrated windows (*1455 Rental*, 100b–102b; and see above). The modern illustrations may therefore be showing the results of post-medieval – presumably eighteenth-century – refurbishment. Only the west tower, built between 1455 and 1472 (*VCH Glos.*, iv, 307), now survives, the Victorian nave and chancel having been demolished in 1956.

The demolition of St Michael's provided an opportunity for archaeological excavation, and the sites of the nave and the small churchyard to the south were trenched (Cra'ster 1961). The walls and internal arcades of the pre-Victorian building were found, conforming to the irregular plan recorded in 1847 (see fig. 3.9). The Victorian building had badly disturbed earlier stratigraphy, and the foundations of the medieval walls had been extensively modified by known mid-seventeenth-century alterations (Cra'ster 1961, 64; *VCH Glos.*, iv, 307). Within the church two short stretches of earlier walls were found, one or both running east–west, 'so disturbed as to be little more than a pile of stones of which little sense could be made; the same applies to several other similar agglomerations of loose stones resting on natural, but seeming to have no plan or purpose' (Cra'ster 1961, 64). These may well – as Heighway suggests (*VCH Glos.*, iv, 10) – have been the remains of the Anglo-Saxon church. In the churchyard to the south, graveyard deposits were machined-off and the forum-area organic deposits found, cut by robber-trenches seeking underlying Roman walls. However, the interpretation of the published pre-churchyard features and deposits and their relationship to others excavated in the vicinity of the Cross remain very uncertain.

Just as the plan of the pre-Conquest church is unknown, so too is its precise relationship to the street frontages to the north and west. The later medieval building projected northwards into Eastgate Street from the adjacent frontage, and a row of shops here represented a further rank of encroachment, as we have seen. If – as seems to be the case – the late fifteenth-century west tower was the first addition to the west gable, then that would originally have lain about 11 metres behind the Southgate Street frontage, which in 1455 was occupied by five small tenements (*1455 Rental*, 2b–4b).

St Mary de Crypt (plate 8)

The church was first recorded in 1139, when Bishop Robert of Exeter (1138–55) granted the nuns of Godstow a perpetual pension of 20 shillings from the church of St Mary, Gloucester (Clark 1905, i, 138). That this was the St Mary's that by the end of the middle ages was usually called St Mary de Crypt is confirmed by the later evidence for this pension, in the thirteenth and sixteenth centuries (Astle *et al.* 1802, 224; Caley 1810–34, ii, 498). The grant has been interpreted as showing that St Mary's then belonged to the see of Exeter (*VCH Glos.*, iv, 300). Between 1141 and 1143, Earl Miles gave Ralph, son of Pichard, a little house or *mansiuncula* before the church of St Mary, while by a separate charter the Empress Matilda allowed him 26½*d* landgable which had formerly been paid to the Crown for land in Southgate Street before the church of St Mary (A5, fo. 3v; Walker 1960, 198). Ralph was a loyal supporter of the Angevin party who had lost all his property in Winchester and was subsequently rewarded by the leaders of his party with the means to resettle his family in Gloucester (Walker 1960). Probably both of these charters referred to the same piece of land, which Matilda described as having formerly been held by Reinald the Janitor, and Miles said he had acquired from Bishop Robert of Exeter – evidently since 1138 (A5, fos 3v, 4; Walker 1960, 195, 198–9).

In 1174x75 Ralph gave his lands to Lanthony Priory (A5, fo. 4; Walker 1960, 200–202). His messuage before the church was promptly alienated in fee by Prior Roger for a rent of 4*s* (A5, fo. 20), and subsequently – and most unusually – disappeared from the Lanthony records, not even being recorded in Steymur and Cole's rental of the 1440s amongst the scatter of properties that had been lost or amalgamated with others (A13, fos 21v–23v, and *passim*). As the later medieval structure of St Mary's, however, was built right up to the street frontage, it is possible to deduce the subsequent course of events. At some time after the 1170s this property must have been re-acquired and any buildings demolished by the priory, to allow the west end of St Mary's to be extended to occupy land which once had belonged to the church. The fact that it was from the Bishop of Exeter that Miles had acquired the *mansiuncula* leaves little doubt that it had been an encroachment upon the original churchyard of St Mary's, sanctioned by one of the church's previous owners.

Within at most a very few years of Bishop Robert's 1139 grant to the nuns of Godstow, St Mary's had come into the possession of Lanthony Priory, together with All Saints. King John's recitation and confirmation of gifts to Lanthony says that both the church of St Mary in Gloucester and the chapel of All Saints were the gift of Bishop Robert of Exeter (Caley *et al.* 1849, vi, 137); certainly St Mary's – and presumably All Saints' as well – had previously belonged to Exeter, as Lanthony Priory felt it necessary in 1241 to secure the Bishop of Exeter's recognition of their rights to the advowson of St Mary de Suthgate, in the form of a final concord (PRO CP 25(1)/73/14, no. 269). The donor of the two churches, however, had been Bishop Simon of

Worcester, according to the cartulary copy of his charter, preserved by Lanthony Priory (A5, fo. 9v). Simon's charter must have been issued before 1150, when he died, and apparently shows that the see of Exeter had relinquished these churches – for whatever reason – to Worcester. This may already have happened by 1139: Bishop Robert's grant of a pension does not prove he still held the advowson in that year, as he may have been doing no more than disposing of what was already a residual right in the church. The 20 shillings pension granted to the nuns may indeed have been the only interest that Exeter retained in 1139, as in 1241 Bishop William of Exeter claimed nothing more for his quitclaim than obituaries and prayers. But a date of 1138 or 1139 for the transference of these churches from the see of Exeter to Worcester is likely, particularly in view of King John's confirmation that specifically mentions Bishop Robert; and the latter's gift of the *mansiuncula* to Miles between 1138 and 1141x43 reinforces the impression that it was in the first years of his episcopacy that he decided to dispose of two of his Gloucester churches, together with any associated secular buildings. Whether he gave the churches to Bishop Simon with the intention that they should be transferred to the new priory, or whether the gift was really Simon's, is uncertain.

As in the case of St Michael's and St Martin's, it seems likely that the bishops of Exeter's ownership of these churches came through their acquisition of the Gloucester property that in 1066 had been held by the thegn Edmer. There is no indication of whether St Mary's might have been one of the 10 city churches recorded in 1100, so that it had not necessarily been owned and built by Edmer or one of his predecessors. Its close association with All Saints' may be significant, in so far as the dependency of that possibly Anglo-Saxon church suggests an early origin for St Mary's; the possibility is not to be excluded, however, that it was St Mary's that was the later church, and that – like St Owen's – it had usurped the parochial rights of a church that thereby became its dependent chapel.

The absence of any later evidence that either of the town's pre-Conquest religious houses had any interest in St Mary de Crypt suggests that it had not been founded by the Old or the New Minster. It could have been founded by a layman; but the burial rights it possessed in the twelfth century, and very possibly earlier, and its unusually large parish, together show this to have always been an important church that is likely to have been a royal foundation.

St Mary de Crypt lies on the east side of Southgate Street between St Mary's Lane and Greyfriars, within a large (*c.* 0.5 acre/0.2 hectare) churchyard that extends back from the built-up frontage, bounded by lanes on either side (fig. 8.4). The church is oriented at right-angles to the street, its west end now on the frontage line. The rectory is recorded in the 1455 rental as being divided into two parcels of land to the south of the church (*1455 Rental*, 10a–12a). It is a large church, consisting of an aisled nave, transepts and a tower over the crossing, a long chancel with north and south chapels, and a two-storey south porch. Part of the west front survives from the twelfth-century church, but there was extensive reconstruction in the late fourteenth century when the nave and chancel arcades, the crossing and the east end of the chancel were rebuilt, and the south porch constructed; windows were also replaced in the west front and in the transepts – in 1401 the church was described as 'new' (*VCH Glos.*, iv, 301; Dancey 1903). This fully transeptal plan was unique amongst the Gloucester parish churches and had been achieved before the end of the thirteenth century. An explanation should probably be sought in Lanthony's acquisition of St Mary's during the twelfth century. With the exception of the dependent All Saints, and St Kyneburgh's, whose parochial functions were taken over by St Owen's outside the walls, St Mary de Crypt was the priory's only intramural city church; this, and its position on the main road leading southwards via Lanthony, made it an essential vehicle for the display of that institution's wealth and status. The crypt, or rather crypts, extend under almost the whole of the church footprint. Burial vaults under the chancel and its side chapels, the transepts and crossing are recorded only after *c.* 1775, but a basement under the nave and north aisle appears to be earlier and may be the space that was occupied by a tavern by 1576; it remained in secular use until the restoration of the church in the 1840s (*VCH Glos.*, iv, 301–302). Another separate crypt or undercroft lies beneath the south aisle but is currently inaccessible; Norman arches are said to survive there (Pevsner 1976, 232). The provision of one or more subterranean spaces in this church is (so far as we know) unique in Gloucester. An explanation may again be found in the church's ownership by Lanthony Priory and that institution's need for the use of an undercroft, a demand more usually accommodated within secular property.

St Mary de Crypt possessed the largest of Gloucester's intramural parishes, covering an area of approximately 17 acres (6.9 hectares). Its western boundary was, in part, a southward continuation of that between the parishes of Holy Trinity and St Nicholas – a boundary suggested (below) to represent a modification of the line of the western fortress wall. That boundary line was continued for only a very short distance before it was deflected by the outer ditch of the second castle, a modification to the parochial geography datable to the first quarter of the twelfth century (Hurst 1984, 105). The southern and eastern parish boundaries followed the town wall, except where interrupted by the intramural salient of St Kyneburgh's parish, which has already been discussed: St Mary de Crypt thus included the sites of the two intramural friaries. The north side of the parish – adjoining four others – was more convoluted. In part it followed two of the city's east–west streets: Longsmith Street in the west, reflecting the course of a Roman street, and Bell Lane in the east, one of the lanes of the suspected planning of the eastern half of the *burh*. However, as fig. 4.1 shows, the central portion of the boundary either side of Southgate Street departed markedly from these lines to embrace ground almost as far north as St Michael's church, generally following property boundaries in this area. It is possible that this irregular northward projection of St Mary de Crypt's parish is a secondary feature, a departure from an original line following the two east–west streets, a situation reconstructed by Heighway (1984b, fig. 7), and possibly an 'organic' growth from, or adaptation of, an original planned allocation of territory by street-block.

The size of the parish is remarkable, even if much of the area is considered to have been but thinly occupied before the Conquest. However, in 1991 a geophysical survey using ground-penetrating radar identified a focus of 'grave-like anomalies' to the south of Longsmith Street, outside the Blackfriars precinct, that may represent the location of a hitherto-unknown church (Atkin 1992a, 37). An unrecorded church must have been a feature of the period before 1200 – and probably considerably before. In fact, the existence of such a church, destroyed by the construction of the first castle during the years immediately following the Conquest, is postulated below in Chapter 9 (on slender evidence). There is, therefore, at least the possibility that the recorded parish of St Mary de Crypt in fact represents two formerly separate parishes divided by Southgate Street, amalgamated at an early date. Equally, it is possible that if the western half of St Mary's parish – west of Southgate Street – was indeed a secondary acquisition, it was made directly or indirectly from St Peter's Abbey which certainly in the twelfth century claimed parochial rights over the site of the old castle (see p. 244, below).

All Saints'

During the twelfth century All Saints' was regarded as a chapelry of the church of St Mary de Crypt. It was described as a chapel in John's confirmation of gifts to Lanthony Priory, and in later centuries it paid an annual pension of two shillings to St Mary's (Caley *et al.* 1849, vi, 137; A12, fo. 54v). Whether its dependent status indicated an arrangement of convenience that was recent in the twelfth century, or whether it originated in the circumstances surrounding the foundation of either church, is impossible to resolve. On the face of it, the evidence of the pension points to All Saints' having been a secondary foundation within St Mary's parish, although the example of St Kyneburgh's and St Owen's – with the subordinate church in fact being the older of the two – demonstrates how unreliable such a conclusion might be when unsupported by other evidence. All Saints' seems always to have constituted a separate benefice, and already had its own parish early in the thirteenth century when it was in dispute with St John's over parochial rights (see below, pp. 255–6). Like St Nicholas's and Holy Trinity (see below), it was described in the early thirteenth century as a *monasterium* (GCL, Abbot Froucester's Register B, p. 7), although it is difficult to see what connotations the term conveyed in this context. Especially in view of its use for these two other Gloucester churches, both argued below to have been foundations of the twelfth century, it implies no ancient minster status.

Despite residual uncertainty concerning its origins, in all likelihood All Saints' was one of the ten churches of 1100. It lay on the corner of Westgate Street and Southgate Street, and shared their orientation. The remains of the medieval church were found and recorded during redevelopment for a bank in 1893–4 (Medland 1894–5): the west and south walls of the nave were found standing to a considerable height where they had been incorporated within the enlarged Tolsey in 1648, and the north wall and those of the chancel were revealed by excavation. The building was very small, with a two-bay nave and square-ended chancel. The sketch at the beginning of the 1455 rental suggests – even if it is not entirely conventional – that the church had a belfry (*1455 Rental*, sketch 8, following xvi). The fabric recorded in the nineteenth century appears to date mainly from the thirteenth century and later, though the published account claimed a pre-Conquest origin for the building from two instances of 'long and short bond' at a level of seven feet below that of the fourteenth-century floor (Medland 1894–5, 153). If Medland's identification was accurate, this may indeed suggest the presence of pre-Conquest fabric, though possibly as late as or later than its use locally in Odda's Chapel at Deerhurst in 1056 (Taylor 1978, 957). Additional evidence of the pre-Conquest origin of All Saints' comes in the form of a carved stone bear's head found on the site, published by Medland as a 'relic of the Saxon period' and subsequently accepted as such (Medland 1894–5, 154; Heighway 1984b, 48; Heighway, pers. comm. quoting Professor R Cramp).

The church's central location within Gloucester is also consistent with a pre-Conquest origin. It occupied virtually all of its street-corner site and appears to have pre-dated the local encroachments on the Westgate Street frontage (see above, p. 50, and fig. 3.8). This suggests that the foundation of All Saints' took place before the town-centre frontages were densely built-up (Morris 1989, 193; Biddle 1976, 334), a process likely to have been well advanced here by the mid eleventh century. The relationship with the frontages was duplicated across the road by St Michael's – whose parochial geography was very clearly that of an early, pre-Conquest, church.

A lay proprietary origin may be suspected for this church, on account of its small size and dependent status, but the extent of any property within which it was founded is entirely obscure. At a smaller scale, the presence of a blocked door in the west wall of the church reveals that the immediate church plot must once have extended further to the west to include the property that is now No.1 Westgate; or, at least, that some means of access existed from that direction in the thirteenth century and – if the published account is reliable – before the Conquest (Medland 1894–5, 153 and plate III). The 1455 rental reveals church property extending to the south in the form of the rectory (*1455 Rental*, 4) which, like the church itself, was separated from the street by a screen of minute commercial encroachments. All Saints' did not have burial rights, and no burials are known from the site. There is no evidence it had a cemetery, and the twelfth-century agreements between St Peter's Abbey and Lanthony Priory leave no doubt that All Saints' was not then regarded as having the right to bury its parishioners.

All Saints' parish, as mapped in the nineteenth century, was the smallest of the city parishes, covering an area of about one acre (0.4 hectare) immediately west of the Cross. All except its eastern boundary followed minor property divisions. Its geography was very similar to that of the larger parishes of St Mary Grass Lane and Holy Trinity to the west: rectangular, with its longer axis north–south, straddling Westgate Street and the properties on each frontage, but extending beyond these to include plots facing other streets, in this case Northgate Street and Southgate Street.

The similarity in the geography of the three Westgate Street parishes that lay within the line of the Roman west wall prompts speculation as to exactly how closely they were originally related; it seems possible that the three could once have formed a single parish that originally covered all of the Westgate Street area within the west wall, from the precinct boundary of St Peter's Abbey on the north to Longsmith Street on the south. The chronology of St Mary Grass Lane and Holy Trinity will be further discussed later in this chapter but, in summary, a strong case can be made for their foundation in the twelfth century, in all probability later than All Saints'. It is possible that All Saints' was the original possessor of this hypothetical parish, but to accept that would be to ignore All Saints' status in the mid twelfth century as a dependent chapel of St Mary de Crypt. It is more likely that the undivided parish belonged directly to St Peter's Abbey, representing perhaps a last vestige of the direct provision of pastoral care within the walls that had elsewhere been taken over by the growing number of new churches, St Mary de Lode fulfilling this function for its extensive parish that included the abbey's estates outside the walls (Heighway in *VCH Glos.*, iv, 10, and see above; see also Heighway 1984b, fig. 7; discussed further in the context of St Mary de Crypt, below).

St Aldate's

Occupying the least prominent site of any of Gloucester's intramural churches, St Aldate's stood on the south frontage of St Aldate's Street; its large churchyard to the rear extended westwards to the back wall of properties on Northgate Street. It was bounded by a lane to the east and south, and its orientation was clearly determined by the prevailing street pattern. The church was first recorded in 1205 when its rector was in dispute with the Rector of St John's over the matter of parochial rights (*Cal. Papal Registers: Papal Letters*, i, 24); the advowson, it was recorded in 1275, belonged to Deerhurst Priory (Bund 1902, 67). Deerhurst, with most of its lands, had been given to the abbey of St Denis, Paris, by Edward the Confessor in or around 1059 (*VCH Glos.*, ii, 103), and the 30 burgesses that Domesday Book records as tenants of St Denis in Gloucester (DB i, 166) were actually Deerhurst's; according to the survey of *c.* 1100, there were then 36 tenants of Deerhurst Priory, which had the third-largest holding after the Archbishop of York (who owned the burgages formerly of St Oswald's) and St Peter's Abbey (Moore 1982, Appendix, Evesham K). Heighway's proposition, in the *Victoria County History*, that this substantial group of 30 or more burgages lay in a coherent block – which by implication St Aldate's had been founded to serve – is interesting, although it cannot be proved (*VCH Glos.*, iv, 11). Nevertheless, it is reasonable to suppose that a holding of this size had not grown through a series of casual acquisitions, but had come about as Deerhurst had systematically developed land that it had been given; and while the area of St Aldate's parish cannot be positively identified as such a development, it is certain that it largely coincided with a district of the Anglo-Saxon town that was developed by a lord other than the King. The 1455 rental records no landgable payments from St Aldate's parish, other than from five tenements lying together on the Northgate Street frontage (*1455 Rental*, 78b–80b; fig. 10.1), so that as a result the north-east corner of intramural Gloucester formed the largest of the areas of streets and houses in which the Crown had either had no interest or had relinquished it at an early date.

St Aldate's evidently had burial rights in *c*. 1280, when a tenement near the north gate was described as extending from Northgate Street as far as the cemetery of St Aldate's (*Cal. Recs Corpn Glouc.*, 668). In the 1440s the tenement apparently next to it, which was held in fee from Lanthony Priory, was described as lying to the south of a curtilage that lay beside the lane that ran within the north wall, with Northgate Street on its west side and the cemetery of St Aldate's church on the east (A13, fo. 70v). When this property had been granted in fee by Lanthony in the 1220s or 1230s no mention was made of the cemetery in describing its location (A5, fos 86–86v); but then neither was the cemetery mentioned when the property was acquired by the Abbot of Gloucester in 1374 (A5, fos 85–85v). There is no reason to believe that this cemetery was new in *c*. 1280, therefore, and its character was such as to suggest that from the time of its foundation St Aldate's may have stood within an area of open ground.

If St Aldate's had indeed been founded to serve the tenants of Deerhurst's urban estate, we might expect it to have been a pre-Conquest foundation, and certainly one of the ten churches of *c*. 1100. Yet its location suggests it was secondary to the overall planning of the area, and that it may indeed have originated as a private chapel attached to a prominent house on the main street close to the north gate. The evidence of dedications is generally of dubious reliability, although in this case it may be of use: the dedication to Aldate is presumably to St Eldad, a British bishop of Gloucester in the fifth century, according to Geoffrey of Monmouth's fanciful history (Farmer 1978, 11; Thorpe 1966, 193–5). Putting aside the improbability that this was a dedication to a saint of whom there was a genuinely early cult in the city, the most likely context for the dedication – if not necessarily the foundation of the church – was the period of the wide dissemination and popularity of Geoffrey's book after 1136 (Thorpe 1966, 28). The occasional designation of this church as 'St Aldhelm's' in the fifteenth and sixteenth centuries (*1455 Rental*, 70 and sketch 16, following xvi; *Cal. Recs Corpn Glouc.*, 1257) probably points, not to its true dedication, but to a tendency for dedications to become misunderstood and corrupt.

St Aldate's parish was a compact rectangular block of just under 5 acres (2 hectares) in the north-east corner of the city. Its boundaries followed the city wall on two sides and Northgate Street on the west side. Its southern boundary, as recorded in the nineteenth century, lay about half-way between Mitre Street (Oxbode Lane) and New Inn Lane (Grant Lane), generally – but not invariably – following the back-property boundaries dividing the north-facing and south-facing plots. The line also represents the course of a minor east–west Roman road.

Heighway, noting the coincidence of the Roman road and the parish boundary, suggested: 'it is possible that the parish unit represents an early urban estate or *haga* originally laid out on a Roman street (1984a, 364)' – the case for an early (eighth-century) date resting on the use of the Roman street rather than a feature associated with the postulated later *burh* replanning in this part of the city. She went on to note that the precise course of the parish boundary, as it is known to us from the post-medieval cartography, was determined by the back fences of the properties facing the two lanes (1984a, 376) – implicitly a further case of the local rationalization and shifting of a parish boundary, as has been proposed here for the line of the Roman west wall. The idea that the parish of St Aldate's represents an early urban – even pre-urban – estate is an attractive one, but two notes of caution should be struck. First, it might be surprising to find that the late ninth-century replanning of the eastern half of the city ignored a large existing property unit which thereby managed to maintain its integrity after the imposition of the new and intrusive street pattern. Secondly, there is the possibility of coincidental replanning: the minor Roman road was laid out half-way between the defences and the axial street underlying Eastgate Street, dividing the north-east quadrant into two *insulae* of approximately equal area. Any subsequent attempt to bisect this land would be likely to re-establish the street line, as could have occurred if there was a planned division of territory between St Michael's and St Aldate's when the latter was founded, probably in the tenth century. There is perhaps insufficient evidence as yet to decide the issue, though the possibility of regular parochial sub-division after the foundation of the *burh* seems rather more likely than the survival of an eighth-century estate.

The church itself was demolished in 1653–5, and nothing is known of its fabric other than that it comprised a nave, chancel and tower (*VCH Glos.*, iv, 296). A commercial excavation in 1934 within the western boundary of the medieval churchyard, identifiable from Lanthony cartulary evidence (A5 86–86v; A13 70v), was archaeologically recorded (Knowles and Fullbrook-Leggatt 1934 [The Bon Marche Site]). Any stratification in the dark soils overlying the Roman buildings went unrecorded, but a group of stone sculptural fragments was recovered. These included a tablet, probably part of a shrine, showing the god Mercury with attendant goddesses, and the well-known carved stone head, regarded for a long time as a prime example of Romano-Celtic sculpture but more recently as a likely Romanesque corbel (Collingwood and Taylor in Knowles and Fullbrook-Leggatt 1935, 80–81; e.g. Toynbee 1962, 8 and 125; Greene 1975). The head bore slight traces of red paint, but the tablet was 'thickly covered with whitewash'; the excavators speculated that they had been found during building work on the church, installed there and dumped when it was demolished (Knowles and Fullbrook-Leggatt 1935, 78). St Aldate's has therefore to be added to the corpus of church sites yielding Romano-British sculpture (Morris 1989, 28–9, 71–2) – if only on account of the Mercury tablet – but its significance here is perhaps only that of the opportunistic re-use of Roman masonry.

St Nicholas's (plate 9)

The cult of St Nicholas had become widely known in the Christian west by the tenth century, and was celebrated at Worcester by the 1060s where St Wulfstan showed a particular devotion to the saint. Greater popularity accrued to the cult with the translation of the relics of St Nicholas to Bari in 1078 (Farmer 1978, 316; Ortenberg 1992, 71).

St Nicholas's church, outside the core area of the *burh*, would seem to have been one of the small number of Gloucester's medieval churches that were founded after *c.* 1100. Before its surroundings were redeveloped in the 1970s, St Nicholas's stood at the front of a large churchyard on the north side of Lower Westgate Street, projecting beyond the building line into the street (fig. 3.14). The orientation of the church is distinctive: more nearly east–west than any other Gloucester parish church, it fits awkwardly into a townscape dominated by the underlying Roman alignment. An explanation may be found in its late foundation, in a period of greater concern for correct liturgical orientation (Morris 1989, 208–209), a concern also visible in the orientation of Serlo's abbey church begun in 1089.

The earliest reference to the church comes in a charter of about 1180, by which Sigar the priest and all the parish of St Nicholas granted a portion of land they had evidently been given (*Cal. Recs Corpn Glouc.*, 85). St Nicholas's belonged to the Crown in 1203; in the same year it was described as 'St Nicholas of the bridge of Gloucester' (Hardy 1835, 31, 34), and presumably was of royal foundation. Its association with Gloucester bridge, and the explicit description of it as the keeper of the bridge in 1221 (*Hist. et Cart.*, i, 322), suggest that influencing the circumstances of its foundation – perhaps early in the twelfth century – was the need to vest responsibility for upkeep of the bridge in a lasting institution. According to the annals of Tewkesbury Abbey, work on the bridge of Gloucester began in 1119 (Luard 1864, 45) – actually on 15 May that year, according to the Gloucester chronicler Gregory of Caerwent, a thirteenth-century monk of the abbey (Hare 1993, 43).

Gregory said this was the 'great bridge' – *pons magorus* – of Gloucester, although it is not entirely certain to which bridge he was referring: whether to the inner or Foreign Bridge, which may in the twelfth century have been already old, or to the outer or Westgate Bridge, which in the mid fourteenth century was believed to have been built only in the reign of Henry II (Fry 1910, 363–4). Certainly, when in 1221 the parson of St Nicholas's as custodian of the bridge claimed certain pasture on either side of the bridge as his, against the Abbot of St Peter's who claimed the land to be of his manor of Maisemore (*Hist. et Cart.*, i, 322), the bridge in question was the Westgate Bridge; that identification does not necessarily hold good for the whole of the period since the church's foundation, however. Because the Severn is a major river, meandering within a wide and marshy flood-plain, the crossing was a composite one with causeways being as important as bridges (*VCH Glos.*, iv, 242–3). As well as the two medieval bridges, therefore, there were two causeways: that which formed the lower part of Westgate Street, beyond the Foreign Bridge, and the causeway beyond the Westgate Bridge that stretched to Maisemore. The appearance of the new arm of the Severn – whenever and by what means this might have occurred (see above, p. 28) – changed the river-crossing only to the extent that it made necessary the insertion of a new bridge into an existing complex of bridge and causeway. Thus 'the bridge' might have carried somewhat different connotations at different periods, while at all times conveying the underlying sense of the complete structure that made up the crossing. It would have been logical had St Nicholas's custody of the bridge extended to the whole crossing, possibly following on an expensive rebuilding when it was clear that new arrangements needed to be made to ensure a continued programme of maintenance; it might also have been that the need for a new bridge to be built – the Westgate Bridge – provided the context either for the church's acquisition of new responsibilities or for its foundation.

According to a local jury in 1356, the Westgate Bridge had been built in the reign of Henry II as an act of charity by a priest called Nicholas Walred. He was said to have gathered together a group of workers, who lived together in a house built for the purpose by William Myparty, a burgess of Gloucester; after the bridge was completed, they continued to live together at William's house under the rule of a priest, taking in sick people. In 1229 the house was formally constituted as St Bartholomew's Hospital by Henry III, who gave it the church of St Nicholas and allowed the brethren to elect a prior to rule them – which they promptly did, choosing one Adam Garon as the first prior (Fry 1910, 363–4; *Cal. Inquisitions Miscellaneous 1348–77*, 219). There are inconsistencies here: certainly Henry III gave St Nicholas's to St Bartholomew's in 1229 (*Cal. Charter Rolls 1226–57*, 98), and there was a Prior Adam in *c.* 1230; but he was succeeded by at least two priors called Walter and John before Adam Garon or Garne – alias Reyner – became prior (*Cal. Recs Corpn Glouc.*, 253, 430, 492, 677, 678). He ruled the house during the 1270s or 1280s, being succeeded by John le Pessover in 1286 (Bund 1902, 292). More seriously, this story conflicts both with St Nicholas's known responsibility for the bridge, and with the surely more reliable date of 1119 supplied by two – possibly quite separate – sources. Furthermore, it is difficult to believe that the initiative to build such an important river crossing could have been taken by a simple priest, while the lack of any hint as to how the work might have been financed is the most powerful reason for regarding the whole story as suspect from beginning to end. Doubtless this was a story concocted to explain – long after the essential facts had been forgotten – how St Bartholomew's had acquired the responsibility for the Westgate Bridge which it retained until the close of the middle ages (*VCH Glos.*, iv, 242).

Yet the myth may preserve, in however muddled a way, details of the events surrounding the building of the bridge. It bears the character more of a rationalization of a scattering of misunderstood memories than of a complete work of fiction. Thus there could have been, in the fourteenth century, a memory that a priest called Nicholas Walred had had a role in the construction – plausibly enough, given what can be deduced about the relationship between St Nicholas's and the bridge; perhaps, too, the institution which would become St Bartholomew's did somehow begin with the building of the bridge. For while it is true that St Nicholas's was said to have the custody of the bridge in 1221 (*Hist. et Cart.*, i, 322), in the same year letters of protection were issued to 'the keepers and preachers of the bridge of Gloucester' (*Cal. Patent Rolls 1216–25*, 320). Whoever these might have been, they can only have derived their title from St Nicholas's; they sound, though, rather like the community of the hospital that only eight years later would be formally given the church, and consequently the care of the bridge (*Cal. Charter Rolls 1226–57*, 98). Certainly St Bartholomew's already existed before that grant in 1229: in 1223 the 'brothers and sisters of the hospital of Gloucester' received letters of protection (*Cal. Patent Rolls 1216–25*, 368). These were not the leper brethren of either St Margaret's or St Mary's which had both been founded in the mid twelfth century (*VCH Glos.*, iv, 15; Kealey 1981, 107–13); both of those hospitals stood outside the limits of the town at Wotton (fig. 4.2).

So it would appear that the hospital already carried some responsibility for the bridge-works before 1229 – and, incidentally, that it had a preaching function as well. It is reasonable to conclude that the association of church, hospital and bridge was already well-established, the new arrangements of 1229 serving only – it may be suggested – to make the parish church subordinate to the institution that had previously been its bridge-chapel. With the numerous endowments that St Bartholomew's had received from the people of the locality since *c.* 1200, if not earlier (*Cal. Recs Corpn Glouc.*, 94, 98, 102, 108, 109, 116, 117, 124, 131, 133, 134, 146 etc.), the increasingly wealthy hospital must have outgrown its dependence on the parish church of St Nicholas. Whether it had already happened in practice, it was now logical that their formal relationship should be reversed: that the church should be brought under the rule of the new prior of what had grown to become a religious house of some importance.

Like All Saints' and Holy Trinity (see below), St Nicholas's was described in a charter of the early thirteenth century as a minster (GCL D&C Register B, 464), a term which in this context may carry no special connotations. It would seem to have enjoyed burial rights from the time of its foundation, if the *atrium* it possessed on its eastern side in *c.* 1210 is to be interpreted as a cemetery, which was how it was described in the 1440s (A5, fos 59v–60; A13, fo. 52). In 1440, one Stephen Baret was stabbed to death in a fight in St Nicholas's churchyard (*Cal. Patent Rolls 1441–6*, 134).

It has been suggested above that St Nicholas's parish, likely to have been a post-Conquest creation, was cut out of the more ancient parish of St Mary de Lode, its boundaries reflecting the main divisions of the built-up area established over the previous century and a half. It was divided into three parts by the east and west channels of the Severn. On the east bank, the parish was fairly precisely co-terminous with Westgate Street and its plots, outside the Roman west wall. For most of its length the northern parish boundary followed the continuous back-fence line, marking the junction of the south-facing Westgate Street plots with the north-facing plots of St Mary's Square and Clare Street. The parish boundary only departed from this line to form a southward-projecting salient where the rear of Westgate Street plots had been laterally sub-

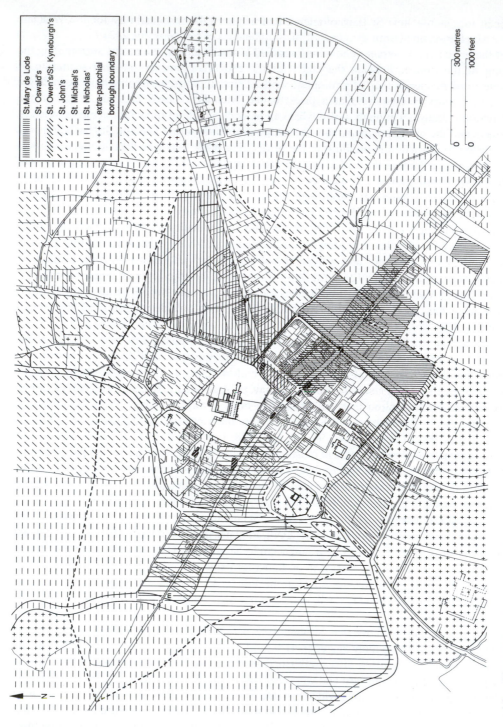

St. Mary de Lode
St. Oswald's
St. Owen's/St. Kyneburgh's
St. John's
St. Michael's
St. Nicholas'
extra-parochial
borough boundary

300 metres

1000 feet

4.2　Gloucester: extramural parishes

divided to form short east–west plots facing Deacon Street (Archdeacon's Lane). The southern parish boundary followed the defences of the later castle. On the west bank, the close association between the parish and Westgate Street was maintained: the parish covered Westgate Island, its northern boundary following the watercourse at the rear of the northern plot-series. South and west of the western channel, the parish covered the substantial area of Castle Mead meadow.

The Norman church of St Nicholas consisted of a nave, chancel and north aisle; the surviving elements – including the south door – date to the first half of the twelfth century and may represent the first building. The eastward extent of the chancel and the original form of the west end are unknown. In the first half of the thirteenth century, perhaps soon after it came formally under the control of the wealthy St Bartholomew's, the church was largely reconstructed. A south aisle was added, and the nave arcade and chancel rebuilt. In the fourteenth century a short north transept and south porch were added. The present west tower was built in the mid-fifteenth century but appears to have replaced an earlier one, a stone-built west bell-tower being recorded in 1347. The fifteenth century also saw large-scale refenestration (*VCH Glos.*, iv, 308–10; Medland 1900; *Cal. Recs Corpn Glouc.*, 938).

St Nicholas's must initially have been built within one or more cleared urban plots, and its churchyard subsequently extended into another. This part of Westgate Street seems to have been built up before the Norman Conquest (see above, p. 80–81) and certainly well before the likely foundation of the church. The reference to the *atrium* of St Nicholas in *c.*1210 (see above) suggests that the church lay within a churchyard, or less specific open space, within a century of its foundation. The churchyard, as mapped in the nineteenth century (see fig. 3.14), had little to distinguish it from the urban plots either side other than its width; like its neighbours, it ended at the common back-fence line (which also carried part of the parish boundary) to the Lower Westgate Street properties. There is some doubt as to the exact relationship of the recorded east and west boundaries of the church plot to their medieval predecessors. In the nineteenth century the western boundary lay within a few feet of the west tower. However, the settlement of a dispute in 1440 over a minor encroachment by the parishioners at the expense of the property next door (*Cal. Recs Corpn Glouc.*, 938), and the 1455 rental (*1455 Rental*, 46b), make it clear that the west boundary in the fifteenth century left room for a range of buildings and a processional way west of the tower; the nineteenth-century boundary may therefore represent a minor contraction of the church plot. The churchyard had been extended – legitimately – westwards before the encroachment recorded in 1440: in 1403 a piece of land next to the church was acquired for the graveyard, ostensibly from St Bartholomew's (*Cal. Patent Rolls 1401–5*, 329).

St Nicholas's is distinctive among the Gloucester parish churches in breaking the rule that later-founded churches were located behind frontages. Perhaps there was an unidentifiable factor: could the disastrous fire of March 1122, which several sources report as having burnt down the abbey and the town (*Hist. et Cart.*, i, 14–15; ASC s.a. 1122; Thorpe 1848–9, ii, 77), have fortuitously made this site available, only three years after building work began on the bridge? Otherwise, there are two reasons which may be advanced for St Nicholas's location. Firstly, by the circumstances of its foundation, it is unlikely to have been subject to the same constraints as a lesser proprietorial foundation, where there was more concern for the preservation of occupied buildings on the frontage and the income to be derived from them. Secondly, to fulfil its role as a bridge church it would have needed to attract offerings from passing travellers to supplement the tolls it presumably collected. Thus a location on, or even projecting from, the frontage would have been advantageous – a location replicated by St Bartholomew's, its associate and successor in the role. The church's apparently aggressive relationship to the street is explicable, then, as the result of the combination of the desire for a 'proper' liturgical orientation, with the church's continuation – in a sense – of the previous commercial use of the plot frontage.

It is perhaps inevitable that such a large plot on a major traffic street would have been subject to pressure for more intensive exploitation. This is apparent in the permission granted in 1347 to the parishioners to erect a building on the tiny triangular space between the street, the west tower and the south aisle, rents from which were to go to the maintenance of the church (*Cal. Recs Corpn Glouc.*, 938). The first-floor chamber over the porch also earned revenue for the parish, and the dispute over the strip of land on the western boundary shows that building had taken place along the western boundary near the frontage before 1440 (*Cal. Recs Corpn Glouc.*, 1115). Nevertheless, space was left for the processional way around each end of the church recorded in 1455 (*1455 Rental*, 46b).

Holy Trinity

Although relatively new when it was first directly recorded in 1176 (A5, fos 70v–71), Holy Trinity church was sufficiently established for the nearby lane that led back from the north side of Westgate Street – later Crafts Lane or College Street – to be known as Holy Trinity Lane in the time of Prior Roger of Lanthony, around 1180 (A5, fo. 61). Like the other church that stood in the middle of Westgate Street, St Mary Grass Lane (below), Holy Trinity was virtually certain to have been – with St Nicholas's – one of the Gloucester churches that were founded after 1100.

Until given to St Peter's Abbey in 1391 (*Cal. Patent Rolls 1388–92*, 406), Holy Trinity belonged to the Crown – as indeed did St Mary Grass Lane (*Cal. Patent Rolls 1225–32*, 425, 438; *1216–25*, 323). Particularly in view of their position on the public highway, there is little doubt that both churches were built either by one of the kings of the twelfth century, or – which is more plausible – by one of the constables, acting in the name of the King. Holy Trinity was called a minster around 1200 (*Cal. Recs Corpn Glouc.*, 112), and indeed Cole so described it in 1455 (*1455 Rental*, 34b), but as with All Saints' and St Nicholas's this should not be taken as implying any special status. There is no documentary evidence of its parishioners being buried there in the middle ages; it never possessed a cemetery, although burials could have taken place within the church.

The parish of Holy Trinity, a rectangular area of just under 6 acres (2.4 hectares), was the westernmost of the three Westgate Street parishes within the line of the Roman west wall. It was bounded by the abbey precinct to the north and Longsmith Street to the south; its boundary with St Mary Grass Lane was irregular and followed minor property boundaries (see below); its western boundary followed the east side of College Street (the medieval Lich Lane) from the abbey gate, and property boundaries on the other side of Westgate Street. The similarity in the layout of this parish, and those of St Mary Grass Lane and All Saints', and their potential original unity, has already been commented upon.

Heighway, as part of her case for an early, pre-*burh*, date for the removal of the Roman west wall, argued that the parish boundary between Holy Trinity and St Nicholas's ignored the course of the west wall (1984a, 367). However, the topographical analysis suggests that the balance of probability is that the western wall survived when the *burh* was established and only began to be demolished in the later tenth century. Does the parochial geography irrevocably contradict this argument? As Heighway's plan shows (1984a, fig. 119 p. 367) the parish boundary followed a staggered course generally parallel to the line of the wall, approximately 12 to 24 metres (40–80 feet) outside it – a line about 9 metres (30 feet) outside the lip of the early medieval ditch away from Westgate Street, but one that coincides directly with it nearer Westgate Street (site 25/76II:

Garrod and Heighway 1984, 28–30; Hurst 1986, 130). In Worcester, various instances will be noted where parish boundaries apparently reflect major pre-Conquest topographical features – such as defences or tenurial boundaries – but are not precisely coincident with them (pp. 247–52, below). These have been interpreted as the adaptation, for convenience, of original parochial boundaries to follow settlement boundaries that have replaced the original features. Such appears to be the case here. Having originally followed either the Roman west wall or the ditch outside it, the parish boundary was – upon the disuse and removal of the defences and the spread of settlement along the newly established Berkeley Street – moved a few yards to coincide with the new properties where these had not themselves been determined by the line of the old ditch.

It is of course most unlikely that, while the west wall still stood, this parish boundary separated (as it did later) Holy Trinity from St Nicholas's, both churches probably being new foundations of the twelfth century (see below). In Gloucester's earliest parochial geography, the west wall is most likely to have separated St Mary de Lode's parish, on the outside, from the original Westgate Street parish – whatever that was – on the inside.

As all but its west tower was demolished in 1699 (*VCH Glos.*, iv, 295), the architecture of Holy Trinity church is largely unknown. Cole's sketch at the beginning of the 1455 rental shows only a conventionally drawn church with a tower (*1455 Rental*, sketch 11, following xvi); the latter survived until the mid eighteenth century and was drawn by Kip on his 1712 plan as a tall, five-stage Perpendicular structure. Archaeological research along Westgate Street, in the form of the monitoring and recording of a service trench and a survey using ground-penetrating radar, has established the church's position and revealed the principal elements of its plan (Atkin 1992b, pp. 45–7; fig. 3.8). These were the west tower, an aisleless nave and a square chancel; the church had an overall length of about 90 feet (27.5 metres). Burials were found outside the church. The site of the Trinity Well was also found, in the street a short distance west of the tower.

St Mary Grass (or Grace) Lane

First recorded in 1176, and then called St Mary in the market – *in foro* (A5, fos 70v–71) – it had been built sometime after 1100 in the middle of Westgate Street, most probably by Walter of Gloucester or his son Miles (see Holy Trinity, above). Its advowson was held by the Crown until 1391, when it was given to St Peter's Abbey; it was then described as a chapel of Holy Trinity, although it retained its own parish into the modern period (Bund 1902, 345; *Cal. Patent Rolls 1388–92*, 406; *VCH Glos.*, iv, 302–3).

The wholly intramural parish occupied an area of about 2 acres (0.8 hectare), sandwiched between All Saints' and Holy Trinity. It also shared those parishes' characteristic layout, straddling Westgate Street and its plots, and additional plots to the south. It might be supposed, given the probable twelfth-century foundation of this church and Holy Trinity, that the parish boundaries would have been fixed immediately and would only reflect the secular geography of the twelfth century or earlier. However, the salient of St Mary's parish that stretched westwards to include a length of frontage on Bull Lane (Gor Lane) appears to reflect property boundaries formed by the division into three, in the late thirteenth or early fourteenth century, of a large block of property held undivided by Benedict the Cordwainer in the reign of Henry III (*1455 Rental*, 34a; Household 1946–8, 42–3): evidently the boundaries of even a relatively late parish could be subject to later adjustment.

The church, which was demolished in the mid seventeenth century, consisted of a nave, square-ended chancel, and a west tower with (if Speed's map is reliable in its detail) a spire. In

1991, the foundations were located by archaeological monitoring of a service trench, and by a radar survey (Atkin 1992b, 46–7; see fig. 3.8). These revealed the church to have been a small one (72 feet/22 metres long, 26 feet/8 metres wide): slightly smaller than Holy Trinity, slightly larger than All Saints' – sizes almost directly proportional to the relative areas of their respective parishes. There seem to have been burials within the church, disclosed by radar signals of what appeared to be skulls lying to the west of the chancel arch (M. Atkin, pers. comm.).

Non-parochial chapels

St Martin's Chapel

This church was first directly recorded in the 1140s, when two shops built against the wall of St Michael's church were described as facing the church of St Martin (Walker 1964, 29). In 1129, however, Richard, priest of St Martin's, witnessed a deed of gift of land in Gloucester to the abbey (*Hist. et Cart.*, i, 81–2). There is no sign that it ever had its own parish or burial rights, and it was described as a chapel of St Michael's in 1285 when both churches were acquired by St Peter's Abbey from the Bishop of Exeter (Walker 1976, 15–16; *Hist. et Cart.*, i, 84). There are no clues to the circumstances of its foundation or to how its dependency on St Michael's began, although it would appear that the Crown felt it had some claim upon the chapel: in 1334, for no clear reason (there was no vacancy at the abbey), it presented a new incumbent (*Cal. Patent Rolls 1330–34*, 565), and when St Martin's was demolished in the 1360s the burgesses were given the site on the grounds that the chapel had been built upon the King's ground on the King's highway (*Cal. Inquisitions Miscellaneous 1348–77*, 791; *Cal. Patent Rolls 1370–74*, 178). The grant was cancelled, however, when the Crown was convinced that the chapel belonged to St Michael's (*Cal. Inquisitions Miscellaneous 1348–77*, 804), and the site was confirmed to the Church for the construction of a house for the parson (*Cal. Close Rolls 1369–74*, 391–2; *1455 Rental*, 86b).

The site of the chapel – said in 1371 to measure 72 feet by 24 feet (21.9x7.3 metres) (*Cal. Patent Rolls 1370–74*, 178) – lay behind the street frontage in 1455 (*1455 Rental*, 86). If this was an early church, as its central position would seem to suggest, encroachment upon its original plot may have begun at an early date; alternatively, St Martin's was founded after the street frontage had been claimed by secular buildings. There is no clue as to whether this was one of the city churches in 1100.

Very little is known of the building. In 1889 'romanesque' masonry was discovered during the northward extension of premises on Eastgate Street near the Cross (W. C. Mann's: now 2–4 Northgate Street and 1–3 Eastgate Street). In 1895 the footings for a doorway and the corner of a masonry building were found 'at the north end of the site'. A manuscript plan of 1889 seems to suggest that the building measured some 24 feet by 72 feet (7.3 x 21.9 metres) ('Dry-as-dust Antiquary' 1895; also photo of MS plan 'site of Roman basilica' sent by G. A. Howitt to C. H. Dancey, in Howitt 1890, Glos. Lib.). While a mistaken identification with a secular building can never be entirely ruled out, both sightings appear to confirm the position of St Martin's behind the street frontage implied by the 1455 rental. Such a location – in addition to its status as a chapel of St Michael's – suggests that St Martin's was the latest arrival of the three churches around the Cross, constructed after the frontages had been fully built up.

St Brigid's Chapel

On 10 October 1184, according to the chronicle of Gregory of Caerwent, Ugoniilus or Eugenius, the Bishop of Ardmore in Ireland, dedicated the chapel of St Brigid, Gloucester (Hare 1993, 43). Eugenius was acting as a suffragan bishop in the diocese of Lichfield at that time (Fryde, Greenway, Porter and Roy 1986, 334), which goes some way towards explaining his presence at Gloucester.

The chapel's location within the abbey's walls dated only from the precinct's final expansion northwards in 1218 (*Hist. et Cart.*, i, 25, 83). Until then, the street, known in later centuries as Bride's Lane but in the thirteenth century as St Brigid's Lane (A5, fo. 91v), presumably connected the chapel with the streets on the north side of Gloucester. The expansion of the precinct, beginning in the time of Abbot Serlo, had been accomplished largely at the expense of St Oswald's. Land belonging to the New Minster had been given by two archbishops of York, Thomas (1070–1100) and Gerard (1100–1108), to enable the construction of a new wall for the abbey (*Hist. et Cart.*, i, 13; ii, 65); more land was required from St Oswald's in 1218 when the abbey again wished to enlarge its precinct. The rent of 20 shillings that in 1222 St Peter's gave in return was to compensate for the loss of land now enclosed within the new abbey wall, as well as to settle a number of other outstanding matters including the church of St John at the north gate and the chapels of St Brigid and St Thomas the Martyr (*Hist. et Cart.*, i, 25, 83). The nature of the priory's grievances concerning these churches is far from clear, although in the case of St Brigid's it may have been no more than its having been built upon the land the priory had lost.

St Thomas the Martyr

This chapel was referred to in the agreement dated 1222 concerning the settlement reached by St Oswald's Priory and the abbey some four years before (*Hist. et Cart.*, i, 25, 83). A possession of St Oswald's, it was described at the Dissolution as standing next to – *iuxta* – the Blind Gate (PRO SC6 Hen VIII 1212, m.5). This description may have been inaccurate: the location of this chapel by the *Victoria County History* beyond the Blind Gate, by the road to Kingsholm on the south side of the Twyver (*VCH Glos.*, iv, 317) is based on later evidence and appears to be trustworthy. This river may have marked a late Anglo-Saxon defensive line, and with the chapel's position next to the lane leading north from St Catherine's Street (Wateringstead Street) towards Kingsholm, it could perhaps be considered as a wayside chapel, at a point half-way between the Kingsholm royal palace and St Oswald's, on a route which whilst the palace remained in use would have had a particular processional significance (see fig. 3.3).

St Thomas the Apostle

A church by this name was recorded before 1179 in two charters, both of which were endorsed 'Kingsholm' (GCL D&C Abbey Deeds, iv, 7, 9). In view both of its general location and of the lack of any further references to it, there is little doubt that it should – provisionally, at least – be identified with the chapel of St Thomas discussed above. Heighway, who also implicitly identifies this church with the later chapel of St Thomas the Martyr (1988, 6) has suggested that it already existed in the tenth century, and may even have been of ninth-century date (1984a, 363, 372, 377). A change of dedication, or attribution, from the apostle to St Thomas of Canterbury in recognition of the importance of the latter's cult after the 1170s is not improbable.

St Thomas

Another chapel of St Thomas stood beside the road to Wotton, outside the outer north gate (GCL D&C Register B, 256). It already existed in *c.* 1300, and in 1454 it was rebuilt by Philip Monger, a prosperous Gloucester merchant and vintner (*1455 Rental*, 98a; Holt 1987, 240).

Chapter 5

Worcester and the Church before 1100

Unlike Gloucester, Worcester did not take shape in the early Middle Ages among the impressive ruins of a major Roman city. Worcester's Roman predecessor had been extensive, it is true, but it had been far from imposing and there is no sign that it had been a centre of authority in the region. The archaeological evidence points to its having been primarily an industrial settlement, concerned with the smelting and forging of iron, and with few if any public or other buildings of a monumental character or built entirely of stone. Only the rudiments of a regular street-grid have as yet been recovered (Barker 1969; Mundy 1989; Baker *et al.* 1992). At the core of the settlement was a small oval enclosure of some 26 acres (10.5 hectares), within substantial earthwork defences (Barker 1969, 15–19, 44–53) which survived into the medieval period (for a fuller discussion of Roman Worcester see below, pp. 143–7). In all likelihood it was that defended circuit which ensured Worcester's local prominence during the post-Roman centuries, rather than any continuation of its economic functions. There are strong indications (albeit from much later evidence) that St Helen's church originated as the principal church of the district during the period before the foundation of the see (Bassett 1989a; 1992, 20–26; and see below, pp. 197–8), which would support the impression that Worcester acted as a centre of secular authority in the post-Roman period. Indeed, it is easy to appreciate how attractive this compact defended area by a major river crossing might have appeared under the changed circumstances of the times. The greater viability of Worcester's defences – in contrast with those of other sites by the Severn that had formerly been so much more important, such as Gloucester or Wroxeter – offered greater protection to those who dwelt within. The two high-status burials from the site of the cathedral, not closely dated but from the broadly post-Roman period, perhaps support this perception of Worcester's importance at that time (Barker *et al.* 1974).

The establishment of the new see of the Hwicce at Worcester, traditionally in about 680 although perhaps as early as 675 or before (Sims-Williams 1988, 168–9), was clearly a recognition of the convenience of its small ready-made defensive circuit. It may, too, have reflected the fact that Worcester was already both an ecclesiastical centre and an important – if secondary – royal centre, dispensable but sufficiently prestigious to give to the Church. A stray find from that period is a coin of the Byzantine emperor Phocas (602–610), by far the latest of the sequence of Roman coins found in 1833 when Castle Hill – the motte of the Norman castle of 1069 – was removed, and the original ground below excavated (Fendall 1969, 105, 112). The circumstances of this find, if Allies (1852, 16) is to be trusted, rule out the possibility of this coin having found its way to Worcester other than during the Anglo-Saxon period. Coins of Edgar, Æthelred II and Cnut were also found under Castle Hill, suggesting that this part of Worcester, overlooking the Severn and within the old Roman defences on the south side of the cathedral complex, may have seen commercial activity before the Conquest.

The Church of Worcester and the early city

The medieval city of Worcester grew up, in due course, beside the cathedral church of St Peter which had been built there by the 690s (B 75; S 77). What evidence there is suggests that the

127

Church of Worcester was the dominant influence on the early city, certainly until the foundation of the borough, or *burh*, in the 890s, and probably for a considerable time thereafter. The topographical analysis of Worcester (Chapter 6, below) – which presents the evidence for the successive phases of its development during the Anglo-Saxon period – as well as the city districts in which pre-Conquest concentrations of Church property can be detected (see Chapter 10, below), suggest that the Church continued to influence the way in which Worcester grew until at least the end of the eleventh century.

In its earliest centuries the Church of Worcester was the city, and the bishop was the lord of Worcester. When in 814 Coenwulf of Mercia remitted to Bishop Deneberht the cost of maintaining 12 men which was due from the city of Worcester, it was clearly the bishop's establishment in Worcester that constituted the city (H 23–4; S 172). And Burgred's charter to Bishop Ealhhun in 857 made the same assumption, when land in London, it was stipulated, was to be held by the bishop 'in his own liberty, or belonging to the city of Worcester' (H 44–5; S 208; Whitelock 1979, 92). The bishop's lordship of Worcester was the lordship of the ancient defended area, which was at once both the city and the cathedral precincts.

But how urban, if at all, was this ecclesiastical city before the 890s? And to what extent was the economic development of Anglo-Saxon Worcester sustained by the presence of the powerful and wealthy community that was resident at the cathedral?

With the exception of finds of coins, there is no archaeological or historical evidence for any commercial or manufacturing activity within the city's defences between Roman times and the last decade of the ninth century. Of course, the general sparseness of evidence for that period does not necessarily rule out the possibility that Worcester had urban, or rather proto-urban, functions during that period of nearly five centuries. And because for two centuries following on the foundation of the Church of Worcester the bishops were lords of the whole area of the city, any economic development of the site would have occurred at their instigation or at least under their authority. But the analysis of the phases of physical development and expansion in Worcester, to be considered in Chapter 6, suggests that the period which saw virtually all of the increase in Worcester's importance as both an economic and a population centre was that which followed on the foundation of the *burh* in the 890s. Any previous urban phase that there might have been left no detectable mark on the series of development phases that began at that time, and which led to Worcester becoming a major town – in contemporary terms – with probably 2000 inhabitants or more by the time of Domesday Book (Clarke and Dyer 1969, 30–32).

The cathedral community was a wealthy one that presumably kept its residence in the same place throughout the year, with the partial exception of the bishop and his personal retinue. The retainers that must have been attached to a community and episcopal household of this importance would thus have generally been resident in the city, and much of the revenue from its estates would have been consumed within Worcester. From the evidence of witness lists, Christopher Dyer has found that the cathedral clergy alone were never fewer than 9 in number, and on occasion there were as many as 25 (Dyer 1980, 28). From the late seventh century onwards, Worcester accommodated these men together with their families and servants, and the specialist craftsmen they employed. Presumably the bishops maintained a military retinue as well. In all likelihood, these people comprised all or most of the population of the defended city that in the eighth century contained – besides the cathedral – the church of St Helen, and possibly already those of St Alban and St Margaret (see below, pp. 200–203).

The essential attribute necessary to turn this concentration of population into a settlement with a truly urban economy would have been a regular market for rural produce, together with resident merchants, craftsmen and petty traders making a living primarily by servicing the needs of the rural population of the vicinity. As a major landowner, the Church of Worcester itself could have provided a stimulus to the local market economy if its practice had been to sell in Worcester any of the large agricultural surplus from its extensive estate. The size of the community and its dependants undoubtedly ensured that a considerable proportion of the estate's surplus could be delivered in the form of food rents and consumed within the city; but we are far from well-informed about the specific nature of any such rents, or of what share of the estate surplus they represented, or whether they really were considered worth bringing from the quite distant lands that the Church of Worcester already owned in the eighth century. Lands on the southern slopes of the Cotswolds, for instance, or the remote holding at Henbury-in-Salt-Marsh, on the Severn estuary, could never have been convenient sources of supply for Worcester. The value of a scatter of estates in supporting an itinerant bishop and his household is obvious; the mechanism by which they provided the sustenance for the resident community at Worcester less so. With regard to food rents recorded as being paid from lands belonging to the Church of Worcester, from Westbury-on-Trim in the 790s, and from Kempsey in 844 or soon after (H 101–103, 564, 562; S 146, 1833; Whitelock 1979, 78; Finberg 1961, 251), Christopher Dyer (1980, 28–30) has drawn attention to their smallness in relationship to the likely yields from those estates. Either (we may suppose) a cash rent was paid in addition, or our expectations of the level of exploitation are simply too high, and Anglo-Saxon lords were content to extract a far smaller surplus from their lands than later lords were. Perhaps, though, there were other food rents from these lands: in the first of these two instances a residual rent only was recorded, which was to be paid to the King after the grant of Westbury to Worcester; the second records items to be supplied to the cathedral community from lands which may have yielded substantial quantities of produce in addition.

Certainly some cash payments were made at this time. A food rent from the Worcester estate was commuted to a cash rent in 803 (H 50–52; S 1431), and charters from 864 and 903 record annual cash rents (H 63–5, 119–21; S 210, 1446). Meanwhile, six charters of lands and privileges from the Mercian kings Berhtwulf and Burgred to the Church of Worcester between 840 and 864 provide details of horses, jewellery, gold and silver given by the bishops in return (H 26–8, 69–70, 70–71, 85–7, 31–3, 63–5; S 192, 194, 196, 206, 207, 210): whether these are to be seen as acts of purchase or as mutual exchanges of gifts is less important than the evidence they provide for the disposable wealth of the bishops of Worcester by this date. Whilst much might have been accumulated over the years from offerings, it was the income from rents, the sale of produce and other commercial activities that must already have been more important as sources of cash revenue.

The commercial interests of the Church of Worcester in the eighth and ninth centuries

The Church of Worcester was drawing resources from non-agricultural sources within a short time of its foundation. In 716 or 717 Æthelbald of Mercia granted it land south of the River Salwarp in Worcestershire for the construction of saltworks in exchange for the church's existing saltworks north of the same river. This had consisted of two salthouses and six furnaces, and the bishop was to replace it by a new saltworks which was apparently comparable in capacity, consisting of three salthouses and six furnaces (H 442–3; S 102; Whitelock 1979, 64). The exchange was undertaken, it was said, because the new arrangement seemed more convenient to both parties, but there may have been more to it than that: the King was receiving an operational saltworks, whilst the bishop got in return only a piece of ground 'on which salt is wont to be made' and would have to construct his saltworks anew. Unless the exchange had been blatantly in Æthelbald's favour, there must have been some other consideration in favour of the Church, the greater potential capacity of the new saltworks being the most likely. At any rate, this was a major enterprise – employing no doubt numerous people and consuming quantities of fuel. Would it have been worked only to supply the church's estates, which at this date were less extensive than they would be by the end of the century (Dyer 1980, 11)? Salt was a major local product, which had a wide distribution, and the Church of Worcester retained an interest in its processing and doubtless its sale: in 956 King Eadwig granted it land and salt furnaces in Himbleton, Worcestershire (H 333–4; S 633).

The extent to which the people of the Worcestershire countryside had recourse to markets during the eighth and ninth centuries remains quite uncertain, although obviously there were particular commodities that were distributed through trade, such as the locally manufactured salt or iron goods. Whilst such trade in itself should not be taken to indicate the existence of regular markets, the need for an agricultural population to obtain cash for purchases perhaps should: the evidence that by this time at least some rents were paid in cash indicates that there were tenants – both of the Church of Worcester and no doubt of other lords – who customarily had to sell a proportion of their produce. Numismatic evidence from the region has been used to advance the view that already during the eighth century the circulation of coinage was an essential feature of the local economy: the *sceattas* that have been found within the area of the kingdom of the Hwicce were perhaps a local issue, and there are indications that this coinage played a role in trade between the region and London, and thus the continent (Metcalf 1976, 64–74). Fundamental questions concerning the volume of the Anglo-Saxon currency – and the implications of that – are, however, still to be resolved (Metcalf 1965; Grierson 1967). Two *sceattas* have been found within Worcester itself: a Frisian-type coin of the second quarter of the eighth century from an unstratified context at 91 High Street (the Guildhall), an interesting location just outside the northern gate of the pre-*burh* city (Fendall 1969, 112); and another nearby to the west, between the High Street and the river, found in the Deansway excavations (Baker *et al.*, 1992, 72).

A significant document from 743 or 745 is a grant by Æthelbald of Mercia to Bishop Milred and St Peter's, Worcester, of the toll due on two ships at London (H 45–6; S 98). This is one of ten such surviving grants of the period, four of which specifically confirm this as a perpetual right to be conveyed to new ships in succession to the original ones (Kelly 1992; Whitelock 1979, 66). Five of the grants were to the abbesses of Minster-in-Thanet; two were to the bishops of London; and one each to the church at Reculver and to the bishops of Rochester and Worcester. The grant to Worcester, whose text survives only in a later and suspect translation into English, might imply no more than that the bishop was being given the right to collect toll from two ships in London – a right he could have farmed to someone resident there. But it is far more likely that, as with the other grants, the bishop was being excused toll on two ships he himself owned and which used the port of London. Early in the twelfth century the cathedral priory believed that Æthelbald, some time between 718 and 743x745, had given Bishop Wilfrid a court or enclosure – a *curtis* – in London, between the streets called *Tiddbertistret* and *Savinstret* (Caley *et al.* 1849, i, 607); whilst the record may be untrustworthy, it is consistent with the reliable evidence from a century or more later that bishops of Worcester maintained commercial premises in London (below).

London's function as a major port was already well established. Bede, writing early in the eighth century, knew of it as 'a market of many nations visiting it by land and sea' (HE ii, 3), and those who kept ships there presumably had dealings with Frisia and Francia. Within decades of its foundation, therefore, the Church of Worcester was apparently participating directly in trade with continental Europe. But what did that trade consist of? In exchange for imported luxury goods for the bishop and his household, what commodities had to be exported? The most likely commodity was perhaps wool; by this time Worcester had acquired lands in the Cotswolds at Bibury, Withington, Batsford and Woodchester (Dyer 1980, 11), and it is not impossible that during the 740s these lands were producing a surplus of wool that was being shipped abroad through London.

Despite such strong indications of a Worcester and London connection during the eighth century, active participation in trade in London by the bishops of Worcester can be confirmed only for a century later, when in 857 Bishop Ealhhun acquired a haw or *haga* near the west gate of London, described as 'a profitable little estate'. Although it was ostensibly granted by Burgred of Mercia, the Bishop appears to have purchased the land from the Reeve Ceolmund, and then had to pay the King 60 shillings for it and the rights which went with it (H 44–5; S 208; Whitelock 1979, 92). These were stipulated to be the rights to use the customary weights and measures of the port, and were evidently commercial privileges. The Bishop was to pay the King a rent of 12*d* for the *haga* – a rent which in the post-Conquest period might be described as a burgage rent.

Then from the 880s and 890s come two charters which are similar in content, but which in providing more details raise even more urgently the question of the active involvement of the bishops of Worcester in regular trade through London. The first, dated 889, was a grant to Bishop Wærferth from King Alfred and from Æthelred, *sub-regulus* of the Mercians, of a *curtis* somewhere in London, described as an old stone building that extended from the street to the city wall, called *Hwætmundesstan* (H 41–3; S 346). As in the earlier grant, the bishop and his people were given the right to free use of the London weights and measures for sales within the property and for their own use. Tolls on sales made within its bounds would go to the bishop, although the grant was careful to specify that elsewhere in the public streets or on the 'trading shore' of London – the Strand – the bishop's men had no immunity from the royal tolls that were due on traded goods. The property was stated to be 26 perches (130.8 metres) in length, 13 perches and 7 feet (67.5 metres) at the upper or northern end, and 11 perches and 6 feet (57 metres) at the lower or southern end. The second charter, dated to 898 or 899, records that King Alfred, Ealdorman Æthelred, Plegmund the Archbishop of Canterbury and Bishop Wærferth of Worcester had met at Chelsea to consider how they might effect the *instauratio* – meaning the restoration, and perhaps laying-out – of the city of London (B 577, 578; S 1628). One of the decisions that the four reached was that Plegmund and Wærferth should each receive a plot of land in London at the place called *Ætheredeshythe* – 'Æthelred's Hythe' – identified with the later Queenhithe. The two plots were either side of a street running northwards from the Thames; streets similarly defined their eastern and northern limits, and permission was granted for ships to dock on their southern sides.

Tony Dyson (1978) argued that the texts of both of these charters are essentially genuine, although it is obvious that the extant texts of the later grant have been corrupted in certain minor details. He also concluded that the two grants to Wærferth are of the same piece of land, which today is bounded by Thames Street on the south, by Bread Street Hill on the west, by Trinity Lane on the north and by Huggin Hill on the east. That must remain conjectural, given the vagueness of the first charter as to the location of *Hwætmundsstan*, and more recently Susan Kelly has dissented from the view that the second charter was in effect a regrant to Worcester (1992, 13n). In favour of Dyson's identification is the certain fact that the proportions of the plot as given in 889 fit that block of property and apparently only that one; and the location of the block is consistent with the later grant, as it lies immediately to the north of Queenhithe.

If in these two charters we really do have two grants to Worcester of the same piece of land, ostensibly made some ten years apart, this might seem at first sight implausible. Yet there are at least two possible explanations of the situation. First, the 889 grant is recorded only in the eleventh-century volume of Worcester material, Hemming's Cartulary (H 41–3; S 346), and that of 898–9 in five separate copies, all with a Canterbury provenance (S 1628). It is at least possible that both charters in fact refer to a single event, their separate wording resulting from no more than the written confirmation of this single grant having been supplied – and thus composed – by the two recipients of the gift. In other words, these two charters are the differently worded versions recorded by the two beneficiaries – Worcester and Canterbury – of a single grant. And if that were the case, it would explain why the Worcester clerks had no record of the supposed second grant, a problem which indeed has been cited as an indicator that it is spurious (Kissan 1940, 227n). That still leaves the problem of the ten-year difference of date, although as neither the Worcester text nor the group of five Canterbury texts is accepted as being entirely authentic in its present form, the discrepancy could be an error in the single Worcester text, or in that from which all five Canterbury texts were ultimately derived. Plegmund became Archbishop of Canterbury only in 890 (Brooks 1984, 153), and so a date after that is indicated.

The second explanation is perhaps more attractive, and supposes that there were indeed two grants to Worcester. That of 889 expects the bishop's men to be using – at least sometimes – the trading shore or *ripa emptorali*; the later grant evidently follows on the construction of a quay named presumably after Ealdorman Æthelred. Perhaps the second charter records a new grant to Christ Church, Canterbury, but is a necessary confirmation to Worcester of its existing land. Whilst we do not know the precise form of the 'restoration' of London, it entailed perhaps a laying-out of a new, regular street pattern as Brooks has suggested (Brooks 1984, 154) and clearly there was commercial regeneration too. The building of a new waterfront, proper quays to replace the previous beach, implies considerable reorganization and investment. Inevitably, existing property rights would have been affected, and Wærferth may have felt the need for such a confirmation.

The 'restoration' was clearly a major refoundation of the *burh* of London, that part within the old Roman walls. New minster churches, it has been argued, were founded in the eastern part of the city and doubtless elsewhere, whose parishes or *parochiae* coincided with a system of wards organized for the defence of the *burh* (Haslam 1988, 35–43). The city's inhabitants – strongly Scandinavian in character if the court of Husting, with its Norse name, was indeed already in existence as Brooke and Keir suggested (1975, 249) – were to be neutralized by means of their conversion to Christianity, at the same time as London's ability to defend itself was ensured and the profits of the city were directed towards the English King and his nobility. The city had been recovered from Danish rule in 886, and the apparent delay of some years before the restoration was undertaken perhaps points to a period during which English authority needed consolidation. These grants of privileged access to the wharves of London, therefore, should be seen in the context of the deliberate policy of reconstruction pursued by Alfred and his associates and successors. Plegmund and Wærferth were close advisers of his in the spiritual and cultural regeneration of the realm (Keynes and Lapidge 1983, 92–3), whilst their presence at the Chelsea conference testifies to their role in secular affairs. These were not simply pious gifts to the Church, therefore, or opportunistic purchases by shrewd men of affairs; rather, they are to be seen as a practical expression of the policy of reconstruction that – although it bears Alfred's name – was evidently also the cause of these Mercian churchmen.

The founding of the *burh* at Worcester

The restoration of London in the 890s had its parallels in the other *burhs* constructed during this period, of which that at Worcester is the best recorded. The report of an agreement made after *c.* 884, and more probably between 889 and 899 – with King Alfred's approval – between Ealdorman Æthelred, his wife Æthelflæd and the Church of Worcester, concerning this most crucial event in Worcester's history, is a remarkable and unique survival, referring as it does to the construction of the city's new fortifications and the arrangements for regulating the *burh*'s affairs (H 3–5; S 223; trans. in Whitelock 1979, 99). The agreement reports that the building of the *burh*, for the protection of the people, had taken place at Wærferth's request; that the royal couple granted to the Church of Worcester half of all their rights of lordship in the city, whether in the market or the street, both within the fortification and outside; and that the profits from the *burh* in the form of land-rents and the proceeds of justice would be shared equally with the Bishop. The sharing of the rights of lordship in the streets and market presumably referred to the tolls on trade (although the customary tolls on wagon-loads and horse-loads of salt passing through the *burh* were to go to the King).

Within the terms of the agreement we can see the workings of a conscious, centrally directed programme. As in London, the aim was to provide strategic fortifications and to enhance opportunities for trade (and profit), but more clearly too to extend royal authority into new areas. The apparent generosity of the half share of the *burh* to be enjoyed by Wærferth and his successors, and the guarantee that outside the market-place the Bishop was to continue to enjoy his lands and his rights, mask the essential point that the lordship of the city no longer belonged to the Church of Worcester as it had done since the Church's foundation. Thus the agreement marks the beginning of the transition from episcopal to state control, for whatever might have been the influence wielded by Wærferth and his immediate successors in this situation of shared lordship, it was inevitable that in time ultimate control over the city would come to lie with the secular authorities. (The question of lordship within the city of Worcester following on the foundation of the *burh* will be discussed further in Chapter 12.)

The agreement can be dated only to the period *c.* 889–99, so that it is not possible to demonstrate a sequence of events with regard to the restoration of London. But clearly the grant of a substantial London property to the Church of Worcester might have been seen as balancing the formal loss of authority in the Bishop's own city. However, the increase of royal authority and interest in Worcester went beyond the formal agreement ordering the *burh*, as in 904 Wærferth granted a riverside haw or *haga* in Worcester to Æthelred and Æthelflæd (H 13–15; S 1280). They and their daughter Ælfwynn were to hold it, together with other lands to the north of Worcester and on the opposite bank of the river, for the duration of their lives, after which it was to return to the Church of Worcester. No stipulation was made concerning the *haga*'s possible use, although unquestionably from its size and position it was intended for commercial development as it gave useful access to the river bank and to the trade on the Severn. It was said to occupy the north-west corner of the new *burh*, its boundary running eastwards 28 rods (140.8 metres) in length from the river along the north wall, then 24 rods (120.7 metres) southwards, and then westwards 19 rods (95.5 metres) to return to the Severn – dimensions which enable it to be located within the street-pattern of medieval Worcester and incidentally to define the exact position of the *burh* defences on their north side (see below, pp. 176–7). The fact that the Mercian rulers could extract such a valuable gift from Wærferth – the *haga*, after all, contained a considerable proportion of the *burh*'s land and most importantly most of its useable river-frontage – demonstrates their continued determination to dominate and profit from their newly acquired city. In the event, however, Æthelred and Æthelflæd may have been unable to initiate any extensive development within the *haga*, and perhaps it was not long before it was returned to Wærferth's successors. By 919 both Æthelred and Æthelflaed were dead and, with Edward the Elder's assumption of power in Mercia, Ælfwynn had been carried off to Wessex; already, then, the property could have been released to the Church of Worcester, although we cannot tell how long Edward and his successors might have attempted to retain the Worcester *haga*.

The Church of Worcester in the tenth and eleventh centuries

Our knowledge of the Anglo-Saxon cathedral buildings at Worcester is slight, and briefly stated. A cathedral dedicated to St Peter was erected apparently soon after the foundation of the see in 680; between the 960s and 983 Bishop Oswald built nearby a second cathedral of St Mary, the older church of St Peter still remaining in use. The present cathedral, which St Wulfstan began to build in the eleventh century, replaced certainly St Mary's and presumably St Peter's as well (Dyer 1968–9), although there is no record of the older church's eventual demolition (Dyer 1969; Bassett 1985, 98 notes 54 and 55). There is, however, considerably more evidence for the community that served the cathedral churches (Atkins 1937, 1940), and recent work has considerably extended our understanding of aspects of the pre-Conquest Church of Worcester (Sawyer 1975; Dyer 1969, 1980; Barrow 1992a, 1996).

From at least the time of Eadmer, who compiled his *Vita Sancti Dunstani* by the second decade of the twelfth century (Stubbs 1874, 197), it was believed that Oswald built St Mary's as part of his programme to reform the Worcester Church. Unable to displace the existing community of clerks by reason of their powerful connections, Oswald accordingly resolved to found a new church that he might fill with monks, he himself to be at their head. Until recently, this version of events was broadly accepted, although there was disagreement about the date when monks were introduced to Worcester, and about how abrupt Oswald's reforms actually were (John 1966, 234–48; Robertson 1956, 360–61; Robinson 1919). Sawyer (1975), however, after a close examination of the 71 lists of witnesses amongst the 79 surviving leases that were issued under Oswald, questioned the nature of the changes at Worcester under Oswald's episcopacy. His analysis does indeed demonstrate a small upsurge in recruitment of personnel to Worcester between 963 and 966, with a probably higher than normal level of recruitment continuing for another ten years or so thereafter. But if a process of gradual change – based upon a high level of continuity – was evidently occurring under Oswald's episcopacy, nevertheless there seems to have been no sign that it was under Oswald that Worcester became one of the leading reformed monasteries of England. There is no evidence that the community became noticeably more monastic during this period. The designation of witnesses as 'monk' rather than 'priest' or 'clerk' was infrequent, and was confined almost entirely to just three individuals; furthermore, a recorded grant of property to the monk Wynsige, the leader of the 'reformed' community, does cast severe doubt on how far matters had changed. In Sawyer's words (1975, 93): 'It is hard to see what difference Oswald actually made at Worcester.' It now seems clear that whilst monastic vows were taken by a few of the community under Oswald, there was no wider reform; that came during the eleventh century, and its attribution to Oswald was essentially a concoction by the Worcester monks of the twelfth century (Barrow 1992a, 1996).

The received tradition, therefore, that Oswald built St Mary's to house a new community of monks, may be founded in the events of the time, but is clearly too great a simplification. Simple piety may have been his prime motivation; yet there could have been a number of contributory factors. Hemming, copying and perhaps embellishing in the 1090s a charter of some three centuries before, goes on to tell how – before St Mary's was completed – Oswald chose to preach from the tomb of two eighth-century benefactors of Worcester, Wiferd and his wife Alta, because the level ground around it would hold the great concourse of people come to hear him and unable to squeeze into St Peter's. Hemming implied that a larger church was needed for what was clearly an energetic mission to Worcester (H 341–3; S 1185). And it is certain that St Mary's church was a new one and not a rebuilding by Oswald of an existing church. Although a number of Worcester charters of earlier centuries record grants of land to St Mary's and to its community, the text of every one of them is suspect. By contrast, those charters which are evidently not forgeries – such as that establishing the arrangements for the administration of the new *burh* in the 890s (H 3–5; S 223; Whitelock 1979, 99) – always refer to St Peter's church alone. The earliest charter reference to St Mary's that seems to be reliable comes in a grant of 967 from King Edgar to his thegn Brihtnoth; Brihtnoth's assignment to St Mary's of the land in question may be contemporary as the charter purports it to be, or rather later. Sawyer suggests that the assignment dates from 973 (H 371–3; S 751). Of the many leases of land issued by Oswald, only one, dating from 982, specifies the eventual return of the land to St Mary's, rather than to the bishopric or the Church of Worcester (H 238–9; S 1344).

St Peter's did not fall from favour, as we should expect it to have done according to the traditional version of events: although we are told that St Mary's was completed in 983, Oswald's throne was still at the older church in about 991 (H 187–9, 232–3; S 1345, 1308. The latter charter is erroneously dated 965: Finberg 1961, 138). There is no record of when the eventual transfer of the episcopal throne occurred, and St Peter's remained in use: the latest date we have for it is the 1030s when its presbytery was enlarged and the tomb of Wiferd and Alta was removed (H 342–3; S 1185). In all likelihood St Peter's was demolished, as we know St Mary's was, when Wulfstan began to build the present cathedral.

Whilst the cathedral priory was evolving under Oswald and his successors, the process of the separation from the bishop's estates of the lands of the cathedral community had begun before his day. From the late ninth century, if not before, the affairs of the Worcester community had begun to be separate from those of the bishops of Worcester. The process of apportioning the revenues was to be a long one – indeed it would not be complete until the twelfth century – and it saw the bishops convey to the monks not only a proportion of the see's rural lands, but eventually also most of their interests in the city of Worcester. As early as 889, the *familia* at Worcester were in a position to grant a lease to Bishop Wærferth of land at Elmstone Hardwick in Gloucestershire which had formerly belonged to the minster church of Bishop's Cleeve (H 118–19; S 1415), and they granted him a similar lease on rural land three years later (B 570; S 1416). In 922, Bishop Wilfrid granted land in Warwickshire, at Clifford Chambers, to the community at Worcester (B 636; S 1289). Thus both parties already had their own lands, but as yet the greater part of the Church of Worcester's lands was held by the bishops. Christopher Dyer pointed to the bishopric of Ealdred (1046–62) as the most likely period when the evolving cathedral priory received the greater part of its lands, although the process of division between the bishop and the monks continued until after the Conquest: in 1089 Bishop Wulfstan gave the priory the 15-hide manor of Alveston in Warwickshire (Dyer 1980, 18–19; Darlington 1968, 3).

The occasion of this last grant was Wulfstan's recent recovery of Alveston from lay control: it was, in effect, a new acquisition from which recent bishops had drawn no revenues. The grant was an act of generosity to the monks he favoured, and Wulfstan boasted in this charter that he had brought the number of monks at Worcester up from 12 to 50 – an achievement that would have been impossible without much greater provision for the priory from the revenues of the see. In the twelfth century Bishop Theulf gave the priory a fishery in the Severn just to the north of Worcester (Darlington 1968, 63), and his successor Bishop Simon (1125–50) made grants to the monks of several churches including Little Malvern Priory, minor pieces of land, and dues such as 20 shillings worth of Peter's pence collected from their lands (Darlington 1968, 61a, 62, 65, 66, 67, 68, 69, 70). The character of these grants suggests that they were no more than adjustments to the balance of revenues between bishop and monks, to take account of the increased needs of a community whose numbers and expenditure had grown.

It has been observed (Barrow 1996, 90) that a number of Oswald's charters, dating from 967 onwards, contain an invocation to St Mary, St Michael and St Peter (H 127–8, 123–4, 193–5, 176–7, 173–4, 139–41, 151–2, 141–2; S 1312, 1317, 1337, 1338, 1355, 1369, 1373, 1374). This perhaps indicates that when work began on St Mary's, Oswald had St Michael, too, honoured in some fashion, conceivably by building the church of St Michael which stood within the precinct, although it is recorded only from the thirteenth century (see below, p. 214). Barrow went on to suggest that the building of a new church or churches in the 960s was the occasion for a major reorganization of the cathedral precinct, intended for the first time to set a firm boundary between the ecclesiastical and secular quarters of the city. Certainly at some time after the foundation of the *burh*, and in all probability during the tenth century, the Church of Worcester did abandon the former line of the old defences to establish a new northern boundary along what would later become Lich Street (see below, pp. 160–61); this was very plausibly carried through by Oswald as part of his (albeit limited) programme of reorganization. The action achieved the separation of the Church from the northern part of the pre-*burh* city, which was the location of St Helen's church, and perhaps St Alban's and St Margaret's, and which might have already been an area of secular dwellings; at the same time it released this area for more intensive and profitable development, evidenced by the deliberate levelling of the old defences and the laying out of new streets.

There were major changes, too, in the physical presence of the Church elsewhere in Worcester at about this time. Contemporary with the building of St Mary's would seem to have been that of St Gudwal's in Sidbury, whilst the tenth century also saw the foundation of All Saints', St Martin's and perhaps also – if it had not been founded already – St Andrew's. St Peter the Great was recorded in 969, although possibly, with St Alban's and St Margaret's, it dated – like St Helen's – from before the building of the *burh* in the 890s. The eleventh century would see the initial construction of St Clement's, St Nicholas's and probably St Swithun's, as well of course as Wulfstan's post-Conquest reconstruction of the cathedral; but it is notable how comparable in scale had been the surge in church-building during the previous century. (For all of these churches, see Chapter 7, below.) If that is an index of Worcester's growing importance as a centre of population and wealth, then the phase of urban development that followed the laying-out of the new streets and defensive circuit of the new *burh* had been a vigorous one.

The city in the tenth and eleventh centuries

It had been under the watchful eyes of Bishop Wærferth and his successors that the city's growth of the tenth and eleventh centuries occurred, and presumably the presence of the large households of the bishops and the cathedral clergy continued to make a substantial contribution to its commercial life. Formally, however, as we have seen, the bishops' authority over Worcester had diminished with the foundation of the *burh* in the 890s when their lordship of the city came to an end and royal authority within the newly enclosed area was clearly recognized. Despite the arrangement for sharing the proceeds of lordship, the administration of the city must have been entrusted to royal officials. A century and a half later it is possible to see how the bishops had lost further ground within the city. A writ of Edward the Confessor, dated probably to 1062, confirms to Bishop Wulfstan on behalf of St Mary's minster the third part only of the *seamtoll* and of the *ceaptoll* collected in Worcester (Harmer 1952, 117; S 1158), for now there was the earl's share to find. Domesday Book confirms that at the Conquest the bishop's interest had indeed been formalized as the third penny of the £10 paid to the King and the £8 paid to the earl as farm of the city. After the Conquest, when the King held the earl's part as well, and the farm – for which the sheriff was responsible – was £23 5*s* by weight, the bishop's one-third share had gone up from £6 to £8 (DB, i, 172a, 173c).

By the eleventh century, therefore, the rights of the bishops of Worcester in the city were little more than those of a major urban lord; they no longer enjoyed the privileged position of sole lordship of the early bishops, or the shared lordship of Wærferth's day. But the town too had developed while these adjustments were being made and by the late eleventh century formed a substantial community. Authority within the city lay – after the Conquest, certainly – with the sheriff, and with the citizens appointed as reeves who appear as the leading witnesses of charters surviving in increasing numbers from the second half of the twelfth century onwards (Darlington 1968, 2 and *passim*). (For further discussion of the seigneurial rights of the Church in Worcester see Chapter 12.)

Interestingly, as if to match their diminished secular role there, the bishops also withdrew from their landed interests in the city in favour of the monks of the cathedral priory. Quite when that happened is not clear: it was by the thirteenth century, certainly, although at the end of the eleventh century the monks' property in Worcester was still far from impressive compared with that of the bishops'. The 40 houses or messuages, according to Hemming, from which they drew rents in 1100 compares with the 90 that Domesday Book recorded as being held from the bishop in 1086 (H 289–90; DB, i, 173c). But then a number of recorded grants of Worcester property from twelfth-century bishops to the cathedral priory give every appearance of a tidying-up process – the disposal of minor rights and revenues that were of relatively little value and difficult to collect. For instance, we are told that Bishop Simon (1125–50) granted the monks land which Roger the baker had held from him in Worcester (Darlington 1968, 65), which does not sound very substantial; on another occasion he gave them 5 marks to be taken annually from the tolls due to him in the city (ibid., 68). The exact nature of the tolls is not specified, although the need to collect them is undoubtedly implicit in the grant, for otherwise there would have been no need to mention the source of the cash. It is suggested in Chapter 10 that it was between 1170 and 1240 that the bulk of the bishops' Worcester rents were transferred to the cathedral priory; the properties the bishop retained, according to a survey made in the 1290s, were almost entirely in the suburbs. So whilst the medieval bishops had a physical presence in Worcester, in the form of their ancient palace which stood to the north of the cathedral precinct, they no longer had an active temporal interest in the city whose early development they had led and indeed for centuries controlled.

Chapter 6

The landscape of medieval Worcester

Introduction

The physical setting (figs 6.1 and 6.2)

The medieval and modern city of Worcester lies on the east bank of the Severn, on a gravel terrace overlying the Keuper Marl at a point where the river, meandering within the 500-metre-wide floodplain, cuts into the terrace, making its banks directly accessible from the high, well-drained ground. Another broader terrace lies beyond the alluvium on the west bank and is the site of the transpontine suburb of St John's. The city site itself is a naturally defensible south-facing promontory defined by the river on the west and the Frog Brook to the east. The brook, now canalized and culverted, joined the Severn at Diglis about 500 metres south of the cathedral, and was flanked by its own narrow belt of alluvium. The medieval (and earlier) High Street and Foregate Street follow the north–south spine of the promontory, rising gradually from about 23.8 metres above Ordnance Datum on the northern city boundary to a peak of about 25.9 metres AOD around St Helen's church, falling gently southwards towards the cathedral before dropping sharply down to the Frog Brook alluvium at Diglis.

The configuration of the promontory's riverside slope was crucial in determining the way in which the site was exploited as the city grew. The width of the promontory was substantially reduced by an indentation some 750 metres from the tip; it was used before *c.* 1200 by the north side of the medieval city wall and its ditch. A spring in the immediate vicinity of the Foregate fed a brook, draining westwards in this indentation and canalized by the city ditch, though it appears to have turned northwards a short distance from the river, flowing into it at Pitchcroft (Richardson 1956, 52). The pre-modern configuration of the terrace-edge immediately to the south of this defile is less certain. Martin Carver thought that the approach to the medieval bridge made use of a westward projecting spit of gravel, though subsequent trial-trenching towards the end of Dolday suggested that this was not the case, and that the terrace-edge sweeps evenly south-west, the bridgehead having been engineered by Roman or later reclamation of the alluvial zone at the foot of the slope (Carver 1980, 19, fig.5; Mundy 1985).

The steepness of the western slope increases from this point southwards. All Saints' church stands on a bluff, marking the point at which the terrace-edge resumes its southerly course, before reaching another defile – less substantial than that to the north but equally significant in terms of its effect on settlement. Richardson and Ewence (1963, 231) identified a former streamlet flowing in and eroding it, rising from a spring at the base of the gravel in the area just north of St Alban's church. The defile was exploited by the northern side of the Roman earthwork defences (see below), and later by Copenhagen Street as the principal means of access to the waterfront from the High Street.

The slope is at its steepest between this point and the west end of the cathedral. Further south, towards the south side of College Green, there is another substantial indentation in the slope, much of it retained by sandstone terrace walls of medieval origin. At the bottom of this indentation is the cathedral priory's surviving water-gate, a fourteenth-century building built across an infilled defile or channel, detected by geophysical survey (Barker 1994, 90). This is now known to mark

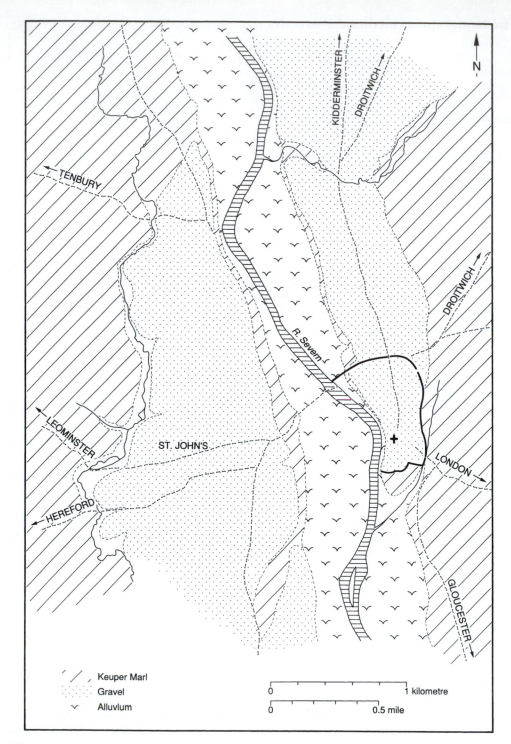

6.1   Worcester: the geology of the city site (showing the cathedral and the outline of the medieval city wall for location)

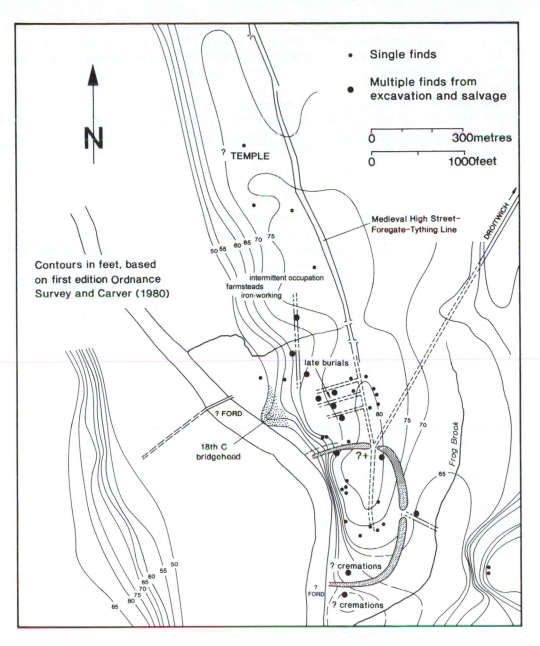

N

? TEMPLE

Single finds

Multiple finds from
excavation and salvage

0   300metres

0   1000feet

Medieval High Street–
Foregate–Tything Line

DROITWICH

50 55 60 65 70 75

Contours in feet, based
on first edition Ordnance
Survey and Carver (1980)

intermittent occupation
farmsteads
iron-working

late burials

? FORD

80

75 70

18th C
bridgehead

Frog Brook

65

?+

50
60 55
65
70
75
80
85

? cremations

?
FORD

? cremations

6.2   Worcester: the Roman settlement and modern contours. Since this plan was compiled excavation
has revealed a marked increase in the density of occupation in the area west of Foregate Street
and the Tything

the return of the former northern perimeter of the Norman motte-and-bailey castle to the river, geophysical survey immediately inland having located a double-ditch system crossing College Green (pers. comm. Professor J. Hunter). When it was built, the castle encroached on the monks' cemetery, the cathedral priory regaining part of its lost ground in the early thirteenth century (see below, p. 158).

The castle occupied almost all of the southern tip of the Worcester promontory, the southern ditch of the bailey curving westwards just short of the very bottom of the gravel terrace and the edge of the Frog Brook floodplain to the south. The line of the bailey defences was almost certainly a re-use of an earlier defensive circuit. The medieval ditch was partly waterfilled, a channel being diverted into it from the Frog Brook at Sidbury, and it was used in the later medieval period to drive a watermill.

The site and its geology were powerful constraints on the form of early settlement at Worcester. Occupation appears to have been largely confined to the gravel terrace in the Roman and Anglo-Saxon periods, only one suburb (Lowesmoor) extending eastwards beyond it onto the marl in the twelfth–thirteenth centuries. Groundwater is retained in the gravel by the underlying marl, and wells for domestic use are widely known from excavations in the Roman, medieval and later periods. The river and minor watercourses were also doubtless exploited, though the cathedral priory must have found its needs inadequately met from local sources as it brought piped water across the bridge from a source in St John's (WCL D&C B1653; Hist. Mss Comm. Report 14, Part VIII, 193).

Communications (figs 6.2 and 7.2)

As a number of writers have commented, Worcester's importance as a town must always have been closely linked to its river-crossing: in the medieval period the nearest alternative bridges were at Gloucester, 25 miles to the south, and at Bridgnorth, the same distance to the north. The only certain natural ford site at Worcester was that known as the Newport ford, immediately adjacent to the site of the medieval bridge (Carver 1980, 19–20), but the wide belt of alluvium on the west bank, still subject to flooding in winter, must have been at least as great an obstacle to traffic as the river itself. The only permanently dry route across this was the Causeway, leading from the ford and bridge to the west bank gravel terrace. The origin of the Causeway has never been established. It may have been newly built in the pre-Conquest period or even later but, if Martin Carver's contention that the medieval bridge (first recorded when it was repaired in 1088) made use of the surviving piers of a Roman predecessor is correct, then the Causeway too is of pre-medieval origin.

Roman roads are known approaching the city from Gloucester to the south, from Droitwich to the north-east, and from Hereford and Kenchester to the west. The course of the Gloucester road is well established until it reaches a point about a mile to the south of the cathedral. Its course northwards from there is unknown: it may have turned east to enter the Roman settlement via the later Sidbury area; it may have carried on in a straight line, crossing the Frog Brook further downstream. Similarly, the course of the Droitwich road is known until it enters the medieval Lowesmoor suburb, after which it is lost beneath the built-up area. There is some evidence that the High Street is of Roman origin, at least within the city, suggested by sightings of the distinctive slag-metalled surfaces at a consistent depth beneath its surface, by its use of the probable gate through the northern Roman defences, and by its axial course along the spine of the town promontory (Barker 1969, 50–51; Baker 1980a, 35).

Further Roman roads have been identified by excavation within the city boundaries but in each case it is uncertain whether or how they continued for any distance beyond the contemporary settlement area. The first of these to be discovered was located by Philip Barker in the Blackfriars area in 1966–8, heading north-north-east. The same road was excavated immediately to the north by Charles Mundy in 1985–6 (Mundy 1986a, 1989), and further north outside the medieval city wall in the Farrier Street area by John Darlington, Hal Dalwood and others (Dalwood, Buteux and Darlington 1994). Martin Carver and John Sawle's excavations on the north side of Sidbury (Carver 1980; Darlington and Evans 1992) discovered another road running south-east away from the cathedral area, off which the road to Gloucester may have branched. The Kenchester road is far more easily identified at that end than in the Worcester area, though the present main road leaving St John's for the Hereford area is recorded as a *straete* route in a charter of 963 (H 133–35, 350–51; S 1303; Hooke 1980, 45–6) and may be of Roman (or earlier) origin.

The road network radiating from the city becomes apparent by degrees in the later Anglo-Saxon period as individual roads are recorded as landmarks in the definition of estate boundaries in charters. From these it can be seen that most of the main roads in use in the modern period were extant before the Norman Conquest (Hooke 1980). Worcester's role as a crossing-point of the Severn seems to have been most important at the intra-regional level; further afield, the fourteenth-century Gough map shows the city on the north–south route following the Severn valley between Bristol, Shrewsbury and ultimately Chester, and as the starting point on this route for roads to the north-east, notably to Lichfield and to Coventry. Whitehead comments on the city's medieval and later role as the port where goods brought up the Severn from Bristol, and iron (from sources which are at present uncertain), were trans-shipped for the road journey to Coventry: the city acting, in effect, as the midlands' outlet to the sea (Whitehead 1976, 30).

Roman Worcester (figs 6.2 and 6.3)

It is not possible in this context to offer more than the briefest survey of the evidence for the Roman settlement at Worcester. Excavations since 1985 have produced much new data, much of which is, at the time of going to press, awaiting final publication.

From the general distribution of excavated and casually found artefacts of Roman date it is becoming clear that the Roman town on the east-bank gravel terrace was much more extensive than its medieval successor, probably covering an area not exceeded until the nineteenth century. Successive excavations have found Romano-British occupation, and iron-working debris, extending in a wide corridor well to the north of the medieval city, west of the medieval suburb of the Tything. At the extreme north end of this is the present Britannia Square where, in 1829, circular masonry foundations and quantities of coins were found, suggesting that it may have been the site of a temple (Barker 1969, 15, n. 36); subsequent finds also point to at least one well-appointed masonry building in the vicinity.

Philip Barker's single most striking contribution to the exploration of the Roman settlement was his definition of a circuit of earthwork fortifications enclosing the tip of the peninsula and the site of the pre-Conquest cathedrals. This was based on what would now be termed a salvage excavation, in 1965–6 on the Lich Street development site. Crossing the site diagonally was a ditch (ditch 'b'), 90 feet (*c*. 27 metres) wide, with a rampart on the inside, seen to be the last in a sequence of superimposed fortifications which, Barker suggested, included an Iron Age and an early-Roman military predecessor (Barker 1969, 44–62). He also proposed that an east–west ditch excavated some years earlier by Peter Gelling (1958) on Little Fish Street was part of the northern perimeter of the same circuit, which was interrupted by a gate on the line of the High Street close by St Helen's church. Barker also found another smaller ditch ('d') on a north-west–south-east course, outside the larger Roman ditch 'b' near the corner of Pump Street and Friar Street. He suggested it was likely to have been later than the larger ditch and tentatively wondered whether it might not belong to the pre-Conquest *burh* – an idea explored later in this chapter.

The south side of the Roman earthwork enclosure remains less clear. Barker proposed that it followed the southern boundary of the cathedral close, immediately outside which lay a probable cremation cemetery, represented by finds made when excavating in and beneath the demolished castle motte in the first half of the nineteenth century (Carver 1980, cat. 12/1). However, the only dramatic change in ground level along the southern boundary of the close (a line established or re-established in 1217) slopes the wrong way (down to the north), whereas the more southerly castle-ditch line is a substantial and archaeologically complex feature – though it has never been fully excavated (see Edwards 1989). Defences on this line would also make sense of a staggered frontage-line and property boundary at the junction of Sidbury and the south side of Edgar Street, suggestive of a fault-line or 'plan-seam' in the later urban fabric. If the earthwork defences were built late in the life of the Roman settlement, they may well have ignored an earlier cremation cemetery if it had gone out of use, and if the natural topography dictated it.

Barker was also able to conduct the first scientific examination of the Roman iron-smelting industry (the Broad Street excavations, 1967–8), whose slag residues had been known over a wide area of the city since at least the mid seventeenth century (Carver 1980, Cat.49/3; Barker 1969, 63–97). The Blackfriars excavation also led to the first recognition and description of a 'dark earth' deposit and a consideration of its implications (see below).

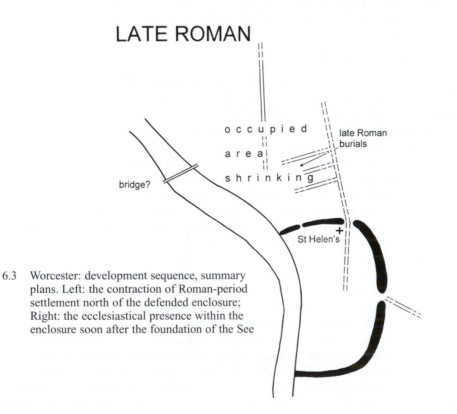

6.3   Worcester: development sequence, summary plans. Left: the contraction of Roman-period settlement north of the defended enclosure; Right: the ecclesiastical presence within the enclosure soon after the foundation of the See

Excavation at Nos 23–29 Sidbury, by Martin Carver and John Sawle in 1976–7, located a Roman road (referred to above) constructed with iron slag, as the Blackfriars road had been, and cut by trenches for wooden water-pipes. These features were buried by a deposit of grey soil containing only fourth-century and earlier pottery (Carver 1980, 154–219) (see fig. 6.16). In 1985 excavations by Charles Mundy began on a site a short distance to the north of Barker's Blackfriars excavations (HWCM 378 T7: Mundy 1986 a and b and 1989) (fig. 6.11). This site straddled the Roman road found previously by Barker and showed that it had been resurfaced on several occasions, latterly with slag. Post-holes belonging to timber buildings were found on the west side of the street. These were replaced by a clay-founded building whose disuse was probably contem-porary with the disuse of the road itself, marked by the dumping of loose slag. Cut into these dumps were the remains of a small ephemeral building associated with late-Saxon pottery. Sealing all these features was a layer of 0.25–0.4 metres of dark soil, interpreted as having been dumped in the early medieval period for agricultural use. A trackway across this continued 'the line of that established at the back of the latest Roman building fronting the main road' (Mundy 1986b, 10–11; Mundy 1989, 35).

The largest-scale excavations that have so far taken place in Worcester were the four sites of the Deansway excavations, completed in November 1989 (HWCM 3899: Mundy 1989; Dalwood, Mundy and Taylor 1989; Baker, Dalwood, Holt, Mundy and Taylor 1992; Dalwood, Buteux and Jackson 1992) (fig. 6.11). Again – as on Barker's Blackfriars and Lich Street excavations – late-prehistoric activity was encountered, here in the form of an animal burial, curvilinear ditch, part of a palisade trench, and other features. Minor features of first-century date may have been of military

origin. A second-century enclosure, metalled surface, and a building may represent agricultural activity. Perhaps the most important aspect of the Roman sequence for the shaping of later settlement was a series of three parallel east–west roads of second-century date, the first evidence for formal planning in the Roman town. Site 4 produced evidence of iron-smelting, and dumps of slag were found on the other three sites. On site 2, a spread of bone on the road surface appeared to represent a change in its use, and was followed by the deposition of a 'dark earth' similar to those on the other sites. On site 4 a late-Roman cemetery was found, probably dating from the third–fourth centuries, containing at least 15 inhumations, including three decapitated burials.

The end of Roman Worcester (see fig. 6.3)

The end of the Roman period is represented in various ways in the archaeological record in Worcester, but the picture that emerges is still substantially less complete than that of Gloucester. The Deansway site 4 inhumation cemetery might be read as a symptom of contraction of the occupied area in the northwards stretching corridor of settlement and iron-working. Reality may be more complex, with intermittent rather than continuous occupation (at least further north) in the settlement corridor and some distinct late-Roman activity well to the north, represented by late fourth- or fifth-century pottery from the Castle Street area, roughly 300 metres outside the medieval city wall (White, in White and Baker 2000). Dark-earth deposits are found everywhere: in the Farrier Street–Castle Street area to the north; Sidbury to the south-east; the Blackfriars and Deansway sites in the northern part of the centre; and the cathedral close to the south. A recent scientific analysis of the dark-earth deposit overlying Roman horizons in the Farrier Street area concluded that it represented the debris of occupation – charcoal, daub, dung and iron slag – re-worked by worm action and by agriculture (MacPhail 1994). The dark-earth deposits on the Deansway sites were found to have originated in a thick layer of mud containing plant remains characteristic of the floodplain, and thought to have been deposited on the site via the hooves of late-Roman cattle. Re-worked by worm action and agricultural activity the mud was gradually transformed into a mature soil. Eventually, with the resumption of intensive human occupation in the area, occupation debris like charcoal, building materials and dung was mixed into it (pers. comm., Hal Dalwood). At Deansway site 1 the late-Roman levels were scored by ploughmarks at the base of the dark earth (Mundy 1989, 6).

This was not desertion – this was reversion to agricultural production, and on more than one Deansway site a continuity in the orderly ownership of land seems to be implicit in the maintenance of boundaries and rights of way (Baker *et al.* 1992, 69). On the Blackfriars site, traffic continued to use a route that had developed at the rear of buildings lining the original Roman road (Mundy 1986b, 10–11; Mundy 1989, 35).

Within what is assumed to have been the core of the Roman town – inside the earthwork enclosure first defined by Barker – excavation has been on an even more limited scale than outside, so neither the character of the Roman occupation nor its fate in the fifth century and beyond have ever been defined. The earliest post-Roman activity detected so far is represented by two east–west inhumations found beneath the cathedral refectory undercroft floor. The most recent calibration of Carbon-14 dates obtained from them suggests that they date from the seventh century (58.3 per cent probability, compared with 22.3 per cent for a pre-600 date and 19.4 per cent for a post-700 date). The probability distribution suggests that they are marginally more likely to pre-date the foundation of the see in 675–80 than to post-date it (pers. comm., Philip Barker and Ancient Monuments Laboratory corresp., April 1995; see also Barker *et al.* 1974). The burials seem, as Barker and his colleagues first suspected, to belong to a Christian community, worshipping within the defended enclosure at Worcester, before the accepted date of the first cathedral. The church of St Helen, just within the northern defences, may also belong in this context, and is discussed further elsewhere (Chapters 5 and 7).

Finally, the defences themselves cannot be ignored. The ditch ('b') excavated by Barker was a substantial one, about 27 metres wide, and it must have had a rampart of similar dimensions. The defences – comparable in scale to those of an Iron Age hillfort – would have been perhaps three or four centuries old when the see was established and would certainly have been an imposing landmark which also retained some military value: they must have been a significant factor in the continued importance of the site in the post-Roman centuries. Ultimately, they did not just weather away, they had to be removed.

An introduction to the medieval urban landscape (figs 6.4, 6.5 and 6.6)

The late-medieval walled city occupied an area of about 85 acres (34.4 hectares) at the southern end of the gravel promontory. The promontory tip was occupied mainly by the cathedral close, though the southern part of this was destroyed by the Norman motte-and-bailey castle and later reconstituted. The late-medieval city-wall circuit was probably established by the end of the twelfth century (Beardsmore 1980); it made use of the castle defences to the south and generally followed a line dictated by the natural topography, with streams canalized in the ditches.

Just as a cursory inspection of Gloucester's town-plan raises the inevitable question: 'What happened to its west wall?' so a similar inspection of Worcester's invites the question: 'What happened to the High Street?' The built-up area to the north of the cathedral was dominated by the High Street, part of the north–south axial routeway following the spine of the gravel promontory, and the wealthiest street of the intramural city throughout the medieval and early-modern periods. The High Street comes to an abrupt end at the northern boundary of the cathedral close, exciting the immediate suspicion that the latter has encroached over the pre-existing through-route. There is, it must be said, no conclusive evidence available that bears upon this problem, though there are a number of significant clues in the landscape and archaeology of the cathedral close and its surroundings.

To the west of the High Street a complicated road network took traffic to and from the twin riverside foci of the bridge and the public quay. The medieval Guildhall occupied a site on the corner of the central section of the High Street and the principal road to the quay. Beyond the walls, suburbs extended along all the approach roads: the Tything and Foregate Street suburb to the north, along the road to the upper Severn valley and one way to Droitwich; the less extensive suburbs of Lowesmoor to the east, and Sidbury to the south-east; and the St John's suburb on the west-bank terrace. The physical evidence for the medieval city survives rather better below ground than above, where much has been destroyed and very little has been recorded. Martin Carver's 1980 assessment of Worcester as an archaeological site identified deep deposits within much of the later medieval walled area, the deepest concentrated mainly along the High Street (Carver 1980, 23–4). Since then, the Deansway excavations have amply demonstrated the potential of the area to the west. However, the percentage of the walled area for which archaeological evidence is available is still extremely small – around 2 per cent – and the suburbs have seen proportionately less archaeological activity.

The visible remains of the medieval city are limited. The street-pattern is largely that established by *c.* 1200, though a few significant changes have taken place. New streets were provided in the eighteenth century: to the new bridge opened in 1781, and across the cathedral close in *c.* 1794. The twentieth century saw the replacement of the medieval Birdport by Deansway, a wide modern road that cut a north–south swathe through traditional street- and building-patterns; the clearance of large areas around Angel Lane and then Dolday for successive bus stations; the notorious destruction of Lich Street and the street-block to the north for a hotel and shopping-centre in 1965–6; the destruction of the street-pattern between Birdport/Deansway and the river for the Technical College; and the dislocation of Sidbury for the City Walls Road in the late 1970s. These changes, and the prosperity of the sixteenth century and later city, have meant that very few buildings of medieval date remain standing. Of the ten medieval parish churches only two survive

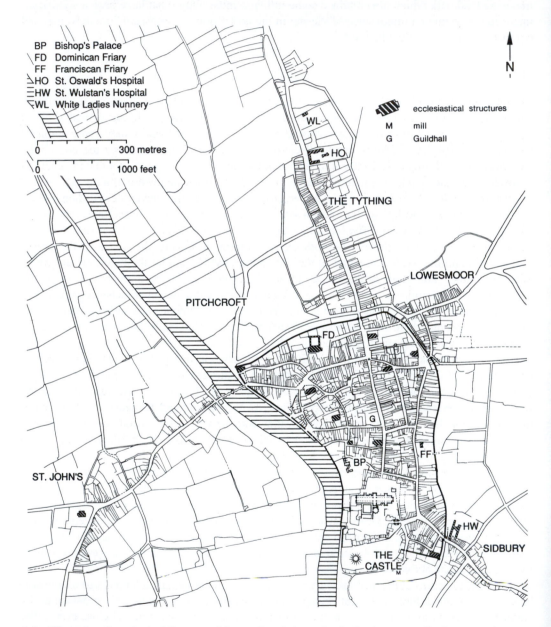

6.4   Worcester: the principal features of the medieval city and suburbs (see appendix for sources)

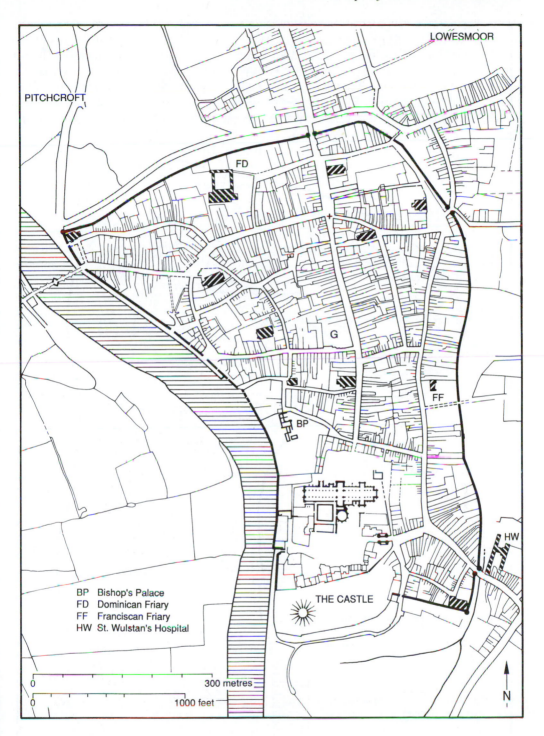

PITCHCROFT

LOWESMOOR

FD

G

FF

BP

THE CASTLE

HW

BP Bishop's Palace
FD Dominican Friary
FF Franciscan Friary
HW St. Wulstan's Hospital

0   300 metres

0   1000 feet

N

6.5   Worcester: the principal features of the medieval intramural city (see appendix for sources)

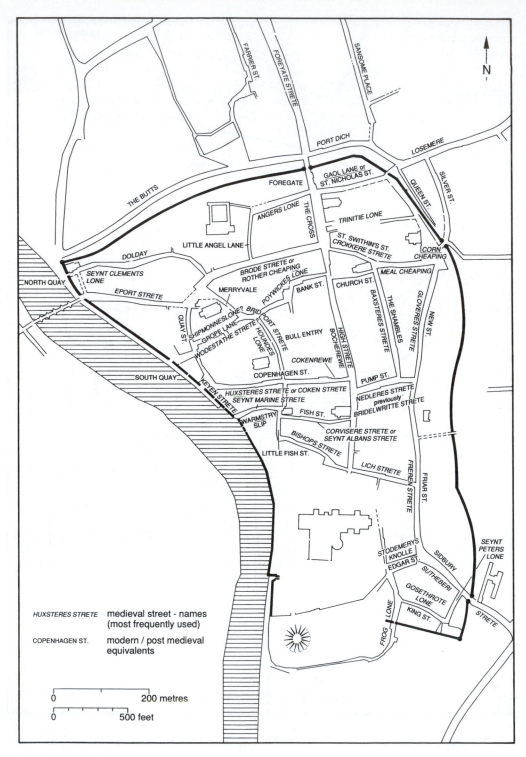

6.6   Worcester: medieval and modern street names (medieval names are *italicised*)

with substantially medieval fabric (St Helen's and St Alban's); four were nearly or totally rebuilt in the eighteenth century (St Nicholas's, St Swithun's, All Saints', St Martin's); three were demolished and rebuilt in the nineteenth century (St Peter's, St Clement's, St Michael's); and one was demolished save for its spire in the post-war period (St Andrew's). While many sixteenth- and seventeenth-century timber-framed buildings survive on Friar Street and New Street and are thinly scattered throughout the rest of the un-redeveloped city streets, a survey in 1980 found evidence of only five surviving medieval secular buildings within the walls (Hughes and Molyneux 1980), to which can be added a single building in St John's.

The city dismantled: approaches to landscape analysis in Worcester (figs 6.7 and 6.8)

It may appear paradoxical that the town-plan of Worcester, with its chaotic appearance, its irregular perimeter and street-pattern, is more susceptible to the disaggregation process of urban landscape analysis than is Gloucester, where very few features of the medieval geography depart from the ruling alignments of the underlying early Roman fortress. But this is no coincidence. Without the rigidly constraining influence of surviving masonry walls, gates and roads, the individuals and institutions that at Worcester promoted or permitted the growth of new housing over the former Roman occupied area could proceed as if on a (more or less) clean slate; the distinguishing characteristics of one local settlement phase or another are more readily apparent and distinct from those of neighbouring areas. Influences transmitted from the Roman geography are apparent in early-medieval Worcester, but are more subtle than those of a straight-jacket of Roman military planning executed in survivable masonry.

Distinctions within the settlement pattern or town-plan of Worcester may first be drawn between the walled city and its suburbs, and between the east and west banks of the Severn. Within the walled city a distinction is first apparent between the largely open space of the cathedral close and the remainder of the built-up area. The size, internal diversity and distinct historico-legal identity of the close suggest that it may, for analysis, most usefully be taken as a plan-region, apart from the remainder of the city – though this is not to deny or forget that the boundary between close and city was, for much of their history, a changeable one. The remainder of the intramural area may be considered as a second plan-region, and within this local variations in the character of the townscape are everywhere apparent. The classic instance of this is the central section of the High Street: marked by a rectangle of streets on its eastern side that takes its alignment from that section of the High Street, and by a distinctive arrangement of long irregular plots or properties that extended to both sides of the street. By their own peculiar street- or plot-patterns and distinctive local alignments, neighbouring areas can be distinguished as in some way different from each other.

These local variations in the character of the built-up area can be identified at a larger scale than the lane-by-lane variations explored in Gloucester's townscape. In Worcester distinct areas can be recognized that, like the High Street, encompass both sides of a major street or two or more contiguous street-blocks, covering areas often 4 to 6 acres (1.6–2.4 hectares) in extent. The reason for this difference in scale has much to do, it will be argued, with the planning history of each place: the different effect, in particular, of speculative development by individuals within a very large and under-exploited planned street-system (Gloucester), and successive, accretionary, modest ventures into planned urban expansion (Worcester). For analysis, the intramural area of Worcester lends itself most easily to disaggregation into plan-units on the lines of Conzen's second-order plan-units (1969, 108–18), with further division into sub-units as a vehicle for the description of smaller-scale changes in the character of the townscape.

The suburbs on the east bank (plan-region III) are individually distinct (even if contiguous as at Lowesmoor–Silver Street) and internally homogeneous, and are likewise treated as plan-units. West-bank suburban occupation took the form of a single, almost continuous ribbon of settlement from the bridge to the outer limits of St John's. The area has been treated as a plan-region (IV), with clear internal landscape variations at plan-unit scale coinciding with changes in the natural topography.

As the introductory chapter outlined, there are fundamental differences in the historical sources available for Gloucester and Worcester, and these materially affect the potential to interpret the

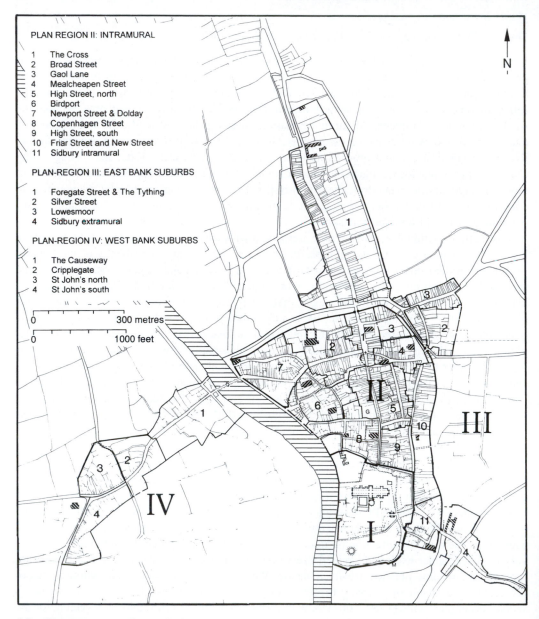

PLAN REGION II: INTRAMURAL

1   The Cross
2   Broad Street
3   Gaol Lane
4   Mealcheapen Street
5   High Street, north
6   Birdport
7   Newport Street & Dolday
8   Copenhagen Street
9   High Street, south
10   Friar Street and New Street
11   Sidbury intramural

PLAN-REGION III: EAST BANK SUBURBS

1   Foregate Street & The Tything
2   Silver Street
3   Lowesmoor
4   Sidbury extramural

PLAN-REGION IV: WEST BANK SUBURBS

1   The Causeway
2   Cripplegate
3   St John's north
4   St John's south

0 _____ 300 metres
0 _____ 1000 feet

N

6.7   Worcester, town-plan analysis: the plan components of the medieval city and suburbs

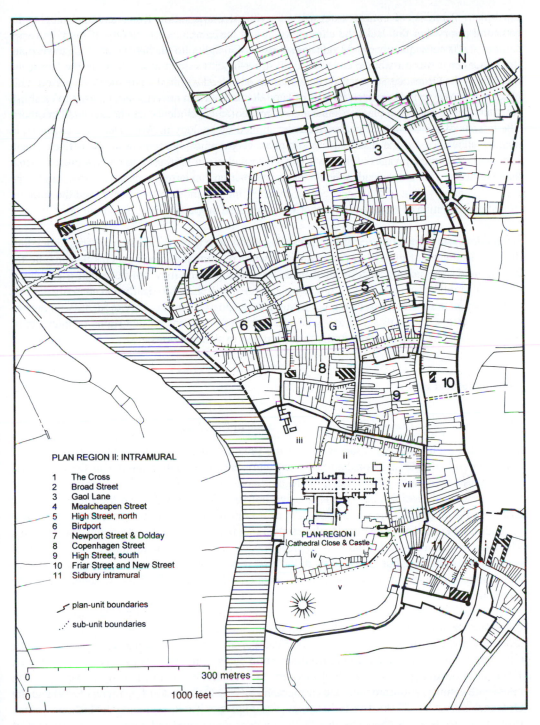

PLAN REGION II: INTRAMURAL

1   The Cross
2   Broad Street
3   Gaol Lane
4   Mealcheapen Street
5   High Street, north
6   Birdport
7   Newport Street & Dolday
8   Copenhagen Street
9   High Street, south
10 Friar Street and New Street
11 Sidbury intramural

plan-unit boundaries

sub-unit boundaries

PLAN-REGION I
Cathedral Close & Castle

0 — 300 metres

0 — 1000 feet

6.8   Worcester, town-plan analysis: the plan components of the medieval intramural city

town-plan. There is, of course, extensive surviving documentation from, amongst others, the cathedral priory, but this lacks the chronological and topographical continuity of the Gloucester sources and is consequently of less value as a source of insight into the behaviour of the town-plan. In Gloucester it was possible to estimate, from street-block to street-block, how far the landscape mapped by the Ordnance Survey had changed from or indeed within the late-medieval period. This is scarcely possible in Worcester, though isolated documents can nevertheless be used to establish whether change has taken place in some areas; archaeological evidence can be deployed in others. The lessons of the Gloucester evidence can be applied by analogy in Worcester – for example, in making allowance for the instability of suburban geographies, susceptible to post-Black Death depopulation and the ravages of the Civil War. Nevertheless, in Worcester to a much greater extent than Gloucester, we are dependent on the basic propositions underlying medieval urban landscape analysis generally: that of the innate conservatism of the pre-modern townscape, and the stability of features common to a number of properties once those properties have been built up.

As in Gloucester, the disaggregation process described here is but a first step towards understanding the sequence of growth of the medieval town and, ultimately, the agencies responsible for it. The landscape components defined in this process may or may not have had a particular historical significance: one might, for example, represent a chronologically and spatially distinct episode of planned urban extension; but in some cases analysis is able only to identify an area as different, or discrete, without in any way being able to comment on its origins or interpret it. Such questions will be explored in the following and in later sections.

The intramural city

Plan-region I: the cathedral close and castle (see also fig 12.1)

The cathedral close at Worcester was, like the precinct of St Peter's Abbey at Gloucester, a dominant and complex part of the town-plan, representing roughly a quarter of the intramural built-up area. But, unlike Gloucester, the legal bounds of the cathedral close embraced not just the ecclesiastical precincts but secular housing bordering on two sides and the site of the royal castle on the third. The area is treated here as a plan-region, not primarily on morphological grounds but because of its distinct legal-historical identity, and separation from the medieval city. The close, as defined by the end of the fifteenth century, was not the product of a single act of ecclesiastical planning but, like the rest of the city, was the outcome of a long process of growth and change. One part only of this process was explicitly documented; others are suggested by the physical evidence.

The earliest surviving record of the close boundaries comes from 1460, when Bishop Carpenter detailed them as relevant to his denunciation of a breach of the monks rights of sanctuary; the city authorities respected, in effect, the same boundaries in a perambulation of the city undertaken in 1497; a more detailed description dates from 1640 (WCL D&C B1648; Green 1796, ii, appendix, lxx–lxxi; *VCH Worcs.*, iv, 383–4); these remained in force well into the nineteenth century, and were recorded cartographically by Doharty (1741), Young (1779) and the Ordnance Survey (1883–6). The 1640 survey was quite specific in excluding the bishops' palace from the close, but it is also clear that the palace was considered to be outside the city, part of the parish of St Michael in Bedwardine (see Doharty and Young's maps of 1741 and 1779).

SUB-UNIT I.i: THE CATHEDRAL CHURCH AND CLAUSTRAL RANGES

The cathedral church and its surviving or known claustral buildings were disposed within a narrow, restricted area measuring less than *c.* 100 metres north to south and *c.* 200 metres west to east, the claustral buildings extending right down the slope to the river. The arrangement is unusually cramped, and the major departures from standard Benedictine planning (the west–east dormitory and reredorter, and the infirmary, all to the west of the cloister) are attributable to the constraints imposed by the castle impinging from the south, the needs for water supply and drainage, and the necessity of public access to the priory complex from the east (see Bowen 1992, 18–20). In brief, the earliest securely dated fabric in the cathedral church and claustral buildings is Romanesque – in the crypt, transepts, presbytery and the west end of the nave – the earliest of which belongs to Wulfstan's building campaign of the 1080s. Most of the cathedral choir belongs to a rebuilding begun in 1224, and much of the nave to a rebuilding commencing in 1317. The cloister is basically Norman with much rebuilding in the fourteenth and fifteenth centuries, though there is also a possibility of earlier fabric (see below). Parts of the east range are attributable to Wulfstan's work, the chapter house being slightly later. The refectory, occupying the south range, has a superstructure of 1372 over an earlier undercroft. Beyond the cloister to the west, running down to the river, are the remains of the Norman dormitory and reredorter. To the east of the cloister are the remains of the fourteenth-century Guesten Hall and the site of the prior's hall, lodgings, chapel and garden (Barker 1994; Gem 1978; *VCH Worcs.,* iv, 402–6; Greatrex 1998).

The limited historical evidence for the form and development of the early-medieval cathedral buildings was presented more fully in Chapter 5 but, in summary, the first cathedral church of St Peter had been built by the 690s. In 961 Oswald became bishop and by 983 had built a church dedicated to St Mary, close to the earlier church and in its cemetery. Oswald's throne was still in St Peter's in 991 and its presbytery was enlarged in the 1030s; the church is assumed to have remained in use until demolition at some stage of Wulfstan's great rebuilding campaign begun in 1084. St Oswald was buried in St Mary's and his relics enshrined there in 1002–1003. Wulfstan became prior in the 1050s and added a belfry to St Mary's which, like St Peter's, he was regretfully to demolish thirty or so years later (Dyer 1969; Gem 1978; Barker 1994, 7–15).

Excavations in and around the cathedral have mostly been on a limited scale, the exception being a campaign over a number of seasons to the east of the chapter house, with significant results (see below). Detailed structural analysis of the buildings progresses alongside the fabric repairs process but is still, overall, at an early stage. The fragmentary archaeological evidence for the pre-Conquest site is therefore, not suprisingly, full of ambiguity, and the form of the pre-Conquest cathedral and the position of its churches has been the subject of scholarly debate for some years (summarized by Carver 1980, 7).

The earliest evidence of post-Roman activity is the pair of probable seventh-century inhumations beneath the refectory, discussed earlier. Circumstantial evidence from the excavation and the apparently high status of at least one of the burials suggests that they may have been in (or at least in close proximity to) an important church – possibly a predecessor of the cathedral church of St Peter or that church itself. Later pre-Conquest inhumations have also been excavated from the eastern end of the refectory and the area outside (Barker *et al.* 1974; Clarke 1980).

Just to the east, a series of excavations have uncovered a circular wall outside and concentric to the Norman chapter house, with clasping buttresses of Romanesque type opposite those of the chapter house. The wall has been shown stratigraphically to be of the same date as, or earlier than, the Norman chapter house. At the time of going to press, no convincing parallels for a Norman chapter house with an external ambulatory-type structure have been found, and the excavators are looking instead at the possibility that the wall represents part of a rotunda added to one of the pre-Conquest cathedral churches (Crawford 1998).

There are other hints of possible pre-1084 features south of the present cathedral. The refectory lies at a very slight angle to the rest of the cloisters and the church. Investigation has shown that its late-Norman undercroft appears to incorporate three earlier buildings on slightly different alignments, and this complex history may be responsible for its odd alignment (Barker 1996 and amendments to Barker 1994).

SUB-UNIT I.ii: THE LAY CEMETERY

The area of the close lying between the cathedral and the city was occupied by the lay cemetery, known in the post-medieval period as College Yard. Within the cemetery stood a number of ecclesiastical buildings, including the church of St Michael in Bedwardine (see below, p. 214), a free-standing octagonal belfry, and the medieval charnel chapel dedicated to St Thomas (Buchanan-Dunlop 1942, 21; *VCH Worcs.*, iv, 406). By the early nineteenth century the area around St Michael's and the adjacent site of the belfry, demolished in 1647, was occupied by a dense cluster of encroaching tenements, removed gradually in the course of the nineteenth century (Noake 1866, 385–96). Access to the lay cemetery from the city was via two entries through the screen of properties to the north along Lich Street: the principal entrance was the College Gate at the end of the High Street; the Lich Gate provided pedestrian access directly opposite St Michael's, the cemetery chapel. In 1271 the bishop was licensed to crenellate the cathedral close (Beardsmore 1980, 60), but just what this implied for the area north of the cathedral is not entirely clear. It is likely that by this date the surrounding street frontages were already built up and that the cemetery must already have been enclosed by buildings. The east side of the cemetery was also in part defined by a wall running from the main gatehouse (the Edgar Tower) to St Michael's; from there its line was continued westwards by the parish boundary between the close and St Michael's in Bedwardine but there is no evidence that the wall itself continued past the church.

A very small sample of the lay cemetery has been excavated in the cellar of No. 5a College Yard, in the north-west corner. This revealed extremely dense, intercut burials of adults and children and a possible multiple grave. Given the cathedral's long-standing burial monopoly within the city (see below, pp. 242–4) such closely packed internments are to be expected, even in the furthest corner of the cemetery; the excavator also suggested that the site, within a few feet of the boundary wall separating it from the bishop's palace, fell within an area of the cemetery used for the poorer section of the city population (Smith 1993, 2–3).

SUB-UNIT I.iii: THE BISHOP'S PALACE

The bishop's palace stands in an enclosure of about 2 acres (0.8 hectare) in the north-west corner of the precinct, on the edge of the slope (here at its steepest) down to the river. The core of the palace comprises a group of adjoining medieval structures, united by an east wing with a formal facade built for Bishop Hough in the early eighteenth century. Preliminary work suggests that the earliest structures survive at the south end of the complex, built in green Highley stone and possibly dating to Wulfstan's episcopate. To the north is the mid-late-thirteenth-century first-floor hall or chamber block, orientated east–west with its vaulted undercroft terraced into the slope, with access by an external stair and a newel turret at the south-east and north-east corners. A chapel stood alongside to the south. The hall/chamber block was flanked by north and south wings (one of them three-storeyed), also with vaulted undercrofts.

The complex stood at the back of a large courtyard entered through a gatehouse at the north-east corner of the palace enclosure on the Palace Yard frontage (Noake 1866, 403); Bishop Giffard was granted a licence to crenellate the palace in 1271. Various ancillary buildings are known to have occupied the enclosure in the thirteenth century (Ronchetti 1991, 10). The greatest uncertainty remains, however, as to whether the thirteenth-century first-floor 'Great Hall' as it is now known was really built as a hall or whether (as is perhaps more likely) it was a chamber block to an even larger ground-floor hall, probably on the level ground adjacent to the south.

It may be significant that the earliest standing elements of the bishop's palace are towards the south end of the complex. The northward projection of the palace enclosure from the line of Lich Street is a notable feature of this side of the close and may represent an encroachment into what is known to have been a relatively poor part of the medieval city. The palace enclosure also represents a partitioning-off of one corner of the close. There is no direct evidence for the date of such a development; it may have taken place in the later tenth century, paralleling similar events in Winchester associated with the reform movement (Biddle 1976, 324); it may equally have been a development of Wulfstan's episcopate in the 1060s.

SUB-UNIT I.iv: COLLEGE GREEN

To the south of the cathedral church and its claustral ranges is an open green lined with buildings along its west, south and east sides. There was formerly a north range also, facing south, stretching from the refectory east to the Edgar Tower. Nearest the gate was the complex of buildings accommodating the prior and his household staff, next to the Guesten Hall, lying south of the cathedral's south-east transept. The Edgar Tower, also known as the great gatehouse or St Mary's Gate, was the principal entrance to the monastery. Building accounts suggest that it may date from 1346–7, somewhat in advance of the licence to crenellate the cathedral priory issued in 1369. Lying as it did within the circuit of the city walls and the castle, it is probable that the gatehouse – a large, crenellated building with corner turrets and elaborate statuary – was of much greater symbolic value than military (Molyneux 1992).

College Green was the outer or Great Court of the medieval priory. The buildings on the south side of College Green probably occupy the site of (and may incorporate the remains of) the priory service and ancillary buildings. Obedientiaries' accounts survive in some numbers from the middle ages and give insights into the number and function of buildings in the close. There is, however, relatively little that can be said of their planning from these sources, other than that the whereabouts and character of the finer detail of the monastic establishment are quite unknown to us: where for instance was the courtyard of the cellarer's stables (Greatrex 1998)?

At the west end of College Green the ground slopes sharply down towards the river, with the surviving monastic watergate building of 1378 at the bottom of a noticeable indentation in the slope. Ground-penetrating radar results show that the watergate is built over an infilled channel, dock or slipway (Barker 1994, 90), adding to the impression that the watergate was built in what was once a considerable defile, whose upper slopes are retained by sandstone terrace walls. The position of this partly infilled defile is consistent with an origin in the north ditch of the Norman castle, and this has been confirmed by geophysical survey on College Green, which located a double-ditch system heading in this direction. The fourteenth-century watergate – where the Priory Ferry landed – may well have been the successor to earlier wharfage developed by the cathedral and by the castle garrison just off the river in the water-filled ditch.

The westernmost building on the south side of College Green (Nos 10–10a) stands on the crest of the slope. Beneath its early eighteenth-century superstructure is a substantial west-facing sandstone wall that retains the higher ground to the east. It is aligned with and on the southern close boundary, thought to have been established in 1217 when the cathedral priory regained ground it had lost to the castle in the 1060s (see below). The sandstone wall incorporates a small cellar or undercroft, and appears to have been both a retaining wall and the sub-structure of an unidentified priory building (Guy 1991, 3–4).

SUB-UNIT I.v: THE CASTLE

The only changes in the extent of the precinct to have been explicitly recorded arose from its relationship with the Norman constable's motte-and-bailey castle to the south. By 1069, the ditch of Urse d'Abitot's bailey had enclosed and cut off part of the monks' cemetery. In 1217, after a careful enquiry, the Crown returned the northern half of the castle to the cathedral priory – partly perhaps to reduce a stronghold that, in baronial hands, had caused the monarchy a great deal of trouble over several decades (Beardsmore 1980, 55–6). The boundary is apparent on the eighteenth- and nineteenth-century maps, and survives today, incorporating sections of stone wall of medieval character. Fig. 6.9 shows the pre-eighteenth-century situation, the curved southern boundary of the close separating College Green from the open ground of the surviving part of the castle bailey to the south. The location and size of the motte overlooking the river is known from early-nineteenth-century sources, including plans and a measured profile; it was levelled between 1823 and 1843. As elsewhere (at Gloucester and Shrewsbury, for instance) the former royal castle had an afterlife as its gaol continued into the nineteenth century: both it and

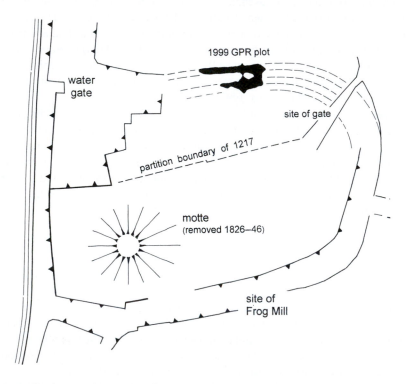

6.9   Worcester Castle: reconstructed outline plan, based on modern and mapped topographical features and geophysical survey

the Bridewell built next to it in the seventeenth century were demolished around the same time as the earthworks (Beardsmore 1980, 57; see also Carver 1980, 22–3). The ditch around the east and south sides of the bailey determined the line taken by Frog Lane, now Severn Street; fragments of sandstone masonry retaining the bank within the former ditch may derive from a stone curtain wall. The ditch was supplied with water from the main course of the Frog Brook via the city ditch around Sidbury, and this drove the Frog Mill, shown on Speed's map of 1610 on the north side of Frog Lane about half-way between the motte and the east end of the bailey. The castle ditch was not fully built over until the nineteenth century and is now marked by a curving series of short properties backing onto a low terrace wall.

Once again, no large-scale archaeological investigation has taken place in this area and some features remain unexplained. Radar survey has, for example, located the probable line of a ditch just inside (west of) the Edgar Tower on a south-westerly course parallel to the close boundary of 1217 (see figs 6.17 and 12.1). What this represents is, without excavation, impossible to determine, though it could be of almost any date, from the prehistoric period onwards.

SUB-UNIT I.vi: THE LICH STREET CEMETERY FRONTAGE

Housing on the south side of Lich Street was of very different character from that on the north side. While the latter occupied long plots of more or less conventional type, the eighteenth-century maps pre-dating the insertion of College Street across the precinct in the 1790s show that the south side tenements were no more extensive than the buildings they contained. They represent a type of building frequently associated with encroachments – in this case onto the Lay Cemetery. They are clearly described in documents of the cathedral priory, and were certainly a speculative venture by the cathedral priory in the thirteenth century to raise rents from the potentially valuable commercial frontage where the cemetery abutted a major through-route (see also pp. 272–7, below).

SUB-UNIT I.vii: THE SIDBURY (WEST) TENEMENTS

Adjoining the south side of the Lich Street properties and lining the east side of the cemetery was (before the insertion of College Street) a block of ground *c.* 170 feet (*c.* 52 metres) deep, with tenements facing outwards to Sidbury and Friar Street and inwards to College Yard. The internal divisions of this street-block are not well recorded, but Young's map of 1779 indicates deeper tenements facing Friar Street and Sidbury, shallower tenements facing the cemetery, and some longitudinal boundaries passing through the block from one frontage to the other. A somewhat schematic plan of 1794, showing the intended construction of College Street diagonally across the precinct (see Appendix) also shows a common straight north–south boundary dividing the outward- and inward-facing tenements towards the south end of this block, and this is consistent with the truncated plot-pattern recorded post-College Street by the Ordnance Survey.

These cathedral close tenements were clearly of a different type from those on Lich Street. The outward-facing plot-series at least was of normal urban type, with buildings on the main street frontage and strip-like plots to the rear, and it is difficult to believe that this block was developed at the same time or in the same way as the Lich Street cemetery encroachments. At least some of the inward-facing tenements (now College Precincts) were built up by the thirteenth century (pers. comm. Pat Hughes). Nevertheless, a find of disarticulated human bone, undated, though almost certainly post-Roman, from the rear of no. 3 College Precincts, one of the inward-facing properties opposite the east end of the cathedral, suggests that the plots were indeed developed over part of the (or a) cemetery (Brown 1991b), though at what date is unknown.

SUB-UNIT I.VIII: EDGAR STREET

Edgar Street (Stodemerys Knolle or La Knole) is the short, wide street connecting the monastery's main gate with Sidbury. The great width (*c.* 50 feet/15.2 metres) in relation to its length suggests that it was a planned formal approach to the monastery gate, though the characteristics of the plots on each side are different. The north side is occupied by plots without well-defined boundaries beyond the frontage buildings, merging with the surviving College Precincts and Sidbury tenements. On the south side is a wedge-shaped block sub-divided into five plots, with an additional large rectilinear plot on the corner of Severn Street (Frog Lane). These plots were clearly separated from those lining the southern section of Sidbury. The corner with Sidbury is curiously staggered, a feature identifiable first on Doharty's map of 1741. This may simply represent a northward encroachment by the corner building; alternatively an explanation may be found in a discontinuity of alignment resulting from the breaking-through of a former barrier, quite possibly the Roman and later defences. This street seems also to have been the principal approach to the castle, whose gate probably lay just to the south of the monastery gate, where a lane now gives access to the King's School yard, on the site of the castle gaol yard.

Discussion: the early development of the cathedral close

The observations from the watching-brief at 3 College Precincts are the only archaeological evidence available from the block of properties on the east side of the close. However, the discovery of the Roman earthwork defences by Barker in the adjacent Lich Street area is directly relevant, and provides a probable context for the post-Roman development of this part of the close (Barker 1969, 50–53). As will be argued later in more detail, the complete disappearance of these massive earthworks from the city landscape north of the close, and signs of regularity and organization in the succeeding layout of streets and plots, suggests that the defences were systematically levelled for planned urban occupation.

This process may be what underlies the formation of the block of properties on the east side of the close. First, from Barker's investigations there can be no doubt that the great late-Roman ditch and rampart continued south into this very area, and the same model should apply: there is now no trace of the earthworks in the surface topography, strongly suggesting that they were levelled in this area too. Second, there are signs that the cathedral close properties here were laid out as part of the same scheme as the Lich Street–Friar Street area. The depth (east–west) of the Friar Street/College Precincts block within the close boundary replicates exactly that of the plots overlying the former defences further north, on the west side of Friar Street. These were between 140 and 170 feet deep (*c.* 42–52 metres), separated from the rear of the plots facing High Street by a continuous north–south fence line, which is effectively continued into the close by the College Precincts frontage (see figs 6.5 and 6.14). In other words the block of plots on the east side of the close may well have been conceived at the same time, as part of the same planned layout, as the plots further north beyond the close. Future contributions to this line of questioning will only come from further archaeological evidence for the extent of burials and the dating of the levelling of the defences in this area.

One further point arises from the observations at no. 3 College Precincts. Towards the bottom of the strata was a sequence of slag-metalled surfaces, certainly of Roman date, and thought by the excavator to belong to an east–west road (Brown 1991b). As the earthwork defences must have run a few metres to the east of this site, and if the excavator's interpretation is correct, it implies the presence of a gate. This supposition is supported by Martin Carver's excavations on the north-east side of Sidbury, beyond the defences, which located a Roman street running north-west–south-east, directly towards the site of this hypothesized gate.

In summary, a critical process in the early development of the medieval cathedral close in the area under discussion seems to have been that by which the former defensive earthworks – presumably serving as the *vallum monasterii* for the early cathedral community – were more or less rapidly transformed and masked by levelling and redevelopment, the recorded late-medieval ecclesiastical boundaries reflecting the outcome of this re-urbanization process. But, in addition, we have to consider the undocumented relationship between the ecclesiastical precinct and the High Street. As the introduction to this chapter points out, the most glaring topographical anomaly in the medieval town-plan is the apparent interruption of the axial through-route by the cathedral close.

There is some evidence that the High Street was, in origin, a Roman road, and it appears to have maintained its course within the northern defences of the Roman earthwork enclosure in the area of St Helen's church. The point at which the High Street stops – its junction with Lich Street – is also the northern boundary of the cathedral close. There is no suggestion from Barker's 1965–6 excavations that the main Roman ditch was diminishing in size as it neared Lich Street (as if approaching a gate) in the way that it did as it approached the High Street near St Helen's. As far as one can tell, the defences would have passed under Lich Street with no interruption until they reached the hypothesized east gate near no. 3 College Precincts. Lich Street is almost certainly a post-Roman street, ignoring the old defensive perimeter, though perhaps functioning as a replacement for the road entering via the hypothesized old east gate. Furthermore, there is evidence to suggest that, west of the High Street, the line of Lich Street formed the base-line for a distinct planned area that represented another phase in the process by which the old defences were levelled for the extension of the built-up area (see below).

It can therefore be suggested that the north and east boundaries of the close were the outcome of the destruction and replanning of the Roman enclosure, and that the truncation of the High Street probably took place as part of the same process. The old earthwork defences were levelled and new streets laid out. The northern boundary of the close was established on one of the new streets, Lich Street, and traffic that had formerly passed down the High Street, through the centre of the enclosure, and out south-eastwards via the east gate, was diverted along Lich Street around the new ecclesiastical perimeter, well away from the cathedral churches.

When might this have taken place? It has to be said that there is no direct dating evidence, either from within the close or from the area to the north. Archaeological dating evidence from the defences themselves (in the Fish Street area: see p. 183) suggests only that the ditch was filled in before medieval pottery types were in circulation. A tentative chronology can be built up for the development of the core of the intramural city following the foundation of the *burh*, and this will be discussed in detail later. In summary, however, it might be expected that such a grandiose re-planning scheme – affecting both the boundaries of the close and the layout of the urban area beyond – would have been associated with a known episode in the development of the cathedral community and its buildings at some time in the early-medieval period. Two notable periods of major change do of course suggest themselves: Oswald's episcopate (961 to 992), and Wulfstan's (1062–95). Of these two, there are some indications that the former is the more likely to have seen this phase of replanning.

How far south the High Street may have continued prior to the suggested replanning is impossible to say. It would be surprising if it had not continued as far as the suspected east–west road and east gate near the no. 3 College Precincts site; possibly it continued further southwards through the enclosure leaving via a lost south gate, but the Norman motte-and-bailey castle effectively disguises the pre-eleventh-century topography of the southern tip of the peninsula. Both the pre-Conquest cathedral churches, as well as the known pre-Conquest burials, could or would have lain just west of the extended line of the High Street – which may, therefore, have marked some distinction in land use within the old Roman enclosure.

In conclusion, there are indications that the late medieval cathedral close boundaries were related, but only indirectly, to the Roman earthwork enclosure in which the first cathedral was built: at least the north and east sides of the close appear to have been associated with the replanning of the area following the destruction of the old defences. The southern boundary was also subject to change as a result of the incursion of the Norman castle, though what the basis of the 'restored' boundary of 1217 was is unknown. Within the precinct, localized changes in land use must have taken place on many occasions, when (we might guess) the Bishop's Palace enclosure was created, and the area of the cemeteries reduced during ecclesiastical building campaigns and the development of lay housing. But throughout the late-medieval and early-modern periods the integrity of the cathedral close remained unchallenged. This began to change with the construction of College Street diagonally across it in the last decade of the eighteenth century, and was more or less ended by the destruction of Lich Street in 1965–6 when, once again, the north side of the close and the southern end of the High Street were united within a large-scale redevelopment programme; ironically, this was to provide the evidence for the one that took place perhaps exactly a thousand years before. Now, only College Green south of the cathedral retains the discrete identity and sense of enclosure that was characteristic of the medieval precinct.

Plan-region II

PLAN-UNIT II.1: THE CROSS

This is a short but quite distinct section of the principal north–south axial street. The Cross takes its name from the medieval Grass Cross which formerly stood at the south end of this part of the street, just before it narrows abruptly to become the High Street. To the north of the St Nicholas's Street (Gaol Lane) and Angel Lane junction the street is again substantially narrowed. These narrowings in the street line are significant: the Cross is that part of the High Street route which lies between the Anglo-Saxon defences and the medieval defences, the narrowings representing the passage of the street through the former gates. The contrasting width of the Cross may be due to the fossilization of frontage encroachments at each gate but it nevertheless seems probable that the Cross represents a section of street deliberately widened to accommodate a market.

The plots on the west side of the Cross are small and shallow and, except in one case, do not exceed 80 feet (*c.* 24 metres) in depth. The plots on the east side are slightly larger, and mostly end on a strongly marked back-fence line about 160 feet (*c.* 48 metres) from the frontage; this line also marks the point at which buildings first oversail the lane known as the Trinity, and the end of the curious unnamed blind alley immediately to the north. The much smaller and shorter plots lining the funnel-like southernmost section of the Cross have been included here as a sub-unit, but they must have originated separately, following the infilling of the *burh* ditch whose position has been confirmed nearby by excavation.

If this area was indeed laid out as a market, the date at which this would have taken place, and the date at which the area was first built up (which need not be the same), are uncertain. The pre-Conquest town can be shown in other areas, Sidbury for instance, to have been outgrowing the *burh* perimeter even before the end of the tenth century, and there is a strong possibility that the Cross was developed before *c*. 1200, perhaps as an extramural market. Some time in the later twelfth century the city's medieval defences were built, and there is a strong probability that by this date the area around the Cross was already developed and that the new defences cut through the existing suburb. This is supported by the observation that the north–south back-fence line to the plots on the east side of the Cross, referred to above, is continued by the back fence shared by the short suburban plots on the east side of Foregate Street and the Tything, beyond the city wall; the situation on the west side is less clear but may be comparable. In short, it is probable that the Cross is in reality the truncated south end of the great, planned, Foregate Street–Tything northern suburb, isolated from it by the construction of the city wall and ditch. This interpretation is not without its problems: the Foregate Street suburb is thought to have been developed by one of the bishops of Worcester, and perhaps during Wulfstan's time as the probable late-eleventh-century St Nicholas's church was apparently part of the foundation (see below, p. 213). Was this really the first development of any consequence outside the pre-Conquest north gate? Or did it clear and replace earlier extramural growth; or is the whole of the Foregate Street–Tything suburb much earlier than has been thought? Archaeology has made little impression on this part of the city and the suburb beyond, and there is as yet no independent dating evidence for the growth of this part of the built-up area.

PLAN-UNIT II.2: BROAD STREET

This area includes Broad Street and its associated plots, and two adjacent areas to the north: the precinct of the Dominican friary founded in 1347, and Angel Street, formerly Angel Lane, with its own associated plots; as a whole it covered approximately 10 acres (4.05 hectares).

Broad Street is about 100 metres long, connecting the High Street route with the main river crossing via All Hallows' Square, the area in front of All Saints' church used as a cattle market in the late middle ages (Buchanan-Dunlop 1936, 16) and probably long before, and the two streets of Newport and Dolday. Broad Street is straight, up to *c*. 40 feet (*c*. 12 metres) wide, and forms a right-angle with the northern section of the High Street and the Cross, characteristics that may suggest a degree of deliberate planning in its development. The plot boundaries, with some notable exceptions, are generally straight and perpendicular to the street, defining plots that are, or were, for the most part fairly wide and long, and subject to longitudinal (and some lateral) sub-division. Historical evidence gives a *terminus ante quem* for Broad Street of 1196–1203 (Darlington 1968, 452), though the archaeological and topographical evidence suggests an origin some time before this as an extramural road along the outer edge of the pre-Conquest ditch (see below); it may possibly have had a still more ancient origin as one of a number of east–west Roman roads in this area.

As a townscape unit, Broad Street with its associated plots has, overall, a clear and discrete identity, although in some areas its boundaries are indistinct. Its easternmost plots are interlocked with those of the Cross, and there is no clear evidence for a chronological relationship between the two areas. The plots on the south side of Broad Street either run, or ran, through to Powick Lane (the eastern part of which is now Old Bank Street) to the south: many of the longitudinal plot boundaries still run through from one frontage to the other, and documentary research has shown that the colonization of the Broad Street plot-tails in this area, to provide properties facing

Powick Lane, was taking place in the early-modern period (Currie 1989b). This has received further confirmation from the excavation of a stone building of probable late-twelfth- or early-thirteenth-century date on one of these plots, straddling the (later) east–west property boundary between the Broad Street and Powick Lane tenements, which was followed by the parish boundary between All Saints' and St. Andrew's. The east–west division was a new development post-dating the demolition of the building in the sixteenth–seventeenth centuries (Mundy 1989 and pers. comm.). Powick Lane can therefore be proposed as the original southern boundary to the Broad Street plan-unit.

The irregular course of Powick Lane itself requires explanation. The lane represents a significant fault-line or seam in the medieval town-plan, marking the boundary between three adjacent but clearly distinct plan-units formed by adjacent streets with their associated plot-series: Broad Street, the High Street and Birdport. The Deansway excavations of the 1980s comprised four sites, two to the north of Powick Lane (sites 3 and 4), and two to the south (sites 1 and 2) – one of these (site 1) on the southern lane frontage. The latter revealed an east–west Roman road a few metres to the south of Powick Lane near its junction with Birdport, and a watching-brief conducted on contractors' excavations immediately north of the site showed that there was a sequence of linear metalled surfaces representing a gradual shift in the line of the Roman road to that of the present-day Powick Lane (Dalwood, Buteux and Jackson 1992). The eastern part of Powick Lane bends northwards from this line, around the north end of the plot-series on the west side of the High Street. It will be argued later that this section of the High Street, including the plots on the west side, may represent a major planned urban extension, precisely the sort of development to require the blocking of the eastern end of the Powick Lane route and its northward diversion around the new plots.

Sub-unit II.2.ii: Angel Lane   The north side of Broad Street was divided into two blocks by Little Angel Lane. The plots to the west were of various depths, forming a staggered back-fence line marking the boundary with the Blackfriars precinct to the rear. The plots to the east back on to properties facing northwards onto Angel Lane. Angel Lane was first recorded in 1496 when it was to be gravelled and gated at both ends to accommodate the cattle market, which was to be moved from All Hallows' Square (Molyneux 1980, 265); there is no direct evidence to show how long the lane had been in existence prior to this. Speed's map of 1610 shows open ground on the north side of the lane, and this is confirmed by the documented location of the friars' orchard here, reaching from the claustral buildings as far eastwards as the rear of the Foregate plots (Hughes 1986, 40). By 1610 the south side of the lane was built up, and the map evidence shows a number of short irregular properties here. One of the property boundaries of the Broad Street plots passes from one frontage through to the other. This – and a sixteenth-century conveyance describing the property immediately east of Little Angel Lane extending between both frontages (Molyneux 1980, 267) – suggests that other Broad Street plots formerly ran through to the lane, and that the plots facing Angel Lane, like those on Powick Lane, represent secondary developments on the tails of the Broad Street plots. It is unknown whether Angel Lane was itself a secondary development to Broad Street or whether it was conceived as a contemporary rear service lane, but it cannot have been (as is sometimes suggested) a relic of a through-route continuing the Lowesmoor–St Nicholas's Street (Gaol Lane) line towards the river-crossing: this has been ruled out by the extensive Blackfriars excavations immediately west of the friary. Possibly the lane was created to give access to the friary from Foregate in the fourteenth century and widened in the 1490s to accommodate the cattle market.

Sub-unit II.2.iii: the Blackfriars precinct   The late-medieval topography of this area has been explored in detail by Hughes and others (1986). The friary church and cloisters lay behind the properties on Broad Street, with access via Friars' Lane, a gated lane leading off the street near its junction with Dolday. The size and position of the church and cloisters are discernible from post-Dissolution deeds and leases, and the north-west corner of the cloisters has been confirmed by excavation (Hughes 1986, 37–9; Mundy 1986a, 1986b, 1989). The layout of the other claustral and ancillary buildings is unknown, as is the use and ownership of the land between the cloisters and Little Angel Lane. On the north side, the friary grounds extended as far as the city wall. The friary was founded in 1347, following the gift of a piece of land, named as 'Belassis', from William Beauchamp. This land was said to measure 100 perches long by 30 perches broad (*Cal. Patent Rolls 1345–8*, 541), dimensions which present an unsolved problem: if the perch in question was the statute perch, the block of land in question would have measured 1650 by 495 feet (503 x 151 metres), a length greater than the distance between the High Street and the river, and broader than the distance between Broad Street and the city wall. This is clearly impossible, particularly as it is known that the friary subsequently acquired further land to the west of the precinct on the north side of Dolday. It is legitimate to question whether such an apparently large area with dimensions expressed in such neatly rounded figures could have had much basis in reality in a part of the town that was already settled (and the measurements seem unlikely, therefore, to be a reliable guide to the use of a 14-foot pole in medieval Worcester: Carver 1980, 214).

The orientation of the friary church and cloisters suggested by topographical and historical research, and confirmed by excavation, was found by excavation (the Blackfriars site: HWCM 378 T7) to be related to the alignment of an underlying Roman road first recorded in the area by Barker during redevelopment in the 1960s (Barker 1969, 63–4, and above), the west range of the cloisters following the eastern edge of the road. Before the construction of the friary in the mid fourteenth century, the area was a field. A path crossing this field perpetuated the line of a small metalled track following the back wall of a clay-founded rectangular building – the latest building constructed by the side of the Roman road while the latter was still in use (Mundy 1989, 35). The 'continuity in the organisation of land use' which Charles Mundy (1986a) identified within the Blackfriars precinct may have applied over a wider area, the orientation of the friary being shared by Little Angel Lane. It could be argued that this lane was a very late development respecting (and secondary to) the planning of the precinct but, if this were the case, it would also be reasonable to expect a feature of such a late date to be constrained by the prevailing orientation of Broad Street and its tenements, which it clearly was not, except very close to the main frontage. The simplest explanation is that the lane reflected surviving earlier (Roman) boundaries or other features, just as the friary itself did.

Broad Street and the pre-Conquest defences (figs 6.10 and 6.11)   A major influence in the development of Broad Street was decisively revealed in the course of the final stages of the excavation of Deansway site 4 in 1990. A trench excavated northwards from the main area towards Broad Street located a levelled earth rampart whose tail had appeared in the main excavated area, covering the remains of a wall of re-used Roman limestone rubble, and extending northwards to the southern edge of a substantial east–west ditch. The wall and rampart were constructed on top of a 'dark earth' deposit, and one of the minor local Roman east–west streets, and the rampart and ditch fill were cut by pits of medieval date, while the main filling of the ditch appeared to have taken place before medieval pottery types were in circulation. Scientific analysis of the 'dark earth' deposits showed that the dark earth sealed by the rampart consisted of a basic agricultural soil devoid of

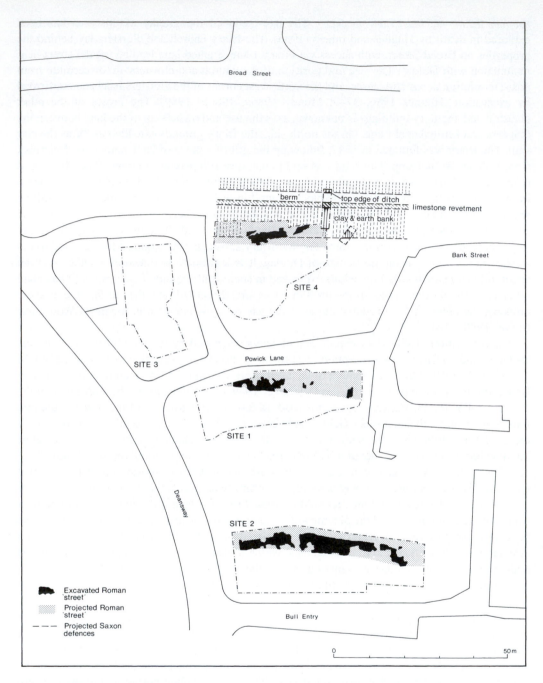

Broad Street

berm
top edge of ditch
limestone revetment
clay & earth bank

SITE 4

Bank Street

SITE 3

Powick Lane

SITE 1

Deansway

SITE 2

Excavated Roman
'street'

Projected Roman
'street'

Projected Saxon
defences

Bull Entry

0   50m

6.10   Worcester: Broad Street and the pre-Conquest defences (Worcestershire County Council
Archaeological Service)

occupation debris; beyond the rampart, the 'dark earth' had been transformed by the mixing in of ash, charcoal, dung and building materials. In other words, the rampart was built after the Roman period but before intensive human habitation recommenced in the area (pers. comm., Hal Dalwood, summarizing ongoing work by R. McPhail). It is therefore fairly certain that these remains represent an early-medieval defensive feature (Baker, Dalwood, Holt, Mundy and Taylor 1992). Furthermore, their position is consistent with documentary and topographical sources for the area

6.11   Central Worcester and the pre-Conquest defences: the archaeological evidence for the Worcester *burh*

immediately to the west that suggest that these defences were in use in the first decade of the tenth century (see above, p. 133, and below, pp. 176–7): they represent the northern defences of the *burh* of Worcester.

A sequence of development for the Broad Street area may now be proposed. The character of the Roman occupation sequences and the deposits north and south of Broad Street have been found to be substantially different, and Charles Mundy (pers. comm.) has suggested that Broad Street may have originated in an east–west Roman road, the northernmost of the metrologically regular series discovered in the Deansway excavations, and forming some kind of land-use division within the Roman settlement. But Broad Street is more clearly related to the pre-Conquest defences, the *burh* ditch lying under its southern frontage; it almost certainly functioned, if it did not originate, as an extramural road connecting the High Street with the access roads to the river crossing and the suspected gate and extramural market by All Saints' church (see pp. 205–7, below). The peculiar north–east south–west orientation of All Hallows' Square is most likely to reflect the course of the defences turning southwards to meet the riverbank at an approximate right-angle.

From the very limited archaeological sample so far explored, it is not possible to say definitely whether the defences in this area were deliberately levelled or allowed to decay and be reclaimed plot by plot over a long period: stratigraphic differences within the excavated (Deansway site 4) area probably indicate piecemeal reclamation of the ditch (pers. comm. Rachel Edwards, Hal Dalwood). The regularity of Broad Street itself is tentatively suggestive of a central authority at work, and it may be that the street was improved and widened before individual plot-holders were left to level the obstacles on their own properties. Although the sample-size was limited, metrological survey suggested that the development of plots was on an individual *ad hoc* basis without regulation of frontage-widths. The date at which Broad Street began to be occupied remains unclear. The site 4 excavations on the south side of the street – well behind the frontage – found pitting from the late eleventh to thirteenth centuries but this may not accurately reflect the start of activity on Broad Street itself. The 1985–6 Blackfriars excavations revealed a corn-drying oven of possibly tenth–eleventh-century as well as a 'small building/shack' of the same date built on the disused Roman road surface (Mundy 1989, 33, 35). Parallels elsewhere suggest that the oven would likely have been situated in open ground behind occupied tenements.

PLAN-UNIT II.3: GAOL LANE

Gaol Lane, now St Nicholas's Street, was a narrow lane in the late-medieval period leading from the Cross to a postern gate in the town wall known as Trinity Gate, first recorded in 1540 (Beardsmore 1980, 62). The street was widened in the early nineteenth century when this part of the city wall was demolished. While Gaol Lane was clearly a minor thoroughfare in the late-medieval period, this was probably not always the case. The development of the north-east quarter of Worcester and its approach roads is obscure, the area having seen little excavation, but there is an obviously strong possibility that Gaol Lane was, before the construction of the city wall in the late twelfth century and the diversion of traffic to St Martin's Gate, a continuation of Lowesmoor and thus the principal means of access from the axial High Street to the road to Droitwich and the north-east. This is not to say, however, that the area was built up at all intensively away from the Cross within the medieval period. On the contrary, documentary evidence shows that empty plots on Mealcheapen Street to the south were still being developed in the thirteenth century (pers. comm. Dr Pat Hughes): in default of archaeological evidence, the north-east quarter of intramural Worcester seems to have been a relatively open, under-exploited area.

PLAN-UNIT II.4: MEALCHEAPEN STREET

This landscape unit contains two main components: St Swithin's Street and Mealcheapen Street, connecting the High Street at the Cross with St Martin's Gate, and the Cornmarket at the east end of the street, inside the city wall. Mealcheapen Street represents an access route of secondary importance, leading into the city from the east via St Martin's Gate and the extramural street of the same name, from the agricultural district around Tibberton, Huddington and Himbleton. When the city wall (or possibly a local boundary ditch preceding it: Bennett 1980, 65–9) was constructed, the line of Mealcheapen Street appears to have been diverted a short distance to the north via Clapgate to the new gate. At least from *c*. 1200 on, Mealcheapen Street also carried traffic to and from the High Street and the Droitwich area, via Lowesmoor and Silver Street.

The plot-pattern, which still survives well, has different characteristics each side of the street and in the small street-block containing St Swithun's church. The plots on the north side have a slight curve, as the longitudinal boundaries come off the curving St Swithin's Street frontage more or less perpendicularly, and then take up the ruling north–south alignment that ultimately derives from the High Street–Cross–Foregate Street line. Trinity Passage, a narrow north–south lane, and several of the plot boundaries, ran from the Mealcheapen Street frontage north through to the lane known as Trinity, and although several of the plots appear to have been laterally sub-divided to provide properties facing northwards, Trinity appears to represent the original rear boundary to the series. The lateral sub-division of these plots is likely to have occurred, at least in one case, within the medieval period: a length of back boundary common to several of these plots coincides with the St Swithun's–St Nicholas's parish boundary, and in one of these north-facing properties on Trinity, between the two buildings shown built over the lane, was the hall and other buildings of the Trinity Gild (Hughes 1980, 277–8; for the Trinity Gild see below, pp. 217–8).

The plots on the south side of Mealcheapen Street were much shorter. A group in the centre, deeper than the others, shared a common back-fence line perpendicular to New Street, the side boundary of one of the latter's plots, to which the Mealcheapen Street plots may have been secondary in date. The smallest plots on the street were those around St Swithun's church, the most constricted parish church site in the city. The relationship of the western Mealcheapen Street plots to those on the Cross is uncertain. The distinct common back boundary to the east-side Cross plots (see above) continues southwards to St Swithin's Street, eventually as a boundary between two of the latter's plots, with the westward curve characteristic of that part of the plot-series. The same line appears to continue south of St Swithin's Street as the boundary of the St Swithun's church-plot – but without further information there is no way of knowing whether this apparent continuation is significant or not.

Elsewhere in Worcester (Foregate Street is the classic case) and Gloucester the provision of common back lanes to a series of plots has been taken as a possible indication of imposed organization, or town-planning – though there will inevitably be cases where main streets and parallel lanes came into existence at different dates. The termination of the north side Mealcheapen Street plots on the east–west lane known as Trinity raises such a question here. It seems entirely possible that the north Mealcheapen Street plot-series represents a discrete planning episode – a series of plots laid out along an existing road (Mealcheapen Street) and serviced by a common back lane laid out at right-angles to the High Street/Cross routeway. It should also be noted that Trinity lies half way between Gaol Lane and Mealcheapen Street; so, if the origin of Trinity was indeed as a service lane within a planned layout, this may originally have included Gaol Lane.

A critical factor in the evolution of this area is the course of the *burh* defences east of the High Street. Archaeological, documentary and topographical evidence converge to demonstrate conclusively that the northern defences of the pre-Conquest *burh* crossed the High Street at the point where it narrows, immediately south of its junction with Broad Street and St Swithin's Street. From there, the line of the ditch, wall and bank may be safely projected into the area of St Swithun's church itself, and two watching-briefs in 1990 and 1992 on the school-room in the churchyard reported the presence of deep organic grey loam with bands of organic material – consistent with the infilled ditch (City SMR sites, WCM 100662, 100663). On present evidence, the most probable scenario is that the curve of St Swithin's Street – as has often been suspected – reflects the southward return of the *burh* defences, St Swithun's church itself being built over the ditch. In this case an evolutionary model for the area may be proposed on the following lines: First, there was a Roman east–west road, on the line of Mealcheapen Street, representing an eastward continuation of the Roman road shown by the Deansway excavations (site 4, see fig. 6.11) to be underlying Bank Street (formerly Powicke Lane); with the construction of the *burh* at the end of the ninth century this road was interrupted east of the High Street, and traffic was diverted around the new obstacle, giving rise to St Swithin's Street in exactly the same way as Sansome Street (Town Ditch) developed later, skirting the late twelfth-century defences. With the growth of the town and the eventual reclamation of the *burh* defences here (see below), Mealcheapen Street was developed as a satellite corn-marketing area and was the subject of a simple town-planning episode to encourage its growth.

The name Mealcheapen – signifying the flour or meal market – may refer to the triangular marketplace at its east end known as the Corn Market, or it may refer to a marketplace function possessed by the street itself before the marketplace was created. There are some grounds for suspecting that the present Corn Market may indeed have been a relatively late arrival on the scene. The triangular shape of the market that can be reconstructed from the cartographic evidence seems to have been determined entirely by the course of the late-medieval city wall which formed its eastern boundary; the marketplace itself may well have been created by the amalgamation and clearance of built-up plots that were being truncated by the new defences. The development of new and secondary marketplaces in this period is paralleled elsewhere – in Shrewsbury, for example, where pressure of space on the old King's Market led to the creation in 1261 of a new marketplace, probably by the clearance of built-up plots, some of which appear to have been the site of private selds (Cromarty 1991, 6). The Worcester Corn Market is dominated by the church of St Martin, extant by 1003x23 (see below, p. 211), which occupies a site in the centre of the west side. If, however, the relationship of the Corn Market to its surroundings has been correctly interpreted, the association of St Martin's church with the marketplace was accidental, and the church's primary context should be seen as the back of one of the plots facing Mealcheapen Street.

Archaeological investigations at various sites around the city wall circuit have, with a single exception, all shown the circuit to have been built *de novo* after the Conquest (Carver 1980, 8). The one exception was a site a short distance south of St Martin's Gate where a ditch, possibly defensive, containing sherds of early-medieval pottery was found, overlain by the city wall; the ditch followed a similar course to the wall but was seen to curve westwards under it at the south end of the trench (Bennett 1980; see fig. 6.11). Hypothetical reconstructions of this ditch as part of a larger scheme of Anglo-Saxon city defences are not supported (though not absolutely refuted either) by other sources (Bennett 1980, 69; Carver 1980, 5). The strongest possibility is that the ditch was part of a more localized scheme, possibly defending or just demarcating suburban development in the Mealcheapen–St Martin's area, in the manner of the short-lived boundaries referred to in contemporary documents as 'the king's ditch' around suburbs such as Barton Street in Gloucester, and possibly the Causeway, on the west bank at Worcester (see above, p. 92; below, p. 194).

PLAN-UNIT II.5: THE HIGH STREET (NORTH)

A cursory inspection of the town-plan of Worcester rarely fails to draw attention to a single recti-linear element at the centre of the street-system: this is the street-block defined by the northern section of the High Street and Church Street, the Shambles (the medieval Baxteres Street) and Pump Street (Nedleres or Bridelwritte Street). The plot-pattern within this area was distinctive. It consisted (before the gross amalgamations of the mid twentieth century) of a dense pattern of long, thin, irregular properties, often interlinked at the rear in a way that suggests the frequent and

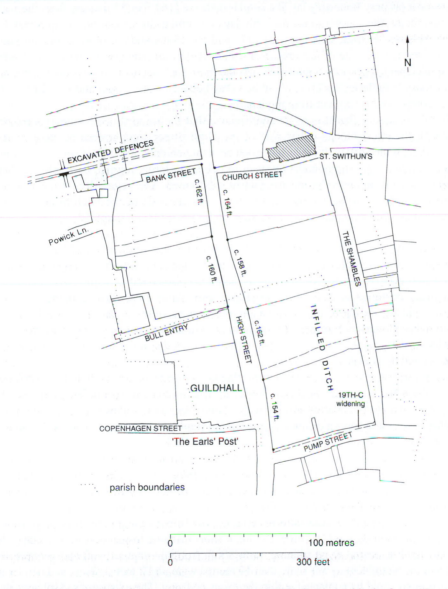

6.12 Worcester: the High Street: the plot-system on the High Street outside the former Roman defences, with measurements between primary (frontage-to-frontage) property boundaries, and the line of the levelled pre-Conquest defences

chaotic exchange of small land parcels for back premises between neighbouring properties. But amongst this chaos can be found elements of an apparently more organized system. This is represented by a small number of straight boundaries, perpendicular to the streets, running from one frontage through to the other without interruption or deflection. These are what have been termed primary boundaries by historical geographers (Slater 1981), and suspicion that they may have been earlier in date than the irregular boundaries around them seems to be supported by their metrology (see fig. 6.12). Three out of four such boundaries on the east side of the High Street were spaced at approximately regular intervals, between 158 and 162 feet (c. 48–9 metres) apart. The northernmost primary boundary lay at a similar distance (164 feet/50 metres) from the north side of Church Street; the southernmost probably lay at a similar distance from Pump Street, but the latter was widened at some date between 1779 and the 1880s and the original measurement has been lost. On the west side of the street is a similar pattern of irregular properties with what appear to be interspersed primary boundaries, and the metrology seems to be repeated there, one of the two primary boundaries occuring about half-way between Bank Street and Bull Entry, 162 feet from the former and c.160 feet from the latter.

It is difficult to believe that it is of no significance that the minority of boundaries passing straight through the street-blocks either side of the High Street were spaced at more or less regular intervals; it is also difficult to see how such an arrangement could have been created once the area had been built up. The boundaries seem to belong to large, regular, early plots of land that were subsequently intensively and irregularly subdivided. The regularity of the frontage measurements, and the rectilinear frame of streets on the east side of the High Street, suggest that this area or plan-unit owes its basic shape to a single town-planning episode.

The High Street and the burh (figs 6.11 and 6.12)   This part of the High Street is, and has previously been discussed in print as, a classic example of a distinct 'plan-unit' within the larger town-plan, brought into being as the result of a localized town-planning episode and remaining a distinct entity in the plan many centuries after its creation (Baker and Slater 1992). There being no direct archaeological evidence of the date of its creation, previous accounts of this area noted its axial position within the city and its confinement within the northern defences of the *burh*, as proved by excavation. Its southern limit (Pump Street) was determined by the ditch of the Roman earthwork defences, excavated by Barker in the 1960s.

The area represented, it was concluded, a town-planning episode associated with the foundation of the *burh* in the 890s. Its eastern limit was, it was argued, the eastern *burh* defences, marked by a series of parallel parish boundaries and property boundaries running down the east side of the Shambles; these seemed to form a distinct 'plan-seam' beyond which the road network spread out, as if free from some constraint. In this situation, it was suggested, the Shambles may have functioned as both a service lane to the High Street and as an intramural street, on the Wessex model, allowing access along the defences (Baker *et al.* 1992). So far, this hypothesis remains untested. No archaeological investigations have taken place that have yielded useful archaeological information from the east side of the Shambles.

In late 1999 a large negative feature, almost certainly an infilled ditch of substantial proportions, was found by excavation on the City Arcades Site, a short distance to the west of – inside – the Shambles. The ditch appeared to be running north–south (roughly parallel with and between the High Street and the Shambles); it was more than 10 metres wide and 2 metres deep, and neither its edges nor its bottom could be contacted within the excavated area. The excavator's suspicions that this was a linear, rather than a local, feature were supported by observations of unusually deep and soft made-ground encountered during foundation works at the rear of a china emporium a few properties to the north. The ditch could not be closely dated: it was late Roman or later, but infilled before medieval (eleventh–twelfth century) pottery types were in circulation; pits containing such pottery were cut into its upper fills.

In summary, it is now believed that this ditch represents the east side of the pre-Conquest *burh*. The line of the City Arcades feature can be extended north, via the deep fills of the Prattley's (emporium) site into the St Swithun's area and thus to the High Street, to connect with the excavated section on Deansway site 4 (see above). The stratigraphic sequence of the City Arcades ditch is similar to that on site 4. The excavator of the City Arcades site also noted that there was a tip of oolitic limestone rubble down the west side of the ditch fill: while this could have been derived directly from Roman masonry structures found to the west, it could equally plausibly, he suggested, derive from the destruction of the *burh* wall fronting the rampart – found on Deansway site 4 to have been built of oolitic limestone rubble derived from the robbing of Roman building foundations (Robin Jackson, pers. comm.).

If the line of the City Arcades feature is extended to the south, the possibility is also raised that it represents a continuation of Philip Barker's ditch 'd', regarded when it was found as a later feature than the (probable) late-Roman massive ditch 'b', and a possible candidate for the pre-Conquest *burh* (Barker 1969, 51). If this is the case, it would suggest that when the Worcester *burh* defences were constructed, they in part formed an outer perimeter reinforcing the old Roman enclosure.

It is quite clear that the town-planning event represented by the High Street plan-unit is later than the ditch found on the City Arcades site – its east–west streets and property boundaries all run across it. If – as is possible on the ceramic evidence alone – the City Arcades ditch was of late-Roman date, the interpretation of the High Street plan-unit as a primary component of the late ninth-century *burh* need not be invalid: it is not impossible, after all, that part of the *burh* was laid out over part of a former, now superseded, defensive circuit, just as later pre-Conquest urban extensions were to be. But, until archaeology locates another major north–south ditch outside the Shambles, the balance of probability is that the City Arcades ditch was indeed part of the ninth-century perimeter. The similarity of the Deansway and City Arcades sequences is striking, and the topography and archaeology of the St Swithun's church area strongly suggest that these two sites encountered the same linear monument. A pre-ninth-century origin – even a late-Roman origin – cannot be ruled out from the archaeological evidence for either the site 4 or the City Arcades ditch, but the former of these at least seems to have been the *burh* ditch of the 890s.

The previously published model – that the High Street plan-unit was an example of a *burh* foundation-period town-planning episode – should therefore for the moment be set aside (see also Baker and Holt 1996). A more complex sequence – one in which, for instance, regular plots laid out on the High Street were extended back as the defences to the rear were colonized and reclaimed – may perhaps have applied. But parallels for the planning of the High Street area should most probably be sought in other instances, where the comprehensive levelling of obsolete defences was accomplished by an overall authority as a prelude to planned urban settlement (see pp. 184–5, below).

Sub-unit II.5.ii: the west side High Street plots: later development   The obvious difference between this area and that on the opposite side of the street is the absence here of a parallel secondary street to the rear. Instead, the plots on the west side of the High Street ended against a staggered and irregular alleyway separating them from the rear of the plots facing Birdport to the west. This alleyway grew slowly, a product of infilling behind the frontages in the modern period. The northern end, Pye Corner, appears for the first time on Doharty's map of 1741. Broad's map of 1768 and Young's of 1779 record two further stages in its development as the lane extended southwards, servicing new infilling and eventually joining up with Bull Entry. The latter was, by the 1880s, an alley linking High Street with Birdport; it does not appear on Doharty's rather schematic map at all, but by 1779 it extended about two-thirds of the way westwards from the High Street towards Birdport. Although, as a thoroughfare, it was a creation of the eighteenth and nineteenth centuries, it is likely to have developed along much earlier property boundaries, as did the alleyway behind the High Street plots.

The staggered boundary between the High Street west-side plots and those on Birdport suggests that land ownership in this area was particularly fluid, parcels being exchanged almost randomly between the two systems according to the workings of the property market over several centuries. The parish boundary between St Andrew's and St Swithun's in this area (see fig. 7.1) also follows a similar but separate staggered north–south line, a short distance from the lane marking the junction between the two plot-systems. This line seems likely to represent an earlier junction between the plot-systems, and excavation across it on one site has demonstrated that, at that point, the line of the parish boundary was apparent as a fence and as a metalled path in the thirteenth century. Before that, continuous spreads of industrial residue suggested that the boundary lay, as it was to do later, closer to the High Street (Deansway site 2: Mundy 1989, 14, and Victoria Bryant, pers. comm.).

The medieval Guildhall, rebuilt in the eighteenth century, occupied the large southernmost plot on the west side of the High Street. The first apparent reference to it is found in 1249, when a charter was witnessed by Richard de la Gyldhall (*VCH Worcs.*, iv, 381). Like its eighteenth-century successor, it was set back from the High Street frontage, behind shops facing the High Street and Copenhagen Street.

PLAN-UNIT II.6: BIRDPORT

This area was characterized by a core of small irregular street-blocks, showing a degree of morphological unity by their common size and irregularity, and in most cases by the limited plot definition in their interiors – short plots with shared yards behind. Each might be considered a plan-unit in its own right (and this area exhibits all the problems of the scale at which town-plan components are defined), but their compact distribution in the central waterfront quarter of the city justifies their treatment as a single localized phenomenon. On the fringes of this area were a number of minor plot-series of more conventional character whose origins arguably had little in common with that of the core area; they were nevertheless generally distinct from the surrounding, larger and more morphologically homogeneous plan-units, and so have been grouped with the core area to form a single waterfront plan-unit, whose internal diversity serves to distinguish it from its neighbours.

Birdport was the principal medieval thoroughfare west of the High Street, carrying north–south traffic along the top of the steep slope overlooking the river and to the river crossing via Newport Street and Dolday. Though definitive archaeological evidence is lacking, Birdport is probably the successor to a north–south Roman street, a southward extension of the road first identified in the Blackfriars area, connecting the regularly spaced east–west Roman streets found in the Deansway excavations (Mundy 1989, 12).

Sub-unit II.6.i: the St Andrew's block   This was an irregular squarish area, sub-divided into four quarters, with steep slopes down to the west and south. St Andrew's church, first recorded in the mid eleventh century but probably rather earlier (see pp. 203–4, below), occupied the south-eastern quarter, bounded by Birdport, Hare Lane to the north, Copenhagen Street to the south, and a block of tenements on the corner of Copenhagen Street and Quay Street to the west. Speed's map of 1610 shows the church separated from the tenements to the west by a north–south road, continuing the line of Hounds Lane southwards to Copenhagen Street. The church stood in the centre of this block within a large churchyard (see fig. 6.13). Its Birdport frontage was taken up by a rectangular block of property, occupied by dense housing and separated from the east end of the church by a narrow alley. The seventeenth- and eighteenth-century maps show all of the Copenhagen Street frontage to the south of the church built up, though by the 1880s housing was confined to a regularly sub-divided plot terraced into the slope in the south-west corner of the churchyard. A charter of 1214–27 refers to land and houses in Huckster Street (Copenhagen Street) in front of the church of St Andrew (Darlington 1968, 406).

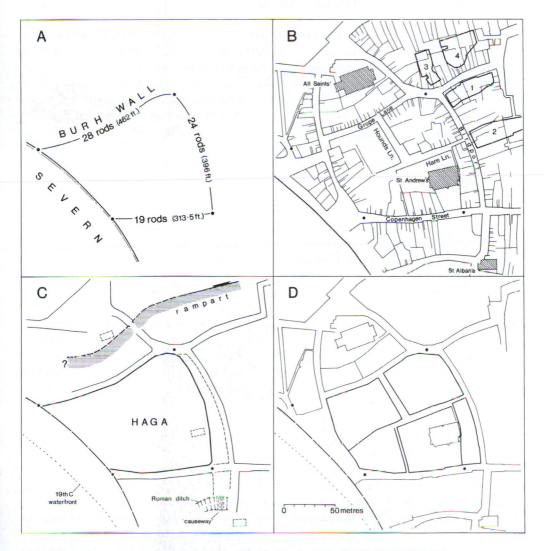

6.13   Worcester: a reconstruction of Bishop Waerferth's *haga*. A: the 904 lease description;
B: the Birdport area, showing the Deansway excavation sites (1-4); C: the *haga* boundaries
reconstructed; D: the suspected initial phase in the *haga*'s sub-division

The north-east quarter of this area was bounded by streets or lanes on all sides. The first edition Ordnance Survey plans show dense cottage development behind the frontages within plots which (with the exception of the two northern corner-plots) had ill-defined boundaries away from the frontage buildings. The north-west and south-west quarters were clearly separated from the areas to the east, but from one another only by a property boundary that appears to have continued the line of Hare Lane westwards. The 1886 plans show a number of short plots facing west onto Quay Street, presumably terraced into the slope, ending at a back-fence line parallel to the street. The corner of Quay Street and Copenhagen Street, and the west end of the latter, were occupied by short, irregular plots, shown by both Young and the Ordnance Survey. Behind the northern end of the Quay Street plots was an area which, in 1779, was mainly open ground with some buildings on the Hounds Lane frontage.

Sub-unit II.6.ii: the Quay The Lower Quay (so called to distinguish it from the Upper or North Quay, by St Clement's church) is approached by two roads: Quay Street, from All Hallows' Square to the north, and Copenhagen Street, carrying traffic from the south end of the High Street via a substantial defile descending the escarpment. In the medieval period the Quay was at least in part closed off from the waterfront by the city wall; there must have been access through one or more gates for the movement of goods, but no gates are recorded. Speed's map shows the wall in this area to be discontinuous – three separate sections with gaps between them, but it is not clear whether these are meant to indicate access points or merely ruination. Inside the wall, Speed's map shows a loose agglomeration of housing encroaching on the open space; this is not shown on the 1651 map, but appears again on Doharty's map (1741) and subsequently, and still survives. The below-ground structure of the Quay has never been explored, but there is some evidence (see below) that the waterfront formerly lay directly at the bottom of the slope beneath St Andrew's church, and that the flat, wedge-shaped open area of the Quay is a medieval creation, possibly the product of gradual waterfront reclamation of the type familiar in London, King's Lynn and a great many other towns. The present surface of the Quay is the lowest-lying area of the medieval intramural city (at about 13.7 metres AOD – 44 feet in the 1880s) and is particularly susceptible to winter floods.

Origins: the episcopal haga What were the origins of this plan-unit? The core is represented by the four small irregular street-blocks on the west side of Birdport, described above, surrounded by peripheral areas occupied by minor plot-series, to be described below. The appearance of the area does not suggest that its development was subject to any obvious form of centralized planning; rather, the landscape appears to consist of a number of discrete blocks of property, incompletely sub-divided internally, one of which contains a parish church of pre-Conquest origin. These four small street-blocks can be shown to represent sub-divisions of a single substantial pre-Conquest property, a *haga* leased in 904 by Bishop Wærferth to Ealdorman Æthelred, Æthelflæd and their daughter Ælfwynn for three lives, together with associated property on the west bank and more to the north of the city. The boundaries of the *haga* were recorded: '28 rods in length from the river itself along the north wall eastwards and thence southwards 24 rods in breadth and thence westwards to the Severn 19 rods in length' (H 13–15; Robertson 1956, 34–9; S 1280). If, as is suggested by the excavations to the east, the north wall of the *burh* lies under or near All Saints' church, the 904 *haga* must have lain somewhere just to the south, within the area under discussion. Assuming that the 'rods' used are equivalent to the statutory perch of 16.5 feet, the recorded dimensions would have been, respectively, 462, 396, and 313.5 feet (140.8, 120.7 and 95.5 metres). While there are inevitable uncertainties – whether the dimensions were precise or schematic, for instance, or measured along curving frontages or in straight lines – the measurements are consistent with the larger street-block bounded by Grope Lane, Birdport, Copenhagen Street and the Quay (see fig. 6.13). The measurement along the north side, from a point westwards from the junction of Birdport, Powick Lane and Grope Lane, extends about 90 feet (27 metres) into the Quay beyond the bottom of the slope. The measurement from the north-east corner southwards to Copenhagen Street is precise. The length of the south side, from the Birdport-Copenhagen Street junction is some 50 feet (15 metres) short of the bottom of the slope and is the only problematic dimension. However, this too can be reconciled if, firstly, the early-tenth-century line of Birdport were following a slightly more westerly course at this end, towards the hollow-ways and brushwood causeway across the Roman defences excavated by Gelling (1958) near St Alban's, and if, secondly, the riverbank formerly lay right at the bottom of the slope – as it still does immediately to the south – prior to reclamation at the Quay.

The core of this plan-unit seems to have originated, therefore, in this *haga* recorded for the first and only time in 904 and thereafter subdivided: first, arguably, into the smaller street-blocks and later into individual strip-type and other house-plots. The chronology of this process is not known, though the Deansway excavations across Birdport and the reference quoted above to land and houses on Copenhagen Street (then Huckster Street) in front of St Andrew's, suggest that the process was complete by *c.* 1200. The origins of the 904 *haga* are unknown. It was more than just a substantial riverside property: it occupied virtually all of the waterfront of the Worcester *burh* outside the old enclosure surrounding the cathedral. It offers a close parallel with the Church of Worcester's riverside properties in London at this time and earlier (see above, pp. 130–32), and like them it had a considerable potential for commerce. How – or whether – this was exploited is unknown, at least until Worcester's waterfront is excavated. Possibly the river frontage too was defended in some way, though if so this is not recorded.

Sub-unit II.6.iii: Birdport (east side)   On the east side of Birdport, between Powick Lane to the north and the properties facing Copenhagen Street to the south, was a group of plots shown on the eighteenth- and nineteenth-century maps with well-defined but very irregular boundaries. The Deansway site 2 excavation within this area covered one tenement and parts of the two adjoining tenements. An east–west Roman road or trackway was found which went out of use, or its use changed, in the late-Roman or early-post-Roman period, when it was covered by stone and slag debris and quantities of unbroken animal bone. It was subsequently buried by a deposit of soil – 'dark earth'. In the late pre-Conquest period industrial debris (lime, ash, charcoal) spread over the course of the road and appeared to be associated with a timber building, possibly related to the Birdport frontage which lay beyond the western edge of the excavation. In the eleventh–thirteenth centuries the medieval and later tenement boundaries were established, first represented by lines of pits, and one of these was found to follow exactly the line of the edge of the underlying Roman road (Mundy 1989, 10–14). Unless this was purely coincidental, it suggests either that the boundary was perpetuated by some archaeologically undetectable means – such as a hedge, for instance – or that its re-establishment resulted from its position relative to adjoining boundaries beyond the excavation, for example by plot amalgamation and redivision (mediation).

This chronology is, though imprecise, revealing. The area lies very close to the geographical centre of the Worcester *burh*, though it seems that its late-pre-Conquest character was largely industrial; it may not have been intensively occupied until after the Norman Conquest, possibly even as late as the beginning of the thirteenth century. The sequence may be taken to indicate an infilling process of the ground between the High Street and the waterfront, and as such it may possibly be analogous to excavated sequences away from the principal through-streets in Gloucester, the Berkeley Street site for example (see above, p.58).

Sub-unit II.6.iv: the All Saints' block   This was (before being largely erased by mid-twentieth-century redevelopment) a small semi-circular street-block occupying a projecting bluff on the escarpment overlooking the river. It was dominated by the church of All Saints', and bounded by Grope Lane, Merryvale, All Hallows' Square and Quay Street. In the late eighteenth and nineteenth centuries it was subdivided into a number of small land parcels; two side-on to Grope Lane were separated from the small plot of land at the back of the church by a long sinuous east–west property boundary that may have reflected former terracing and possibly the line of a component of the Anglo-Saxon defences. The foot of the slope in front of the church was, before the eighteenth century, occupied by an island of housing representing market encroachment onto All Hallows' Square. Although the *burh* wall may reasonably be expected to lie at the top of the slope, its precise course and its relationship with the church fabric are not known; there are tantalizing nineteenth-century reports to the effect that the church tower was built on top of the 'Saxon wall', and it was said to have been seen last in 1913 when the tower was restored (Buchanan-Dunlop 1936, 15; Sheppard 1910, 593; see also below, pp. 206–7).

Sub-unit II.6.v: the Warmstry House block   This was the squarish block of land defined by Warmstry Slip, Palace Row, the bishop's palace and the river. Large industrial premises including the porcelain manufactory had destroyed the plot-pattern within it by the 1880s, but Young's and Broad's maps show Warmstry House occupying a large plot adjoining Warmstry Slip running down to the river, with three further small plots adjoining to the south. Warmstry House appears to have originated as a substantial house in the later middle ages (pers. comm. T. Bridges). Its inclusion within the Birdport plan-unit (from which it was separated by the course of the Roman defences and the plots between Warmstry Slip and Copenhagen Street that eventually colonized them) is based on the dissimilarity between this block and its immediate surroundings (the Copenhagen Street plan-unit), and on documentary evidence for its parochial geography. The area can be identified as containing the site of the church of St Margaret (also known as St Marina), one of the two churches recorded by the later-medieval Evesham Abbey chronicle as a gift to that abbey in 721 (p. 200, below). St Margaret's had a parish that later amalgamated with that of St Alban's: the geography of the latter is such that it is virtually certain that St Margaret's parish must have been coterminous with this street-block, an area of only an acre, though possibly reduced in size by the northward encroachment of the Bishop's Palace (see p. 202, below). The street-block itself appears to have been a discrete landscape feature, and if as suggested it also formed a separate parish, it is difficult to see it as anything other than, in origin, a single block of property – a riverside enclosure perhaps, resembling the *haga* to the north, and the secondary enclosures that appear to have been carved out of it.

Further small blocks of land on the margins of the core-area of the plan-unit will not be described further as there is little information regarding them. They comprise a small group of tenements on the east side of Meryvale, adjoining the rear of Broad Street properties, and plots on the west side of Quay Street adjoining the rear of properties on Newport.

PLAN-UNIT II.7: NEWPORT STREET AND DOLDAY

These two streets, although in many respects different in character from one another, have been defined as constituents of a single plan-unit by virtue of their common function as approach-roads to the river crossing, and the shared plot-series between them. They represent the most eccentric element in the medieval intramural town-plan, departing from the general north–south alignment of the streets around the High Street in a way similar to New Street, which veers off to the east, and arguably also outside the *burh* defences. The streets carried traffic between All Hallows' Square (and the probable pre-Conquest gate close to All Saints' church), and the river crossing.

Dolday, to the north, was a strikingly sinuous road, narrow at both ends and wider in the middle, that left Broad Street just short of All Hallows' Square and ended at the North or Upper Quay, opposite St Clement's church. The medieval bridge stood at the bottom of Newport Street, known earlier as Eport, which runs in a straight line from the west side of All Hallows' Square opposite All Saints'. Both roads took traffic off the edge of the gravel terrace onto much lower ground around the waterfront: in the nineteenth century Dolday dropped by 21 feet (*c.* 6.5 metres) from south to north, Newport Street by 13 feet (*c.* 4 metres). Trial excavation on the north side of Dolday in 1985 revealed strata containing Roman material descending sharply to the west, buried by a mass of undated but probably post-Roman tipped material (Mundy 1985). It is very likely that both streets represent the result of local reclamation, at least near the river, the counterpart in function if not necessarily in date to the causeway leading to the bridge on the west bank (see pp. 193–4, below).

The whole area has been subject to extensive clearance, road-widening and redevelopment, and although Newport Street and the southern end of Dolday survive in recognizable form, the plot-pattern has been almost totally obliterated. The 1886 Ordnance Survey shows that in the block between the streets, except near the east end, many of the plots' boundaries ran through from the north side of Newport Street to the south side of Dolday. The boundaries appear irregular, and the plots of varying widths and subject to varying degrees and depths of sub-division. At the east end the arrangement was more complicated, with shorter sub-divided plots facing both streets and others facing All Hallows' Square. Doharty's map of 1741 suggests that the group of tenements on the corner of Newport Street and All Hallows' Square had encroached forwards onto the open space, matching the island encroachments of minute premises on the slope below All Saints' church. The strange orientation of the frontage here is likely to parallel the course of the *burh* defences on the slope across the square.

The plot-pattern on the south side of Newport Street was very largely destroyed without record by the construction of Bridge Street in 1771–80 (Whitehead 1982). The fragmentary boundaries surviving in the nineteenth century at the west end of Newport Street curved strongly south-east, as if to bring the plot-tails parallel to the waterfront. An explanation for this is not immediately apparent, though it may represent the result of successive westward reclamation and terracing. This pattern would not give rearward waterfront access to more than a very few plots, and contrasts with areas in other towns on the Severn where plot-patterns developed that provided river access to large numbers of industrial and mercantile tenements (Baker, Lawson, Maxwell and Smith, 1993). The industrial character of All Saints' parish (largely Newport Street and its surroundings) was however well established by the fourteenth century, when it was populated by tanners, dyers and fullers (Barron 1989, 12). The plots on the north side of Dolday were, in 1886, generally parcels of land of squarish proportions, intensively subdivided on the frontage and occupied by densely packed court housing to the rear. The plots were of varying depths, those towards the east end of the street separated by back-lands from the city wall, though a number of primary boundaries may be observed passing from the frontage through to the wall. Property in this area was acquired by the Dominicans in 1391 (Hughes 1986, 13).

The most obvious question regarding this part of the city is why there should be two streets giving access to the river crossing: what was the relationship between them? There seem to be three possible answers. The first is that the site of the crossing shifted. The medieval bridge at the bottom of Newport Street which was demolished in the eighteenth century had been built in 1313–28 (Beardsmore 1980, 61–2). It is not known for certain whether this bridge was, in reality, a rebuilding of the existing bridge first recorded in 1088, or a new structure on a different site. A rebuilding is more likely, given that the site of the bridgehead on the west bank must have been fixed by the Causeway. An alternative model might be that the bridge replaced or supplemented a diagonal ford, but while there is some evidence for a ford in the Newport Street area there is none known further north (Carver 1980, 19–20). The most likely explanation is implicit in later medieval deeds showing a great difference in character and status between Newport Street and Dolday, the former being a fully built-up commercial street, the latter a sparsely occupied back-lane (Currie 1989a). Newport Street was the straight, principal approach-road and Dolday a service lane at the rear of its northern plots. St Clement's church – dating apparently from the mid eleventh century – stood at the bottom of Dolday, a less imposing public site than one on Newport or by the bridge would have been. Whether the location was determined by the circumstances of this church's proprietorial origins, or reflected an association with the quay, is unclear (see below, pp. 207–10).

PLAN-UNIT II.8: COPENHAGEN STREET

The core-area of this plan-unit is represented by the central part of Copenhagen Street, the western and central part of Fish Street, and the area to the south of Fish Street backing onto Palace Yard. Much of this area was destroyed in the 1920s by the construction of Deansway, but the street-plan and plot-pattern can be reconstructed from the usual sources. Copenhagen Street (formerly Huckster Street or Cooken Street) was the principal access to the Quay from the High Street and the central-southern part of the city. Fish Street runs on a course not quite parallel to it, 50–60 metres to the south, bending northwards at its junction with the High Street opposite St Helen's church. Whereas Copenhagen Street gave access directly to the waterfront, Fish Street stopped at Little Fish Street, the southern extension of Birdport; access from there to the river was down Warmstry Slip, a short distance to the north. The line of Little Fish Street continued southwards from the staggered junction at St Alban's church as Palace Row, where it met the northern boundary of the bishop's palace and Palace Yard.

   The Ordnance Survey and Young's map of 1779 show the plot-pattern in the core area to have been of a regular appearance, generally formed by properties with straight boundaries perpendicular to Copenhagen Street and Fish Street. The tails of the plots on the north side of Copenhagen Street were deflected slightly westwards, following the grain of Birdport and the natural topography. By the late eighteenth century the western plots ended against narrow properties fronting the alley which became known as Bull Entry; those to the east ended against a wedge-shaped property in the angle of Bull Entry and the High Street. The boundary between this property and those on Copenhagen Street was followed by the parish boundary. No evidence survives of their earlier arrangement, though it is probable that Bull Entry represents the original, more regular back-fence line to the Copenhagen Street plots. By the late nineteenth century the finer details of these had been destroyed by a hair-cloth manufactory.

   The plots on the south side of Copenhagen Street had straight north–south boundaries, several of which passed through to Fish Street. However, Young's map shows that the majority of plots stopped short, ending against a narrow band of housing on Fish Street without differentiated boundaries other than a straight back-fence at the eastern end parallel to Copenhagen Street. The latter was clearly the more important street and, behind its frontage, ancillary buildings stretched down the plots nearly all the way to Fish Street. The plots on the south side of Fish Street, similarly, had straight north–south boundaries passing through the block to Palace Yard; the frontage buildings faced Fish Street, with very little development of the plot-tails and southern frontage, even by the 1880s.

To the west of Little Fish Street, the eastern part of the street-block between Copenhagen Street and Warmstry Slip shared the basic characteristics of the core area, consisting as it did of straight-sided north–south plots running between the two streets. Young's map shows that in this block too, Copenhagen Street was the more important, with the frontage buildings mostly facing north, though with irregular development also on Warmstry Slip. By the 1880s, most of the plots here had been amalgamated to form St Alban's Square. The plots further west on the steep gradient down to the river were much more irregular and had more in common with those on the opposite side of Copenhagen Street (and have been treated as part of that area).

Sub-unit II.8.ii: the High Street (south-west)   The north–south plots in the core area of the plan-unit abutted plots facing eastwards onto the High Street. The rear boundary of the Guildhall plot formed the east boundary of the end-plot on the north side of Copenhagen Street, on which it was perpendicularly aligned. Between Copenhagen Street and Fish Street is a series of High Street plots, most of which average about 145 feet (*c.* 45 metres) deep, ending against a straight north–south back-fence line that similarly forms the side boundary of one of the Copenhagen Street plots. The northern end of this line also carried the parish boundary between St Helen's and St Alban's. St Helen's church itself occupies the southernmost plot in the High Street series, with one small tenement apparently cut out between the church and the next primary boundary to the north. The Ordnance Survey shows the churchyard sharing the straight north–south back-fence line with the adjoining plots, as it does today. Young's map is ambiguous, implying deeper High Street plots and no clear boundary to the rear of the church. The northern three plots in the series, as shown by the Ordnance Survey, were only half as deep as those to the south, probably having lost their rear halves to short plots facing Copenhagen Street. The junction between the Fish Street plots and those facing the High Street to the east is much more irregular. The Fish Street plot-series ended, in the 1880s, about 120–130 feet (*c.* 38–40 metres) west of the High Street. The eastern plots in the series seem to have lost ground to a garden behind a large house lying behind the High Street frontage.

This plan-unit, from the cartographic evidence alone, appears to possess some characteristics that might suggest that it had originated in a planned urban development, though the destruction of much of its core area since the nineteenth century rules out the possibility of supporting data from metrological field survey. The area was dominated by the two east–west streets, Copenhagen Street and Fish Street, which are nearly parallel to each other and perpendicular to the southern half of the High Street; they converge slightly towards the west to conform to the natural topography. Palace Yard to the south may once have been similar, in that there is some possibility that the bishop's palace enclosure has encroached northwards from an earlier position, possibly from a continuation of the line of Lich Street. If this were the case, before its diversion, the predecessor of Palace Yard would have been roughly parallel to the other streets, again converging slightly towards the west. Another possible east–west thoroughfare or perhaps just a boundary may be found in the line of Bull Entry, probably the original termination of the plots on the north side of Copenhagen Street. Bull Entry, Copenhagen Street, Fish Street and Palace Yard may therefore all be elements of the same system, forming a simple three-block grid distorted to fit the westward curve of the High Street and the natural site (figs 6.14 and 6.15).

There were irregularities in this street-system: the staggered junction by St Alban's church, and the abrupt northward deflection of Fish Street by St Helen's at its junction with the High Street. The northward deflection of Fish Street opposite St Helen's could be attributable to northward encroachment into Copenhagen street at the High Street corner, particularly if there was once an open churchyard around St Helen's. If this possibility is entertained and the line of

Fish Street continued eastwards in a straight line, the resulting junction with the High Street would lie precisely mid-way between Copenhagen Street, 74 metres to the north, and the end of the High Street, the same distance to the south. The southern side of Bull Entry was also about 76 metres north along the High Street frontage from Copenhagen Street. What these measurements suggest is that these streets were indeed probably laid out as a unitary system, a simple grid based on three or four east–west streets, covering an area of about 6.5 acres (2.6 hectares) on the west side of the High Street.

Excavated evidence gives support to the hypothesis that the landscape of this area was deliberately shaped over a short period of time. The Roman defences, a wide ditch and rampart, ran through the area immediately to the north of St Helen's, St Alban's and Warmstry Slip. A 'brushwood causeway' found crossing the lower fills of the ditch in Peter Gelling's (1958) excavations west of St Alban's seems most likely to represent a phase in the life of the Birdport–Palace Row route. The line of the defences is, however, completely unrepresented in the later landscape of the area, except in so far as it apparently influenced the siting of these churches, both of which, together with the lost church of St Margaret, may be considered pre-urban foundations. If such a major obstacle had remained in place when the area was being built up, it would be odd if it had not influenced the formation of the topography of the area, affecting the lines followed by property boundaries or by the streets. That it did not suggests that the defences were not allowed merely to decay by neglect – that and the simple fact that they no longer exist in relief. It

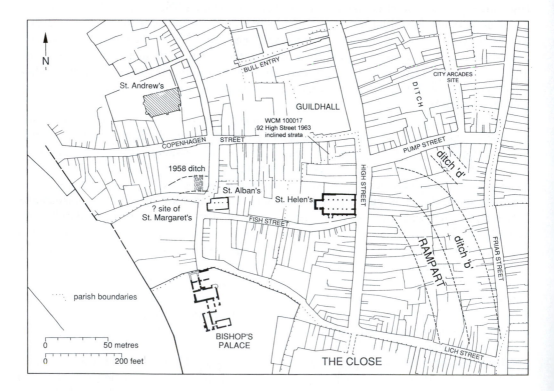

6.14   Worcester: the Copenhagen Street–Friar Street area, based on the first edition Ordnance Survey plans, showing the location of the underlying former defences (after Barker, Gelling, Jackson and others)

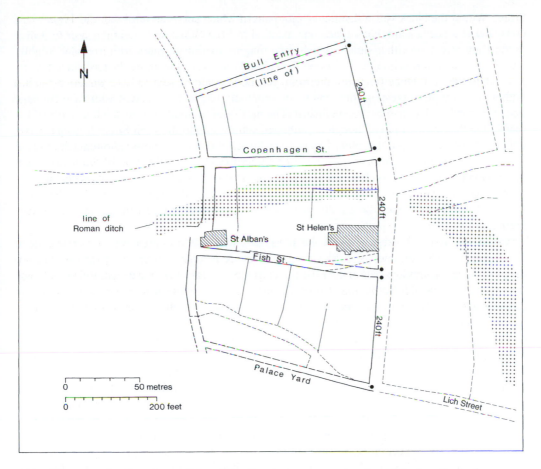

6.15   Worcester: the Copenhagen Street–Friar Street area, a reconstruction of the hypothesised
        planned street grid, with principal measurements

suggests that they were levelled by the time settlement began, most plausibly as a prelude to
further activity – in modern terminology, as the groundworks for an urban redevelopment. This
idea is supported by the sequence of ditch-fills excavated by Gelling in the 1950s, the primary
slow-silting and the causeway being covered by 'back-filling containing layers of marl, sand, loam
and slag, with Roman pottery' (Gelling 1958; Carver 1980, 302); no medieval pottery was seen,
so the back-filling may well have taken place in a period before common medieval pottery types
– such as eleventh–twelfth-century cooking pots – were in general circulation. Modern property
developers would also acknowledge the potential of the area thus reclaimed, linking the city's
principal street and market with the waterfront.

PLAN-UNIT II.9: THE HIGH STREET (SOUTH)

Morphologically, this area was entirely dissimilar to the previous plan-unit, but archaeologically
there were close parallels. The plan-unit, at least in its late- and post-medieval state, was defined
by clear boundaries: the rear of the Pump Street plots, Friar Street, Lich Street and the High

Street. Within the block was a distinctive plot-pattern which survived until the mid 1960s. This consisted of a north–south back-fence line, parallel to Friar Street and slightly nearer to it than to the High Street, on either side of which were roughly rectilinear plots with irregular, slightly wavering boundaries. While many longitudinal boundaries were shown by the Ordnance Survey to reach to the back-fence line from the frontages, none could be said to have passed through it without deflection, suggesting the separate development of plots associated with each frontage once the dividing line had been established. The north–south dividing line stopped short of the rear of the Pump Street plots, though it continued southwards to the Lich Street frontage. Here, either side of it, were similar plots facing Lich Street, the deepest plots adjoining the central dividing line. At the southern end of the High Street frontage the direction of the longitudinal property boundaries changed from the prevailing orientation to that of Lich Street, with a wedge-shaped tenement (Newdix Court) at the junction. By the 1880s all the plots in this block had been subjected to intensive irregular subdivision, with cottage developments in rear courts being a particular feature of the Friar Street plots.

Given the apparent irregularity of the plots, to claim that this area was a planned urban development would seem perverse. Metrological evidence is largely absent, with the exception of the plots along the northern half of the Friar Street frontage. These were measured, and no evidence of regularity was found. But like the Copenhagen Street area, archaeological investigation during redevelopment showed that this landscape was superimposed over the flattened Roman defences, here consisting of the ditch 'b' 90 feet (*c.* 27 metres) wide with a large earth rampart, curving diagonally across the street-block and out under Friar Street (Barker 1969, 44–62; figs 6.14 and 6.15). If such a substantial earthwork had been left to weather naturally, it would have persisted in the landscape and must surely have had some detectable influence; yet the only sign of it is a slight eastward bulge in the line of Friar Street. This again suggests a deliberate levelling campaign, a major piece of work that only makes sense as reclamation prior to redevelopment. Of the surrounding streets, only the High Street is likely to pre-date the proposed reclamation and re-development, and may, within the defences, be of Roman origin: Barker (1969, 50–51) noted the narrowing of the ditch near the north-west corner of the street-block, and suspected the presence of a gate; metalling with Roman characteristics was also found beneath the High Street at this point. Friar Street is likely to have been of late pre-Conquest origin, given its – at least partial – super-imposition over the Roman ditch, and also over Barker's ditch 'd', which it has already been suggested is likely to represent a continuation of the ditch found on the City Arcades site in 1999 and part of the *burh* perimeter. There is no direct evidence for the origin of Lich Street, though its line west of the High Street has been interpreted as part of the redevelopment of the reclaimed defences there. Here too, Lich Street cuts across and certainly post-dates the Roman defences (which approach it with no sign of narrowing for a gate), and appears to have been another component of the replanning process following the levelling of major earthwork defences that were evidently felt to be obsolete. Lich Street may have been planned as a replacement for the east–west Roman road excavated by Carver and Sawle under Sidbury and suggested earlier to have led to a gate opposite the present east end of the cathedral. In summary, we seem to have here another town-planning episode that not only followed the levelling of the Roman defences but also those now thought to be part of the *burh* as well. Lich Street was one of the components of this episode, which arguably included the reorganization of the north side of the cathedral close where again the defences have been levelled and replaced.

PLAN-UNIT II.10: FRIAR STREET AND NEW STREET

New Street (formerly Glover Street), Friar Street's northern extension, stands out from the other city streets in its easterly divergence from the prevailing north–south orientation. Arguably outside the constraints of the *burh* perimeter, it was free to adopt a course best suited for taking traffic from the south and south-east, via Sidbury, by-passing the centre, to link up with the main road from the Droitwich direction, represented by medieval Lowesmoor.

The plot-pattern associated with New Street and Friar Street can be divided into three areas; the plots occupying the block between Lich Street and Pump Street have been dealt with as part of a separate plan-unit (see above). Further north along the western frontage between Pump Street and Mealcheapen Street, the first edition Ordnance Survey shows a number of short, wide plots ending against the back-fence of the Shambles plot-series. At some points plots fronting the Shambles have broken through to the New Street frontage. The frontages of the wide, block-like New Street plots were intensively subdivided by the time cartographic evidence becomes available. The east side of New Street and Friar Street are rather different, with tenements of various proportions, again with subdivided frontages, and straight primary boundaries running from the frontage to the medieval city wall at the rear. Medieval deeds for properties in this area invariably use the city wall as one of the boundaries but it cannot be said with certainty that these properties therefore post-date the city wall. The ditch beyond made use of and canalized the Frog Brook and it is not impossible that the tenements originally took this as their back-boundary and suffered marginal truncation with the construction of the city wall.

With the exception of the area destroyed by the Lichgate Development in the 1960s, Friar Street and New Street have escaped large-scale redevelopment and the traditional plot-pattern remains largely intact, with a large number of surviving sub-medieval timber-framed buildings. The frontage widths of the plots were measured. Although some plots were laid out in perch-based units, there was no evidence of regular planning throughout the street, and settlement would appear to have been on a piecemeal basis. There is little dating evidence for the chronology of settlement on these streets. The foundation of the Franciscan friary here in the early thirteenth century with its long unexploited frontage need not imply that the land was unoccupied, but might instead suggest that property here was relatively cheap and not in great demand. Towards the south the Friar Street plot-series is continued down Sidbury and there occupation is datable from as early as the tenth century; however, while Sidbury may be considered a major early approach road to the city and to the cathedral, the same cannot be said of the northern section of Friar Street or of New Street, both of which may have been built up much more slowly and appear to be a later component of the town-plan.

The origins of Friar Street and New Street appear to lie in the post-*burh* period, in that the ditch ('d'), excavated by Barker and now thought to represent part of the circuit in use by 900, intersects with Friar Street and runs under it – a relationship confirmed by the identification of the ditch close to the Friar Street frontage in a watching-brief by Charles Mundy in 1993 (City SMR site, WCM 100632). Friar Street may have had a prehistory as a narrow track skirting the outer edge of the ditch, but as a street in the form in which we know it today it must post-date the infilling of the ditch, and it forms the eastern side of the redevelopment episode that followed (plan-unit II.9, above).

The Franciscan friary   Around 1226 a Franciscan friary was founded on the east side of the street, and in 1231 the friars received permission to make a postern gate through the city wall, enlarging it in 1246 (Beardsmore 1980, 62). The friary site is now represented by Nos 11–15 Friar Street, a frontage of about 278 feet (85 metres). Little is known of the internal arrangements other than that, in the sixteenth century, the frontage was occupied by a stone wall pierced by a gate giving access to a lane leading to the postern. At the northern end of the site was a large hall with an oriel window: this survived the Dissolution and was finally demolished in 1822; the arrangement of the church and claustral buildings are unknown, but they stood on a separate plot of land outside the wall. Institutional use of parts of the site persisted long after the Dissolution. The Corporation used friary buildings outside the wall for a pest-house in the seventeenth century, and in 1724 they rented the hall at the north end of the intramural plot for use as the city gaol. A purpose-built gaol replaced it in 1822. This was turned into an almshouse in 1867 and remained in use until 1912, when new almshouses were built; these remain today (Hughes and Molyneux 1984, 8–9).

PLAN-UNIT II.11: SIDBURY (INTRAMURAL)

In the medieval period Sidbury gave access to the city from the south and the south-east; beyond the medieval gate lay the junction of major routes to London, Gloucester and the lower Severn valley. Sidbury is a post-Roman street. Excavations at 23–9 Sidbury located a Roman road orientated north-west–south-east, possibly associated with an entrance through the Roman

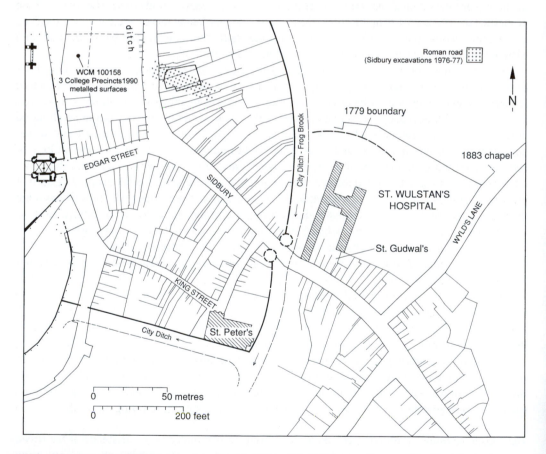

6.16   Worcester: the Sidbury area: based on the first edition Ordnance Survey, showing principal archaeological features and St Wulfstan's Hospital (the Commandery)

defences to the east of the present cathedral (Carver 1980, 161–3). The course of the Roman road eastwards from the excavated area is unknown but it may well, over a short distance, have run roughly parallel to Sidbury and into the area occupied by St Wulfstan's Hospital beyond the city wall. Beyond the Frog Brook it would probably have avoided the steepest gradients of Fort Royal Hill and been deflected to follow London Road, Sidbury's extramural extension, recorded as a *straete* in a charter of 983x985 (H 156–7, 359; S 1361; Hooke 1980, 43).

The earliest post-Roman activity identified by the excavation took the form of a series of pre-Conquest pits, probably of tenth–eleventh-century date, though conceivably of the ninth, aligned approximately along the later tenements'. The evidence was unfortunately insufficient to prove that the mapped and surviving property boundaries were in place at this time; it was not until the fourteenth century that the tenement divisions were unambiguously reflected by the excavated features (Carver 1980, 165). The archaeological evidence of pre-Conquest secular occupation is consistent with the documentary evidence for the existence, by the late tenth century, of both the church of St Peter the Great and the chapel of St Gudwal (see below, pp. 211, 215): the sources point to Sidbury – *suthan byrig* – developing as a distinct suburb outside the south wall of the *burh* in the middle years of the tenth century.

The tenement pattern in this area was distinctive, the property boundaries on the north side of the street in particular exhibiting a noticeable eastward curve towards the Frog Brook. The same feature was apparent on the south side, but to a much less marked extent, and may not be significant. Two possible interpretations can be offered. The first and most plausible is that the plots were laid out in this way to give them all access to the running water of the Frog Brook, probably for industrial purposes, before they were separated from it by the construction of the city wall; the same arrangement can be found in riverside situations in a number of other towns and elsewhere in both Worcester and Gloucester (Baker, Lawson, Maxwell and Smith, 1993; see above, p. 79). The second, and less probable, explanation arises from the observation that the curving line of one of the north-side plot boundaries appears to have been continued beyond the city wall and the Frog Brook by the pre-Victorian northern boundary of St Wulfstan's Hospital precinct: a curving boundary there – a hedge or ditch – is very clearly shown on Young's map of 1779 (see fig. 6.16). This is most easily explained as an accidental coincidence, but given the probable early foundation of St Gudwal's chapel on the hospital site frontage, the possible presence of some sort of enclosure, even one that straddled the Frog Brook (and was thus bisected by the medieval city wall) should not be dismissed completely.

Sub-unit II.11.ii: King Street   The principal arm of King Street runs parallel to Sidbury about 200 feet (*c*. 60 metres) to the south; it returns north-east to the main street as St Peter's Street. The streets survive but the church of St Peter and the surrounding plot-pattern have been destroyed and replaced by car parks. The north side of King Street was formerly occupied by slightly curved plots created by the sub-division of the Sidbury plot-tails. The plots on the south side of the street, a mixture of narrow plots and much wider plots, all crammed with cottages within courts, backed onto the city wall. As St Peter's church was established by the mid-tenth century it is likely that one or perhaps both arms of the street were in use by this time to give access to the church from the main road. King Street, parallel to Sidbury, is an obvious candidate to be considered as a planned rear service lane associated with the deliberate laying out of the plots on the south side of Sidbury. This seems the most likely explanation of its origin, though this archaeologically unexplored corner of the city could have some surprises in store – such as, for instance, an alternative early approach to the cathedral area via a ford across the Frog Brook.

The suburbs

Plan-region III: the east bank suburbs

INTRODUCTION: THE MEDIEVAL CITY DEFENCES

Before turning to the extramural built-up areas, it may be useful to briefly review the historical and archaeological evidence for the medieval defences that separated them from the areas already described; much of this information has already been collected and synthesized by Beardsmore (1980). Although the course of the late-medieval city wall is known in some detail, archaeological investigation of it has been almost entirely restricted to the east side of the city; and the question of undocumented predecessors following the same line still, in places, remains open.

The three principal medieval gates (North, St Martin's and Sidbury) were all recorded for the first time in the second half of the twelfth century, and there is circumstantial evidence for an effective circuit by 1216. Murage grants suggest periods of intensive wall-building activity in 1224–39, in 1252–1310 and 1364–1411 (Beardsmore 1980, 58–63). These periods of activity have yet to be correlated in detail with the known structural remains. Excavations in the Greyfriars area to the east of Friar Street located a thirteenth-century (or later) bank built on cultivation soil and cut by the foundations of the city wall from the fourteenth century or later; results consistent with these also came from excavations further south, between the Greyfriars and Sidbury Gate (Carver 1980, 8). At only one site, a short distance south of St Martin's Gate, has a probable defensive feature thought to have been found substantially earlier: this was the ditch, containing sherds of 'early-medieval' pottery, overlain by the city wall (Bennett 1980); this may have been a local feature associated with the Mealcheapen Street suburb. Excavations in the Blackfriars area on the north side of the city located a bank and quarry-ditch of the Civil War period just within the wall-line (Mundy 1989, 34).

Beyond the city wall was a substantial ditch. This was sectioned at a point between the Greyfriars and St Martin's Gate, and found to have been flat-bottomed and over 30 feet (*c.* 10 metres) wide, with no evidence of recutting in the Civil War, although the documentary evidence suggested that there should have been (Barker 1969, 102–3). Broad's map of 1768 shows the ditch generally free from encroachment, except for the north-east quarter between Foregate and St Martin's Gate. This part is known to have been subject to encroachments within the Middle Ages, particularly as the stretch between Foregate and Lowesmoor provided a valuable short-cut between those streets (see below).

PLAN-UNIT III.1: FOREGATE STREET AND THE TYTHING

This was the medieval city's most extensive suburb, a linear settlement along the principal approach-road from the north and east, extending for a distance of about 600 metres from the north gate. The suburb can be subdivided into four main areas. The west side of the street is characterized by short rectilinear plots backing onto a rear access lane *c.* 100–170 feet (*c.* 30 to 50 metres) to the west. Most longitudinal plot boundaries run straight through from the frontage to the rear lane, where secondary development has taken place on the plot-tails. By 1741 the southernmost plots had almost doubled in depth, taking over land beyond the rear access lane and encroaching over it.

The east side of the street is different, many of the plots ending at back-fence lines *c.* 115–150 feet (*c.* 35–45 metres) from the frontage, with some longitudinal boundaries running through to

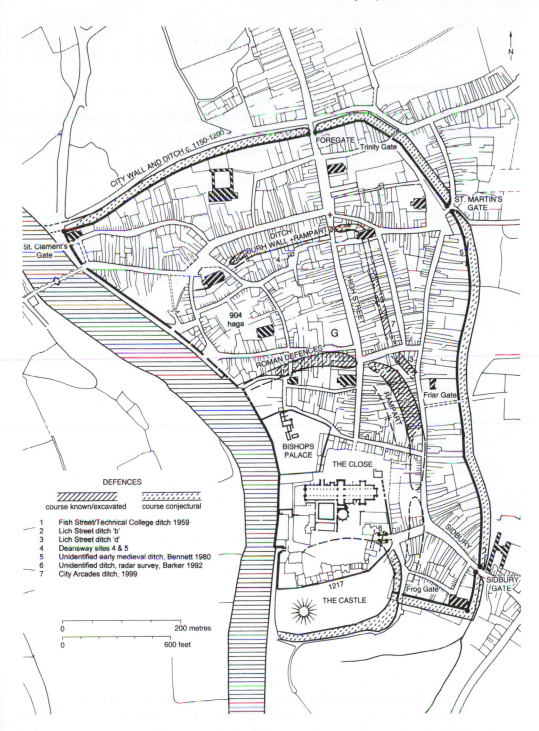

Labels within the figure:

N

CITY WALL AND DITCH c. 1150-1200

FOREGATE
Trinity Gate

ST. MARTIN'S GATE

St. Clement's Gate

DITCH
BURH WALL +RAMPART
4

HIGH STREET

904 haga

G

5

ROMAN DEFENCES

3

RAMPART

Friar Gate

BISHOPS PALACE

THE CLOSE

SIDBURY

6

1217

THE CASTLE

Frog Gate

SIDBURY GATE

DEFENCES

course known/excavated   course conjectural

1 Fish Street/Technical College ditch 1959
2 Lich Street ditch 'b'
3 Lich Street ditch 'd'
4 Deansway sites 4 & 5
5 Unidentified early medieval ditch, Bennett 1980
6 Unidentified ditch, radar survey, Barker 1992
7 City Arcades ditch, 1999

0 ————— 200 metres
0 ————— 600 feet

6.17   Worcester: an archaeological summary plan of major defensive features around and underlying the medieval city

Sansome Walk, an access lane about 360 feet (*c.* 110 metres) to the rear. The depth of the frontage-plots here mirrors that of the plots across the street. Between Sansome Walk and the frontage-plots were larger rectangular parcels of ground that probably represent contemporary garden crofts. In the modern period the more extensive plots available on the east side of the street attracted institutional and larger commercial occupants, the nineteenth-century Shire Hall and Public Library for example, in contrast to the west side where medium- and small-scale commercial premises still predominate. There is also some distinction to be made between the northern half (the Tything) and the southern half (Foregate Street) of the suburb. The plot-pattern recorded in 1886, and still largely intact, shows that the Tything, beyond the city boundary, was characterized by more intensively subdivided plots, occupied by smaller buildings, than the area within. This is particularly obvious on the west side of the street, but to a lesser extent also applies to the east side.

St Oswald's Hospital and the Priory of Whistones   At the far end of the suburb stood two medieval institutions: the hospital of St Oswald, of obscure origin though probably a twelfth-century foundation, and next door the nunnery of Whiteladies (the Priory of Whistones), founded between 1237 and 1255. St Oswald's hospital is first referred to in *c.* 1200 by Gervase of Canterbury, and then again in 1268 when William de Beauchamp bequeathed ten shillings to its infirm residents. Another bequest was made to the 'brothers of St Oswald' in 1291, and in 1296 William de Molendiniis – also a substantial benefactor of St Wulfstan's Hospital – died before he could complete the church he was building for St Oswald's (Molyneux 1981; Edwards 1992). The dedication was entirely appropriate to a foundation on the bishop of Worcester's manor, and the foundation itself may well have been episcopal. Small-scale excavation on the site found moulded masonry fragments of Romanesque character (Morris, in Edwards 1992, 188). Possibly the foundation of the hospital was contemporary with the establishment of the suburb, or may have taken place in its earliest years. The nunnery of Whiteladies was founded by Bishop Walter Cantilupe (1237–65) on a site adjoining the north side of St Oswald's cemetery. Never richly endowed, and despite gifts and bequests of lands and tithes in the thirteenth and fourteenth centuries, it was often in financial difficulties (*VCH Worcs.*, ii, 154–6).

The layout of the medieval hospital is almost completely obscure – particularly so since excavations near its present southern boundary showed that the present and previous post-Reformation courtyard plans probably bear no relation at all to the layout of the medieval buildings. The excavations encountered the end of a substantial late-medieval masonry building aligned approximately north-west to south-east, the present ranges being more nearly east–west, perpendicular to the street. The excavated building had decayed and been robbed in the sixteenth century, at a time when the hospital avoided suppression by leasing out its property, but suffered neglect and despoliation at the hands of unscrupulous lay leaseholders (Edwards 1992; Hughes 1980, 274–6). More is known about its cemetery, which was extensive, and covered a large area of ground up to the site's eastern boundary: it had been used by the city in 1349 and during other epidemics (see below, p. 243) and was later to be used as an overspill burial ground by city churches with inadequate churchyards.

The planning of the Whiteladies' nunnery is equally obscure. There are few records of the nunnery's internal workings, order or buildings, save for a well-known account of the election of a prioress in 1349, which mentions a chapter house. The thirteenth-century chapel survives, built over a vaulted undercroft, and in the eighteenth century Valentine Green described what he thought was the refectory 'nearly in its primitive state, a spacious and handsome apartment'. This is probably identifiable with part of the present house (now a school) on the site, what was in the nineteenth century a kitchen, with a panelled chamber above (Goodrich 1994; Green 1796, i,

241–2; Lees 1866, 355–64). To the north of the chapel (shown in fig. 6.4) was the convent's cemetery and, beyond that, a fish-pond and tithe barn.

These religious houses together occupied a block of land nearly 300 metres long at the outer end of the suburb. The 'White Stane' cross which gave its name to the nunnery and, according to Valentine Green (1796, i, 242), once stood somewhere in the vicinity, may once have marked the beginning of the bishops' suburb, giving the nunnery a classic peripheral-suburban setting. The common eastern boundary to both institutions was a field boundary that continued the line of the service lane, Sansome Walk, northwards, suggesting that St Oswald's and the adjoining nunnery were probably established within the plot-system or the framework to accommodate it, and that they subsequently encroached over the lane.

Discussion   There is little doubt that this extensive suburb originated as a single design, as a planned episode of urban expansion. This is clear from the provision of parallel rear service lanes to both series of plots, and by the more or less equal depth of the frontage-plots on each side of the street. It might be argued that the difference between the simple plot-series on the west side and the combined frontage-plots and garden crofts on the east side indicates that they were developed at different dates. However, the common depth of the frontage-plots suggests that they were laid out as part of the same scheme; furthermore, there are examples elsewhere of what appear to be unitary planned developments with provision for a mixture of plot-types, presumably to cater for a wide spectrum of prospective settlers with varied mixtures of craft, trading, horticultural and livestock-related interests. A metrological survey was carried out where enough of the traditional plot-pattern survived for the plot frontages to be measured, but the results were inconclusive. At least the inner part of the suburb was razed in the Civil War – 'burnt by the Cavaliers' – and the rest was badly damaged (Hughes 1980, 288); such an event would be likely to have left the framework of streets and lanes intact but may well have resulted in the reorganization of cleared plots and the loss of any original regulated system of land division.

There is no direct documentary or archaeological dating evidence for the foundation of this suburb, though circumstantial evidence points to an early post-Conquest origin and a close association with the church of St Nicholas, a probable foundation of the later eleventh century (see below, pp. 213–14). The southern half of the suburb lay within St Nicholas's parish, the northern half in that of Claines, though the suburb's inhabitants worshipped at the chapel in St Oswald's Hospital. St Nicholas's church in Gloucester, similarly, served the post-Conquest suburb on Westgate Island. Superficially, the Foregate Street/Tything suburb appears to post-date the medieval city defences, the service lanes on either side ending at the lane following the outer edge of the city ditch. But as discussed earlier, unless the suburb was laid out after the late twelfth century, it is probable that it was bisected by the construction of the defences some time after its inception, leaving the Cross and Foregate within the walls. If this is what happened, one possibility is that the service lanes originally led to Gaol Lane (St Nicholas' Street) east of the High Street and Angel Lane to the west (see fig. 14.6).

PLAN-UNIT III.2: SILVER STREET

Silver Street ran on a curving course northwards from St Martin's Gate to a right-angled junction with Lowesmoor, and before the demolition of the city wall was the principal entrance to the town from the Droitwich direction. The street itself now survives as an insignificant loop off the City Walls Road; the tenement pattern survives on its east side, in a highly degraded state, but has been destroyed on the west side. The cartographic evidence shows a series of short plots on the west side ending at Watercourse Alley, on the site of the medieval city ditch. On the east side the plots were larger and of more irregular outline, with a slight southwards curve to accommodate the angle between the street and St Martin's Gate. On the 1886 Ordnance Survey, the majority of the plots were about 130–180 feet (*c.* 40–55 metres) deep, but there was no common back-fence line to the whole series, blocks of two to four plots sharing shorter common rear boundaries. By 1886 the area to the rear of the eastern plots had largely been destroyed by the Worcester Vinegar Works, though several boundaries can be observed continuing eastwards into the industrialized areas beyond the boundaries at the rear of the housing. The explanation is provided by Young's map of 1779 which shows a number of garden crofts, behind the street-plots, ending at a continuous north–south rear boundary running from the end of Lowesmoor to St Martin's Gate (the street), a line followed in part by the nineteenth-century St Martin's Street. Silver Street had an industrial character in the medieval and early-modern periods, characterized by activities such as tile-making and bell-founding.

PLAN-UNIT III.3: LOWESMOOR

This suburb, which takes its name from the badly drained ground in the area, stretched for a distance of about 200 metres from the city defences. Young's map depicts it very clearly as a widened street, narrowing abruptly at the point where the rear boundary of the Silver Street garden crofts meets it, and although this feature is not as marked in the modern landscape or on the nineteenth-century maps (probably due to the widening of the road beyond the boundary), it offers a clue to the development of the area. The suburb consisted of two separate components or sub-units, one each side of the street.

Sub-unit III.3.i: the north plot series   These plots are shown by Young's map and by the 1886 Ordnance Survey as subdivisions of fairly regular appearance within a back-fence line parallel to the street. This also carried the parish boundary between St Martin's and the extramural portion of St Nicholas's. A metrological survey undertaken in 1990 showed no signs of regularity in the frontage measurements: this may reflect post-medieval amalgamation and redivision (Young's 1779 map shows a carpet manufactory occupying the eastern plots), or the plots may have been individually developed without regulation.

Sub-unit III.3.ii: the south plot series   The cartographic evidence suggests that settlement on this side of the street was secondary to the establishment of the plots and garden crofts on Silver Street. The short Lowesmoor plots used one of the extended tenement-croft boundaries running at an angle to Lowesmoor as their back-fence line, with the result that the Lowesmoor plots to the west are much shorter than those to the east. The still-extant kink in the frontage about 190 feet (*c.* 60 metres) east from Silver Street marks the former back-fence line of the most northerly Silver Street plot, subdivided into short north-facing plots.

PLAN-UNIT III.4: SIDBURY EXTRAMURAL

Some aspects of the early development of the Sidbury area in general have already been covered in the context of the intramural street. The extramural suburb – an area cut off and excluded by the construction of the city wall, or later grew outside it – was of quite limited extent, with plots lining Sidbury and London Road, its south-eastern extension, for a distance of about 350 metres beyond the medieval gate. The plots were irregular, their shape conforming to the steep gradients and becoming smaller further out, towards the top of Fort Royal Hill. Bath Road, leading south-west towards Gloucester, was virtually undeveloped when mapped in the eighteenth century, and a similar extent of settlement is represented by Speed's map of 1610.

St Wulfstan's Hospital, the Commandery, occupied a precinct of about two acres (0.8 hectare) in the angle of Sidbury and Wyld's Lane, with the Frog Brook, canalized in the city ditch, forming its western boundary. The north boundary was, according to Young's map of 1779, a curving length of hedgerow or ditch (see also above). The fifteenth-century hospital buildings took the form of a double quadrangle set back behind shops on the frontage, and are discussed elsewhere in greater detail (below, pp. 323–4). The hospital used as a chapel the probable pre-Conquest church of St Gudwal, which stood on the Sidbury frontage (see below, pp. 215–17).

Somewhere to the rear of the hospital – not precisely located but *c.* 100 metres to the north – was what was said to have been another chapel with pre-Conquest features (possibly that recorded as St Catherine's), discovered by workmen digging foundations next to Wyld's Lane in 1883. They found the footings of an east–west stone building, measuring 25 feet by 16 feet (7.6 x 4.8 metres), the masonry courses of which were interspersed with 'thin layers of tiles' in the Roman tradition. Two skeletons were also found, one north–south, the other east–west, though these were inevitably interpreted as casualties from the adjacent Civil War battlefield (*Worcester Herald*, 17th February 1883). While the location close to the northern boundary of the hospital precinct is consistent with that of the documented chapel of St Catherine (Marsh 1890, 20n; Baker 1980b, 122), other possibilities – that it was actually a Roman building for example – need to be considered (and see below, p. 218).

Plan-region IV: the west-bank suburbs

Settlement on the west bank was essentially linear, extending westwards from the bridge along the floodplain causeway, up onto the gravel terrace and south-west along the road to Hereford. With each change in terrain the settlement character varied; four plan-units can be defined, one in the floodplain, one on the escarpment and one on each side of the road on the gravel terrace. Almost no archaeological excavation has taken place on this side of the river and the chronology of the built-up area is very uncertain. There are, however, a couple of documentary landmarks. First, settlement had begun by the late eleventh century, five houses 'across the Severn' being included in a list of the monks' urban property contained in Hemming's cartulary (H 290); second, the architecture of the church of St John in Bedwardine suggests that, although it did not then have parochial status, its congregation was sufficient to require at least a north aisle by the late twelfth century; parochial status finally came in 1371 by which time its rural predecessor (St Cuthbert's, Lower Wick) was virtually deserted (*VCH Worcs.*, iii, 501–2).

PLAN-UNIT IV.1: THE CAUSEWAY

As the name suggests, the axis of this zone, which was wholly within the floodplain, was the raised road approaching the medieval bridge. On Doharty's map it is labelled Causeway along the western, undeveloped stretch, and Turkey in the built-up area around the bridgehead. By the 1880s the whole street was known as Tybridge Street. The difference in level between the road surface and the surrounding land is clearly marked on the Buck brothers' eighteenth-century view of the city from the west; today, the difference has disappeared as completely as the rest of its historic landscape. This was inevitably doomed after the area was isolated by the removal of the bridge further downstream in the eighteenth century; industrialization was already a marked feature of the area by the 1880s, with tanneries on the north side of the road and a distillery to the south. While the tanning premises largely respected the existing plot boundaries, they were replaced in the twentieth century by a power station which removed the last traces of the medieval landscape.

The plot-pattern was irregular and is likely to have been created by a piecemeal process of reclamation and enclosure, possibly adapting pre-existing boundaries belonging to the local floodplain drainage. Whitehead (1979) drew attention to two thirteenth-century documents referring to the 'town ditch' and 'the King's ditch' in this area, a feature which cannot be identified from the cartography. It was suggested that this may have been a defensive feature enclosing the bridgehead, of the kind seen, for example, in Hereford and Bedford (Haslam 1983). However, as there is no trace of an enclosing defensive work in any of the cartographic sources, it is possible that the references were to boundary features that had a legal and jurisdictional significance but physically were no different from others in the area; the Barton Street suburb of Gloucester offers an example of this (see above, p. 93). The 1651 map of Worcester shows, in typically schematic form, a hexagonal defensive earthwork on the west bank of the river at the end of the bridge, though this has the appearance of a Civil War feature.

One distinctive feature of the plot-pattern on the south side of the Causeway was a long boundary with a pronounced eastward curve. There is no way of knowing whether this was an isolated feature or a relic of a more extensive system, but it appears to be related to the category of riverside settlement patterns characterized by plot-series curved towards the river to facilitate waterfront access at the back of the plots. These can be identified in areas that were built up and occupied by water-using crafts in the early-medieval period, but also in urban and suburban contexts where the grazing and watering of livestock was important (Baker, Lawson, Maxwell and Smith 1993; see pp. 79 and 187 above). Either case could apply here, though by the mid-thirteenth century the tail of the plot thus bounded was used by the cathedral priory as an orchard (pers. comm., Pat Hughes).

PLAN-UNIT IV.2: CRIPPLEGATE

Cripplegate was the name applied to the road from the bridge where it climbed the edge of the gravel terrace. The area was distinguished by an unusual arrangement of westwards curving property boundaries on the gradient either side of the road, probably formed as a result of different processes of partitioning larger land parcels, and accommodating plots to the gradient, and to the framework of streets and earlier boundaries.

PLAN-UNIT IV.3: ST JOHN'S (NORTH)

The plot-series to the west of Rosemary Lane was also strikingly irregular, with long, thin westwards curving tenements, intensively and in some cases eccentrically subdivided. The series occupies the top of the slope, and some of the frontage buildings are rather above the level of the street which has had a hollow-way effect, cutting into the gradient. The prevailing westward curve of the plot-tails is a reflection of the formative frame of Rosemary Lane. Its very narrow width in the built-up area belies its significance as part of an early, strategic north–south routeway following the edge of the gravel terrace along the west side of the river valley; it appears in a charter of 851 as the *folc hearpath* (H 416–18; S 201; Hooke 1980, 46). In view of this, its erratic course (followed by the parish and city boundary between St Clement's and St John's) through the built-up area both north and south of Cripplegate, is all the more surprising and demands an explanation. One possibility is that its course was determined by or diverted around a large earthwork enclosure – presumably of prehistoric date, if it existed. The outlines of the east and south sides of this possible earthwork are suggested first of all by the apparent eastward deflection of Rosemary Lane around the built-up plots on both the north and the south sides of the main road. A south side to this earthwork may be implicit in the curving footpath returning westwards to the south end of the St John's plots, accompanied by a second, parallel lane. It also happens that the footpath forms a substantial terrace on the slope, marking an abrupt change in ground level downwards to the south.

There is, it must be emphasized, currently no supporting archaeological evidence for such a monument, and no evidence of a west or north side on the flat ground of the gravel terrace. If this enclosure existed, it would have been about 350 metres north to south, straddled the main roads on the edge of the terrace and would have covered an area almost as large as the Roman defences across the river; the church of St John would fall more or less in its centre.

PLAN-UNIT IV.4: ST JOHN'S (SOUTH)

This area comprises two plot-series to the south of the road: a long eastern series ending against a straight back-fence line running north-east–south-west; and a western series of plots representing subdivisions of a triangular block in the angle of St John's and the east–west lane known as Powell's Row. The plots of the long eastern series are of fairly regular appearance, but no metrological work has been done to determine whether there was any degree of regulation in their layout. The seventeenth-century maps treat the whole of the western suburb very schematically and are of little use. In the eighteenth century, when cartographic evidence becomes available, the north side of St John's south of the church was not built up, apart from a single large house. There is no evidence available to indicate whether the medieval settlement was of similar extent.

The basic framework of roads through the township was established in or by the late pre-Conquest period, most of the approach roads being recorded in charters. Bromyard Road leading west from the north side of the churchyard appears as a *stræte* in 963, and Bransford Road, also leading west, with the long St John's Green on its south side, appears as *suth stræte* (lies at the junction of two roads each recorded as a *stræte* in 963) (H 133–5, 350–1; S 1303; Hooke 1980, 43–6). Malvern Road, the southern continuation of St John's towards Lower Wick, may be later – a replacement for the *folc hearpath* which rejoined it to the south as Bromwich Lane.

Plates

1 Medieval Worcester: a reconstruction model of the thirteenth-century intramural city

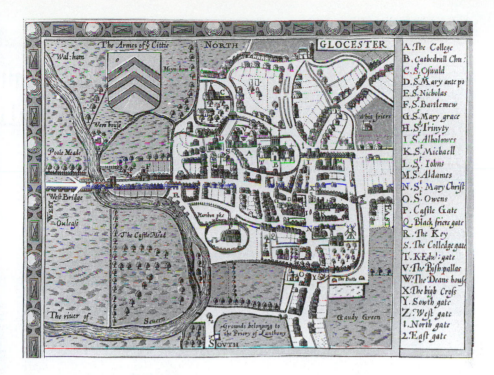

2   John Speed's map of Gloucester, 1610

3   The New Inn, Gloucester

4   Hall and Pinnell's map of the City of Gloucester, 1780 (Gloucestershire Record Office)

KINGSHOLM CLOSE

ster

STER

U
N
D
S

M O N K L E I G H T O N

LOWER NORTHGATE STREET

NORTHGATE STREET

FALLOW GROUND

BARTON HILL

STILE
ROUNDS

R. HALL AND T. PINNELL.

G.L.C.S 51(2)

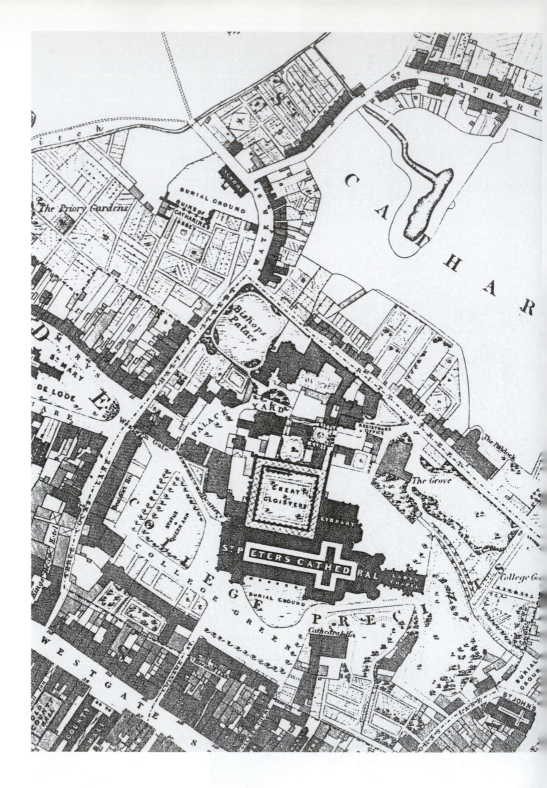

5   Arthur Causton's Map of the City and Borough of Gloucester from a survey of 1843. Sample extract at a reduced scale (Gloucestershire Record Office)

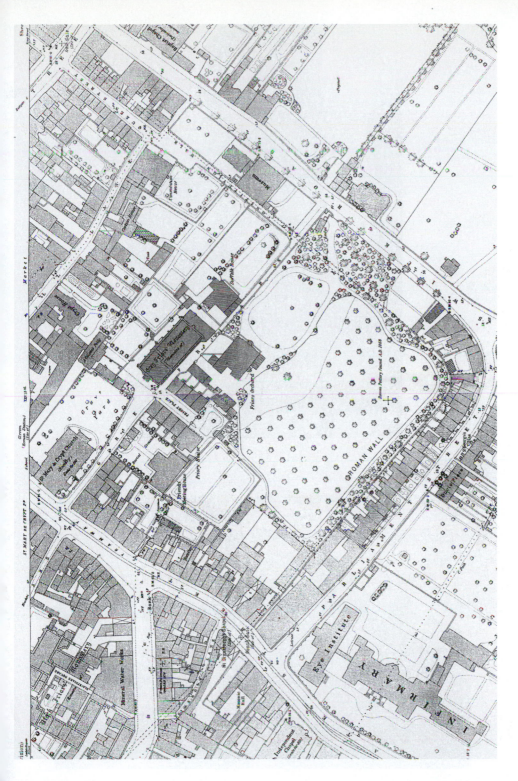

Ordnance Survey first edition 1:500 plan of Gloucester, published in 1884 (XXV.15.21). Sample extract at a reduced scale showing the south-east corner of the walled city

7   St Michael's, Gloucester

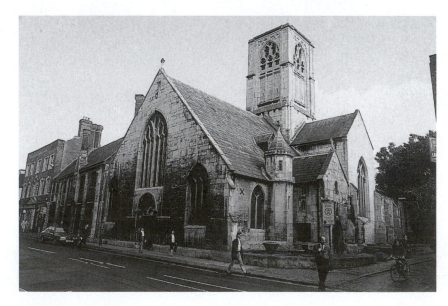

8   St Mary de Crypt, Gloucester

9   St Nicholas's, Gloucester

10   Air photograph of central Worcester in the late 1980s, looking west. The Deansway excavations are
in progress, centre right. (C F Mundy/Worcestershire County Council)

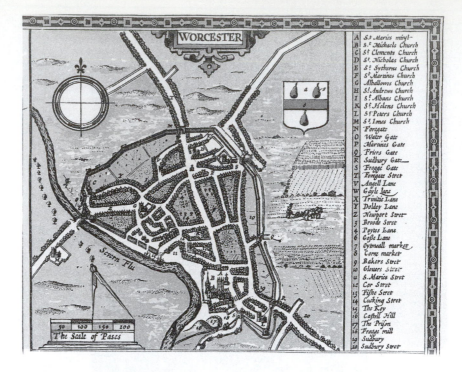

11   John Speed's map Worcester, 1610

12   St Helen's, Worcester. The bend in the line of the High Street marks the site of the gate through the Roman defences

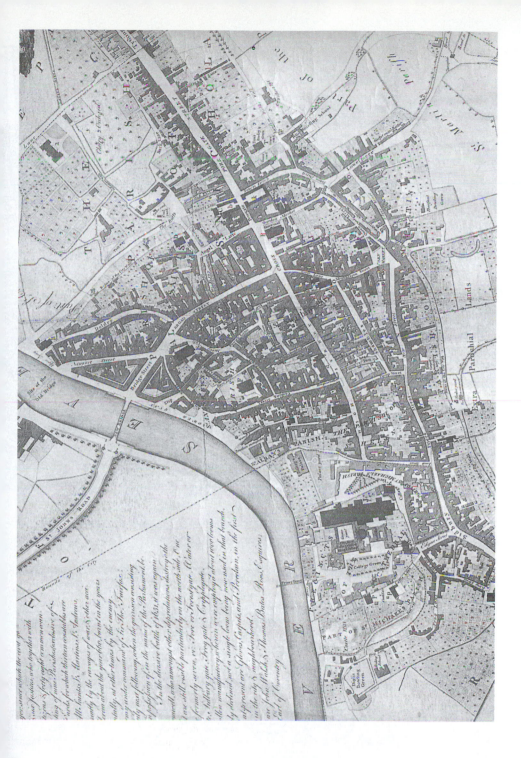

3   George Young's Plan of the City and Suburbs of Worcester, 1779 (Worcestershire County Record
Office)

14   John Doharty's Plan of the City of Worcester, 1741 (Worcestershire County Record Office)

Block house Fields

DIGLIS.

Meadows belonging to the Rev.d The Dean & CHAPTER of WORCESTER

A PLAN of the CITY of WORCESTER with References. J. Doharty Fec.t 1741.

1	The White Ladys	25	Angel Lane	49	Road to Cotheridge	73	New Street	97	St Peters Church	A	Cathedral (St Marys) College Precincts
2	St Oswalds Hospit.	26	Goal Lane	50	St Johns Church	74	Madams Vine	98	Church Street	B	The Deanary
3	The Tything	27	St Nicholas Church	51	Leven Street	75	Pump Street	99	Sidbury Gate	1	Prebendal House
4	Stewing Hospit.	28	The Trinity	52	All Saints Church	76	High Street	100	The Commandry	2	Prebendal house
5	The Liberty Post	29	Market Cross	53	Mercy Vale	77	Guild Hall	101	Union Lane	3	Prebendal house
6	Salt Lane	30	The Broad Street	54	Greyse Lane	78	St Helens Church	102	London Road	4	Prebendal house
7	Foster Lane	31	Little Angel Lane	55	Hounds Lane	79	Great Fish Street	103	Glocester Road	5	Prebendal house
8	Ingleborne Hospit.	32	Fryars Alley	56	Powykes Lane	80	St Albans Church	104	Fort Royal	6	Prebendal house
9	Foregate Street	33	Dolday	57	Bird Port	81	Wormstry Slip			7	Prebendal house
10	Town Ditch	34	Beast Market	58	Cooken Street	82	Leech Street	105	Bishops Pallace	8	Prebendal house
11	The Malt house	35	Newport Street	59	St Andrews Church	83	City Goal	106	The College Gates	9	Prebendal house
12	The Quakers Meet.	36	Beans Entry	60	The Key	84	Block House	107	College Church Yard	10	Prebendal house
13	Anabaptists Meet.	37	Seven Bridge	61	City Water Works	85	Wyatt Hospital	108	Leech Gate	B	The Library
14	Silver Street	38	St Clements Gate	62	Little Severn	86	Fryars Street	109	Old Tower	C	Cloysters & Garden
15	Lonye moor	39	St Clements Church	63	Goose Lane	87	Sidbury	110	St Michaels Church	D	College School
16	Blew-Coat hospit.	40	Turkey	64	The Dish Market	88	Knowles End	111	Talbot entry	E	College house
17	Bowling Green	41	Hinton Lane	65	St Swithins Church	89	Edgar Street	112	St Marys Steps	F	
18	City Work house	42	The Pound	66	The Shambles	90	Fog Lane	*	King Charles IIt	G	King Edgars Tower
19	Berkeleys Hospit.	43	Causeway	67	The Meal elengin	91	Digley Bowling G.		took Post and went	H	Register Office
20	Gardiners Lane	44	Cripple Gate	68	Corn Market	92	Castle Hill		to Robold after the	I	The College Green
21	The Butts	45	Rosemary Lane	69	St Martins Church	93	County Castle		Battle fought and	K	The Oven
22	Frightenan Meet.	46	SwanPost Lane	70	St Martins Gate	94	Bride well		lost Sep.t 3.d 1651	L	The Water Gate
23	Picks Cold Bath	47	St Johns	71	Queen Street	95	Castle Lane		when the entry	M	The Priory Post
24	Whites Par. Groab.	48	Road to Powyke	72	Nashes Hospital	96	Little King Street		Fryars Street	N	The Infirmary

1740 Sold by T. Jefferys at the Corner of St Martins Lane, London.

John Doharty Jun.r Delin.

15   St Alban's, Worcester

ALL SAINTS CHURCH, WORCESTER. AND THE ENTRANCE INTO THE CITY FROM THE BRIDGE AS IT IS.

16   All Saints' Worcester and All Hallows Square. An engraving pre-dating the clearance of the houses
     in front of the church in the early nineteenth century (Worcester City Museums)

7   St Peter the Great, Worcester. The medieval church, painted by H H Lines before its demolition in
1835 (Worcester City Museums)

8   The Edgar Tower, Worcester – the Great Gate of the medieval Cathedral Priory.

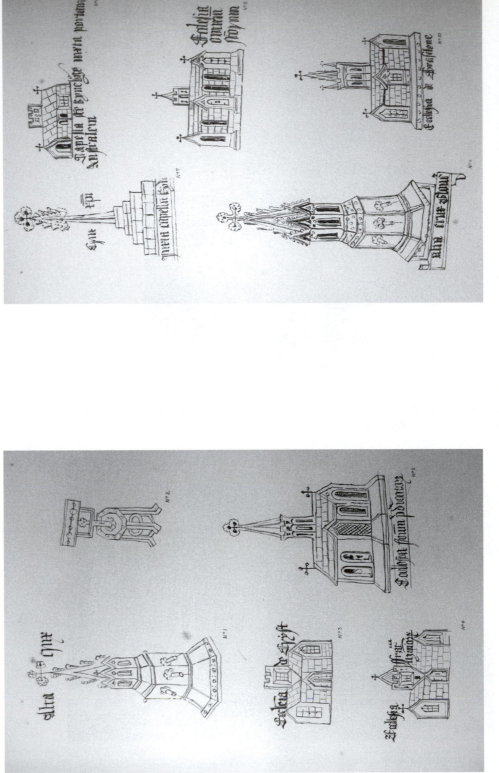

19   Sketches from the 1455 town rental of the principal landmarks of fifteenth-century Gloucester. The sketches were used as locational landmarks within the rental; the High Cross appears four times because the renter, Robert Cole, drew it each time he passed it during his perambulations (Birmingham University Library, Special Collections)

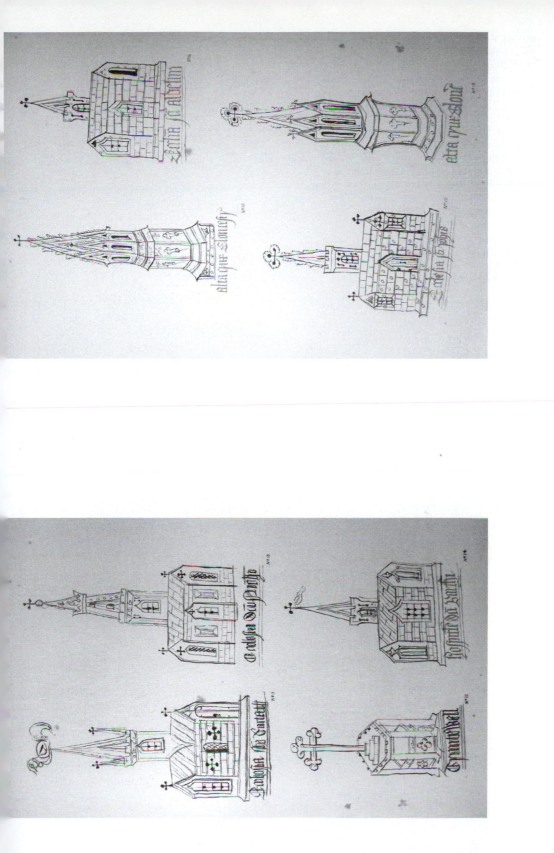

KEY TO PLATE 19

1 High Cross
2 The pillory (not named)
3 St Mary de Crypt
4 Greyfriars (The Friars minor)
5 Blackfriars (The Friars preachers)
6 Chapel of St Kyneburgh
7 Christ's Cross, next to the chapel of St Kyneburgh
8 Church of All Saints
9 High Cross
10 Church of St Mary, Grase Lane
11 Church of Holy Trinity
12 Trinity Well
13 Church of St Nicholas
14 Hospital of St Bartholomew
15 High Cross
16 Church of St Aldate
17 Church of St John
18 High Cross

Chapter 7

Worcester: churches, chapels and parishes

As in Gloucester, there were ten parish churches in late-medieval Worcester, as well as a number of non-parochial chapels. The obvious difference between the towns, however, was the way in which the Worcester parishes were dominated by the cathedral. In Gloucester, it was the Crown that had originally been the patron of at least four and perhaps more of the parish churches, St Peter's Abbey anciently possessing only St Mary de Lode; of the city of Worcester's ten parish churches (excluding St John in Bedwardine), apparently as many as nine had originally been dependent upon the bishop or the priory, or would become so. Only St Alban's seems never to have come under the cathedral's authority.

The earliest foundations

St Helen's (plate 12)

An early origin is claimed for St Helen's in the purported report of the 1092 synod, a document composed apparently in the mid twelfth century (Barrow 1992a, 69 and *passim*). According to this source, the synod was called to settle a dispute between the priests of St Helen's and St Alban's. The synod arrived at the conclusion that the church of St Helen had been a vicarage of the mother church – the cathedral – from the days of King Æthelred and Archbishop Theodore, who founded the cathedral in 680 and made Bosel its first bishop. It was further claimed that in the 960s Wynsige, the priest of St Helen's who was the vicar installed by the mother church, surrendered his church on going to St Oswald's recently founded abbey of Ramsey to become a monk. On his return three years later he was chosen by Oswald to become the first prior of the new cathedral priory (Darlington 1968, 52). What is to be made of this concoction is uncertain, although recent research has suggested that the claims made for the antiquity of St Helen's were not exaggerated: there are indications that it pre-dated even the foundation of the see in 680, and the possibility of a Roman or sub-Roman origin for this church has been seriously proposed (Bassett 1989a; Baker 1980a). The vast extent of the original parish of St Helen's, a large and coherent block of land surrounding Worcester which by the twelfth century had been subdivided into the parishes of a dozen rural churches, is the starting point of a series of arguments leading towards the conclusion that this was likely to have been the primary church of the region before 680. In origin, indeed, St Helen's may have been the seat of a British bishop serving the Christian population of this region during the period that saw the transition to English rule (Bassett 1992, 20–26).

The church stands directly on the western side of the High Street, just within the course of the Roman earthwork defences identified by Barker in the mid 1960s (Barker 1969): the earliest church must have lain hard against – or actually been cut into – the rampart (see above, fig. 6.14). Barker's work strongly suggested the presence of a gate through the defences at this point, and – consistent with an early foundation – St Helen's was clearly sited in relation to the gate. The present eastern end of the church lies directly on the west frontage of the High Street; and whilst it is not certain that this section of the High Street is of Roman origin – it might be replacing an earlier road heading for the gate on a different alignment – the probable early date of the church strengthens the possibility.

The present churchyard is a small walled area beyond the west end. Although it is likely that the use, or resumption of use, of this area for burials is late in date (see below, pp. 242–4), it is suggested (see above, p. 181) that the church formerly lay in a larger rectangular open area, the southern part of which disappeared as Fish Street encroached northwards into it. The western boundary of the churchyard is also the back boundary of the three High Street plots adjoining the church to the north. It is possible that these plots all represent encroachments on the early curtilage around the church (covering about half an acre/0.2 hectare), which was laid out, like the surrounding area, following the levelling of the Roman defences (see fig. 6.15). In a document of about 1100 recording the appurtenances of St Helen's Fritheric, its priest, included nine houses lying around the church (Darlington 1968, 53). It has been suggested that these were built on the church's ancient precincts, and that they were an indication of St Helen's having originated probably as a Celtic church, served by a monastic community living round about it (Bond 1988, 130; Whitehead 1976, 18). The topographical evidence for the existence of a formerly larger church plot seems clear enough, though Bond's conclusion that 'this bears all the hallmarks of a *clas* church' is an unwarranted assertion quite at odds with the rectangular form of the enclosure. Fritheric said that part of the property he had acquired by purchase or gift and by hard work, and that if the damage it had suffered by fire were to be repaired it would be worth 40 shillings or more a year (Darlington 1968, 53). So was this plot put together as an act of speculative investment, involving the purchase of land lying around the church following a major disaster? Or do Fritheric's words imply that these were houses anciently held from St Helen's, and whose tenancies had been surrendered or bought when they burnt down?

Despite the extensive discussion there has been concerning St Helen's extramural rights and possessions, their origins, and their implications (Baker 1980a; Bassett 1989a), the geography of the intramural parish has received less attention. The medieval and later parish, some 10 acres (4.05 hectares) in extent, covered the area within and on top of the Roman earthwork defences thought to have been replanned when they were levelled, possibly in the mid to late tenth century. The parish also extended over the southern half of the High Street outside the old defences.

As recorded in the eighteenth century (fig. 7.1), the parish was irregular in plan. The southern boundary with the Cathedral Close followed Lich Street and Palace Yard. The western boundary with St Alban's followed one of the primary north–south tenement boundaries between Palace Yard and Fish Street, and thereafter continued northwards on a line not marked as a property boundary in the eighteenth or nineteenth centuries. The northward course of the boundary was then, according to Young's map of 1779, interrupted by a westwards projecting salient of St Andrew's parish, discussed below. To the north of Copenhagen Street, the boundary passed diagonally across the rear of the Guildhall plot, on a course that appears to reflect standing buildings lining the rear in 1779. It then turned westwards to include a wedge-shaped block of land facing Bull Entry that probably represents the alienation of the rear of a number of the Copenhagen Street plots, following the transition of the Bull Entry line from a property boundary defining the rear of the plots into a thoroughfare. The northern boundary of the parish with St Swithun's followed the Bull Entry line before stepping slightly northwards to follow property boundaries of what are interpreted as secondary sub-divisions within the larger primary plots on both sides of the High Street. The eastern boundary of the parish followed the Shambles before turning eastwards to incorporate the junction of Pump Street and Friar Street. The latter was followed southwards to the Cathedral Close, excepting the inclusion of the Greyfriars precinct on the east side of the street.

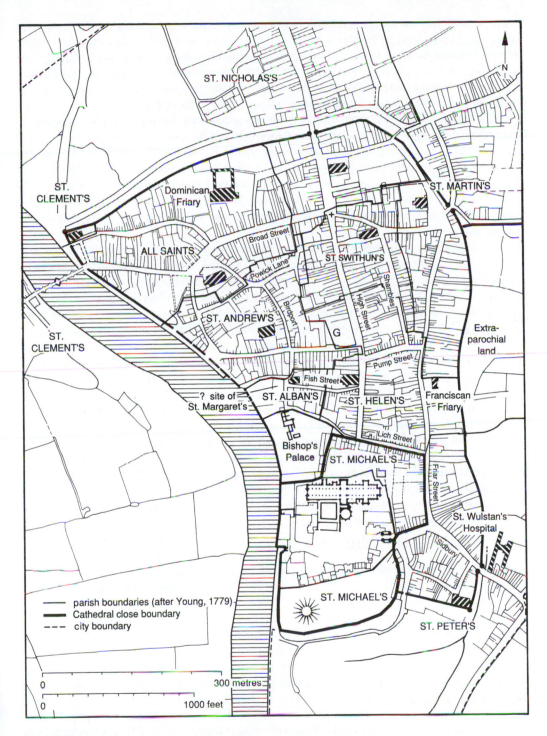

7.1   Worcester: intramural parishes and ecclesiastical geography

The western boundary with St Alban's parish appears to represent a straightforward partition between the two churches of the planned area within the former Roman defences, on a line roughly mid-way between the High Street and Palace Row /Little Fish Street. To the east, St Helen's was co-extensive with the adjoining area (plan-unit II.9) which has again been interpreted as planned urban growth over the flattened defences; the inclusion of the Greyfriars precinct within the parish is most likely to have come about immediately after the friary's dissolution.

The behaviour of the boundary with St Andrew's parish was the most complex: it seems to have reflected changes in the property boundaries between the plots facing Copenhagen Street (plan-unit II.8), those facing the High Street (plan-unit II.7), and Birdport to the west (plan-unit II.6). It is probable that the projecting salient of St Andrew's at the junction of Copenhagen Street with the High Street was a late-medieval or post-medieval feature (discussed further with St Andrew's parish, below). In general, it may be said that the northern half of St Helen's parish respected the western and eastern limits of the planned area represented by the High Street and its plots outside the Roman defences.

The boundary between St Helen's and St Swithun's followed secondary elements of this plot-pattern. It is certainly possible that subdivision of the suggested primary plots in this area could have taken place by the time the parish boundaries were established: the demonstrably early subdivision of the large primary plots in Winchester provides a parallel (Biddle 1976, 341). It is perhaps equally likely that there has been a minor shift in the parish boundary, subsequent to the subdivision of the primary plots, from an original line following the precursor of Bull Entry, across the High Street to the primary boundary dividing the two southern primary plots from the two northern plots (see figs 7.1 and 6.2). Just as that part of the proposed Copenhagen Street planned area that had lain within the Roman defences was divided in two between St Alban's and St Helen's, so this planned area was divided in two between St Swithun's and St Helen's.

St Helen's, now the County Record Office, is by Worcester standards a relatively well-preserved medieval church consisting of a nave and chancel, their full length flanked by aisles, and a west tower. Most of the church is Perpendicular, though the north chancel aisle was built in 1288 to house a chantry, and much of the south wall and the tower are nineteenth century. During the rebuilding of the south wall in the 1870s Norman features were uncovered and recorded. No recording work or excavation took place when the church was converted to house the Record Office (Buchanan-Dunlop 1939, 14–26; Baker 1980b, 115–16).

St Alban's and St Margaret's (plate 15)

St Alban's was first recorded as a possession of Evesham Abbey during the time of Abbot Æthelwig, 1059x1077, when it rendered 3*s* annually to the abbey (BL Cotton MS Vesp. B xxiv, fo.13), and like St Helen's it was named in the dubious account of the proceedings of the synod of 1092 (Darlington 1968, 52). The thirteenth-century chronicle of Evesham Abbey, however, relates that both it and the church of St Margaret were chapels given to the abbey – together with many houses lying round about – in 721 by Æthelbald of Mercia (Macray 1863, 73). Before considering St Alban's further, it is necessary to examine the evidence for this church of St Margaret which did not survive the medieval period, and about which virtually nothing has hitherto been known.

Dedications to St Margaret of Antioch appear also as dedications to St Marina, and in England her cult can be traced back to before the Norman Conquest (Farmer 1978, 281–2; Ortenberg 1992, 120). Well over 200 ancient English churches were dedicated to her (Farmer 1978, 282), and the confusion with St Marina of Alexandria – also by repute a late-Roman virgin and martyr and commemorated in the Greek church – was evident in the Roman church by the ninth century, although elements of the romantic stories attached to St Marina had already been attributed to St Margaret by the fifth century (Arnold-Forster 1899, i, 130).

The Worcester church of St Margaret already existed in 1059x1077, when Evesham Abbey granted it to the rector of St Andrew's in return for an annual rent of a pound of incense (BL Cotton MS Vesp. B xxiv, fo.11v); it was then said to stand 'opposite Wodestathe' (uncharacteristically, Stenton misread the letter *thorn* in this name, which he gave as 'Wodestape': *VCH Worcs.*, iv, 411). St Andrew's belonged to the cathedral priory (H, 290). We next hear of the church as 'St Marina's': in 1149 it was listed with the other churches in Worcester that Bishop Simon confirmed to be the property of the monks (Darlington 1968, 73), and in the 1190s Roger of St Marina appeared with the other incumbents of the priory's Worcester churches as a witness to a gift of land to the monks for the celebration of an anniversary (WCL D&C B1450, 1451; Darlington 1968, 340). The parish of St Marina was given as the location of property, formerly belonging to Thomas of Malmesbury, clerk, from which Juliana de Branesford in the early thirteenth century gave the priory a rent of 6*s* (WCL D&C B1690); and this seems to have been identical with the property described in the published edition of the priory rental of 1240 as being formerly of Thomas the clerk, and lying in the parish of St Alban and St Mary (Hale 1865, 107b). Hale in fact misread the entry, which clearly reads: 'in parochia sancti Albani et sancte Marine' (WCL D&C A2, 107b). Similarly, under the entry of another rent drawn from the same property, we are told it lies 'in parochia sancte Marine', which Hale again transcribed as 'S. Mariae' (WCL D&C A2, 108; Hale 1865, 108).

According to this source, then, by 1240 St Margaret's or St Marina's parish had been merged with that of St Alban, and indeed there are no more references to the church. But references continue to Saint Marina's Street on which it evidently lay or had lain, and we find that in the middle of the thirteenth century land was conveyed in *Seintemarinestrete* (WCL D&C B1385). By the end of the century this had been corrupted in common usage to St Mary Street, the form used in several other thirteenth-century conveyances of land there (WCL D&C B1028, B1386, B1387, B1388). We can identify St Mary Street with the street later called Warmstry Slip, which led from St Alban's church to the river (Bloom 1909, xii; Baker 1980b, 122, citing Speed's map of 1610; pers. comm. from Dr Patricia Hughes).

So there was by the early eleventh century a church of St Margaret or St Marina, which in time was said to be an ancient foundation, and which had parochial status in the twelfth century. Its separate parochial status had apparently gone by 1240, and the church itself would seem to have gone too. The fact that after the middle of the century 'St Marina Street' was becoming corrupted in popular usage to 'St Mary Street' is a sign that the church itself no longer existed and its dedication had been forgotten. As for its location: the eleventh-century description of the chapel as lying 'opposite *Wodestathe*' confirms that it was near the river; it is far from safe to assume, however, that this is the Wodestathe Street (modern Quay Street) of the later middle ages, as the stathe where wood was landed was liable to have moved over the centuries. The granting by the Crown in 1588 of an unlocated chapel of St Margaret to Charles Baghot has been cited as evidence that the church still existed in the middle of the sixteenth century, and this has been tentatively identified with the remains of a medieval building seen early in the present century in Grope Lane (Baker 1980b, 117); but this does not agree with the evidence for the church's demise in the thirteenth century, nor with the position of St Marina Street /St Mary Street /Warmstry Slip. There are two other indicators that St Margaret's was indeed in the vicinity of St Alban's: firstly, the statement that the churches were conveyed to Evesham Abbey *cum pluribus domibus circumiacentibus* (Macray 1863, 73) which suggests the two churches lay together; second, and more importantly, the fact that it was with St Alban's parish that St Margaret's was combined – indicating that they were adjacent.

The late-medieval and post-medieval parish of St Alban was a roughly rectangular area covering 2 acres (0.8 hectare), between St Andrew's to the north – beyond the former Roman defences – and the Cathedral Close to the south. The former parish of St Margaret's was almost certainly represented by the square riverside street-block to the west of Palace Row. In their earlier medieval form, St Alban's and St Margaret's can therefore be reconstructed as tiny, wholly intramural, areas of about one acre each. St Alban's parish lay entirely within the suggested planned area within the former Roman defences; the riverside street-block that included St Margaret's, and was probably coextensive with its parish, has or had a marked similarity to the riverside enclosures of the Birdport area. The precise course of the parish boundary between St Alban's and St Andrew's along Warmstry Slip is not entirely certain: Young's map of 1779 shows it following the road, and the Ordnance Survey shows it to the north of the road. The Roman ditch which the line of the boundary follows seems likely from Gelling's excavations to have actually coincided with the curved western section of Warmstry Slip. The site of St Margaret's therefore almost certainly lay within the square street-block on the south side of the road, probably within the northernmost of the plots – the Warmstry House tenement, later the porcelain manufactory.

The siting of St Alban's church has parallels with that of St Helen's. Gelling's excavations on the west side of Little Fish Street (Gelling 1958) located the Roman ditch (explored later to the east by Barker) about 20 feet (6 metres) north of the church. Like St Helen's, the earliest church must have been cut into the back of the rampart. Yet unlike St Helen's, this church does not fit easily into the surrounding street-pattern, and its orientation may well reflect the line of the defences: it was some degrees from the alignment of Fish Street to its south, and the angle thus formed was used as a tiny triangular churchyard. Like St Helen's, it apparently stood by a gate in the Roman earthwork defences. Gelling's excavations found a 'brushwood causeway' across the ditch about 33 feet (10 metres) west of Little Fish Street, held in place by stakes driven into the primary silts. This feature was secondary to the construction of the ditch, and though it was associated with Roman pottery, could have been either Roman or post-Roman in date. The west end of St Alban's projected well to the west of Little Fish Street, and it is possible that the church site was determined by a post-Roman breach in the defences represented by the causeway. However, if Charles Mundy's contention that Anglo-Saxon and medieval Birdport was the successor to a north–south Roman road following the terrace edge (see above, p. 174) is correct, there should then have been a primary gate through the defences in this area, either under – and thus blocked by – the church, or immediately to its east.

Evesham Abbey retained the advowson of St Alban's church until the Dissolution, when it passed to the Crown (Buchanan-Dunlop 1950, 6). The date of 721 which the abbey chronicle claimed for the grant of these two churches from Æthelbald is inevitably suspect, and can neither be confirmed nor dismissed. But there is rather more to recommend the chronicle entry than is at first obvious: given the position of the churches, and the surrounding houses that went with the grant, this was an important piece of riverside property which constituted an unusually generous gift, and one which was entirely in keeping with the lavish grants made to Evesham during the twenty years following on its foundation in 701 (*VCH Worcs.*, ii, 113). Even if the circumstances of the grant were not quite as they are recorded, the essential fact – that Evesham Abbey acquired these two churches as a grant from a king of Mercia, and did so at an early date – is entirely plausible.

It is significant that, alone among the older of Worcester's parish churches, the cathedral had no claim upon St Alban's, although the Church of Worcester jealously guarded its property; when

Bishop Oswald granted out his own churches of St Peter the Great and – apparently – All Saints', it was for a limited period only, and to men who were dependent upon him. Leaving aside St Helen's, with its early origins quite separate from the Anglo-Saxon Church of Worcester, all of the other Worcester churches believed to have been in existence before 1000 evidently were founded by the bishops of Worcester: certainly they belonged to the bishops at an early date. That St Alban's and St Margaret's were exceptions to this pattern means either that – like St Helen's – they had been founded before the See of Worcester itself, or alternatively that they were lay foundations dating from after *c.* 680. If the judgment attributed to the 1092 synod was historically correct, that there was indeed but one parish in Worcester, and all the churches were no more than chapels of the one mother-church, then that would imply that the two churches were not minster foundations, but were early examples of proprietary churches.

Little can be deduced from the fact of the dedication to St Alban. Frances Arnold-Forster noted only nine ancient examples in England, and said that this was the only one in Mercia. In fact London – which had St Alban's, Wood Street – became a Mercian city, but it is true that the Worcester example is the only one in the midlands (Arnold-Forster 1899, ii, 294–9). She argued that Offa had a special affection for St Alban, a view supported by more recent research (Biddle 1977); Buchanan-Dunlop's insistence that this was shared by the Mercian kings in general, and by Æthelbald in particular, rests only on this one royal grant of dubious authenticity (Buchanan-Dunlop 1950, 1), and is entirely at odds with the rarity of the dedication.

Due no doubt to the limited resources of its small parish (Caley 1810–34, iii, 232), St Alban's church has survived relatively intact in its twelfth-century state. It is a small single-aisled building of very irregular plan and a continuous nave and chancel (fig. 8.3). The nave arcade suggests that the north aisle was a later twelfth-century addition to the structure; the prevalence of green Highley sandstone at the west end, in contrast to the red sandstone that is most frequently used in the rest of the building, suggests that the nave has also been extended. A number of writers have suggested that the church contains pre-Conquest features. During restoration in 1919 removal of rendering from the south wall revealed a narrow blocked door and window – both still visible – with flat monolithic lintels, and 'over the doorway several layers of the early tilework commonly called Roman bricks' (WCRO BA3762/32 899:31). The window and door lintels are probably Cotswold limestone, and may be re-used Roman masonry, though that over the window does not pass through the thickness of the wall; these 'early' features are at least as likely to be of eleventh- or twelfth-century date as earlier. Later structural modifications to the church, before restoration in the nineteenth century, appear to have been restricted to fifteenth-century windows and a piscina (Buchanan-Dunlop 1950, 1–2).

Probable later pre-Conquest foundations

St Andrew's

The earliest reference to the church is its acquisition of St Margaret's from Evesham Abbey, which occurred in the mid eleventh century when Reyner was the incumbent (BL Cotton MS Vesp. B xxiv, fo.11v); by 1100 it was held by Uhtred, according to Hemming's rental of the monks' Worcester property (H 289). There is no documentary evidence to suggest how much earlier than this St Andrew's had been founded: the site of the church was within the *haga* granted by Wærferth to Æthelred, Æthelflaed and Ælfwynn in 904 for their lives (see above, pp. 175–7), but if this church had already existed then, would it not have been specified in the grant?

With Æthelflaed's death in 918 and Ælfwynn's involuntary transfer to Wessex, it may be that the lease fell in; alternatively the *haga* passed into the hands of Edward the Elder and his successors. It is unclear when – or if at all – it reverted to the bishops of Worcester, although St Andrew's church was the property of the cathedral in the eleventh century. Presumably Æthelred and Æthelflaed required this land for urban development, within which context the foundation of a new church by them or by their successors, the Wessex kings, would be a definite possibility; otherwise St Andrew's was founded by one of the bishops at some time after the recovery of the *haga*. This was a popular saint of the Anglo-Saxon period (Farmer 1978, 18), and by the late tenth century there may have been a cult of St Andrew at Worcester: in the 950s Dunstan was comforted by visions of the saint whilst at Ghent, according to his biographers, and it is perfectly feasible that he might have wished to express a devotion to St Andrew as soon as an opportunity arose with his appointment to Worcester (Stubbs 1874, 60, 193, 285: the story was already current when Adelard of Blandinium was writing, between 1006 and 1011: ibid., xxx, 60).

The medieval church (now demolished, apart from the west tower) consisted of a nave flanked by aisles, and a chancel flanked by side-chapels roofed continuously with the aisles. The nave and tower were both of fifteenth-century date, although the chancel was twelfth century, heavily restored in the nineteenth (Buchanan-Dunlop 1937, 18–20; Baker 1980b, 117). The church occupied an imposing site right on the edge of the gravel terrace, overlooking Copenhagen Street in the defile to the south, and the Quay at the bottom of the slope to the west. The church's surroundings have already been described (see above, p. 174 and fig. 6.13): a small squarish street-block of about one acre, not much larger than the churchyard itself – a subdivision of the 904 *haga*.

The parish of St Andrew's corresponded roughly in extent with the plots fronting both sides of Birdport, together with an area of the Copenhagen Street south-side plots laid out over the former Roman defences. In fact, St Andrew's incorporated nearly all of the area that lay outside the line of the Roman defences, which in general terms determined the line of the boundary between this parish and those to the south. Young's map of 1779, and later maps, show an eastwards projecting salient incorporating the south frontage of Copenhagen Street as far as its junction with the High Street. This however does not seem to reflect the late-medieval situation as early-modern property records for the tenement known as the Earl's Post, and for surrounding plots, show no such parochial allegiance (pers. comm., Dr Pat Hughes).

Further north along the east side of the parish, immediately north of Bull Entry, the line taken by the parish boundary (as mapped in the eighteenth century) was investigated archaeologically by the Deansway excavations (Mundy 1989, site 2). The boundary between St Andrew's and St Swithun's did not appear in the excavated sequence until the late fourteenth or fifteenth centuries, when its course first became apparent as the edge of a zone of pit-digging. It is unlikely that this line was in use as a boundary before that date as the excavation revealed a sequence of deposits laid without interruption across the area, representing activities associated successively with the plots on Birdport to the west and the High Street to the east. The ground at the rear of the two plot-series was swapped, piecemeal, between them (Mundy 1989, 14). This fluidity, or random exchange of land parcels, between the two plot-series produced the staggered course of the lane (Chapel Walk–Pye Corner) that separated them by the late eighteenth century, and which has been taken as the boundary between the two plan-units (II.5 and II.6). The parish boundary recorded in the eighteenth century had clearly been subject to the same local fluidity, responding to changes in the plot-pattern, and it seems highly probable that when it was first defined it followed the back-fence line separating the High Street plots from settlement fronting onto Birdport.

The boundary between St Andrew's and All Saints' is generally explicable only in terms of the relationship of the respective churches to the excavated Anglo-Saxon defences that separated them, and will be discussed below with All Saints'.

All Saints' (plate 16)

The first documentary reference to this church comes in the charter of Bishop Simon which confirmed and enumerated the possessions of the monks. Dated 1149, the charter names All Saints' as one of the five churches – with St Andrew's, St Marina's, St Martin's and St Swithun's – that belonged to the cathedral priory (Darlington 1968, 73; Buchanan-Dunlop 1936, 16, in error attributed the charter to 1125). However, in the case of All Saints' this would seem to have been the registration of a historical claim rather than a record of what was in fact true at that time, for the advowson of the church of All Saints' was held in the twelfth and thirteenth centuries by the lords of Richard's Castle, Herefordshire. In 1175 the cathedral priory arrived at a settlement with Osbert son of Hugh, the patron of All Saints', by which it recognized the right of his family to hold the advowson in perpetuity; the pension of 6s 8d he agreed to pay annually to the monks was doubtless in recognition of what must have been an historical claim to the church on the priory's part (Darlington 1968, 177). The descent of the advowson to Osbert's successors as lords of Richard's Castle is confirmed by inquisitions *post mortem* of members of the Mortimer family, when it was always adjudged to be worth 100s per annum (Bund 1894, 21, 22, 28; Bund 1909, 30).

However, it would be wrong to conclude that the advowson was necessarily attached to the lordship itself; the evidence, indeed, indicates it to have descended with the manor of Cotheridge in Worcestershire. At the time of the Domesday survey, Cotheridge was held by Osbern son of Richard, the lord of Richard's Castle; it was assessed at one hide, and was one of eight manors which made up the eleven hides or so held from the Bishop of Worcester's manor of Wick (DB, i, 172d). This was the only manor that Osbern held in the county, although he also held eight of the bishop's houses in Worcester. All of the bishop's houses in tenancy were in fact held by four men – Osbern, Urse the sheriff, Walter Ponther and Robert the Bursar; and these men were also the tenants of all but one of the hides held from Wick. So although Domesday Book records that these houses in Worcester were held from the bishop's manor of Northwick, there must be a strong suspicion that originally they had all been attached to the lands appurtenant to Wick. In other words, we might conclude that if Osbern's houses were appurtenant to any rural manor, it was to his single Worcestershire manor of Cotheridge. And indeed, the inquisition *post mortem* of Hugh de Mortimer of Richard's Castle made in 1304 confirms the relationship, saying that the ten houses that Hugh held in Worcester of the bishop, and for which he owed one-fifth of a knight's fee, pertained to his manor of Cotheridge (Bund 1909, 9).

What cannot be conclusively demonstrated is that All Saints' church, too, was historically part of this family's Worcestershire estate and that it had belonged to Osbern in the 1080s. However, only 90 years later his family were adjudged to be its ancient patrons, and in all probability it had been acquired together with Cotheridge and the manor's appurtenant houses in the city.

Fortunately something is known about the previous history of this manor. This was not one of the spoils of war and conquest, but had passed smoothly into the hands of its Norman owners before 1066 (DB, i, 252d). Hemming explains that Cotheridge had been granted by Edward the Confessor to Richard Scrob, Osbern's father, following its confiscation from the exiled king's clerk, Spirites or Spiritus. He in turn had been given the property by his brother Earnwi, described as a wealthy reeve (H 254; for Spirites' career, see Barlow 1963, 131–2, 174–5). A century before these events, in 963, Cotheridge had been given by Bishop Oswald to his *minister* or thegn, Ælfric. The grant was for three lives, Ælfric's successors being nominated as his son Æthelsige, and then his male heirs (H 133–5, 350–1; S 1303). Whether this Earnwi was the next heir of Æthelsige we cannot tell; if he was, then the terms of Oswald's grant were still being observed. Only with the king's grant to Richard Scrob did the land pass beyond hope of effective recovery by the Church, and it is noteworthy that Hemming should have remarked that it was indeed only then that Cotheridge was lost to Worcester (H 254).

Without any firm evidence for the date of All Saints' foundation, its initial construction by any one of these men who held Cotheridge and presumably its appurtenant land in Worcester cannot be ruled out. But its position, just within or even upon the probable gateway of the *burh* constructed in the 890s (below), points strongly to its having been built at that time or shortly after. There are parallels from elsewhere of the possible erection of gate churches as part of the process of *burh* foundation during the late ninth century (Haslam 1988, 35–43), and it remains the most likely explanation of All Saints' origins. Furthermore, and more certainly, the cathedral priory's success in the twelfth century in establishing its right to an annual pension in the church indicates how likely it is that it was founded by the Church of Worcester. There is no certainty of when All Saints' became linked with Cotheridge, but most plausibly it was in 963 when Oswald might be presumed to have tied this hide of land to suitable city property with which to endow an important retainer (see below, pp. 262–4, for a discussion of the policy of Oswald and other bishops with regard to this practice).

The discovery of the ninth-century defences by excavation at the Deansway site 4 (figs 6.10 and 6.11), 100 metres to the east, has transformed understanding of the church's early context. It is now clear, as we have seen, that All Saints' was situated immediately behind or actually on the defences. Given the arguments for the early origin of Birdport and the bridge approach roads (Newport and Dolday) extending from it, there is little doubt that All Saints' was, in origin, a gate-church marking an important entrance to the city. This explains the parish's geography. In late-medieval terms, after the building of the post-Conquest city wall, it was wholly intramural – the largest intramural parish; but originally it would have been almost entirely extramural, lying outside the gate with which the church was associated and incorporating the roads that led from it. The only part of the parish which lay within the *burh* wall was a tiny area enclosing the church itself.

The parish as recorded in the eighteenth century was a roughly rectangular area of about 15 acres (6 hectares) in the north-west corner of the city, covering the Newport and Dolday area and the western half of Broad Street. The southern boundary with St Andrew's followed a north-easterly course from the river, excluded the large plot immediately south-west of the church (in what was perhaps a post-medieval diversion), and then followed Grope Lane which marked the north side of the episcopal *haga* leased in 904, with what appears to have been a cleared zone or strip immediately behind the defences. Further east, the parish boundary followed the backs of the Merryvale plots before adopting a straight, eastward course between Powick Lane and Broad Street. Excavation across its line at this point (Deansway site 4: Mundy 1989) showed that the parish boundary lay about 10 feet (3 metres) to the south of, and parallel to, the *burh* rampart. While the line of the parish boundary seems initially to have been determined by the position of the rampart, when that was levelled all physical manifestation of the boundary disappeared for a while from the excavated sequence; indeed, a late-twelfth or early-thirteenth-century stone building was built across it at the rear of a plot extending back from Broad Street. With the differential robbing of the stone building in the later middle ages and the division of the plot into two, the boundary line re-appears in the archaeological record. The eastern parish boundary with St Nicholas's followed plot boundaries northwards to the city wall: why it took this particular line is not at all clear, as the line is a short distance to the west of the plots facing the Cross that were specifically associated with St Nicholas's parish and church.

A greater problem is posed by the north boundary, which followed the city wall. There is no archaeological evidence from this part of the circuit, but the wall may be as late as the early thirteenth century. However, the circuit here follows a natural break in slope and canalizes a stream rising immediately west of the Foregate, and it is possible that the parish boundary was determined by these natural features and then reorganized when the wall was built, as appears to have happened on the east side of the city. The existence of a boundary between All Saints' and St Clement's dates presumably from 1175, when the independence of the latter church was recognized (see below); that does not mean, of course, that the demarcation line followed then was the same as that of later centuries, which was the line of the city wall. Beyond the wall there lay also the extramural part of the parish of St Nicholas, probably a post-1050 creation (see below). The possibility must be considered that All Saints' parish was originally more extensive and lost ground to St Nicholas's in a later re-organization, perhaps post-city wall.

Most of the fabric of the present church dates from its rebuilding between 1738 and 1742 by Thomas White, a pupil of Wren; only the west tower and the south wall of the medieval building survive. The base of the tower may be earlier than its fifteenth-century superstructure, and from the tower projects part of an earlier north wall to the nave containing part of a blocked round-headed arch. F.T. Spackman is said to have 'found in the tower and (south) wall many traces of Norman work' (Buchanan-Dunlop 1936, 15). Part of a 'Saxon' wall claimed to have been part of a defensive circuit was observed in the mid nineteenth century and during restoration in 1913, but has not been seen since (Buchanan-Dunlop 1936, 15; Sheppard 1910, 593). The church is oriented slightly north-east–south-west in conformity with the edge of the prominent gravel bluff on which it is sited, the present building being 'built with the east end pointing slightly south of the old foundations' (Buchanan-Dunlop 1936, 17). It overlooks All Hallows' Square – the medieval cattle market – and the site of All Hallows' Well. Until redevelopment in the 1960s, All Saints' was surrounded by housing: to the south, built on short, wide plots fronting Grope Lane, and to the north by a block of commercial encroachments projecting into All Hallows' Square: an early illustration shows what appear to be tall, one-room deep, timber-framed buildings accommodated into the slope below the church.

St Clement's

We have already seen that the advowson of the church of All Saints' was held in the twelfth and thirteenth centuries by the lords of Richard's Castle, by virtue of their lordship of their Worcestershire manor of Cotheridge, and that in 1175 an agreement was reached with the cathedral priory by which the monks recognized Osbert son of Hugh's right to the presentation whilst he in return promised that each parson he appointed should pay an annual pension of half a mark to the priory (Darlington 1968, 177). But there was more to the agreement than that, for the bishop's adjudication between Osbert and Prior Ralf also concerned the advowson of St Clement's (Darlington 1968, 182). The prior had claimed that St Clement's did not pertain to All Saints', nor was it in any way subordinate to it. Osbert agreed, and quitclaimed St Clement's to the prior, whilst Hugh Poer, the lord on whose fee St Clement's had been founded, also conveyed all his rights in the church to the monks. The bishop declared St Clement's free of any subjection to All Saints', and to be the monks' own demesne chapel. Clearly the judgment that All Saints' had no rights over St Clement's is not to be taken as a statement of historical reality, but was part of the compromise agreement which had been reached. Had St Clement's indeed never been a chapel of All Saints', the question would hardly have arisen; in acquiring St Clement's from its secular patron the monks had also had to free it from its historical dependency on All Saints' and the patron of that church.

The association between the river crossing and church is even more marked in the case of St Clement's than in the case of All Saints'. This church lay at the riverside end of Dolday, by the North Quay, a short distance from the medieval bridge. Its parish was divided into three parts. Within the city walls it was restricted to the area of the church itself and its presumably post-medieval burial ground adjoining to the east. Beyond the wall, the parish consisted of an irregular area of meadowland of about 11 acres (4.45 hectares) bounded by the city boundary to the north and the watercourse draining the city ditch to the east. However, the bulk of the parish lay across the river, included the Causeway suburb, and extended westwards to the north–south Rosemary Lane which followed the edge of the gravel terrace and also marked the city boundary. The southern city and parish boundary here was mapped by Doharty and Young as a straight line extending across the fields to Rosemary Lane, though it is clear from the 1497 perambulation that the medieval boundary followed field boundaries between distinct landmarks (Green 1796, ii, lxxi). The parish also extended north of the Causeway and incorporated a long northwards projecting spit of the floodplain extending beyond the return of the city boundary. Apart from this northward extension, there is a possibility that the west bank parish was actually co-extensive with an area leased by the Bishop of Worcester to Æthelred and Æthelflaed, together with the *haga* on the east bank. Given the original dependency of St Clement's on All Saints', it would seem that the east bank parish of St Clement was alienated from that of All Saints'. But can the same also be assumed for the west bank? Had All Saints' parish, which included the river crossing and its associated roads, also included originally the Causeway across the river?

The dedication to St Clement can be paralleled in transpontine and waterfront contexts elsewhere, for example in Cambridge and Rochester; its Scandinavian associations have led to the suggestion that its occurrence marks the presence of racially distinct immigrant communities settling outside predominantly Anglo-Saxon *burhs*. It has also been speculated that the Worcester St Clement's served a Hiberno-Norse population (presumably on account of Worcester's western location) dwelling on the west bank of the river (Haslam 1985, 27–8). However interesting this idea may be, it has yet to receive support from archaeological or numismatic sources – or indeed any other source. It is perhaps more likely that the dedication of the parish only reflects a concentration of maritime occupations close to the river and its quays and has no racial connotations: Hemming records tenements held by boatmen on the west bank in the eleventh century (H 290). Yet direct Scandinavian influence is not to be ruled out, for there is at least a possibility that the founder of St Clement's had strong Danish sympathies.

Some clues to the circumstances of the church's foundation are to be found in the structure of its parish. The church itself lay within the late-medieval city wall, and that part of the parish that lay beyond the walls on the east bank of the Severn was meadowland, and liable to flood. Only that part of the parish on the west bank of the Severn was populated, and so St Clement's church was in the somewhat anomalous position of serving a population dwelling on the other side of a major river. Had its foundation been prompted in the first place by a desire to serve this transpontine community, and certainly had it been brought about by those who were subsequently to be its parishioners, then surely it would have been built where they lived, on the west bank of the Severn. The implication of its position seems to be that it was built where it was purely as an act of piety, with no intention of its serving any particular group of people, and certainly not the suburb across the bridge. Its subsequent acquisition of this district as a parish came about because there was no nearer church for these people to use; it was not part of any original plan.

In 1175 St Clement's was said to be sited in the fee of Hugh Poer and Richard of Grafton, from which Darlington inferred that the church therefore pertained to the manor of Grafton (Darlington 1968, 183). In 1086 Hugh's ancestor, Walter Ponther, had held seven hides at Grafton Flyford from the Abbot of Westminster (DB, i, 175a); it thus seems likely that it was indeed rights in Grafton that gave both men a legitimate claim to St Clement's in 1175. The link between the church and the manor cannot be established any more firmly than that. Which of Grafton's earlier lords might have founded St Clement's? Or during which period might a previous lord have acquired the church? Grafton Flyford was one of the ancient possessions of Pershore Abbey, until Edward the Confessor gave it to Westminster (*VCH Worcs.*, iv, 86). No Worcester property was attached to it, according to Domesday Book, neither the seven hides held by Walter nor the two hides held by Urse (DB, i, 175a). Both men held houses in the city, but they were held from the bishop and were said to pertain to his manor of Northwick – although it has already been argued, above, that they would in fact have been held from Wick. How can the link between Grafton and St Clement's, evident by the twelfth century, be explained?

Given the absence of any known link between Grafton and Worcester before the Conquest, a foundation by any lord of that manor is unlikely. Equally unlikely is an act of foundation by Westminster Abbey in a city where it owned no property that we know of, and for the same reason Pershore Abbey, too, is an improbable founder. Therefore some other person or institution would seem to have been responsible for building St Clement's, which only subsequently became associated with Grafton. This might have happened in one of two ways. As tenants both of Grafton and of property in Worcester, Walter Ponther or one of his heirs could have founded the church within the existing parish of All Saints', and then attached it to the manor of Grafton. Alternatively, there is the possibility of a pre-Conquest foundation by someone with interests in Worcester: St Clement's might subsequently have been acquired by Westminster Abbey, and attached to Grafton – perhaps even at the time Walter Ponther took possession. It is easy to see how a man who already had property in Worcester would wish to extend his interests there by acquiring a church, and how the transfer might be arranged if he already held a manor from Westminster Abbey.

If Westminster Abbey had not received St Clement's as part of the grant of Grafton Flyford from Edward the Confessor, then it had been by a separate grant, although this too had presumably been from the King who so comprehensively endowed the abbey. But how might St Clement's have come into the Crown's possession? One possible route we already know of: the confiscation of the lands of Spirites, the cleric who held the manor of Cotheridge with the church of All Saints', and who fell from royal favour in 1065 or thereabouts. Spirites is certainly a plausible candidate for founder of St Clement's: All Saints' was his own, and so no problems would arise from the placing of a new church within an existing or a developing parish. He was a wealthy churchman, who might be expected to have founded new churches where he could, and perhaps especially in a rapidly growing town where he owned land. His career had begun at the courts of Harald and Harthacnut, and a dedication to a saint apparently favoured by the Scandinavian community would have been appropriate. Finally, we know that his lands were confiscated by King Edward; and whilst Cotheridge and All Saints' went to Richard Scrob, at least some of his property would very probably have been given to the Church. Spirites served at Court from before 1040 until his exile in about 1065 (Barlow 1963, 132); if he was indeed the founder of St Clement's, then we should look for the origins of the church within that period.

Evidence that might support that dating emerged from the demolition of St Clement's in 1823 (when it was replaced by a successor on the other side of the river). An extremely rare gold coin of Edward the Confessor was recovered, minted about 1050 by the Warwick moneyer Lyfinc (Allies 1852, 14; Stewart 1978, 155–6). The nature of the coin points to a special minting and likely ritual deposit perhaps at the time of the church's consecration, rather than accidental loss.

The structure of the demolished church was reported to have been mainly Norman in style and consisted of a nave, chancel and north aisle. A stone tower that had been bonded into the city wall was demolished during the Civil War and later replaced in wood: the 1651 map suggests it to have been a small fourteenth- or fifteenth-century addition to the earlier church structure (*VCH Worcs.*, iv, 409–11; Baker 1980b, 120–121).

St Swithun's

St Swithun's was first recorded in 1125x49, when Bishop Simon, at the petition of Eudo the dean, granted the churches of St Martin and St Swithun to the monks, along with some land in Worcester that Eudo held of the bishop (Darlington 1968, 64; and see Hale 1865, 91a). Eudo had evidently just become a monk, and this was confirmation of the disposal of his assets: St Martin's, which he had held from the monks, he had restored to them on joining their number, whilst St Swithun's was described as having been founded upon Eudo's own fee. This has been taken to read that Eudo was himself the founder of St Swithun's (for instance by Baker 1980b, 118), but that is not necessarily implicit in the wording of the grant. St Swithun's had been founded by the second quarter of the twelfth century, but there is no indication of how much earlier it was founded, or whether Eudo was the founder or not.

While the topography – particularly the curving line of St Swithin's Street – is suggestive, it is the excavations at Deansway Site 4 to the west, and the City Arcades site to the south, that show that St Swithun's must have been founded in the immediate vicinity of the late-Saxon defences, most probably on the actual line of the (backfilled) ditch (see above, pp. 172–3). There is a lack of reliable archaeological evidence from the immediate vicinity to confirm this, though watching-briefs in the early 1990s on the former school-room in the churchyard found an organic silt deposit that would be consistent with the fill of a ditch (City SMR records). St Swithun's parish is intimately associated with what has been interpreted as the replanned High Street area, and a plausible sequence can be suggested whereby St Helen's, the original intramural 'High Street parish', was divided and reduced when St Swithun's was founded to serve the newly laid-out area. The west and east boundaries of St Swithun's parish were extensions of those already discussed between St Helen's and its neighbours to east and west. The southwards projecting salient of St Swithun's on the east side of the Shambles can be accounted for in terms of the rational apportionment or re-apportionment of properties between the two churches (see below, p. 250). The northern boundary followed the back of the northern Mealcheapen Street plots, or the boundaries to the secondary plots developed on their tails, facing northwards onto the Trinity. To the west of the High Street the boundary seems to have followed the *burh* ditch for a short distance.

In its present form St Swithun's is substantially eighteenth century, having been rebuilt in the 1730s by the Woodwards of Chipping Camden. They retained and refaced the medieval west tower, and were unable to rebuild the medieval north wall that then supported a number of buildings. The rebuilding was too early in date for illustrative evidence of any value to record the church's previous medieval appearance; the 1651 map shows it schematically but puts the tower at the wrong end. Of all the Worcester parish churches, this is the most characteristically 'urban' in its setting. It occupies the eastern end of the small triangle of land defined by the Cross, St Swithin's Street and Church Street, and is still hemmed in by dense building. The 'churchyard' to the north of the church is minute, and largely built over.

St Martin's

The church was first recorded by name as the property of the cathedral priory at the end of the eleventh century (H 290). It is also virtually certain that St Martin's was the church mentioned in a charter of 1003x23 as lying just beyond the boundary of the manor of Perry – a manor which formed part of the later parish (H 358; S 1385; Clarke and Dyer 1969, 30).

St Martin's, like All Saints' to the west, was associated with a market, the Cornmarket, lying outside the *burh* defences and immediately within the medieval city wall. As the town-plan analysis emphasized, this is perhaps the least well understood part of the town and the layout of the district before the construction of the city wall is not at all clear. It is probable that the Cornmarket was a very late feature in the landscape, possibly contemporary with the construction of the city wall. In that case, St Martin's was not originally built on the frontage of the Cornmarket, but set back from the Mealcheapen Street frontage, possibly within an extant plot.

An extramural church in relation to the *burh* defences, St Martin's had a wholly extramural parish. A small part of it – New Street, the Cornmarket and the eastern half of Mealcheapen Street – was enclosed by the later medieval city wall. The much larger extramural part covered an area of undulating clayland stretching for about a mile and a half eastwards from the city, but included the Lowesmoor/ Silver Street suburb. The parish was laid out as a roughly triangular area, with its apex at the church and its north side following minor streams and, in part, the Tolladine Road which appears as the *port stræte* in a charter of 969 (H 136–8; S 1327; Hooke 1980, 45). The southern boundary with St Peter's mostly ran along or closely parallel to the road running eastwards from Sidbury, recorded as a *stræte* in 974 (H 155, 358; S 1329; Hooke 1980, 45), although a short distance east of the city boundary it swung north to leave Sidbury and the fields east of the city wall in St Peter's. Close by was an extra-parochial area known as Blockhouse Fields, immediately outside the city wall: this was land belonging to the Greyfriars, taken over by the dean and chapter of the cathedral at the Dissolution. The base of the triangle was formed by north–south field boundaries.

Like most of its neighbours, this church was rebuilt in the eighteenth century, between 1768 and 1772, by Anthony Keck. Its medieval form is known only superficially. It was illustrated by Valentine Green in 1764 as an aisled building roofed with separate gables over each aisle bay, and with a west tower and two-storey wooden porch.

St Peter the Great (plate 17)

Without question, this was the St Peter's church outside the south wall of the *burh* which, with the manor of Battenhall and a *haga*, was granted by Bishop Oswald for three lives to the priest Wulfgar in 969 (H 136–8; S 1327). Between 1204 and 1234 its advowson was granted by John Poer, Lord of Battenhall, to Pershore Abbey (*VCH Worcs.*, iii, 517). The topography of the surrounding area has already been discussed. In brief, the church lay set back from Sidbury, the main through-road, on the corner of King Street. The *haga* conveyed with St Peter's in the Battenhall charter was not measured, and there is no way of knowing how extensive it was or how it related to the mapped topography.

St Peter's lay outside the *burh* and, like St Martin's and possibly All Saints', had a large extramural parish only part of which was enclosed by the medieval city walls. Within the walls, the parish encompassed Sidbury and the lower part of Friar Street as far as the Greyfriars precinct which was absorbed by St Helen's at the Dissolution (see above). If, before the foundation of the friary in the thirteenth century, the parish had extended to the precinct's northern boundary, the

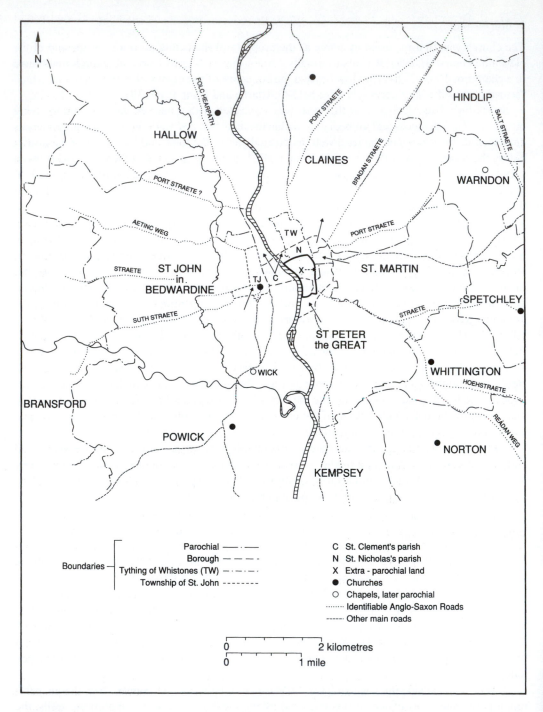

7.2   Worcester: extramural parishes, with Roman and other roads represented in pre-Conquest charters (after Hooke 1980)

length of the Sidbury/ Friar Street/ New Street 'by-pass' outside the presumed *burh* wall would have been divided equally between St Peter's and St Martin's. St Peter's parish also included Edgar Street and the properties on its southern frontage; the inclusion of these within St Peter's parish was most probably a post-*burh* or post-Conquest parochial re-organization following on the disuse and reclamation of the ninth-century defences in this area.

The rural parish was not unlike St Martin's. It occupied a similar area, triangular in shape, with the apex represented by the church site just outside the Anglo-Saxon town, and its west side formed by the Severn. Its eastern boundary with St Martin's and Whittington followed the *readan wege* or 'red way' as it was called in 983x985, diverging to the south-west from the *stræte* out of Sidbury (H 156–7, 359; S 1361; Hooke 1980, 43), and its base was formed by east–west field boundaries. It contained the manor of Battenhall, represented in later medieval settlement by scattered, moated farms.

The medieval church, demolished in 1838, consisted of a nave flanked by separately roofed aisles – the north aisle timber-framed, and a small tower attached to the north-west corner. Illustrations published in the nineteenth century show the west door and a blocked window to have been of Norman date (Baker 1980b, 119; Society of Antiquaries of London, Prattinton Collection V, 6, no. 21: see plate 17).

Post-Conquest foundations

St Nicholas's

This church was first recorded in 1256 (*Cal. Patent Rolls 1247–58*, 492). The advowson always belonged to the bishops of Worcester (*VCH Worcs.*, iv, 411). Examples of the dedication to St Nicholas in other towns suggest that the church was likely to have been founded after the middle of the eleventh century (Brooke and Keir 1975, 138), and certainly that was the period when the cult of Nicholas was being promoted in England, under the influence of the Lotharingian bishops (Ortenberg 1992, 72). Bishop Wulfstan of Worcester shared their enthusiasm for the cult (ibid.), and could well have taken the opportunity during his long episcopacy, from 1062 to 1095, of dedicating – or re-dedicating – a Worcester church to this favoured saint.

Like All Saints' and St Martin's, St Nicholas's church was associated with a market area developed just outside the *burh*. The church is on the east side of the Cross, some yards to the north of the site of the medieval Grass Cross. The Cross and its plots appear to represent the original southern end of the planned Foregate Street–Tything suburb, isolated from the rest of the suburb by the construction of the new city wall before *c.* 1200: whether the Cross had an earlier existence as an extramural market while the *burh* defences were still in use is uncertain (see above, pp. 162–3). The parish was closely related to the northern suburb: it extended beyond the city wall, its eastern boundary running parallel to and a short distance east of Sansome Place, the rear service lane behind the eastern Foregate Street plots and crofts; the western boundary included the fields to the west of the suburb. The parish extended northwards as far as the city boundary. The Tything, the northern half of the suburb, lay within the rural parish of Claines though the inhabitants chose to worship – 'being verie seldome god knowes' – at the chapel in St Oswald's hospital (which lay to the north of Worcester) rather than the distant parish church (Roy and Porter 1980, 206). It is always possible that St Nicholas's was founded within a much earlier suburb, but rather more likely that church and suburb were contemporary creations of the late eleventh century. The parish of St Nicholas in Gloucester, which covered the outer half of

Westgate Street and its planned suburban continuation across the river channel, offers a close parallel.

The present building dates mainly to *c*.1730 when the medieval church was rebuilt by Thomas White (Walker 1858, 333); its crypt – described as a 'vault for burial' by Valentine Green in 1764 – is built of sandstone and contains two blocked doors possibly of late-medieval or sixteenth-century date. Otherwise nothing is known of the medieval church, beyond the inadequate sketch in the 1651 map of Worcester.

St Michael in Bedwardine

This church, which stood outside the north-east corner of the Cathedral, was first recorded only in 1268 at the earliest (*VCH Worcs.*, iv, 411n; Buchanan-Dunlop 1942, 19–24). Julia Barrow, however, has drawn attention to the addition, after 966, of St Michael's name to the invocations of charters issued by Bishop Oswald. This, she argues, indicates the building of a church or chapel of St Michael at this time, as part of the re-organization of the northern part of the cathedral precinct which she proposes happened during the early part of Oswald's episcopacy (1996, 90; see above, p. 136).

The architecture of the medieval church was 'of Early English character' with later windows; a wooden tower stood to the north of the west end of the nave, probably a replacement for the cathedral bell-tower of 1320 (demolished in 1648) which had been built against St Michael's west end (Buchanan-Dunlop 1942, 21–2). Both its position and its dedication are consistent with its use as the cemetery chapel, St Michael being regarded as the conductor of departed souls (Ortenberg 1992, 108–13); but in time it came to serve as the parish church for the increasing numbers of people resident in houses encroaching on the area of the cemetery, particularly along the Lich Street frontage. 'The parish was the Sanctuary, with the addition of the Bishop's Palace and the Castle' (Buchanan-Dunlop 1942, 23), and its boundaries can be accurately followed from a series of perambulations of the precinct, as well as from the eighteenth-century maps.

St John in Bedwardine

This church lay at the very edge of Worcester's transpontine suburb, and in the middle ages was never considered to be a city church. Apart from the loss of one aisle, the medieval church survives intact, and lies at the junction of two roads each recorded as a *stræte* in 963 (H 133–5, 350–1; S 1303; Hooke 1980, 45–6) on the edge of the west-bank gravel terrace. It consists of a nave with a west tower and chancel, and the surviving south aisle is extended by a chapel adjoining the chancel. The earliest surviving fabric is the late-twelfth-century north nave arcade, which is consistent with the first reference to St John's in the 1190s (Darlington 1968, 340) and shows that the building was of some size long before it had parochial status. This it acquired only in 1371, at the expense of St Cuthbert's in Lower Wick which by then was already 'half deserted and attended by very few' (*VCH Worcs.*, iii, 501–10).

The essentially rural parish was, by Worcester standards, very large, covering an area larger than all the east-bank extramural parishes put together, extending from the River Teme on the south to erratic western and northern boundaries defined by minor watercourses and field boundaries between the radiating *stræte* routes.

Non-Parochial chapels

Of the several non-parochial institutions, including minor religious houses, situated in and around Worcester, four may have been of particular importance.

St Gudwal's chapel (see fig. 12.7)

This was the chapel of St Wulfstan's Hospital, situated in Sidbury outside the medieval city walls; there is reason to believe, however, that the chapel had an independent existence before the hospital's foundation. The generally accepted account of the foundation of St Wulfstan's Hospital by the saint himself (Marsh 1890, xii, 1; *VCH Worcs.*, ii, 175) is clearly a fiction, without any basis in fact. Had Bishop Wulfstan II of Worcester (1062–95) indeed founded and endowed a minor religious house dedicated to the care of the sick, his monks and their successors would have remembered it as one of his most pious acts; yet William of Malmesbury's *Vita*, written within a few decades of Wulfstan's death and based on the biography produced by Coleman, Wulfstan's chaplain for 15 years and who himself died only 18 years after the bishop (Darlington 1928, viii), does not mention the hospital. William's life of Wulfstan is both laudatory and lengthy, and loses no opportunity to tell of the sick people he cured, amongst his countless good deeds; it is unthinkable, therefore, that he could have neglected to mention the foundation of a hospital had he known of it. Nor is any reference made to a hospital in other accounts of the life, miracles, canonization and translation of the saint before an anecdote firmly dateable to 1221. Wulfstan's recent biographer devoted a single sentence to the hospital and evidently could see no reason to associate its foundation with Wulfstan himself, beyond the general belief to that effect in Worcester (Mason 1990, 190).

The origins of the hospital should be sought, therefore, during the 120 years or so following Wulfstan's death – probably, indeed, after the 1140s, for had an institution associated with his name been recently founded when William was writing, it is likely that he would have alluded to it. As it was always in the patronage of the bishops of Worcester (Marsh 1890, 2) it was evidently founded by one of Wulfstan's successors after the mid twelfth century. The logical time for such a foundation was when there was heightened interest in the saint, beginning with an unusual number of attributions of miracles to his relics after January 1201; after a year of seeming hysteria during which as many as 15 or 16 sick were cured each day, a deputation of monks was sent to Rome to secure Wulfstan's canonization, which was duly approved in 1203 (Darlington 1928, 115–88; *VCH Worcs.*, ii, 98). Certainly this would have been a fitting occasion for Bishop Mauger to found a hospital associated with Wulfstan's name and reputation as a healer; Mauger himself was an appropriate founder of a hospital, having been physician to Richard I before becoming Bishop of Worcester in 1199 (*VCH Worcs.*, ii, 11).

The hospital was a flourishing institution by 1221, according to a story in the compilation of St Wulfstan's miracles composed at Worcester by about 1240. This tells how a man called Thomas, sentenced to be castrated and blinded after losing a judicial duel on open ground outside the Sidbury Gate, had his sight and his virility miraculously restored by the intercession of the saint and through the tender care of a sister of the hospital, called Ysobel; her usual task was to lay out and pray for deceased paupers, but she surreptitiously tended this grievously wounded man after the master had refused to admit him. After his recovery, Thomas was more acceptable to the brethren, and he showed his gratitude to the saint by becoming a brother of the hospital (Darlington 1928, 168–75). The basic circumstances of the case are independently attested to in the surviving roll of the eyre (Maitland 1884, 21–2).

The new hospital's chapel lay close to Sidbury Street, according to the details of a corrody grant of the fifteenth century that stipulated the chamber to be occupied as one between the great entrance of the hospital and the chapel (Marsh 1890, 82). It was dedicated to St Godwald or Gudwal, a Breton saint of the sixth century (Farmer 1978, 197) whose cult in the diocese of Worcester was unique in England. Two possible dedications to him in Cornwall have now been discounted (Ekwall 1960, 207), leaving only that at St Wulfstan's Hospital, and the chapel of Finstall in the parish of Stoke Prior, Worcestershire – which belonged to Worcester Cathedral Priory (Arnold-Forster 1899, iii, 124, 365). Four references to Gudwal in medieval liturgical literature all come in Worcester manuscripts: in a calendar of the early thirteenth century contained in the Worcester Antiphonar; in a calendar of the same period and a Litany, both part of a Worcester Psalter at Magdalene College; in the calendar of a thirteenth-century psalter originally used at St Helen's Church, and now at Exeter Cathedral; and in a fifteenth-century Litany attached to a thirteenth-century commentary on the Psalter (Molyneux 1981, 4, citing WCL D&C F160; Floyer and Hamilton 1906, 90–93; Magdalen College, Oxford, MS 100; Turner 1916, lxiii, lxvi–lxvii; Exeter Cathedral Library 3508; Morgan 1978, 100; Bodleian Library 862, fo. 201v).

The dedication to Gudwal, rather than to Wulfstan, implies that the hospital – or at least the chapel – was already in existence when the latter was canonized in 1203. Interestingly, the use in several charters of 'St Gudwal's' as a topographical location suggests that the chapel was already well established when the hospital was founded, and that its name remained in common use for some time. In the 1240s, John Payn sold his windmill outside the Sidbury Gate to the cathedral priory, when it was described as being built outside Worcester towards St Gudwal (WCL D&C B1316, 1317; Hale 1865, 105b–106a). John had inherited the mill from one Robert of St Gudwal, a prominent Worcester citizen of the early years of the century (WCL D&C B1316; 1012, 1014, 1015). Such continued use of the chapel's name, rather than the hospital's, is an indication of its former individual identity and that it had been an established place in the locality, and so presumably points to its antiquity: as late as 1294, agricultural land situated on the south-east side of Worcester in the manor of Battenhall was described as lying next to land of St Gudwal (WCL D&C B1440).

Whilst the evidence of dedications is a most untrustworthy source for the study of early churches (see, for instance, Butler 1986, 44–50, and pp. 228–31, below), nevertheless the decision to dedicate two Worcestershire churches – alone in England – to this unlikely saint requires explanation. Historically, Gudwal is known to have been a prominent figure in sixth-century Brittany (Farmer 1978, 197), from whence his relics were removed during a period of Viking activity. They were translated with due ceremony in 959 to the Abbey of Mont Blandin, Ghent, where subsequently his feast was kept on 6 June (Bolland 1695, Junii 1, 728–42). Doubtless it was from Ghent that his cult – presumably with appropriate relics – came to Worcester, but not later than the early twelfth century, as Gudwal's feast was already being celebrated in 1125x49 under Bishop Simon (Darlington 1968, 65). If the cult had been introduced by one of the French bishops who occupied the see after the death of Wulfstan in 1095, then only Simon or one of his two predecessors were possible candidates. Samson (1096–1112) and Theolf (1113–23) were both canons of Bayeux, appointed to Worcester for political reasons; Simon, too, was a courtier, and was still only a deacon when he was elected to the see (*VCH Worcs.*, ii, 9). Neither man appears a strong candidate for the introduction of a new continental cult to Worcester.

A more credible context for the introduction of the cult is that brief period in the tenth century when contact between Worcester and Ghent was particularly close. The near coincidence in time with the translation of St Gudwal, moreover, points to this as the moment when the saint became known in England. After his exile by Eadwig in 955, it was to Mont Blandin that Dunstan retreated, and where he saw for the first time a great reformed monastery (Farmer 1975, 13). The reform of Ghent had occurred not long before Dunstan's exile (Bullough 1975, 31), and in the two years before his recall to the see of Worcester he had leisure to experience at first hand what before he had only heard of. Dunstan's stay at Ghent was thus of crucial importance to the subsequent course of the Reform Movement in England, and he himself must have regarded his experience there as a formative influence on his life. Monks from Ghent were present at the assembly held at Winchester around 970, and advised Dunstan and Æthelwold in the composition of the *Regularis Concordia*, that 'most characteristic document of the revival' (Symons 1975, 45–59; Farmer 1975, 13). Whilst at Ghent, Dunstan must have heard of Gudwal: the preparations for the translation would have been under way before Edgar summoned him to Worcester. That Dunstan returned to England with a devotion to Gudwal is possible; what is virtually certain is that he would have left Mont Blandin with valuable gifts and relics suitable for the endowment of churches in his new diocese. The monks of Ghent would not have let such a great man, restored to power and influence in England, depart empty-handed.

Dunstan remained at Worcester only until 959, being succeeded in due course by his close associate Oswald, whose own experience of a reformed continental monastery had been at Fleury (Farmer 1975, 13). Dunstan himself could have founded the two churches of St Gudwal during his brief spell at Worcester; alternatively, the responsibility was his successor's, perhaps during the 960s. In any event, a single guiding hand should be looked for in the dedication of both churches of St Gudwal: although it was recorded no earlier than the fourteenth century (*VCH Worcs.*, iii, 531–2), the foundation of the Finstall church ought surely to have happened before the division of the Church of Worcester's estates and financial affairs between the bishop and the priory led to a clear demarcation of spheres of interest. Arguably, the most serious objection to the dedication of both these churches in the post-Conquest period is the improbability that both bishop and priory would have felt moved to honour the same unusual saint.

The failure of St Gudwal's at Worcester to acquire parochial rights suggests that it was founded to serve some specialist purpose, rather than as a place of worship for the local lay population. That function was served by the nearby church of St Peter the Great, already in existence in the mid tenth century. As St Wulfstan's Hospital this would be the property of the bishops of Worcester; its brethren, sisters and inmates were maintained presumably from alms as well as from the income from its endowments, which even by 1232 were considerable (*Cal. Charter Rolls 1226–57*, 172–3; Marsh 1890, *passim*). Much of the hospital's land had evidently been given since its re-foundation; but it is significant that there is no record of its acquisition of the substantial number of houses which it owned in the 1480s in Sidbury, scattered around its buildings (Marsh 1890, 111–25, and *passim*). This was property whose unrecorded acquisition might be presumed to have dated from an early phase of the hospital's history; in all likelihood this was land around the precinct of St Gudwal's, given by whichever of the bishops had founded the church. Even in the later middle ages the hospital lay outside the city walls, and so St Gudwal's had been founded on the very fringe of the *burh* of Worcester: it has every appearance of having begun as a minor religious house of some kind – a suitable undertaking for the reforming Dunstan or Oswald.

Holy Trinity chapel and the Trinity gild

According to the chantry returns of 1548 for the parish of St Nicholas, the parish church housed an altar service worth around £4; but far more valuable – worth more than £22 annually – were the chantry and gild of the Holy Trinity (PRO E301/60). These institutions maintained their own chapel situated in Trinity Passage and quite distinct from the church (Hughes 1980, 277–8; and see above, p.169); technically it was the chantry that owned the chapel of Holy Trinity and the gild that owned the adjacent Trinity Hall (PRO E315/374, ff.1v, 3), although in practice it would surely be wrong to regard chantry and gild as separate bodies. The chapel was first mentioned in 1240 (Hale 1865, 105b), and nothing is known of its early history; its physical separation from St Nicholas's points to a foundation unconnected with the parish church. In later centuries it was independent of St Nicholas's: the contemporary rental of ex-chantry and gild lands draws a distinction between the altar service of the Virgin Mary, entered under the parish of St Nicholas, and both gild and chantry of the Holy Trinity, which are entered together at the beginning of the document, and are described simply as being in the city of Worcester (PRO E315/374, fo.1).

The Trinity gild most plausibly originated as a means of providing a priest for the non-parochial chapel of Holy Trinity – a function that gilds elsewhere performed (Rosser 1988, 32 and *passim*; and see, for instance, Smith 1870, 258–61). Perhaps the chapel was built by the people in that part of Worcester, who formed themselves into a gild so that they could maintain it; alternatively this was in origin a proprietary chapel, and the gild emerged only as a response to the owners' failure to provide a priest.

St Catherine's chapel

In 1883, workmen building new houses in the field to the rear of the buildings of the former St Wulfstan's Hospital, in the angle of Wylde's Lane and the Birmingham–Worcester canal, discovered the remains of a stone structure some 16 feet by 25 feet (4.8 x 7.6 metres), lying 7 feet (2 metres) below the ground surface. Stone built, with alternating layers of thin tiles probably of Roman origin, it was oriented east–west (Marsh 1890, 20n and p. 193 above). This would appear to have been a small church, and from its reported fabric one of Anglo-Saxon date. Possibly it was the original St Gudwal's chapel – as was believed at the time – although the chapel of the later middle ages can be shown to have stood very close to the edge of the street in Sidbury (see above). It is more likely that this structure was the chapel of St Catherine that in 1544 was said to stand upon the pasture around the prominent hill just to the south, now known as Fort Royal Hill (Baker 1980b, 122). The circumstances of the discovery discourage too much trust in the reports of the building's fabric; nevertheless, the possibility cannot be dismissed that this small area of suburban Worcester contained – with St Peter's and St Gudwal's – a cluster of three Anglo-Saxon churches.

St Peter the Less

So-called to distinguish it from the nearby parish church, this chapel stood within the castle bailey. First mentioned in 1276, and in a number of late-thirteenth-century deeds, it was last referred to in 1402. It was presumably built as the castle chapel (*VCH Worcs.*, iv, 411; WCL D&C, B987, 990, 992, 1061, 1391).

Chapter 8

The lesser churches and chapels of Gloucester and Worcester: conclusions

The foundation of the parish churches

The chronology of church-founding in both Gloucester and Worcester, in so far as it can be reconstructed, mirrored national trends. National trends were not apparent, however, in the identity of those who founded these churches.

With the exception of the friaries, the establishment of new churches in both towns had ceased by *c.* 1200 (see table, fig. 8.1). In Worcester, possibly only a single church out of a total of eleven within the city had been built in the preceding century. This was the church of St Michael in

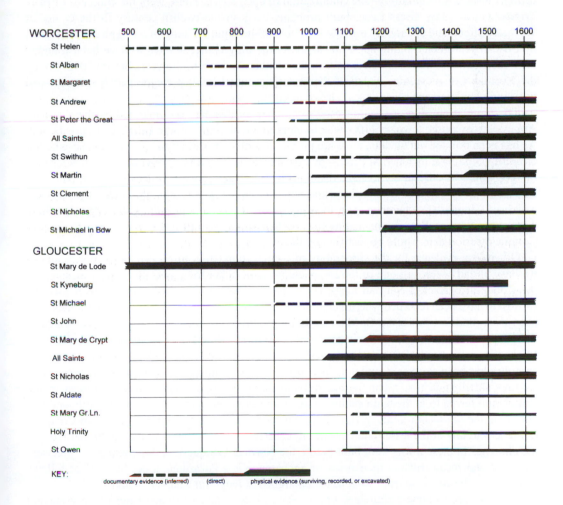

8.1   Gloucester and Worcester: the chronology of parish church foundation

Bedwardine, which stood within the cathedral close, serving as a cemetery chapel but additionally providing pastoral care to the inhabitants of the housing recently built on the edge of the lay cemetery. Alternatively, this church was in fact a much older foundation, of the tenth century, in which case the latest of Worcester's parish churches was St Nicholas's, serving the new Foregate suburb from around or shortly before 1100. If St Michael's was a post-Conquest church, then both churches can be seen to have been associated with the final stages of the expansion of the medieval built-up area: St Michael's with the intensification of settlement and the internal colonization of valuable open space, and St Nicholas's with the creation of a new suburb.

The latest churches founded in Gloucester are directly comparable. Of eleven lesser churches in *c.* 1200 (including St Kyneburgh's, which had lost its parish to St Owen's a century earlier), three had been founded in the preceding century. Again there was a church of St Nicholas, datable perhaps to the first quarter of the century, and associated not only with the creation of a new western suburb but also with the building of a new bridge, for whose upkeep it was to be responsible. The other churches were both associated with the intensification of settlement in the form of inward growth through the colonization of open space. These were the churches of Holy Trinity and St Mary Grass Lane, built probably early in the twelfth century in the centre of Westgate Street, and apparently the first elements of the rapid infilling of the centre of that street by officially-promoted buildings. Prior to these, the only church known to have been founded after the Conquest was St Owen's, built in the southern suburb in the years before 1095. So, by the Norman Conquest, nine or ten of Worcester's eventual total of eleven parish churches had been built, and perhaps seven out of eleven in Gloucester.

The foundation of most of Gloucester's churches by this date is confirmed by the Evesham Abbey Survey of the town, *c.* 1100, which refers to ten churches in the King's own jurisdiction. As has been pointed out already, there are problems with using this figure. It is not clear whether or not it would have included St Peter's, by now a great Benedictine abbey; nor should we expect the compilers of this survey to have distinguished between those churches enjoying parochial rights and those that did not. For these and other reasons, it is not possible to identify precisely which of Gloucester's churches were founded before 1100, although the knowledge that there were at least ten of them means that more churches can be assigned with confidence to the pre-Conquest period than would be justified by the available evidence.

Otherwise, evidence for the chronology of church foundation in either town is uncertain. As we have already seen, not one of the lesser churches of either town contains visible masonry of pre-Conquest character; Norman fabric is the earliest that survives and, almost universally, the earliest to have been recorded where a church has been rebuilt or demolished. Three churches have been excavated in Gloucester: St Mary de Lode produced conclusive evidence of pre-Conquest structures; All Saints', less certainly pre-Conquest fabric; while the excavations on the site of St Michael's yielded only fragmentary structures of very uncertain date. Not one of Worcester's churches has been excavated, and documentary evidence generally furnishes first references that are undoubtedly much later than the actual foundation of the relevant churches. In Worcester, one church is referred to in the tenth century, three more in the eleventh, five in the twelfth, and two not until the thirteenth century (fig. 8.1). There are no direct, contemporary, pre-Conquest references to any of the lesser churches of Gloucester. So, while there is little doubt that most of the churches in these towns were built before the Norman Conquest, dating them more precisely than that and reconstructing their order of appearance is a hazardous procedure. What follows summarizes the conclusions to what has been argued at length in Chapters 4 and 7.

Of these pre-Conquest churches, one in each place appears to have been of very ancient foundation. St Helen's in Worcester and St Mary de Lode in Gloucester were both very probably pre-Anglo-Saxon in origin. In Worcester, St Alban's and – less probably – St Margaret's may have been founded in or by the early eighth century, though the evidence for their existence at this date is contained in a much later source. At the other end of the period, a mid-eleventh-century date has been deduced for St Clement's in Worcester. Between the eighth century and the early eleventh, documentary sources allow the identification of two more Worcester churches: St Peter the Great, conveyed as part of a suburban property in a lease of 969; and St Martin's, occurring as an unnamed but easily identifiable boundary landmark in a charter of 1003x1023. To these we may add the church of All Saints', broadly datable by its likely foundation by the Church of Worcester, apparently before 963, and by its topographical context. It appears to have been a *burh* gate-church and should have been founded within the lifetime of the Anglo-Saxon defences, after the 890s and probably before 963. St Andrew's, likewise, has a good burghal context in the form of the 904 *haga*, though there is no proof of their contemporaneity.

In Gloucester, the church of St Michael, it has been suggested, was founded soon after the creation of the *burh* there: its occupancy of the corner-site frontages overlooking the central crossroads makes it unlikely that it was a feature inserted after the area was fully built up. The same may also be true of All Saints' on the opposite side of the street. St Kyneburgh's, a minster church with extensive rural dependencies, was located in or next to the Roman south gate. First recorded in 1095, it was without doubt a pre-Conquest foundation. It may have been founded soon after the creation of the *burh*, but an earlier origin cannot be ruled out. St John's, Gloucester's other gate-church, is argued to have been a tenth-century foundation. Despite indications that St Aldate's was a new foundation of the twelfth century, circumstantial evidence points to a likely origin as a private chapel in the tenth century. The church of St Mary de Crypt is one of the least well understood in the town; a pre-Conquest date is likely but cannot be proved, let alone refined, on the available evidence.

The evidence for the chronology of church-founding in the two towns is summarized in fig. 8.1. Three main points can be stressed. First is the paucity of all of the sources of evidence that are available to us. Second is the overwhelming impression that the founding of lesser churches was almost complete by 1100. Finally, it is clear that the tenth century, even more than the eleventh, emerges as the period that saw by far the greatest number of new churches – although, given the uncertainties of the evidence, final proof of this is lacking.

Previous work on the origins of English urban churches has suggested that churches in pre-Conquest towns were usually founded by laypeople (e.g. Morris 1989, 171). This conclusion emerged, for instance, from Keene's work on Winchester, where 'most of the parish churches in the city were probably essentially lay foundations set up as chapels for the owners of substantial houses and their families or in the service of more extensive local communities with common social or trading interests' (Keene 1985, 113). The same was true of London, Brooke and Keir concluding that the 'London churches were proprietary, whether built by particularly rich land-holders or by groups of citizens' (Brooke and Keir 1975, 143). A similar pattern has been noted in Lincoln, York, and other towns in eastern England, from the evidence of foundations by wealthy laymen, from inscriptions, and from surnames attached to churches (Morris 1989, 171–5).

It is clear that neither Worcester nor Gloucester followed this model. Only a single church – St Clement's – out of a combined total of 22 lesser parish churches in the two towns appears certain to have had a private, non-institutional origin, and its proposed founder was not a layman but a priest. A private, lay origin for All Saints' in Gloucester has been very tentatively suggested, and the siting of St Mary de Crypt in Gloucester and St Martin's in Worcester may possibly suggest a similar origin. St Swithun's, too, could have been built as a private church (although its likely association with the replanning of the High Street area perhaps suggests an institutional founder). By contrast with the pattern elsewhere, then, the majority of foundations in the two towns were royal, or the responsibility of royal officials – in Gloucester, the hereditary constables of the castle. Five or six churches can be shown to have been episcopal or other ecclesiastical foundations; two churches – St Helen's and St Mary de Lode – were of probable pre-Anglo-Saxon origin (though here, too, ecclesiastical origins have been argued).

Not that there was a pattern of foundation that was common to both Worcester and Gloucester. In Gloucester, most lesser church foundations are attributable to the King or his agents (5–7 out of 11). Four of these were post-Conquest foundations: St Owen's, St Nicholas's, St Mary's Grass Lane, and Holy Trinity. St Owen's is directly attributable to Roger de Pistres, sheriff and castellan of Gloucester; the other foundations were most probably the responsibility of his son, Walter, or perhaps of Walter's son, Miles of Gloucester. Amongst the pre-Conquest churches, St Kyneburgh's – which was to become the property of the constables – was an integral part of the defences, and its parish included land that may have been alienated from the royal estate of King's Barton. There is no comparable evidence for the origin of St Michael's. But if, as seems likely, it was founded in the earliest years of the *burh*, it may well have been a royal foundation accompanying the replanning of the eastern intramural area or the central crossroads. St John's, the other gate-church, was founded on royal property and was probably a royal foundation. Of the remaining Gloucester churches, St Aldate's was the only one that seems to have been founded by a religious house – Deerhurst Priory. The origins of St Mary de Crypt are too obscure to allow a founder to be identified, although if it was founded before 1086, it may then have been in the hands of Edmer the thegn. Its site is compatible with a proprietary origin (see below).

Worcester, by contrast, was dominated by episcopal foundations (4–5 out of 11). St Nicholas's was certainly a post-Conquest foundation, associated with the development of the Foregate suburb on the bishops' manor of Northwick. St Michael's, too, was founded either by one of the pre-Conquest bishops or by the cathedral priory during the post-Conquest period. Of the churches known to be pre-Conquest, St Peter the Great was episcopal property and was leased with other property by Bishop Oswald in 969; an episcopal origin is suggested for All Saints' too, because of the residual rights that the cathedral priory was able to prove in the late twelfth century, and because of its location at the entrance to the western half of the *burh* adjacent to the 904 *haga*. Within the *haga* stood St Andrew's. Despite its belonging to the cathedral priory in the eleventh century, the possibility that St Andrew's originated as a royal church is an alternative to its having been an episcopal foundation.

Thus the responsibility for church-founding in each of the two towns was very different, yet consistent with what is known about the different course of their development in the tenth–twelfth centuries. In Gloucester, a royal centre, royal foundations predominated as successive kings and their agents controlled or promoted urban development, and ecclesiastical involvement was limited. The contrast with Worcester, where ecclesiastical influence predominated, was a consequence of the roles played in each town by the respective mother-churches and their clergy. The vigorous involvement in Worcester of successive Anglo-Saxon bishops was not matched in Gloucester, where the moribund Old Minster appears to have taken no interest in founding new churches, just as it apparently remained detached from the rest of the process of urban development.

One characteristic common to both towns, then, was that in neither was there any significant degree of church-founding by the wealthy laity, the process that appears to have been predominant in London, Winchester and the larger towns of the east of England. An explanation may be that the major lords in Worcester and Gloucester – the Bishop and the King respectively – played more dominant roles amongst the smaller urban populations here than was the case in larger, more populous and wealthier towns. Gloucester's population in *c.* 1100 can be estimated to have stood, perhaps, at 3000; a figure for Worcester is more difficult to calculate, but a minimum of 2000 has been suggested (Holt 1987, 154–5; Clarke and Dyer 1968–9, 31–2). Compared with places like Lincoln and York, with estimated populations in excess of 6000 and 8000 respectively (Morris 1989, 176–8), it may be that our two towns were less socially diverse, and simply did not contain individuals who were sufficiently wealthy to contemplate founding churches.

Church buildings

Of the 22 lesser city churches in Gloucester and Worcester that were parochial at one time or another during the middle ages, only 5 (St Mary de Crypt, St Nicholas's and St Mary de Lode in Gloucester; St Alban's and St Helen's in Worcester) now remain as complete structures or retain substantial amounts of their medieval fabric. Five more (St Michael's and St John's in Gloucester; All Saints', St Swithun's and St Andrew's in Worcester) preserve their medieval west towers and little else, whilst 12 – the majority of these churches – have been demolished or entirely replaced in the modern period. Some sort of illustrative evidence showing something of their medieval form survives for five of these lost churches. All Saints', Gloucester, was excavated in the nineteenth century, and more recently an excavation took place within the demolished St Michael's, Gloucester, although the results were less than conclusive. Excavations have also taken place more recently within the surviving church of St Mary de Lode. Finally, the ghostly outlines of the foundations of two further Gloucester churches (St Mary Grass Lane and Holy Trinity) have been detected by ground-probing radar. Given the poor survival of medieval fabric and the limited extent of archaeological investigation, therefore, the conclusions to be drawn from a study of the buildings of the parish churches will necessarily be limited – as, too, will be the possibility of comparing trends in the architectural development and building chronology of the lesser churches with the great, senior churches.

Excluding the New Minster church of St Oswald (which lies outside the scope of this chapter), it is possible to discuss the form of only two pre-Conquest churches, both in Gloucester. The excavations at St Mary de Lode (Bryant 1980; reviewed more fully p. 98, above) took place within and towards the west end of the standing Norman and later building; they were necessarily limited, and consequently there is more to be said about the sequence of buildings on the site than about the development of their plans (fig. 8.2). It was shown that the late-Saxon church, possibly of ninth-century date and wholly or partly timber-built, replaced an earlier masonry structure. The nave was possibly 10 metres wide internally, and a slot parallel to the west wall was interpreted by the excavator as either a screen wall or a supporting wall for a western gallery (Bryant 1980, 9). A final pre-Norman building phase saw the construction of a tower-like masonry structure against the west wall, characterized as a 'western annexe' and interpreted as the base for a more substantial first-floor gallery or chapel. Alterations to the nearby New Minster church in the tenth century also appear to have been associated with the provision of a tower or of an upper floor (Heighway and Bryant 1999, 12–13).

All Saints' – if Medland was correct in his identification of pre-Conquest characteristics – was much smaller. It was a two-cell building consisting of a nave about 5 metres wide internally, and a square-ended chancel (fig. 3.8); the building was about 17.5 metres long including the chancel (Medland 1894–5). It was in the same size-range as other small, late-Saxon two-cell churches and chapels, both urban and rural – such as Odda's Chapel at Deerhurst; its nave floor area of about 50 square metres compares closely with the very smallest Norman two-cell buildings in the region (Bond 1988, 141–2). The proportions of its nave, in a ratio of 1:2.5, were perhaps rather longer and

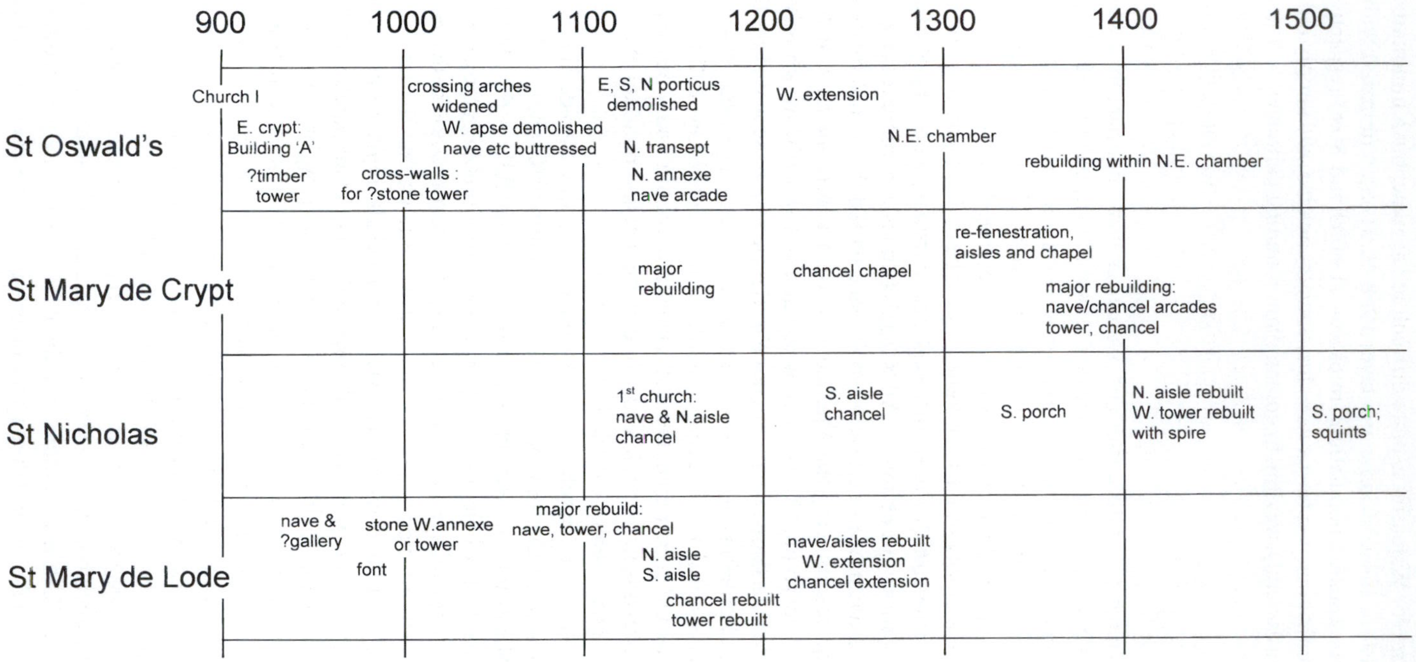

St Oswald's
Church I
E. crypt: Building 'A'
?timber tower
cross-walls for ?stone tower
crossing arches widened
W. apse demolished
nave etc buttressed
E, S, N porticus demolished
N. transept
N. annexe
nave arcade
W. extension
N.E. chamber
rebuilding within N.E. chamber

St Mary de Crypt
chancel chapel
major rebuilding
re-fenestration, aisles and chapel
major rebuilding: nave/chancel arcades tower, chancel

St Nicholas
1st church: nave & N.aisle chancel
S. aisle
chancel
S. porch
N. aisle rebuilt
W. tower rebuilt with spire
S. porch; squints

St Mary de Lode
nave & ?gallery
stone W.annexe or tower
font
major rebuild: nave, tower, chancel
N. aisle
S. aisle
chancel rebuilt
tower rebuilt
nave/aisles rebuilt
W. extension
chancel extension

900   1000   1100   1200   1300   1400   1500

8.2   Church-building in Gloucester: chronological development diagram of construction activity

narrower than most (Taylor 1978, 1033). As discussed earlier, its west wall contained a centrally placed door that appears to have belonged to the pre-Conquest structure and would have given access to ground that was later to become a separate plot. The position of other doors is not known for certain, though by 1455 there was a public entrance in the north wall towards the chancel.

Few if any of the lesser churches in Gloucester or Worcester can have been left unaltered in the century following the Norman Conquest; there were Norman features in every church for which there is any information relating to the medieval fabric. Nevertheless, for only a tiny minority of churches can their Norman plans be recovered. The most intact surviving building of that period is St Alban's, Worcester, originally an unaisled single-cell building with no structural division between the nave and chancel; it was extended a few feet westwards possibly within the twelfth century. It doubtless owes its survival to the small size and limited resources of its parish which discouraged later rebuilding. At St Mary de Lode, the late eleventh and early twelfth centuries saw the entire church rebuilt, save for the late-Saxon western annexe. The new church was an aisleless building with a central tower and a rectangular chancel (Bryant 1980, 10).

St Nicholas's, Gloucester, was probably founded in the early twelfth century, and the surviving Norman fabric – which belongs to the first half of the century – may be a relic of the first church. Its original size is unknown, but it was provided with a north aisle from the beginning (Medland 1900). The addition of aisles to existing buildings – and north aisles, wherever they occur singly – appears to be a phenomenon that begins at this time. It was paralleled at the New Minster by the construction just after *c.* 1150 of a 'north annexe', or a long two-cell structure reached from the nave via a single door, and subsequently by the construction of a true aisle communicating with the nave through an inserted arcade. These events may have been associated with the Minster's refoundation as the Augustinian priory of St Oswald in 1152–3 (Heighway and Bryant 1999, 17). St Mary de Lode was also rebuilt at this time, acquiring nave arcades and north and south aisles (Bryant 1980, 10). In Worcester, the nave arcade and north aisle of St Clement's were of early-twelfth-century date. At St Helen's 'remains of the Norman capitals and dog-tooth enrichments' found by Aston Webb in the nineteenth century imply that the church was aisled before 1200; at about that time a north aisle was also added to St Alban's (Baker 1980b).

In the second quarter of the thirteenth century, St Nicholas's, Gloucester, was substantially rebuilt, becoming fully aisled. By the end of the middle ages, all of the Worcester churches for which there is evidence were fully aisled with the exceptions of the single-aisled St Alban's and St Clement's. The acquisition of aisles by the Gloucester churches was, however, less straight-forward. An interesting group of churches remained unaisled or single-aisled – not a sign that their parishes were poor but a consequence of their occupying constricted sites in the town's commercial centre. Thus the two twelfth-century street churches, Holy Trinity and St Mary Grass Lane, had of necessity to retain their original two-cell plans as any lateral expansion would have blocked what little remained of the public highway (fig. 3.8, based on radar survey by M. Atkin). All Saints' was rebuilt in the thirteenth century, and again in the fourteenth, when the wealth of its parish or its patron was reflected in the evident quality of its masonry, but not by any increase in its ground area. Completely hemmed-in by built-up frontages, a property boundary to the west, and probably by its rectory to the south, the only way to go was up – and the result was a fine and very lofty thirteenth-century church on a tiny, probably Anglo-Saxon, ground-plan. Similar problems faced St Michael's too. It was able to build a south aisle or chapel only in the early fourteenth century, when the opportunity arose to acquire extra ground from the next-door plot. Construction of a north aisle was not possible – not because the burgesses would necessarily have objected to another encroachment onto the street, but because the opportunity had already gone, commercial buildings having been erected there in the twelfth century.

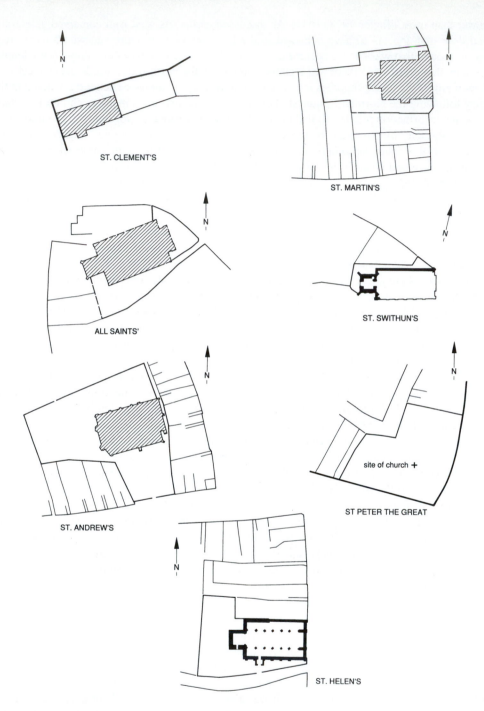

8.3   Churches and church-plots: comparative plans, Worcester

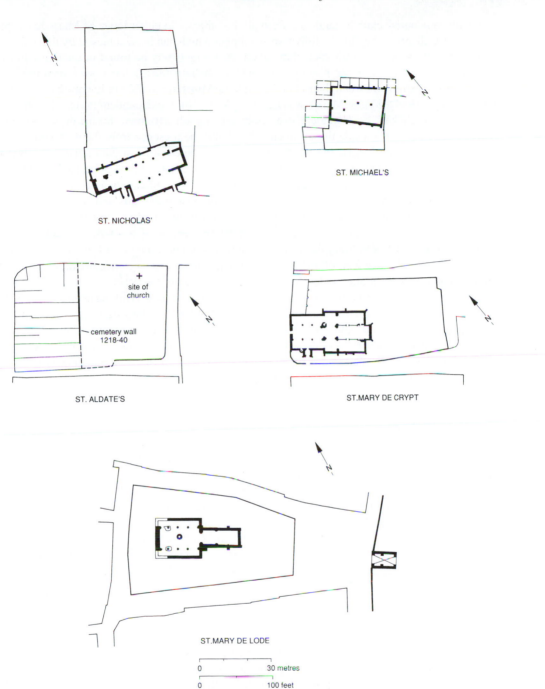

ST. NICHOLAS'

ST. MICHAEL'S

site of
church

cemetery wall
1218-40

ST. ALDATE'S

ST.MARY DE CRYPT

ST.MARY DE LODE

0   30 metres

0   100 feet

8.4   Churches and church-plots: comparative plans, Gloucester

Finally, one parish church stands out from all the others – in either town. St Mary de Crypt in Gloucester is distinguished by the fully transeptal plan which had been achieved by the end of the thirteenth century. A reason for such elaboration can undoubtedly be found in Lanthony Priory's acquisition of St Mary's in the mid twelfth century. Richard Morris has drawn attention to the 'cruciformity' exhibited by daughter churches of York Minster, possibly in imitation of the parent house (Morris 1989, 283). St Mary's was Lanthony's only fully independent parish church within the city, and would have been an ideal, even essential, city advertisement for the priory, which lay on a secluded site well outside the south gate. No doubt the presence from the thirteenth century of the friaries, lurking behind the Southgate Street frontages, was an additional incentive: the Dominicans at least made sure that passing traffic would be aware of their presence by placing the gatehouse of their precinct on the frontage, opposite St Mary's. Directly behind St Mary's was the precinct of the Greyfriars. It is difficult to avoid the conclusion that this parish church's splendid thirteenth-century and later architecture was a direct result of intense competition between rival religious houses, thrown together within the restricted length of a single city street. A not dissimilar role to that of St Mary de Crypt was being played in London for Canterbury Cathedral Priory by St Mary le Bow. This church's most distinctive feature is its enormous vaulted eleventh-century undercroft, extending under the nave and aisles. Later, this was the setting for the Court and Deanery of Arches; possibly its original uses were more prosaic (Brooke and Keir 1975, 283; Schofield 1984, 44). Apart from the elaboration of its plan, St Mary de Crypt's most unusual feature was the eponymous undercroft beneath its west end. It is not impossible that this common feature of their structures points to an intended similarity of role for both churches, and that the Gloucester church performed some of the logistical functions for the extramural priory that might have been discharged by a town-house with an undercroft.

Church dedications

In only one of the studies of the churches of Worcester or Gloucester has a dedication been taken to constitute decisive evidence for the circumstances of a church's foundation. Because of the precise coincidence of the origin of the cult of St Gudwal at Ghent and the period of Dunstan's residence there, together with the fact that in England the cult was observed only at Worcester, the unusual dedication of the chapel of St Wulfstan's Hospital to Gudwal has been advanced as indicating a probable foundation date in the late tenth century, following on Dunstan's appointment to the see of Worcester. Otherwise, when a dedication has been cited it has been to inform a discussion of evidence rather than to conclude it. Most obviously, certain dedications establish a probable – though seldom a certain – *terminus post quem* for the naming of a church. In the case of the two churches dedicated to St Nicholas, the beginning of this cult's widespread popularity in the west only during the eleventh century is a powerful indicator of the earliest likely date for their foundation. Similarly, the dedication of a church to St Aldate, it has been argued, presumably post-dated the wide dissemination of Geoffrey of Monmouth's *History of the Kings of Britain* after 1136 – a dating that does, of course, rest upon the identification of Aldate with Eldad (Thorpe 1966, 28; Farmer 1978, 11), Geoffrey's surely mythical fifth-century Bishop of Gloucester.

It may also be remarked how appropriate some dedications were to their setting, or to some other identifiable circumstance of their foundation. Churches of St Clement have a tendency to maritime or waterfront associations, as is the case at Worcester (Morris 1989, 175; Arnold-Forster 1899, i, 286). The commemoration of an Irish saint in St Brigid's chapel at Gloucester becomes more easily understood when we see that the act of dedication in 1184 was carried out by an Irish bishop working in England at that time. The church of St Owen, or Ouen, built by the Norman constables of Gloucester and dedicated in 1095, commemorated a suitably Norman saint, whose cult came from Rouen (Farmer 1978, 332). Even when a dedication is less obviously appropriate, whether in spatial or chronological terms, it may open up a new route into a church's history. Dunstan's known devotion to St Andrew should certainly not be allowed to influence unduly the discussion of when St Andrew's church was dedicated or who might have been the founder, but it does point to what might have been the beginning of a period during which the community of the Church of Worcester are likely to have favoured a dedication to St Andrew.

How far were there detectable trends in dedication, either before or after the Conquest? The fondness of church-builders of the early Anglo-Saxon centuries for dedications to St Peter is amply confirmed, with two known churches in each city dedicated to the apostle by the tenth century. In Gloucester, an Anglo-Saxon preference for dedicating churches to the apostles and to certain traditional saints (Butler 1986, 44) seems to be borne out, with dedications to All Saints, St John, St Michael and two to St Mary; the chapel of St Thomas the Apostle may be Anglo-Saxon, or may be no earlier than the twelfth century. There was a single dedication to an Anglo-Saxon saint, to St Kyneburgh, a local saint whose cult was presumably kept at the Old Minster. Probable post-Conquest dedications drew on a wider range of sanctity, commemorating as they did St Mary, the Holy Trinity, St Aldate, St Martin, St Brigid, St Ouen, St Nicholas and St Thomas the Martyr. In Worcester, the founders of pre-Conquest churches were rather more inventive: in addition to St Peter, there were dedications to St Andrew, All Saints, St Martin, St Clement, St Helen, St Alban, St Gudwal and perhaps St Margaret. The date of St Michael's church is very uncertain; churches which are possibly or probably post-Conquest were dedicated to St Swithun and St Nicholas, whilst non-parochial chapels of uncertain date were dedicated to the Holy Trinity, St Catherine and St Ursula.

Yet, however much we might know about the pattern of dedication, it cannot be used as a reliable aid to dating either the churches themselves or the date of development of their surroundings. With the exception of the single dedication to St Gudwal, none of the church dedications of Worcester or Gloucester has been found acceptable as having any intrinsic value as evidence for a church's date of foundation, and each one of these churches has been dated by using other evidence. The knowledge that a particular choice of dedication might have been favoured during a particular period is insufficiently firm ground on which to base an assessment of a church's antiquity, and might indeed be wholly misleading. There are 'early' dedications, such as that to St Martin in Gloucester, which are attached to what seem to be late churches; and because of the general lack of evidence for the early years of many churches, in Worcester and Gloucester and elsewhere, the possibility that some examples of 'late' dedications might appreciably pre-date the period of their greatest currency is not to be excluded. The establishment by the mid-tenth century of a cult of Ouen at Christ Church, Canterbury (Rollason 1989, 36), means that the dedication could conceivably have been attached to English churches well before the Conquest. And after a particular saint had become fashionable, of course, a dedication to them can only be precisely dated by other means. Furthermore, observed associations cannot work in reverse: apostolic dedications certainly do not have to be Anglo-Saxon, just as churches of St Clement need not be located by waterfronts and have Scandinavian connections.

Most difficult to assess is how many dedications were in fact rededications of older churches. Existing churches were undoubtedly rededicated more frequently than known examples might suggest; and whilst there would appear to be no case in either Worcester or Gloucester quite as emphatic as that of St Nicholas's in Leicester, which combines early Anglo-Saxon fabric with a dedication usually attributed to the post-Conquest period (Morris 1989, 37), nevertheless the possibility of such major discrepancies can never be excluded. The churches of St Nicholas in both towns have been dated within a relatively narrow chronological range, from the late eleventh century to the mid twelfth; but that is a judgment in each case based on topographical and historical evidence, and the dedications are merely consistent with that conclusion. The only certain rededication that we know of in either town, the dedication of St Peter's, the New Minster, to St Oswald, has misled historians into believing that this church must have been founded after 909 and the acquisition of St Oswald's relics. The fact of its rededication has hitherto obscured the earliest phase of the church's history as well as that of the *burh*; for although it was clearly still a relatively new church in 909, its earlier foundation has important implications for Æthelred's and Æthelflæd's activities in and around Gloucester during the preceding years, and for the date of the refurbishment and laying-out of the *burh*.

Of the other Gloucester churches, St Aldate's is – on the face of it – the most likely to have been rededicated. As argued above, an association with St Eldad, Geoffrey of Monmouth's fictional bishop of fifth-century Gloucester, points to a dedication after 1136, a date quite in keeping with the first reference to the church in the early years of the thirteenth century. But on other grounds a twelfth-century date seems too late for this church. Edward the Confessor gave Deerhurst Priory to St Denis in Paris, which seems an unlikely founder of a church in a faraway town in which it can have had little interest; moreover St Aldate's position, at the rear of what appears to have been the capital messuage of Deerhurst's block of Gloucester property and close to the north gate, points perhaps to its having originated as the private chapel of its important patron. Both strands of evidence, therefore, indicate this to have been a foundation by Deerhurst Priory before the Conquest – and perhaps well before. St Aldate's possession of parochial rights over this block of property is also more consistent with a foundation earlier than the twelfth century, when different criteria for the establishment of parish boundaries would have applied (see Chapter 9, below). Together, this other evidence for St Aldate's antiquity is far more persuasive than its late dedication.

The dedication of the church at Gloucester's south gate to St Kyneburgh is undatable, and provides an illustration of some of the complexities that surround even a dedication to an entirely local saint. Even if we are correct in identifying this saint with the reputed first abbess of the Old Minster, the period during which the association was made can be narrowed down only to the four centuries between *c.* 700 and 1095, the earliest reference to the church. Thus the dedication alone can tell us very little about the antiquity of either the church or of the cult, and demonstrates only that the cult was not confined to the Old Minster where it must have originated. The commemoration of the saint at a lesser church of the town – albeit apparently a minster church – is unlikely to have been based upon the possession of any significant relics, despite the claim for the rebuilt church of St Kyneburgh in the late middle ages that it possessed the corpse of a saint who was now presented as a mythical princess. It is not even clear, therefore, whether the dedication should be attributed to a period when Kyneburgh's cult was flourishing locally; it may, alternatively, date from a time when the Old Minster was in eclipse, and was no longer prominent as the focus of the cult. The need to create a mythical identity for St Kyneburgh in later centuries suggests that her true identity had been forgotten during a period in which her cult had been neglected, with only her name – and perhaps her royal associations – remembered.

Yet however uncertain their usefulness as evidence, church dedications are not to be dismissed out of hand. The choice of patron saint for a new church or a re-foundation can never have been an entirely random matter, but on every occasion reflected some deeper consideration – whether of deep personal devotion, the opportune possession of relics, a symbolic attribute of the saint, close local association, or simply current fashion. And whilst it is inevitable that in most cases it will be impossible to identify a specific reason for a dedication, nevertheless a potential value as evidence always remains. It is quite clear from the examples of the Worcester and Gloucester churches that in a few instances a clearer understanding of the significance of a dedication can add a great deal to our perception of the circumstances under which a church was founded; it is equally clear, however, that only in the most exceptional of cases will a dedication be understood without good, additional evidence. The problem of rededication adds further complications, which are least serious when other evidence exists to show that this might have occurred, as in the case of St Aldate's. Few saints, however, are so conveniently dated as is St Eldad, and for most churches rededication is an unquantifiable possibility, of which there is no indication but for which allowance must always be made. A church's dedication is not, therefore, a short cut into its early history, an easy way of approaching its origins. There is every prospect that in time we shall understand much more about both church foundation and dedication in the Anglo-Saxon period; but that will be achieved only through a wider study of the evidence for church origins, in which the enigmatic evidence of dedications may find its place.

The distribution and siting of the lesser churches

Research in a variety of towns has shown that parish churches were seldom evenly distributed within early-medieval built-up areas. In particular, some towns, such as Winchester, Exeter and Colchester, reveal concentrations of churches along their High Streets, a distribution pattern widely accepted as a reflection of the early medieval geography of wealth and population in those places (Keene 1985, 114–15; Allan *et al.* 1984, 398–9; Morris 1989, 192–3). The distribution patterns of lesser churches within Gloucester and Worcester were markedly dissimilar, Gloucester following the High Street model closely, but Worcester scarcely at all.

The effect of the surviving Roman fortress walls on the subsequent development of Gloucester's town-plan has already been commented upon: briefly, it is argued that the most striking effect of this morphological frame was the restriction of through-traffic passing across the urbanizing site to the four great streets converging on a central cross-roads, and a consequent restriction of the total length of intramural main-street frontage that was available for development. This guaranteed that an enormous differential in status and value would exist between the frontages of the principal streets and those of the minor streets that did not carry through-traffic. The distribution of the lesser churches in Gloucester reflects this directly: only one parish church out of the eleven extant by *c.* 1200 was not associated with one of the four main streets. The exception was, of course, St Mary de Lode, whose site was determined by wholly extraordinary and pre-urban factors. Two of the churches, and one non-parochial chapel, occupied what have been characterized as 'carfax sites' on opposite corners of the central cross-roads. St Michael's is likely to have been the first and, as a public church that was probably of royal foundation, it occupied a site that may well have been earmarked for the purpose when the planned street-system was laid out over the eastern half of the *burh*, or, more likely, when the central crossroads were reorganized slightly later. All Saints' stood opposite to the west. Its small size and dependent status strongly suggest that it was, in origin, a private chapel later appropriated for public worship. The same may well have been true of St Martin's in the north-east quadrant, which never achieved parochial status, was set back farther from the frontages, and may have been the latest arrival of the three. In its partly proprietorial origins, this group of carfax churches differs somewhat from that in Bristol, which may have been planned as a group to serve respective quarters of the town – 'each ward's church visible to the others, like opposing pavilions at an international exhibition' (Morris 1989, 210).

Both St Kyneburgh's and St John's can reasonably be argued to have been gate-churches. The former was located in, on or next to the Roman south gate, and the latter stood immediately opposite the north gate; the interests of both were largely extramural. Both churches were very probably in place before the end of the tenth century. While Westgate Street may have been the principal commercial and market street of the *burh* (Hurst 1986, 129), the Northgate–Southgate route through the town was part of the long-distance strategic north–south route along the east bank of the Severn, commemorated by the name Hare (*here* = army) Lane beyond the walls; it also connected the town to the royal palace at Kingsholm. It was also the axis of the *burh* street-system. It may, therefore, have had a special political, symbolic and processional significance that was additionally recognized by the foundation of churches at the gates at each end.

Holy Trinity and St Mary Grass Lane, both apparently early-twelfth-century foundations by the constables of the castle, were sited in the middle of Westgate Street and were almost certainly primary components of the officially promoted central block of street encroachments. Their construction marks the increasing importance of Westgate Street as Gloucester's connection with Wales and the Marches developed, and emphasizes the re-orientation of the town-plan from the old, Anglo-Saxon, north–south axis. To incomers to the town from the west, these churches were prominent, even obstructive, presences, and may when built have represented a very direct way for the constables to display their town's prestige. Perhaps, too, they had some stational significance. The cross formation of Gloucester's main streets has obvious symbolic associations, and it would perhaps be surprising if the processional potential inherent in it was not realized and adapted as more churches were founded. More prosaically, we may suppose that the population of commercial Westgate Street was expanding, maybe rapidly, in the early twelfth century: the foundation of these churches can also be seen in this context of intensifying settlement and an enlarged local population.

St Mary de Crypt and St Nicholas's, probable pre-Conquest and early-twelfth-century foundations respectively, also had direct main-street associations. Both were sited on commercial frontages, St Mary's within the walls, St Nicholas's on Lower Westgate Street, outside the old west wall but within the linked enceintes of the post-Conquest town. It is also the case that each of these churches had a distinctly secular – even commercial – element to it: St Mary de Crypt had what appears to have been an undercroft, while St Nicholas's played a role in the construction and maintenance of the Gloucester bridge.

St Aldate's lay some distance from Northgate Street on an intramural lane and, at first sight, appears unassociated with the main street. However, a case has already been made for suggesting that the church lay within, and was in origin a part of, a large rectilinear plot or *haga* belonging to Deerhurst Priory. That this property originally extended westwards to embrace the Northgate Street frontage can be argued from the inclusion of the frontage properties west of the churchyard within St Aldate's parish, despite their proximity to St John's. The location of the Deerhurst property on Northgate Street just within the north gate is particularly appropriate as this was the gate leading to the parent house, and recalls the location of the pre-Conquest properties of *Staeningahaga* and *Basingahaga* in London near the road to their respective parent rural manors (Dyson and Schofield 1984, 306–7). The late-eleventh-century St Owen's church stood in the Southgate Street suburb behind the western plot-series; it was the pastoral successor to St Kyneburgh's and the place of worship for the inhabitants of the Southgate suburb; excavation has located the winding metalled surface of St Owen's Lane leading from the Southgate Street frontage to the church behind the plots (Atkin 1991b, 14). The rationale for the location of the church on that particular site at the rear of the plot-series is, however, less than certain and may have been determined by a pre-existing cemetery serving St Kyneburgh's parish (see below).

The distribution of churches in Worcester was very different. The early medieval town was dominated by the axial north–south High Street, and this can be seen to have been the wealthiest part of the town as soon as its economic geography becomes apparent. Yet out of the eleven city churches extant by *c*.1200 – and probably a century earlier – only two were located on the High Street itself, with a third near Sidbury, which in effect was its southern continuation. But of even this small group of churches, the site of one – St Helen's – was determined by pre-urban criteria, specifically, by the course of the Roman earthwork defences, and the presence of a probable gate through them on the line of the High Street (fig. 6.17). The origins of St Helen's should, as discussed before, probably be sought in the period before the foundation of the Worcester see. Its peripheral location next to the Roman north gate suggests that it may from an early date have been closely identified with the High Street route that was to form the core of its later medieval intramural parish. This may explain why no further churches were founded along the High Street within the lifetime of the *burh*. When (or after) the High Street north of the Roman enclosure was redeveloped, a new church – St Swithun's – was founded and its parish came to share the High Street with St Helen's. St Swithun's itself was not founded on a High Street site, but on what seems to have been newly won ground behind it, reclaimed by the levelling of the defences. Only St Nicholas's, a foundation almost certainly of *c*. 1050–1100 associated with the Grass Market outside the old defences and the Foregate suburb beyond, complemented St Helen's in terms of physical proximity to the High Street.

St Peter the Great was loosely associated with the axial north–south routeway. Extant by 969, it occupied a site on the corner of King Street and St Peter's Street behind the plots on the south side of Sidbury. It was leased along with the *haga* by the southern wall described in the Battenhall charter (H 136–8, 357–8; S1327). The extent of this property is unknown, and there is no evidence to suggest how long the church had existed before its appearance in the documentary record. Its siting may have been determined by purely secular demands arising from the development of the Sidbury suburb, though as an episcopal foundation it may have had a particular liturgical significance, and possibly even an association with St Gudwal's across the road.

The siting of most of the remainder of Worcester's lesser churches can be shown to have been dependent on other through- or main-traffic streets passing across the town site. The location of All Saints' was that of a gate-church marking the entrance to the *burh* of the roads coming up from the river crossing and ultimately from Wales and the Marches. St Martin's, perhaps newly-established in 1000, is argued to have been associated not with the Cornmarket – which was probably a post-Conquest development – but with one of the suburban properties facing Mealcheapen Street; this road, heading east into agricultural countryside, was more directly overlooked by St Swithun's and may have been regarded as much the latter's natural constituency as was the High Street.

St Alban's is a difficult case. The immediate determinants of its site may have been the Roman defences immediately to the north, and a probable passage through them for the wandering escarpment-top road eventually fossilized as Birdport, but these factors cannot be invoked with absolute conviction as so much uncertainty surrounds the church's origin. But the balance of evidence points to a relatively early pre-Conquest date for its foundation, almost certainly anterior to the establishment of the planned street-grid over the levelled Roman earthworks; this would explain the church's peculiar relationship to the adjacent street frontages. As an outpost of Evesham Abbey within the Roman enclosure it is likely to have been attached to a larger piece of city property, presumably once in royal hands (as the thirteenth-century Evesham Abbey chronicle claims). If St Alban's was founded by Evesham, then the location of the church is likely to have been determined by the location of this property.

St Andrew's was located within the area of the bishops' riverside *haga* recorded in 904. Unfortunately, there is as yet no way of knowing how long the integrity of this property, as measured, was maintained – nor, with any precision, the date at which this church was founded. It is certainly possible or even likely that St Andrew's was founded in the tenth century as a chapel within the *haga*, but this cannot be proved. In general terms it can be safely concluded that the church's location was determined by the 904 *haga* or one of its immediate successor-plots (see fig. 6.13) and, ultimately, by proximity to an accessible waterfront and access to Birdport.

The church of St Michael in Bedwardine, though fully parochial, was an exceptional case and, strictly speaking, falls outside the scope of this discussion. Within the cathedral close and in the lay cemetery, its location would have been determined by the close's developing liturgical geography – whether St Michael's was of Anglo-Saxon origin or a new foundation of the late twelfth or thirteenth century. Its site suited its known or assumed functions in the thirteenth century, as a chapel for the lay cemetery and as a place of worship for the residents of the plots and encroachments around the north-east quarter of the precinct.

Finally, there is the problem of St Clement's. Its siting has been discussed at length already without any firm conclusions being reached. In summary, its detachment from the parish it served was anomalous: the church lay on the east bank of the Severn and its parish mainly on the west. The location of St Clement's may have been determined solely by the location of its founder's property, the church acquiring its parochial functions at a later date: it was regarded as being dependent upon All Saints' until the settlement of 1175; the maritime associations of its dedication are consistent with its waterfront siting.

In conclusion, it appears that the distribution of churches within early-medieval Gloucester and Worcester was influenced by very diverse factors: by pre-urban constraints, mainly surviving elements of the Roman landscapes; by the respective geography of each *burh* – most obviously by the defences, but also perhaps by less tangible factors to do with symbolism and procession; by the distribution of high-status properties where church- or chapel-founding and maintenance was both economically possible and socially or spiritually necessary; and, to a lesser extent, by the development of early-medieval suburbs. The distribution pattern of churches in Gloucester was simple because the secular occupation pattern was simple: wealth, high-status properties, traffic and population were concentrated on the four main streets. The churches were almost entirely intramural, in Roman and late-Saxon terms – another reflection of status, wealth, politics, and the relative chronology of church-founding and population. The contrast between Worcester and Gloucester suggests that the distribution of churches – referred to at the beginning of this section – seen in Winchester, Exeter and Colchester, should be regarded as typical not of early-medieval towns but of early-medieval towns growing up within Roman walls. The distribution of churches in Worcester was so different because its early-medieval secular geography was so much more complicated. The one main traffic street that dominated the site may itself have been dominated by St Helen's, the oldest foundation, which prevented the multiplication of later foundations along it. Instead, in Worcester, the more amorphous pattern of lesser through-streets, with a multiplication of junctions as potential foci, provided competing locations for church-founding. The distribution of high-status properties, where they can be identified, was also more amorphous than that in Gloucester, influenced not only by secondary through-streets but by the availability and competing pull of the river frontage, and this too complicated the physical patterning of church-founding.

Churches and church-plots (figs 8.3 and 8.4)

It has been said that both Worcester and Gloucester were to some extent typical of medieval towns in the west of England in that their parish churches grew up in the shadow of great churches that claimed burial monopolies; the lesser churches were thus usually unaccompanied by graveyards. This in turn significantly affected the choice of sites for church-founding, leading to a significant proportion of foundations on carfax, street-corner and street-encroachment sites (Barrow 1992b). As noted above, Gloucester in particular exemplifies this trend, with three carfax foundations (including the non-parochial St Martin's) and two in the middle of Westgate Street. In Worcester, however, the association is far from valid, only St Nicholas's and St Swithun's occupying restricted corner sites, though the cathedral sought to maintain its burial monopoly until the end of the middle ages. In Worcester, the absence of burial rights does not seem to have been a determining factor in the location of the lesser churches. It can also be argued that when burial rights were acquired – whether in the late middle ages or subsequently – the majority of the lesser churches already had open space available for burials. Others may once have had it, and one of the corner-site churches was able to acquire it.

In Gloucester, the churches of St Nicholas, St Mary de Crypt and St Aldate all stood in open plots that, sooner or later, came to be used for burial. St Nicholas's stood right on the frontage of a plot that closely resembled those of its secular neighbours, the kind of site that has been described as an 'ecclesiastical burgage' though this was not a local proprietorial foundation (Morris 1989, 195). Parishioners were buried within the plot perhaps from the foundation of their church in the late eleventh century: it had an *atrium* in *c.* 1210, and by 1403 the churchyard needed to be enlarged. The church almost certainly post-dated the plot. Its position on the frontage is interpreted as a product of its association with the nearby bridge and its need to attract offerings (if not actually to collect tolls) from passing traffic; it must have replaced earlier secular buildings, and in a way it maintained the commercial function of the plot-frontage. Its orientation was less than ideal for its surroundings, but it was liturgically proper for the date at which it was founded.

St Mary de Crypt stands on the Southgate Street frontage at the head of a plot which, while larger than most, was not out of place among its commercial neighbours; it was used for burial by the 1190s (see below, p. 245). Frontage buildings appear to have been demolished for the extension of the church in the late twelfth century, though whether the church had been built behind a built-up frontage, or the frontage left open and then encroached upon, is unknown. St Aldate's stood on open ground that was described as a cemetery by *c.* 1280, but it may not always have been used as such. The church's origins may, as discussed, have been as a private chapel within a large plot belonging to Deerhurst Priory, with a built-up commercial frontage on Northgate Street. If this interpretation is correct, then the location of the church away from the main street may be attributable to its proximity to a former hall complex; if instead St Aldate's was indeed the new twelfth-century foundation that its dedication might suggest, then its location would be explicable in the usual way as being on open ground away from the frontage.

Because of its twelfth-century reconstruction and the subsequent redevelopment of the area, there is no way of knowing whether St Kyneburgh's church at the south gate possessed any sort of attached curtilage. It did, however, have rights of burial in the eleventh century, and a cemetery outside the wall that was first recorded in 1377; the cemetery may, by analogy with Winchester, by then have been an extremely old one (Keene 1985, 108). The cemetery may also have determined the site of the later church of St Owen. St John's, at the north gate, had no attached plot that can be seen in the later cartographic record though it possessed burial rights in 1197–8;

in 1407 it acquired a 'new cemetery' across the lane, just within the city wall. Where it buried its twelfth-century parishoners is not clear: there is no archaeological evidence for an early extramural cemetery, so it may be that an original open plot around the church has been obscured by encroaching properties.

Even All Saints' on its carfax corner-plot seems originally to have stood in a rather larger curtilage than that required for its own footprint. Its west wall latterly formed part of the boundary between the church plot and no. 1 Westgate Street next door, yet the nineteenth-century records of the rediscovery of the church show its west wall to have been pierced by a blocked door associated with the church's lowest floor levels, which were thought to be of late-Saxon date. Again, we seem to be seeing evidence for the disintegration of a larger plot that contained the church and may once have contained other, secular buildings as well. There is no evidence that burials ever took place here. Well before 1455 ecclesiastical use of the plot was probably confined to the church itself and to the rectory immediately to its south, and the alienation of pieces of land for commerce had extended to the point where the church itself now lay behind a continuous screen of commercial frontage encroachments.

St Michael's was – except for the street-churches – the only Gloucester church without an associated curtilage from its foundation. The stages by which the church was enlarged and an open plot acquired at the expense of its neighbours are well recorded (see above, p. 110). First, in 1321, it acquired the tail of an adjoining plot to the south so that an aisle could be built: at that time there was no burial ground. Second, in 1368, the tail of a further plot was acquired for burials, the right to which had only recently been won. The final episode in the expansion of the church and its plot took place with the construction of the west tower in the mid fifteenth century.

There is, finally, the case of St Mary de Lode. Excavation has established the presence of burials around this church by the ninth century, against a background of sub-Roman burials within what had, in the Roman period, been an open metalled area. The date by which the cemetery assumed the form of the churchyard represented in cartography of the eighteenth century and later is not known; the possible co-existence here of burial and market functions cannot be ruled out.

In Worcester, St Helen's church – though on a High Street corner site – retains an open area around its west end that may well represent the surviving portion of a much larger church plot. It shares a common back boundary with the adjoining secular plots to the north, and it is not improbable that these represent former church property, the descendants of the nine houses, appurtenant to St Helen's, that lay around it in *c.* 1100. The whole series fits unobtrusively into the general landscape of the west side of the High Street suggesting that (as the church is of ancient, pre-urban, origin) St Helen's surroundings were subject to the replanning of the area that is argued to have taken place in the late-Saxon period, possibly the mid tenth century.

St Andrew's was a notable example of a church sited within a large churchyard which has the appearance of being an early feature of the local landscape, but which nevertheless was not consecrated for burial until 1635 (Baker 1980b, 122). It is perhaps conceivable (just) that the churchyard was newly created in the seventeenth century by the unrecorded acquisition and clearance of surrounding plots, but virtually certain that the church had always had an open plot around it. More specifically, the St Andrew's church plot appears to represent a substantial relic of the episcopal *haga* recorded in 904, with a regular strip of urban properties along the Birdport frontage (on the line established after the early tenth century but before the twelfth–thirteenth) and an irregularly bounded series of plots more obviously cut out of the church-plot on its southern, Copenhagen Street, frontage.

St Martin's church occupied a rectilinear churchyard on the west side of the medieval Cornmarket. However, while the church is likely to have been founded by *c.* 1000, there are indications that the Cornmarket was a much later feature, created by the clearance of plots adjoining the line of the new city wall in *c.* 1200. If so, St Martin's must originally have been located at the rear of a plot facing south onto Mealcheapen Street and backing, as the neighbouring plots did, onto the lane known as the Trinity. This context tends to suggest that the church was of proprietary origin, but by the end of the eleventh century it was the property of the cathedral priory: whether this is a true reflection of its foundation, or whether it was given to the Church at an early date, remains uncertain. The original lateral extent of the church plot is uncertain: the post-medieval graveyard around it may have been enlarged by the acquisition of land from the surrounding properties.

At least in its later life, St Peter the Great also had a churchyard around it, in the angle of the city wall. In the 969 Battenhall charter (H 136–8, 357–8; S1327) the church was leased to a priest along with a *haga* by the south wall of the *burh*, suggesting that the church may have been contained within the property; its dimensions are, however, unknown.

Finally, All Saints' has the ironic distinction of at once having one of the most confined sites of all the Worcester churches and the only medieval reference (from 1405: see p. 242, below) to an attached cemetery, likely to have been in the narrow strip of ground along its south wall.

In conclusion, despite the existence or claims of burial monopolies by the senior churches, and the absence of cemeteries associated with many of the lesser churches until the end of the middle ages, about half of the lesser churches in each town certainly occupied plots – or churchyards – that were significantly greater in area than the church building itself. Some that we can recognize may have originated in remnants of early (pre-eleventh-century) town properties of high status, of greater or lesser extent according to their location and other factors. Others, of the type sometimes described as 'ecclesiastical burgages' have little to distinguish them from their neighbouring urban strip-plots, and may well have originated as ordinary domestic and commercial properties. The case of St Nicholas's in Gloucester warns against the assumption that churches occupying frontage sites necessarily pre-date the development of the frontage in that area.

Some churches may have been provided with precinct-like curtilages in which the church was, at least at first, the only or the dominant building. But how were church-plots used before burial rights were devolved from the senior churches? A full answer will remain elusive until further excavation of urban church sites and their surroundings has taken place. Some of the churches under discussion may have begun life in association with high-status building complexes – hall-garths – and their households. Others, possibly including St Peter the Great in Worcester where the *haga* was leased with the church to a priest, may have been founded on properties that contained the priest's house and little else. An open space around a church may well have been held to be appropriate to the dignity of the building, and desirable for aesthetic reasons, as a setting in which its architecture could be seen and appreciated. An open space would certainly have been useful for public gatherings, whether associated with worship or not. From the late middle ages there is also evidence from two sites for processional ways around churches: at St Andrew's, Worcester (pre-dating its acquisition of burial rights), and at St Nicholas's, Gloucester (post-dating its burial rights).

The intrusion of commercial functions onto church-plot frontages by encroachment cannot easily be distinguished from cases where churches (like St Aldate's Gloucester and perhaps St Martin's, Worcester) were founded, possibly to serve as a household chapel for a high-status dwelling, behind frontages that were already built up. Nevertheless, several cases of straight-forward commercial frontage encroachments can be recognized. Those of All Saints' and St Michael's at the Cross in Gloucester are clear enough, the process datable to the mid twelfth century at the latest; St Nicholas's in Gloucester provides documentary evidence for building by the parish on a minute plot of land in front of the church in 1347, with further rents derived from letting the chamber over the church porch. Excepting the much larger-scale enterprise by the cathedral priory along the Lich Street frontage of their cemetery, there is no comparable, reliable evidence from Worcester. Probably this is in part a reflection of the surviving sources, but also perhaps a reflection of the less pressured frontages in that town.

Church-plots resemble their secular counterparts in their behaviour as well as in their physical form. As pieces of urban property, they were not static: they could be reduced by encroachment and alienation, or they could be enlarged by the acquisition of land from their neighbours – whether in tiny strips or extensive parcels. The behaviour of St Michael's plot in the centre of Gloucester is a classic example, one that was not so very different from that of its prosperous secular neighbours. It may be, as Richard Morris (1989, 197) suggests, that the large cemeteries surviving around urban churches in eastern England have, through progressive enlargement for burials, ceased to resemble the original church-plot; but it is also the case that the smaller plots around the urban churches of the west of England have undergone transformations too.

Chapter 9

The development of the parishes

Introduction

The main outlines of the process by which rural parishes and their boundaries developed have become fairly clear and are now widely accepted. Between the tenth and twelfth centuries there was a rapid proliferation of local, 'private' churches with resident priests. These began to eclipse and eventually replace the smaller number of senior churches – the 'old minsters' and 'lesser minsters' – staffed by communities of priests serving large dependent territories which historians have often referred to as *parochiae*, but now more usually as minster parishes. Within these – according to legislation by Æthelstan (926–30) and Edgar (960–962) – the minsters had the right to extract a number of dues, including tithe, soul-scot (burial fees), church-scot, and plough-alms (Liebermann 1903–16, vol. 1, 146–9; 196–7). As local lords founded their own churches, these rights were either delegated by agreement, or were appropriated: the new local churches were able to extract some or all of these dues from their own much smaller dependent territories – parishes – that were frequently coterminous with the property of their founder. The resultant rural parochial system had been completed within fossilized boundaries by the thirteenth century (Blair 1988; Morris 1989, 128).

These processes – baldly summarized – appear consistently across most of the country. But investigators of urban parishes have, in contrast, no such common ground to work from: no obvious consensus has emerged from the study of the development of urban parishes and their boundaries; the experience of every town that has been studied appears to have been different.

One of the most influential studies of town parishes has been Alan Rogers' 'Parish boundaries and urban history' (1972). Rogers was in no doubt as to the origin of urban parishes. Having discussed the origin of rural parishes he noted: '… the private origin of churches was the same in the towns (where many parish churches began life as private chapels) and in the country. Urban parishes thus reflect property divisions, although perhaps not such early ones as in rural areas, for urban properties probably changed relatively more frequently than did rural property.' After considering evidence for the long-term stability of parish boundaries, Rogers used two case studies to demonstrate his main theses, that:

> Parishes which include large areas of the town's lands would seem to be early; those which are purely urban in character came later and were cut out of existing parishes. Again, early parish boundaries would seem to lie along natural features and pre-existing landmarks like roads; later ones relied upon property divisions and frequently run, not along roads but along the backs of tenements.

The link between an early parish and the possession of rural or extramural territory, and the contrast with two later, purely intramural, parishes was demonstrated very clearly by the example of Nottingham. This relationship was also postulated in Stamford. But here, amongst a much larger number of urban churches, the correlation between early foundations and the possession of rural territory was less certain; all the 'early' churches with a stake in the town fields lay on the periphery of the pre-Conquest fortified area (Rogers 1972, 48, 63, 51–6, 58–9), though subsequent work has amply demonstrated the early, pre-urban, origins of one of these (Mahany and Roffe 1982, 200–204). As we shall see, this was a pattern repeated at Worcester.

The relationship of urban parishes to early private properties was pursued by Brooke and Keir in their work on London (1975). They distinguished two types of parish: first, those that originated in the property – the *soke* – of a church-founder, his tenants worshipping in the church and contributing to its maintenance, and the priest being his chaplain; and second, parishes that originated in neighbourhood communities of 'pious craftsmen', such parishes distinguished by their geography – 'in every case a major thoroughfare runs through their midst; sometimes an important cross-roads forms their centre. They are thus natural units, not formed by artificial frontiers'. The territorial definition of parishes, the authors suggested, was largely a question of the allocation of tithes: 'London citizens had the privilege to be buried where they liked; burial privileges were therefore not of the essence of London's parochial rights'. Some intramural parishes were still being defined in the early twelfth century, but the pattern was fully formed by 1200 (Brooke and Keir 1975, 130–33).

More recently, a different and very precise mechanism for the determination of parish boundaries has been proposed to have been used in Winchester and London and, implicitly, much more widely. The lesser churches of Winchester lacked the rights of baptism and burial – amongst the normal characteristics of a parish church – until the very end of the Middle Ages, these being the prerogative of the cathedral. They did, nevertheless, acquire other attributes of parochial status and appear to have had territorially defined parishes by the middle of the twelfth century (Keene 1985, 107, 116).

Working from the boundaries recorded on eighteenth-century and later maps and from surviving fifteenth-century property records, Keene deduced that the principle that had been used to determine parochial limits was simply that of the nearest church to any given property:

> What mattered in the definition of the parish boundary was the relationship of the church to a particular house or household from which payments were made rather than to an area of land. The distance between the front door of the house and the door of the church was the critical factor in determining to which parish a house belonged and physical obstacles to movement, such as the city or precinct walls, had a marked effect on the pattern.

The operation of this principle was deduced solely from the boundaries themselves in Winchester, but it also appears to have operated in London, for a lease of 1566 stipulated that the position of the tenement's front door, nearest the church of St Pancras, be maintained, and with it the parochial loyalty of the property's inhabitants. Even notable eccentricities in Winchester's parochial geography were explicable in terms of the operation of this principle; only in a single instance was there 'a direct correlation between the parish boundaries and a unit of land ownership, in this case the bishop's demesne land administered as the manor of Wolvesey' (Keene 1985, 124–6). Nevertheless, connections between early units of land tenure and urban parochial geography have been observed or proposed elsewhere: in Chichester, for example, where the parish of All Saints' in the Pallant appears to perpetuate a pre-Conquest soke belonging to the archbishops of Canterbury (Peckham 1933, 68; Munby 1984, 327–8); and also in London, where the parishes of St Mary Staining and St Michael Bassishaw have been identified with the pre-Conquest *Staeningahaga* and *Basingahaga* respectively (Dyson and Schofield 1984, 306–7).

In some towns, the creation of planned parochial units and hierarchies has been suggested. In Hereford, a planned reorganization of parishes in the mid twelfth century has been tentatively proposed, the churches centrally placed within their parishes (Pearn 1988). Morris has suggested that there may have been 'an element of formal parochial apportionment' in the arrangement of the three churches and their parishes at the central cross-roads in Bristol (Morris 1989, 210). And in London, Jeremy Haslam has suggested that the restoration at the end of the ninth century was accompanied by the creation of wards in the eastern part of the city, each centred on a gate, and each provided with a new minster whose minster parish was coterminous with the ward (Haslam 1988).

So it is that a number of serious individual studies have presented very diverse hypotheses and evidence for the origins of urban parishes: in the fragmentation of large tenurial units, the earliest of which can be recognized by their maintained rural territory; in lesser tenurial units (sokes); in collectives of pious craftsmen; in the rational apportionment of clerical catchment areas; and in acts of ecclesiastical planning. The only unifying factor amongst these disparate theories is the universal acknowledgment that urban parochial systems had fossilized or at least reached completion by *c.*1200.

Parochial rights in Worcester and Gloucester

Turning now to Worcester and Gloucester: we have seen in Chapter 8 that the period of church foundation was substantially finished in each town by 1100. But to what extent did all or some of these churches have full parochial rights in 1100, and how early can distinct parishes, or districts within which those rights were exercised, be identified? From both Worcester and Gloucester come references to parishes in documents purportedly from the 1090s, though in each case probably dating from the mid twelfth century (see below). Central to any discussion of the origins of the parochial topography must be a consideration of the role played in each of these towns by the ancient mother-church (Brooke 1970, 76–7): in Gloucester by St Peter's Abbey, the Old Minster, and in Worcester by the cathedral churches of St Peter and of St Mary. As both towns at an early date contained additional churches, it follows that the minsters had no local monopoly of pastoral care; the view that before 1000 the urban minsters were largely unchallenged in their role by local churches built mostly between that date and 1150 (Rosser 1992, 274) is rather at odds with the certainty that in the tenth century there were already several churches in Worcester, and probably in Gloucester too. Of crucial importance is the question of how far these lesser churches enjoyed parochial rights: of baptism, burial and the collection of tithes. Nothing is known of tithe payments in either town during the early middle ages; baptism was apparently performed at the lesser churches of Worcester during the eleventh century, however, whilst the Old Minster in Gloucester may never have been able to insist on a monopoly of burial even within the walls of the *burh* (see below). Perhaps some of these early churches were private chapels, like the examples cited by Rosser: All Saints' and St Martin's in Gloucester, if they were early foundations, might have originated in that way. But we have already seen that the churches of Worcester and Gloucester were for the most part located upon prominent sites, whether on the main streets or at the gates – locations more in keeping with their foundation, not by private citizens, but by the ecclesiastical or secular authorities. There is little doubt that the churches of Worcester and Gloucester were designed in the first place for public devotion, providing the citizens with an alternative to the minsters.

That is not to suggest that the local churches of either town had entirely supplanted the mother churches during the eleventh century. Illustrations of the saintliness of St Wulfstan from his twelfth-century *Vita* (Darlington 1928) assume that the mother-churches of both towns still acted during Wulfstan's lifetime as centres of the Church's pastoral activities, although the evidence is indirect. We are told that the saint – both as prior and as bishop – would preach to the people on Sundays and at the greater festivals, although as he was portrayed as diligent in visiting his diocese, such preaching was not necessarily to a Worcester congregation. Anecdotes to illustrate his piety, however, often allude to citizens' regular attendance at the cathedral: for example, the story of the wife of a wealthy citizen who harboured a passion for Wulfstan and who, whilst in church, promised him both sexual favours and sufficient wealth to redeem his guilt through alms-giving; or that of a mason of Worcester who apparently came frequently to worship at the cathedral, and whose hatred of a fellow citizen always led him to walk out when the congregation were enjoined to be at peace with their neighbours (Darlington 1928, 13, 51–3, 11–12, 40).

Having performed the morning offices, Wulfstan would often stand at the door of the church and receive the poor of Worcester and the vicinity, who would come to him when they required help and guidance. As other priests – by implication the parish priests of Worcester – were now refusing baptism without payment, the people would bring their children to Wulfstan to be baptized, a service he performed out of charity but also as a rebuke to the priests. The custom of receiving baptism from the bishop quickly spread to the rich of the region as well, baptism by a lesser priest being popularly held to be of less merit. Wulfstan was just as scrupulous in the performance of his episcopal duty to confirm children, and one anecdote illustrates the continued role of St Peter's Abbey as Gloucester's mother-church. It describes how the common people of Gloucester waited in the abbey cemetery with their children for Wulfstan to come out to them. Although having said mass, Wulfstan on this occasion failed to go straight out to the children as was his custom but had been persuaded by Abbot Serlo to dine with the monks: the delay brought on unseemly scenes among the many waiting people which incurred appropriate divine punishment – not on the dilatory Wulfstan, perhaps surprisingly, but on those who had been impatient and indecorous (Darlington 1928, 12–13, 86).

The *Vita*'s depiction of the leading role played by Wulfstan and his principal church in the religious life of the diocese is not to be accepted uncritically (and for a fuller discussion of this matter see Mason 1990). It was clearly a concern of Wulfstan's biographers to emphasize his unusual dedication to all of his flock; other priests were not so favoured, however seriously they might in reality have taken their responsibilities. The pastoral role of the local churches is recognized only incidentally, as with the case of Wulfstan's taking upon himself their baptismal functions; and in this important matter the impression is given of a bishop prepared to go beyond the letter of his duties to restore something of the prestige of his own church at the expense of the local churches. The judgment of the synod, reportedly held at the cathedral in 1092, was that there was no parish in Worcester other than that of the mother church, a statement which Brooke felt was not to be interpreted as the literal truth (1970, 64). The account of the synod has now been shown to be one of a number of forgeries by the Worcester monks of the mid twelfth century (Barrow 1992a); and whether or not the statement did indeed accurately represent the historical situation, it can only be safely interpreted as a statement of what the twelfth-century monks felt ought to be the relationship between their church and the city churches. The latter had undoubtedly for a long time asserted their independence of the cathedral – as in the matter of baptism, despite the best efforts of Wulfstan to reverse that particular trend and recover from the churches a valuable source of revenue.

The antiquity and development of the churchyards and precincts of Worcester and Gloucester have already been discussed in Chapter 8. But what evidence is there for the legal right of burial in these towns? By contrast with their apparent surrendering of the right of baptism, when it came to burial Worcester Cathedral and – to a much lesser extent – Gloucester Abbey maintained something of their mother-church status throughout the middle ages. A deed transferring a plot of land beside All Saints' church, Worcester, in 1405 describes it as lying in Newport Street, and extending along the side of the cemetery of the church as far as All Saints' Stair (WCRO X496.5 BA9360 CAB 14, unnumbered box/unnumbered deed). With that exception, there is no reference to any of Worcester's parish churches having a cemetery in the medieval period, and there are no tombs or other signs of medieval burial in any of the surviving churches. Of the 54 extant wills of Worcester citizens from before 1500 (PRO Prob.11; WCRO Probate Register 008.7 BA3590/1; D&C B class; WCRO 850 St Swithin BA1026, parcels 1, 2, 4, 9, 10, 17; WCRO St Martin BA8502/7, parcel 7; WCRO X496.5 BA9360 CAB 14, unnumbered box; Marsh 1890), six contained instructions for burial in the church of the Greyfriars; three in the church of the Blackfriars; one in the cemetery of the hospital of St Oswald which, located to the north of Worcester, served at least part of the Tything suburb outside the city limits; and two testators willed that they should be buried wherever they died. Forty-one – 29 men and 12 women – were to be buried at the cathedral, 9 inside the church and 31 in the cemetery, whilst one, Henry Newdyke (WCRO Probate Register, 21), left his widow to decide whether he was to be buried beside one former wife who lay inside the cathedral, or beside another who lay outside. The remaining testator was to be buried within the church of St Michael, which of course also lay within the area of the cathedral cemetery.

Thus the evidence from these 54 Worcester wills – of which all but 9 are from the fifteenth century – is that the cathedral priory had a virtual monopoly of burial in Worcester. During the Black Death, burials were ordered to be held outside the city walls in the cemetery of St Oswald's Hospital (*VCH Worcs.*, ii, 32), and Leland in the sixteenth century also reported the use of St Oswald's as a public cemetery for the city during periods of plague (Smith 1907–10, v, 91); but under normal circumstances only the two orders of friars resident in the city could provide an alternative place of burial, and it may be significant that, in each of the nine cases of burial by the friars, the place of burial is specified as the inside of the church, rather than in a cemetery. A burial ground belonging to the Dominicans was consecrated in 1350, three years after the initial grant of land on which the order could build their Worcester house (*VCH Worcs.*, ii, 167), but it was not necessarily intended to be used for the burial of lay people.

William Beauchamp, the Lord of Elmley, had been buried in the Franciscans' church in 1268, but his son so mistrusted the monks of the priory that he had the grave opened in 1276 to satisfy himself that the corpse was still there (*VCH Worcs.*, ii, 17). This sounds as if it had been an isolated burial, and we know that the Worcester friars had to fight for the right to bury members of their flock: in 1290 there was a celebrated quarrel between the Franciscans and the cathedral priory over the corpse of one Henry Poche which the monks – apparently using some force – seized from the friars and buried in the cathedral cemetery. Archbishop Peckham intervened, ordering the exhumation of the corpse and its return to the friary; and although a formal enquiry into the affair by Bishop Giffard found that Poche was known to have expressed a desire to be buried at the cathedral, Peckham insisted and eventually the monks relented. The friars made the most of their victory, digging up the corpse as ostentatiously as they could, and explaining the facts of the case to the large crowds that gathered. Subsequently the two parties agreed that in future those who had expressed a wish to be buried by the friars could be so buried, as long as a mass was said for them at the cathedral first, and providing that there was no pecuniary loss to the Priory (*VCH Worcs.*, ii, 170).

What remains unclear is whether the friars were attempting to establish – in effect for the first time – the right of burial, or whether the monks were attempting to put a stop to a practice that had grown up since the arrival of the Franciscans in Worcester between 1225 and 1230 (*VCH Worcs.*, ii, 169). The agreement reached in 1290 would seem to have held, although as the testamentary evidence for burial at the friaries is much later – all after 1450 – further disagreement of which we know nothing cannot be excluded. Certainly all but one of the nine testators expressing a preference for burial by the Dominicans or the Franciscans made a cash bequest to the cathedral, of the same order as those made by the people who were to be buried there.

Yet it is possible that the available evidence for burial in medieval Worcester provides a misleading picture. In particular, the wills that provide almost all of our information on this matter are by their nature a biased sample, coming as they do exclusively from the upper ranks of Worcester society. All of the testators had at least modest property, and most had land as well as chattels and cash to dispose of. That the cathedral priory should wish to reserve its right to bury them – and to receive the associated mortuary payments and gifts – is understandable; but would the monks have been so zealous when it came to the burial of the Worcester poor? The few possessions of the city's artisans, let alone those of its poor labourers, would have had little attraction for the monks; the paupers – both old and young – can only have been buried by the charity of others. Perhaps, then, throughout the medieval period there were burials at parish churches with cemeteries: at All Saints', for instance, or at St Andrew's, St Helen's or St Peter the Great, at all of which the local topography suggests there may have been open ground before the general acquisition of burial land by the Worcester churches during the post-medieval period. In the friary cemeteries, too, the poor may have been able to find a resting-place, as it is now suspected that they did in Gloucester (see below).

By contrast with the situation in Worcester, it is recorded that in Gloucester most of the parish churches were in time able to establish their own cemeteries (see Chapter 4). However much St Peter's Abbey might have insisted upon its rights of burial during the twelfth century, there were even then too many exceptions for it to be able to defend its position for very long. In 1143 there was controversy following the burial of Miles, Earl of Hereford, at his own foundation of Lanthony. In order to retain his corpse, the canons acknowledged before the Bishop of Worcester the right of the abbey in future to bury members of Miles's family and any other lords of Gloucester castle, anyone dying at Gloucester castle – whether the old castle or the new – and every burgess of Gloucester within the city walls, all of whom the abbey claimed to be its parishioners (*Hist. et Cart.*, i, lxxv–vi).

The qualification that the abbey's parish was restricted to the intramural area of Gloucester was an important one: the extramural St Owen's church already had a cemetery in the 1130s, evidently having acquired the right to bury its parishioners at its foundation in 1095 or before with the grant of the gate-church of St Kyneburgh's and its mainly extramural parish. Lanthony's rights of burial over the inhabitants of the southern suburb pre-dated its own foundation in 1136, therefore, having been acquired at that time together with these earlier churches and their parish. According to the foundation charter of St Owen's, Walter of Gloucester, the castellan and Miles's father, granted to the new church the existing church of St Kyneburgh together with its parish both inside and outside the south gate (Walker 1964, 37–8; and see above, p. 104). St Owen's was dedicated, reportedly, in 1095, and certainly it was given St Kyneburgh's, but there is no original of Walter's charter, and it is quite possible that the wording of the deed of gift was composed at Lanthony Priory during the following century. But there is no reason to doubt that St Kyneburgh's had indeed anciently possessed burial rights, if only for its extramural parishioners.

Walter was not buried at Gloucester, for in old age he had retired to Llanthony Priory in Wales – later to be known as Llanthony Prima – and was buried there. The abbey's claim to his son's corpse, it was reiterated before the bishop in 1164x79, was based upon its insistence that the site of the castle had always been within St Peter's parish: the first castle had been built on land that had been the abbey's garden, and the people who had previously lived in that part of Gloucester had been served by the abbey's chaplain. Ostensibly, that is a reference to a now lost pre-Conquest church somewhere in the vicinity – though not necessarily on the site – of the castle. (This possibility is discussed at greater length below.)

Consequently, the abbey had had parochial rights over all that area, including the right of burial: this had continued to apply to the residents of the castle – to Roger of Pistres, the first constable, to Durand his brother and successor, and to all the family of Walter of Gloucester (*Hist. et Cart.*, i, lxxvi–vii). The abbey therefore extended its claims both to the area of the first Norman castle, as well as to its successor of the early twelfth century. Interestingly, in 1143 the abbey had asserted its right to bury all the town's intramural population, as its parishioners; it had not pressed this as the basis of its claim to Miles's corpse, however, nor did it repeat the assertion on this later occasion. Evidently the claim that the whole of intramural Gloucester was its parish was not one the abbey felt it could sustain.

In 1197 a new agreement was reached with Lanthony, which it was thought necessary to confirm formally before the Bishop of Worcester (*Hist. et Cart.*, i, lxxvii–lxxviii; ii, 8–9). By now the monks had retreated even further from their original position that they enjoyed a monopoly of burial within the town, and the agreement eventually reached was that Lanthony's parishioners – defined as being of its churches of St Mary de Crypt and of St Owen – could be buried at St Peter's if they so chose, whilst parishioners of the abbot – now defined as of the churches of St Mary de Lode, St John 'and other churches lacking cemeteries in the town of Gloucester' could likewise be buried at Lanthony. The choice had to be expressed before witnesses, it being the duty of any monk or canon present to remind the individual of his parochial loyalty to the appropriate religious house. Significantly, the difference in terms between this agreement and that occasioned by Miles's death includes the abbey's recognition that the parishioners of St Mary de Crypt belonged to Lanthony. Possibly the priory had already owned this church in 1143 (see above, pp. 111–12), in which case Lanthony did not then claim burial rights there, or at least was prepared to promise to forego them; if, on the other hand, it had not yet acquired St Mary's, then that church's right to burial had been a matter between its patron, the Bishop of Exeter, and St Peter's, and had had no bearing on what Lanthony was at that time prepared to agree to.

The abbey's earlier insistence, therefore, that it had the right to bury not just those dwelling at the castle but also all the burgesses of Gloucester when they died was evidently no longer realistic by the 1190s, when burial could take place at Lanthony's church of St Mary de Crypt, with its wholly intramural parish. And, as we have seen, the claim was largely incidental to the agreement of 1143 when, to retain the corpse of its founder, a newly founded and vulnerable Lanthony Priory would have had little choice but to make concessions to its powerful neighbour. It may be concluded, therefore, that in the early twelfth century the abbey's claim to a legal monopoly of burial within Gloucester had already become difficult to maintain, and had little force in the 1190s.

But we may also question whether this record of a private dispute between St Peter's Abbey and Lanthony Priory is, in some respects, misleading. All three of these agreements, and in particular that which the abbey reached in 1197 with the now wealthy and influential Lanthony, concerned only their rights *vis-à-vis* the other, and perhaps have nothing to say about the burial rights which the patrons of other Gloucester churches – the bishops of Exeter, Deerhurst Priory or the Crown – might have claimed during the twelfth century. Had the abbey disputed the right to burial with anyone but Lanthony, and won their case, then we should expect some record of this to have been preserved with the Lanthony agreements; had the abbey been unsuccessful, however, this is likely to have been quietly forgotten. It would be mistaken, therefore, to conclude that no party other than St Peter's Abbey and Lanthony Priory had any interest in burial in Gloucester, especially towards the end of the twelfth century.

Besides the evidence of the 1197 agreement, it can be shown that other Gloucester churches did indeed have cemeteries by that date. Given its antiquity and early prominence in the region, it is not surprising that the church of St Mary de Lode should have possessed burial rights by the late ninth century (Bryant 1980, 8–9), and by inference from long before. The minster church of St Oswald's, too, must always have had the right to bury those who dwelt in its large extramural parish. The statement in the 1197 agreement that St John's church possessed burial rights suggests a parallel with St Kyneburgh's, Gloucester's other gate-church. The two stood at either end of the north–south street that was planned as the main thoroughfare of the *burh*; both had parishes that were largely or almost entirely extramural. The historic right claimed by St Peter's to bury all the intramural burgesses – that is, from the area of the *burh* – would not have prevented these gate-churches from having always enjoyed the right to bury their own parishioners, or at least those of them from the extramural parts of their parishes. Doubtless the Old Minster's right of burial had once been real enough and, significantly, a prominent town-centre church such as St Michael's had been founded without any provision for a cemetery. But the decline of the monopoly was reflected in the provision of burial grounds at the churches of St Nicholas and St Aldate, both apparently foundations of the early to mid twelfth century – though St Aldate's may have been founded earlier and only rededicated then. The parish of the former lay outside the *burh* defences, its boundary following approximately the line of the old west wall; the latter, though, had a wholly intramural parish.

During the thirteenth century and after, as we saw in Chapter 8, most of the remaining intramural churches acquired cemeteries; as the pieces of land they could acquire within the residential and commercial districts were necessarily restricted in size, parish burial may never have become common and for many burgesses could not have been a realistic alternative to burial at St Peter's. Even wealthy burgesses and their widows, such as Thomas Crook, William Crook and Joan atte Noke might choose to be buried at St Peter's, in 1349, 1401 and 1375 respectively, although all three belonged to the parish of St Nicholas (A3, fos 143, 143v; *Cal. Recs Corpn Glouc.*, 996). And as a timely reminder that available documentary sources may fail to convey a wholly accurate picture, a large number of late-medieval burials have recently been identified by both excavation and ground-probing radar in and around the site of the house of the Gloucester Blackfriars (Atkin 1992a, 35–9). In all, there were an estimated 2000 burials on the site – and that in a cemetery which is otherwise virtually unrecorded. Its existence was known from leases of 1391, 1484 and 1497 of a piece of land lying between Southgate Street and the Blackfriars' cemetery (*Cal. Recs Corpn Glouc*, 1025, 1177, 1188), but such a large concentration of burials over so extensive an area was unexpected. Men, women and children were buried here during the fourteenth and fifteenth centuries, although in the later phases of the cemetery the corpses buried were mostly those of elderly men. The very high proportion of skeletons showing the effect of serious diseases is in marked contrast with the significantly healthier skeletons recently excavated from the nearby but extramural site of St Owen's church (Atkin 1992a, 35–9, and pers. comm.), giving rise to the suspicion that the Blackfriars cemetery served either a large – and entirely unrecorded – hospital, or more probably that it had become the customary place in which the town's poor and destitute were buried. It is quite possible that the cemetery of the Greyfriars on the other side of Southgate Street, recorded in 1436 (*Cal. Recs Corpn Glouc*, 1108), served a similar function.

Whatever the abbey might have pretended in 1143, therefore, the evidence suggests that by that date – and certainly by the 1190s – for a Gloucester church to enjoy burial rights it had only to possess a cemetery. The twelfth-century monks of Worcester said that the whole city was the cathedral's parish, and could point to their monopoly of burial; their Gloucester counterparts knew they were on very weak ground if they asserted parochial rights over the whole of Gloucester, and wisely restricted their claim to the right to bury the parishioners only of those churches that both lay within the area of the old *burh* and had no cemeteries of their own. They recognized, in effect, that each of these churches had its own defined parish, and that the parishioners of the intramural church of St Mary de Crypt owed an allegiance to the recently founded Lanthony Priory.

Parish boundaries: Worcester

A detailed description of each parish and its boundaries is to be found in Chapter 7; the task now is to interpret the parochial geography and the processes behind its formation. First of all, it is necessary to compare the pattern of parish boundaries with what other sources have to say about the development of the secular and ecclesiastical landscape. But Keene's model, based primarily on the Winchester evidence, suggests that parish boundaries could be determined quite independently of tenurial boundaries above the level of the individual plot. It is also necessary, therefore, to assess whether the layout of Worcester's parishes could indeed have been determined by the operation of this principle.

At a few points within Worcester the line followed by a parish boundary has been dated; wherever this has been done, the parish boundary in question has been found to reflect a late, post-twelfth-century, feature. It is, however, arguable that this has been a limited sampling of a system that was always subject to a degree of mobility, and does not imply that the parochial structure was, throughout, of late-medieval date. The latest large-scale pre-nineteenth-century adaptation of the parochial geography probably occurred at the Dissolution: the preservation within St Helen's parish of the outline of the Greyfriars' precinct on the eastern edge of the city must imply that the parish boundaries were modified when formerly extra-parochial land was taken into a city parish. This should occasion no suprise, and it has echoes in Gloucester (see below) and also in Winchester (Keene 1985, 125). In part, the later-medieval city wall also carried parish boundaries, and it seems likely that the parochial geography was modified when it was built. But it is not possible to be precise as to when most of the circuit was constructed.

Rather more precision is possible in two instances where the line of a parish boundary has been excavated. The north–south boundary between St Andrew's and St Helen's ran on a staggered or dog-legged line to the west of the High Street, reflecting but never coterminous with the junction between the High Street plots and those facing westwards to Birdport. At the point at which it was excavated, the line that was followed by the parish boundary was shown to have been newly established in the late-medieval period. However, it has been suggested that the staggered back-fence line of the High Street plots is indicative of the plots' fluid, and to an extent random, extension and retraction as ground was exchanged with the plots at the rear-facing Birdport, according to the vagaries of the local property market. It is likely that the parish boundary represents no more than a tide-mark left by an essentially transitory situation. A comparable process was revealed between Broad Street and Powick Lane. In this instance, the boundary between All Saints' and St Andrew's followed a property boundary dividing plots fronting onto Broad Street from the plots behind fronting onto the lane. At the point where it was excavated, this boundary was found to have been inserted at the end of the medieval period, the plot having formerly stretched from one frontage to the other. Before the plot's lateral partitioning, the parish boundary is likely to have followed Powick Lane, the plot as a whole lying within All Saints' (see below); earlier than this, there are some indications that the first boundary between the parishes may have been the standing *burh* defences that ran across this area.

The possibility of localized mobility in urban parish boundaries (excluding gross movements through parochial amalgamation) appears to contradict the prevailing orthodoxy of their relative antiquity and post-twelfth-century stability (e.g. Rogers 1972, 49; Brooke and Keir 1975, 129–30). But mobility in parish boundaries has been seen before. In Norwich, Alan Carter noted that fluctuations in parish boundaries 'were a result not only of medieval and post-medieval parish amalgamations … but also of eighteenth- and nineteenth-century adjustments to "fit" boundaries to newly constructed buildings' (Carter 1978, 194). A similar process is implicit in Derek Keene's description of the parochial attribution of a vacant plot according to its attachment to a particular house (1985, 125). In Shrewsbury, a parish boundary was found to have shifted away from a medieval property boundary to a demonstrably new alignment at the end of the Middle Ages, as the property was reorganized following the demolition of its principal building (Baker, Lawson, Maxwell and Smith 1993). A case in Gloucester in which a boundary was moved – first in the early thirteenth century by agreement, and again later by a less transparent process – is described below.

At first sight there is no strong correlation between Worcester's parochial geography and the structure of the town-plan, at least as it has been broken down into its constituent parts or plan-units (figs 6.8 and 7.1): the planned High Street area (plan-unit II.5) is, for instance, bisected by a parish boundary. However, there is an undeniable relationship at a general level between the parochial geography and what has been deduced of the layout of the post-890s *burh*. This is most strongly apparent at the margins, there being a clear distinction between the central block of parishes – St Helen's, St Alban's, St Andrew's and St Swithun's – that were entirely intramural in late-medieval terms, and an outer ring of churches with sometimes very extensive extramural and rural parishes (see fig. 9.1). The extent of this central block of parishes corresponds approximately with the limits (as far as they are known) of the *burh*. Around this block lay the churches and parishes of St Clement, St Nicholas, St Martin and St Peter the Great. Only St Nicholas's might have been a post-Conquest foundation. St Clement's – whatever the circumstances of its foundation around the middle of the eleventh century – originated as a chapelry dependent upon All Saints'. The latter, identified as a probable gate-church, had a parish that was almost entirely extramural in terms of the *burh*, and it is possible that St Clement's parish on the west bank of the Severn annexed territory belonging to All Saints'. St Martin's and St Peter's were both outside the Anglo-Saxon defences, though later brought within the medieval circuit, and both had extensive rural parishes (see fig. 7.2); St Peter's, at any rate, was in use during the period of the *burh* and while its defences were still standing.

Two points arise from this. The first is that some elements of the parochial geography may have been determined within the lifetime of the Anglo-Saxon defensive circuit – as a landmark or administrative barrier if not still a military one. This is not, perhaps, enormously helpful for establishing a chronology of parochial development, as the demise of the *burh* defences in Worcester cannot yet be dated; it may, however, indicate some form of parochial territorialization well before, say, the twelfth century. The second point that arises is that this pattern appears to duplicate that in Stamford, described by Rogers (1972), while also suggesting very strongly that the equation between the earliest parishes and the possession of rural land is far from universally valid, or at least needs qualification (see below).

Further correspondence between the pre-Conquest secular geography and the parochial geography could be argued within the central block of parishes covering the former *burh* area. For an undetermined period, but perhaps until the 960s (see below), Worcester was divided between the old Roman earthwork enclosure and the northward extension of the 890s, which itself was divided between the High Street on the east, and the 904 *haga* between Birdport and the river on the west. The boundaries of St Andrew's parish reflect, in a very general way, the location of the *burh* defences to the north, the Roman defences to the south, as Baker (1980a) argued, and the High Street plots to the east. The High Street was represented parochially by the extension of St Helen's northwards beyond the Roman defences and its continuation by St Swithun's. Rarely, however, is the correspondence precise, though this is not suprising – local mobility in the precise line of parish boundaries following the expansion and contraction of individual properties has already been described and could, at least in part, provide the necessary explanation.

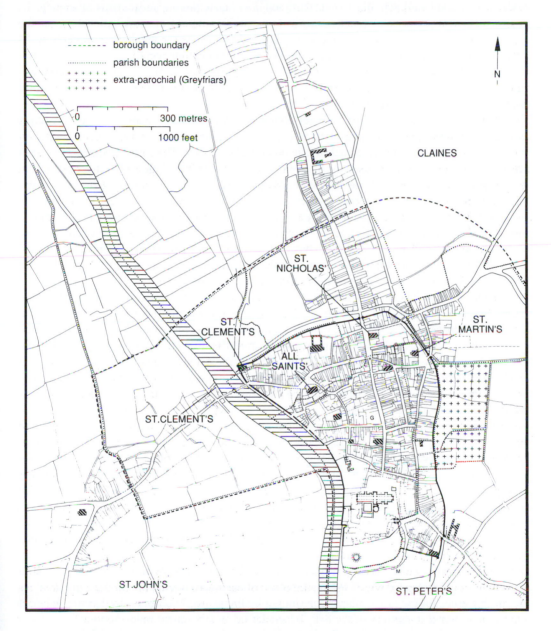

9.1   Worcester: selected parochial boundaries, emphasizing the junction between wholly intramural medieval parishes (those within the former *burh*) and those with extramural territory

But could Worcester's parochial geography have been determined by any other factors? Derek Keene's 'nearest church-door' hypothesis for Winchester and London represents a strongly argued model that can actually be tested against the parochial geography of other towns.

Fig. 9.2 is a map of Worcester showing hypothetical parishes determined solely by the operation of the nearest church-door principle. It contains some problems and imponderables, notably the lack of information regarding the position of the doors of churches demolished before they could be reliably illustrated. This, and doubt as to the medieval status of some paths or alleyways, leaves a degree of uncertainty as to the precise placing of some boundaries, but the churches were generally so widely and evenly spaced that the error involved is unlikely to be critical – involving at most the attribution of one or two contiguous plots.

With this reservation in mind, the correspondence that can be observed between the theoretical and actual pattern of parish boundaries is often extremely close. A few instances are worth drawing attention to: the southward extension of St Swithun's parish along the Shambles (Baxter Street), which offers a particularly close correlation; the division of the properties on Fish Street as closely as possible half-way between St Helen's and St Alban's; and the general degree of similarity between the latter's actual and hypothetical parishes. The correspondence between actual and theoretical boundaries in the St Alban's area casts doubt on Baker's (1980a) observation that the parish boundaries were determined by the course of the Roman defences.

There are also, of course, notable discrepancies, although some can be accounted for. St Clement's never acquired an intramural parish of the extent of its hypothetical parish: this is surely a reflection of its original status as a dependent chapel of All Saints'. Similarly, St Michael in Bedwardine should, in a 'free market', have taken control of the plots on the north side of Lich Street and on the northern part of Sidbury; it did not, because as a cemetery chapel its parish boundaries were determined by the extent of the cathedral close.

The eastern boundary to St Swithun's, parallel to the Shambles, is anomalous in that it did not follow the backs of the plots – which formed a continuous parallel back-fence line – but cut across them closer to the street. This, it has been argued, may accurately reflect the course of the *burh* defences. A particularly important departure from the theoretical boundary is to be found close by. According to the nearest church-door principle, St Helen's should have had a substantial block of its parish on the east side of Friar Street, sandwiched between St Martin's to the north and St Peter's to the south – by virtue of the easy communication between this area and St Helen's via the east–west Pump Street. In reality, it did not; the parish boundary followed Friar Street, at least before St Helen's took over the former Greyfriars precinct (which it may well have acquired on the basis of this principle). Friar Street formed the eastern limit of what has been argued to be the area redeveloped following the levelling of the Roman earthwork defences (plan-unit II.9). St Helen's parish boundary may at first, therefore, have followed the defences, being adapted later to encompass the plots laid-out over their levelled remains. Alternatively, the parish boundary may simply not have existed before the levelling and redevelopment had taken place. Julia Barrow has suggested that those events may be dated to a possible reorganization of the cathedral precincts by Oswald in 966 (1996, 89–90); Steven Bassett has suggested that the area covered by St Peter's parish represents an estate that became associated with St Peter's 'shortly after 969' perhaps having earlier been served by the church at Whittington, which was a dependency of St Helen's (Bassett 1989a, 235). In short, the intramural parochial geography does not, in this area, appear to have been determined by the principle outlined by Keene; rather, it appears to preserve a memory of the 890s perimeter or its subsequent redevelopment.

Other anomalies – the eastward projection of St Andrew's parish into the High Street, for example – remain unexplained, and there is a recurrent loose or inaccurate correlation between

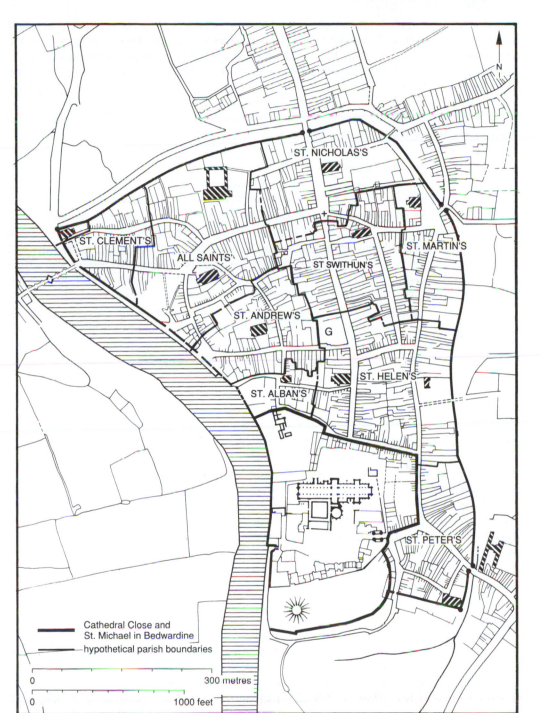

ST. NICHOLAS'S

ST. CLEMENT'S

ALL SAINTS'

ST. MARTIN'S

St SWITHUN'S

ST. ANDREW'S

G

ST. HELEN'S

ST. ALBAN'S

ST. PETER'S

Cathedral Close and
St. Michael in Bedwardine
—— hypothetical parish boundaries

0   300 metres

0   1000 feet

9.2   Theoretically-determined (nearest church door principle) parish boundaries – Worcester

the theoretical and actual boundary positions that defies interpretation. The division of the High Street between St Helen's and St Swithun's for example: was the known boundary of the eighteenth century identical to that of the middle ages, or had the nearest church-door principle not been applied, or had it been applied inaccurately? In this instance the positions of the church doors are not in doubt.

Parish boundaries: Gloucester

A detailed description of each parish and its boundaries is to be found in Chapter 4. As with Worcester, insights into the development of Gloucester's parochial geography are to be gained by comparing it with what is known of the developing secular landscape, and with changes in the town's ecclesiastical establishment. Again, the map of historic parishes can be compared with a hypothetical parish map drawn according to the nearest church-door principle, the convergences and divergences analysed, and an assessment made of the role of this principle in the parochial evolution (see fig. 9.3). The 1455 rental also provides further comparative information of the greatest value, revealing some of the town's most fundamental tenurial divisions through the distribution of landgable payments.

The long-term stability of most of Gloucester's defensive perimeter simplifies the analysis of its parochial system. Just as in Worcester, a fundamental distinction can be drawn between the churches beyond the walls, or having substantial extramural parishes, and those within. Outside the walls there is now very little doubt that the most ancient ecclesiastical foundation was the church of St Mary de Lode: its antiquity has been established by excavation, and Steven Bassett has suggested that its early history was analagous with that of St Helen's in Worcester as a British church – that it pre-dated the English ecclesiastical presence of *c.* 679 when the Old Minster was founded (Bassett 1992, 26–9). Archaeological evidence shows that burials were taking place around it by the tenth century at the latest. Inside the walls the Old Minster would have been responsible for the pastoral care and burial of whatever intramural population there was.

This appears to be the earliest stratum of ecclesiastical provision in and around Gloucester. A second, later, stratum is represented by the fragmentation of St Mary de Lode's extramural minster parish, a process perhaps commencing with the foundation of the New Minster, later St Oswald's, at the end of the ninth century. St Kyneburgh's too, in or next to the south gate, had some of the characteristics of a lesser minster, but its origins are unknown and the date at which its extensive minster parish to the south of the city was created is obscure; as we have seen, St Kyneburgh's had the right to bury its parishoners in the 1090s, and may possibly have done so from a much earlier date. The church of St John, a probable tenth-century foundation by the north gate, had the right to bury its extramural parishoners by 1197 but like St Kyneburgh's may have had this right much earlier. At Winchester, the development of cemeteries in the suburbs much earlier than within the walls has been noted (Biddle 1976, 332).

A third stratum of parish formation, but one which would have overlapped chronologically with the second, was represented by the fragmentation of the Old Minster's minster parish and the gradual demise of its intramural monopoly of ecclesiastical provision. The process by which this happened is more complicated and obscure than the process outside the walls, but a few clues suggest that there were two principal stages, divided chronologically by the Norman Conquest and separated geographically between the western and eastern halves of the intramural area.

From its location on a corner site on the central cross-roads, St Michael's is argued to have been an early foundation, quite possibly contemporary with the planned street-grid occupying the

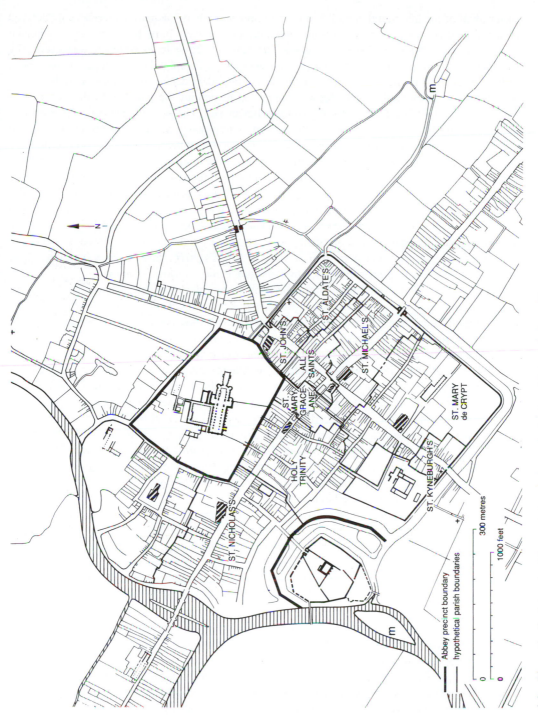

9.3   Theoretically-determined (nearest church door principle) parish boundaries – Gloucester

eastern half of the intramural area. It is uncertain how and when it acquired a territorially defined parish, but there are some grounds for thinking that it may have been an act of planned ecclesiastical provision. St Michael's parish – at least in the state in which it was eventually recorded – was closely related to the planned layout of the *burh*, and it does not appear to have been influenced at all by the nearest church-door system of boundary demarcation. Its western boundary was the main north–south street; this was also used to delimit the parishes to the north of St Michael's and, it will be argued, possibly to the south as well. The use of the street as St Michael's boundary with All Saints' suggests that the nearest church-door principal was not employed, and that other factors determined the layout of the parish. The hypothetical configuration of parishes determined by the nearest church-door principle cannot be predicted with absolute certainty or accuracy in this area because of the proximity of the two churches to each other and uncertainties as to the position of their doors, but it is likely that All Saints' would have commanded properties on both sides of Northgate Street – which, historically, it does not appear to have done – and St Michael's would have had rights over the properties immediately south of All Saints' that were almost opposite its own front door. St Michael's southern boundary also followed a street until deflected by the northward projection of St Mary de Crypt's parish: this was very probably a later diversion to encompass properties owned by Lanthony Priory, St Mary's patron.

St Michael's was the only intramural church other than the gate-churches to have had extra-mural land as part of its parish. This was restricted to Eastgate Street and may have been a relatively late accretion, coincident with the development after the Conquest of the Barton Street suburb, St Michael's being the nearest place of worship for the inhabitants.

St Aldate's parish, to the north, also had the appearance of a planned territorial unit, representing exactly half of the north-eastern quadrant. St Aldate's parish was, additionally, very closely coincident with an area of the town that did not pay landgable to the Crown, evidently owing chief rent to another lord: the parish can be claimed with some confidence to have been coeval with a pre-Conquest estate belonging to Deerhurst Priory (see p. 115–17, above). In part, the extent of the parish also corresponded closely with the hypothetical parish predicted with the nearest church-door model, but only along Oxbode Lane, away from the frontage, where St Aldate's would have had little competition. The crucial area of the Northgate Street frontage was also in St Aldate's parish, though it was directly opposite the east end of St John's: here, at least, proximity was of no account in determining boundaries.

The origins of the church of St Mary de Crypt are obscure. Its parish was remarkable mainly for its size, though there are slight indications that this may have been a relatively late feature. Towards the end of the eleventh century, St Mary's may have acquired rights to the land on the opposite – west – side of Southgate Street from a lost chapel, whose existence as we have already seen is implied by the abbey's claim in 1164x79 to have formerly had a chaplain serving the inhabitants of that district of Gloucester and which was cleared for the building of the old castle soon after the Conquest, and from the archaeological hints of an otherwise unexplained concentration of pre-Conquest burials in that area. St Mary de Crypt's parish may also, therefore, have been confined before the twelfth century to the area east of Southgate Street.

On the opposite side of the axial north–south road, in the area apparently not subjected to major replanning, the Old Minster's parish may have been maintained intact until much later. Holy Trinity and St Mary Grass Lane were almost certainly twelfth-century foundations, and it is surely no coincidence that the boundary between them, and with All Saints', appears to have been determined on the nearest front-door principle. Not so the boundary between Holy Trinity and St Nicholas's, however. This boundary instead reflects, close to Westgate Street, the line of the infilled western city ditch and, further away from Westgate Street, the back-fence line of properties built over the ditch – in other words, it was determined by the western defences (*contra* Heighway 1984a) and their successor-features. Before the twelfth century, this boundary would have separated St Mary de Lode's extramural parish from the Old Minster's intramural parish. Possibly, therefore, the area covered by the combined parishes of Holy Trinity, St Mary Grace Lane and All Saints' represented the last vestige of the old intramural minster parish, finally subdivided on the Winchester model in the course of the twelfth century.

St Nicholas's was founded in the early twelfth century. As it lay outside the old intramural area, it probably met no opposition from the abbey in burying its late parishioners from the time of its foundation. Its boundary with St Mary de Lode – out of whose minster parish it would have been formed – followed an evidently long-established property boundary dividing the Lower Westgate Street plots, which paid landgable to the Crown, from the abbey's tenants around St Mary's Square.

Finally, the gate-churches' intramural parishes remain to be considered. St Kyneburgh's, as recorded, may bear little relation to its pre-twelfth-century form. The foundation charter of St Owen's shows St Kyneburgh's to have had an intramural parish by the end of the eleventh century. But the mapped boundaries of the parish respect the friary precincts either side of Southgate Street and so must have been redrawn in the thirteenth century. The north side, at least in part, coincides exactly with a boundary determined by the Winchester model and so may also represent a rationalization of an earlier boundary. St John's intramural parish has been discussed very briefly above. It was confined by the boundary drawn along the middle of Northgate Street and was unable to command the plots lying immediately opposite its east end. Nevertheless, an unusually detailed account has survived of adaptations of its southern boundary and in this process at least, plot to church proximity played a part.

An ordinance of Bishop W of Worcester, attributed by its editor probably to 1186x90 (Walker 1976, 15) but more probably dating from 1218x36 (see note at the end of this chapter), records that a dispute arose when two neighbouring houses on the west side of Northgate Street were made into one. They had formerly belonged to Ailwin the Mercer and to Osbert the Cellarer, and had lain in separate parishes, in St John's and All Saints': to which of these parishes should the new house be assigned? Lanthony Priory and Gloucester Abbey, to whom the churches belonged, agreed that since the house's principal entrance lay in the parish of All Saints' and, furthermore, since that was the church that Richard Rufus, the new tenant, already attended, then it should lie in All Saints'. However, it was also agreed that one-third of the oblations should continue to be paid to St John's; and the abbey had evidently been able to insist that its rights in the matter should not be alienated in perpetuity, for it was stipulated that should the houses ever be divided again, then each would revert to its original parochial allegiance.

Richard Morris has presented the terms of this agreement as a demonstration of how the concept of the parish originated in a system of personal allegiances, and of how parish boundaries came to be defined (1989, 226). But the evidence does not necessarily point to that conclusion. The bishop's solution to the dilemma implies that a convention for dealing with such disputes already existed, whilst the abbey's insistence on continued payments to its church of St John similarly suggests that parochial rights were well entrenched, and that those rights had been defined within a framework of firm boundaries. Furthermore, the provision allowing for the eventual restoration of the parish boundary must mean that even if the boundary was not held to be immutable, nevertheless the existing rights of both churches were not easily to be set aside.

As it turns out, not only can this property be identified, but its subsequent history can be traced. The Lanthony Priory records show that the amalgamation of the two houses took place under Prior John (*c.* 1218–45): both Ailwin and Osbert had granted their respective houses to

Lanthony, and it was from Prior John that Richard Rufus took a lifetime lease on the property, with its shops and other buildings, for the considerable rent of £2 10*s* (A5, fos 78–9). The lease did not expire on Richard's death and his successor as tenant, Ralph of Cornwall alias Vintner, added small parcels of land to the property in 1232 and 1240 (A5, fos 76–76v; A13, fos 66–66v). Ralph's son and heir – also Ralph – relinquished all this tenement to Lanthony and in 1244 the priory granted it, together with some adjacent shops it had acquired, to Herbert the Mercer, to hold in fee (A5, fos 80–82). In all these transactions, no reference was made to the parochial location of the property nor to the obligations of its tenants. Having been held by a succession of tenants (A13, fos 64v–67v), during the reign of Edward III the property came into the possession of Nicholas Bursy and Henry Drapere who, with Lanthony's permission, divided it: Nicholas, it was reported, received the part in the parish of All Saints', and Henry that within St John's (A13, fo. 64v, 65v.) (Nicholas's portion was the tenement held by Thomas Byseley in 1455: *1455 Rental*, 70–72). So the terms of the agreement of more than a century before had been remembered, and were adhered to in preference to any other method of determining the parochial allegiance of the two new tenements.

But parochial adjustments might still be made. For in 1363 the Abbot of Gloucester bought Henry's portion – John Pirie, Thomas Baverton and John Godwot having acted as intermediaries (A13, fos 65v, 68; *Cal. Patent Rolls 1361–4*, 401). By the 1430s a great inn had been built here by John Twynnyng, who had been the collector of the abbey's rents, and who had similarly built the New Inn on the opposite side of the street; in 1455 the inn was leased to Philip Monger (*1455 Rental*, 72, 84). In the 1440s Robert Cole described this tenement as lying not within St John's but within St Michael's parish (A13, fo. 65v), and although the means by which the change had come about is unknown, it is surely no coincidence that both St John's and St Michael's belonged to the abbey. Evidently it had suited the abbey to divert – or to allow to be diverted – this wealthy tenant's tithes from his historic parish church to another, admittedly slightly nearer his front door. There is no other evidence for St Michael's parish ever having included houses on the west side of Northgate Street.

Conclusions

A general *caveat* is necessary before we begin to draw conclusions. We have seen, in Chapters 4 and 7, and above, that both Worcester and Gloucester apparently had medieval churches that are now lost. In the case of Worcester, the church of St Marina is recorded and furthermore we can be certain that on its disappearance its parish merged into that of St Alban's. In Gloucester, however, the existence of a lost pre-Conquest church destroyed by the first Norman castle cannot be proved, and the annexation of its parochial area by St Mary de Crypt can only be postulated. In neither case has the received plan of medieval parishes been distorted by very much, although both of these examples do demonstrate the possibility that lost churches might affect the parochial geography of any major early town. We must therefore be wary of assuming that urban parish identities necessarily began to evolve within the relatively stable pattern of ecclesiastical provision which we might deduce from later records. Where settlement came early in the Anglo-Saxon period the ecclesiastical geography might have been even more fluid: in *Hamwic*, early medieval Southampton, for instance, the inhabitants of the eighth and ninth centuries used a number of small, short-lived cemeteries, of which at least nine have been identified. Their relationship to the minster church of St Mary or other unknown churches is unknown but, whilst St Mary's later exercised a burial monopoly in Southampton, that was apparently not the case earlier (Morton 1992).

The pattern of parish boundaries in Worcester was evidently a palimpsest, the result not of a single period of agreed boundary demarcation, and certainly not of a single act of ecclesiastical planning by a central authority. But neither does it wholly or accurately reflect tenurial patterns and the secular landscape of the tenth century. Instead, it appears to contain a number of chronological components. During the modern period and at least the later middle ages, we may envisage a continuous process of very small-scale change that only becomes visible under exceptional conditions: a relationship with a known and datable feature (a friary precinct for example); the survival of unusually complete documentation; or evidence from excavation. The earliest chronological component of the Worcester system appears to be the distinction between those parishes that were wholly intramural and those that were partly extramural – in late-medieval terms. The distinction between them, and the determinant of the boundaries between them, was arguably the *burh* perimeter or the replanning episodes that directly followed its levelling. The chronology of parish formation is little clearer outside the town than in, but it is possible that, for a while, the *burh* defences formed a boundary between the cathedral parish or *parochia* within, and St Helen's minster parish without, the latter subject to a steady process of fragmentation as territory was annexed by the cathedral and as chapelries sought independence. Parish formation (or minster parish fragmentation) may have taken place or been allowed to take place a good deal earlier outside the walls than within, where the process is likely to have been retarded under the watchful eye of the cathedral.

In part, this supports Rogers' (1972) hypothesis that the earliest parishes were those with a share of the town fields. Two qualifications are necessary. First, what is meant here by 'parish'? St Helen's parish was purely intramural in the late-medieval period but there is little doubt that its once extensive rural minster parish was extremely ancient (Bassett 1989a). Second, whilst this hypothesis may in some circumstances have applied to parish formation – or acquisition – it did not apply to the sequence of church-founding. Those churches with extramural parishes in the later-medieval sense were, like those in Stamford, peripheral to the *burh*, at least in part associated with suburban growth, and far from being the earliest stratum of foundations.

Two distinct views of the origin of the wholly intramural parishes may be argued, neither of them at all decisively. The first would stress the general correspondence between the broad divisions of the post-890s town-plan and the parochial geography, and thus claim that parish formation, patently in progress by at least the mid twelfth century, in fact began early enough in Worcester to reflect the tenurial landscape of the tenth century. Departures from this relationship could be explicable in terms of the mobility of property boundaries and thus of the parish boundaries that followed them. This is the more radical view – given the cathedral's powerful presence and undeniably jealous and monopolistic tendencies – and demands a higher level of proof than is currently possible.

In opposition to that view, the close overall relationship between the historical parishes of Worcester and a parochial map determined by the nearest church-door hypothesis can be cited. First evidenced in Winchester, could this particular phenomenon be characteristic of late (maybe twelfth-century) parochial organization under monopolistic conditions? There seems little doubt that some boundaries were determined using this method – the southward projection of St Swithun's parish into St Helen's provides a fine example of this principle in operation.

The truth may lie somewhere between these extremes. The correspondence between the late-Saxon town-plan and the parochial geography may be explicable simply in terms of the distribution of churches around the street-system and the gradual formation of natural constituencies amongst the inhabitants of the adjoining streets. The nearest church-door principle evidently played a part in the determination of parish boundaries, but so too did other factors: the influence of the pre-Conquest defences has been noted, as also have those instances where the extent of parishes was determined by known legal-ecclesiastical constraints. The inaccuracies also give pause for thought, but inconclusively in the absence of information as to the accuracy of the prototype system in Winchester. Possibly it was used as a method for rationalizing existing boundaries and settling disputes rather than in creating parishes where none had existed before, or rather in determining the outcome of minster parish fragmentation.

The parochial geography of Gloucester leads to rather different conclusions. The principal difference with that of Worcester is that in Gloucester there is more unambiguous evidence of planned parochial provision reflecting major secular boundaries. This appears to have been characteristic of the first stage of the fragmentation of the Old Minster's intramural minster parish and was confined to the eastern half of the city. There is evidence that the simple proximity principle was employed – both from the boundaries themselves and from documentary evidence (above), but it appears to have been less influential, and particularly characteristic of a late phase of development, by which time much of the historic boundary pattern had already been established.

From these two towns some more general conclusions may be reached regarding the development of urban parishes and their boundaries. Urban parishes were just like rural parishes in that they were formed by the process of minster parish fragmentation, acquiring rights at the expense

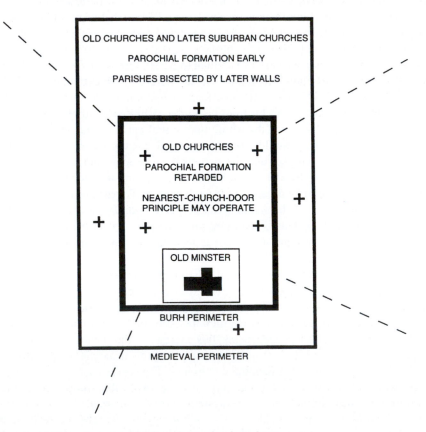

9.4   Urban parish formation: a model for minster-dominated towns

of an older minster church. But in these towns, at least, fragmentation was delayed or retarded by the proximity of their respective minsters and doubtless also by their ownership of property. Beyond the walls, fragmentation could advance and rights be acquired more speedily than within. So, whereas rural parishes may often be found to have been coterminous with large tenurial units or estates, urban parishes will, under these conditions, show such correlations much less frequently: parish formation was delayed, and therefore liable to post-date the subdivision of large early plots or *hagas* into a multitude of smaller plots.

In Gloucester, some evidence has nevertheless been found for a parish based on a large tenurial unit – St Aldate's; and there is some evidence for deliberate, planned, parochial provision. There is also extensive evidence of the use of Keene's nearest church-door principle. But this was certainly not the only mechanism that determined boundary positions; rather, it appears to have been strongly characteristic of situations where rights were acquired late and needed definition in an already densely populated landscape; it was also particularly appropriate to the settlement of disputes between existing parishes and the rationalization of earlier arrangements. It would, for example, have had no place (and it can be shown not to have operated) in a town like Shrewsbury, territorially divided between minsters of equivalent status (Bassett 1991).

The most intractable problem remains that of chronology. The documentary evidence from both Worcester and Gloucester appears to show the respective mother-churches attempting to halt the fragmentation of their intramural minster parishes in the middle of the twelfth century. Suspicions that the intramural parishes in Worcester had begun to have some kind of territorial definition within the tenth century remain unconfirmed, due to the level of coincidence between the known parish boundaries and the predictive model based on the nearest church-door principle: the possibility that they were substantially freshly defined in the twelfth century cannot yet be completely ruled out. The evidence for an earlier start in Gloucester is more secure (though hardly incontrovertible), resting on the preservation in parochial form of what appears to have been a pre-Conquest estate, and the evidence for 'planned' parishes closely associated with the planned area of the *burh*, and not responding to the Winchester model of boundary determination.

Note
The dating of the agreement as to Richard Rufus's parochial allegiance would seem in fact to date from the time of Bishop William de Blois (1218–36): for whilst Ailwin the Mercer might temptingly be identified with the Gloucester burgess of that name, named in the Pipe Roll of 1165 and fined in 1171 evidently as the leader of what seems to have been an illegal attempt to establish a commune (Pipe Roll 11 Hen. II, 12, 14; Pipe Roll 16 Hen. II, 79), his grant of this property to Lanthony was witnessed by Gloucester burgesses prominent in the decades 1210–40, such as Richard Burgeys, David Dunning and William Sumery, as indeed was Osbert the Cellarer's grant (A5, fos 78–78v; *Cal Recs Corpn Glouc., passim*). The grant to Richard Rufus was from Prior J, which places the grant within the successive priorates of John and of John of Hempstead, *c.* 1217–45+. Adam Keyl, whose land was next to Osbert's and who was first witness to Osbert's charter to Lanthony, sold his land on 1 April 1240 to Ralph of Cornwall (Cornubiensis), who had himself witnessed both Ailwin's and Osbert's charters (A5, fos 77+, 77+v).

Chapter 10

The major religious institutions:
their lands and their role in urban growth

Introduction

In Gloucester, and especially in Worcester, the period before 1200 saw the greater churches make a distinct contribution to the physical character of the developing town. To what extent, though, did they continue to influence the pattern of settlement in a later period when change came more slowly and was constrained by the existing urban topography? As the towns ceased to expand, the opportunities for major new development drastically diminished, and the small areas of new settlement were confined largely to the suburbs – a theme to be examined at length in Chapter 13. As a consequence, the physical impact of the greater churches on both towns became most marked through their accumulation of real property scattered throughout each town. As far and away the greatest landlords of their towns, their ability to influence the developing character of the urban environment at the level of the individual plot or property was unparalleled. The rental of all the houses in Gloucester made in 1455, for instance, shows the three great religious houses of the town as the immediate owners of some 250 properties. Most were single houses, although there were also blocks of residential property which could be extensive: Robert Cole described Lanthony Priory's adjacent properties of Ratoun Row and Asschewelle's Place as a single street-corner block occupied by various tenants, when his more detailed Lanthony rental of ten years previously had enumerated 21 separate tenements here (*1455 Rental*, 46b; A13, fos 51–3). There is no way of checking the size of similar blocks belonging in 1455 to St Peter's Abbey, such as the two blocks that occupied a considerable proportion of Abbey Lane (*1455 Rental*, 44b–46b). It is apparent, though, that these 250 properties totalled at least 270 separate dwellings and doubtless well in excess of 300 – that is, at least one-third of the 900 or so houses that, it can be deduced, Cole was describing in 1455 (Holt 1987, 48–52). And taking into account the suburban districts that Cole omitted, the proportion of Gloucester's total housing stock controlled by the three religious houses was even larger. He ignored the southern suburb, virtually all of which belonged to Lanthony, and failed to draw attention to the numerous houses and cottages belonging to St Oswald's Priory in the streets around its precinct (see pp. 326–9, 331–5, below).

The size of these fifteenth-century urban estates prompts a range of questions. Did they coincide at all with the lands the churches held perhaps four or five centuries earlier? If they did not, how and when had so much property been acquired? And a further question: how far did the different institutions follow a conscious policy of development, beyond the inexorable accumulation of property whether by gift or purchase? Or, by implication, what was the continued impact of the great churches on the ways in which the mature town was changing and growing during the medieval centuries?

A notable difference between the two towns was the number of greater churches. In Worcester, the dominant ecclesiastical presence had always been the cathedral, although in institutional terms there was change as the Church of Worcester divided its affairs and estates between the bishops and the cathedral priory – which itself remained Worcester's only significant religious house and became, by 1200 or so, the city's only great ecclesiastical landowner as the bishops relinquished their city property. Gloucester, by contrast, had both Old and New Minsters – later to be identified as St Peter's Abbey and St Oswald's Priory – and acquired during the twelfth century a third major religious house, the new foundation of Lanthony Priory. Established in 1136 as a temporary refuge for the Augustinian canons of Llanthony in Wales, it quickly acquired substantial holdings of land; after the re-occupation of the original house it remained in being, and in 1205 it became an independent priory (*VCH Glos.*, ii, 87–8). Although both Worcester and Gloucester were to acquire hospitals and friaries during the thirteenth century, the topographical impact of these minor institutions and their property holdings was small and localized; the greater institutions continued to have by far the most considerable presence in the two towns, within and outside their own precincts.

The comparability of the wealth and influence of the cathedral priory and St Peter's Abbey does not, however, extend to the surviving documentation for their temporal affairs. St Peter's has left no rentals from which the exact state of its holdings may be calculated; the only surviving descriptions of the abbey's lands in Gloucester – those of *c.* 1100 and 1455 – come from documents compiled by others, and designed to serve another purpose. We cannot arrive at a precise figure for how many houses the abbey owned in 1455, nor do we know their rents; nor, moreover, does the 1455 rental identify the numerous houses held in fee from the abbey or from the other religious institutions, houses which they did not directly control but from which they drew rents, and which they had granted to tenants in heredity during previous centuries (see below). By contrast, the Worcester properties of the cathedral priory are listed in four of its own rentals, well spaced chronologically and so allowing the growth of this estate to be measured and to some extent understood. With the proviso that the development of the Gloucester estate must have differed in important respects, nevertheless what can be learnt of the ways in which the Worcester monks amassed their property and sought to maximize its potential, must also provide insights into the evolution of a similar estate in a similar city. As for Gloucester's two Augustinian priories: very little can now be known about the properties of St Oswald's during much of the period, although there are interesting conclusions to be drawn concerning their extent before the Conquest and at the end of the middle ages. The excellent documentation for Lanthony Priory, on the other hand, illustrates the process by which a great and relatively late ecclesiastical estate was put together.

Because a more coherent analysis is possible of the urban property interests of the Church of Worcester, as compared with those of the two older Gloucester houses, the Worcester material will be presented first and in greater detail. For the late-medieval period this will be a study of the lands of the cathedral priory although, as the priory's lands were initially scarcely separable from those of the bishops, it is the Worcester interests of the bishopric that must be examined first.

The city property of the bishops of Worcester

The land – not necessarily in a single block – that Bishop Wærferth held in the new *burh* of Worcester was broken up and granted out to tenants by him and his successors. His lease of a considerable part of it to Æthelred and Æthelflæd in 904 (H 13–15; S 1280) was evidently the most important of such grants, both in terms of its size and in the status of its recipients, and may be taken to indicate that the Church of Worcester was unable to dispose of its land without having regard to the wishes and interests of the secular authority. Perhaps Wærferth's willingness to alienate such a large and well-placed block of urban land – between the new High Street and the riverside landing-place – may be interpreted as an act of generosity to the Mercian royal house, or was prompted by the promise of reciprocal gifts; but the context of the grant would surely have been his need to ensure he retained the favour of his overlords. As a lease for the lives of Æthelred, Æthelflæd and Ælfwynn their daughter, the *haga* should in time have returned to the church, perhaps as early as 919 when Ælfwynn was deposed and taken into Wessex (ASC s.a. 919); whether, in fact, it was ever wholly recovered is unclear.

During the tenth and eleventh centuries the church's remaining lands within the *burh* came to be attached to rural estates. Domesday Book (i, 173c) recorded the bishop's holding in Worcester as 90 houses appurtenant to his own manor of Northwick, of which half were held directly from the church and half from intermediate lay tenants; but the link with Northwick, the manor from which the land directly to the north of the city was held, had clearly been established for the convenience of the bishop's administration. Unnoticed by Domesday Book were other urban plots held from the Church which – certainly within the previous century – can be shown to have had tenurial links with rural manors; and whilst these links may in certain cases have come about through the deliberate policy of successive bishops, for the most part they are likely to have originated with the continued need of the Church's aristocratic tenants to maintain town-houses. Several of the surviving leases of rural lands issued by St Oswald as bishop make specific mention of accompanying properties within Worcester: a lease of 963 to Cynethegn of land at Oddingley and Laughern was accompanied by a haw or *haga* in Worcester measuring 12 yards by 8 yards (11 x 7 metres) (H 160–61; S 1297); a lease of 969 to Wulfgar, *clericus*, of a *haga* by the south wall – presumably of Worcester – accompanied a grant of St Peter's church and land at Battenhall and in Perry (H 136–8; S 1327); in 985 Oswald leased to perhaps the same Wulfgar, *clericus*, land at Clopton and a *haga* described as lying within the minster towards the town (H 135–6; S 1352); to Ælfsige his *cliens* he granted a *haga* and a croft in Worcester (H 158; S 1367), and to Goding, a priest, land at Bredicot and elsewhere and a *haga* before the gate – presumably of Worcester (H 139–41, 357; S 1369).

What is implied by such grants is that whilst Oswald was seeing to it that these clerical and lay-members of his household had the means to provide for themselves, he was also making provision for their continued residence in Worcester. Whatever his motives in extending their relationship with the Church, so that they became tenants as well as retainers, it was not his intention thereby to release them from his service: their town-house was to be as essential to them as their rural estate. And this was as true of other recipients of Church land, even though there may be no surviving record of a grant of a house in Worcester. For example, in 961x972 and 991 Oswald made grants of rural land, the first unidentified and the second in Ashton-under-Hill, Worcestershire, to Wulfhelm and to Æthelmær, each of them described as his *artifex* or craftsman (B 1184; H 131–2; S 1375, 1365). These were skilled men for whom Worcester must have been their customary workplace; probably they worked with jewels and precious metals, and indeed it is surely the very same Æthelmær who appears as a Worcester moneyer in the 990s (Robertson 1961, 868; Galster 1966, 1300, 1301). It is unthinkable that Oswald gave such men estates with the intention that they should live, in Æthelmær's case, almost 20 miles (32 kilometres) from Worcester; and if neither of the leases mentions a town-house, it can only be because that was conveyed separately, or more probably because both men and their families were already settled in houses they had been given earlier. In the same way, the thegns that Oswald rewarded with land cannot have been expected as a consequence to have removed themselves from the city on any permanent basis.

There is further, if indirect, evidence to support the proposition that the bishops of the tenth century used their city land to house and reward their retainers. It has already been suggested (see above, pp. 205–6) that All Saints' church, the advowson of which descended with the manor of Cotheridge, was built by the Church of Worcester before Cotheridge was leased out by Oswald in 963 to Ælfric, his minister (H 133–5, 350–51; S 1303), and further that the eight houses in Worcester which the lord of this manor held of the bishop in 1086 had in all probability been associated with the tenth-century grant.

The monks of the priory, too, held houses in Worcester that were appurtenant to two of their manors. Of the 40 houses listed by Hemming in the 1090s (H 289–91), 12 were said to lie *in burgo regis*, or 'in the king's borough', and paid a chief rent to the king of a penny or two; the other 28 paid rent only to the priory and were held of Hallow and Teddington, two priory manors. Hallow had belonged to the Church of Worcester since the early ninth century or before (*VCH Worcs.*, iii 367; S 179, 180; H 1–3, 337–40, 381–3, 556), and may have been given to the monks by the end of the tenth century. Edgar's forged charter of 964 generally known as *altitonantis* (Darlington 1968, 21–4; S 731) lists Hallow as one of the possessions of the monks, which implies that the monks of the twelfth century – whose work the charter was (Barrow, 1992a, 69–71) – believed the manor, together with its appurtenant land in Worcester, had been theirs for some considerable time. Teddington, by contrast, was a recent acquisition on their part. In 969 Bishop Oswald granted land in Teddington to Osulf, a kinsman of his and described as a *cniht*, for three lives (H 177–9; S 1326), and the Church seems not to have recovered this land until the reign of Edward the Confessor, when it came to Worcester under the will of Toki. It was then that Bishop Ealdred gave it to the monks, and we are told that land – *curtem unam* – in Worcester went with the grant as pertaining to the estate (H 395–8; S 1408; *VCH Worcs.*, iii, 470). The descent of the rural manor with the urban plot suggests that they had been associated since the time of Osulf, although whether under the terms of Oswald's lease or by a separate grant of a house in Worcester is unclear.

Property in Worcester continued to accompany grants of rural lands made by the eleventh-century bishops. In 1017 Wulfstan I gave a lease on land at Bentley in Holt to his brother Ælfwig, together with the *haga* said to pertain to it; 25 years later Bishop Lyfing granted the same land and *haga* to Æthelric, elsewhere described as his thegn, the *haga* being identified now as lying within the *port* or town (Hooke 1980, 48; S 1384; 1395; 1394). Wulfstan I, at some time between 1003 and 1023, leased land at Perry Wood to Wulfgifu, together with a *haga* held formerly by one Eadwerd (H 358; S 1385); in 1038 Lyfing gave a lease to Earcytel of land at Tapenhall accompanied by two *hagas* within the gate (Hooke 1980, 48; S 1393); and between 1038 and 1046 Lyfing sold the manor of Bushley in Worcestershire to Brictric for 3 gold marks, along with a house in the city of Worcester that paid a rent of a silver mark (DB, i, 180d).

Either explicitly or implicitly, the terminology of the eleventh-century grants conveys the sense that in each case *haga* and rural land were already associated – that the initial matching of rural estates with town-houses had taken place during an earlier period. On the evidence we have, that had occurred during the tenth century, following the establishment of the new *burh*; nevertheless, the possibility cannot be ruled out that the Church of Worcester had already followed the practice of leasing rural land with appurtenant town-houses to its retainers before the *burh* foundation, the houses lying either within the old defences of the city or in an extramural location.

It is important to note that the practice of linking urban with rural holdings was not confined to the church. A lifetime lease from King Æthelred II to Ælfric, Archbishop of York and Bishop of Worcester, was of land at Dumbleton, Aston Somerville and Flyford Flavell, with a *haga* within the *port* (Hooke 1980, 48; S 901); between 1052 and 1057 Earl Leofric gave the Church of Worcester land at Wolverley and Blackwell, also with a *haga* within the *port* (H 408–10; S 1232). According to Domesday Book, in 1086 there were – in addition to the bishop's manor of Northwick – 11 manors with appurtenant burgages in Worcester: Bushley, sold by Bishop Lyfing to Brictric 40 or more years before and now held by the King; Halesowen; Astley; Pedmore; Witton; Osmerley; Upton Warren; Chaddesley Corbett; Martley; Hollow; Suckley; and Coddington (DB, i, 180d, 176a, 176b, 177b, 177c, 177d, 178a, 180c, 180d, 182b). Except for Bushley, there is no indication that any of these manors had ever belonged to the Church of Worcester; Witton, Chaddesley Corbett and Hollow, however, had all been held before the Conquest by thegns of King Edward, whilst Queen Edith had held Martley and Earl Edwin had held Suckley. Upton Warren had been held by Evesham Abbey, and Coddington by the Church of Hereford. The Worcester burgages, we may surmise, had become attached to these manors by the King or by other great lords, acting in the same way as bishops of Worcester had done to provide their retainers both with a means of support and a base within the shire town.

The presence within the Domesday boroughs of these 'contributory burgesses', as Adolphus Ballard called them (1904, 14), has for long awaited a satisfactory explanation. F. W. Maitland's persuasive argument in *Domesday Book and Beyond* (1897, 172 ff.) that they were a relic of an ancient pattern, the tenurial descendants of the retainers kept by lords of the countryside to perform their military obligations to the *burh* – the so-called 'garrison theory' – was swiftly disposed of by James Tait in his review of the book (1897, 768–77), although the matter continued to be debated (Tait 1936, 26n). Tait himself, however, was unable to advance any alternative explanation for the existence of Maitland's 'tenurial heterogeneity' in the county boroughs, beyond general observations to the effect that it might have originated with royal grants of proprietary or jurisdictional rights, or even with the persistence of seigneurial rights over unfree migrants to these towns (1897, 775). Most later historians have followed J.H. Round in his belief that the lords of rural manors kept establishments in towns for commercial reasons (for instance: *VCH Herefs.*, i, 297; *VCH Worcs.*, i, 268; Hilton 1992, 43). In the case of Winchester, it has been pointed out that the economic advantages of privileged access to the urban market might have been substantial (Biddle, 1976, 382–3). It was also suggested that the urban properties attached to Hampshire manors were perhaps the means by which the inhabitants of the countryside were guaranteed accommodation within the defences of Winchester in time of trouble.

Yet Round himself also proposed that pre-Conquest thegns might have maintained houses in the boroughs because they themselves lived there (*VCH Surrey*, i, 286), and surely that is the inference to be drawn from the Worcester evidence: that significant numbers of the aristocracy of tenth-century Worcestershire, principally the important retainers of the bishops of Worcester and those of the King, formed what was essentially – and however temporarily – an urban class. They might depend upon their rural estates for their sustenance, but their service to their lord – whether military, ecclesiastical or administrative – was to be performed within his *burh*. Oswald's tenants would have had the produce of their estates delivered to their houses in Worcester, both for their own consumption but also so that they themselves could oversee the sale of the surplus. It was not the town-house or burgage that was initially appurtenant to a manor, but rather the manor that had been assigned to support an urban household. Moreover, from the evidence of burgesses or burgages in Worcester, held in 1086 by lords whose antecedents had had no obvious connection with the Church of Worcester, but rather with the Crown, it would seem that royal thegns, too, had been based within the *burh* during the tenth century.

Interpreted in this way, Domesday Book confirms that before 1066 the thegnly class had routinely owned urban land in the greater boroughs, and involved itself in urban affairs – a theme recently explored by Robin Fleming (1993). There were at least superficial parallels, therefore, between England at that time and the more urbanized parts of Europe such as Italy or Flanders where the ruling class was at home in both town and country (Wickham 1981, 85–8; Hilton 1992, 88–91). The likely participation of townsmen in royal administration as well as in commerce has also been commented on, for instance by James Campbell (1987, 209–10). By 1086, however, the link between urban and rural estates was changing, as the castle rather than the borough became the focus of public authority. The service owed by the new aristocracy to their superior lords no longer required them to retain their own permanent base in the shire towns, and their town-houses were of importance perhaps only in conferring privileged access to the market on the same terms as other burgesses, or more tangibly as sources of rental income. It would have been natural for the earlier blocks of urban property to have been subdivided and redeveloped, the presumably grander halls and associated buildings of the previous occupants being replaced now by more characteristically urban houses.

Within a relatively brief period much of its land within the area of the *burh* of Worcester must have been effectively lost to the Church, to become permanently attached to rural estates which in turn were lapsing into hereditary tenure. It is difficult to see how in fact the Church might have retained effective control of this land, to direct the future course of its development; for whatever precautions successive bishops might have taken, once the land was securely occupied by tenants the prospect of the Church's being able to profit from it further was remote. The Church might later claim that it retained jurisdictional rights over its ancient lands in Worcester, but other evidence suggests that in practice such rights were conveyed to the tenants along with the land. Chief rents or landgable, presumably, remained the Church's only interest in its original city properties. When eventually these lands came to be redeveloped, therefore, to accommodate a growing commercial population, the Church played no part in the process and drew no profit from it.

In 1086 the Bishop of Worcester had 90 houses in the city pertaining to his manor of Northwick, of which 45 were retained in his demesne and owed suit of court and 45 were held by other lords. Urse d'Abitot held 24 of these, presumably to be identified with the separately listed 25 houses that he held of the bishop in the marketplace, and from which he received 100 shillings a year (DB, i, 173c). A survey of the bishop's manors made around 1170 (Hollings 1934, 30–32, 37–8) confirms the extent of this holding in Worcester and provides more details. Of the total of 90 houses pertaining to Northwick, 43 were held by other lords from the bishop and he himself was said to hold 65 in demesne, although this latter figure may be a misreading (either by the editor or by an earlier transcriber). The detailed account of the bishop's houses actually lists 55 separate holdings, containing some 38 houses and cottages and 42 closes or lands: there seems no way of telling how many of the latter were in fact built upon, and no indication is given of the locations of these properties within Worcester, beyond the statement that two houses and an empty plot lay in Lowesmoor. A cash rent was specified for 39 properties: one was a rent of 4s 6d for 12 houses, another of 6s for land, and two were rents of 5s for land. Of the remaining 35 there were 12 (34 per cent) of 1s and 11 (31 per cent) of 6d. And these were not all of the bishop's houses in Worcester. There were said to be ten tenements belonging to his manor of Wick, which when listed totalled 18 houses, closes and lands – 6 of them paying a rent of 1s (Hollings 1934, 31). Also pertaining to Northwick were rents of assize of 30s said to be due to the bishop from Worcester, which would seem to be identifiable with 27 rents listed as *de burgagio Wygornie*, and which totalled 26s 8d (ibid., 31, 37). Three of the burgage rents were stated to be for land; the remaining 24 properties were described as closes. Ten of the latter (42 per cent) were rented for 1s, four for 6d, four for 1s 4d, three for 8d, two for 1*s* 8*d* and one for 2*s*. The only identified location was of one of the shilling rents, which was drawn from a property in *Brupord* – presumably Birdport (Hollings 1934, 37).

At some time during the century following 1170, the bishops of Worcester divested themselves of the 27 burgage rents held of the manor of Northwick, for when the manor was surveyed again, in the 1290s, this distinctive group of rents had disappeared (Hollings 1934, 6–13). The bishop's Worcester lands consisted now of half a dozen rents drawn from free tenants, and 72 customary tenancies, nearly all of single messuages. These evidently included or were identical with the 55 holdings consisting of some 80 houses and pieces of land that had been recorded in the mid twelfth century, and which had appeared in Domesday Book as the 45 houses in the bishop's demesne. A location was given for each, thus revealing a distinctive distribution pattern: only 22 or 23 of these properties were in the city itself, most being situated in the suburbs. There was a messuage in the otherwise unrecorded Yngrith Lane, which may or may not have been intramural, and there were single messuages in the High Street and Birdport. Two messuages were in Sidbury, two in Crocker Street/St Swithin's Street near St Nicholas's church, and two in Angel Street. The only concentrations of intramural property were 7 messuages belonging to the bishop in Broad Street, and 7 in Needlers Street/Pump Street. Suburban locations included Foregate Street (13 messuages), 'next to the Port ditch' (2), Lowesmoor (12), and outside Sidbury Gate (2). Fifteen properties were just said to be in the suburbs. A broad range of rents was paid, in addition to minimal labour services on most of the properties, so that although shilling rents made up the largest single group with 12, and both 6*d* and 2*s* rents followed with 11 each, there were 20 separate levels of rent, between 3*d* and 8*s*. The total of 1*s* and 6*d* rents is identical with that recorded for the bishop's 55 tenements of the mid twelfth century.

The city property of Worcester Cathedral Priory

The pre-Conquest separation of the lands of the cathedral priory from those of the bishops of Worcester has been discussed in Chapter 5. There is no indication of when a formal division of Church lands in Worcester itself might have occurred, although any such division was at best an unequal one. The large number of rents the eleventh- and twelfth-century bishops drew from Worcester contrasts with the 40 properties in the city that the monks owned in the years before 1100 (H 289–91).

It is the survival of lists of rents, beginning with that in Hemming's cartulary, that makes it possible to study the evolution of the urban estate of Worcester Cathedral Priory. The most detailed rental is that made in 1556 of the city properties of the newly created Dean and Chapter of Worcester (Canterbury Cathedral Archives, Literary Mss E29). As the priory's Worcester properties had been transferred complete to the new body at the Dissolution, the rental is in effect a record of the final location and value of its city lands. It is not a complete record, unfortunately, as the cathedral close parish of St Michael – where other evidence indicates the heaviest concentration of cathedral priory properties to have been – was omitted from the survey. Otherwise, all the Worcester rents that the priory received are here – rents described as chief rents as well as rents from properties leased or let at will, or held by copyhold tenure. In all, 133 houses had belonged to the priory, and there were 29 pieces of ground described as gardens or closes. In addition, chief rents totalling £10 0*s* 11*d* were drawn from a further 57 or more properties.

A conclusion to be drawn at once is that probably throughout the middle ages the priory had followed a policy of disposing of fixed rents of assize – presumably those of little value, or which were inconvenient to collect. The priory's cartulary of 1240 (Darlington 1968, *passim*) and surviving deeds in the collection of the Dean and Chapter (WCL D&C, principally B961–1699) together record 78 separate acquisitions of rent in Worcester, virtually all before the fifteenth century and with a total annual value of £19 3*s* 10*d*. As the surviving deeds are certainly not a complete record of transactions during the period after 1240, then this figure must underestimate the real total by an unknown amount; even so, it is itself considerably in excess of the £10 that the rents of assize inherited by the Dean and Chapter from the priory were worth in 1556. Such rents were easily lost, or rather became impossible to collect, usually when the buildings from which they were collected were demolished, fell empty, or otherwise changed in status. Frequent changes in ownership, and cases of disputed ownership, must have disrupted the easy collection of rents that were often so small that expensive legal action for recovery could be justified only on exemplary grounds. Even so, a reduction of this order could have come about only through a policy of alienation.

Further evidence for the turnover in these chief rents comes from a damaged rental of 1384 (WCL D&C C869), and a rental of the priory's properties made in 1240 (Hale 1865, *passim*, and particularly 105a–117b). Despite being damaged at the head, so that only the heading of 'Wygorn' and the date of 'April, 7 Richard II' are legible, the 1384 rental is evidently a list of the rents to be paid to the prior and omits the obedientiaries' properties. This rental is, therefore, not the exact counterpart of that made in 1240 which lists separately not only the prior's rents but also those assigned to the priory officials; thus a comparison is possible only with the prior's rents in 1240, the Worcester rents paid to the obedientiaries in that year being excluded. In 1384 the prior drew rent from 52 properties in eight parishes, and from an illegible number in St Helen's, in all worth £10 13*s* 7½*d*. Those in St Helen's were the most valuable group, worth together £4 9*s* 4*d*. Judging by the range of the 52 legible rents – as high as 11*s* but most less than 3*s* and 14 of 1*s* or less – these were mainly free or quit rents. By comparison, in 1240 the prior had drawn rents from 130 separate properties, totalling £10 3*s* 3*d*. The total value of his Worcester rents had remained quite stable over the period, therefore, showing only a small increase; what had changed, quite clearly, was that by 1384 there were fewer rents, and each must have had a higher average value. Of the 130 rents in the earlier year, the highest was a rent of 10*s* in St Helen's parish, and 67 rents were of 1*s* or less.

It is impossible to be sure of the total value of rents that the priory acquired during the period between the two rentals, but on the evidence of the surviving deeds of gift in the cathedral Dean and Chapter archive the monks acquired 56 rents or blocks of rents within the city of Worcester with a value of £15 9*s* 10*d* (or an average value of 5*s* 6*d*) between the mid-thirteenth century and 1384. The total agrees closely with that taken from the licences for alienation in mortmain enrolled on the patent rolls, according to which the priory acquired Worcester rents totalling at least £15 6*s* 4*d*, and perhaps as much as a further £1 10*s*, between the passing of the Statute of Mortmain in 1279 (designed to restrict further gifts of land to the Church) and 1378, the last year for which any acquisition is recorded (*Cal. Patent Rolls 1281–92*, 474; 1313–17, 80; 1330–34, 338; 1340–43, 6; 1358–61, 88; 1367–70, 258; 1377–81, 211). We cannot tell how far these figures may under-estimate the true total, or in what proportion these rents were assigned to the prior or to the obedientiaries, but the evidence of acquisition on such a scale leaves little doubt that an approximately equal value of rents was at the same time being sold. It is impossible to measure the exact individual value of the prior's rents in 1384 because we do not know how many were collected from St Helen's parish – in 1240 it had been 15 worth £1 3*s* 6*d*, and in 1384 all we know is their appreciably greater total value which was £4 9*s* 4*d*. Probably a greater number of rents came from St Helen's parish in the latter year and doubtless their average value was greater.

At the same time the prior had apparently relinquished all of the 19 rents which he had drawn from St Peter's in 1240 and which had been worth just £1 3*s* 4*d*, or less than 1*s* 3*d* each. There seems to have been a tendency, therefore, for smaller rents to have been sold or granted away whilst those that were more valuable were retained.

Evidence for earlier planning in the records of the cathedral priory

One effect of the priors' policy of realizing the capital value of fixed assets is that the contents of the 1384 rental can apparently tell us nothing about the priory's city lands in earlier centuries. But how far is that also true of the 1240 rental? The details of rents recorded in that year suggest that the process of alienation had not yet been so extensive as to obliterate the remnants of a pattern which perhaps had once been more coherent. For instance, of the 130 rents owed to the prior in 1240 – or rather of the 121 whose value is given – as many as 36 (30 per cent), were rents of exactly 1*s*. Their distribution varied widely from parish to parish: there was a 1*s* rent among the 11 from St Martin's (9 per cent); 3 among the 19 from St Clement's (15 per cent); 3 among the 17 known rents from St Peter's (18 per cent). In three parishes the incidence of shilling rents was much more pronounced: in St Helen's it was 5 out of 13 known rents (38 per cent); in St Swithun's it was 8 out of 20 (40 per cent); most markedly of all, in St Alban's 8 of the 14 rents (57 per cent) were of 1*s*. Furthermore, there was a certain regularity of the remaining rents that was more pronounced in some parishes than in others. Only 6 rents are recorded for St Nicholas's: 2 were of 6*d*, 2 of 1*s* and 2 of 2*s*. In St Helen's only 2 rents out of 13 were not multiples of 6*d* or 1*s*. In all, 77 of the prior's 121 known rents (64 per cent) were multiples of 6*d* or 1*s*. How far can this pattern have arisen by chance? Alternatively, should we not expect an overwhelming proportion of rents to be multiples of these basic sums? Apparently not, for in two parishes in particular the pattern is hardly in evidence: in St Martin's 6 out of 11 rents were of sums such as 5*d*, or 1*s* 2*d*, or 1*s* 8*d*; in St Clement's 11 out of 19 (58 per cent) were not based on the 6*d* multiple. Nor did they follow any alternative pattern, consisting as they did of 10 different amounts – 8*d*, 9*d*, 1*s* 1*d*, 1*s* 2*d*, 1*s* 3*d*, 1*s* 4*d*, and so on, up to 5*s* 8*d*.

Thus the 1240 rental appears to preserve evidence for earlier acts of planning, if that is indeed the implication of these instances of what seems to have been a standard burgage rent. One shilling was frequently chosen to be the burgage rent in new towns of the twelfth and thirteenth centuries, although it was less characteristic of older established towns such as Worcester (Hemmeon 1914, 61–77). The rents acquired by the priory during the thirteenth and fourteenth centuries – some large, some insignificant – came overwhelmingly by gift or purchase from Worcester burgesses: they were new charges, or had arisen through comparatively recent acts of sub-infeudation. Only a lord in receipt of a burgage rent, however, could have granted it to the priory. What we see in 1240, then, is a collection of rents of all sorts, including a significant number set at regular levels – undoubtedly chief rents which in origin, and still in theory, carried rights of lordship. These chief rents, moreover, will have become the priory's property in one of two distinct ways: either they were ancient rents, paid to the priory in token of grants of tenements made by the Church of Worcester long before; or they were relics of similar grants made by other lords, and which had subsequently been given to the monks in pious donation. It goes without saying that in the case of any individual rent nothing certain can be said of its origins nor of how it came to the priory; nevertheless, the greater part of these rents of 1*s* and its multiples are likely to have originated as burgage rents.

It is not merely the concentrations of the shilling rent in at least three of the parishes, and particularly in St Alban's, that lead to this conclusion. Burgage rents from Worcester of 6*d* and

1*s* were indeed being paid – to other lords – during the eleventh century. A significant proportion of the houses belonging to the bishop, for instance, can be shown to have been paying these rents at that time (see above). Domesday Book clearly fails to list most of the other Worcester burgages, but Evesham Abbey had 28 houses in the city, 23 of which rendered 20*s*; 11 other lords were recorded as holding 18 burgages, 5 of which were said to render 1*s*, 2 rendered 2*s*, and 2 rendered 6*d* (DB, i, 175d, 176a, 176b, 177b, 177c, 177d, 178a, 180c, 180d, 182b).

The monks themselves, on the other hand, had fewer Worcester rents at that time. It was presumably by an oversight that Domesday Book makes no mention of any houses in Worcester that belonged to the priory, as within 10 to 15 years their property in the city consisted of the 40 houses recorded by Hemming in the rental included in his cartulary (H 289–91). Of these, 8 were held by servants of the priory, and paid no rent. A further 4 pertained to the church of St Helen. Sixteen, of which 5 were beyond the Severn, paid rent only to the monks: 6 paid 2*s*, 4 paid 1*s*, 2 paid 1*s* 4*d*, 1 paid 1*s* 2*d*, 2 paid 10*d*, and 1 paid 6*d*. A further 12 houses were held by the monks *in burgo regis* – although whether that implies a distinct district of Worcester that was identifiably the King's, or simply means that these properties were held from the King, is left unclear. All 12 paid a chief rent to the King, generally of 1*d*, 1½*d* or 2*d*, although one paid 7½*d* and another 1*s* 3*d*. Seven of the houses paid no additional rent to the priory (one because it was waste). In total, the value of all these rents to the priory came to no more than £1 6*s*. This was a relatively small urban estate and there is certainly no sign of a standard burgage rent.

The shilling rents owned by the priory in 1240 had been acquired, therefore, since 1100. And rather than having been acquired piecemeal, through a multiplicity of grants, the indications are that they had come to the priory probably as a single donation. That can be seen from a comparison between the rents to be paid to the prior in 1240, and those to be paid to the almoner and sacristan. Of the sacristan's 27 rents, 5 were of 1*s* and 5 were of 6*d* – a pattern not dissimilar to that of the prior's rents. But the almoner had no shilling rents, and only three sixpenny rents, among his 28 rents; the commonest rent, paid in five cases, was 1*s* 7*d*. In all, 16 different amounts were paid to the almoner in rent, 11 of them only once, suggesting that these properties – like those of the prior's in St Clement's parish – had come to the monks through a number of individual acts of piety. The contrast with the regularity of the prior's rents emphasizes how different had been the way in which the latter had been acquired. But is it possible to determine who gave these rents to the priory? No grant by any secular lord of a large number of rents is recorded during this period – a period which moreover is well documented in the folios of the priory's cartulary of about 1240; the only possibility that presents itself is the relinquishing by one of the bishops after 1170 of the 24 or more burgage rents previously held of the manor of Northwick.

Certainly the twelfth and early thirteenth centuries saw the bishops make several grants of lands and rents to the monks of Worcester, as well as compromises and adjustments by both parties as they agreed on the continuing process of separating their interests (for instance, Darlington 1968, 54–75). In this context the transference to the priory of these burgage rents in Worcester, with an annual value of £1 10*s*, would have been a relatively minor matter. It is true that the priory cartulary, containing material going back to around 1100, makes no explicit reference to any such grant; perhaps, though, it followed on – or is concealed within – another grant, such as that made before 1149 by Bishop Simon of £3 6*s* 8*d* annually from his tolls from Worcester. There is no clarification of what those tolls might have been, or in what way the bishops collected them (Darlington 1968, 65, 73). Payment was to be made to the monks at fixed times of the year, and it is far from impossible that by subsequent agreement these or similar payments were replaced by a transference of rents.

Returning, then, to the rents paid to the cathedral priory in 1240: the frequent occurrence of rents of 1*s* and associated sums indicates that a proportion were in origin burgage rents; this was the sum most often paid by the bishops' tenants, and the concentrations observable in 1240 – most notably in St Alban's parish – are too great to admit of their having arisen through anything but a regular rent charged on a planned development at some previous time. It is unlikely that the priory itself had been the developing agency: it did not own these rents in 1100, and the central parts of Worcester had been developed in major schemes long before then. Therefore the priory had been given these rents, and given them by the successors of the lord or by the institution that had initiated the development some centuries before. That the donor was the bishop and thus the developer had been the pre-Conquest Church of Worcester, cannot as yet be demonstrated, but the undoubted dispersal of the bishops' burgage rents does lead most strongly to that conclusion.

The cathedral priory's management of its Worcester estate

By the time of the Reformation the cathedral priory had built up a substantial estate within Worcester of houses and other properties that were let by lease or by other renewable tenure. In 1556 a total of 134 houses and cottages recently belonging to the priory was recorded in eight of Worcester's parishes (Canterbury Cathedral Archives, Literary Mss E29). As usual, the basically rural parish of St John was not included, and the absence of the tiny parish of St Alban evidently means that at its dissolution the priory had owned no property there of any sort, neither lands nor rents. The exclusion of St Michael's parish was presumably a consequence of the legal status of the sanctuary area: the cathedral authorities asserted that their ancient precincts were not part of the city of Worcester, and so it is logical that a rental of their Worcester property should have omitted St Michael's.

The largest recorded concentration of the former priory's houses in 1556 was in St Peter's parish, where there were 25 tenements or houses and 10 cottages; in both St Helen's and St Clement's there were 23 houses, and in St Nicholas's 14 houses and a single cottage. Twelve houses were in All Saints', 11 houses and a cottage in St Martin's, 8 houses in St Andrew's and 6 in St Swithun's. In addition some 28 gardens and other plots of land were listed, 12 of them in St Peter's within the walls and a further 5 in the suburb there. In terms of value the ranking was rather different, as we might expect. Including the gardens (which were generally let for a shilling or so), the St Helen's properties were worth £20 16*s* 8*d* annually; the greater number of properties in less-favoured St Peter's were worth £18 10*s* 7*d*. Rents worth £9 13*s* 0*d* were drawn from the late priory's property in St Clement's; £8 14*s* 4*d* from St Nicholas's; £7 0*s* 4*d* from St Martin's; £6 8*s* 11*d* from All Saints'; £5 8*s* 10*d* from St Andrew's; £4 6*s* 4*d* from St Swithun's. The total of rents from houses and gardens in Worcester let on lease, by copy or at will was £80 19*s* (Table 10.1).

Table 10.1
Dean and Chapter: value of houses and lands let on lease, by copy or at will in 1556

Parishes	Number of houses and gardens	Value of houses and gardens	Average value of houses and gardens	Total per parish as % of city total	Value per parish as % of city total
St Peter	52	£18 10s 7d	7s 2d	32	23
St Helen	27	£20 16s 8d	15s 5d	17	26
St Clement	28	£9 13s 4d	6s 11d	17	12
St Nicholas	16	£8 14s 4d	10s 11d	10	11
All Saints	12	£6 8s 11d	10s 9d	7	8
St Martin	13	£7 0s 4d	10s 10d	8	9
St Andrew	8	£5 8s 10d	13s 7d	5	7
St Swithun	6	£4 6s 4d	14s 5d	4	5
	162	£80 19s 0d		100	101

The rental also separately listed rents of assize – described as chief rents – paid to the new Dean and Chapter. Their total value was far less, at £10 8s 11d, and their distribution among the Worcester parishes significantly different. St Helen's parish again produced the largest share of the total, some £3 9s; but St Swithun's contribution was scarcely less, at £3 5s 8d. Small or negligible amounts were drawn from properties in the other parishes, and seemingly no assize rents at all came from St Clement's. Assize rents in the remaining parishes were: St Peter's £1 3s 9d; All Saints' £1 2s; St Nicholas's 10s 4d; St Martin's 10s 2d; St Andrew's 8s (Table 10.2).

Table 10.2
Dean and Chapter: value of chief rents in 1556

Parishes	Number of rents	Value of rents	Average value of rents	Total per parish as % of city total	Value per parish as % of city total
St Helen	17	£3 9s 0d	4s 1d	29	33
St Swithun	16	£3 5s 8d	4s 1d	28	31
St Peter	8	£1 3s 9d	3s 0d	14	11
All Saints	8	£1 2s 0d	2s 9d	14	10
St Nicholas	3	10s 4d	3s 5d	5	5
St Martin	5	10s 2d	2s 0d	9	5
St Andrew	1	8s 0d	–	2	4
St Clement	0	–	–	–	–
	58	£10 8s 11d		101	99

How much property did the priory own in the parish of St Michael – that is, within its own precincts? The 1563 ecclesiastical census (Nash 1799, ii, appendix, p. cxvii) recorded a total of 48 households for St Michael's, a figure which if correct could admit of a maximum of 48 inhabited houses there and perhaps fewer in practice – and how many of them belonged to the priory? To establish some sort of a figure for that we need to begin with evidence from a century later. The parliamentary survey of 1649 (Cave and Wilson 1924, *passim*) recorded 57 houses as belonging to the late Dean and Chapter within the sanctuary or cemetery of the cathedral – that is, St Michael's parish – 23 of them held by lease and 34 by copy of the court roll of the manor of Guestenhall – the manorial court of the priory and subsequently of the Dean and Chapter to which it was claimed their Worcester tenants owed suit. The totals of houses for each of the other parishes were largely unchanged since 1556, except in the case of St Clement's where the 23 houses of a century earlier were now just 7. If both the 1563 census and the 1649 survey are correct, then the number of houses in St Michael's parish had increased; but comparison of the two totals leaves little doubt that the Church held most if not all the property there in 1649, as it presumably had also done in the sixteenth century.

If, then, to the total of 134 houses belonging to the Dean and Chapter in 1556 in the rest of Worcester, a further 40 for the parish of St Michael were cautiously to be added, this would not be to overestimate the size of its holding in that quarter, nor to underestimate it by very much. This means that the distribution of the cathedral priory's Worcester property had been even more uneven than the 1556 rental suggests. With practically a quarter of its properties sited within what had once been indeed the cathedral's cemetery, over half of the total number were either here or in one of the two adjoining parishes. Otherwise the only other notable concentration of lands was in the city's suburb across the bridge.

This was not an ancient distribution pattern. The evidence that the priory followed an active policy of disposing of its less desirable rents at the same time as it gained new ones, should counsel against too-hasty a conclusion that the houses it was letting on economic rents in the late middle ages had been in its hands for centuries. Indeed, the evidence is clear that this estate was slowly assembled, presumably from the time that the cathedral priory began to hold property in Worcester separate from that of the bishop. And while the priory could have had little choice in what property was offered to it in acts of charity, it was nevertheless able to discriminate in acts of purchase, and more importantly in deciding whether to retain or sell individual properties it had received by gift. This has already been recognized in the case of the priory's fixed rents, where it is clear that the continual process of acquisition – by whatever method – was matched by a compensating policy of disposal, keeping the total value of these rents roughly constant from the thirteenth century onwards.

The total in 1556 of 134 houses, together with an estimated 40 houses in St Michael's, represented an increase of some 135 or so over the 40 that Hemming recorded in 1100 (H 289–91). This of course was the net gain during those four centuries, a period during which we may be sure the priory was buying and being given houses, as well as building new houses on land in and around Worcester it had owned for centuries, or which it had recently acquired. At the same time – at least until around 1300 – it was granting out houses and land in hereditary tenure, in fee. Sixty-five separate acquisitions of real property in Worcester and the suburbs by the cathedral priory are recorded, consisting in all of some 52 houses, messuages or tenements plus two other grants of an uncertain number of houses. There were in addition 5 shops, 20 curtilages or other pieces of land, and a windmill – all acquired between the late twelfth century and the end of the fifteenth (Darlington 1968, *passim*; WCL D&C, principally B961–1699). Only five of the grants were made evidently before 1200 (Darlington 1968, 368, 392, 402, 443, 452), a reminder of the wholly inadequate nature of the documentary record: undoubtedly the twelfth century would have seen the priory acquire much more property than that. These early grants are known from the cartulary into which details of the priory's affairs were entered until perhaps 1240, so that the scarcity of early documentation is not to be attributed to poor survival

Rather, it is a reflection of the infrequency with which small land transactions were recorded in writing before 1200, even by the largest ecclesiastical institutions (Clanchy 1979, 38).

Having been acquired, how many of these properties were alienated in fee by the priory – let on hereditary tenure for a fixed rent – is impossible to tell, although it would appear to have been a minority after 1200. Six grants in fee of houses and land in Worcester are recorded for the period before and around 1200 (Darlington 1968, 440, 441, 443, 452, 453, 454), a further 4 from the thirteenth century (WCL D&C B929a, 1079, 1662, 1683), and the last such grant from 1304 (WCL D&C B1553). The small number from the twelfth century is comparable with the equally meagre total of recorded grants of land made to the priory at the same time, and again reflects how such transactions were recorded only exceptionally. The handful of grants in fee made after 1200, however, compares with the 44 acquisitions of property during the same period. Such a large discrepancy is not the accidental result of capricious record survival, but indicates that alienation in fee was far from being the obvious choice of the priory by the thirteenth century. The shift in emphasis away from such tenancies thus came long before the Statute of Quia Emptores of 1290 (Luders *et al.* 1810–28, i, 106) made further acts of sub-infeudation illegal.

As no leasing agreement is known from the thirteenth century, the priory may have let perhaps as many as three-quarters of its new properties at will, or by some other form of precarious tenancy. The earliest lease for a term of years to survive comes from 1303 (WCL D&C B1020), and 11 further leases date from the fourteenth century (WCL D&C B1039, 1056, 1084, 1248, 1249, 1341, 1509, 1537, 1573, 1668). Two can be readily identified as leases of newly acquired property (WCL D&C B1077/1341, 1668/1669); the remainder are of property previously let at will, presumably, or whose acquisition is unrecorded.

The great majority of recorded grants of land and houses to the priory come from the thirteenth century – 44 out of a total of 65. Six grants of land were made to the priory between 1300 and 1350 and a further 8 between 1350 and 1400. Two grants of plots of land in 1483 and 1498 complete the total. Licences for alienation in mortmain tell the same story: no licence for the acquisition of land – as opposed to rents – in Worcester was granted to the priory until 1314, and the last was granted in 1392, during which period the priory was given property amounting to at least 9 messuages, 9 shops, 5 cottages and 3 pieces of land in Worcester and its suburbs (*Cal. Patent Rolls 1313–17*, 80; *1330–34*, 338; *1340–43*, 6; *1350–54*, 500; *1367–70*, 258; *1391–6*, 148–9). The sharply reduced numbers of grants after 1300 cannot be attributed to lack of documentation, as the later centuries were as likely to be properly documented as the thirteenth was. Nor is accident of survival to be blamed, for although time has clearly taken its toll of the Worcester deeds, the most serious damage would seem to result from modern neglect of the whole collection – which presumably affected deeds indiscriminately from all periods. The evidence for the drastically reduced scale of property acquisition after 1300 – which became even more marked in the fifteenth century – reflects the reality of the situation, with the very real restrictions imposed by the Statute of Mortmain serving to reinforce a reducing inclination on the part of the laity to make pious donations to large religious houses. Grants of rent to the priory (above) show the same pattern, so that of the total of 57 there were 4 from before 1200, 41 from the thirteenth century, and 12 from the fourteenth century – and none after 1378.

The economic profile of each of the parishes helps explain the distribution of its lands and rents of assize that the priory had arrived at by the sixteenth century. That St Helen's parish should appear as the largest single source of both types of rent is not surprising in the light of its commercial pre-eminence: centred on the High Street, this was a high-rent district, and we should expect the cathedral priory over a long period to have sought – and retained – valuable investments in land there. The scarcely smaller rental income the priory drew from the property it owned in St Peter's, however, demonstrates that the investment policy was not simply one of relying on intrinsically valuable property to produce a good return. For although there were some better houses in this parish, along the lower part of Friar Street in particular, St Peter's was nevertheless in the main a district of cheap housing. The priory's substantial rental income here was possible only because of the very large number of houses it owned in St Peter's, far more than in any other city parish. Of its 134 houses and cottages in Worcester, over a quarter – 35 – were in St Peter's. Similar substantial holdings by the priory of cheaper property accounted for the appreciable income from St Clement's – the third largest total for any parish. There the priory owned 23 houses – as many as it owned in St Helen's – producing rents totalling £9 13s, or rather less than half of the sum it drew from the richer parish. The size of these holdings in St Clement's and St Peter's contrasts most markedly with the much smaller numbers of houses owned by the priory in St Swithun's (only 6) or in St Andrew's (8), St Martin's (12), All Saints' (12), or St Nicholas's (15) (Canterbury Cathedral Archives Literary Mss E29).

Interestingly, the attractiveness of property in the commercial centre was not reflected in the priory's acquisitions. Between the twelfth century and 1359 only 7 tenements and 2 plots of land situated in St Helen's and St Swithun's are recorded as having been bought or given to the monks (Darlington 1968, 402, 409; WCL D&C B1028, 1043, 1213, 1217, 1571). Possibly, therefore, many of the 29 houses it owned in these two parishes in the sixteenth century had been acquired before 1200, and indeed may have been among those that Hemming listed around 1100. Neither did the priory's purchasing policy extend to the cheaper property in St Peter's, so that another explanation is needed for its large estate there. Acquisitions of only 3 tenements or messuages, all in Sidbury, are recorded for the period before the mid thirteenth century, and no more than 2 thereafter (Darlington 1968, 380; WCL D&C B986, 1571, 1578). Yet the dissolved priory had owned 35 houses – described mostly as tenements or cottages – in this parish, together with a considerable number of plots of ground. Twelve gardens within the town walls and 5 closes outside the walls were listed for St Peter's in 1556, a much larger number than in any other parish, bringing the Dean and Chapter's separate properties there to a total of 52. Even having regard to the inevitable loss of documentation since the middle ages, this figure is quite disproportionate to the number of known acquisitions: one is forced to the conclusion that a considerable proportion of the St Peter's properties already belonged to the priory before the effective beginning of the documentation of their estates in the late twelfth century. Again, some may have been among those listed by Hemming, whilst others could have been built on land owned by the priory – extramural land before the building of the city wall during the twelfth century.

During the thirteenth century the priory's clear preference was to acquire suburban property in St Clement's. Fourteen of the 44 grants were of houses or land across the Severn, 7 being messuages or tenements in Cripplegate, with the others being houses or land in locations closer to the river or the bridge. Subsequently, there was little acquisition of lands in this suburb: only 2 shops in St Clement's Lane in the years around 1300, and 2 plots of land in 1483 and 1498. After 1300 the priory's attentions quite clearly shifted towards property around the cathedral, the remaining 5 of the 6 acquisitions between 1300 and 1350 being all of tenements built within the precincts or cemetery along Lich Street. Whatever the nature of earlier acquisitions – whether they had been pious donations or purchases by the priory – the similar location of every one of this latter group leaves little doubt that now there was a single-minded policy of purchase, and that the citizens of Worcester had ceased to give land in the city freely to the monks. It is also the case, though, that a factor contributing to the priory's preference for properties within its ancient cemetery area is that all must have been held in fee from the prior or perhaps the sacristan as lord: under the provisions of the Statute of Mortmain – admittedly never strictly observed –

the priory was supposed to restrict its acquisitions to such properties, rather than to lands held from other lords.

It is possible to achieve some measure of the proportion of the housing stock the priory had acquired in each parish. The census of households compiled in 1563 – only seven years after the Dean and Chapter's rental – can be used for purposes of comparison (Nash 1799, ii, appendix, cxvii). For whilst one records houses and the other households, and moreover the totals of households recorded for each parish may not be entirely reliable – a household, after all, under circumstances of multi-occupation being sometimes difficult to define – nevertheless these are factors common to each parish. The ratio of the 134 houses belonging to the Dean and Chapter to the number of households in Worcester was 1 : 6.6, but behind this figure lie great variations from parish to parish. For St Peter's the ratio is 1 : 2.3, for St Clement's it is 1 : 2.4, and for St Helen's it is 1 : 5. For the other parishes it is less than the overall figure, declining to a ratio for St Swithun's of 1 : 18 (these ratios are presented in Table 10.3, where they are also expressed as percentages).

Table 10.3
Comparison of the number of houses belonging to the Dean and Chapter in 1556 with the total of city households in 1563

Parishes	(a) Dean and Chapter houses in 1556	(b) City households in 1563	Ratio of (a) to (b)	(a) as % of (b)
St Peter	35	82	1 : 2.3	43
St Clement	23	55	1 : 2.4	42
St Helen	23	115	1 : 5	20
St Nicholas	15	158	1 : 10.5	9.5
St Martin	12	88	1 : 7.3	17
St Andrew	8	116	1 : 14.5	7
All Saints	12	149	1 : 12.4	8
St Swithun	6	106	1 : 17.7	6
St Alban	0	20	–	0
St Michael	–	(48)	–	–
Total	134	889 (+48)	1 : 6.6	15

Recalculating percentages, and allowing for the estimated total of 40 houses in St Michael's parish to add to the 134 owned by the Dean and Chapter in the rest of Worcester: in 1556 St Michael's contained 23 per cent of the houses belonging to the dissolved priory, and as many as 56 per cent were to be found in the parishes of St Michael, St Peter and St Helen. The priory's presence as landlord in these three parishes had been massive, with 98 houses in a district of 245 recorded households; the ratio of the Dean and Chapter's houses to the total number of households as recorded in 1563 was thus exactly 1 : 2.5.

Whatever the degree of multi-occupation in sixteenth-century Worcester, it is clear that in the three parishes the Dean and Chapter (and previously the priory) was landlord to a substantial proportion of the population, unlike the situation particularly in St Swithun's, St Andrew's and All Saints' where the small numbers of houses belonging to the Church really were no more than a marginal local presence. So the cathedral priory had over a long period managed its Worcester property towards two ends. First, it had followed the policy already identified, of rationalizing its fixed rents of assize by shedding – where possible – those of little value, whilst retaining rents of greater value. As a result, by 1556 as much as 65 per cent – virtually two-thirds – of the income from what were described as chief rents was drawn from the two wealthy High Street parishes of St Helen's and St Swithun's, and none at all from St Clement's or St Alban's. Second, it had concentrated those properties which it actually owned into particular parts of the city, poor as well as wealthy. The very small number of houses the priory owned in certain parishes – in particular in St Swithun's – contrasts significantly with the concentrations of its property in St Helen's, St Michael's and St Peter's, close to the cathedral, but also in transpontine St Clement's with its mean housing.

The Gloucester lands of St Peter's Abbey

The surviving documentation for St Peter's Abbey is so different in character from that for Worcester Cathedral Priory that any comparison between their urban estates must be superficial at best. Because there are no surviving rentals compiled by the abbey's servants, reliable estimates of the size, nature and value of the abbey's urban estate during different periods cannot be made. Cole's town rental of 1455 – however important a document it may be for the overall view it gives of a fifteenth-century town – provides details only of the intramural tenements leased or held at will from the abbey, and even then is not very informative about those areas where the abbey was apparently the only landowner and from which no landgable was due. Furthermore, at no point in time after 1100 is there any evidence for the number of properties held in fee from the abbey, nor is there any indication as to the true extent of its suburban holdings.

But despite the accident of survival which has led to this disparity of documentation, we might expect these two estates to have shown many similarities. According to the *Valor Ecclesiasticus*, St Peter's Abbey had in the 1530s an income from all sources of £1430 4s 3d, and the priory slightly less at £1386 9s 9d. Of these totals, the abbey drew a greater proportion from property in Gloucester than did the priory from Worcester property: rents and tenements yielding £145 3s 5d a year or 10 per cent of the total, compared with the latter's £98 17s 4d or 7 per cent (Caley 1810–34, i, 417, 418; iii, 220, 225). The difference is not great, and probably reflects medieval Gloucester's greater size and overall value.

According to the brief survey of Gloucester made in about 1100 and preserved in the Evesham Abbey cartulary (BL Cotton Vespasian B xxiv fo. 57r; text edited by H.B. Clarke in Moore 1982, appendix), after the King the greatest landholder in the town was the Archbishop of York with 60 burgesses – evidently the urban properties of the recently acquired St Oswald's. Then came the Abbot of St Peter's with 52 burgesses. Of a total of 506 recorded burgesses in 1100, therefore, the abbey was lord of slightly more than 10 per cent. St Peter's had existed for more than three centuries as a minster, and for perhaps the last 80 years as a house of Benedictine monks; the relative decline it had suffered since at least the early tenth century had been reversed only with Serlo's appointment as abbot in 1072. Unlike Worcester, where there are firm indications that the Church participated in the foundation and planned expansion of the *burh* after the 890s, there is no such clear evidence connecting either of the Gloucester minsters with urban development in the tenth century. Both minsters' ownership of so many burgages in 1100 may indicate an involvement only in relatively recent acts of development.

It is not possible to tell whether these 52 burgages were scattered throughout the town, or whether they were in the concentrations that might point to the abbey's having developed a block or blocks of its own land. Later evidence suggests that a substantial proportion of the abbey's houses had formerly lain together around the church of St Mary de Lode, indicating that St Peter's had indeed developed an urban estate to the west of its precinct – although whether before 1100 as seems likely, or later, remains uncertain.

Cole's rental identifies rather more than 300 properties that had been noted as paying landgable to the Crown, in rentals going back to the 1220s or before (see above, p. 2); it preserves, therefore, something of the pattern of lordship over the Gloucester burgages as it was early in the thirteenth century, and perhaps considerably earlier than that. When mapped, a pattern emerges of clear concentrations of royal lands, but also of districts from which the Crown drew no chief rents at all (fig. 10.1). One of the more obvious of these latter districts was the whole of the parish of St Mary de Lode, from which not a single tenement paid landgable to the bailiffs. As the area around the church, in particular, shows some signs of planning and organization, this points to a phase of development in which the secular authority had not been involved. Its long and close relationship with St Mary's leaves little doubt that it was St Peter's which had been responsible, either as minster or as abbey: supporting evidence for the abbey's role in developing the district is to be

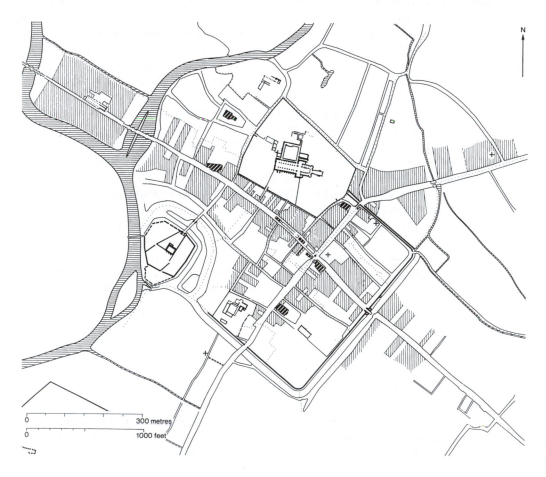

10.1   Gloucester: properties paying landgable in 1455

found in the scatter of references in charters of the thirteenth century that conveyed property here, and which stipulated that landgable was to be paid to the abbot of Gloucester or that the tenants owed suit to the abbey's Gloucester court (*Cal. Recs Corpn Glouc.*, 272, 329, 687; *Hist. et Cart.*, ii, 236, 242, 244–5). In all likelihood the development of housing here outside the walls of the *burh* had been a response on the part of St Peter's to the growing number of people living along the main streets of the town during the tenth and eleventh centuries.

Even had rentals of the abbey's Gloucester properties survived, it is possible that few of its 52 houses in 1100 would have remained identifiable through the centuries. In Worcester the burgages belonging to the Church in the eleventh century – and which similarly had originated in earlier phases of development initiated by the bishops – returned fixed rents that, as we have seen, were apparently given to the cathedral priory during the twelfth century, and subsequently disposed of in a gradual rationalization of the priory's urban estate (see above). Whether the ancient chief rents of St Peter's, Gloucester, were similarly sold off is unknown.

Incidentally, the fact that the town's bailiffs had followed no such policy of alienating or commuting the langable payments owing to them is not surprising: worth notionally more than £10, this rent made a principal contribution to the annual fee-farm of £65 they and their successors had to deliver. Traditionally this had been made up from the former royal perquisites they had been given the right to collect, including chief rents, market tolls and court proceeds; and as long as these sources of revenue remained more than adequate to pay the fee-farm – as they did until the mid-fifteenth century (Holt 1987, 296–300) – the bailiffs were unlikely to have made any radical changes to the system. Furthermore, they would not have sold on their own initiative what remained in legal reality – with all that that implied – a chief rent owed to the King.

According to the *Valor Ecclesiasticus*, at the time of its dissolution the abbey was drawing £145 3s 5d in rents from its Gloucester properties, of which £17 5s 4½d was described as 'free' rents, or rents of assize, and the remaining £137 1s 6½d must have been drawn from properties leased for term of years or let at will (Caley 1810–34, ii, 417). The only source that can indicate the number and distribution of properties represented by this overall figure is Cole's rental of 1455. In that year more than 130 houses within the walls of Gloucester were rented from the abbey, either by lease or at will, of which 107 were described as tenements and 11 as cottages; Cole also recorded the abbey as the owner of 9 blocks of houses along Gloucester's minor streets and back lanes, which together may have accounted for substantial additional numbers of tenements and cottages. Thirteen buildings described as stables belonged to the abbey, and there were 6 vacant pieces of intramural land important enough for Cole to record. In addition, in those parts of the suburbs described in the rental – that is, where there were properties owing landgable to the bailiffs or which came within the jurisdiction of the borough court – the abbey owned 28 separate tenements and 6 cottages, with a further 5 blocks of tenements and 5 pieces of land (*1455 Rental, passim*). In total, the abbey must have owned close to 200 houses in Gloucester. Undoubtedly there were in addition many properties held from the abbey in fee from which it received only a chief rent, but Cole did not record the superior lords of any messuages other than those held from the Crown.

By the early fourteenth century, as we have seen, Worcester Cathedral Priory had stopped granting out its urban property in hereditary tenure, favouring instead leases for terms of years; this may be a guide to when a similar change occurred in Gloucester. Certainly during the thirteenth century the abbey commonly granted its houses and plots to tenants in fee, sometimes with the stipulation that they or their heirs should not alienate the property without permission; on other occasions the grants were to assigns as well, as if in recognition that in practice there was little obstacle to the free sale of such land (*Hist. et Cart.*, i, 184, 318; ii, 15, 117). Alienation in fee was favoured by Abbot Reginald de Homme (1263–84) (ibid., i, 194, 195; ii, 237, 238, 241, 242, 244), but his successors decisively turned away from ensuring fixed rents in perpetuity in favour of leases for limited terms which, as well as offering the prospect of periodic review of the rental level, conformed with tenurial law following the Statute of Quia Emptores of 1290.

Lifetime tenancies had not been unknown in Abbot Reginald's time (GCL D&C Abbey Deeds, i, 3), and from at least 1301 the abbey was regularly leasing its Gloucester tenements: at first for the lifetime of the lessees (ibid., v, 6; viii, 3, 4), although after the first decade of the fourteenth century the lifetime term was invariably limited by a term of years – usually 60 or 70 (ibid., iii, 17; v, 22; vi, 3, 11, 14, 20; ix, 5). Leasing allowed the abbey to retain the option of enhancing future rent values through investment, by means of redeveloping land when it became available on the surrender of a lease. Whether or not this was a factor influencing the change of practice, a century later the abbey was embarking upon a number of ambitious schemes designed to increase the rental yield from certain of its sites (see below). Fixed-term tenancies enabled it – if it wished – to take better advantage of changing patterns of demand for land within the town.

It was concluded that many of the properties acquired by the cathedral priory during the twelfth and thirteenth centuries must always have been let at will. This, too, points to the way

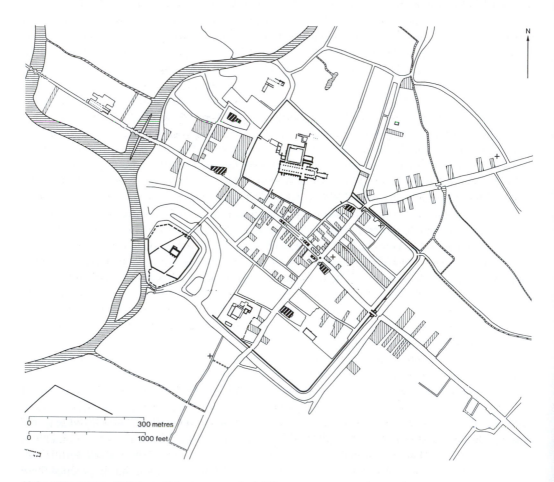

10.2   Gloucester: St Peter's Abbey property in 1455

in which Gloucester Abbey had exploited its lands during the same period. By analogy with the experience of Worcester Cathedral Priory, the impressive number of houses leased for term of years or held at will that the abbey had accumulated by the mid fifteenth century was composed of lands acquired at different times. Some, no doubt, had been acquired relatively recently and had been promptly leased out; others had belonged to the abbey for much longer, and although once let in fee had returned to the abbey by default of heirs or other cause. Yet others had always remained in the abbey's control, having been let at will. Perhaps among its virtually 200 houses recorded in 1455 there still remained a remnant of the 52 burgages held by the abbey's tenants in the eleventh century, although for the most part the Gloucester estate of the pre-Conquest minster and abbey would have long constituted no more than a collection of small fixed rents which – again by analogy with Worcester Cathedral Priory's experience – would have been lost over the years, or might well have been disposed of when they became irksome to collect.

Both its acquisition of suburban tenements and the development by the abbey of areas of suburban housing had been on a more ambitious scale than the evidence of the 1455 rental would suggest. A late-thirteenth-century rental of the manor of Abbot's Barton listed the customary tenants of 24 messuages in the 'New Land' outside the outer north gate, with a further 26 in Barton Street outside the east gate (*Hist. et Cart.*, iii, 155–8). Ten customary tenants held messuages along Brook Street (ibid., iii, 154–5), which was then the smallest and most recent of the Gloucester suburbs (see below, p. 331). It is not possible to suggest a date for the original development of Barton Street, although the presence here of properties paying landgable to the bailiffs (*1455 Rental*, 102b–110b) points to its having taken place already by 1200 (see below, pp. 485–6); the Brook Street houses, by contrast, may have been developed by the abbey only after the building of the Almesham postern, not long before 1253, gave access to intramural Gloucester (*Cal. Recs Corpn Glouc.*, 492).

By 1300, therefore, the abbey had some 60 customary tenants in these districts of the town that lay outside the bailiffs' jurisdiction, in addition to its suburban houses within the liberty, which totalled some 40 or more in the fifteenth century (*1455 Rental, passim*). Furthermore, hidden in the Abbot's Barton rental were the suburban tenants who held their lands freely from this extensive manor; it is not possible to tell how many there were as the rental followed the usual pattern of totalling rents of assize. In 1310 the abbey purchased or was given two messuages in Abbot's Barton (*Cal. Patent Rolls 1307–13*, 282) which must have been held freely from the abbot as lord; in 1317 the abbey likewise acquired as many as eight messuages in Brook Street in a single transaction (*Cal. Patent Rolls 1317–21*, 47), which suggests that in this suburb, too, the abbey had numerous free tenants. But clearly the growth of the abbey's suburban estate followed closely the overall pattern for its Gloucester properties: initial development of its own lands was followed by a long period – lasting into the fourteenth century – in which it purchased houses held in fee from itself or from other lords.

The abbey continued to acquire new property in the town until the fourteenth century. Licences issued under the Statute of Mortmain show that between 1303 and 1374 the abbey acquired by gift or purchase as many as 51 messuages and shops in Gloucester and its suburbs (*Cal. Patent Rolls 1307–13*, 282; *1313–17*, 206; *1317–21*, 47; *1327–30*, 484; *1330–34*, 326; *1345–8*, 369; *1348–50*, 493; *1361–4*, 401; *1364–7*, 218; *1374–7*, 25), far more than the cathedral priory acquired during the same period. After the middle years of the century the estate ceased to expand, however, either as charitable donations ceased or as the abbey found itself with insufficient surplus funds to invest in the purchase of property. The licence it was given in 1329 to acquire lands with an annual value of £10 was effective until 1374, after which date there were no more recorded acquisitions of property in Gloucester or elsewhere until the very end of the fifteenth century, when the abbey again entered the property market (see below).

Late-medieval investment by St Peter's Abbey

By 1400, therefore, the abbey could increase its income from Gloucester property only by investing in property it already owned – a policy it was indeed following in the fifteenth century, and which gave late-medieval Gloucester at least four major new buildings. Even today, the New Inn in Northgate Street is a large and impressive building. Cole described it as 'newly-built' in 1455 (*1455 Rental*, 84), but it was evidently then at least fifteen years old: the monk responsible for its building, he said, had been *laudabilem virum* John Twynnyng – who had not been a monk at Gloucester since 1441 at the latest (*Cal. Patent Rolls 1441–6*, 29). Twynnyng, as collector of the abbey's Gloucester rents, had also built another inn virtually opposite the New Inn, on the other side of Northgate Street, on land held in fee from Lanthony. Cole, writing in the 1440s about this second inn, had not then been so complimentary about Twynnyng, for the otherwise 'praiseworthy man' had contrived to block up a small lane at the side of the property, making access difficult to a tenement of Lanthony's at the rear (A13, fos 65v–66).

The New Inn replaced a tenement and six shops that had occupied the corner of Northgate Street and Grant Lane, and which the abbey had acquired sometime between 1263 and 1284 (*Hist. et Cart.*, ii, 198). Redevelopment of the site must have required a major investment of capital, but was to prove profitable. In 1455, unusually, the New Inn was not let to a tenant, but remained in the abbot's hand and may have been managed by an employee; when it was leased in 1508 for a term of 31 years the rent was set at the high level of £9 10*s* (GCL D&C Register C, fo. 86). The inn on the opposite side of the street was apparently comparable in scale and value, and represented a similar investment: in 1455 it was let to Philip Monger (*1455 Rental*, 72; A13, fo. 65v), a prosperous merchant who the previous year had completely rebuilt at his own expense the chapel of St Thomas which stood outside the outer north gate (*1455 Rental*, 98). He was alone among the Gloucester merchants of his day in having his merchandise carted overland from Southampton, including nine pipes of wine in 1439–40, and ten in 1443–4 (Bunyard 1941, 77, 136, 156; Coleman 1960, 1, 13; Coleman 1961, 153). As with the New Inn opposite, the abbey's intention in building this second inn was clearly to capture the lucrative business of the wealthiest visitors to the town.

A third inn was built by the abbey during the early years of the sixteenth century, following on its acquisition of a tenement in Westgate Street near the King's Board in 1498 or shortly before. This was the inn later known as the Fleece, which was leased to a tenant by 1534 (Household, 1946–8, 44). The site was a large one, and had access at the rear to Gore Lane (*Cal. Recs Corpn Glouc.*, 1189); it can be identified with a block of three properties held by the countess of Shrewsbury in 1455 (*1455 Rental*, 24, 30–32). The abbey acquired four separate tenements at this time, securing a confirmation of their title from the mayor and burgesses as superior lord – evidently each of the tenements owed landgable to the town authorities (*Cal. Recs Corpn Glouc.*, 1189). It would appear, therefore, that the abbey had taken advantage of a slump in property values associated with the widespread dereliction the burgesses complained of in 1487, and for which there is supporting evidence (Stevenson 1891, 406–7; Holt 1990, 157–9; Holt 1987, 287–318). Thus the decline in Gloucester's fortunes at this time might not have been regarded by everyone as a disaster; the abbey – and perhaps others – saw the opportunity for rich pickings. That the Fleece was built within so few years of this prominent site's acquisition points to the dilapidation of the existing buildings when they were purchased, and leads to the conclusion that it was the potential proceeds of redevelopment that attracted the abbey to this particular property.

Yet however profitable such great inns might have been, there was a limit to the number that Gloucester and its visitors could support – and the 1455 rental lists at least 10 in addition to those the abbey had built. But redevelopment of other types of commercial property could also, apparently, produce a satisfactory return on investment, despite the contemporary reports of a surplus in the town's housing stock that showed itself in the dereliction of a large number of properties.

The evidence for the abbey's replacement of at least one of a group of small tenements or selds on the west side of Northgate Street, extending northwards from the Cross (*1455 Rental*, 66b; Moss and Spry 1972; and see above, p. 49 and fig. 3.8), during the latter part of the fifteenth century indicates that – whatever the situation with regard to poorer property elsewhere in the town – demand for good quality premises in the centre of Gloucester may have remained buoyant. Cole described this part of the street as the Cordwainery, a traditional description that, if it did not still hold good when this tenement was renewed, is at least consistent with its obviously having been intended as working and living accommodation for a craftsman who required little working space, and who sold his products retail. If the abbey considered it worthwhile to rebuild this seld (and doubtless the others in the row) this would be a clear sign of its confidence in an investment in rents for craft premises.

And a further indication, perhaps, of the abbey's commitment to replacing its ageing town-centre tenements with larger and better premises was its rebuilding in 1498 of another, more important, block of selds nearby (fig. 3.8). This was the tenement block in the middle of Westgate Street, between the Mercery and the Butchery. Described as reaching from the church of St Mary of Grass Lane towards the High Cross, the new block was 21½ feet (6.5 metres) wide, and extended for some 77½ feet (23.6 metres); at its end towards the Cross the building was carried on for a further 9 feet 5 inches (2.9 metres) upon posts. Whilst being built it was the subject of a dispute between the abbey and the town authorities, who protested that it was higher than the building it replaced; after arbitration between the parties the abbey was allowed to proceed (*Cal. Recs Corpn Glouc.*, 1187, 1369). The site itself and the buildings on it, according to Robert Cole, had in 1455 only recently been recovered by the abbey after legal action against the tenants for non-payment of rent (*1455 Rental*, 26): it looks very much, therefore, as if by the middle years of the century this block in the main commercial quarter was losing its value, and may already have been on its way to dilapidation. That it should have taken the abbey another 40 years or more to replace it shows, perhaps, the limits to its investment policy during a time of economic uncertainty, falling population and a reduced demand for housing and commercial premises. It was as early as 1447 that symptoms of decline had been reported by the burgesses (*Cal. Patent Rolls 1446–52*, 70), and it may only have been in the 1490s that the abbey felt confident enough to make such a large investment. Coming as it did when the abbey was purchasing land in Gloucester for the first time in nearly 150 years, and preparing to build another inn, this may suggest that by the 1490s there were clear signs of the town's economic recovery.

The Gloucester lands of St Oswald's Priory

The survey of *c.* 1100 goes to confirm the New Minster's pre-eminence within Gloucester since the foundation of the *burh*. After the Crown's holding, the largest – of 60 burgages – was that of the Archbishop of York, which obviously had been recently acquired with St Oswald's (BL Cotton Vespasian B xxiv fo. 57r; text edited by H.B. Clarke in Moore 1982). Thus St Oswald's had derived marginally more benefit from the urban development of the previous two centuries than had its sister institution of St Peter's, with its 52 burgages.

Just as St Peter's, perhaps after 1100, seems to have laid out areas of its own land for housing, so St Oswald's did likewise with its land to the north of the *burh*. Again, the most telling evidence comes from the 1455 rental. As with the parish of St Mary de Lode, there were no payments of the royal landgable from any properties in the parish of St Oswald: the first houses here, therefore, had been built on non-royal land. It must be presumed that just as the Gloucester part of St Mary de Lode's parish had been entirely the Old Minster's land, so likewise had the New Minster at its foundation been given the land that constituted its own parish, on the north side of St Peter's, together with the detached section that lay immediately to the east of walled Gloucester, wedged between the parishes of St Michael and St John (fig. 4.2). When the now flourishing St Peter's felt the need to expand its precinct northwards early in the twelfth century, and again a century later, it could do so only by acquiring the land it needed from St Oswald's (*Hist. et Cart.*, i, 13, 25, 83; ii, 65). Either on its own initiative or with the co-operation of other authorities, St Oswald's had evidently been responsible for laying out and developing the early-medieval streets here: the western side of Hare Lane, St Brigid's Lane (generally known later in the medieval period as Bride Lane) and Wateringstead Street, as well as the tenements along the southern side of the street between the inner and outer north gates (see above, pp. 85–90; and below, pp. 326–9). There is no conclusive evidence that all this development had already taken place by 1100, and no information as to how many of St Oswald's 60 burgages lay within its own parish or how many were to be found lining Gloucester's intramural streets.

The few surviving references to payments of landgable to the Archbishop of York are all consistent with these streets having been laid out on land of St Oswald's. Two thirteenth-century charters conveying tenements in Bride Lane to Lanthony Priory both specify rent – of 2½d and 5s 8d respectively – to be paid to the Archbishop of York (A5, fos 91–91v; 92–93); the charter, by which Robert Bay of Gloucester in the 1220s gave the canons of Cirencester his free land in Hare Lane, specified a chief rent of a halfpenny to St Oswald's (Ross 1964, 390).

Despite the lack of evidence, it must be assumed that – like St Peter's – during the twelfth and thirteenth centuries St Oswald's Priory was acquiring houses in Gloucester by gift or purchase, and then letting them to tenants in hereditary tenure, in fee. The effect was to leave the priory by the fifteenth century in direct possession of very few properties in the town: in 1455 it had only 11 tenements and 6 cottages within the walls (*1455 Rental, passim*). Numerous other properties would at one time have been obliged to pay small rents to St Oswald's in perpetuity but, like those of Worcester Cathedral Priory, they had by the end of the middle ages long since been lost or sold for ready cash. The rental of St Oswald's properties made in 1536 records only 9 rents of assize, worth only £1 11s 2d or less than 5 per cent of its gross receipts from Gloucester of £33 9s (PRO SC6 Hen. VIII 1212, mm. 4–6).

Much of the property the priory owned in the fifteenth and sixteenth centuries had been acquired relatively recently. Between 1290 and 1355 it purchased or was given the surprisingly large total of 45 messuages and shops, most in the suburbs but at least 10 and perhaps 15 or more of them in the intramural part of Gloucester (*Cal. Patent Rolls 1281–92*, 47; *1301–1307*, 396; *1330–34*, 256; *1338–40*, 157, 248, 419; *1340–43*, 409; *1348–50*, 280; *1354–8*, 278). Unless some had been alienated before 1455, this would seem to account for virtually all the priory's intramural houses in that year.

Both the evidence for fourteenth-century acquisitions and the distribution of the priory's lands at the end of the period demonstrate a marked preference for suburban property. Over half of the houses and shops it acquired between 1290 and 1355 were reported to be in the suburbs, and subsequently – if not before – its lands were concentrated overwhelmingly on the north side of Gloucester. In 1455 it had 11 tenements in Hare Lane and a further 3 outside the north gate (*1455 Rental*, 80–88, 98, 102); but most of its suburban property was excluded from Cole's rental, either because it lay in streets that were outside the jurisdiction of the borough or because Cole simply ignored the extramural districts from which no landgable was to be collected. In the 1530s the priory had 9 tenements or cottages in Hare Lane and 3 cottages outside the outer north gate, but it had a further 35 tenements and cottages in Wateringstead Street, and 9 blocks of land; 6 houses and 2 gardens in the street that lined the north wall of the abbey; 4 pieces of land in Bride Lane or St Brigid's Lane; and 2 houses and a parcel of land in the otherwise unrecorded *Buckestrete* (PRO SC6 Hen VIII 1212, m. 4). In all, there were 53 inhabited dwellings which, together with over 30 pieces of land recorded as gardens, closes or orchards were rented for a total of £19 14s 2d, or 6s 11d per tenement, 3s per cottage and 2s 4d per piece of land. This compared with an average of 17s 9d for the 12 dwellings which contributed virtually all of the £11 3s 8d the priory received from intramural leases in 1536; quite clearly, then, the greater value of the suburban houses reflected only their far greater number and emphatically not their quality.

With only single tenements outside the south and east gates, the priory's preference for property close to its own precinct is apparent. And these were houses in its parish, on land it had been given at its foundation. So how far was this concentration relatively recent, the result of a policy of selective purchase? Or how far was it an ancient pattern, pointing to St Oswald's having been responsible for the initial development of the district? The two possibilities are not incompatible, in that the acquisition of large numbers of suburban houses by St Oswald's in the fourteenth century may have been the recovery by purchase of properties previously granted out in fee. We have already seen how Worcester Cathedral Priory, having released the northern and western sides of its own precincts for housing, found itself in the fourteenth century re-establishing its control of this property by means of purchase. But the concentration of houses belonging to St Oswald's in Wateringstead Street in particular suggests that the priory had always retained a proportion of properties here in its own hand, presumably by letting them only at will.

The Gloucester lands of Lanthony Priory

Beyond the south gate of Gloucester stood the Augustinian priory of Lanthony, often in the medieval period known as Lanthony Secunda, to distinguish it from its parent house Llanthony Prima, or Llanthony in Wales. Established originally in 1136 as a refuge for the canons of the Welsh house who had fled a politically unstable situation, Lanthony by Gloucester soon became a permanent institution. When it became safe for the canons to return to Wales, many chose to remain in Gloucester and the two houses coexisted under a single prior (Langston 1941, 1–7).

As Gloucester had already become an established and thriving town, the priory had no role in its initial stages of development. Its intramural lands came to it already built up, it would seem, and most of them as pious donations from the wealthier burgesses. Consequently, its influence on the shape the medieval town took was restricted to the area of the Southgate Street suburb – and even there it may have done no more than inherit an already developing district (for a discussion of this suburb, see pp. 331–5). As much as its late foundation, it is the remarkable survival of so many of the priory's cartularies and registers (Jack 1970–73, 370–83) that has ensured that its early history and its accumulation of property are relatively well documented. The key to any analysis of Lanthony's Gloucester properties is the extensive rental summarizing all that was then known (and thought to be worth recording) of the tenurial history of each tenement that brothers Richard Steymur and Robert Cole compiled in *c.* 1445 (A13; Jack 1970–73, 378).

Between 1136 when he founded Lanthony and his death in 1143, Earl Miles of Hereford richly endowed the new Gloucester house (Caley *et al.* 1849, vi, 136). Amongst the gift of lands and tithes scattered throughout Gloucestershire was the large tract of land outside the south gate of Gloucester on which the priory itself was built, together with Gloucester's southern suburb. This land already belonged to the Church: Miles's father, Walter of Gloucester, had granted it some forty years previously to his own father's foundation, the church of St Audoen or Owen which had been built just outside the walls of Gloucester and consecrated in 1095. Now St Owen's was granted to the new priory, together with all its lands – just as, in its turn, St Owen's had been given the existing gate-church of St Kyneburgh with all its possessions. So, despite Lanthony's having acquired all of its property after 1136, it was in this respect the heir of older ecclesiastical institutions.

A measure of how successfully Lanthony Priory established itself in Gloucester is the contrast with the fortunes of St Oswald's. Despite its having been reformed as an Augustinian priory within 20 years of Lanthony's foundation, St Oswald's apparently was never able to match the newer church's place in local affections – certainly it was never the recipient of charity on the same scale. Although only the end result can be measured, St Oswald's was given less property and must have had fewer resources with which to purchase lands: as both houses faced dissolution in the 1530s, Lanthony's Gloucester rents of £76 9*s* were worth twice as much as St Oswald's which amounted – as we have seen – only to some £33 9*s* (PRO SC6 Hen. VIII 1224, mm. 2d–5d).

Nearly all of Lanthony's acquisitions of property came during the priory's first century, following on Miles's initial endowment. But while Miles's family continued to exert great influence in Gloucester until at least the death of his daughter Margaret de Bohun in 1197 (Walker 1964, 1–11), they themselves were to give the priory no more property in the town. At the same time, though, a number of significant donations came from Miles's family's retainers – in one case specifically with his lord's permission (A5, fos 83v–84v; 60v–61; 67; 70v–71; 109–109v, A13, fo. 85; A5, fos 3–4v; Walker 1960, 195–202). By means of these and other such gifts, the priory had by 1200 acquired a substantial estate within Gloucester.

Writing in the 1190s, Gerald of Wales praised the saintly existence of the canons who had returned to Llanthony Prima in Wales, and contrasted it with the worldliness and wealth of the Gloucester house whose very existence he regretted. Perhaps his low opinion of Lanthony had been formed during the period of his education at St Peter's Abbey in the 1150s and early 1160s, although he may have exaggerated his disgust at Lanthony Secunda simply to draw the greatest possible contrast with the natural beauty and healthiness – both physical and spiritual – of the mother-house deep in the Honddu valley. But his judgment that within a short time of its foundation the rich and powerful daughter-house had 'odiously and enviously supplanted its own mother' (Brewer *et al.* 1861–91, vi, 37–41; Thorpe 1978, 10–12; 99–101) was evidently justified as the two priories eventually found it impossible to continue their association. The long-overdue formal dissociation came in 1205, when they decided each to elect their own prior and to divide their common property (Langston 1941, 34–7). As part of the settlement the Gloucester rents worth £24 10*s* were shared, with Llanthony Prima receiving slightly more than half of the gross value as its moiety (A6, fos 192v–195v). But the Welsh house must have encountered problems in managing a distant urban estate, and in 1251 was willing to transfer its Gloucester lands to Lanthony Secunda in return for what looks like a low annual pension of £5 6*s* 8*d* (Langston 1941, 48).

Analysis of the cartulary entries shows that by 1200 at least 35 separate properties – 19 of them described either at the time or later as tenements, 3 as cottages, 3 as shops and 3 as selds

– had been acquired from 16 individuals. Perhaps as many as a further 14 or so properties of a similar kind had been acquired from unknown individuals, their earliest appearance in the Lanthony documentation being their granting to tenants by the priors of the twelfth century. Taking these properties as a whole, there was no obvious pattern to their distribution: 16 were situated on one or other of Gloucester's main streets; 25 were scattered throughout the back streets and lanes of the town; a further 8 or so were suburban (A5, *passim*).

Doubtless these totals are incomplete, as there is nothing in the Lanthony records to show how it came by 53 of the properties it held in 1445, as well as 11 of its former holdings before the castle which were cleared in 1265 when the Bareland was made. Certainly these 53 properties had been acquired by Lanthony by the mid thirteenth century, but their earliest history consists of no more than the names of previous tenants cited by Steymur and Cole – although in virtually every case they were quoting from rentals dating apparently from 1270 or before (A13, *passim*). Perhaps these lands had been conveyed to the priory orally or by charters that were subsequently lost, although they must then have been let to tenants at will, or by oral agreement, or in some other way that has failed to be recorded. More likely, though, the lack of any record to indicate when they first came into Lanthony's possession points to their having been the lands transferred from Llanthony Prima in 1251 – and transferred, quite clearly, without associated documentation. If that explanation is correct, then many if not all of these properties, too, would have been acquisitions made before 1205.

Lanthony's rapid acquisition of property continued until well into the thirteenth century. This is well attested to by the numerous identifiable grants of land it received: charters dated or which can be assigned to the period between 1200 and 1250 conveyed a further 35 tenements, 2 shops, 8 holdings described simply as 'lands', and 15*s* rent to the priory (A5, *passim*). But during the last decades of the thirteenth century such grants virtually ceased, in marked contrast with the rate of acquisition of previous years. The change came very quickly: in grants dated or attributable to the 1250s and 1260s the priory acquired 13 tenements, 2 shops, 4 cottages, 5 curtilages or other plots of land, and a total of 38*s* rent (A5, *passim*). Yet between the 1260s and 1300 only two more properties – a piece of land inside the west gate and a close of meadow or pasture outside it – were added to the priory's Gloucester properties (A5, fos 52v–53; 54v–55). Whilst the change coincided with the passing of the Statute of Mortmain in 1279, which was designed to control transfers of property to religious institutions, it seems unlikely that Lanthony's phase of expansion should have been brought to such an abrupt end simply as a result of legislation. Nevertheless, the passing of the act was doubtless effective in hastening the process.

Whether the priory just ceased to purchase lands, or whether the burgesses of Gloucester no longer looked to it as a suitable recipient for pious donations intended to ease the burden upon their souls, remains unclear. Nor is it possible to tell how far the new legal restrictions effectively discouraged any return to the pattern of acquisition. Certainly, unlike the two other major Gloucester houses and unlike Worcester Cathedal Priory, Lanthony would not increase its holdings of urban property by any appreciable amount after the thirteenth century. Between 1300 and 1445, the date of Steymur and Cole's rental, Lanthony acquired 2 tenements, some cottages in Gore Lane, 3 shops, a garden, some lands outside the south gate, and 11*s* rent – a negligible total for a period of virtually 150 years (A13, fos 36v, 60v–61; A5, fos 34v, 46v, 66; A12, fos 23v–24, 30). And most of that property, moreover, came as a single pious donation in 1369 (A12, fos 23v–24, 25v, 30; A5, fo. 46v), as is confirmed by the enrolled licences for alienation in mortmain (*Cal. Patent Rolls 1367–70*, 238; *1391–6*, 416).

Lanthony Priory's management of its urban land

Interestingly, the methods chosen by Lanthony Priory to exploit its urban property differ in certain respects from those of Worcester Cathedral Priory. Like the monks of Worcester, Lanthony sold off rents it was given: every one of the tenements from which the priory drew rent in *c.* 1445 either belonged to the priory and had been let at will or for term of years, or had previously been granted out in fee by the priory itself. Equally clearly, however, and in contrast with the policy pursued by the cathedral priory, Lanthony had not sold the rents from the tenements held of it in fee: comparison of the rental with the priory's cartularies shows it still receiving rent in the 1440s from all the lands it had ever owned – with a single exception, a rent of 3*s* from a tenement within the south gate granted to be held in heredity apparently in the mid twelfth century, and which was itself alienated either by Prior Geoffrey (*c.* 1189–1203) or by Prior Gilbert (*c.* 1207–*c.* 1216) (A5, fos 20v–21). Any lost or disputed rents were still meticulously recorded in *c.* 1445.

Until the 1260s, successive priors made numerous grants of tenements – particularly those newly acquired – in fee. Some favoured this form of tenure more than did others: Prior Roger (*c.* 1170–*c.* 1189) made 32 recorded grants in fee, Prior John and his successor John of Hempstead (*c.* 1217–45+) together made 42, and Godfrey (1245+ –1264) made 17, whereas only single alienations in fee are recorded for Geoffrey (*c.* 1189–1203), and none for Martin (*c.* 1203–*c.* 1205), Walter (*c.* 1205–*c.* 1207) or Gilbert (*c.* 1207–*c.* 1217) (A5, *passim*). Prior William (1264–83) made three recorded grants in fee, a reflection perhaps of the much smaller number of new properties acquired by Lanthony during that period rather than of a change in policy; his successor, Walter (1283–1300), also made three such grants, but made Lanthony's first recorded written grant for the term of the grantee's life (A5, *passim*; fos 111–111v). Thus the priory's practice would seem to have fallen into line with the law against sub-infeudation after 1290, so that by the beginning of the fourteenth century only grants for limited terms are recorded, such as a lifetime grant dated to 1310 and a grant for two lives dated to 1335 (A5, fos 112, 112v). By the time of the earliest of the surviving registers of the priors, that of Simon de Brockworth (1362–77), leases were almost invariably being issued for three lives, with a maximum term of 49 years (A12, *passim*), a practice which continued certainly until the middle years of the fifteenth century (A7, *passim*; A3, *passim*).

At first, therefore, the greater part of the priory's lands were held in fee, with precarious tenancies far less important: in 1205, when the Gloucester properties were temporarily divided between the two priories, rents from lands described as being at fee-farm totalled £18 3*s* 3*d* – 74 per cent of the total – while other lands were let, presumably at will, for £6 6*s* 9*d* (A6, fos 192v–195v). Yet, despite the persistence of the practice of granting out lands in fee for at least another three-quarters of a century, the value of these hereditary rents eventually fell back to something like its 1205 level. In *c.* 1445 the priory received rents of assize worth £17 10*s*, a slight reduction on the figure for two centuries before; but the rental records numerous examples of lands held in fee which had for whatever reason reverted to Lanthony's ownership. Some rents had become impossible to collect, moreover, and these alone totalled rather more than £4. By now, most importantly, the overall value of the Gloucester properties had increased, so that rents from properties held in fee accounted for only 23 per cent of the total.

Despite the prominence of leasing agreements in the priors' registers, their importance to Lanthony should be put into perspective. In *c.* 1445 leasehold rents produced £8 4*s* 10*d*, or just 11 per cent of Lanthony's Gloucester rents. The figure does, however, conceal two other factors which are less quantifiable: in the first place, some of the leasing agreements of the fifteenth century – though not of the fourteenth – specified that an entry fine was to be paid, most often of £10 but as high as £20 (A3, fos 2, 3, 90, 186, 200); secondly, and much more importantly, under the terms of all of the recorded leases the tenant accepted responsibility for the fabric of his tenement. At the least he had to maintain its present condition, whilst in a significant number of cases he undertook to rebuild it within a short period of the commencement of the lease. Twice it was agreed that this would entail a complete rebuilding from the foundations, the rooms and dimensions of the new tenement being carefully specified (A3, fos 61v–62v; 65v–66); thus the annual rent each of these tenants was to pay – *7s* with an entry fine of £6 13*s* 4*d*, and 3*s* 4*d* and an entry fine of £5 – was only one element in the value of the lease to the priory.

The alternative to granting out land in fee, or by lease for prescribed terms, was to let it at will. In *c.* 1445 it was the revenue from rents of properties let at will that had accounted for the overall growth as compared with 1205, standing now at £48 15*s* 9*d* or 65 per cent of the total. In 1205, by contrast, rents from precarious tenancies had amounted to only 26 per cent of the total. Tenements held at will – and in fee – were scattered throughout Gloucester, but there were obvious concentrations: tenements that Lanthony had alienated in fee had been in the main prominent and well-situated, occupying the frontages of the principal streets of the commercial centre; those at will, on the other hand, were cheaper residential property, and included all of the houses described as cottages. By far the greatest concentration of tenancies at will covered all of the southern suburb, and extended into the area of mean housing that Lanthony owned within the south gate. Their tenurial history as recorded in Steymur and Cole's rental suggests that most of these houses had always been let at will (A13, fos 2v–20), this suburban land and intramural land around St Kyneburgh's having been Lanthony's since its foundation. (These figures are summarized in Tables 10.4 and 10.5, below.)

This original endowment of land continued to be an important constituent of Lanthony's Gloucester estate, therefore; but to what extent had its character been deliberately planned, and then consciously maintained? It is still not clear whether the priory had itself been responsible for the initial development of the suburb, or whether its planning had in part pre-dated Lanthony's own foundation: some development here seems to date from before the Conquest, and at least some responsibility for its planning may have lain with the constables of the castle who, from the 1060s, had owned both the extramural manor of the Hide and the intramural block of land around St Kyneburgh's. But as Lanthony's property since 1136, the priory had not lacked the opportunity to influence how this part of Gloucester developed – even though, as a fringe area whose economic focus remained the intramural centre of Gloucester, it was never likely to attract wealthier residents in any numbers. There is no obvious sign, however, that the priory ever had any ambition other than to maintain the suburb's character as a district of poor housing, an easy policy to follow and one which called for a minimum of investment; significantly, the contraction of settlement here which was apparent by 1400 had prompted no response on Lanthony's part other than to clear the derelict houses and let their sites as gardens (see below, pp. 334–5).

Perhaps this show of inactivity indicates not inefficiency but a shrewd appreciation of the property market. For the priory's management of its Gloucester estate as a whole during the difficult conditions of the fifteenth century was far from inept. By contrast with the threefold growth in the value of Lanthony's Gloucester properties after 1205, the final century of the estate until the priory's dissolution in 1539 was a period of stability. Not of stagnation: behind the modest rise in the total of rents from £74 9*s* 10*d* in *c.* 1445 to £76 9*s* 1*d* in 1539 lay wider changes that point to genuine shifts in the way the urban estate was managed. The value of rents of assize had fallen appreciably, to £12 13*s* 5*d*, suggesting not only that more of them had become impossible to collect or perhaps that some of these properties had reverted to Lanthony as superior lord, but also that the priory had at last agreed to sell a certain number to realize ready cash. The decrease continued the decline in the overall contribution made by such rents, from 23 per cent of the total to 17 per cent. But rents from tenancies at will fell too, to £37 5s 8d, and now constituted slightly less than half the value of the priory's rents, compared with the virtually two-thirds of a century before. The greatest change, however, had come in the value of rents for tenements leased for term of years. Twenty-two leases – by coincidence the same number as in *c.* 1445 – produced rents in 1539 amounting to £26 10s, or 35 per cent of the total compared with 11 per cent contributed by the leases of a century before (Tables 10.4 and 10.5). Evidently, whilst the value of properties let at will had remained static or had even declined, the value of these leased properties had remained buoyant – at any rate had been so during the 1520s and 1530s when virtually all of these leases were granted (PRO SC6 Hen. VIII 1224, mm. 2d–5d).

Table 10.4
Values of different types of rent paid to Lanthony Priory

	At fee	Lease	At will	Total
1205	£18 3s 4d	–	£6 6s 9d	£24 10s 1d
1445	£17 10s	£8 4s 10d	£48 15s 9d	£74 9s 10d
1539	£12 13s 5d	£26 10s	£37 5s 8d	£76 9s 1d

Table 10.5
Values of different types of rent paid to Lanthony Priory, expressed as percentages

	At fee	Lease	At will	Total
1205	74	–	26	100
1445	23	11	65	99
1539	17	35	48	100

The greater value of its leased property is the firmest indication that Lanthony Priory had taken positive measures in response to changing economic circumstances. As we have seen the priory had often used leasing agreements as a way of arranging the replacement of derelict buildings without any outlay of capital: in return for a reduced rent, the new tenant would put up at his own cost the building that Lanthony specified. And even when the terms of the lease did not require the tenant to rebuild within the first two years, his responsibility to maintain the existing tenement kept Lanthony's liabilities, in theory, to a minimum. But on occasion the priory could respond to change in a way that it had failed – or refused – to do in the southern suburb in the decades around 1400. By the end of the fifteenth century Gloucester's population had fallen to the extent that in 1487 the burgesses could claim that 300 of the town's houses now stood empty. Perhaps they did not exaggerate, for during the 1490s the rents from many of the houses belonging to the corporation had fallen or were proving difficult to collect. Of the 14 poorer houses the corporation owned in and around Walkers' Lane, for example, 11 were now apparently empty or derelict, and the corporation would own only 4 low-rent cottages here in 1509 (GCRO, GBR 1306; 1313). Nearby was the warren of 18 small tenements called Ratoun

Row on the corner of Westgate Street and Abbey Lane, which altogether had produced rents totalling £7 6s 8d in the 1440s (A13, fos 51–2), and which had evidently been a useful revenue earner since this land was given to Lanthony around 1210 (A5, fos 59v–60). Demand for houses there must also have been waning, for when we next catch sight of this property, in 1535, all the low-value tenements had been cleared away to make room for a single grand mansion, which Alice Messynger was leasing for term of years for £6 10s (GCRO GBR 1368). Thus Lanthony had responded positively to the reduced demand for cheaper housing by replacing perhaps its least desirable dwellings with a single house that must have been as grand as any in Gloucester.

Conclusion

The chapter began with a series of questions about the ways in which the urban landholdings of the greater religious houses developed through the medieval centuries, and how far the policies of these religious houses affected the changing shape of the growing town. The extent to which the evidence from Gloucester and Worcester can provide answers varies from institution to institution, at the same time as we can see that the separate history of each introduced its own peculiarities to the way their urban estates were managed. Taken together, however, the coherent quality of the evidence is impressive; both similarities and divergences of policy become apparent in such a way as to greatly extend our understanding of ecclesiastical landholding in English towns.

The history of Lanthony Priory's Gloucester lands informs and illuminates what can be perceived of similar movements at the albeit much older religious foundations of Worcester and Gloucester. During the twelfth and thirteenth centuries every one of these houses shared in the great increase in urban prosperity and population when it was given, or purchased, urban property in approximate proportion to its overall wealth and importance. At first Lanthony let those tenements that it could in hereditary tenure, in fee, so that in 1205 only a small proportion of its urban rents came from properties in precarious tenure. Its continuing with this policy until *c.* 1300 meant that the enormous increase in the value of Lanthony's estate by *c.* 1445 had been brought about partly through the increase in its size during the thirteenth century, but mainly through a massive rise in the value of those tenements that had been let at will, and whose rents were thus sensitive to price movements. A lesser factor was the policy followed since 1300 of leasing a proportion of its properties for term of years. What can be deduced of the ways the other religious houses exploited their urban properties suggests that Lanthony's experience stands as a model: identified differences were minor differences of chronology, as each house moved away from sub-infeudation in favour of leasing during the latter years of the thirteenth century.

After 1300 there was a marked divergence of attitudes to the acquisition of new property – a situation that must have had much to do with the increased cost of acquiring lands following the Statute of Mortmain. St Oswald's Priory and Gloucester Abbey continued to invest heavily in new property when, by contrast, Worcester Cathedral Priory and Lanthony had virtually ceased to do so. Whether this implied no more than a different approach to investment on the part of the latter institutions is doubtful; Lanthony certainly showed no sign of diverting resources it might otherwise have expended upon purchasing property into the improvement of its existing estate, preferring instead to leave that to its lessees. On the other hand, Lanthony's policy – which meant that the priory accepted a low rent in the short term as an alternative to laying out large sums in cash on necessary rebuilding – might have seemed to the canons the best way of enhancing the overall quality of their Gloucester property.

Until the fifteenth century none of these houses seems to have followed a very active policy of investment and improvement, to substitute for the amassing of suitable tenements as the opportunity arose or the slow improvement of a small range of properties on a piecemeal basis. The closest they came to a recognizable policy for their urban estates was the concentration on cheap housing, to be seen most obviously in the cathedral priory's purchasing of tenements in St Clement's parish, the major interest in cheap suburban housing shown by St Oswald's, and Lanthony's firm hold on its own suburb.

Only the Church of Worcester under the pre-Conquest bishops took an active part in planning the early phases of the emerging town. The Gloucester minsters had clearly played a less active role, as we should expect given their different history and local standing. The reduced influence – and interest – in Worcester of the bishops of the eleventh century, however, left the cathedral priory in a position increasingly indistinguishable from that of the two – and later three – Gloucester religious houses. There is no sign of any of them in the post-Conquest period having promoted any extensive building schemes within the walls of either Worcester or Gloucester. Re-development of intramural church lands, when it came, was in every recorded case confined apparently to the replacement of standing buildings, one by one.

Suburban development was another matter. All of the religious houses had a more positive policy in that respect. Just as the pre-Conquest bishops had taken the initiative in planning the Foregate surburb on the north side of Worcester, so ecclesiastical planning was also a factor in the development of the Barton Street suburb of Gloucester (where St Peter's Abbey owned so much land and had clearly taken a leading role) and of the western part of Gloucester's northern suburb (which seems to have originated as an enterprise of St Oswald's Priory on its own land). The initial planning of Gloucester's southern suburb may have only been accomplished after Lanthony Priory acquired all of it in 1136, and here the canons were careful to retain control of as much of this property as they could. Worcester Cathedral Priory, perhaps, initiated no schemes of large-scale suburban planning, but placed a high value on its property in St Peter's parish, and followed a policy of acquiring property in transpontine St Clement's. The common factor is each religious house's awareness, apparently, of the advantage of cheap property: despite the low individual rents, maintenance costs were probably much lower than that of the better intramural properties they owned, and low-status suburban houses – even slum property perhaps – evidently produced a higher return relative to their capital value.

Finally, at the end of the middle ages, there may have been the beginnings of a change of attitude on the part of at least two of these religious houses. The redevelopment of single sites was perhaps on a more impressive – and costly – scale: there were the inns built by Gloucester Abbey in the fifteenth and sixteenth centuries, its replacement of the tenement block in the centre of Westgate Street in the 1490s at the same time as it was rebuilding blocks of nearby selds, and there was Lanthony's ambitious rebuilding of Ratoun Row. It may be that together these are signs of a new approach to urban property, the product of a new willingness to invest in high-quality property as a way to commanding a greater share of urban wealth.

Chapter 11

The major religious institutions: their relationship to urban secular authority

As Worcester and Gloucester grew as centres of commerce and population, the ecclesiastical institutions there were also evolving – partly in response to urban growth, but perhaps mainly as their standing in the wider world changed. For instance St Peter's, the Old Minster, clearly stood in one relationship to the tenth-century *burh* of Gloucester and St Peter's Abbey had quite another relationship to the mature medieval town of three centuries later. The size and nature of the urban community had changed, whilst the Anglo-Saxon minster had become a great Benedictine monastery, living by the intensive exploitation of its wide rural estates. As predominantly urban institutions, with relatively few rural parishioners, the parish churches might be said to have been more successful in retaining their original identity; but even they had had to adapt to population change and to new styles of observance and liturgy. Most parish churches underwent successive phases of rebuilding in response to such changes, so that their late-medieval form must have been far removed from anything envisaged by their founders.

The developing relationship the urban Church had with townspeople went beyond its pastoral role, of which there have been several notable studies (Brooke 1970; Campbell 1979; Rosser 1992). In the towns founded by ecclesiastical lords, there was the secular relationship of lord and tenant which so often turned to disagreement and conflict (Hilton 1973, 198–207; Fuller 1884–5; Lobel 1935; Street 1915–17; Green 1894, i, 277–308); far more widespread was the relationship between great ecclesiastical institutions and the lay people of the older towns they dominated – or had once dominated (Green 1894, i, 333–83; Rosser 1998; Tanner 1984, 141–54). In Worcester the cathedral priory inherited, perhaps, a memory of the bishops' historic lordship of the city to add to their pre-eminence as urban property owner; in Gloucester, St Peter's could make no such claim, although it too was the greatest of the town's landed magnates and had constructed around itself an extensive precinct within which it exercised the juridical privileges of lordship. Lanthony Priory, and St Oswald's too, were the lords of substantial suburbs – economically part of Gloucester – over which they could claim ancient rights to temporal authority.

Yet the relationships between these houses and the secular community came into prominence only when they deteriorated to such an extent that disagreements became documented. Generally these were fundamental differences, and obviously of long standing, although just as interesting were the petty grievances that might be expressed at times of stress and which indicate how a tight-knit, literate, religious community could bear a grudge for a century or more – in a way that was perhaps beyond the comprehension of a secular community with a far shorter collective memory. Whether the record of disputes truly reflects reality, however, or if instead it accentuates the exceptional and atypic, remains open to question. We might suspect that for most of the time these relationships were more constructive, if distant; even so, it is through the accounts of disagreements that we can perceive the shifting balance of power between religious house and urban secular authority.

St Peter's Abbey, Gloucester

It is virtually impossible to make any firm statement concerning the role of the Old Minster within pre-*burh* Gloucester. Later evidence indicates that the prominence of St Mary de Lode had had the effect of restricting the minster's pastoral functions to the limited population dwelling within the walls. With the founding of the New Minster, and of the *burh* with its new churches, the pastoral role of St Peter's is likely to have remained a marginal one; with its reforming as a Benedictine house in 1022 it began to take on a new character which became progressively more pronounced as the century progressed. The great rebuilding begun by Serlo, the recruitment of large numbers of new monks, and the acquisition of new estates, marked the final phase of its transformation into one of the country's great religious houses. In the early twelfth century, and again in the early thirteenth, it enlarged the area of its precinct (see below, pp. 311–13), thus emphasizing its isolation from the town in which perhaps its most active role had been that of landlord.

It has been pointed out that the abbey of the late-medieval period must have seemed to the burgesses of Gloucester an alien intrusion rather than an organic part of their community (Hilton 1966, 26, 33–4). The sense of separation can only have been reinforced when, by the charter of 1200 and succeeding charters, the burgesses were formally granted the rights of ordinary jurisdiction that had previously been the Crown's (*Cal. Recs Corpn Glouc.*, 5, 6, 7, 13, 20). These extended to those parts of Gloucester which had been held by the Crown: ancient areas of immunity from the portmoot, it later transpired, continued to exist, to become a potential source of friction. How many such franchises or exceptions to the community's jurisdiction there were is not clear, nor how likely it was that any great secular lords attempted for a while to exercise jurisdiction over their own tenants; certainly from the fourteenth century onwards only the great religious houses were coming into conflict with the burgesses over this matter.

Despite the tenuous nature of the evidence for serious and prolonged contention between the abbey and the town it is clear there was a long history of friction. By the time a dispute entered a violent phase, the underlying disagreements may have been quite obscured behind an ostensible *casus belli*: for instance in 1449 the burgesses, suspicious of the part that Abbot Reginald Boulers had played in acting for the Crown in negotiations with Charles VII, accused him of taking bribes to sell out English interests in France, and attacked abbey property outside Gloucester. What is impossible to determine is how far their dissatisfaction with the abbot's political role stemmed from a general animosity towards the abbey (Kingsford 1913, 355–7). A succession of minor disputes may have been no more than isolated incidents: the inevitable, petty quarrels between neighbouring bodies keenly aware of their own interests. Nevertheless, the vilification and even violence that could occur, and more frequently the recourse that was had to the highest authorities to settle ostensibly unimportant matters, point to the possibility – at least on occasion – of deliberate harassment by the burgesses.

Disputes such as that over the rights to the water of the stream alternatively called the Fullbrook or Weaver were understandable enough: in 1221 the abbey complained that the stream was being diverted, and fifty years later it was itself being accused of diverting it to the detriment of others (Maitland 1884, 109; GCRO GBR 637, published in Stevenson 1891, 412–13). Similarly, the dispute over common rights in the meadows along the Severn was a straightforward clash of interests, with the abbot in 1236 recognizing – in return for a payment of £23 6s 8d – the rights of the burgesses to common on his meadows after the hay had been cut. The burgesses remained content with the settlement for two centuries or more (see below). Of a similar nature was the question of fishing rights in the Severn, over which the abbey came to an agreement with the burgesses in 1414. This must have been of some importance locally, as Prior John Wyche of Lanthony had it recorded in his register (A3, fo. 76v). Saving the rights of the abbey to its particular weirs and a fishery called *Abbotspulle*, the burgesses were themselves to have the right to fish anywhere in the Severn from the town as far north as the lordship of Ashleworth, whilst the same right was confirmed to the common fishermen of Gloucester who caught fish for sale, on payment each of a penny a year to the abbey. There is no way of telling if this was in effect no more than a recognition of existing practice, or whether it represented a new concession by the abbey which evidently claimed the sole liberty of fishing in the Severn.

A dispute with the burgesses over whether the abbey was exempt from tolls in Gloucester was, however, more fundamental to their relationship. The claim of the monks to hold the right by royal charter of Henry II (*Hist. et Cart.*, i, 353) evidently was respected until 1247–8, when the bailiffs levied a distress upon the abbot for unpaid toll on horses, oxen, sheep and corn which had been bought and sold in the market. In court both parties claimed that their respective royal charters empowered them to act as they did (*Hist. et Cart.*, iii, xxiii); and whilst no more is heard of the dispute, the matter seems to have been determined in the abbey's favour. The burgesses were never able to sweep aside the commercial privileges claimed by the abbey, if that remained their intention: part of a general agreement between the two parties drawn up in 1518 was a recognition that the abbot and his successors continued to enjoy all the liberties of a burgess of Gloucester – which can only mean that the abbey retained the right to trade freely in the town without paying toll (*Cal. Recs Corpn Glouc.*, 1197).

It was perhaps during the latter part of the fourteenth century that the behaviour of the burgesses became deliberately provocative. Evidence is slight and largely circumstantial; most crucially, however, the better Lanthony Priory evidence shows a similar unmistakeable heightening of friction at the same time (see below), whilst certainly during the 1370s the royal officials resident in the castle, too, felt themselves subjected to prolonged harassment. The overall impression is that – as Lanthony Priory claimed – the town authorities had embarked upon a concerted campaign to increase their power and influence at the expense of their neighbours. In 1372, for instance, the monks were forced to complain to the Crown to secure the removal of a communal privy which had been set up over the Fullbrook, above the point where it ran through the abbey precinct. The stream was so polluted, they said, that the stench put them off their prayers (*Cal. Patent Rolls 1370–74*, 240). The quarrel with the castle officials centred around the dumping of noxious refuse before the castle gate, first reported in 1373 (ibid., 293) – another minor matter which, even so, had still not been resolved in May 1381 when the Earl of Buckingham was authorized to intervene (*Cal. Patent Rolls 1381–85*, 22). The concern expressed at that time for the safety of the castle 'in the event of insurrection', the Peasants' Revolt in southern and eastern England during June and July which Buckingham did so much to suppress, and his swift return to Gloucester by the middle of July to stifle what appears to have been a dissident faction in the ruling oligarchy, all together suggest that the burgesses' treatment of the castle – and indeed of the abbey and Lanthony Priory – constituted but one part of a campaign that had serious political objectives (Holt 1985).

The same techniques of harassment were possibly being used again during the first decade of the fifteenth century, when the abbot petitioned the court of Chancery for a writ to restrain the burgesses from dumping ordure against the abbey wall in Grass Lane (PRO C1/4/176). Once more, this would seem to have been an excessive (and expensive) way of dealing with an annoying but minor matter; the abbey must have tried to settle it more expeditiously but had obviously failed. It was the historical immunity of the abbey and its tenants from the borough court that the burgesses were challenging by this time, if they had not been doing so previously. When they received a new royal charter in 1398, augmenting the already extensive legal powers of the bailiffs, the final provision enabling the arrest either of individuals or their chattels during the course of actions for debt, detinue and other trespasses was specifically stated not to apply to the Abbot of Gloucester, his servants or his tenants (*Cal. Recs Corpn Glouc.*, 13; *Cal. Charter Rolls 1341–1413*, 371–2). Anxious not to find itself at even more of a disadvantage in its relations with the burgesses, the abbey had evidently petitioned or paid for the exemption. It was not an imaginary threat that the monks feared, and in 1414 the abbey considered it expeditious to pay the Crown £26 13*s* 4*d* for a confirmation of its ancient rights of jurisdiction. Since time out of mind, it was affirmed, the abbots of St Peter's had held courts within the abbey to which their tenants in Gloucester owed suit, and which dealt with all matters arising within the abbey precincts. Recently, however, the burgesses had wrongfully been interrupting the exercising of these liberties, their officers having entered the precincts bearing their maces to make arrests, and were now commanded by the Crown to desist (ibid., 471).

How seriously the town authorities took the order can only be conjectured; the issue would not go away and arbitration was resorted to in 1429, when it was agreed that borough officials could enter the precinct but were still bound by the charter of 1398 (GCRO GBR 1375, fo. 195v). By 1447 the monks had conceded even more ground, accepting now that the precinct was part of Gloucester and subject to secular authority: the bailiffs could make arrests for felonies there and could hold coroners' inquests whilst the abbey renounced its right to harbour criminals who claimed sanctuary. The agreement was intended to be a working arrangement that would last and, as an indication that both parties were in a constructive mood, the opportunity was taken to settle several other outstanding matters, such as the ancient dispute over the waters of the Fullbrook (ibid., fos 196–8).

But despite such agreements, it was perhaps impossible for a corporation as wealthy and as powerful as St Peter's Abbey to retain at all times the goodwill of a vigorous public authority. However permanent and binding a settlement seemed when it was made, the original point at issue was liable to be revived by the burgesses in every generation. The agreement on grazing rights made in 1236 had simply been forgotten by the burgesses of the late fifteenth century who had obviously already lost their earlier records, including their court rolls: they had no copy of the incompletely dated agreement until supplied with one – doubtless by the abbey – and they were quite unable even to identify the parties to the agreement as prominent burgesses of the early to mid thirteenth century. Their response to the document was to search the Crown's judicial records to establish if the agreement was genuine, a sure sign of how suspicious they were of this proof that their ancestors had approved an arrangement that they now considered unjust (for further discussion of this document see Note 1, below). There is no indication of when this matter again became contentious, although in the summer of 1513 it turned to violence, with bands of armed townspeople physically driving the abbey's cattle and servants from the meadows. The role of the mayor and aldermen in all this was clear enough, as they were said to support the actions, and were presumably responsible for supplying the food and the barrels of ale that the burgesses, returning at nightfall 'with taburs and hornys bloing and piping', consumed at the High Cross 'with grete shoutes and cryes in maner of tryhumphe'. Following the intervention of the Crown, the matter was submitted to independent arbiters who insisted that established procedures for the use of the pastures should be followed by both parties (*Hist. et Cart.*, iii, xxxix–xlvii).

The cathedral priory, Worcester

Superficially, the relationship between the secular authorities in Gloucester and the monks of St Peter's Abbey had many parallels with the situation in Worcester. There the cathedral priory in the late-middle ages found itself confronting the citizens over the same sorts of issue, most particularly that of the precinct's immunity from their jurisdiction. Yet historically the priory's position was quite different from that held by St Peter's in Gloucester: the Church of Worcester from its foundation had been the lord of the city, and even after the *burh* was built it remained probably the dominant power in the district.

Sir Frank Stenton suggested that the route of a perambulation of the city's boundaries in 1498 indicated that a memory then persisted of a distinct ecclesiastical quarter of Worcester within which the Church had been the civil authority (*VCH Worcs.*, iv, 383–4), and whilst his interpretation of the reasons for taking that particular route was mistaken (see Note 2, below) his suggestion demands attention. Is it possible that at the *burh*'s construction the newly defended area was divided between the Crown and the Church, each to hold its own sector in lordship? We know that after the construction of the *burh* the rights of the Church were guaranteed by the Crown, and the charter of Æthelred and Æthelflæd (H 13; S 223; Whitelock 1979, 99) goes on to confirm that the bishops were to enjoy half of the profits arising from the new enterprise; it also makes it clear, however, that Æthelred and Æthelflæd made the grant by virtue of their lordship of the whole burh. That is not to say that the Church was not allotted a proportion of the land within the new defences – or rather, perhaps, that it retained some of its own land at the same time as it granted the rest of the site of the *burh* to the Crown. The *haga*, for instance, that Bishop Wærferth leased in 904 to Æthelred and Æthelflæd was inside the north wall of the *burh*, and was a valuable property occupying the gently sloping land between the High Street and the river, with a useful stretch of the riverfront. The *burh* charter specifies that the Church was to receive a half-share of the profits of justice, and half of the *ceapstowe* or marketplace: so although Æthelred and Æthelflæd asserted their lordship over the whole of the *burh*, it would have been consistent for them to have allowed the Church to keep half of the newly defended land.

Outside the *ceapstowe*, they said, the bishop was to enjoy his lands and all his rights as he always had done. The extension of royal lordship did not extend to the previously defended area of Worcester: for a long time the Church could successfully claim rights of jurisdiction over its own precinct, and this self-evidently was the substantial remnant of the enclosure held by the early Church. The *ceapstowe* of the charter was therefore, as we might expect, that part of the *burh* which was newly enclosed in the 890s. This area contained two plan-units (II.5 and II.6): one was the block of properties that after the removal of the defences was laid out in a regular pattern, presumably by a single owner, along both sides of the High Street; the other was the more haphazardly planned district between the High Street block and the Severn. It was this district that contained Wærferth's *haga* of 904 – which indeed alone constituted virtually half of it. And so it is likely to have been the western side of the *burh* (plan-unit II.6) that was the land retained by the Church in the 890s.

The area of the *burh* did not long remain static. It has been pointed out (pp. 269–71, above) that there were signs still in the thirteenth century that much or all of the property in the parish of St Alban had originally belonged to the Church of Worcester. This district – and part of the parish of St Helen – had not been part of the *ceapstowe* of the 890s because it lay within the old defences of the city. When their northern side was subsequently removed, perhaps as early as the 960s if the cathedral precinct was indeed re-modelled by Bishop Oswald, the way was cleared for the land of the bishops at either side of the southern end of the High Street to be physically incorporated into the new Worcester. Now, without a physical barrier to separate the streets and houses subject to two distinct authorities, the *burh* and the bishop, the possibility of disagreements over jurisdictional matters was greatly increased. However, Hemming in the 1090s could still distinguish between those properties the monks held in Worcester *in burgo regis*, and those held of their manors of Hallow and Teddington in which they had *sac* and *soc* and over which the King's reeve had no authority (Hearne 1723, 289–90). Perhaps it was only subsequently, therefore, that the monks of the cathedral priory – who had by then inherited the authority of the bishops over the cathedral and its surroundings – found themselves no longer able in practice to assert their legal authority over this district. Possibly, though, the distinction Hemming drew had already ceased to be of more than historical significance.

A century later a claim by the Church to jurisdictional rights within Worcester was challenged by the citizens, who in 1220 took the case to the Curia Regis (*Curia Regis Rolls of the Reign of Henry III*, vol. 9, 353–4). The bishop was summoned by the city's bailiffs, who complained that he had wrongly arrested a citizen, one Henry son of Geoffrey, and detained him until he was freed by the sheriff. They said that the bishop had usurped the authority that was properly theirs, as the King's officials in the city. It was for them to arrest criminals, and for their hundred court to try them. In reply, the bishop defended his action in arresting Henry and another named man by saying that the bailiffs had spoken wrongly in insisting that only they had judicial authority within Worcester. He had arrested the men within the liberty of Walter de Beauchamp, which was Walter's by virtue of the fact he held from the bishop; and in token of his own judicial authority the bishop himself had one-third part of the farm of the city, or £8 a year. (To demonstrate further his rights of jurisdiction, the bishop pointed out that from each woman who brewed within his fee he received a penny in toll, just as the constable of the castle had a tine of ale worth fourpence from each brewing.) The arrests had been made because the men were dangerous criminals who had been caught red-handed, and they had been handed over to the sheriff when he came for them. The bailiffs' response was to deny the bishop's claim to jurisdiction, saying that the £8 the bishop received was of no importance, being alms from the King that was paid in the first place to the Crown from its own men.

Both parties were mistaken in their assertions. The bishop would seem to have been claiming the right to jurisdiction over all his Worcester tenants and their sub-tenants, which was unjustifiable. Despite his profits from the *burh* land, its lordship remained with the Crown, and historically the bishop's authority should have extended only to those parts of the city which had been built within the line of the old defences. The bailiffs, too, were quite wrong to deny that he had ever had any authority in the city. In all probability, by the early thirteenth century both parties had long ago forgotten the true extent or limitations of their ancient rights, if of course they cared; what was happening now was a struggle to assert the rights each party felt it ought to have in the present and in the future. It is uncertain how this particular case was resolved, although the apparent absence of any subsequent actions indicates that it was the rights of the bailiffs which had been upheld. The bishop's basic claim surfaced again a year later but in a very different way, and in its judgment the court did little to resolve the issue. At the eyre of 1221 the jury alleged that two houses built by the Sidbury Gate – one by the city wall – were purprestures that had been built without permission (Stenton 1934, 1262). The defence was that they were not on the King's land at all, but were built on the bishop's fee and were therefore nothing to do with the borough. The verdict that the houses should be removed avoided the rights of the matter, as it was their detrimental effect on the city's defences to which the court took exception.

The insistence from this time onwards, however, that the cathedral precinct and the bishop's palace were enclaves immune from the actions of the city authorities demonstrates that the cathedral priory and successive bishops refrained from claiming any wider authority. The bishops claimed suit of court from those Worcester tenants they retained after 1200, who continued to hold from the manor of Northwick (Hollings 1934, 5–7 *et seq.*). But in practice their rights of lordship were no more than the right to a small chief rent, itself often difficult to collect and eminently suitable for alienation for cash or as a pious gift. With the effective limitation of the monks' judicial rights to the area of their precinct, they found themselves in a parallel situation to that of their brothers of Gloucester, and that despite the very different histories of the precincts. Worcester's was the remnant of a large fortified enclosure of which the Church had been indisputably the lord; Gloucester's had grown by recent accretions from the originally small cemetery area of a minster church (see below, pp. 311–13). But by the thirteenth century such historical considerations counted for little, and in both towns the claim of these great churches to jurisdiction over their precincts was based on the reality of their prestige and power as regards the local secular authority, and on their influence with the Crown. Whether or not they would be able to maintain their claims depended in each case on their continued ability to defend their position. In Gloucester the burgesses were successful by the middle of the fifteenth century in their efforts to overcome the juridical independence of St Peter's Abbey; in Worcester, the citizens would find that the rights of the cathedral priory – backed by the bishop's authority – could not be so easily overturned.

Within the liberty of the cemetery, the cathedral priory could challenge the authority of any city official seeking to exercise his office. The numerous houses which by the fourteenth century had been built around the edges of the cemetery were, in the seventeenth century, recorded as being held from the manor of Guestenhall, to which their tenants owed suit (Cave and Wilson 1924, 169–220). It might be expected that this alone would be a major cause of trouble between cathedral and city, as the population of this enclave lived in the heart of the city whilst apparently contributing as little to its common liabilities as any inhabitants of the suburban fringe. The existence of an area of private criminal jurisdiction, furthermore, is unlikely to have been seen by the citizens as contributing very much to public order. Whatever the events that triggered any particular dispute between the priory and the city, the question of the precinct's legal status was likely to become a matter of contention.

This was certainly the case when, in 1348, during a period of disorder in the county, the legal status of the cemetery became an issue. For some years the patent rolls had contained reports of the activities in Worcestershire of what was described as a band of outlaws and troublemakers; the description of their criminal acts perhaps gives a one-sided picture of what may have been serious political unrest (*Cal. Patent Rolls 1345–8*, 108, 118, 386–7; see also *VCH Worcs.*, iv, 450–51). In 1345, for instance, William de Beauchamp was prevented by William le Cartere and others from acting as Justice of the Peace in Worcester (*Cal. Patent Rolls 1345–8*, 35). But the mob that assailed Beauchamp and his retinue had been raised and was led by the city bailiffs, it was said (ibid., 97), and evidently there was more at stake than just a few trials of common criminals. The cathedral priory became involved when John le Cartere, William's son, was found murdered within the precinct in 1348. Nothing is known of the events that led to his death, or of the identity of those responsible, but feelings were running high, and a large crowd gathered by the bailiffs forced their way into the cathedral to claim the corpse. Carrying it off, they had the city coroners hold an inquest, although the prior complained that the place where John had died lay outside their jurisdiction, being within the hundred of Oswaldslow (*Cal. Patent Rolls 1348–50*, 245–6).

Whether truthfully or not, the prior insisted that the citizens had been armed and had used considerable force in effecting an entry to the precinct – a sign of the poor state of relations between the two parties. And he went on to complain that this was not the first such infringement by the bailiffs; indeed, he said:

> ... at divers times they have usurped cognisance of pleas and matters emergent in the priory, without the liberty of the town, that by such continued usurpations they might draw to themselves the places of the priory, churchyard and precinct, which are within the liberty of the church, a liberty far older than the liberty of the town, and subject these to their liberty. (ibid.)

A determined campaign by the bailiffs of the mid fourteenth century to overturn the prior's authority within the area of the precinct sounds plausible enough, and would have led to numerous disagreements. Even so, a breakdown of relations of the magnitude of that of 1348 was an unusual occurrence. For most of the time a *modus vivendi* prevailed, if the infrequency of recorded disputes are any guide. The surviving records of three sessions of the cellarer's court of Guestenhall provide some information as to how an uneasy truce might have been maintained, whilst at the same time a necessary degree of order was enforced. At the court held on 9 October 1411, it was presented that Hugh Sampson and Thomas Buttere had illegally taken a bow and 12 arrows worth 2*s* from the goods and chattels of a certain felon captured in the house of John Flecchere within the cathedral precinct (D&C C82). Until less than a month before the court, Hugh had been one of the two city bailiffs (WCRO X496.5 BA9360 CAB 14, Unnumbered Box, 4), and the facts of this case were quite obviously that he had been acting in an official capacity in seizing the goods of a convicted felon. The priory denied his right to do so, but had been unable to prevent him exercising his office. That is not to say that the city authorities by this time customarily ignored the priory's rights, however, and on other occasions the monks were evidently still able to compel respect for them. At the following court, held on 23 April 1412 (D&C C82, dorse), it was presented that Philip Ewyas, the claviger or mace-bearer of the city, had illegally arrested one John Goldsmythe within the cathedral cemetery, and had had him imprisoned in the city gaol. Again the priory had not been able to stop the action, if indeed it had wished to do so. But the court roll records that afterwards Philip had agreed to pay the prior a fine of 40*d* for the trespass, from which we might deduce that both parties had been satisfied: the city officers had made their arrest, and the prior had drawn a profit from enforcing his rights within his liberty.

Disputes of this sort were as likely to be matters of profit as of principle. On this particular occasion the prior himself presumably had no wish to arrest John Goldsmythe, whatever his crime; neither, we may suppose, did he have any objection to seeing him in gaol. But the very act of Goldsmythe's arrest infringed a right which was a source of profit, and which therefore had to be defended. As long as the citizens were prepared to pay for the privilege, the prior may – in practice – have been content for them to police the cathedral precincts. And most importantly it would be simplistic and mistaken to see this issue of jurisdiction as one between Church and city: between entrenched privilege and public order. For meanwhile the prior had a similar problem with another neighbour. At the same court that had seen Philip Ewyas presented for arresting John Goldsmythe, it was presented that William Nashe, the bishop's under-bailiff, had likewise arrested Robert Wateley within the prior's liberty, and had illegally imprisoned him in the bishop's gaol in the palace. This – so much more clearly a dispute between two neighbouring feudal and indeed ecclesiastical magnates – puts that with the citizens into greater perspective.

The circumstances of a subsequent dispute over the cathedral precinct's immunity from the legal powers of the city officials illustrates that perhaps later in the fifteenth century the determination of the city began to harden. It may be that the citizens were less willing to pay for the privilege of maintaining order around the cemetery than they had been. For the priory had found it expeditious to cease to press the claim that the cemetery was its liberty, and thus immune from the attentions of a neighbouring authority; now it stressed its right of sanctuary, insisting that the precincts of the cathedral were free from the representatives of any secular authority – and in this it was able to enrol the support of the bishop. The event which sparked off the dispute was the escape of some prisoners from the castle, which served as the county gaol; having taken refuge in the house of John Hylle in the cemetery, they were forcibly removed – presumably by the city bailiffs – and returned to the castle. Prompted no doubt by the monks, Bishop Carpenter in May 1460 denounced the action as a breach of the right of sanctuary, and called for the prisoners' return to the cathedral (D&C B1648). He then proceeded to recite the boundaries of the cathedral precincts (which included his own palace) so that nobody should be left in any doubt as to where the edge of the sanctuary area lay.

The terms of a settlement made eighteen months later between the prior and the bailiffs, and witnessed by Bishop Carpenter and leading men of the county, demonstrate how far the question of sanctuary had been raised to buttress the priory's ancient rights of jurisdiction (D&C Cathedral Priory Register i, 1458–98, A6, fo. 21). The apparent contrast with Gloucester is very marked: there the right of the secular authorities to enter the precinct to arrest felons had been recognized, and by 1447 the abbey had renounced its rights of sanctuary (see above). At Worcester, the Church was prepared to admit only that in future the city's bailiffs could have their maces borne before them within the cemetery and within the parish of St John, and that their servants could carry their maces beneath their belts if their masters were not present. The bailiffs and their servants had no power or authority – 'nor never hadde' – to make any arrest, or execute their office in any way within the cemetery, which was within the franchise, jurisdiction and liberty of the prior and convent. Any servant breaking this agreement was to be dismissed by the bailiffs; should they fail to do so, and it were to be proved before the sub-prior, the cellarer, four monks and six representatives of the citizens (should they choose to attend), then the bailiffs' right to have their maces borne before them within the cathedral precincts would cease.

Reality, however, may have been rather different from the priory's view of what was appropriate. If the denial of the bailiffs' ceremonial privileges within the precinct was the only sanction the prior could call upon to defend his rights of jurisdiction, it is not surprising that he should have begun to stress the cathedral's sanctuary rights. Without more evidence, it would be wrong to conclude that the liberty of the cemetery, still a reality in 1412, had – as in Gloucester – in practice come under the jurisdiction of the town authorities by the end of the century; but the practice of allowing the bailiffs to make arrests within the precincts on payment of a fine was always a dangerous one for the priory. It was inevitable that in time it would become an established practice, and then a right for which the citizens would refuse to pay; and that time would seem to have come by the 1460s.

St Oswald's Priory, Gloucester

The fifteenth-century quay in Gloucester owed its position north of the castle to the silting and diminishing in importance of the channel of the Old Severn; the immediate reason for the removal from the vicinity of St Oswald's Priory, however, was as told to John Leland in the later 1530s 'strife betwixt the towne and the house of St Oswald' (Smith 1907–10, ii, 57). The fact itself seems improbable, but conveys a local memory of disagreement and bad feeling between the burgesses and the priory. This was unlikely to have been on the scale of the recurrent disturbances with St Peter's Abbey; after its short-lived prominence in the tenth and eleventh centuries, St Oswald's was too small and poor to have been able to assert extensive rights over a large precinct, or to have demanded suit of court from large numbers of urban tenants. But the fact that such a story was still current in Leland's time indicates that the memory of conflict came from the not-too distant past. The priory was a large suburban landlord, holding at its dissolution some 51 houses in the streets to the north of the town (PRO SC6 Hen. VIII 1212, mm. 4–5d), and questions of jurisdiction over these tenants would undoubtedly have arisen during the fourteenth and fifteenth centuries if the experience of Lanthony Priory is any guide.

Lanthony Priory, Gloucester

The dispute between Lanthony Priory and the Gloucester authorities is well recorded in the priory's own cartularies and registers. We see this affair, therefore, through the eyes of the canons, and can follow their reactions to what they felt was the hostility and duplicity of their opponents. Looking back from the 1450s, Prior Hayward was convinced that the burgesses had begun to demonstrate a new assertiveness in their dealings with the priory in the immediate aftermath of the Black Death of 1349 (A11, fo. 12v). He noted that during the Black Death 19 of the Priory's 30 canons had died, and to make the catastrophe even worse those who survived were young men who had neither the knowledge of the muniments nor the experience to defend the priory's rights. Promptly seizing their opportunity, the bailiffs had by various arbitrary acts inconvenienced the priory in unspecified ways, and had even sold property belonging to Lanthony. The wrongs and errors of that time had continued ever since, said Hayward (A11, fo. 12v).

If we are to accept Hayward's interpretation of events – formed, surely, as much by oral tradition handed down among the canons as by written records – the town authorities had seen their chance in 1349 to take advantage of an adversary they had previously been wary of, and on meeting with success they had continued to apply pressure. In addition to the burgesses' expropriation of disputed lands such as those in the Bareland to the north and north-west of the castle, obliquely referred to by Hayward and detailed in the priory's rental of *c.* 1445 (A13, fos 42v–45), Lanthony's jurisdictional privileges came under attack. Individual burgesses, acting one must suppose in concert, had for many years before the compilation of the rental been denying that their tenure of properties held in fee from Lanthony entailed suit of court (A13, *passim*); during the 1370s a more audacious assault was being launched on Lanthony's claims to jurisdiction over its own precincts and over the suburb outside the south gate. This lay within the priory's manor of the Hide, given at its foundation in 1136, and the tenants of which owed suit to Lanthony's court of St Owen for which there is evidence from the 1170s or earlier (A5, fo. 15).

The route through the suburb that the burgesses planned to take in a perambulation of the bounds of the town in 1378 was taken by Lanthony as an intentional affront; the priory thereupon complained to the Bishop of Worcester, whose response was to instruct the Archdeacon of Llandaff, Robert More, to collect together the evidence for the priory's rights over the southern suburb (A11, fos 10,10v). More presented the evidence to the bailiffs, and when Prior Cheryton made a conciliatory and deliberately ambiguous statement that the priory had no intention of impeding them in the exercising of their legitimate powers of jurisdiction, the perambulation was called off (ibid.). The bailiffs went away convinced that the priory had conceded the legitimacy of their claims to administer at least a part of the southern suburb – and in truth it was probably only Lanthony that believed otherwise. As we know about these events of the 1370s not because they were reported in Prior Cheryton's register, but because eighty years later Hayward saw fit to enter them into his – complete with the evidence assembled by the Archdeacon of Llandaff – it is clear that the fifteenth-century canons believed their legal right still stood; it is equally clear that the burgesses would have disagreed.

This was not simply a matter of the prestige of either the town or the priory, and perhaps more was at stake than the profits of justice. Alongside the tale of the priory's lost rights, Hayward claimed that merchants had always come to Lanthony to buy and sell freely, without hindrance by the town authorities, and without paying Gloucester's tolls (A11, fos 11v, 13). A claim to a presumed right to hold an extramural market in competition with the town market – and one, moreover, ideally placed to attract Severn-borne trade – can only have strengthened the resolve of the burgesses to extend their authority over the whole of the suburb. Whether or not there was any substantial extra revenue to be drawn from commercial transactions outside the walls, it was not in the urban mentality to tolerate a potential commercial competitor.

In this connection, the question of the personal status of the inhabitants of this suburb must from time to time have arisen. The privileged position the merchant guild had held in Gloucester since 1194 (*Cal. Recs Corpn Glouc.*, 3, 5) ensured that only enrolled burgesses and those who paid an appropriate annual fine could work as master craftsmen in the town or sell their manufactured goods retail. All other men of the town had to pay to acquire the status of *portman*, which by the thirteenth century carried no privileges and served as a means of registering the male inhabitants and generating a limited revenue, although through an oath of loyalty to the community it also entailed a recognition by the portman of the authority of the borough court (Holt 1987, 181–92). There is no indication that the men of the southern suburb were at any time in practice able to avoid these requirements, that the market rights Lanthony claimed made the suburb in any way a separate economic community; indeed Hayward's silence on this matter of the status of the suburb's inhabitants is significant. He would say only that the inhabitants of the priory itself did not become either burgesses or portmen, an admission that the other inhabitants of the southern suburb did so by the mid fifteenth century, and undoubtedly had done so for a long time (A11, fo. 12).

The matter of how far the suburban population shared in Gloucester's taxation burden may also have arisen. Hayward reported triumphantly that the town officials appointed to collect the poll tax of 1381 had attempted to take the tax from the people at the priory, including the servants of the Earl of Buckingham who happened to be there at the time, and that they had been rebuffed (A11, fo. 11). This implies that the secular inhabitants of the suburb contributed to the poll tax with the people of Gloucester, and presumably also contributed to the lay subsidies that the town authorities had to collect.

The low point of the relationship between Lanthony and the town came perhaps in the 1390s, when a disagreement with the burgesses came before the courts. This was a dispute over the priory's alleged acquisition of property in Gloucester without licence, which the bailiffs had accordingly seized. In 1391, Lanthony brought a charge of novel disseisin, the case resting at least in part on the claim that, as the priory was not part of Gloucester, the property lay outside the bailiffs' jurisdiction, despite being situated within the walls (*Cal. Close Rolls 1389–92*, 249, 264). It was presented in Chancery that an inquisition had found that Lanthony had indeed acted illegally in acquiring a piece of land in Southgate Street, between the town wall and St Kyneburgh's, but the priory insisted in court that they had owned the land since at least the early thirteenth century, and that the bailiffs had misled the escheator so as to secure a false verdict. A second inquisition was ordered (Stokes 1914, 165; *Cal. Patent Rolls 1388–92*, 444), and a month later the case again came to court, concerning now not only this piece of land but also six other tenements in Gloucester. Again the report of the inquisition was that the prior had acquired the land illegally (ibid., 173), although as an interim measure the court allowed Lanthony to retain the seven tenements (*Cal. Fine Rolls 1391–99*, 1). Victory for the priory followed, and it was recorded that the burgesses had even resorted to bribery to secure favourable findings from the different inquisitions (A13, fo. 21); but the canons had less success with their claim for compensation. An award of £50 made against the bailiffs and community in 1391 had still not been paid in 1457, by which time it had become only one, and not the most important, of the priory's tale of grievances and complaints against the burgesses (A11, fo. 16v).

What the Lanthony evidence makes abundantly clear is that – like the disputes already considered – this history of disagreement is not intrinsically one of Church and secular authority. It is more realistic to see it as a dispute between neighbouring authorities, one of which – the community of burgesses – was growing in authority after 1200 and was thus well placed to erode the legal authority of its rivals. Quarrels of the sort that took place in Worcester and Gloucester were unexceptional in this context, although of interest inasmuch as they demonstrate how far the citizens and burgesses were able to make good their claim to jurisdiction over all of the members of their growing communities. Other urban communities – the citizens of Exeter especially, but also those of Winchester or Canterbury, for instance – were less successful (Green 1894, i, 321–30; 338–82). Prior John Hayward's decision to devote a large section of the earlier part of his register to the dispute with the burgesses of Gloucester shows the extent to which this had become an obsession of the priory by 1457, but also reveals the fact that by then the canons had lost (A11, fos 9–16v). The specific grievances included several that were petty, but of real substance was the matter of the property in the Bareland that Lanthony had lost in 1265, and from which the burgesses were now drawing rent. Altogether this land had previously paid to the priory annual rents in excess of £7 (see above, p. 80). Together with statements that the burgesses had never paid the £50 damages incurred in 1391, and more importantly that the bailiffs exercised their office over all the southern suburb, the details of the lost rents and lands convey both the indignation the canons felt but also their impotence before their now much more powerful neighbour (A11, fos 16,16v).

Note 1

The *Victoria County History* is mistaken in its assertion (based on a misinterpretation of the endorsements on the copy of the 1236 agreement in the Gloucester borough archives) that the meadows were again a matter for dispute in 1292–3 and 1347 (*VCH Glos.*, iv, 60). The fifteenth-century copy of the agreement, which was all that the bailiffs had, was dated in the 21st year of an unnamed king who, from the names of the early-thirteenth-century burgesses who were parties to the agreement, can easily be identified as Henry III. As W. H. Stevenson pointed out in 1893, the endorsements recommending that searches of the Crown's judicial records for the years 20 and 21 Edward I, 21 Edward III and 21 Richard II be made, and confirming that the searches were carried out, indicate simply that on some occasion there was a determined effort to establish the date of the agreement and to confirm its validity (*Cal. Recs Corpn Glouc.*, 347 and p. 163n; *Hist. et Cart.*, iii, 240–41; *VCH Glos.*, iv, 60). The town authorities' inability to identify the prominent burgesses of the thirteenth century demonstrates that Gloucester's court rolls and other muniments had already been lost at the end of the Middle Ages. The large number of thirteenth-century deeds, now in the Gloucester collection and calendared by Stevenson, belonged to the Gloucester hospitals which came under the control of the burgesses at the Reformation.

Given the fifteenth–century date of the town's copy of the 1263 agreement – which presumably had been helpfully supplied by the monks – and the subsequent searches, the burgesses had again begun to pursue this matter of common rights some time before the recorded renewal of the quarrel in 1513 that, as we have seen, gave rise to serious disturbances.

Note 2

Sir Frank Stenton, in his survey of the medieval city of Worcester in the *Victoria County History*, suggested that the memory of a dual lordship in the early medieval period might indeed have survived until the end of the fifteenth century. He drew particular attention to what he saw as the unusual and significant details of a perambulation of the city boundaries conducted by the civic authorities on 12 April 1497 (*VCH Worcs.*, iv, 383–4. Stenton miscalculated the date, which he gave as 1498). The route which had been followed was recorded in the volume containing the contemporary city ordinances, and was accurately transcribed and printed by Valentine Green (H&W RO BA 9360 X496.5 C2; Green 1796, ii, appendix, lxx, lxxi). In Stenton's view the boundaries of the city as defined by the perambulation are very strange, for a large part of the central district was, he said, excluded from the area claimed by the bailiffs as being under their jurisdiction. His interpretation was that 'the borough boundaries are deliberately drawn so as to omit the populous district to the north of the priory which is roughly enclosed by the Severn, Broad Street and High Street'. He went on to infer that this was part of the town that was still traditionally regarded as belonging not to the citizens but to the Church of Worcester: that although there could be no question at this late date of the district lying outside the bailiffs' jurisdiction, nevertheless the perambulation preserved an ancient memory of the former division of authority in the city.

Given the basic purpose of such a perambulation, which was to establish unambiguously the precise bounds of the territory over which the civic authorities exerted jurisdiction, the notion that they might have continued to respect the bounds of an ancient immunity or liberty long after it had disappeared seems most implausible. Even if such a district had really existed, one would expect the course of events to have long since obliterated all memory of it. But Stenton's suggestion remains intriguing and indeed provocative; it is not to be dismissed without careful consideration of the circumstances.

In the first place, what indeed was the route followed by the citizens, and how was the perambulation conducted? Proceedings began at the Guildhall with the bailiffs' swearing-in of seven men to lead the procession. They swore to put aside their love and affection for the city, and any hatred or malice they might feel for the Cathedral Priory or any other institution, and so to follow the boundaries they had followed – and knew to have been followed – in the past. Then starting from the Cross outside the Guildhall, the citizens proceeded to walk north along the High Street as far as the Grass Cross, and then turned along Broad Street to the bridge. Crossing the river, they walked southwards along the bank of the Severn until they reached a ditch situated opposite the Quay; they followed it away from the Severn, and kept to the city boundary by means of landmarks, many now impossible to identify. But clearly they walked in a clockwise direction around the transpontine part of the city, crossing the river again (presumably by boat) to Pitchcroft meadow on the north side of the city. Proceeding east and then south, the perambulation curled round the city, eventually reaching the Severn again at a point south of the castle; turning north, they followed the river bank as far as the castle ditch, and then turning to the east followed it – and then the precinct wall of the cathedral – up the Knowle to Lich Street, and so to the High Street and back to the Guildhall.

The line is the same as that marked on the eighteenth-century maps of Worcester, except that the westward boundary from the river as far as St John's parish appears to take a more northerly route than that marked at a later date, and so enclosed a somewhat smaller area. On Young's map of 1779, for instance, the city boundary is shown as running straight across the meadowland opposite Worcester, whereas the description of the perambulation at this point shows it to have followed a route marked by a succession of meadows, stiles, trees and such landmarks. In fact, the route followed seems more likely to have been the footpath that George Young's 1777 map of the properties of the Dean and Chapter in the parishes of St John and St Clement (WCRO 971.2 BA 1691/43) marked as running from virtually opposite the site of the new bridge, curving round to Cripplegate. This was the route soon to be taken by St John's Road, which Young in 1779 (WCRO 2960 r726) marked as the new road built to bring traffic from the west bank to the new bridge, and which thus followed an ancient pathway and the city's ancient boundary.

It seems to have been Stenton's interpretation of the route of the perambulation that was at fault. As he saw it, it excluded from the area of the city all that part that was bounded by the High Street on the east, Broad Street on the north, the Severn on the west and the Bishop's Palace on the south. But the more rational interpretation is to ignore those sections of the route that passed through the city: these formed part of the itinerary, it can be argued, only because this ritual occasion with its sworn oaths, and no doubt its convivial consumption of food and drink both before and after the proceedings, had of necessity to start and finish at the Guildhall. The procession through the city streets which began and ended the perambulation was simply the ceremonial element of the real business of the day, which was the tour around the boundary between the city and neighbouring jurisdictions. The true perambulation thus began on the west bank of the

Severn, and ended on its east bank, and followed the whole length of the city's external boundary, whilst neglecting to follow its internal boundary – that between the city and the cathedral. Given the disputes over rights of jurisdiction within this part of the city, it would hardly be surprising if the citizens forbore to trace, publicly, the limits of their authority; the boundary, too, was fiercely guarded by the cathedral priory and well defined both by its walls and by an inquisition of 1460 (D&C B1648; published by Bloom 1909, 183–4).

Chapter 12

Ecclesiastical precincts in the urban landscape

Calculating the proportion of the late-medieval built-up areas of Worcester and Gloucester under the direct control of the Church is an imprecise exercise. To begin, we have to accept that any estimate of the built-up area itself is likely to be somewhat notional as it clearly varied through time. One or two areas – like Severn Street in Gloucester – that were once built up reverted to agricultural use before precise cartography became available, and it is unlikely that the occupation of some suburbs – like Newland in Gloucester – was ever continuous to the far end of the enclosing 'urban fence'. In some quarters of Gloucester, even the distinction between what was intramural and what was extramural is to some extent subjective: urban merged with suburban and suburban faded into rural. Further, as will have become clear from earlier discussion (Chapters 3 and 6), ecclesiastical precincts of all sorts expanded (and sometimes contracted) through time and – except for the great minster churches and one or two hospitals – their precise extent is not always apparent. Neverthless some statistics, however impressionistic, may not be out of place as an introduction to their geography and to their physical impact upon their respective towns.

The walled city of Worcester, including the cathedral close but excluding what remained of the castle after 1217, covered an area of about 79 acres (32 hectares); with its suburbs (including those on the west bank), its total urbanized area at the end of the middle ages is likely to have been about 143 acres (57.9 hectares). About 18 per cent of this (*c.* 26 acres/10.5 hectares) was under the direct control of the Church – occupied by churches and their plots and ecclesiastical precincts. Within the walls the presence of the Church was stronger, church-plots and precincts accounting for about 27 per cent (*c.* 21 acres/8.5 hectares) of the intramural area. Gloucester was not dissimilar. Of a probable total urban area of *c.* 168 acres, about 17 per cent (*c.* 29 acres/11.7 hectares) was ecclesiastical. In Gloucester, similarly, the Church's presence was proportionately higher within the walls: about 33 per cent of the intramural area of *c.* 72 acres (29.2 hectares) was occupied by the Church (this area includes St Oswald's and St Peter's Abbey but excludes the castle and the Northgate and Hare Lane suburbs). The stronger Church presence inside the walls in each place is not in the least surprising, and can be accounted for very simply in terms of the chronology of settlement and church-founding, the extensive precincts of the mother-churches (Worcester Cathedral and St Peter's Abbey), the availability of open land within the walls for the foundation of the friaries in the thirteenth century (and the friars' preaching mission and their need for close contact with the urban populations), and the relatively modest scale of suburban hospitals.

The minster churches

The senior churches of Worcester and Gloucester can be divided into three chronologically distinct strata. The earliest comprises St Helen's in Worcester and St Mary de Lode in Gloucester. Both were 'normal' parish churches in the late-medieval period but there is persuasive evidence for their early, probably pre-Saxon foundation, and for their former possession of extensive dependent rural territories. The second stratum comprises the late-seventh-century foundations of Worcester Cathedral and the Old Minster at Gloucester. The third and final stratum comprises

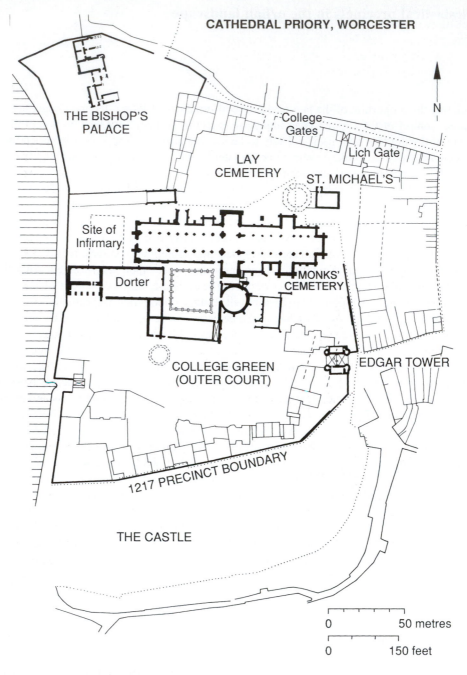

CATHEDRAL PRIORY, WORCESTER

N

THE BISHOP'S
PALACE

College
Gates

Lich Gate

LAY
CEMETERY

ST. MICHAEL'S

Site of
Infirmary

Dorter

MONKS'
CEMETERY

COLLEGE GREEN
(OUTER COURT)

EDGAR TOWER

1217 PRECINCT BOUNDARY

THE CASTLE

0   50 metres

0   150 feet

12.1   Worcester Cathedral and its precinct

a single foundation: Æthelflæd's New Minster at Gloucester, subsequently known as St Oswald's. All of these churches are likely to have been associated with some kind of topographically discrete precinct or curtilage. The task of this section is to compare the available evidence for their origin, behaviour, internal planning and effect on adjacent secular settlement, as well as the ultimate fate of these precincts.

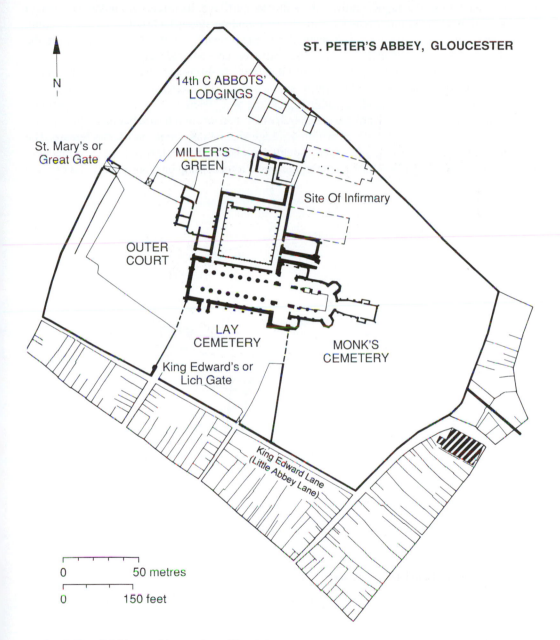

12.2   St Peter's Abbey and its precinct, Gloucester

The earliest precincts

Of all these foundations, it is the settings of the earliest that are inevitably the most obscure. St Helen's in Worcester was founded just within the defences of the Roman earthwork enclosure. Around the church by *c.* 1100 were, we are told, nine houses appurtenant to it (see above, p. 198); neither the form nor the origin of this property was recorded. The cartographic evidence shows that the St Helen's church-plot fell within a series of plots sharing a common rear boundary that may once have formed a single, undivided, rectilinear curtilage. Its origins are unknown, though it is likely to have come into existence with the surrounding streets and plots after the levelling and redevelopment of the former Roman defences, probably in the tenth century; of the immediate context of the church in its earliest years, we have no evidence.

The development of St Mary de Lode in Gloucester is discussed elsewhere but the points relevant to its surroundings may be briefly summarized. The church developed from a well-appointed Roman building standing within a metalled area. There is no evidence for a precinct or substantial curtilage as such around the church other than its churchyard, but this – by the later middle ages – stood centrally placed within a wedge-shaped open area, St Mary's Square. The latter has the appearance of a marketplace, though there is no direct evidence for such a function. It is perhaps possible that St Mary's Square represents a replanning or replacement of a discrete

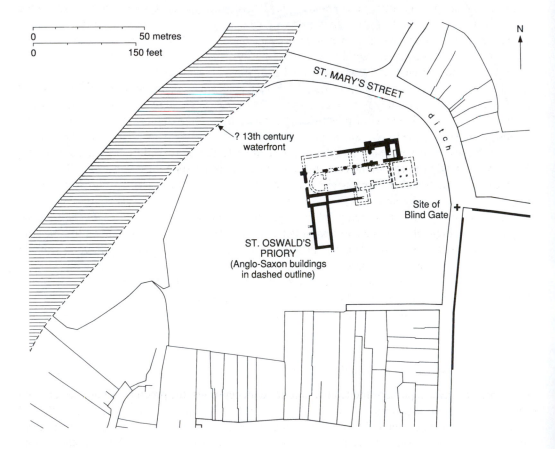

12.3   St Oswald's (the New Minster), Gloucester (after Heighway and Bryant 1999)

ecclesiastical enclosure that became redundant as the Old Minster eclipsed St Mary's control over its rural hinterland. But there may have been some overlap in function between early precinct, cemetery and marketplace. Such functions were certainly mixed in the combined minster cemeteries of St Alkmund's and St Juliana's in Shrewsbury, which accommodated the King's Market before 1261 (Bassett 1991).

The precinct of the late-ninth-century New Minster at Gloucester is a shade less obscure. The church and its detached eastern chapel lay just within the north-eastern boundary of a D-shaped precinct enclosure on the east bank of the eastern Severn channel. The church was perhaps sited thus to avoid land prone to flood and to allow room for its cemetery and associated domestic ranges (later a cloister) to the south. The landward boundary of the enclosure appears to have been defined by a substantial but as yet undated ditch followed by the curving line of St Mary's Street, and later – as St Oswald's precinct – by a stone wall. The southern boundary of the late-medieval precinct followed the back-fence of the tenements on the north side of St Mary's Square; before these were developed, the boundary between the precinct of the New Minster and whatever lay around St Mary de Lode may have followed the Fullbrook, or one channel of it, on a similar line.

The sites of the late-seventh-century minsters, and the precincts that had developed around them by the late-middle ages, had some features in common, but were nevertheless very different in their evolution and in their eventual form. Both were founded within pre-existing Roman enclosures – but of very different character. The Old Minster in Gloucester occupied a site in the north-west corner of the fortress. It has been argued that its first precinct is likely to have been an insula defined by surviving Roman streets (Heighway 1983a). The cathedral in Worcester was placed more or less centrally within the Roman earthwork enclosure, which it shared with the marginally sited church of St Helen. Whether the cathedral was given the entire enclosure which thus became its primary precinct, or whether there was an inner enclosure around the cathedral and its community, is unknown. One possibility that has been suggested is that the earliest precinct was confined to an escarpment-top site between the river and a southward continuation of the axial High Street. The apparent centrality of the cathedral in relation to the Roman enclosure does, however, make an interesting contrast to the more widely paralleled marginal location of the Old Minster in the corner of the (much larger) walled fortress area in Gloucester; interpretation is, however, impossible with so little information regarding the state of the respective town sites in the late seventh century.

There is equally little information regarding the minster churches themselves. Both, it seems, began with a single church dedicated to St Peter; only in Worcester was this joined by a second church dedicated to St Mary. The architecture – even the precise location – of the church in Gloucester is unknown. In Worcester, excavation and geophysical survey are, at the time of writing, beginning to suggest that the church of St Peter lay under the east side of Bishop Wulfstan's cloister. The church of St Mary's probably lay parallel to and to the north of St Peter's, under the present cathedral nave, and was the first to be demolished by Wulfstan's rebuilding in the 1080s (Guy 1996).

Change and expansion in the minster precincts

In the period between perhaps the tenth and fourteenth centuries, the precinct of Gloucester's Old Minster underwent a process of substantial expansion. The precinct of Worcester Cathedral certainly changed in extent and form in the same period and – beween the late eleventh and early thirteenth centuries – was reduced and then expanded again. Whether its final late-medieval area represented an increase or a reduction in its original, late-seventh-century form, however, is

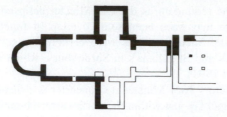

St Oswald's, Gloucester
(period IV: e.11th-C)

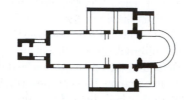

St Mary's, Deerhurst

St Mary's, Shrewsbury
(obsv. 1864)

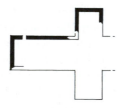

Stanton Lacey, Shropshire

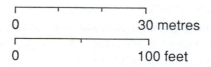

0   30 metres

0   100 feet

12.4   Major pre-Conquest churches in western England: comparative plans

uncertain. In Gloucester, with the passage of time, the street that had probably determined the Old Minster's eastern boundary shifted, adopting a new, shorter, route to the north gate across the levelled remains of the Roman buildings; as the road shifted eastwards, so too – it is argued – did the precinct boundary (Heighway 1983a). The precinct probably also expanded southwards before the Conquest to a new line at a slight angle to the prevailing Roman orientation, though exactly what determined that line or its orientation remains unknown. The precinct may have expanded westwards simultaneously, breaking through the west fortress wall for the first time. In Worcester, the abrupt ending of the axial High Street at the cathedral precinct boundary has suggested to several writers that the High Street was truncated by a phase in the expansion or definition of the cathedral precinct. Such a process is most likely to have been associated with Bishop Oswald's reorganization of the community in the 960s, and appears to have been part of a more general replanning of the cathedral's surroundings (see above, pp. 161–2).

The post-Conquest period certainly witnessed changes in the extent of both precincts. At Gloucester a precinct wall was built in 1104–13 when at the same time land was acquired to the north of the precinct from St Oswald's, which may have been the first stage in the breaking-through of the Roman north wall. The final phase in the expansion of the abbey precinct took place in 1218, land again being acquired from St Oswald's. If, therefore, the hypothesis that the Old Minster had first occupied a single insula is correct, the area of the precinct must have approximately quadrupled between the late seventh and early fourteenth centuries, achieving a final area of about 12.5 acres (5.06 hectares). Much of this expansion was accomplished by the breaking-through of the constraining Roman fortress walls, away from the built-up area. In Worcester, the cathedral precinct site near the peninsula tip had obvious defensible qualities, and its proximity to the main north–south through-route ensured that, soon after the Norman Conquest, it would be forced to share its site with a castle. This was occupying part of the monks' cemetery by 1069 and would continue to do so for about a century and a half, until the area was returned to the priory in 1217. This was of course a period of intense building activity for the cathedral priory, commencing with Wulfstan's campaign of the 1080s. As a result, the presence of the castle doubtless constrained the planning of the priory's domestic ranges (see below). The cathedral close boundaries were recorded in a perambulation of 1497 which shows them to have been coterminous with the boundaries mapped in the eighteenth century; by then the precinct (excluding that part of the castle within St Michael's parish, but including the Bishop's Palace) covered an area of approximately 13.5 acres (*c.* 5.4 hectares).

Perimeters and external relationships

The two senior minster precincts – Worcester Cathedral and St Peter's Abbey – were very different in their spatial relationship to the evolving towns beyond their boundaries, the difference in crude terms being respectively that between separation and integration. St Peter's Abbey stood apart from its town. Its precinct lay on the edge of the medieval built-up area, was well defined and (eventually) geometrically regular. Its jurisdictional and parochial boundary followed the precinct wall, and the wall offered an absolute division between the secular and the ecclesiastic: there was no secular housing within the precinct, although there are indications that the southern perimeter was established as part of the same scheme of planning as the series of secular plots that lay outside. While a minor gate and a postern communicated with the town centre, the abbey's main gate faced west, towards St Mary's Square, part of its own estates. In Worcester, the cathedral close occupied a much more irregular area and its boundaries represented a far less absolute divide between the Church and the town. In particular, it had within its bounds two quite distinct areas of secular tenements. One of these – the cemetery encroachments on the Lich Street frontage – is closely datable and explained in terms of the creation of new rents in the thirteenth century. The other is the series of more conventional burgage-type plots on the west side of Friar Street whose dimensions seem to replicate those further north, outside the precinct boundary. The origin of these plots appears to lie (as in Gloucester) in the replanning of the area around the cathedral and the re-organization of its precinct boundaries, probably in the tenth century, though there is a possibility that these tenements too occupy ground that once formed part of the cathedral cemetery (see above, pp. 159–60, and Brown 1991b).

Whatever their origin, in episcopal Worcester – in contrast to the royal town of Gloucester – there seems to have been less reluctance to incorporate parts of the city within the bounds of the cathedral. It is only at first sight that the precinct gates tell a similar story. As at St Peter's Abbey in Gloucester, Worcester Cathedral Priory's principal entrance, the Edgar Tower, did not face the city centre: it faced east, providing a truly imposing entrance to the monastery from Sidbury via the wide and clearly 'designed' approach offered by Edgar Street (plate 18). Here, however, no other arrangement was possible as the monastery was cut off from a direct approach from the city to the north by the great bulk of the Norman cathedral church. Meanwhile the northern half of the precinct, dominated by the lay cemetery, was easily accessible from the city both via the College Gate at the end of the High Street, and via a postern (the Lich Gate) from Lich Street. The incompletely walled and distinctly permeable precinct perimeter at Worcester thus contrasted with the impermeable walled perimeter at St Peter's Abbey, which much more obviously turned its back, so to speak, on the town outside; the separation of St Peter's precinct from its surroundings may also be viewed as an accurate reflection of the detachment of the abbey from any urban pastoral mission or involvement – other than as a landlord – in Gloucester's affairs.

The enclosure in stone of the Worcester precincts came later than that of Gloucester, where walls were built in 1104–13. The Bishop of Worcester was instructed to crenellate his section of the riverside wall (presumably a retaining and boundary wall) in the 1230s, and in 1271, at the time of Welsh attacks, he received a licence to crenellate the cathedral close (Beardsmore 1980, 60). In 1368–9 the prior was given a licence to crenellate the cathedral priory. By then, just over twenty years had passed since the Great Tower or St Mary's Gate, known more recently as the Edgar Tower, was built (Molyneux 1992). This massive but amply fenestrated construction has some features of potential defensive value, at least in terms of coping with local disturbances, but the overwhelming impression derived from its crenellation and octagonal corner turrets is that its primary function was to act as a very conspicuous symbol of the lordship of the cathedral and its priory. The enclosure of the close and cathedral priory may have begun as an earnestly defensive measure in the thirteenth century, but it seems that a century later such activity was of greater symbolic than military value. St Peter's Abbey, again, offers a contrast. The northern half of its precinct enclosure was an integral part of the town defences, a component in a chain of linked *enceintes* that was still current in the sixteenth century: the castle, the eastern half of the Roman fortress, the abbey and St Oswald's (Hurst 1986). There was even some doubt as to whether the north wall of the precinct belonged to the abbey or was truly part of the town wall: the question was resolved in 1447 when the burgesses relinquished their claims to it and the abbey undertook to stop making new entrances through it (*VCH Glos.*, iv, 244). St Peter's precinct walls had a more serious military value than those of Worcester cathedral, which lay within the protection of the city walls and the surviving part of the castle.

Internal planning

The internal planning of these precincts is evident only in the post-Conquest period. Both sites saw extensive building campaigns starting in the 1080s that effectively obliterated all recognizable evidence of their earlier organization. Both communities adopted standard Benedictine arrangements for their conventual buildings, adapted to the particular circumstances of each site. In each case the cloisters were planned so that they lay away from the town and the lay public: in Gloucester they were on the north side of the church, where the braided course of the Fullbrook offered the additional convenience of a water-supply to the domestic offices. In Worcester the cloisters lay south of the church but the dorter was unusually placed, projecting westwards from the west claustral range: this appears to have been so as to make use of the Severn to flush the attached reredorter, but the unwelcome presence of Urse d'Abitot's castle to the south may have been an additional factor, preventing the building of any substantial ranges projecting south of the refectory. It may also have been the castle that limited the size of the cloister, which was substantially smaller than that at Gloucester although the church was proportionately larger. Immediately north of the dorter, just outside the cathedral's west end, lay the monastic infirmary. In both Worcester and Gloucester the lay cemeteries were placed nearest the town, and the monks' cemeteries segregated to the south-east of the churches' east ends.

The outer court at Worcester (now College Green) lay south of the claustral area, away from the town; at Gloucester it lay to the west of the church, but its relationship to the town was not dissimilar. The precinct at Gloucester appears to have been more compartmentalized than that at Worcester, additional segregation being apparent in the form of Miller's Green, an additional court in the precinct's north-west corner that was home to a water-mill, kitchens and other service buildings. The siting of the accommodation for senior ecclesiastics was somewhat different in each place. At Gloucester, the Norman abbot's lodgings appear to have been in a tower-like structure in the west claustral range and then, at some time after 1329, they were moved to a far more secluded site towards the northern boundary of the precinct. At Worcester, the Bishop's Palace lay within a physically (and jurisdictionally) discrete enclosure in that precinct's north-west corner. It took the form of an ecclesiastical salient projecting into the town. The prior's lodgings lay to the east of the chapter house, adjacent to the Guesten Hall, and close to the priory's principal gate.

The Friaries

Foundation, location, and expansion

By the mid fourteenth century, Worcester contained two friaries and Gloucester three. The establishment of the mendicant orders in these towns took place over more than a century, spanning the 1230s to the 1340s. The Franciscans were the first to arrive: their house in Worcester was founded in *c.*1226, and that in Gloucester about five years later. The Dominican friary in Gloucester followed in *c.*1239, though their Worcester house was not founded until 1347. A Carmelite friary in Gloucester was established in *c.*1268. The Friars of the Sack had, very briefly, a house in Worcester: its existence was recorded only once, in 1271–2, two years before the suppression of the order (see Chapters 3 and 6; *VCH Worcs.*, ii, 167–73; *VCH Glos.*, ii, 111–12).

In each case the friars' precincts were established on sites on the edge of the contemporary built-up area. All but two lay in districts that can be characterized as intramural fringe-belts, to use the terminology developed by Conzen (1969, 110). The exceptions were the Worcester Franciscans (whose first precinct lay in just such a situation, immediately within the city wall, but was later extended by the addition of a second precinct outside the wall) and the Gloucester Carmelites (whose precinct occupied a gap, created by watercourses, in the plot-series of the Northgate Street suburb). All of the precise sites were determined by the location of their benefactors' undeveloped land. Of the five principal foundations (excluding the Friars of the Sack) one (Gloucester Dominicans) was established on royal land, and two (Gloucester Franciscans and Worcester Dominicans) on land belonging to prominent county families (the Berkeleys and the Beauchamps). The Gloucester Whitefriars' house was 'probably founded with the help of Queen Eleanor, Sir Thomas Giffard, and Thomas II of Berkeley' (*VCH Glos.*, ii, 112).

The Gloucester Blackfriars' precinct lay behind the built-up frontages in the city's south-west quadrant, its site determined by the availability of surplus royal land – that occupied by the first castle, redundant or at least little used by the 1230s. Comparable sites were made available a few years later to the Franciscans in York, and to the London Dominicans in the 1290s when they moved from Holborn to Baynard's Castle (Dobson 1984, 113). Like the Gloucester house, the Worcester Dominicans' site lay behind an established plot-series within the town-wall. The Gloucester Franciscans occupied a plot of land donated by the Berkeleys on open ground in the city's south-east corner behind the built-up Southgate Street frontage. The Worcester Franciscans' precinct is more problematic. They were originally established, probably by 1226, on an intramural site: in 1231 on the orders of Henry III a postern was enlarged to allow the friars to import firewood and other necessities. In 1236–9 they moved to an extramural site and were later (1246) granted permission for the construction of another postern. It cannot be proved that their first site was adjacent to their new site, but it is likely that they simply moved from one side of the city wall to the other, the second permission for a postern relating to an enlargement of the earlier one. Their first site is probably represented by the walled precinct on the east side of Friar Street; this was bisected by a lane giving access, via a postern, to the friary buildings and cemetery beyond the wall (*VCH Worcs.*, ii, 169; Hughes and Molyneux 1984).

A similar fringe location appears to have been adopted by the Friars of the Sack in Worcester, their house lying on Dolday in the city's north-west corner, close to the site later taken by the Dominicans. In 1272 they were granted permission to enlarge their plot by the enclosure of part of Dolday itself (*Cal. Pat. Rolls 1266–72*, 633). Monastic life at the very smallest scale may perhaps be represented by Juliana, the anchoress of St Nicholas's, Worcester. The location of her plot (donor unknown) is again comparable: it almost certainly lay on Foregate, just within the city wall. In 1256 she received a licence to extend it by the addition of a narrow strip of land abutting the wall – possibly this had previously been left vacant for access to the wall or the gate (*Cal. Pat. Rolls 1247–58*, 492).

While the mendicant orders were at least theoretically forbidden from holding property beyond that which was necessary for the most immediate needs of their houses, it is nevertheless true that nearly all of the friary precincts in Worcester and Gloucester can be seen to have been growing in the course of the thirteenth and fourteenth centuries. The most substantial acquisitions were often made very soon after a new house was founded, with more modest additions thereafter. The move by the Worcester Greyfriars to an extramural site within their first decade has already been described. The Gloucester Greyfriars were at first allowed to accept only a small part of their founder's gift of land; about eight years later (1239) they found they needed a larger area and, with the approval of their Provincial Minister, accepted the remainder (*VCH Glos.*, ii, 111). The Blackfriars, on the other side of Southgate Street, was founded at about this time. There is some doubt as to the state of the old castle that formed the core of their original gift. The surviving church and claustral area were built right on the castle's eastern boundary, spanning the infilled ditch; perhaps part of the bailey remained in use, with the friars temporarily housed in buildings within the bailey which thus had to be left standing while the new ranges were completed. Whatever the reason, within about seven years of the foundation the Dominicans sought to acquire additional land to the east for the construction of their church, the extension of the cemetery and the construction of a new access lane (fig 3.11). Similarly, the Worcester Blackfriars received an additional two acres (on which they built their gatehouse) adjoining their house in 1351, four years after their arrival, though the title to this land was to be disputed (Hughes 1986, 13–14).

All of these houses went on to acquire further land around their precincts. The Gloucester Greyfriars leased a turret on the city wall in 1246 in which to hold their school; in 1285 they sought permission to acquire a plot of land near their church; and in 1365 they acquired a final half-acre lot, possibly to extend their cemetery (*VCH Glos.*, ii, 112). In 1292 the Blackfriars acquired a frontage plot (a messuage and land) on Smiths (Longsmith) Street, and two further plots, probably behind the frontage, either side of Satires Lane (Ladybellegate Street). Together, these made a substantial addition to the precinct; they were associated with the enclosure of Satires Lane and, probably, with the construction of the north gate. A final plot measuring 6 by 1 perches was acquired to the south of the claustral area in 1364–5 'for enlarging their homestead' (Palmer 1882, 298–9). In 1391, forty years after their two-acre extension, the Worcester Blackfriars were granted a property called Pynnokeshey, between Dolday and the city wall, for the enlargement of their garden, and in 1405 a further piece of land along the city wall was leased to them by the city (*VCH Worcs.*, ii, 167; Hughes 1986, 13–14). The Gloucester Carmelites too, enlarged their suburban premises with the gift of a 'curtilage with stews, hays, dikes, walls, and trees' in 1321, and an additional 3.5 acres (1.4 hectares) in 1343 with a messuage 'for the enlargement of their manse' (*VCH Glos.*, ii, 112).

Internal planning (figs 3.11 and 12.5)

The details of the internal planning of the friary precincts are in most cases unknown to us, except in outline. Only at the Gloucester Blackfriars have the conventual buildings survived and the remainder of the precinct been investigated as well. The planning of this site reveals a number of features that are characteristic of the mendicants in general, and which may also be detected in the other friary sites in the two towns. First, the church was directly accessible from the principal entrance to the precinct. It lay on the south side of the inserted lane off Southgate Street; what may have been an external pulpit was built in the north wall of the nave, perhaps overlooking a preaching-yard outside the church (Knowles 1932, 176). Secondly, the claustral ranges lay to the south of the church, away from the public traffic; more domestic and ancillary buildings probably lay further to the south (Knowles 1932). Thirdly, excavation and radar survey have now shown that the majority of the walled precinct area to the north was given over to use as a cemetery – far more extensive than could have been predicted from the evidence of surviving wills expressing peoples' preferred place of burial. Fourthly, the precinct was walled and gated; but, as it lay well behind the built-up frontages and was hidden from the outside world, for the friars' preaching mission to be successful their presence had to be advertised. The friary gates were therefore located on the frontages, beyond the precinct boundaries, and – at least on the north side – on land specially acquired for the purpose.

The Worcester Blackfriars' site, though known (literally) only in outline, bears close comparison. There the church was similarly sited for easy access, its west end lying on the alleyway leading from Broad Street. The claustral ranges were sited to the north of the church, away from the public. The lane predated the friary, but with the first extension of the friars' land a gate was built on the Broad Street frontage and again this seems to have had more to do with advertising the presence of the house behind the frontage than with questions of security. A cemetery (perhaps one of several) lay south-west of the church, easily accessible from the main street. Still less is known for certain of the Worcester Greyfriars, though there are indications that domestic and liturgical functions were separated. The church, chapter house and cemetery all appear to have stood within the extramural precinct, though whether accompanied by a cloister-garth and the other associated ranges is unknown; at least some form of high-status domestic accommodation remained within the earlier intramural precinct (Hughes and Molyneux 1984, 8–9). As noted earlier, a gateway in the otherwise blank precinct wall announced the way through to the church and cemetery beyond the city wall. The arrangement of the Gloucester Greyfriars' buildings is not known, beyond the siting of claustral ranges to the south of the church and a cemetery to the north; the west end of the church would have been approached directly from the entry alongside the churchyard of St Mary de Crypt from the Southgate Street frontage.

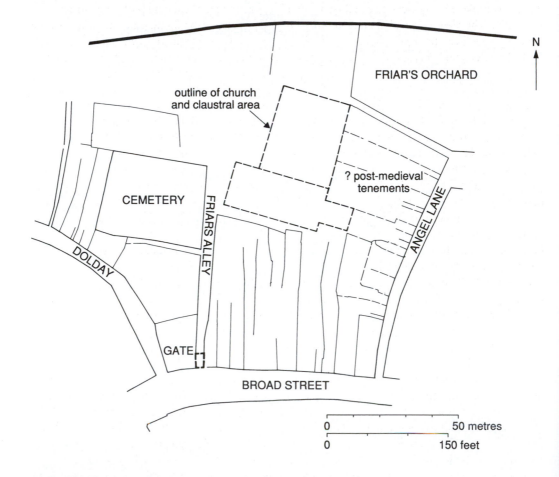

12.5   The Dominican Friary, Worcester (after Hughes 1986 and Mundy 1989)

The morphological impact of the friaries

As we have seen, most of the friaries occupied vacant land behind existing plots; this, and the fact that the mendicant orders were not significantly involved in the development of town property for commercial gain, ensured that the impact of these precincts on their surroundings was not particularly strong. However, the development of precincts on such backland sites not infrequently required improvement to access arrangements, and friary sites were thus frequently distinguished by the insertion of new lanes through existing plot-series, and posterns through city walls. The Gloucester Dominicans created a new way through to the principal (Southgate Street) frontage in 1246 in the first phase of the development of their precinct; Satires Lane, which gave access northwards to Smiths (Longsmith) Street may already have been in existence to serve the castle. A similar pattern of development would be suspected at the Worcester Blackfriars had excavation not shown that Friars' Alley, which gave access to the precinct from the Broad Street frontage, had in fact evolved from a former Roman street – from which the fourteenth-century church and claustral ranges derived their orientation. The Worcester Greyfriars' premises was unusual in that the intramural part of the precinct occupied part of the Friar Street frontage, presenting a blank wall to the street and interrupting the plot-series (Hughes and Molyneux 1984). It is possible that it actually replaced – by clearance and amalgamation – a number of existing plots at its foundation in *c*. 1226. The clearance and amalgamation of built-up plots for the foundation of a friary would certainly have been unusual – but not unheard of (e.g. the later Carmelite house in Corve Street, Ludlow: Klein and Roe 1987). The intramural precinct was bisected by a lane, approached through a gated entry, that gave access via the inserted postern-gate to the extramural part of the precinct. The insertion of new gates through the town walls, and the use of the town walls to form one side of the precinct enclosure, was also a feature of the Franciscan, Dominican and Augustinian houses at Shrewsbury (*VCH Shrops.*, ii, 89–96; and Baker, forthcoming).

No common thread appears to run through the post-Dissolution histories of the friary sites, unless it is that their fate was decided by the economic condition of their surroundings. In Worcester, the Blackfriars' buildings were demolished almost to ground level, the site split up, and parcels leased out by the city. The boundaries of the parcels were determined by the walls of the main ranges, and their outlines were preserved by successive, generally poor, buildings until comprehensive redevelopment took place in the 1960s (Hughes 1986). On the eastern side of Worcester, the Franciscans' church outside the walls was demolished immediately. Domestic buildings within the intramural precinct evidently survived, and saw a succession of uses before being acquired by the City in 1724 for use as a gaol. Friar Street appears to have had a socially and economically mixed population at the time of the Dissolution, and the site was at least in part redeveloped with relatively wealthy buildings (Hughes and Molyneux 1984). In Gloucester, the Blackfriars' conventual buildings were bought by Thomas Bell, an alderman and a wealthy clothier. The church was converted into his mansion and the claustral ranges accommodated his weavers. The remainder of the precinct was left as open ground, though there appears to have been some encroachment by tenements to the east of the precinct over the line of the precinct wall where it ran closest to the street. The Greyfriars' precinct survived in a much less complete state, despite having undergone substantial rebuilding not long before. The church accommodated a brewhouse from immediately after the Dissolution until the mid eighteenth century. By 1721 the chancel and most of the claustral buildings had gone, in part due to bombardment in the Civil War (*VCH Glos.*, iv, 291–2); much of the precinct area away from the frontages remained open ground into the twentieth century. The Whitefriars' buildings in the Northgate Street suburb were described as a small house 'in decay, and some houses taken down and sold' at the time of their surrender in 1538 (*VCH Glos.*, ii, 112). Most of the buildings are said to have been demolished in *c.* 1567; one survived to be converted into a barn, which lingered until the late seventeenth or eighteenth century. The precinct area remained open ground and was used as a cattle market from the 1820s (*VCH Glos.*, iv, 292).

Hospitals and nunneries

Foundation and siting (figs 3.3 and 6.4)

The number of hospitals fluctuated through time in both towns: each had a number of long-lived institutions, and each had one or two more ephemeral ones, perhaps known only from a single reference. In Gloucester there were three long-lived hospitals. Two stood at the far end of the Newland suburb, the continuation of Lower Northgate Street: St Margaret's, a house for male and female lepers founded before 1158, and – at the very end of the suburb – St Mary Magdalen, a leper hospital for women probably founded soon after the mid twelfth century (*VCH Glos.*, ii, 122). The third permanent hospital was St Bartholomew's, a twelfth-century foundation in the Westgate Island suburb. There is also a single reference in the 1455 rental to a tenement of the abbot of St Peter's on the south side of Eastgate Street just within the town wall, 'where divers poor and infirm persons lie' (94b). In Worcester, there were two long-lived institutions: St Oswald's hospital, towards the far end of the northern suburb, founded as a leper house before *c.* 1200 (Stubbs 1880, 435) and St Wulfstan's hospital in Sidbury, the southern suburb, founded before 1221 (see above, pp. 215–16). St Wulstan's hospital seems to have taken over the functions of a short-lived hospital of St John, first referred to in 1189–99, but defunct some time between 1221 and 1240 (Holt, forthcoming). There was, in addition, a leper house of St Mary somewhere outside Worcester in 1264, known only from a single reference (*Cal. Pat. Rolls 1258–66*, 394).

Worcester also had two nunneries. The Priory of Whistones, also known as the nunnery of the Whiteladies of Aston or the house of St Mary Magdalen at Whistones, was founded before 1255 on a site at the furthest end of the Tything suburb to the north of the city. There is also a single reference to the Penitent Sisters of Worcester who were granted £2 and six oaks by Henry III in 1241 and £5 in 1245 for the works of their church, but were not recorded again under that name (*Cal. Lib. Rolls 1240–45*, 30; *1245–51*, 6; *VCH Worcs.*, ii, 173). The location of their house (if this was not indeed the Whistones house) is unknown.

The siting of the hospitals and the single known nunnery was identical in both towns: all, without exception, were located within suburbs, usually at the very end of the built-up area, and usually within an existing plot-series. The marginal siting of the *leprosariae* (St Margaret's and St Mary Magdalen's, Gloucester) is of course very widely paralleled. Their peripheral, or liminal, situation has been interpreted as having less to do with concerns for public health than with the medieval view of leprosy as a divine punishment for sexual misconduct, the hospital inmates assuming the role of the religious penitent and being condemned to a marginal existence, undergoing purgatory on earth; their location on main roads was to keep them in the public mind, to assist in the chantry process (Gilchrist 1992, 113–16). Liminal siting was also a characteristic of nunneries, and may be observed in the Priory of Whistones in Worcester. In two cases, hospitals appear to have been founded on sites with some kind of shadowy former ecclesiastical function. The possible prehistory of St Bartholomew's Hospital, Gloucester, has already been discussed (see above, p. 119); St Wulfstan's in Worcester was founded on a site that contained the probable pre-Conquest chapel of St Gudwal.

There is very little information regarding the precincts and internal planning of most of these institutions. St Oswald's in Worcester occupied a curtilage of about 1.5 acres (0.6 hectare) when first mapped in the eighteenth century; the building ranges within had been replanned in the 1630s and were again rebuilt in 1873. The rear boundary to the site continues the line of the rear access lane from the south (now Sansome Walk), which appears to have been closed and diverted around the rear of both St Oswald's and the nunnery to the north; the implication is that both the hospital and the nunnery were founded within the plot-series of the planned suburb. A reference to the Whistones nunnery on the north side of the cemetery of the hospital of St Oswald suggests that their sites actually adjoined and formed the last two plots of the suburb (*VCH Worcs.*, ii, 154). Limited excavation on the southern side of the St Oswald's precinct revealed the end of a substantial buttressed stone range, function unknown, of possible fourteenth-century date, extending towards the centre of the site on an orientation completely different to the mapped and surviving post-medieval ranges. There was also evidence of earlier (late twelfth- or thirteenth-century) buildings and burials (Edwards 1992).

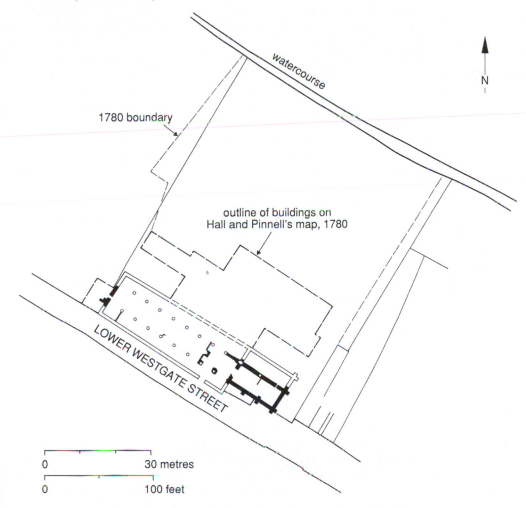

12.6   St Bartholomew's Hospital, Gloucester (after Hurst 1974)

While the detached chapels survive, in whole or in part, from St Margaret's and St Mary's in Gloucester, little is known of their other conventual buildings. St Margaret's, when first mapped, occupied an irregular close within a larger plot on the south side of the street; St Mary's chapel stood isolated on an island site in the middle of the road, a narrow thoroughfare dividing it from the site of its conventual buildings in an enclosure within a larger plot, confined by the continuous back-fence line to the plot-series as a whole.

Buildings

It is possible to comment in detail on the internal organization of only two hospitals in our towns – St Bartholomew's in Gloucester and St Wulfstan's in Worcester. They could scarcely have been more different, illustrating as they do contrasting traditions in the planning of English medieval

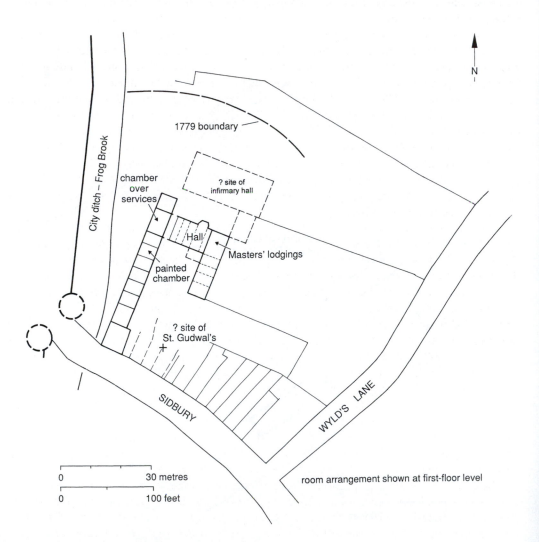

12.7   St Wulfstan's Hospital (the Commandery), Worcester

hospitals: the Gloucester hospital adopting a plan-form ultimately derived from the monastic infirmary, while the later Worcester hospital buildings most closely resemble a wealthy private town-house.

St Bartholomew's was located in the centre of the northern plot-series of the Westgate Island suburb; one of its buildings is known from excavation and from cartographic and illustrative evidence. The principal building lay right on the Westgate Street frontage and even projected slightly into it. This was an aisled infirmary hall of seven bays, continuous with a church at the east end consisting of a two-bay nave and a two-bay chancel, aisled only on the north side; the structure was built in the early thirteenth century and may have been complete by 1232 when permission was given for services to be held in the church. A royal grant of a small piece of land for the enlargement of the chancel in 1265 probably refers to land adjoining the latter's south wall, and the intention to add a south aisle, but this seems never to have been built. The infirmary hall was separated from the church nave and probably partitioned into individual cubicles in the 1560s (Hurst 1974, 41–6). Little appears to be known of the other buildings on the site. In 1333 there were 90 sick inmates, 'including the lame, the halt, and the blind, both men and women'; the hospital's finances suffered gravely from maladministration in the mid to late fourteenth century, and in 1381 accounts refer to the poverty of the inmates and state that 'a great building in the hospital set apart for the benefit of the poor had been unroofed, and the timbers and tiles taken for other purposes' (*VCH Glos.*, ii, 120–21). The hospital survived the Dissolution and was granted to the mayor and corporation in 1564. Hall and Pinnell's map of 1780 shows a substantial block of buildings behind and parallel to the thirteenth-century frontage range, but too close to it to represent a former claustral arrangement; the character of these other buildings is unknown. The location of the infirmary hall and church projecting into the street is undoubtedly significant: it appears to duplicate the position of St Nicholas's church and may, like the church, reflect an association with the suburb's bridges, and the collection of tolls – and not just charitable offerings – from passing traffic (see above, pp. 117–22).

The first reference to St Wulfstan's hospital comes from 1221, and it was most likely founded some 20 year earlier. The hospital was served by the chapel of St Gudwal, probably a pre-existing foundation. At first a mixed community with a master, brethren and sisters, and inmates described as 'infirm', the community may have been re-organized *c.* 1250 (Holt, forthcoming). In 1294 there were 22 sick inmates in the infirmary (*VCH Worcs.*, iv, 4), but by the late fourteenth century at least some of the inmates bought admission with gifts of property (Holt, forthcoming). The hospital was reformed and reconstituted in 1441 with a master, two chaplains, five poor brethren and two sisters (*VCH Worcs.*, ii, 176). The earliest structural evidence comes from the excavation *c.* 1840 of three pier bases and columns of thirteenth-century character, discussed by Marsh (1890) as belonging to the chapel of St Gudwal but more likely from an infirmary hall that was probably located in the back garden of the present buildings on the site of the north courtyard ranges shown on Doharty's (1746) map which were demolished by 1779 (Young's map). Some remains of the north courtyard north range were still standing in 1818 when they were thought to represent the remains of a chapel (Laird 1818). The surviving late-medieval hospital ranges of St Wulfstan's form an H-plan, the Great Hall forming the cross-bar, with chambers over the services to the west and the Master's Lodgings to the east.

The precinct containing St Wulfstan's hospital (the Commandery) has been commented upon elsewhere. In brief, it was a substantial, irregular parcel of land developed at the rear of the secular plots and the roadside chapel of St Gudwal in the pre-Conquest suburb of Sidbury. The earlier eighteenth-century maps of Worcester (Doharty 1741, Broad 1768) reveal a double courtyard arrangement, of which only the southern courtyard ranges remain, though these buildings, dating from the second half of the fifteenth century, survive in a fine state of preservation. The Great Hall, of four and a half bays, lay across the site parallel to Sidbury; its high end lay to the east, the master's lodgings housed at first-floor level in the adjacent wing, running south towards the street. The opposite (west) wing, off the low end of the hall, probably functioned as the infirmary, providing individual chambers in a block-like arrangement. Beyond the hall lay the now demolished north courtyard. Early nineteenth-century accounts of the ruins of an ecclesiastical-type stone building there, and discoveries of thirteenth-century column bases in the garden in the 1840s suggest that the north courtyard may once have been dominated by an aisled infirmary hall, like that of St Bartholomew's. This may have stood opposite an earlier version of the Great Hall, providing a claustral-like arrangement in which the hall was substituted for a common refectory.

The hospital underwent a number of substantial evolutions in its function and in its constitution. Reformed after a corrupt episode in the fourteenth century, the institution's buildings that survive today date from the final phase of its existence and most strongly resemble the ranges of a wealthy urban secular mansion (see e.g. Pantin 1962–3, 223–8). In 1294 there had been 22 sick inmates in the infirmary but, in the fourteenth and fifteenth centuries, the charitable work of the hospital was restricted to a single dole of bread and the care of only seven inmates. These made little impression upon the substantial revenues from the hospital's lands, the remainder of which went to the bishop. He, in turn, appointed the master from amongst the high officials of his household and the surviving buildings would have provided a suitable residence for such a person (Holt, forthcoming; Marsh 1890; Molyneux 1978).

Chapter 13

The suburbs and the Church

The long-term trend of economic and population growth makes it certain that both Worcester and Gloucester were experiencing rapid expansion during the eleventh and twelfth centuries. It was within this context that in each town settlement spilled out beyond the line of the defences established around 900, in time extending well beyond the subsequent enlargement of the defended area.

In this respect Worcester and Gloucester resembled other successful English towns; also – as frequently happened elsewhere – the new phases of extramural settlement remained distinctly marginal to the established urban communities. Already by the time of Domesday Book a considerable degree of suburban growth is recorded, in the form of settlements of cottagers around several of the larger towns (Dyer 1985); in the centuries that followed, such peripheral settlements came to contain a significant proportion of the urban population, with often a quarter or more of a town's inhabitants living in its suburbs by the end of the twelfth century (Keene 1990, 114). Extramural development, therefore, contributed significantly to the form of these greater cities as it developed after the initial planning of their intramural districts; and with it came fundamental social change as the urban poor emerged to be a distinct class beside the burgesses. Their preference for suburban dwellings (Keene 1990, 115–16; MacCaffrey 1958, 250–51) reflected for the most part no more than the greater availability of land and thus the lower rents to be had outside the town walls; what perpetuated the social pattern was the tendency for commercial activity to remain concentrated within the central zones of medieval towns throughout the middle ages, and the consequent unattractiveness of the outlying streets to any townsman wishing to trade retail (Langton 1977).

The suburbs had no monopoly of urban poverty, it must be stressed. It is abundantly clear that in every town poor dwellings were to be found scattered amongst even the fine houses and shops on the principal streets: in Gloucester, for instance, Ratounrewe – the rat-infested row – was a block of 18 small, low-rent houses fronting on to the Westgate Street and Abbey Lane corner to the east of St Nicholas's church (A 13, fos 51–51v; *1455 Rental*, 46); in Worcester, at the end of the middle ages, much of the area of St Andrew's parish was one of general poverty, despite its proximity to the High Street (Dyer 1973, 177–8). Meanwhile in the suburbs there might be better quality houses, particularly along the main roads approaching the town gates; whilst a minority of suburbs such as Redcliffe outside Bristol or Wigford in Lincoln could evolve into notably wealthy settlements (Keene 1990a, 112–13, 115, 117).

Nor, it must be stressed, were medieval suburbs in any sense useless appendages, unimportant to the urban economy. Braudel's description of them as the shoots at the foot of a strong tree, the manifestations of a town's strength however wretched they might be (Braudel 1974, 391), acknowledges their essential function as the residence of much of the labouring workforce but emphasizes also their dynamic role in urban development. If other circumstances were favourable, suburbs could provide the space for new commercial and industrial enterprises. Some towns found it convenient to move their cattle and horse-markets to extramural locations, and industries such as smithing, potting, fulling and tanning were often strongly represented in the suburbs where available space and water supplies gave a commercial advantage, and where they might be acceptably remote from the better streets (Keene 1990a, 110, 116). On occasion, as at Hereford or

Northampton (Keene 1990a, 115), so successful were these offshoots in attracting a range of activities that they became new commercial centres to rival and even replace the existing market districts. Thus the suburb might cease to be suburban, losing entirely its marginal character.

Inevitably, much suburban development is poorly represented in the surviving record. Often it is only modern topographical analysis that can indicate the full extent of a town's suburbs, when both historical and archaeological evidence are insufficient to allow an outline of their chronology and evolution to be deduced. Nor is it clear how often suburbs originated as planned schemes of far-sighted lords in possession of appropriate tracts of extramural land, or alternatively how far they emerged from a process of unco-ordinated and opportunistic property development by a multiplicity of landholders. Ecclesiastical institutions with their large urban and rural landholdings were better placed to take advantage of urban expansion than were secular lords; were they prominent in initiating the development of suburban property or did they do little more than react to an increased demand for extramural plots of land?

A study of the Worcester and Gloucester suburbs can go some way towards addressing the general questions surrounding suburban development. In particular, it is possible to assess the extent of the Church's contribution to this aspect of urban growth. Of necessity, what is known about each suburb has to be presented at length as the only way of countering the unevenness of the sources: if poorly documented suburbs are to be understood at all it will only be in the light of deductions concerning the overall pattern of suburban development both in the same town and in comparable towns. Thus by taking together Gloucester and Worcester – neighbouring communities of reasonably similar size – the body of relevant evidence increases, and conclusions can be reached with greater confidence. The much better documentation for the Gloucester suburbs provides an overall chronology that, if not directly applicable to any specific phase of Worcester's extramural growth, nevertheless acts as a general guide to the periods of expansion; the evidence from Gloucester of the Church's involvement in the suburbs informs and extends the more impressionistic evidence from Worcester.

Gloucester

The northern suburb (fig. 3.16)

The earliest of Gloucester's suburbs was the complex of new developments to the north and north-east of the *burh* walls. Here an extensive suburb grew up, apparently in four phases: first, the length of Lower Northgate Street outside the north gate and as far as the outer north gate; second, the Newland beyond the outer north gate; third, Hare Lane, as far as the Alvin Gate; finally, the streets further to the west, towards St Oswald's Priory, and particularly Watering Street (fig. 3.16). In time most of this district came to be enclosed within a new ditch whose purpose may have been more to control the movement of people and merchandise than to defend the population from attack; the original north wall was maintained as the true line of the town's defences, and the suburb remained essentially extramural.

The Anglo-Saxon names of some of the suburb's streets and features point to its pre-Conquest origins: Fete Lane and Hare Lane are Old English, and the Alvin Gate was Ælfwine's gate (Smith 1964, 126–7, 128–9). By the early tenth century the New Minster – later St Oswald's Priory – had been built to the north of the *burh*, although this did not imply the existence yet of any secular settlement in the area; suburban development probably began with the streets immediately outside the north gate. It has already been remarked (see above, pp. 85–8) how the distinctive shape of

Hare Lane in particular suggests this to have been an area laid out to accommodate markets like those observed outside the gates of other towns, and the same would appear to be true of the unusually wide Lower Northgate Street. Both lay within a ditched extension to the previously defended or delimited area of Gloucester, an extension datable from the name of one of its two principal gates. The Ælfwine from whom Alvin Gate was named was evidently a prominent figure, perhaps the public official responsible for building the gate – and thus the ditch as well.

If the Ælfwine of the gate is to be identified with the Alwin (Alwi or Alwinus) whom Domesday Book records as having been Sheriff of Gloucestershire in King Edward's day, and who died some time after the Conquest still in possession of his lands (DB i, 162d, 167b), then a date around the middle of the eleventh century – and presumably at any rate before the Conquest – can be assigned to both the gate and the ditch (DB i, 162d, 167b.) It is not clear whether or not this Gloucestershire Alwin is to be identified with the Æthelwine also recorded as serving as sheriff, probably in Warwickshire where his family were important landholders (Williams 1989, 279–95).

The landgable rents payable to the Crown from Lower Northgate Street (fig. 10.1) identify the developer there as the civil authority in late Anglo-Saxon or early Norman Gloucester; Hare Lane and the streets to the west, on the other hand, were by the same measure developed separately by another landowner. Everything points to this having been St Oswald's Priory. The large number of houses the priory owned here late in the middle ages can be attributed only in part to its proximity to these streets; all of this district to the west of Hare Lane lay within the parish of St Oswald's, and it seems certain that the priory had once owned it all, presumably from the time of its foundation. The precinct of St Peter's Abbey could be extended northwards in 1104 and 1218 only by taking in land belonging to St Oswald's (*Hist. et Cart.*, i, 25, 83); subsequent development along the new north wall of the abbey, therefore, certainly took place on land belonging to the priory. The concentration of houses belonging to St Oswald's in Watering Street, in particular, suggests that this had always been priory property, and that the priory had taken the initiative in developing it. The role taken by St Oswald's in planning Hare Lane can be similarly demonstrated. It is noteworthy that the boundary between St Oswald's parish and St John's runs down the eastern – and apparently original – arm of this dual roadway; the remodelling of the street with the addition of a second, parallel road some 50 feet (15.25 metres) or so to the west can only be interpreted as an attempt to divert traders and their merchandise along St Oswald's own street. In thus promoting a new commercial thoroughfare on its own land, the priory's purpose may have been not only to enhance its rental income, but also perhaps to divert a proportion of the market tolls collected by the Gloucester authorities at the town gates. In which case, the effective incorporation of Hare Lane into Gloucester with the building of the Alvin Gate by the 1060s may have been prompted as much by the town's reeves' decision to impose their authority over the priory's street as by a need to give physical protection to the growing suburb.

There is some confirmation of the initiating role of St Oswald's Priory in the evidence of payments of landgable. According to the 1455 rental no landgable was owed to the town bailiffs (acting on behalf of the Crown) from any part of St Oswald's parish. From other sources, however, there is evidence for the chief rents paid by three properties – in each case to St Oswald's Priory or to the Archbishop of York, the beneficiary of so much of the priory's property in 1070. The thirteenth-century charters conveying two tenements in Bride Lane to Lanthony Priory both specify landgable to be paid to the archbishop (A5, fos 91–91v; 92–3); the charter by which Robert Bay of Gloucester in the 1220s gave the canons of Cirencester his free land in Hare Lane specified a chief rent of a halfpenny to St Oswald's (Ross 1964, p. 390).

The street-pattern in the western part of this suburb was fully established only during the thirteenth century, as the layout of this district was affected by the extension made to the precincts of St Peter's Abbey in 1218. St Brigid's chapel – to which St Bride's or St Brigid's Lane had evidently led – was incorporated within the new precinct, and a new street was laid out (or established itself) to run along the new abbey wall. It is not impossible that this street had already existed in 1218, and formed a line up to which it was deemed possible to expand; more probably, though, the straightness and regularity of the abbey wall points to its having been laid out across open ground, with the road to its north being therefore a subsequent development. Until this street existed, Bride Lane must indeed have been the main route of access to St Brigid's chapel; it is also possible that there was an earlier road which ran from the foot of Hare Lane to St Oswald's, via St Brigid's. The change in direction taken by the street as it leaves the south-western corner of Hare Lane is very noticeable, and may be the result of the necessary redirection of the road towards St Oswald's after 1218.

The description of the suburb in the 1455 rental is mixed, with more attention being paid to Lower Northgate Street than to the Newland or Hare Lane, while Watering Street is ignored altogether (*1455 Rental*, 78–108). Robert Cole's comparative neglect of the district is explained by the small number of properties here that paid landgable to Gloucester's bailiffs; even so, the information Cole provides, when supplemented from other sources, points to the whole suburb containing in the order of 200 houses at the end of the medieval period, with a further 25 gardens and curtilages that had formerly been built upon – and this latter total, in particular, may be a considerable underestimate.

Forty-six tenements were listed for Lower Northgate Street, 26 on the north side and 20 on the south (*1455 Rental*, 88–96, 104–108). Outside the gate Cole recorded a further 15 along the north side of the main road, and 6 in Fete Lane; his work here was evidently less precise, however, as he recorded no tenements along the south side of the street, and was clearly only interested in locating beyond dispute the 8 properties whose liability to pay landgable he could still demonstrate (*1455 Rental*, 98–104). It is impossible therefore to estimate the size of this furthest suburban district from the evidence of the 1455 rental. A late-thirteenth-century rental of the manor of Abbot's Barton listed customary tenants of 24 messuages in the New Land (*Hist. et Cart.*, iii, 155–6) but, again, that should not be taken as other than a proportion of the total: St Oswald's had 3 cottages and 3 gardens here in the sixteenth century (PRO SC6 Hen. VIII 1212, m. 4). Between the north gate and the foot of Hare Lane Cole counted 10 blocks of property that paid – or had once paid – landgable (*1455 Rental*, 78–82, 86), although for Hare Lane itself, from which no landgable was due, he hardly did more than name a sequence of tenants in order: 11 tenants with 19 separate blocks of property on the west side; 5 tenants holding the land in the middle called 'the Hurst' as 7 properties; 13 holding 18 properties along the east side (*1455 Rental*, 84–6). Some of these properties may have been substantial: Cole recorded St Oswald's Priory as the holder of 2 on the east side of the lane (*1455 Rental*, 86), lands which at the time of the priory's dissolution eighty years later were described as 6 houses and 2 gardens (PRO SC6 Hen. VIII 1212, m. 4). Properties further to the west were left out of the 1455 rental altogether, but in the 1530s St Oswald's Priory had 35 tenements and cottages in Watering Street, and 9 further blocks of land; 6 houses and 2 gardens in the street that lined the north wall of the abbey; 4 pieces of land in Bride Lane or St Brigid's Lane; and 2 houses and a parcel of land in the otherwise unrecorded *Buckestrete* (PRO SC6 Hen. VIII 1212, m. 4).

Yet by 1455 this was a suburb that was already in decline. Its greatest extent had been reached, it would seem, by 1300; indeed, some contraction of settlement already during the fourteenth century can be detected. In the fifteenth and sixteenth centuries all of these streets on the northern fringe of Gloucester saw an appreciable retreat of settlement, characterized by the conversion of house-plots to horticultural use. Lanthony Priory, for instance, had owned four houses in Bride Lane in the thirteenth century (A5, fos 91–94v; A13, fos 74v–75), and a house along the street that followed the north wall of the abbey (A13, fo. 74); only one of these was still standing in the 1440s, however, the others being used as curtilages and gardens. In Hare Lane a plot of the priory's was let in fee for 6s rent and a 6s 8d entry fine in the 1220s or 1230s (A5, fos 90v– 91), and was evidently built up; in the 1440s Lanthony could only let it at will as a curtilage for 2s 6d rent (A13, fo. 73v). Nearby, a tenement with an oven was divided between two tenants in the 1440s (A13, fo. 73), but by 1535 was let as three gardens (GRO GBR 1314). Land outside the Alvin Gate was let in the 1170s or 1180s for 6s – again, a sign it was already built upon. In the thirteenth century a new tenant took it for 4s rent, and rebuilt it; but by the first decade of the fourteenth century it was described simply as land, and let for 4d – a state of affairs that continued for some time until, in the 1440s, it was untenanted (A5, fo. 95v; A13, fo. 76). The plot next to it had likewise been let for 8s rent in the twelfth century and was then given to the Abbot of Gloucester in 1192 in satisfaction of rents totalling 7s 3½d; again, however, by the fifteenth century, and perhaps long before, it had lost its buildings and now the abbot's tenant held it as a piece of land (A5, fo. 95v; A13, fo. 76). At Tullewelle, towards Kingsholm, a tenement of the thirteenth century was two cottages in the fourteenth, with cottages owned by others on either side; in 1445 a tenant held it from Lanthony as a curtilage, and both the neighbouring properties had suffered a similar decline (A13, fos 76v–77). Beween the north gates a tenement held in fee from Lanthony in 1445 and still paying 5s rent was in 1535 a garden, held at will for 2s 8d (A13, fo. 79v; GRO GBR 1314); beyond the north gate, in the 'New Land', a tenement purchased by Lanthony in the thirteenth century was still built up in 1445 but had become a garden by 1535 (A5, fos 101–101v; A13, fo. 80v; GCRO GBR 1314).

The Lower Westgate Street suburb (figs 3.3 and 3.4)

Suburban expansion to the west of Gloucester was limited to the relatively small area between the two channels of the Severn, as beyond that the low-lying marshy ground was unsuitable for settlement. It is not certain when the later main channel of the Severn established itself, or was deliberately cut (see above, pp. 27–9), although in the Roman and Anglo-Saxon periods it is quite clear that the effective westward limit of Gloucester was the line of what would become known as the Old Severn. The Foreign Bridge that spanned this older channel was the only Gloucester bridge until the building of the Westgate Bridge, reportedly in 1119 (Luard 1864, 45). How far the fourteenth-century foundation myth of St Bartholomew's Hospital embodies some memory of the true course of events is unknown (see above, pp. 117–18); according to that source, the hospital originated to house those who built the bridge as an act of piety, and was founded on land belonging to a burgess called William Myparty and which he held in chief from the Crown – that is, as a burgage. Whether, by implication, the plots of the western suburb had already been defined when the bridge was built is not clear. In any case, little trust can be placed in the details of the story.

The Lower Westgate Street suburb can be seen to have developed in an orderly fashion: the regular structure of plots running back from the street to the river on the south, and to the well-defined ditch line on the north, was evidently the result of a single act of planning. In 1455 there were 26 tenements on the south side of the street, and 13 on the north – including the substantial piece of ground on which St Bartholomew's was built. Cole established the liability of all but three of these properties to pay landgable to the bailiffs (*1455 Rental*, 52–6; 60–70); like Myparty's house was said to have been, they had been held in chief from the Crown – and, indeed, St Bartholomew's did pay 1s 3½d landgable for its own site (*1455 Rental*, 56). That it was the secular authority in Gloucester that took the initiative in planning this suburb is, therefore, beyond question. A little archaeological evidence suggests that occupation on one plot began in the late twelfth or early thirteenth century (Heighway 1984b, 45), although this may of course have been atypic; the building of the Westgate Bridge and a consequent increase in the traffic taking this route through Gloucester would in the early twelfth century already have had the effect of enhancing the desirability of property along Lower Westgate Street.

But with its ready access to water, property here was intrinsically desirable; the southern plots backed onto the Severn, and the northern plots onto the ditch which took the earlier course of the river, before its diversion. In addition to the fisherman and the brewer who dwelt there in 1455, the south side of the street held a particular attraction for dyers and tanners: a tanner and a dyer were named as occupants of tenements, whilst two men bore 'dyer' as a surname, and another was called 'tanner'. Three dyers and two tanners were named as former tenants (*1455 Rental*, 60–70). A charter of *c*. 1180 is witnessed by 13 parishioners of St Nicholas's, including three men – Jordan, Ælured and Wlierd – identified as *ultra pontem* (*Cal. Recs Corpn Glouc.*, 85). So the suburb did have inhabitants by that date, but dwelling 'beyond the bridge' rather than 'between the bridges', the formula of later centuries (*1455 Rental*, 52). That is not to be taken as a sign that – contrary to other indications – the Westgate Bridge had not yet been built; rather, it points to the incomplete development of the suburb, so that the new bridge was regarded as lying beyond the bounds of the town. In *c*.1210 the inner or Foreign Bridge could still be called simply 'the bridge of Gloucester', although perceptions were changing quickly, so that by *c*.1220 St Bartholomew's Hospital could be described as lying between the bridges of Gloucester (*Cal. Recs Corpn Glouc.*, 119, 161).

Barton Street

The 1455 rental lists perhaps 50 houses lying outside the east gate, between 25 and 30 on the north side of Barton Street and 20 or so on the south (*1455 Rental*, 102–10). Of these, a total of 13 were liable for landgable. Cole also listed at most a further half-dozen houses located to the south of the street, strung out along the town ditch which at this point was called the Gooseditch (*1455 Rental*, 110–12). That was far from being the full extent of the suburb. Beginning his itinerary at the east gate, Cole evidently did not reach the end of the built-up area, remarking after his last entry for the north side of the street 'and from there the abbot of St Peter's holds everything' (*1455 Rental*, 106). In the late thirteenth century, 26 messuages in Barton Street were held from the manor of Abbot's Barton (*Hist. et Cart.*, iii, 156–8).

It is not certain when or how this suburb originated: the landgable payments to the Crown, like those in the western suburb, could date from as late as 1200. They can hardly have originated later than that, however; for here, as elsewhere, whenever he wished to establish the historic liability of a tenement to pay the rent, Cole cited the evidence of earlier landgable rolls, and on the evidence of the tenants' names his earliest roll had been made no later than the 1220s. The fact that part – and perhaps the greater part – of this suburb was on land belonging to St Peter's points to its having been the abbey that laid it out in such a classic fashion; however, the commencement of the suburb right at the gate, within what was obviously the jurisdiction of the borough, and the landgable payments to the Crown, suggest at least the involvement of the lay authorities. In all likelihood this suburb had originated in an act of co-operation between St Peter's and the reeves of Gloucester during the twelfth century or before .

Brook Street

Apparently the latest – and certainly the smallest – of the suburbs was along Brook Street, outside the Almesham Postern at the north-east corner of the town wall which was described in 1253 as the new east gate of Gloucester (*Cal. Recs Corpn Glouc.*, 492). Brook Street itself was recorded in *c.*1240 and in 1261 (*Cal. Recs Corpn Glouc.*, 367, 570), and whether the gate had been built to permit easy access to the town from an existing extramural street and suburb, or whether the new gate had provided the opportunity for suburban development, is unclear. Perhaps the gate had been built to give the inhabitants of that part of Gloucester direct access to the waters of the Twyver; it is certain, however, that it was not built for the convenience of the Carmelites, whose Gloucester house was founded in Brook Street only around 1268 (*VCH Glos.*, ii, p.112). Their choice of site was obviously influenced by the proximity of this existing entrance to the intramural part of the town.

Brook Street ran along the south side of the Fullbrook, to the north of which was land that came within St Oswald's parish, and so presumably belonged to the priory. There were no houses here belonging to St Oswald's in the early sixteenth century (PRO SC6 Hen. VIII 1212, mm. 4–5d), and so it seems that at the end of the middle ages only the south side of the street was built up. This lay within the manor of Abbot's Barton, and St Peter's Abbey was thus the beneficiary of the suburban growth; how far it encouraged settlement along Brook Street, however, cannot be known. There is little information on the size of the suburb, which – because no tenement here owed landgable – was not included in the 1455 rental; in the late thirteenth century, tenants of Gloucester Abbey held 11 tenements here for rents of several shillings, and in one case for 8*s*, a level that reflects their semi-urban character (*Hist. et Cart.*, iii, 154–5).

The southern suburb

Because there were no landgable payments here for the bailiffs to collect, Cole's 1455 rental gives no hint that there was a substantial suburb outside the south gate. Consequently, the very fact of settlement here has often gone unrecognized – for instance, both Langton and Fullbrook-Leggatt were unaware of it (Langton 1977, 259–77; Fullbrook-Leggatt 1952). The unpublished rental of Lanthony Priory's Gloucester properties (A 13; Jack 1970–73, 375–8), however, that Robert Cole and his fellow-canon Richard Steymour made some ten years earlier, during the 1440s – on internal evidence around 1445 – provides in copious detail the information for this suburb that Cole's 1455 rental lacks. The quality of the Lanthony evidence makes this the best-recorded of any of the suburbs of Worcester or Gloucester: consequently, it can be considered in significantly greater depth than is possible for the other suburbs, and it provides a coherent model of suburban development.

In the streets and lanes of the southern suburb, a total of 48 separate properties belonging to Lanthony were recorded (A13, fos 2–17v) – some developments of a single house, others comprising a number of houses, and yet others consisting only of land, which in most cases had formerly been built upon. As a result it is more meaningful to count the total of recorded houses, which appear to have included virtually all of the houses in the suburb. Sixty-two belonged to Lanthony Priory, and a further 14 were built on land held of the priory in fee and so were entered into the rental. There were other houses, too, that fell into neither category, which the rental, nonetheless, mentions in passing. Common practice in urban rentals was to name the tenants of abutting properties, and whilst the overwhelming majority of Lanthony's houses abutted onto other houses held of the priory, we learn of a further five – and only five – tenements evidently not subject to the priory's lordship. Together this was probably all the land in the southern suburb that was not Lanthony's, and it may be significant that each of the tenements lay on the main highway. A note in Prior Hayward's register, added in the 1450s, recorded that all of the southern suburb – the main street outside the south gate, Sudbroke Street, Severn Street, Small Lane and the alleyway of St Owen – belonged to Lanthony's manor of the Hide, with the exception of certain tenements which were of the liberty of King's Barton (A11, fo. 10). These, presumably, were the five tenements on the main street, together with any others that conceivably went unrecorded in 1445.

The Lanthony documentation provides more than just a description of the state of the suburb at the mid-point of the fifteenth century. Cole was the collector of the priory's Gloucester rents, and had collaborated with Steymour in his meticulous archival work into each of Lanthony's properties (Jack 1970–73, 375–9), so that the rental of *c.* 1445 gives, wherever possible, the names of previous tenants with their tenures dated, not precisely, but by reference to the reigns in which they lived. Disputes over property are recorded and information is generally referenced, either to other cartularies of Lanthony Priory, or to the lost rolls of Lanthony's court of St Owen. The wealth of documentation makes it possible to identify with confidence the land that was the subject of each of the grants and leasing agreements contained in the cartularies and registers, and thus to augment the already full details of the rental – which required a total of 86 large folios to describe the 239 properties in Gloucester that belonged to Lanthony or were held from the priory in fee. Yet, however rich the information for the development of the suburb, there is very little material here that relates directly to its origins.

The existence of a degree of suburban development outside the south gate was noted first in 1095 when Walter of Gloucester, the constable of the castle, endowed the newly founded church of St Ouen or Owen with a substantial income from the tithes owing from his estates, including from the parish of the existing church of St Kyneburgh (Walker 1964, 37–8). The act of founding a new church does not necessarily mean that it was needed by an existing local population: this was not a church built to serve a new parish, but was a secular college intended to accommodate Walter's personal chaplains. Its position – opposite the old castle within the town wall, and in the vicinity of the houses of other of Walter's servants (see below) – reinforces the assumption that these men were expected not only to pray for Walter's soul, but also to serve in his administration. The description of the church in the period 1143–55, as *sancti Audoeni sub castello Gloucestrie* (Walker 1964, 36), emphasizes its close relationship with the castle. Its position, however – set well back from Lower Southgate Street – is of further interest: the choice of such a site for a new church might indicate that in 1095 the main street frontages had already been built up. But only settlement along Shipsters Lane (fig. 3.4) is recorded for the late eleventh century: this was described (A11, fo. 9) as a lane running from the south gate as far as the castle ditch – presumably the old castle, which within 15 years would be replaced (Hurst 1984, 73–132). There in Shipsters Lane was built the house of the priests of St Owen's, and between that and the Severn there were six houses and six tenants living, of whom four were in the service of Walter of Gloucester: a certain smith called Seulf, Aldewyn, Walter of the Fenne, William Butor, Godewyn son of Frye and Turkill. On the other side of the house of the priests, towards the south gate, were another six houses, held by tenants: Richard Pyncum, Wihtric, Sebricht, Milet, father of Richard, Baldewyn Wevecok and Froda, Walter the constable's huntsman. And at the end of the lane towards the Severn, Walter had the barns for his hay, stables for his horses and the kennels for his dogs (A11, fo. 9). There is no evidence for more extensive settlement outside the south gate in 1095, although in the light of the Anglo-Saxon origins of the northern suburb, the possibility that this suburb, too, was pre-Conquest in origin cannot be ruled out.

The substantial grant to the priests of St Owen's church in 1095 included the tithes of the Hide, Walter's manor outside the south gate (A5, fo. 9; Walker 1964, 37–8; for the Hide, see *VCH Glos.*, iv, 61–2, 69, and p. 106, above). When Miles of Gloucester endowed the new Lanthony Priory outside Gloucester with the church of St Owen and all its property in 1136, he included the whole manor of the Hide, thus giving Lanthony both the suburb and the rights of jurisdiction over it (A5, fo.1v). And with the documented acquisition and granting out of lands by Lanthony Priory, beginning soon after the house's foundation, there is more substantial evidence for the extent of settlement. Miles himself, before his death in 1143, granted further small pieces of land outside the south gate to the priory, including land formerly of Sawin the baker for the purpose of enlarging the cemetery of St Owen's, and land formerly of Redmer the brewer (Walker 1964, 18). Their occupations were not necessarily urban, although undoubtedly both Sawin and Redmer had lived by serving the urban market; but it was the need to enlarge the cemetery of a church consecrated only 48 years before that suggests this had become a populous district by the middle decades of the twelfth century. Archaeological evidence points to the planning of this suburb occurring only in the years after Lanthony Priory's foundation. Yet it seems unlikely that development on this scale could have been entirely a phenomenon of the few years since 1136.

As virtually all of the land outside the south gate was held from Lanthony's manor of the Hide, recorded twelfth-century donations to the priory of plots in the southern suburb were of lands evidently held from the manor in free tenure; by inference, these were messuages that had been earlier granted out by the priory or by its predecessors. It is not made clear whether or not these lands were already built up when Lanthony re-acquired them. For instance, Robert son of Seward gave the priory all his land outside the south gate when his son Maurice entered religion there: the land in question extended from the great street as far as the land of the canons and lay between the lands of William Pranchedene and Adam de Aula Regis. As the charter was witnessed by Osmund the reeve, it can presumably be dated to the years between 1165 and 1176 when Osmund was accounting for the farm of Gloucester at the exchequer (A5, fo. 13; *Pipe Rolls* 1165–76). It is not specified whether or not this land was built up, or how extensive it was, except in so far as the circumstances of the gift might imply it to have been a grant of greater value than just a small plot of vacant ground. When this same land was granted out in fee by Prior Roger (1174–*c.*1189: Knowles, Brooke and London 1972, 172–3) to William Tailifer, it was to be held in heredity for a rent of 1*s* 10*d* (A5, fo. 14). Similar properties were let for rather higher rents: land that the same Prior Roger granted to Maiehel of the Castle, and which had been received with one of the canons, Roger son of Alured Cape, was to be held for 3*s* a year (A5, fo. 13). A similar grant in fee, to Alured Bule in 1154, was of land next to that of Reginald the shoemaker, and described as lying in the corner of the lane leading towards Gooseditch and Ticedeswelle. Its rent of 3*s* 6*d* was in marked contrast to that of the plot next to it, a vacant piece of land granted to Dobbin the farrier soon after 1154 for a rent of only 1½*d* (A5, fo. 15; Dobbin is elsewhere identified, rather more formally, as Robertus *marescallus*: A13, fo. 14). The land next to Dobbin's was granted out in fee at about the same time, but for a rent of 1*s* 10*d* (A5, fo. 15).

If vacant land, therefore, could be rented for such a small amount as Dobbin paid, and if these plots were comparable in size, then rents of 3*s* 6*d*, 3*s* and even 1*s* 10*d* would appear to have been for land and buildings. On that interpretation, by the middle years of the twelfth century these were indeed house-plots that were being conveyed, and not curtilages or gardens. But the examples are too few, and perhaps too unrepresentative, to be used as a very accurate guide to how far the suburb had developed. Nevertheless, in the 1440s, Robert Cole could trace the history of these and most other plots through to his own time: seemingly, the messuages of the twelfth century had been identical with those recorded in the fifteenth century. And although little of the medieval plan of the suburb survived the devastation of the siege of Gloucester during the Civil War and subsequent replanning, both the known dimensions of some of the plots and recent archaeological evidence of their shape and relationship to each other and to the main street (personal communication from Malcolm Atkin) indicate them to have been laid out in a regular fashion.

The different strands of evidence, however weak, are consistent in that they point in the same direction: that the southern suburb was already planned and settled during the twelfth century; that by the 1140s its population had outgrown its cemetery; and that the suburb had originated before Lanthony Priory's foundation in 1136. Responsibility for laying out the suburb had, therefore, lain with Lanthony's predecessors as lords of the Hide: perhaps by the priests of St Owen's, although in that case we might expect the initiative to have been taken by Walter of Gloucester or by Miles, the church's lay patrons. Alternatively, the plan of the suburb had been conceived prior to 1095 by Walter or by one of the former sheriffs. Whether or not the houses along Shipsters Lane in 1095 constituted the sum of extramural development at that time cannot be resolved, however, except by excavation. What is certain is that whilst Lanthony Priory may have contributed to the course of development the suburb was to take, it originated as a lay enterprise rather than as an ecclesiastical one.

This is the only suburb of either Gloucester or Worcester where the documentation allows the reconstruction of a profile of settlement from the twelfth century until the sixteenth, demonstrating first the period of suburban growth and then the onset of contraction. Steymour and Cole's practice in their rental of dating previous tenants by reference to reigns is, where it can be checked, reliable, except for their curious attribution of twelfth-century tenants to the early thirteenth century – a sign, perhaps, that they were using a misdated list of rents. Their evidence shows that the suburb had reached its greatest extent during the thirteenth century. For a single site tenants were first named only in the reign of Edward I (A13, fo. 5), which may simply mean it had previously been let at will; otherwise all the lists of earlier tenants and the rents they paid show that expansion had ceased by the end of the reign of Henry III in 1272. Like Gloucester as a whole, and like other similar English towns, the southern suburb reached its greatest population level in the years around 1300; thereafter followed a long period characterized by short phases of steep decline, with perhaps some recovery of population only in the sixteenth century (Holt 1990, 142, 156–8; Palliser 1988; Dyer 1991). From the details of the *c.* 1445 rental, there appears to have been some contraction of settlement already in the years before 1350, although it is the disappearance of houses in the years following the Black Death that is most striking. More than thirty houses vanished during that period, mostly the poor cottages that had lined Severn Street (A13, fos 2v, 3). Whilst this might also be attributed to a growing propensity for the Severn to flood as the climate worsened, for which there is some archaeological evidence from around Gloucester (pers. comm. from John Rhodes), that only explains why these were the particular houses that people chose to abandon as the population fell. Only low-rent cottages had ever been built there, and the district had never been regarded as a salubrious one.

The consequent reduction in the number of houses in the suburb was not to be made up, signifying that the fall in population had been permanent. Nevertheless, the evidence of the Lanthony rentals of the fifteenth and sixteenth centuries is that – perhaps contrary to our expectations – there was to be no further drastic contraction of settlement. The number of houses in *c.* 1445 was, significantly, neither greater nor less than that of seventy years before, indicating that the southern suburb shared in the prosperity that Gloucester continued to enjoy until the middle years of the fifteenth century (A13 fos 2–16v; Holt 1990). Yet even in the period that followed, when Gloucester's population fell from its 1455 level of around 4500 to below – perhaps well below – 4000 in the 1520s (Holt 1987, 151–7, 289–301), the suburb held its position, both with regard to the number of houses there and the rents that tenants were willing to pay. A Lanthony rental of 1535 (GCRO, GBR 1314; Jack, 1970–73, 378) is cross-referenced to Steymour and Cole's *c.* 1445 rental, thus enabling a positive identification for each tenement with those of 90 years before. This provides only a limited sample, as the rental is of the lands of only two of the obedientiaries; nevertheless, an exact comparison is possible for a total of 14 of the 45 holdings in the suburb separately listed in *c.* 1445. Despite the smallness of the sample it is not necessarily misleading: the 24 dwellings paying rent of £9 8s 4d that these 14 holdings contained in the mid fifteenth century had become 25, rented in all for £9 8s 0d, during the sixteenth century. There had been changes both in the use of the holdings and the number of dwellings each tenement contained, and in only two cases had rents remained constant; overall, however, the consistency of the settlement pattern between the two dates is very striking.

Worcester (figs 6.4 and 6.6)

Unlike Gloucester, where the Roman walls survived to be re-used for the *burh* and continued as the effective defensive line on three sides of the town, medieval Worcester was surrounded, successively, by three separate defensive circuits. Only to the south of the cathedral were the Roman defences re-used, firstly for the *burh* and then for the more extensive medieval defences. Thus at Worcester what was 'extramural' was periodically redefined, as previously suburban districts were brought within the intramural area.

By comparison with Gloucester, there is much less to say about the suburban growth outside the gates of Worcester; we do not have rentals of Worcester property that are at all comparable with the Gloucester evidence. Nevertheless, it is clear that the Worcester suburbs were smaller than Gloucester's, and – with one single exception – were less obviously the result of major acts of planning. Worcester's population – estimated to have been between a half and two-thirds that of Gloucester until the mid sixteenth century when it began to increase rapidly (Holt 1987, 149–57; Hoskins 1959, 236–41; Clarke and Dyer 1969, 31–2; Dyer 1973, 19–32) – was perhaps more easily accommodated within the walls. Even in the 1340s there was a large enough piece of open ground within the north wall to accommodate the newly founded Dominican friary (*VCH Worcs.*, ii, 167). Consequently, there was less demand for the owners of extramural land to convert land in agricultural and horticultural use to messuages.

The Sidbury suburb (fig. 6.16)

At least one of the Worcester suburbs had early origins. The Sidbury district outside the south or Sidbury gate was already unusually prominent in the tenth century, although there is no direct evidence of secular settlement from that period. The church of St Peter the Great was referred to in 969, and there is nothing to indicate that it was then a recent foundation; the church of St Gudwal was founded near to it, most probably in the 960s or soon after. The name 'Sidbury' itself is of Old English origin, and is a reference to some form of fortification (Mawer and Stenton 1927, 22). Presumably it refers to Sidbury's position on the south side of the *burh* of Worcester although a less likely explanation of the name is that it refers to Sidbury as 'the south *burh*', implying that the suburb originated within its own enclosure. In any event, there are strong indications here of tenth-century settlement well ouside the *burh* defences of the 890s. Even after the line of the later city wall was established, much of Sidbury remained extramural, and the part that was incorporated into the intramural area perhaps remained suburban in character.

No very reliable estimates can be made of the extent of suburban growth here. Several of the surviving Worcester lay subsidy returns were compiled by parish: St Peter's parish included the lower part of Friar Street, but otherwise approximated closely to the Sidbury suburb as it existed before part of it was enclosed by the medieval city wall. But none of these subsidy returns can be regarded as entirely reliable, since they are all distorted by evasion and corruption; all property-based taxes, moreover, excluded the unknown proportion of the population who fell below the tax threshold. In 1275 some 39 individuals from St Peter's paid the subsidy, or 12.5 per cent of the total of 314 for the whole city (Bund and Amphlett 1893, 1–6). This was perhaps less than 10 per cent of Worcester's population at the time, judging by the fact that a century later, in 1377 – when urban populations generally had suffered some reduction – the city's population can be estimated to have been close to 3000 (Dobson 1983, 57; Palliser 1988, 9). By that measure, then, St Peter's parish contained at least 390 people in 1275, of whom perhaps most, though not all, were resident in Sidbury. That suggests that the parish contained around a hundred households, if we apply the figure of 3.8 for average household size shown to be the appropriate one for late-medieval Coventry (Phythian-Adams 1979, 238–48).

By 1379, according to the poll tax returns of that year (for this dating and other discussion of this evidence see note at the end of this chapter), the parish contained only 23 households – each consisting of a married couple – from which the tax was collected. But this figure is particularly suspect. Presumably as a result of mass evasion, the number of Worcester people paying the tax – 849 – was scarcely more than half the total who paid the first poll tax of 1377 (PRO E179/144/6, printed in Barron 1989, 19–23; Hoskins 1959, 238). Nevertheless, even if the 1379 figures were to be doubled to bring them into line with the overall figure for 1377, they would still indicate a considerable reduction in the parish's population. By the sixteenth century there may have been a recovery to the level of the thirteenth century: in 1545 the taxpayers of St Peter's numbered 78, or 15 per cent of the total – 507 – for the city (PRO E179/200/162); in 1563 there were said to be 82 households here (Nash 1799, ii, appendix, cxvii). Given the uncertainty as to the number of parishioners who lived on Friar Street, perhaps all that can be concluded is that the medieval suburb may have reached its greatest extent in the thirteenth century, after which it went into decline; and that at no time during the middle ages would the population of the suburb have gone beyond a hundred households.

It is uncertain how far the suburb's development was affected by the strong ecclesiastical presence in Sidbury. Both the cathedral priory and St Wulfstan's Hospital owned numerous houses in St Peter's parish at the end of the middle ages: in the 1480s the hospital had some 33 houses in the Sidbury district (Marsh 1890, 111–14), whilst the 34 houses the priory held in the sixteenth century were perhaps distributed more evenly throughout the parish (Canterbury Cathedral Archives, Lit. Mss E29). It is not possible to say how many of these houses lay in Sidbury itself, although clearly the two institutions owned a significant proportion of the houses there. There is no indication either as to whether the priory had taken any active part in developing the Sidbury district, or if its properties there had been acquired at an early date, as and when they became available (see above, pp. 274–5); the substantial block of houses belonging to St Wulfstan's, on the other hand, seems more certainly to have originated with a policy of development. The concentration of many of the hospital's houses close to its own building, outside the Sidbury gate, is not matched by any indication that St Wulfstan's acquired property here in the decades after its refoundation in the early thirteenth century or, indeed, subsequently (*Cal. Charter Rolls 1232*, 172–3; Marsh 1890, *passim*; Holt, forthcoming). So it is likely that the concentration came about through the hospital having developed its own land – land it had been given early in its existence, presumably at its original foundation in the tenth century as St Gudwal's church. When suburban development began, however, and how far it was encouraged by St Gudwal's, are questions that remain unresolved.

The transpontine suburb

By 1100 there is evidence, in Hemming's list of properties belonging to the monks of the cathedral priory, of settlement beyond the Severn. Crucial to the chronology of the growth of this suburb must have been the existence of a bridge, and there is no earlier evidence for the Worcester bridge than 'Florence' of Worcester's reference to the city's defenders crossing it in 1088 to attack the rebels on the other side of the river (the statement that it had been repaired may imply age, or simply that the rebels had damaged it (Thorpe 1848–9, ii, 24–5). Details of the construction of its piers, however, as reported when it was demolished in 1781, suggest that it may have survived from the Roman period (Carver 1980, 20–1). The city church of St Clement, built apparently around the middle of the eleventh century, included the eastern part of the transpontine district within its parish; the furthest settlement in the suburb clustered around the church of St John in Bedwardine, and thus lay in a parish that was never part of the medieval city. For that reason, the St John's part of the suburb is scarcely documented – being excluded from the cathedral priory's city rentals, for instance, and from the Worcester lay subsidy returns – so that there is no indication as to how extensive settlement was in that quarter.

By contrast, some population data exist for that part of the suburb that lay within St Clement's. As the half of the parish which lay on the east bank of the Severn consisted of meadows and other non-urban land, information about the parish's taxpayers may be regarded as applying to the suburb alone. In 1275, there were 12 taxpayers here, or 4 per cent of the total for Worcester, but this was the poorest area of the city with its taxpayers paying less than a third of the city average. Perhaps, then, the named taxpayers may have represented rather less than the suggested proportion of 10 per cent of the local community (above), in which case the population of St Clement's in 1275 would have been considerably in excess of 120. Like Sidbury, however, St Clement's was apparently to lose a significant number of its parishioners by 1379. However distorted by evasion the poll tax return for that year might be, the meagre total of 29 men and women taxpayers recorded in St Clement's must point to a substantial reduction in the population of this suburb during the fourteenth century. But again, the sixteenth century saw a recovery: in 1545 there were only 29 recorded taxpayers although, as this was still the poorest district of Worcester (see below), the total of 55 households recorded in 1563 provides a more realistic measure of population. The large number of houses the cathedral priory owned here at the end of the middle ages (Canterbury Cathedral Archives, Lit. Mss E29; and see above, pp. 275–7) appears to have been accumulated as a result of the very cheapness of the property; there is no evidence that the priory had any significant holding here at a much earlier date, or took any part in the suburb's development.

The northern suburbs

The suburban development outside St Martin's Gate and along Silver Street and Lowesmoor, whilst topographically distinguishable, has left little trace in the records. There are no indications as to its extent or indeed its origins – unless the concentration of a dozen or more houses in Lowesmoor belonging to the Bishop of Worcester at the end of the thirteenth century (Hollings 1934, 6–13) is to be taken as a sign that the bishops had initiated the development here.

Far more important was the suburb that grew up outside the north gate, which was both the largest of the Worcester suburbs and the most regular in its plan. Topographically this was a classic linear development; in its origins it was evidently a suburb of the *burh* of the 890s, which subsequently was bisected by the later city defences – in place along the north side of Worcester by 1175 at the latest, when the parish boundary between the churches of All Saints and St Clement's must have been defined. Whilst not necessarily planned in a single phase, therefore, this suburb began as a development of the tenth century or of the eleventh at the latest. Responsibility for its planning lay apparently with the bishops of Worcester, who continued to own a considerable amount of the property here. In 1086 the Bishop of Worcester had 90 houses in the city belonging to his manor of Northwick, half of which were in his own demesne and half held by other lords (DB i, 173c); further details from about 1170 show that the Domesday Book account of the bishop's Worcester property is incomplete, having ignored 10 houses held of the manor of Wick, and 27 properties held of the bishop in burgage for rents totalling 26*s* 8*d* (Hollings 1934, 30–32, 37–8). The properties now held of Northwick included 43 held by other lords, and 55 separate holdings paying rent to the bishop; by the 1290s, all but half a dozen of the rents from free tenants had evidently been disposed of, leaving only the 55 holdings – consisting in all of 72 customary tenancies of messuages and curtilages (Hollings 1934, 6–13). Locations were now given for some, though not all, of these properties, revealing that an unknown number – but possibly as many as 50 – were in the suburbs: 12 in Lowesmoor, 13 in Foregate Street and 2 next to the Port Ditch along the north wall. A further 15 were just said to have been in the suburbs.

The emphasis on suburban property by the late thirteenth century was only in part the result of the shedding of rents of assize since 1170. The large number of properties that in 1086 had been held from the manor of Northwick, to the north of the city, suggests that this was more than just an administrative convenience: that already the major part of the bishops' Worcester houses were to be found here, as they certainly would be by the 1170s. That would lead to the conclusion that the bishops' suburban properties – particularly the concentrations to the north of the city – had come about through a conscious development of their own lands during the period before 1086.

Evidence from the immediate post-medieval period shows that the southern part of the north gate suburb, or Foregate Street, was distinct from the Tything to the north (fig. 6.4). Here, beyond the city's jurisdiction, had grown up a community which in the seventeenth century consisted largely of labourers and small craftsmen, with a significant element of poor immigrants and transients (Roy and Porter 1980, 203–17). Messuages in the Tything were more intensely subdivided than those in the Foregate, an indication both of greater density of settlement and of poverty. Unlike the Foregate, the Tything was not served by one of the city churches, but instead lay within the rural parish of Claines: until it fell into ruin in the sixteenth century, the chapel of St Oswald's Hospital which lay at the north end of the suburb was the inhabitants' customary place of worship (Roy and Porter 1980, 206). With St Wulfstan's Hospital and the nuns of the Priory of Whistones, St Oswald's held a portion of Claines (Caley 1810–34, iii, 234), and had evidently collected the tithes from the Tything. A census held in 1631 to establish the need of the

Tything's inhabitants for a new chapel counted 350 individuals living in 72 households (Roy and Porter 1980, 207), a surprisingly high number. Without medieval evidence for the Tything's population, it is impossible to say whether this was greater than the population in earlier centuries. But as it can be shown that the population of the rest of this suburb was growing in the sixteenth century, it is likely that at the same time the population of the Tything, too, exceeded its medieval level.

The population evidence for the southern half of the northern suburb, Foregate Street, comes from the same sources that supply data for the population of the other Worcester suburbs. The populated area of the parish of St Nicholas was made up of Foregate Street and the intramural district that had originated as suburban development outside the *burh*; and as the parish was taxed separately on several occasions its population can be estimated, and provides a guide to the fortunes of the extramural area. In 1275 there were 25 people who paid tax in St Nicholas's parish, or 8 per cent of the total for the city; as we have seen, this was unlikely to have been more than one-tenth of the parish's population at the time. In 1379, when the city's poll-tax payers were recorded as barely more than half the total of two years earlier, there were 57 taxpayers in St Nicholas's living in 26 households. Perhaps this total of taxpayers should be multiplied by four to reach anything like a realistic population figure of somewhere between 200 and 250 – giving a result not so dissimilar to the postulated total of a century before, when allowance is made for the crude and scarcely rational nature of these calculations and the uncertainties of the original sources. As the parish was divided approximately equally between its intramural and extramural areas, some half of this population may have been suburban.

By the middle of the sixteenth century, the northern suburb of Worcester had attracted a considerably larger population. As the city's population was to double between 1540 and 1640 (Dyer 1973, 26–7), every part of Worcester, presumably, was growing by this time; but expansion may have been more marked in the suburbs. With 158 households in the 1563 census, or 17 per cent of Worcester's total, St Nicholas's was now the most populous parish in the city (Nash 1799, ii, appendix, cxvii) – its prominence contrasting with its lack of importance in the thirteenth century. The ecclesiastical census was a very different exercise from the lay subsidy of 1275, when the concern had been to identify those citizens wealthy enough to be taxed; even so, when taken with the indications of expansion in the Tything, it is clear that the sixteenth century was seeing a genuine shift of focus in the city towards its northern suburb.

Gloucester and Worcester: the character of the suburbs

By its nature, suburban growth was peripheral to the established urban community – in a figurative as well as the literal sense. For whilst they grew up as newly settled districts beyond the walls that marked earlier town limits, the suburbs, with their cheaper housing, were generally sought out by those on the social fringes, the poorer and weaker inhabitants of the town (Keene 1990a, 115–16). In time, what had been the margin might be transformed into a new commercial centre, although this did not happen at either Worcester or Gloucester where all of the suburbs remained distinctively peripheral in character. Only Westgate Street between the bridges may have shed enough of its early marginal character to have appeared by the end of the middle ages to be as typical a town street as any in Gloucester, its residents working at a range of occupations, and paying rents that appear comparable with those charged for properties in the other town streets (*1455 Rental*, 52–6, 60–70; A13, fos 45v–48).

The variety of rents to be paid in Gloucester's southern suburb (A13, fos 2–17), and the evidence of the different lay subsidy returns, confirm that within each suburb there were marked social variations. To regard them all as no more than haunts of the poor, therefore, would be an oversimplification of their social structure. Nevertheless, some might have come close to having that character: the wholly suburban population of St Clement's was the poorest of any parish in Worcester in 1275, and by such a margin that it must have been a notable centre of poverty, even by comparison with the other suburbs. With a tax assessment of 1*s* 9*d* on average, its taxpayers – numbering no more than 12 – were far poorer than the 25 of St Nicholas's parish, each taxed on goods worth 3*s* 7*d* on average, and poorer even than the 39 taxpayers of St Peter's, taxed on their average wealth of 2*s* 7*d*. Evidently these two parishes, and particularly St Nicholas's, contained a wider social mix than did their transpontine counterpart. But the overall contrast between the suburban districts and the city is equally marked. Of the wholly intramural parishes, All Saints' was the poorest, but even so, its 64 taxpayers had goods worth on average 3*s* 6*d*; an average wealth of 5*s* 10*d* was recorded for St Andrew's, and the wealthy High Street parishes of St Helen's and St Swithun's contained 78 taxpayers worth on average 9*s* 11*d* (these details are presented in Table 13.1).

Table 13.1
Comparison of tax assessments in Worcester's parishes in 1275

Wards	Persons taxed	Tax assessment	% of city taxpayers	% of city assessment	Average assessment per person
St Clement	12	£1 1*s* 4*d*	4	1	1*s* 9*d*
St Nicholas	25	£4 10*s* 3*d*	8	5	3*s* 7*d*
St Peter	39	£5 3*s* 4*d*	12.5	6	2*s* 7*d*
St Martin	44	£13 11*s* 3*d*	14	15	6*s* 2*d*
St Andrew + St Alban	52	£15 3*s* 6*d*	16.5	17	5*s* 10*d*
All Saints	64	£11 3*s* 10*d*	20.5	12	3*s* 6*d*
High Ward (St Helen + St Swithun)	78	£39 10*s* 0*d*	25	44	9*s* 11*d*
	314	£90 3*s* 6*d*	100.5	100	5*s* 9*d* (city average)

For the most part, these patterns persisted through the middle ages. According to the subsidy return of 1545, when the average taxed individual wealth in Worcester was £7 12*s* 5*d*, in St Clement's it was £2 15*s* – again less than half the average for any other parish, suburban or intramural (PRO E179/200/162). But there was now no marked distinction between the wealth of the taxpayers of St Nicholas's, St Peter's, St Martin's and the wholly intramural St Andrew's, whose average assessment came in each case close to £6. The greatest contrast was now between these parishes and the central parishes of St Helen's, St Swithun's and All Saints', where the average assessment was close to £10 (these details are presented in Table 13.2).

Table 13.2
Comparison of tax assessments in Worcester's parishes in 1545

Wards	Persons taxed	Assessed wealth	% of city taxpayers	% of city assessment	Average wealth per person
St Clement	29	£81	6	2	£2 15s 10d
St Nicholas	55	£331	11	9	£6 0s 4d
St Peter	78	£464	15	12	£5 19s 0d
St Martin	79	£457	16	12	£5 15s 8d
St Andrew + St Alban	50	£346	10	9	£6 18s 5d
All Saints	121	£1259	24	33	£10 8s 0d
High Ward	95	£925	19	24	£9 14s 9d
	507	£3863	101	101	£7 12s 5d (city average)

The relative poverty of the Worcester suburbs, therefore, is not in doubt; nor is there any reason to suppose that the Gloucester suburbs were any less disadvantaged by comparison with the central districts. In the case of Gloucester, the evidence of rentals – although limited in scope – provides for two of the suburbs information not to be had from taxation data: for that part of the northern suburb that belonged to St Oswald's Priory, and more especially for Lanthony Priory's suburb outside the south gate. In the 1530s, St Oswald's had 51 houses here (PRO SC6 Hen. VIII 1212, mm. 5, 6), leased for terms of years or rented out at will: 16 were clearly poor dwellings, described as cottages and let for an average rent of 3s 3d. But if the houses described as tenements were clearly superior, that was only in relative terms: there were 35 of them, 28 in Watering Street where the greatest concentration of the priory's Gloucester property was to be found. These 28 were let for an average rent of 6s 2d, less than one-third of the rent generally prevailing within the walls during the later middle ages (see below).

There is more extensive evidence for the suburb outside Gloucester's south gate. As virtually all of the houses in the southern suburb belonged to Lanthony, the character of the whole suburb can be deduced from what is known about the priory's houses. Of the 76 houses belonging to Lanthony in c. 1445 or from which the priory drew a rent, 54 were described as tenements and 22 as cottages (A13, fos 2v–17, from which the following details are taken). The distinction was a real one, judging by the levels of rent that were paid for those held by lease or at will: tenements were rented in one or two cases for a pound or more, whilst the most expensive cottage was 4s and the cheapest 2s 6d. There was a clear social zoning in the suburb between the better houses along Sudbroke Street and Lower Southgate Street – all of which were described as tenements – and the poorer dwellings particularly along Severn Street and Small Lane, where all of the 22 cottages were to be found in the fifteenth century. Significantly, the 18 tenements here were let for rents almost as low as those of the cottages: their rents ranged between 3s and 12s, and averaged only 6s, compared with an average of 8s 6d for the tenements on the main road. They thus fell mid-way in quality between these better tenements and the cottages, which were rented for an average of 3s 7d.

Even the better tenements, however, were worth far less than the houses within the walls. Rental values increased dramatically towards the centre of the town, with houses at the lower end of Southgate Street rather more expensive than the suburban houses, and those near the High Cross worth at least a pound a year and usually much more. Moreover, many of these town-centre properties were very small, offering little more than a shop and one or two cramped upper rooms (Holt 1987, 54–60). What made them so desirable was their location in the prime retail quarter of Gloucester: craftsmen selling directly to the public, and those providing a service – such as cooks with their takeaway shops selling hot food – needed to congregate along the streets their customers frequented. Evidently the economy of the southern suburb was very different. The suburban population obviously felt it unnecessary to pay the high rents demanded for the better commercial premises, or in many cases were unable to do so. Only ten tenants were identified by occupation in 1445, but they consisted of three corvisers or shoemakers, three weavers, two glaziers, a carpenter and a brewer. With the possible exception of the shoemakers, none of these sold a product retail from their houses; brewers sold to tapsters or alewives, the weavers supplied the merchant drapers and dyers who controlled clothmaking in every town, and the other three were building workers who would have worked away from their homes. Other evidence suggests that bakers were to be found here. Before 1143, land that was evidently next to the church of St Owen had been held by one Sawin the baker (Walker 1964, 11), and during the reign of Henry III a baker called Adam Bromere had a lease on the tenement which stood on the northern corner of Lower Southgate Street and St Owen's Lane (A5, fo. 13; A13 fo. 11). His contemporary and neighbour was Margery the baker (A13, fo. 11v), who was also named in the abbey's records as the tenant of the same house, backing onto the cemetery of St Owen's, between 1263 and 1284 (*Hist. et Cart.*, ii, 241; A13 fos 11v–12).

Of the fifty tenants of Lanthony's houses in *c.* 1445 who were named, nine were women – presumably widows. Without landed wealth to sustain them, they would have made a living in the traditional ways open to urban women: as hucksters or petty retailers, as brewers or as alewives retailing ale purchased from the common brewers, or by letting cheap lodgings, or by prostitution (Hilton 1985, 205–15; Hilton 1990, 71–96).

Conclusion

In both Worcester and Gloucester, ecclesiastical institutions were closely involved in suburban development. The classic linear form of the Foregate Street and Tything suburb of Worcester can be attributed to episcopal enterprise of the tenth, or more probably the eleventh, century; the similarly distinctive Barton Street to the east of Gloucester may have originated with an act of planning by St Peter's Abbey – although the presence here of properties paying their landgable to the Crown suggests some degree of secular co-operation. Part of the northern suburb at Gloucester lay within the parish of St Oswald's, on land that had belonged to the priory or to the New Minster, and which it had developed; the southern suburb had been Lanthony Priory's since 1136, although it began as a secular estate before that date.

Elsewhere the ecclesiastical presence in the suburbs was late and opportunist. The concentration of houses the cathedral priory owned in St Clement's parish in the sixteenth century came about through a policy of acquisition of cheap housing, and implies no initial involvement in laying out previously agricultural land as house-plots to encourage settlement. Its holding in the Sidbury district, too, seems to have been the result of no more than a preference for suburban rents. But perhaps the suburb had seen an element of ecclesiastical planning during an earlier period: St Wulfstan's Hospital – or more properly St Gudwal's, its predecessor – may have developed its original precinct for housing.

Other planned suburbs were emphatically the result of lay initiative. Most of the plots along both sides of Lower Northgate Street, between the north gates, paid landgable to the bailiffs, suggesting that the secular authorities of the town had encouraged and planned the extent of this suburban development. Similarly, the houses on Westgate Street, with scarcely an exception, paid landgable to the fifteenth-century Gloucester bailiffs, as they had done certainly since the early thirteenth century and, by inference, since these properties had been newly laid-out – perhaps by the mid twelfth century. The twelfth-century constables of Gloucester, Walter and his successors, would thus seem to have been responsible for the orderly nature of this colonization of the land beyond the Foreign Bridge. The implied association between the foundation both of the church of St Nicholas and St Bartholomew's Hospital and the building of the Westgate Bridge during the early part of the twelfth century may indicate a context for the planning of the suburb.

The different Church institutions, therefore, did not play any distinctive role in the suburban growth of either Worcester or Gloucester. Certain of the suburbs were developed by the Church, because the extramural land belonged to bishop, abbey or priory; where it belonged to laymen, suburbs grew up in the same way. The impression that the Church made a special contribution to the medieval town-plan by encouraging suburban growth stems from nothing more profound than the fact that Church institutions frequently held extramural land.

Note
The account of the 1377 poll tax entered at the exchequer recorded 1557 taxpayers for the city of Worcester (Dobson 1983, 57), a figure that may include those living in the cathedral precinct (St Michael's parish) which was technically distinct from the city. The flat rate tax of 4*d* was collected from everyone over 14, except presumably the indigent, and allowing for a degree of evasion the figure probably needs to be doubled to provide a realistic population estimate (Palliser 1988, 9; Postan 1966, 562). By this reckoning, Worcester's population in 1377 stood at 3114. There is also a fragmentary list of Worcester citizens who paid the 1381 poll tax, 932 in all according to the total at the foot of the roll, although fewer than half that total of names remain (Dobson 1983, 57; Barron 1989, 1–2). A further, undamaged, roll provides data of a higher quality, whilst presenting some minor problems of dating. Listing a total of 845 inhabitants of Worcester – including unnamed wives – with only a few names illegible, but carrying no heading other than a faint rendering of *Wyg'* for Worcester, it has in the past been attributed to London. In fact its Worcester provenance is demonstrated both by the close similarity between these names and those of the 1381 list, and because the names are enrolled parish by parish – the parishes in question being the ten parishes of Worcester, including St Michael's (Barron 1989, 2).

Both this roll and that from 1381 were the subject of an important and scholarly article by Caroline Barron (1989), analysing the economic and social profiles of the Worcester parishes. The article may be deficient in one detail, which has a bearing on our appreciation of the proportion of Worcester's population dwelling in the suburbs. Professor Barron believed that the undated roll recorded the names of the taxpayers in 1377; that the 845 named taxpayers were those from the intramural part of the city, and that the missing 712 taxpayers – 46 per cent of the recorded total of 1557 – must have been extramural residents (ibid., 5). It was because the roll contained no occupational designations, and gave no details of the tax paid, that Barron was convinced that here was a list of the flat-rate taxpayers of 1377 (ibid., 2). But her conclusion seems to be incorrect. The inclusion of the parish of St Michael means that areas outside the bailiffs' jurisdiction were entered onto the undated roll; more importantly, the inclusion of the wholly extramural St Clement's parish must invalidate the argument that the suburban population are missing from the roll. Even if the people of the remaining suburbs, in the parishes of St Peter, St Nicholas and St Martin, were indeed not listed with the residents of the intramural parts of these parishes, it is most unlikely that they could have amounted to 46 per cent of Worcester's total population as Barron said they did – a figure at which she herself confessed surprise (ibid., 3–5).

If this roll was compiled in connection with the 1377 poll tax, therefore, it is not clear on what basis these 845 people were named, and 712 others excluded. No firm evidence connects it with the 1377 assessment rather than with any other; might it not, then, have been compiled at the time of the collection of one of the two later poll taxes? As Barron was able to show that there were significant differences between this and the 1381 roll (ibid., 5–7), that date can safely be ruled out. She seems not, however, to have considered whether this might be a list of taxpayers compiled in 1379. The inconsistencies she identified between this list and the 1377 returns from other towns, and which she attributed as possibly due to the absence – as she saw it – of the suburban population (ibid., 16), would certainly be more easily explained if this was a list compiled at a different time and under different circumstances. In 1379 the tax was a graduated one, with widely varying rates laid down for a range of estates; in Worcester, apart from any men adjudged to be 'sufficient merchants', 'lesser merchants' or hostelers, most people would have paid the 4*d* rate stipulated for married men, their wives and single people (Dobson 1983, 105–11). The higher age at which the tax was charged – 16 years – might alone account for some of the oddities that Barron remarked upon, such as the virtual absence of young people living with their parents, and the unusually low proportion of single adults in the population when compared with figures for other towns in 1377. In that year the single adults who were taxed included all those aged 14 and above, and for that reason should be a more prominent sector of the population; one might expect, as well, that more of them would have been recorded as still living with their parents. To add to the discrepancies between the data from this roll and that from the surviving 1377 rolls, a greater degree of evasion of the tax is likely to have occurred in 1379, as occurred generally in 1381 (Dobson 1983, 54).

In provisionally assigning this roll to 1379, it is recognized that two important questions remain unanswered. Firstly, can evasion in 1379 really have been so severe that the total number of people taxed, at 845, was actually lower than the figure for 1381? In that year, when the collection of the poll tax in much of England was disrupted by disturbances connected with the English Rising, and when evasion was apparently rife, there were 932 recorded taxpayers in Worcester. And second, why were no tax assessments entered onto a roll that was sent to the exchequer? Even if most people would have paid at the basic rate, there were others who should not have: the draper Rober Stevenys and the butcher Robert Baret, for example, who each paid 7*s* in 1381, were recorded as taxpayers in the earlier roll (Barron 1989, 27, 28). This would seem not to have been intended as a final account roll, but perhaps as a list of all those liable for poll tax, the individual assessments to be submitted separately. Nevertheless, the attribution to 1379 seems to be more satisfactory than an attribution to either 1377 or 1381.

Chapter 14

The Church, town-planning and public works

The planning of English medieval new towns has received much scholarly attention over the last thirty years from historians, geographers and archaeologists. Professor Beresford set the agenda for the study of post-Conquest town-founding with *New Towns of the Middle Ages* (1967). M.R.G. Conzen's work on Ludlow and Conway (1968, 1988) revealed hidden chronologies within towns previously considered to have been simple single-phase plantations, and T.R. Slater's research has explored the ideals and working methods of post-Conquest town-planners and the way in which they adapted the layout of new-town foundations to the topographical constraints of their sites (e.g. Slater 1987, 1988). Martin Biddle and David Hill's article 'Late Saxon planned towns' (1971) laid the foundations for the study of town-founding in the pre-Conquest period, to be followed by Phillip Crummy's (1979) metrological analysis of a number of late-Saxon town-plans, and numerous studies of individual towns, of which the collection gathered together by Jeremy Haslam (1984) remains one of the most useful. Much of this body of work has direct relevance to Gloucester and Worcester in the pre-Conquest period and the provision of regulated frameworks for settlement in each; neither, however, was ever – fully – what we would call a 'planned' new town.

The greater part of the identifiable late-medieval town-plans of Gloucester and Worcester was formed by a long process of sequential outward extension. Analysis of each town-plan has identified a number of distinct component areas or zones, some of which appear to be the result of distinct, discrete episodes of urban growth. In many cases the physical characteristics of particular areas have been interpreted as evidence of 'town-planning': in other words, either or both of the preparation and organization of land for urban settlement. But in the urban extensions identified in these towns, there was rarely the scope or the necessity for the provision of the full range of features or facilities usually taken to be indicative of 'planned' urban settlement. Organized urban extension appears to have assumed many different forms, representing very different degrees of investment in and regulation of the process of growth. In order to recognize and quantify the role of Church institutions in the physical growth of Gloucester and Worcester, the degree to which their growth was designed – or 'devised, ordered, and arrayed' as Edward I would have put it – must itself be quantified (Beresford 1967, 14). How 'planned' were they?

Defining town-planning

In the absence of documentary evidence for the foundation or plantation of a new town (or the extension of an old one), deliberate foundation is most commonly interpreted from the presence of certain physical characteristics, foremost among which is, of course, the rectilinear street-grid or 'chequerboard' arrangement. But Beresford and subsequent writers have appreciated that the process of medieval town-founding involved a range of activities far more diverse, and possibly much more expensive, than the deployment of a small number of clerks or *locatores* armed, as we know from their accounts, with a length of rope and pegs, and a knowledge of elementary geometry. Beresford, for example, noted that the principal expenditure on Edward I's new foundation at Rhuddlan was on the wages of ditch-diggers and carpenters working on the defences (1967,

37). Where the defences were built in stone, costs soared accordingly. He went on to list the range of civil engineering work that might be commissioned by a town-founder to prepare the site for a new venture, to ensure its economic viability and to attract prospective settlers: the construction of new bridges and causeways, the diversion of access roads, the widening of streets to form markets, the improvement of river navigation, the founding of new churches and the provision of facilities such as quays, toll-houses, bake-houses, prisons, wells and mills (Beresford 1967, 169, 175–7).

Such civil engineering and building projects are generally noted in association with town-founding in the high middle ages but some were equally applicable in the late ninth and tenth centuries. The provision of new streets would usually have entailed the laying of metalled surfaces, making heavy demands on labour and transport. Martin Biddle has calculated that the creation of the new street-system in Winchester in *c.* 880–6 would have required the transportation and laying of nearly 8,000 tons of flint cobbles (Biddle 1976, 450). The new *burh* at Gloucester, and that at Worcester, was conceived on a much smaller scale (see fig. 14.5), though the construction or renovation of defences and the provision of new streets may nevertheless have made demands on manpower, transport, materials and organizational skills that were without local precedent. Manpower and transport may have been extracted from the local community and landowners as a common obligation (Stenton 1971, 291–2).

Beresford also recognized the existence of much less ambitious town-founding activities than those represented by fully gridded plans preceded and supported by a complex infrastructure. He noted the widespread existence of the 'market based' plan, simply composed with plot-series surrounding marketplaces of various shapes (1967, 155–6). Preparatory work in such cases could involve the diversion of roads to a new market site, or the widening of an existing road, or nothing more than the provision of a back lane behind the burgages. 'Town-planning' – at this reduced scale – was not only applied to the founding of minor market towns, it was, as we shall see, equally relevant to the extension of old towns.

Obviously, then, to be able to recognize and quantify instances of institutionally promoted urban development or town-planning in Gloucester and Worcester, we need to define with some precision what range of attributes indicative of a 'planned' origin are present in any particular area. It would be misleading to search only for areas displaying the full repertoire of planned characteristics – street-grids, metrological regularity of plots and so on – as to do so would be to ignore the possibility of smaller-scale organized urban extensions, perhaps disclosed by little more than the provision of a back lane to a series of plots.

Given that, in some instances, the commitment of resources required in the preparation of a site – for groundworks and associated construction projects – will have been far greater than those required to create a geometrically regular framework for settlement, such activities (where they can be detected) must be taken fully into account. To a degree, such an exercise is bound to be flawed at the outset by the limited extent of the available archaeological data, usually the only source able to comment on, for example, large-scale earth-moving episodes. But there seems no alternative. It would also be misleading to concentrate solely on a search for geometrically regular plan-forms. Rectilinearity (often invoked in support of a 'planned' origin for urban landscapes) has, for example, little or no meaning in medieval Gloucester, where the inherited rectilinear pattern of Roman walls, gates and streets conditioned the morphology of nearly all subsequent developments. Analysis of urban landscapes elsewhere also suggests that evidence of a 'planned' origin may occur in superficially unpromising contexts, as in early medieval Shrewsbury where plots of highly 'irregular' form were found to have metrologically regulated frontages and to have achieved a rational apportionment of scarce environmental resources (Baker, Lawson, Maxwell and Smith 1993).

It is also true that in assessing the contemporary significance of an urban extension, the importance even of metrological regularity may easily be over-emphasized. Such an attribute need not have been the sole preserve of kings or bishops – 'higher-order decision making' (Slater 1989) – it might have been achievable by any individual or community with access to the range of basic mathematical skills commonly employed in, for example, the division of agricultural holdings or setting out the foundations for a parish church. The twentieth-century example of illegal urban extensions (*barriadas*), in places as diverse as Athens and Peru, laid out with immaculately regular grid-plans by the first title-less squatters, offers a useful reminder of the socially diverse levels at which urban society may order its affairs spatially (Mangin and Turner, 1969; Romanos 1969).

Town-planning and public works in Gloucester and Worcester: the foundation of the *burhs*

There is no doubt that Gloucester was a *burh* by 914 at the very latest; its surviving Roman fortress walls had apparently been refurbished in the 880s. So far, however, physical evidence for the repair of the walls and gates, or for the recutting of the ditches, is absent.

Within the restored fortress, new streets were laid out to a rectilinear plan that covered some 17.5 acres (*c*.7.1 hectares), about half of the area available. The street system was based on surviving Roman streets: the north–south axis (Northgate and Southgate Streets) and the Roman predecessor to Eastgate Street. From this base a series of minor lanes were laid out at intervals along the north–south axis of either 4, 8 or 16 statute perches; the measurement of the northernmost block seems to have corresponded to 10 perches, an irregular element fitted into the Roman *enceinte*, in a system that otherwise appears to represent another example of planning based on the four-perch module detected in Winchester, Colchester and London by Crummy (1979). Though the metrology as well as the morphology of the minor lanes suggests that they were conceived as a single system, archaeological dating evidence cannot yet point to any lane metalling that need be earlier in date than the eleventh century – perhaps only the main streets were originally metalled. None of the property boundaries recorded in this area of Gloucester in the nineteenth century appear to fit within this metrological scheme, and they presumably represent later sub-divisions. In terms of its general layout, as well as its metrology, the Gloucester street-system resembles that at Winchester more closely than any of the other disparate if generally rectilinear street-systems attributed by Biddle and Hill (1971) to Alfredian-period planning.

The identification of a single street of primary importance is not so easily made in Gloucester as in Worcester, but it can be argued that the north–south axis of Northgate Street and Southgate Street first served this function. The distribution of pre-Conquest churches is more heavily weighted towards the north–south axis than to the Westgate Street–Eastgate Street axis. The relative width of Gloucester's main streets may also be significant: the maximum width of the north–south axis (*c*.59 feet/18 metres across Southgate Street) was about two metres wider than that of Westgate Street, the principal street of the later medieval town, and Northgate and Southgate Streets narrowed appreciably as they approached the central Cross. The implication appears to be that the north–south streets were originally laid out to a greater width than the others, that they formed the principal market street, and were affected more seriously by encroachment before frontage-lines were finally established. The width-range of the north–south street corresponds fairly closely with that of the High Street in Winchester (10–18 metres in Gloucester, *c*.9–16 metres plus, in Winchester), and contrasts greatly with the 6.4 metre width of the Roman predecessor to Westgate

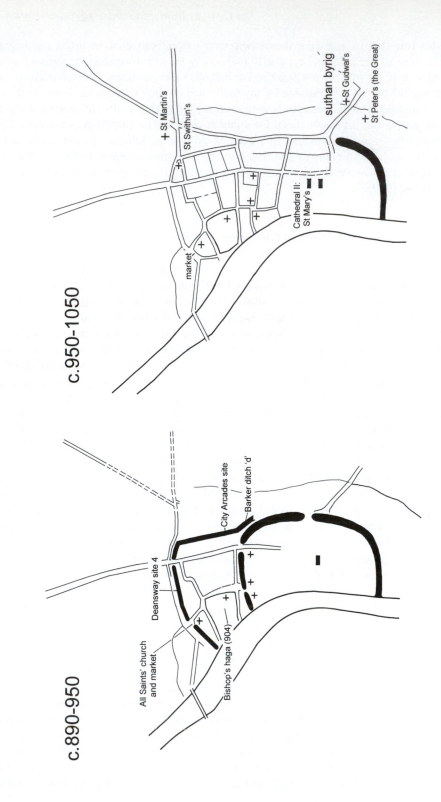

14.1 The Worcester *burh*: a schematic reconstruction

Street (Heighway *et al.* 1979); Roman and Anglo-Saxon planners evidently had very different functions in mind for their main streets.

At Worcester, the charter of 889–899 refers to the city's contemporary fortification. Defences of post-Roman, pre-medieval date have now been found by excavation in two places. One of these is consistent with contemporary documentary evidence for the location of the 'north wall' of the *burh* in 904; the other makes perfect sense as part of the eastern perimeter, and the two are linked by disparate archaeological observations and a convincing topographical framework. The defences consisted of a ditch, and a rampart revetted (from the beginning) with a mortared limestone rubble wall about 1.2 metres thick, probably supported at intervals by vertical timber posts. The limestone used to build the wall was salvaged from the footings of former Roman buildings in the interior of the newly defended area, and perhaps further afield (hardly any Roman masonry superstructures are known from the wide area of the former Roman town), and implies a clearance and recycling operation on a very substantial scale.

The *burh* at Worcester added an enclosure of about 17 acres (6.9 hectares) to the existing Roman earthworks surrounding the cathedral and the other churches; the old defences were presumably restored and strengthened at the same time. The newly defended area appears to have been divided between a riverside zone dominated by a single, substantial, high-status property, and the High Street – the market street or *ceapstowe*. But in complete contrast to Gloucester – and contrary to previously published accounts of the city (e.g. Baker *et al.* 1992) – the creation of the *burh* at Worcester does not seem to have been accompanied by the provision of a planned internal street-system. Though some kind of ordered division of space along the pre-existing but newly defended market street is certainly possible, it cannot yet be demonstrated in this phase, and a new street-system was definitely not yet on the episcopal agenda.

But this is not to say that the *burh* was without, or was not intended to accommodate, a permanent population. The charter of 889–899 explicitly states that the *burh* was founded to provide protection 'for all the people'. But who were these people? Were they, as Nicholas Brooks has asked, the inhabitants of the new borough, or of 'the burghal territory that was to become Worcestershire' (Brooks 1996, 143)? The answer may well be both. Borough-dwellers were certainly expected or already present, as the charter specifies payments that were to be extracted from properties on streets within and without the walls: *landfeoh* (the equivalent of the later chief rent or landgable), and payments for the maintenance of the defences. In Gloucester we cannot yet identify or map any properties or plots originating in the earliest years of the *burh* there; in Worcester the only plot that can be located and mapped is the *haga* on the Severn waterfront that Bishop Wærferth granted to Ealdorman Æthelred and Æthelflæd in 904.

In Gloucester, it is reasonable to say that (to quote Martin Biddle) the new street-system 'not only organized the interior space in relation to the defences, but also reflects the division and apportionment of the area for permanent settlement' (1983, 123). However, the relationship between military requirements and the internal arrangement of the new *burhs* should not be over emphasized. A wall-street or intramural street running along the inside of the defences to permit rapid movement of the garrison around the perimeter was identified as part of the primary layout in Winchester, and has been perceived as one of the defining features of the 'Alfredian' planned *burhs* (Biddle and Hill 1971, 76). But in Gloucester there was no wall-street. None was found inside the western defences on the Berkeley Street excavations; and inside the northern defences, the first metalling of the intramural street (St Aldate's Street) was of eleventh-century date – though Hurst was led to postulate unmetalled intervallum 'areas' (Hurst 1986, 129). Intramural zones kept clear of obstructions have, however, been suggested elsewhere. Within the western section of the London city wall was a pit- free zone; there may have been one within the riverside wall, but there was no pre-Conquest wall-street (Vince 1990, 87–9). In Cricklade there was a wall-street within the defences, and there was an additional clear strip bounded by stones that may have marked the 'official' extent of the defences and defined a limit to building in proximity to them (Haslam 1984, 109). In Worcester, excavation within the northern defences found no evidence of a street or contemporary metalling but, just to the west, the recorded boundary measurements of the episcopal *haga* in 904 suggest that there too was a strip of land immediately within the *burh* rampart (north of Grope Lane) that was considered to be part of the defences and not part of the conveyed property (fig. 6.13).

Finally, one aspect of the planning of the *burhs* remains to be commented upon: the question of associated public works taking place outside the defended areas, specifically bridge-building. A close association between *burhs* and bridges has been appreciated for some time (Brooks 1979), and it is possible that the foundation of the *burhs* in Gloucester and Worcester was accompanied by the building or rebuilding of bridges over the Severn and the provision of whatever causeways were necessary on the approaches. It might reasonably be assumed that military and commercial considerations would have made bridges essential: that neither town could have been left cut off from the west bank of the Severn for several weeks in each year, and that neither town would have neglected the opportunity to control river traffic – whether hostile or commercial – that a defended bridge would have afforded. There is, though, no unambiguous evidence from either place. That Worcester did have a bridge before the Conquest is evident or probable from the account of its repair in 1088; it is also the case that the street-system shows that a river crossing on the site of the medieval bridge was in use while the *burh* defences were either still in use or remained influential in the landscape. But these difficulties are not particular to Worcester or Gloucester. Lack of archaeological evidence for the development of the river crossings impedes research equally in Roman Wroxeter and medieval Shrewsbury: it is a general problem for the Severn valley (see Baker, forthcoming).

The *burhs*: extramural and post-mural growth

Plotting the growth and change of the two *burhs* from their foundation up to the Norman Conquest is a difficult process, bedevilled as it is by the problem of establishing fixed chronologies. The problem is most acute where dating is solely dependent on archaeological ceramics. If (to take an example now common throughout the region) Stafford-type ware is the only pre-Conquest pottery present, we may have to resign ourselves to being unable to distinguish between events taking place in the early ninth and early eleventh centuries (Ford 1995, 29). Relative chronologies too are problematic, though there are a number of instances where physical superimposition shows quite conclusively that some episodes of urban growth must have post-dated the disuse, and in some instances the deliberate dismantling, of *burh* defences. And it is these episodes where the hand of the Church, and other institutional agencies, is most clearly apparent.

Post-mural redevelopment (fig. 14.5)

This is a term we have coined to describe episodes where urban development was achieved by the deliberate removal of defensive structures. There are examples from both Worcester and Gloucester of the disappearance of archaeologically attested defences without leaving any trace above ground, and overlying their known course are urban landscapes showing signs of organized or planned origins. While the possibility of extended chronologies cannot be ruled out (where there was a significant hiatus between getting rid of part of an old defended perimeter and building over it), in each case it seems more probable that redundant defences were levelled as the first stage – the groundworks – in the preparation of an area for organized urban settlement within a planned framework. In several cases it appears that these episodes not only served the needs of enlarged urban communities, but that they also reformed, or at least re-organized, ecclesiastical communities.

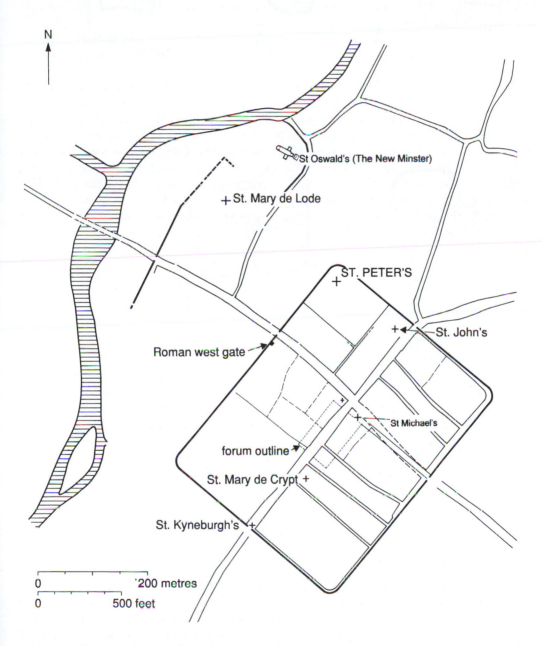

N

St Oswald's (The New Minster)

+ St. Mary de Lode

ST. PETER'S
+

+ — St. John's

Roman west gate

+
+ — St Michael's

forum outline

St. Mary de Crypt +

St. Kyneburgh's +

0   200 metres

0   500 feet

14.2   The Gloucester *burh*: a schematic reconstruction

HEREFORD

BATH

OXFORD

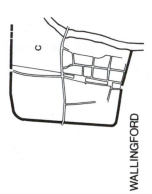

WORCESTER

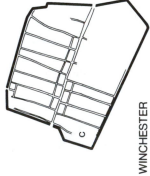

WALLINGFORD

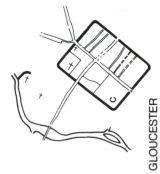

GLOUCESTER

WINCHESTER

c castle

0   1000 metres

14.3   Comparative plans: Worcester, Gloucester, and other western English *burhs*

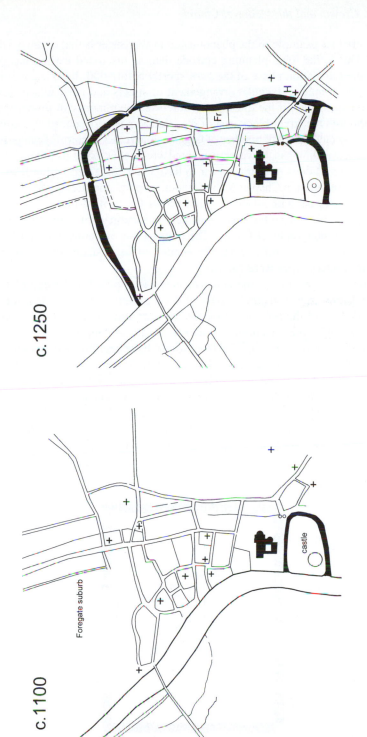

c.1250

c.1100

Foregate suburb

castle

14.4 Worcester: the early Norman city, and the newly-defended medieval city

The most obvious example of the phenomenon in Worcester is that of the northern half of the High Street. This is the town-planning episode that, as discussed earlier, has previously been attributed to the foundation phase of the *burh* shortly before 900. Its existence and integrity are fairly clear – the simple rectangular arrangement of streets and particular property boundaries are an outstanding feature of the town-plan. Moreover, the minority of property boundaries that run straight through the street-block east of the High Street were spaced at regular intervals and appear to have bounded a small number of large (*c.* ¾ acre/0.3 hectare) rectangular plots. Recent archaeological excavation has, however, prompted a re-evaluation of its relationship with the pre-Conquest defences. It does not now appear to have been contained within them, but instead to overlay them. As reported in Chapter 6, the component parts, the streets and property boundaries, of the planned area pass without interruption across the infilled ditch. The latter, though it is wide and deep and must have been accompanied by a rampart of similar dimensions, does not exist in relief as a topographical feature. The rampart has evidently been pushed back into the ditch, which moreover was infilled rapidly enough to be virtually filled up before eleventh–twelfth-century pottery types were current.

The organized demolition of the defences here (as opposed to *ad hoc* plot-by-plot action) cannot yet be demonstrated on purely archaeological grounds – the sample is too small – though the short chronology of the infilling of the ditch points strongly in this direction. But episcopal and royal interest in Worcester's principal market street is undoubted, and the improvement of it, or at least the properties on its east frontage, would have been to their advantage. The primary plots of the newly planned area were clearly different in function and in status from the narrower, more irregular strip-plots or burgages into which they were partitioned in later centuries. They seem rather to be the equivalent of the *hagas* of the documentary evidence – apparent first in Worcester in 904 with the lease of the bishop's riverside property to the Mercian royal house, and later in the tenth century in the leases of rural property with appurtenant urban *hagas* to Bishop Oswald's retainers and household. The care taken in the equal apportionment of the market-street

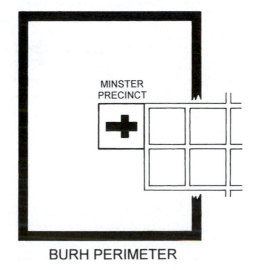

14.5   A model of post-mural redevelopment in minster towns

frontage between these large tenements seems to reflect an expectation that their tenants would exploit the frontage commercially.

The north side of the Roman earthwork defences surrounding the cathedral has similarly left little trace in the historic landscape, arguably a result of their having been deliberately levelled over a short period of time (see above, pp. 160–61). Such an operation would have required a substantial workforce, involving the filling of a ditch about 90 feet wide and 20 feet deep (*c.* 27.4 x 6.1 metres), presumably with material derived from the levelling of its rampart, along a perimeter up to *c.*500 metres long. The total volume of earth that had to be moved can be calculated to have been somewhere in the region of 41,000 cubic metres – about half the volume of material required to metal Winchester's streets, but without the same transport requirements. The only likely rationale for works on such a scale is that the land was required for some other purpose, and the presence (overlying the flattened earthworks) of urban landscape with signs of regular planning is surely more than mere coincidence.

West of the High Street, an area of about 6 acres (2.4 hectares) was occupied by a simple street-grid of three, possibly four, east–west streets spaced at regular intervals (*c.*240 feet/74 metres) along the High Street; the streets converged slightly towards the west in conformity with the local natural topography (fig. 6.15). Copenhagen Street (Huckster or Cooken Street), the route between the High Street and the Severn waterfront, was probably the principal street. Plots recorded much later in this area generally ran north–south from one street frontage to another.

The southernmost street of this grid was Palace Yard. This street was continued east of the High Street by Lich Street, which also quite clearly overlay the infilled Roman ditch and its levelled rampart (see fig. 6.15). North of Lich Street was a street-block containing a plot-pattern with some signs of symmetry in its plan (plots of equal depth terminating at a north–south back-fence line in the centre of the street-block), but again showing not the slightest evidence of any lingering influence, distortion or deflection, that might have arisen from the slow decay of the substantial earthwork defences. This area covered *c.* 4 acres (*c.* 1.6 hectares). The common southern boundary to these two areas, Palace Yard and Lich Street, also formed the northern boundary of the medieval cathedral close. On its east side too, the cathedral close boundary followed the outline of a street-block that reproduced the dimensions of the eastern plot-series on the east side of the High Street, and replaced the old Roman defences and the postulated eastern gate.

On present evidence it appears that the cathedral's surroundings were replanned and provision made for new urban settlement, in place of the old defences following their very deliberate and costly levelling. The question that now arises is that of chronology. Stratigraphically, the events described are post-Roman and pre-Conquest. Given the location of these phenomena between the *burh* and the cathedral, and their extent, they must have taken place at a fairly early stage in the development of the medieval built-up area. Julia Barrow has suggested that they were most probably linked with a re-organization of the Worcester cathedral precinct and the building of the cathedral church of St Mary by Bishop Oswald in the 960s–980s (Barrow 1996, 90). Though this conclusion is inevitably very tentative, Oswald's episcopate was generally coincident with a period of relative political and economic stability that might be considered to have provided a plausible context for such a process. And it is also true that elsewhere a close association is often observable between the reform and rebuilding of monastic communities and the re-organization of their estates – including their urban foundations (Slater 1998).

Aside from the question of absolute chronology, there is the problem of relative chronology and the way in which Worcester was developing – or was developed – in the late-pre-Conquest period. There seems at the moment no way of determining the order in which these town-planning events occurred. If military considerations were paramount, it would be logical to assume that the north side of the Roman enclosure was redeveloped first as it lay within the protection of the *burh* perimeter. If economic considerations were what mattered most, then the east side of the High Street could have been seen as an obvious priority. To complicate matters further there is the question of suburban, extramural, development happening at the same sort of time: this will be considered below.

Comparable events helped transform the *burh* at Gloucester. A probable post-mural development episode may be discerned in the wedge-shaped block of land lying between Westgate Street and the precinct of St Peter's Abbey, the Old Minster. The area is bisected by the course of the west wall of the Roman fortress but, as in the abbey precinct itself, its course is not reflected in the recorded or surviving topography. The date at which the Roman wall was demolished and the precinct extended over it is not certain, though it was most probably before the Conquest and possibly in the late tenth century: archaeological evidence from sites to the west and south suggest that this was also when Westgate Street was being built up. The southern precinct boundary was separated from the rear of the plots facing Westgate Street by a narrow lane, known as King Edward Street by the nineteenth century. This lane was not itself part of the precinct, and may best be explained as a service lane associated with the provision of a series of new plots on Westgate Street, covering an area of about 3 acres (*c.* 1.2 hectares). The lane was also laid out at an early date: a small excavation found tenth- to early-eleventh-century pottery on its lowest metalled surface, and the lane was remetalled on four further occasions before the first stone wall was built along the precinct boundary, possibly as early as the first decade of the twelfth century.

Once again there is no guarantee that the demolition of the Roman defences both inside the abbey precinct and outside, and the creation of a new plot-series serviced by a back lane, were simultaneous events; an extended or more complex chronology cannot be ruled out. But the systematic levelling of the Roman defences must – as in Worcester – have been no casual undertaking, particularly if it is assumed that the wall would have been restored at the foundation of the *burh* and had not yet been significantly damaged by robbing: its demolition is most likely to have been a prelude to other necessary activities. The presence of a back lane to a series of plots is, as discussed already, a widely paralleled indicator of planned provision for urban settlement. The dating of the back lane (though still tentative) is consistent with its having been laid out at the time that this part of Westgate Street was being built up. The extension of the Old Minster precinct and the demolition of part of the town's defences would undoubtedly have required royal sanction and possibly assistance, and it is not impossible that the opportunity was taken to create a new source of rents to the Crown in the form of new landgable-paying plots on Westgate Street. We may be seeing here a co-operative venture between the Crown and the Minster, but was it associated with an episode of monastic reform or re-organization? A possible candidate (and one that would not be inconsistent with the available archaeological dating evidence) could be the reported reformation of the Minster as a house of Benedictine monks by Bishop Wulfstan I in 1022 (see above, p. 25).

Suburban growth

Meanwhile, urban growth was taking place outside the defences or perhaps where they had until recently been. As far as we know, this was linear growth along the principal through-routes, presumably commercially driven, displaying the obsession with a prime frontage that was to be the principal characteristic of the urban properties of later centuries. The best known in Worcester is Sidbury. '*Suthan byrig*' was a district name by the middle years of the tenth century. St Peter's church and a *haga* 'by the south wall' were recorded in 969; the enigmatic chapel of St Gudwal was probably founded around this time, and excavations at 23–9 Sidbury found evidence of occupation dated by ceramics somewhere between the early ninth and early eleventh centuries. The plot-pattern on the north side of the street is arranged to permit access to a watercourse at the rear; the arrangement is paralleled in a number of late pre-Conquest extramural industrial districts in Gloucester (see below) and much further afield. The south-side plots were furnished with what served as and may have been designed as a rear-access lane (King Street). The suburb has then some signs of careful design in its morphology. A series of watered plots could have been contrived by the first occupiers of the land acting in concert, or at a much higher level by the bishop (or his agent) directly. An equivalent riverside system in Shrewsbury shows evidence of carefully regulated plot-frontage widths, suggesting – but not conclusively – the involvement of the civic authority (Baker *et al.* 1993). King Street – the back lane – may again be indicative of higher-order decision-making in this suburban growth, but our ignorance of the archaeological background to this side of the street urges caution.

Newport Street, with Dolday, in Worcester, is another example of what was undoubtedly a suburban extension of the *burh*, but one for which there is no excavated evidence and no way of telling when or how fast it was built up. The streets appear to have been laid out or formed in relation to the defences in use in *c.* 900: they extended from the site of the gate and extramural market at All Hallows' Square down to the river crossing. From their morphology alone there is little sign of organization or regularity. However, from the lower (northern) end of Dolday comes evidence of post-Roman reclamation activity, and this is likely to have extended to the bridge approaches at the end of Newport Street as well. Dolday functioned as a back lane to Newport Street. It would be rash to claim that the two streets were planned together – again the archaeological background to the area is too obscure – but it is a possibility, and whether or not there was any institutional control of the arrangement of plots and the process by which the area was first built up, the basic infrastructure of the river crossing would have been very much the concern of the civic authorities.

Broad Street, from its width and its perpendicular approach to the High Street, appears to be a planned landscape feature. The reality is that it probably originated in a minor Roman road and continued in use as a road following the edge of the *burh* ditch. After the latter's disuse the street was widened and plots formed or laid out over the former defences. Field survey showed no evidence of any metrological regularity in the plot boundaries, and the extent to which the street was indeed planned remains uncertain, and difficult to quantify without further archaeological evidence.

In Gloucester, Lower Westgate Street offers another example of what appears to have been a pre-Conquest suburb, at least part of which was provided with waterfront acccess. This street extended from the western wall of the fortress to the crossing over the eastern channel of the Severn, and seems to have been built up well beyond the fortress wall in the late tenth century. From the cartographic record of this street and its settlement pattern, the only indications of higher-order decision-making in its morphology are the approximately equal depths of the plots either side. But, while the first *c.* 250 metres of this street west of the defences would have run across dry land, at that point the street (which did not overlie its Roman predecessor) would have passed the Roman riverside wall and proceeded for another *c.* 40–50 metres over what had, in the second–third centuries, been open water. Although archaeological data are lacking it seems certain that the development of this street must (like Newport Street in Worcester) have commenced with some kind of reclamation and causewaying activity. Thereafter, the archaeological record suggests plot-by-plot reclamation progressing further and further away from the main-street frontages. The settlement sequence resembles that of the Grandpont on the Thames crossing at Oxford, where the early Norman causeway came to be built up on either side as individual plots became inhabitable by silting, or by reclamation – principally by the larger religious houses in the later twelfth and thirteenth centuries (Durham 1984). The curved plots on the south side of Westgate Street close to the river are indicative of the situation discussed already in the Sidbury context, and the same arguments apply; here, however, documentation is available from the late twelfth century, and shows fullers in particular congregating in this area, with some dyers and a boatbuilder. Lower Westgate Street, in short, may have developed from a complex amalgam of activities organized at different levels: causewaying, most likely undertaken as part of the public works associated with the foundation of the royal *burh*, further reclamation on the basis of individual plots, and either communal or centrally organized apportionment of waterfront access among a group of plots on the south side.

Extramural markets

Another aspect of pre-Conquest urban growth that may be identified – but not closely dated – is the phenomenon of the extramural marketplace or market street. Two or possibly three such markets are known or suspected in Worcester. All Hallows' Square lies before All Saints' church and the site of a gate through the *burh*'s northern defences. Its location suggests that it was established while the defences were still current; it was a cattle market by 1496 and this may possibly have been its traditional and original use. All Hallows' Square is simply an irregular open area at a street junction; there are no indications of a planned origin in its physical form, and no specifically associated plot-series, though the establishment of the market (the activity rather than the place) may be indicative of planning in a broader sense (see below). Many of the same points could be made about the Cross, immediately outside the pre-Conquest north gate on the axial High Street: the street here is wider than within the defences and was possibly – though not demonstrably – widened to create space for a market. Mealcheapen Street may represent another extramural market street, approaching the Cross from the east and bending around the *burh* defences. The street name (O.E. meal market) suggests that it may already have been associated with the medieval Cornmarket at its eastern end. St Martin's church appears to have been built on one of its north-side plots by the beginning of the eleventh century; the street may have begun to be built up around that time, though there was still scope for development there in the early thirteenth century. Once again, Mealcheapen Street has one characteristic of a planned origin, namely the provision of a lane to the rear of the plots on its north side; however, much about this quarter of the city is obscure and the possibility that the lane may belong to a separate development episode has to be considered.

In Gloucester there are two possible pre-Conquest marketplaces lying outside the fortress/*burh* perimeter, though in neither case is there any documentary evidence to demonstrate that they were actually used as markets. The first is St Mary's Square, the wedge-shaped open area surrounding the church of St Mary de Lode. The evidence for a planned origin rests mainly on the marked symmetry of its plan: the open area around the ancient church, and the plot-series of about equal depth to the north and south. St Mary's Square appears to be the only example in Gloucester or Worcester of a market developing at the gate of an ecclesiastical precinct, a phenomenon that may best be exemplified in the region by Merstow Green, at the gates of Evesham Abbey, interpreted by Bond (1975, 56–7) as a pre-Conquest market, or by Coventry, where the triangular marketplace at the gates of the priory has been suggested by Lilley to have been founded at the same time as the monastery itself in the 1040s (Lilley 1998).

St Mary's Square, Merstow Green and the Coventry market bear a strong resemblance to one another in terms of their shape, relationship to the abbey precinct, and marginal relationship to the built-up area of the town as a whole (or in Coventry's case, to the axial east–west street). St Mary's Square may, therefore, have originated as a planned marketplace, but there are complications. As a public open space, it could possibly have originated long before the foundation of the *burh* (and even before St Peter's) in the late-Roman metalled area surrounding the building from which the church evolved, continuing in the fifth or sixth century as a paved area used for burials. The importance of the early church and its large rural hinterland suggest the possibility that it continued to attract public gatherings and perhaps trading activity, and its location on what was for some centuries the Severn waterfront makes this all the more plausible. Possibly St Mary's Square, in its recorded form, was developed by the Old Minster after its precinct had been extended this far west (over the Roman defences), to formalize and exploit the traditional use of the area. This is, of course, pure speculation: the chronology of the precinct's development is still tentative, and virtually nothing is known of the square's development apart from the structural sequence revealed by the excavations in the church's interior.

The second probable extramural market was Hare Lane. There is little archaeological dating evidence for the earliest levels of Hare Lane itself, though there is sound evidence of pre-Conquest activity in its vicinity, and it lay within a probable pre-Conquest defensive perimeter. It appears to have consisted of two streets (Hare Lane and Back Hare Lane) bounding an open metalled area known as the Hurst. There is strong evidence of a carefully planned origin. The street name ('army street') derives from the route north from the city to the Kingsholm palace site: Hare Lane appears to represent a diversion of the original Roman road, the new course being brought within the defensive perimeter based on the Twyver. The elongated rectangular form of the open area strongly suggests a planned market street, and Bride Lane (running parallel to it to the west) may have been created as part of the same scheme. The provision of watered plots on the east side of Bride Lane could be seen as an accident of topography, but it is equally possible that the location was valued for precisely this facility. Most of the area lay within the parish of St Oswald, the New Minster, and if Hare Lane was a market it may have been promoted by and yielded revenue to St Oswald's. However, the eastern plots lay within the parish of St John and owed landgable to the King; this, and the apparent diversion of the original street, strongly suggest that the Crown was also involved in its creation.

The provision, or development, of extra-mural marketplaces, whether displaying signs of a planned or organized lay-out or not, raises the larger question of town-planning in the sense of the management of functions within an existing town. From – we assume – a single marketplace or market street in *c.* 900 in Worcester and one or perhaps two in Gloucester, by *c.* 1300 Worcester and Gloucester, like other towns, contained a number of specialist markets and retailing areas distributed around their streets. To what extent was this process of market dispersal promoted or controlled? To a large extent there seems, as yet, no answer to this question. Streets, districts or rows of houses appear for the first time in the twelfth or thirteenth century to be associated with particular trades, and there is no evidence of the process by which, for example, cordwainers or bakers came to congregate there or why milk or geese came to be sold in that particular street. To some extent the location of retailing activities was economically determined by competition for the best frontages, but this does not explain the location and grouping of economically comparable trades. The location of some trades was, of course, determined by geographical factors, commonly the need for access to running water. In Gloucester the concentration of fullers and dyers in areas where the plots had access to a watercourse is apparent by the early thirteenth century. Gloucester's iron industry too was, by the twelfth century, concentrated in the town's south-west quarter, arguably drawn towards the supply from the quays of raw materials and fuel; the proximity of the castle – a major customer in times of unrest – may have been an additional factor (*VCH Glos.*, iv,

26); so too would have been the avoidance of the high-rent built-up main-street frontages, as well as fear of the very real risk of fire.

In part, this question is related to that of the zoning of urban functions that represented some sort of nuisance to the community as a whole. Of all the trades in a *burh* market street, the buying and selling of livestock must have been the most demanding to accommodate, on account of the space taken up, the waste left behind, damage to metalled surfaces and the need to feed and water the animals. It is not suprising then to find examples elsewhere of extramural cattle markets at an early date, as if this trade was amongst the very first to be expelled from the interior of the settlement. At Canterbury, for example, the cattle market or *ryther ceap* was outside the east wall by 923 (Urry 1967, 108). In south-west England, extramural markets are found by the *burh* defences at Barnstaple and Totnes, for example, and it has been claimed that such provision is 'a general phenomenon shown by the larger *burhs* in Midland England' (Haslam 1984, 256). Hare Lane in Gloucester was not conclusively either a market or a cattle market – though from its long broad rectangular space and watered plots the chances are that it was both. If, as suggested, it was laid out as a joint venture by the Crown and by the New Minster (later St Oswald's Priory), it is unlikely to have been conceived as a venture in competition with the town's markets. Much more likely it was intended to improve living and trading conditions in the town as a whole, as well as a means of providing the New Minster with revenue. A similar sequence has been proposed in Shrewsbury, where a widened street (Pride Hill) provided with watered plots may have been planned as a secondary marketplace, possibly for livestock (Baker *et al.* 1993). The same may also have been true of All Hallows' Square in Worcester, though here there is no evidence of any degree of planning in its morphology and it may instead have developed 'organically' from *ad hoc* trading activities outside the gate, along the lines of Wincheap at Canterbury (Keene 1990a, 110).

It is likely that even in the tenth century there was some concern with, and control over, the spatial organization of urban activities. The provision of extramural markets may, as discussed, have represented such a concern in our study towns, and other places in the region provide further evidence. Excavations in Stafford, for example, have consistently shown contrasting activities in the western and eastern parts of the site. To the west of the north–south axial street, open metalled areas and structures associated with agricultural produce have been found; the area to the east seems, in contrast, to have been dominated by the potting industry. This basic zoning of functions – concerned perhaps with keeping the fire-risk and smoke nuisance of the pottery kilns down-wind – is certainly apparent in the tenth century, and may have been established by the early ninth: the earliest kilns are of that date and located on the same side of town as the later ones. All that is in doubt is to what degree the settlement was in fact urban, though (at a guess) the answer to this may yet be found by sampling the frontages of the axial High Street (Carver 1987, 56; Ford 1995, 29–31). In Hereford in the tenth and eleventh centuries the concentration of iron-working on the town's margins may have been the result of a comparable policy (Shoesmith 1982, 100).

Post-Conquest development

The decades that followed the Norman Conquest saw an explosion of building activity and public works in Gloucester and Worcester, as elsewhere. The construction of earthwork castles in each town in the 1060s–70s was followed by the commencement of unprecedented building campaigns on the major churches: Wulfstan's rebuilding of Worcester Cathedral in 1084, and Serlo's rebuilding of St Peter's Abbey in 1089. While this work was still at an early stage, the secular authorities turned their attention to the towns' communications or, to be specific, the river crossings. Worcester's bridge was apparently first, a bare reference to its repair before 1088 giving no clues to the extent of the work involved – or indeed the age of the bridge being repaired. According to both Gregory of Caerwent and the annals of Tewkesbury Abbey, work on 'the bridge at Gloucester' began in 1119 but, again, the implications of this reference are not quite clear. It may refer to the construction, or reconstruction, of the Foreign Bridge over the eastern channel of the Severn; it could possibly refer to the construction of the Westgate Bridge over the central channel; or it may be a catch-all description of the whole of the Severn crossing at Gloucester, including the Foreign Bridge and 'Over Causeway'. The latter was described by Leland as 'a great Causey of stone' stretching for a quarter of a mile west from the Westgate Bridge across the floodplain meadows with several 'double arched bridges to drain the meadows at floodes'; limited excavation in the 1970s revealed three round sandstone arches belonging to it (Hurst 1974, 51).

The improvement of the river crossings at Worcester and Gloucester may be seen as standard practice in the Normanization of English towns. For comparison, the first reference to the Severn bridges at Shrewsbury – both of them – comes from 1121, in a context that suggests that they were then newly built, or newly built in stone (Baker (ed.) 2002). The Grandpont at Oxford, an enormous arched stone causeway two to three times as long as Gloucester's, was built across the Thames floodplain by Robert d'Oilly, the first Norman Sheriff, before 1091–2 (Durham 1984). But it is perhaps debatable how far such works were inspired by the desire for economic growth rather than the requirements of the military and the state.

It has been suggested that Gloucester was comprehensively refortified under early Norman rule (Hurst 1986). The first castle, which stood in the south-west corner of the fortress, was replaced in 1108–1109 by a new castle outside to the west; a (or the) wall around St Peter's Abbey precinct was built in 1104–13; and excavation showed that the first metalling laid down behind the Roman defences, where a Saxon intramural street might have been expected, was probably laid after the middle of the eleventh century. The north and east gates, and part of the north wall were also rebuilt in the early Norman period (Hurst 1986, 129–32). Whether this amounts to a deliberate campaign of general refortification, or the maintenance of the defences and the co-incidental move of the royal castle to a much more spacious site, is uncertain. Whatever the intent, there is no doubting the extent of public works being undertaken in the first half of the twelfth century.

The same period also saw the creation of new, planned, suburbs to accommodate urban growth in both towns. As ever, the evidence for their chronology is imprecise and it is difficult to say to what extent the post-Conquest suburbs truly represent (as they seem to) a fresh burst of urban growth as opposed to a continuation of much longer-term trends.

New suburbs

Lower Southgate Street was Gloucester's medieval southern suburb. The area was occupied by buildings in the tenth–eleventh century, but was open land for a time before suburban development with some signs of organization in its plan took place. The area was acquired by Lanthony Priory at its foundation in 1136 and, whilst there are signs of earlier settlement, it remains unclear how far it was Lanthony that initiated development here. Ignoring (for reasons already explained) the rectilinearity of the surburb's morphology, the main reason for deducing that the suburb originated as a planned development is the provision of a back lane to the western plots. This, known as Small Lane, was itself built up with cottages before depopulation set in and it was eventually lost to encroachment by the main-street frontage plots. The southernmost plots on this side of the road were laid out to the same depth as those to the north but were not provided with a back lane. Little is known of the east-side plots, though a short series surviving into the nineteenth century towards the southern end suggests that they were of the same depth as those on the west side. The church of St Owen stood behind the west-side plots close to the town wall; the church was founded and endowed by Walter of Gloucester *c.* 1095, but appears to have been intended primarily as a place of worship for the castle household, and not the inhabitants of the suburb. Its site, in close proximity to the contemporary suburb, may be explicable in terms of a pre-existing feature (a cemetery of St Kyneburgh's, its predecessor, for example) or it may be that both it and the suburb – whilst separate – were seen as components of the constables' estate.

The creation of the Westgate Island suburb in Gloucester was an act that involved much more than turning over good grazing land to housing and staking out a few plots. The development of the suburb was preceded by and may have been intimately connected with public works on the Severn channels and bridges in the first half of the twelfth century, probably under the orders of the constables of the castle. The uncertain but possibly substantial amount of work undertaken on the bridge(s) and causeway has already been described. But in addition, if Rowbotham's (1978) model is correct, Westgate Island (*Inter Pontes* in the documentation) was an artificial creation resulting from the diversion of the middle channel of the Severn, from a line to the north of the Westgate Street–Over Causeway road to a new line to the south. This would have involved the excavation of about 450 metres of new river channel, together with the construction of the Westgate Bridge, an undertaking closely comparable to and perhaps exceeding in scale the more widely known diversion of the River Frome by the Bristol burgesses in 1240. The new Gloucester suburb covered an area of about 10–12 acres (*c.* 4–4.9 hectares), and provided *c.* 1600 feet (*c.* 480 metres) of main-street frontage that could be divided into plots which all had a water channel to the rear, for industrial purposes or for access.

Barton Street, located outside Gloucester's east gate, was also a suburb whose layout has characteristics of a planned origin. Its boundary was demarcated by a feature known as 'the king's ditch' in the documentary record, and the street appears to have been widened within the boundary. The plots on the north side of the road still preserve a regular appearance, running back to a common boundary parallel to the street, though, again, the limited significance of rectilinear forms in Gloucester (where everything is rectilinear) has to be taken into account. What makes this suburb different is that the plots on the south side were originally of a similar depth, and that each series of plots can be seen to have been an accurate reproduction of the much earlier plots lining Eastgate Street within the walls: the suburb appears to have been quite specifically designed as a matching extension to the intramural street.

The provision of a rear service lane to a series of plots has generally (though there are certainly some doubtful examples) been taken as an indicator of a degree of organization in their origin and, as we have already seen, Beresford noted it as a recurrent feature of the smallest newly founded post-Conquest towns (Beresford 1967, 153). Such features also appear in Gloucester's intramural area, though their meaning is not always quite so clear. For example, Cross Keys Lane (the medieval Scruddelone) lay *c.* 120 feet (*c.* 35 metres) to the north of and parallel to Longsmith Street, a series of whose plots probably ran back to it. Cross Keys Lane may therefore have been laid out as a rear service lane at the same time as the series of plots were laid out, perhaps in the mid to late eleventh century. However, in a congested area such as this – particularly one where perpendicular or parallel alignments were predetermined and not necessarily of any contemporary significance – to place too much reliance on such a hypothesized relationship between one street and another would clearly be unsafe, at least without further evidence for the simultaneous development of a number of the plots. Nevertheless, as settlement intensified within the defended area, the speculative development of small groups of plots here and there, by the great landowners and by lesser entrepreneurs as well, is only to be expected. Such may be the origin of, for example, Sheep Lane, lying behind a minor plot-series only *c.*100 feet (*c.*30 metres) long, between Southgate Street and the Franciscan friary. Such examples may be seen as the lowest level of planning activity applied to the preparation of a site, as opposed to the speculative construction of new buildings for rent.

The largest single act of planning in either of the study towns, in any period prior to the nineteenth century, was the foundation of the Foregate Street and Tything suburb on the Bishop of Worcester's manor of Northwick, probably in the late eleventh or early twelfth century. The suburb extended for over 600 metres from the north gate, and its streets and plots covered a total area of around 33 acres (*c.*13.4 hectares). The series of plots on the west side of the main street were provided with a back service lane, those on the east side with garden crofts behind and a service lane to their rear. The plots may have been laid out to a metrologically regular scheme but, if so, field survey has been unable to identify it, possibly on account of the razing of the suburb in the Civil War. A road diversion which would have had the effect of diverting traffic to and from the Droitwich direction through the new suburb can be identified 3 miles (*c.*5 kilometres) to the north-east of Worcester; it involved the closure of the old Roman road from Droitwich, the *port straet*, first recorded in 1038 (S1393; Hooke 1980) that entered the city via Lowesmoor (fig. 7.2). The diversion of traffic into newly founded towns, even at some distance, is a familiar feature of medieval town-founding and planning (Beresford 1967, 156) and this diversion may well have been associated with, and designed to ensure the success of, the Foregate suburb.

The provision of separate garden crofts at the rear of one of its plot-series raises a number of issues: how these were used, what sort of tenants they were designed to attract, and why they were provided for only one of the plot-series. Garden crofts behind frontage plots are also found in Worcester on Silver Street, and elsewhere in the region, on the west side of Bridge Street, Pershore, for example (Slater 1980). The significance of the presence of these crofts on only one side of the street is not altogether clear. In Pershore, where they also occur on one side only, a chronological difference in the plot-series either side of the street was proposed, and backed by metrological evidence (Slater, ibid., 61–3), but there is no indication that the Foregate Street–Tything suburb was anything but a single-phase development. It is perhaps just as likely that the provision of extra land attached to the plots on one side of the street was a deliberate policy, followed by the founder of the suburb, to enlarge the possible market for his urban venture by offering plots with different facilities. Possibly the additional land parcels were designed to appeal to artisans or traders with a side-line in horticulture or livestock; possibly the separate garden crofts were intended and expected to be immediately sub-let, to local butchers for example, but there seems to be no further relevant evidence. Other apparently single-phase urban developments in towns elsewhere show similar variability in the facilities accorded to plot-series on opposite sides of a street – as, for example, with the provision of a rear service lane: on Southgate Street, Gloucester (above), at Corve Street, Ludlow, at Lower Rushall Street, Walsall (Baker 1988) or the High Street, Much Wenlock.

What might the implications of the new suburb have been for Worcester as a whole, as a centre of population? Only very crude estimates are possible but they may nevertheless be instructive. Lacking data as to any original regulated plot-widths, one could nevertheless propose (for the sake of argument) that a standard plot-width of 3½ statute perches (as used in the bishops' venture at Stratford-upon-Avon in the 1190s) was adopted. Within a total new main-street frontage of around 3,800 feet (1158 metres), therefore, and excluding that which was set aside for, or was soon occupied by, ecclesiastical precincts (*c.* 550 feet/168 metres), about 65 new plots could have been accommodated. If (again for the sake of argument) it was assumed that each of these plots was taken by a single household, a conservative multiplier of four would suggest that this one suburb could have added more than 10 per cent to the city's estimated population in 1086 (Clarke and Dyer 1969, 32). There are, of course, many imponderables, notably the speed at which plots were actually taken up and built upon. If the velocity of settlement increase was anything like that later on in Stratford, it is possible that within fifty years the number of plots had been doubled or trebled by sub-division (Slater 1987, 195–6), with a proportionate increase in the suburban population. It can be no coincidence that among all the pre- and post-Conquest planned urban extensions in Worcester, only this one is likely to have been contemporaneously provided with a new parish church (St Nicholas's) by a common founder.

No other suburban developments in post-Conquest Worcester approached Foregate Street in terms either of size or in the sophistication of their design – where there was any. The bishops' suburb of Lowesmoor was a tenth of the size (*c.* 3 acres/1.2 hectares), merely a collection of plots within a rectangular land-parcel on one side of the street and a sub-divided former garden croft on the other; the street may have been widened, but even that is uncertain. Suburban growth on the west bank shows little or no evidence of an organized layout, and much stronger evidence of the adaptation of urban plot-series to the irregularities of the site – mainly gradients and watercourses.

Urban infill

Post-Conquest growth in both towns took the form of inward colonization as well as outward accretion. Though much smaller in scale than the suburban extensions considered above, there is evidence that such colonization was organized, required an adequate level of investment and could in return yield substantial new rents: it therefore requires some attention as an example of 'town-planning', even though it might once have been regarded as the antithesis of that.

Street encroachments appear in Gloucester in the mid twelfth century, some as islands in the middle of Westgate Street, some as excrescences clustering around the walls of the churches at the central crossroads. The reason they were there was in part the shortage of intramural frontage space on the four main streets; but they were not, it seems, by any means examples of successful squatting, developed slyly from temporary stalls. First into the street were churches of royal foundation (or if not royal, then by the Crown representatives, the constables of the castle), followed by the mint. Commercial buildings followed; Lanthony Priory was given land in the central strip in the 1170s, and a row of selds, which were owned by St Peter's Abbey in the early thirteenth century, appeared at the east end of Westgate Street.

In Worcester, the cathedral priory sought to capitalize on the traffic passing its precinct by developing their cemetery frontage on the south side of Lich Street; the buildings they built brought in new rents in the thirteenth century and their successors preserved the plotless arrangement characteristic of encroachments onto public open space, whether markets or cemeteries.

Chapter 15

Conclusion

This study was devised as a way of assessing the contribution made by the medieval Church to the developing form of English towns. Specifically, we set out to answer fundamental questions concerning the extent and level of the contribution that existing churches made, both to the early phases of urban growth, and to the continuing development of the physical structure of two neighbouring towns – Gloucester and Worcester.

To achieve that end it was necessary to examine the early Church in each town, through studies of the major churches that were already established long before the phases of sustained urban growth began, and through studies of the lesser churches whose foundation accompanied urbanization and which were nearly all in place by 1100. We also set out to assess how far the different institutions of the Church continued to influence the more stable urban form of the period after *c.*1200, principally through the large urban estates that the greater churches had by this time accumulated but also through the continued development of distinct precincts which collectively came to occupy around a third of each walled city. At the same time it was necessary to extend our understanding of the whole series of processes by which the topography of each town developed, each study being based on a close analysis of the surviving and recoverable medieval form and on the archaeological and historical evidence for the chronology of the changing town-plan.

In the course of this study we found that our different approaches might support each other in unexpected ways. For example, excavation rarely takes place on a large enough scale to reveal lordship at work as a town-planner; in Worcester, however, excavated evidence proved to be the only way of detecting major earth-moving operations that are cartographically – and historically – invisible, yet which had been a precondition for the creation of a new townscape. Excavation thus proved itself – for the first time – to be an essential component of urban landscape analysis, rather than just an alternative or at best a supplementary approach.

It goes without saying that the conclusions we have reached are strictly applicable only to the two towns that have been studied; nevertheless, the questions that have been asked and the issues that have been discussed are of more than local importance, and it was always intended that this work should inform and extend the several lines of current research – from whatever discipline – into the early development of the greater English towns.

In Chapters 2 and 5 we showed that Worcester and Gloucester shared fundamental characteristics during the post-Roman centuries. Whilst little conclusive evidence can be cited, it is most likely that both were already established central places in the Hwiccian kingdom of the seventh century, and subsequently. The deduced prominence of St Helen's church in the region around Worcester, and the similar local importance of Gloucester's St Mary de Lode, points to both having been the superior churches of regions likely to have had a secular identity during the immediate post-Roman period; the foundation during the last decades of the seventh century of a new see in the one city and a major minster in the other reinforced the importance of both in the new religious hierarchy that was being established to serve the English kingdoms.

Both cities had proto-urban functions during the period before their refoundation as *burhs* during the last two decades of the ninth century. The pre-borough phase saw the principal local churches dominating sites otherwise characterized by surviving Roman features and providing a setting for indeterminate commercial activities.

The eighth- and ninth-century bishops of Worcester were lords of their city and clearly active in secular affairs at all levels; their deep involvement in commerce, involving them in trade with the Continent, through premises they owned in London (and probably their own ships), may perhaps offer only a superficial contrast with the apparent inactivity of Gloucester's Old Minster. That too was richly endowed with wide estates, and the abbesses and clerks of the Church would certainly have sought to exchange their agricultural surplus for imported goods – whether directly or indirectly – as did their counterparts of Worcester. The survival of so many Worcester charters from the pre-Conquest period inevitably distorts a comparison between the early history of these two institutions; it is important always to allow for that very different quantity and quality of surviving evidence. We simply do not know whether or not the Old Minster took part in international trade – the greater aristocracy may habitually have made use of the *wics* or coastal trading places in ways that we can hardly appreciate in the present state of our knowledge – but its interests in the products and process of commerce cannot be doubted.

Nor can we be certain to what extent the Old Minster took an active role in the planning and early development of the *burh* of Gloucester. The Old Minster's apparent lack of vigour in secular affairs might be, again, an impression formed largely by the lack of documentation for the period. Nevertheless, due weight must be given to events of the late ninth century. The Church of Worcester was spared the disaster of the Danish occupation of Gloucester during the winter of 877–8 which can only have been severely detrimental to the Old Minster, with the inevitable destruction, loss of records and impoverishment that must have ensued. The foundation within twenty years or so of the New Minster and the royal favour it received over a considerable period would have continued to ensure the older house's eclipse until its regeneration in the second half of the eleventh century. These circumstances brought about, or at least reinforced, the Old Minster's lack of influence within the early *burh* during a crucial period of its development. The perceived contrast between the active role taken by the Church of Worcester, and the apparently lesser role played in Gloucester by the major churches during the period of the planning and construction of the boroughs, thus seems to have been real enough: moreover, political circumstances ensured that the state would afford more respect to the authority of Bishop Wærferth within his own city – and to his successors – than it would to the clerks of the Old and New Minsters of Gloucester.

There is no historical evidence, and as yet no archaeological evidence, for any reconstruction or refurbishment of these two cities that might be attributable to one or other of the Mercian kings. The early defensive sequence and planned street-grid of middle-Saxon Hereford are still without any identified parallel in the other west-Mercian proto-urban places. It was only in the late ninth century, with Alfred's Wessex asserting its rising authority over western Mercia, that we can detect moves to redesign both Gloucester and Worcester. And despite their apparently near-contemporary construction, what is now apparent – and most remarkable – about these two *burhs* is how fundamentally different they were in their conception.

When the *burhs* were founded in the late ninth century, neither was a completely planned new foundation. Gloucester, though, came closer to that than Worcester. There is no close chronology of its refurbishment and replanning, although the establishment of a mint there in the 880s – minting coins of Alfred – and its subsequent prominence under Æthelred and Æthelflæd point strongly to this work having been at least begun by the mid 880s. The close resemblance of the geometry of its new street-system to that of Winchester, the prototypical Wessex *burh*, adds to the perception that this new royal city was intended for a range of urban functions but, more crucially, to play a central political and military role in consolidating Alfred's authority – through Æthelred – over the area of western Mercia. The foundation of the New Minster, perhaps intended from the beginning to be a new royal burial place, reinforces the impression of Gloucester's importance in Alfred's new State.

Worcester, by contrast, was refortified perhaps some years later – not certainly but probably in the 890s – in a much less ambitious operation. It was a smaller foundation, and the recognition of Bishop Wærferth's joint lordship by Æthelred and Æthelflæd in effect confirms this as most likely an episcopal enterprise. However onerous the task of its fortification, and despite the presence of occupied plots, the new *burh* at Worcester now appears to have been little more than a defended enclosure, without the provision of a planned street-system. The planned High Street area came into being only with the removal of the eastern side of the *burh* defences, perhaps within a century of their construction. This clearer than hitherto perception of what was actually done at Worcester throws a little new light on the wording of the charter to Wærferth: in the absence of any planned provision for urban growth, the division of the profits from the marketplace and from passing trade was presumably no more than a new arrangement for an existing situation. The new defences for the first time protected the existing north–south road (perhaps already a marketplace though clearly not yet a High Street) and the waterfront; possibly, though, their most urgent function was – as the charter itself says – the protection of the *folce* or people. Worcester comes considerably nearer to the historians' traditional perception of the *burh* as an emergency military centre and refuge than Gloucester does.

The growth and transformation of each *burh* in the later pre-Conquest period was achieved in part by extramural growth, and in part by what we have termed post-mural redevelopment. This could be described as a species of inward colonization or intensification of settlement achieved by the organized levelling of redundant defences and their replacement by planned urban growth (fig. 14.5). Such a process required both authority and resources. In Worcester, it was successive bishops who shaped the pre-Conquest town. And it may be that it was in the dissolution of the *burh*, the progressive removal of what were perceived to be physical obstacles to urban growth, that the bishops first became involved with the design of a new townscape on their own doorstep, so to speak. A number of episodes have been identified: the improvement of the marketplace, and the creation of new streets and plots in the area around the cathedral precinct – which was itself reshaped as a continuation of the same landscape, the humps and bumps of now redundant defences steam-rollered. Chronology remains a major problem, and the attribution of these events to the period *c.* 960–80 and Oswald's episcopate remains speculative (though attractive). The likelihood is that these events took place at the same time as the cathedral community was itself reformed and reorganized, and that the two – as with any monastic estate – were economically related.

And if Bishop Oswald did indeed lie behind the dissolution and replanning of his predecessors' *burh*, it is likely that he was able to draw on their experience of landscape management and planning exercised elsewhere on their estates. The charter evidence suggests that the best agricultural land of Worcester's estates had already been laid out with open, co-operatively farmed, fields before the process of administrative reform implicit in Oswald's leases took place (Dyer 1996, 179). It may well be that the great landscape changes that appear to be characteristic of late ninth- and tenth-century England were, on Worcester Cathedral's estates at least, a protracted enterprise that began in the countryside and was only later applied to the principal town.

In Gloucester, the disappearance of part of the west wall of the Roman fortress may be traced to a comparable development, as the Old Minster precinct was replanned alongside new urban plots. That process rendered the old Alfredian *burh* indefensible, by the loss of much of its western defences.

This is not, of course, to deny the role of small-scale piecemeal encroachment, robbing and levelling in causing the disappearance of pre-Conquest defences from the urban landscape. However, it may well be that the mechanism proposed here for their partial disappearance is much more widely paralleled than has been appreciated. It seems possible that scrutiny of other English medieval towns would find more signs of pre-Conquest town-planning activity where gaps are apparent in burghal circuits of the late ninth and early tenth centuries.

The expansion of each of our towns after *c.* 900 was also achieved by more conventional linear outward growth – the development of suburbs. These, on close examination, appear to have been formed by a complex amalgam of processes, subject to varying degrees of higher-order decision-making. Bridge-works and causeways would have been a necessary precondition to the development of *burh* suburbs approaching the Severn crossings, and such civil-engineering enterprises were part of the legitimate business of lordship. So, too, may have been wetland reclamation, but this could also be left to individual plot-holders. Suburbs that grew up by the river or by lesser watercourses were the natural home for a range of water-using craft activities. So far, this is scarcely apparent from the excavated archaeological evidence, though it does show up in the historical record later on, after the Conquest. It is most strongly apparent, however, in the morphology of many suburban plot-systems, where rear access to running water was often a priority and plots were carefully contrived, and watercourses large and small diverted to maximize such access. The contrast between episcopal Worcester, whose plots virtually ignore the river, and industrial Gloucester, almost surrounded by watered plots, is very plain to see.

The development of extramural marketplaces was another phenomenon in the pre-Conquest growth of our towns. Some appear to have been individually and carefully planned – notably the great Hare Lane development north of Gloucester – others not. But implicit in all was the zoning of urban functions and nuisances as the urban economy expanded. The early expulsion of livestock markets from the busiest streets seems to have been a universal obsession of pre-Conquest English urban authorities. Church institutions were active in this respect. The New Minster in Gloucester probably had a hand in the creation of the Hare Lane market and suburb; the Old Minster may have established St Mary's Square as a formalized marketplace outside its own precinct.

The later of these phases of planned urban growth can be understood within the general context of an accelerating urbanization in most of England, the effects of which by 1086 are amply illustrated in Domesday Book. But what of the earlier phases, associated either with the foundation of the *burhs* or – in both Gloucester and Worcester – with the subsequent removal of defences now evidently seen to be redundant? In Chapter 10, in the discussion of what the bishops of Worcester did with their city lands, evidence was presented for what seems like a consistent policy over at least a century of granting house plots to the Church's greater retainers. This in turn, it was suggested, is to be seen as closely related to the rewarding of these same retainers with substantial rural landholdings. If it was under Oswald that we see the process most clearly, this may indeed reflect a more determined reorganization of the Church of Worcester's affairs, at the same time as new haws or *hagas* were being made available in the city through systematic levelling and replanning. Our perception of Oswald's activities may, however, reflect no more than the greater mass of documentation surviving from his time at Worcester; and indeed both later bishops and the great secular lords, including the King, similarly gave their thegns the means to settle or remain resident in Worcester. This granting of property in the new *burhs* to the emerging landholding aristocracy, it was suggested, brought about the curious phenomenon of Domesday Book's 'contributory burgesses', to use Ballard's inappropriate name for them which has nevertheless stuck. The large number of town-houses attached to rural manors in 1086, in all of the old *burhs*, points to a widespread practice giving urban society, in its earliest phases, a strongly aristocratic flavour with all that that implies for the nature of the buildings and activities we might expect to find in the towns of the tenth and eleventh centuries.

Accompanying the rapid development of urban communities in both towns was the appearance of lesser churches, most of which came in time to take on parochial functions. In Chapters 4 and 7 their origins were examined critically and at length, with a view to establishing a chronology of foundation in both towns and an appreciation of the identity of their founders: the conclusions from both of these chapters were discussed in Chapter 8. The origins of the lesser churches were diverse, and an uncertain number pre-dated the *burh* phase. But the number of lesser churches whose foundation can be plausibly placed before 1000 suggests something of the vigour of the initial phases of urbanization. In neither town do we see individual or collective lay piety as the decisive force in this series of foundations, by contrast with the situation as reported from some other towns; in fact where a founder could be identified – or more often where one was suggested – greater churches or the state and its officials were shown to be most prominent. The contrast between Worcester, where the cathedral was clearly the main driving force in church foundation, and Gloucester, where neither Old nor New Minster played the same role, is clear and lends some support to the perception of the much more active participation of the Church of Worcester in the several aspects of the development of its city.

An incidental feature of our investigation of church origins was a consideration of the matter of dedications, discussed in Chapter 8. Often we found that a church had an 'appropriate' dedication – one that fitted the period of its foundation, for instance; but in only two cases, that of St Gudwal's at Worcester and St Aldate's at Gloucester, did we feel justified in citing the dedication itself as evidence either for the foundation or for the date of dedication. Clearly dedication evidence can supplement a wider discussion of a particular church's origins, but only under the most exceptional of circumstances can it be used as primary evidence.

The same sort of conclusion was reached in Chapter 9, the study of parish boundaries, where again a close study, together with the consideration of other topographical evidence and evidence for the foundation of these churches, proved to be illuminating. At the beginning of the project, we proposed that analysing parish boundaries might prove to be an important ingredient in understanding the way in which the urban Church – and the older, multi-parish towns themselves – developed. Yet the study amply demonstrates that on its own parish boundary evidence cannot be used to identify – much less define – features or events in the developing urban landscape. Despite the quantity of different types of evidence, uncertainty remains – and will remain – as to the ways in which the parishes of Gloucester and Worcester were formed, or when. The disintegration of the earlier urban minster parishes was a gradual process, just as the construction of lesser churches was a process drawn out over a period of several centuries during all of which, perhaps, the parochial geography was taking shape. What is clear is that, within this prolonged period in which territorial parochial rights were being defined, different influences predominated at different times – and a major, constant difficulty remains the chronology of any particular boundary line. The study has shown that the parish maps of our town are palimpsests, like most other maps. From at least the late middle ages there was a continuous process of small-scale change to parish boundaries, occasionally visible in documentary sources, or from excavation, or where they follow a major datable feature like a town wall or an ecclesiastical precinct. The principle of the nearest church door played a role in the determination of parish boundaries, probably in the post-Conquest period, by rationalizing existing boundaries and settling disputes. But other, more ancient, determinants underlie the pattern of parishes. The earliest chronological component of the Worcester system appears to be the distinction between those parishes that were wholly intramural and those that were partly extramural – in late-medieval terms. The distinction between them, and the determinant of the boundaries between them, appears to have been the *burh* perimeter, or the replanning events that brought about its dissolution. In Gloucester there are also clear signs of planned parochial provision reflecting major secular boundaries in the eastern, planned, half of the *burh*. From these two towns some more general conclusions may be reached regarding the development of urban parishes and their boundaries. Urban parishes were just like rural parishes in that they were formed by the process of minster parish fragmentation, acquiring rights at the expense of an older minster church. But in these towns, at least, fragmentation was delayed or retarded by the proximity of their respective minsters and doubtless also by their ownership of property. Beyond the walls, fragmentation could advance and rights be acquired more speedily than within.

The same period between 900 and 1200 that saw the construction of most of the lesser churches was also a period of great change for the major churches of Gloucester and Worcester (as discussed in Chapters 2, 5, 10 and 11). By 1200 the cathedral priory and St Peter's Abbey had come to take on a similar relationship to the growing urban communities. Under the agreement between Bishop Wærferth and Ealdorman Æthelred, the bishops of Worcester ceased to be lords of the city as they had been since the foundation of the see. In practice, we suggest, for perhaps another century their local (and indeed national) prominence ensured their continued influence over the way the town developed to accommodate the growing community, but erosion of their position during the eleventh century – doubtless reinforced by the circumstances of the Norman Conquest – left St Wulfstan and his successors as spiritual lords of their city, and the monks of the cathedral priory as a major owner of urban land, but no more than that. In Gloucester, meanwhile, the more vigorous and active of the minsters – the New Minster – fell under the control of a succession of proprietors until it finally lost the major part of its property and independence to the archbishopric of York. Little remained of its former estates in Gloucester to demonstrate its possible major role in earlier phases of the evolution of the town-plan. At the same time, the reform of the Old Minster and its reinvigoration under French abbots saw St Peter's Abbey emerge as the leading religious house of the region.

We have been unable to assess the degree of control exercised in Gloucester and Worcester by the pre-Conquest state, although aspects of the planned development of the northern suburb at Gloucester associated with the construction there of the defences and the Alvin Gate suggest an active civil administration. But clearly the Norman Conquest and subsequent developments had a profound effect on both towns and their institutions – as they did on other, similar towns. Most obviously, there was the construction of castles, a physical intrusion into the established urban landscape and pattern of settlement and, more importantly, a mental intrusion into the urban order. Castles were built to control and dominate and were doubtless a compelling visual reminder that surveillance was constant. By the later 1060s the conquerors had emphatically asserted their presence in both towns in typical fashion: Urse, the new sheriff of Worcestershire, constructed the castle in Worcester on land confiscated from the Church of Worcester and in defiance of the bishop, whilst in Gloucester the constables of the new castle established a powerful dynasty that would dominate the town and the region for a century. A number of planning events in Gloucester during that century – the apparent diversion of the Severn to a new channel and the presumed associated building of the new bridge in 1119, the development of the suburb outside the west gate, the construction of the street churches and commercial encroachment on the frontages of buildings, including churches, at the centre of the town – were attributable to Walter of Gloucester and his successors (Chapters 4, 7, 13, 14).

By the early thirteenth century, secular authority within both towns belonged effectively to the burgess administrations whose right to self-government was recognized by the Crown. In both Worcester and Gloucester the following centuries saw the town governments in dispute – generally over rights of jurisdiction – with the greater religious houses. Both the cathedral priory and Gloucester Abbey increasingly emphasized the integrity of their own precincts as areas quite distinct from the secular space of the townspeople, and by the fifteenth century both claimed their precincts to be sanctuaries immune from the authority of the town courts (Chapter 11). The process of physically separating these churches from their towns, therefore, reflected not only a spiritual need for isolation from the secular world but was also driven by the need for a line of legal demarcation that was firm enough to defend. Perhaps as early as the 960s the Church of Worcester saw fit to draw a clear line between the ecclesiastical area and the developing urban community, although it was Gloucester that saw the first stone precinct-wall, around St Peter's Abbey, probably in the early twelfth century. Symbolically, the abbey's new main gate faced west, away from the town. Worcester Cathedral Priory, too, felt the need in the fourteenth century to assert its independence from the city as well as its own importance with an impressive gate, the Edgar Tower.

However, as the greatest landowners in the towns (Chapter 10), the major churches continued until the end of our period to contribute in some measure to the character of the townscape: this is best seen in Gloucester, where both St Peter's Abbey and Lanthony Priory seem by the late fifteenth century to have adopted a policy of improvement of at least some of their property. Their willingness to invest during a period often characterized as one of overall urban decline is a further illustration of the uneven experiences that have been noted (Palliser 1988), and goes some way towards balancing the claims of its burgesses that Gloucester underwent a considerable degree of impoverishment and contraction. Yet the contrast between this policy and that of earlier centuries emphasizes the general reluctance of the religious houses since the thirteenth century to invest in anything other than the acquisition of new properties, and that in turn contrasts with the broadly earlier period when several of these churches were actively involved in the planning of their extramural lands for suburban development. Only there, at the town margins, where expansion of settlement was still being recorded in the thirteenth century, did the major churches – as great landholders – maintain a potential to substantially influence the urban form (Chapters 10 and 13). The post-Conquest suburbs display a mixture of planned and less well-organized development, although generally speaking those furthest from the centre, or on the less important approach roads, are the least likely to display signs of the involvement of a higher authority in their conception. In part this might, of course, be an issue of chronology – as the returns on investment in future urban growth diminished.

The bishops of Worcester were responsible for the most substantial of the post-Conquest planned urban additions: the Foregate Street suburb, a giant, 13-hectare affair, with 600 metres of new frontage, back service lanes, and a variety of plot types to attract new tenants. The classic shape of this development to the north of Worcester shows that an overall plan was followed over perhaps an extended period by the succession of bishops who owned all of this land. Other suburbs, although largely owned by the Church, showed less sign of a single planning influence. Lanthony Priory may have been solely responsible for the layout of Gloucester's southern suburb (although that conclusion rests on evidence from only one area of the suburb); in the case of the northern suburb of Gloucester and the Barton Street suburb, the pattern of ground ownership points to participation in the planning process both by the Church and by agents of the Crown. The transpontine suburban area of St Clement's parish in Worcester came in large part into the hands of the cathedral priory, but only because of its cheap housing which the priory evidently regarded as an expedient investment. It proved impossible, therefore, to detect any strong impulse on the part of church institutions to develop new suburban areas, nor was there any consistent pattern that might have distinguished the efforts of the church from those of other great landholders.

In both towns the Church's dominating physical presence was inescapable. Besides the visual impact of the great churches and parish churches on urban landscapes composed of one-, two- and (from the fifteenth century) three-storey buildings, the precincts of church institutions accounted for a huge amount of urban space. Within the medieval walls of Worcester ecclesiastical precincts took up rather more than a quarter of the available area; in Gloucester it was a third. When the medieval suburbs are taken into account, about 18 per cent of the total built-up area of Worcester was ecclesiastical, as was about 17 per cent of Gloucester. The stronger Church presence within the walls had, as might be expected, much to do with the extensive precincts of the senior minsters, but it was also a product of the relative chronology of settlement and church-founding, and the success of the friaries (and their patrons) in finding vacant intramural sites close to the urban population.

It would, however, be a mistake to think of ecclesiastical precincts as unchanging features in an evolving urban landscape. The evidence is clear that ecclesiastical precincts – the larger ones in particular – grew, and sometimes contracted, and could be replanned, just like any other urban real estate. Insofar as its development is known, the precinct of the Old Minster in Gloucester probably quadrupled in area between *c.* 700 and 1500. The form of the earliest precinct of Worcester Cathedral remains obscure, mainly because both it and the adjacent quarter of the city were replanned together, probably in the tenth century. The loss of a large part of it to the castle in the 1060s had an enduring impact on its internal organization and architectural form, even though its land was restored to it within two centuries of the event.

Similarly, ordinary parish church plots resembled those of their secular neighbours, as well as the great precincts, in their behaviour as well as their physical form. They could be reduced by commercial encroachments and the alienation of property; they could be enlarged by the acquisition of adjacent land. Some church-plots appear to have begun life as secular plots. But churchyard archaeology remains undeveloped in both towns, and there is much left to learn about the use to which church plots were put before the great churches lost their monopolies – actual or theoretical – of burial. Of church buildings, this volume has had little to say. This is in part because our central concerns lay elsewhere, but it is also an indirect tribute to the active urban parish communities in the eighteenth century (and to a lesser extent the early nineteenth), whose vigorous rebuilding ensured that so little medieval parochial architecture has come down to us. A skeletal chronology of church-building trends after the Norman Conquest can be discerned (Chapter 8), but the finer details of art, architecture, liturgy and patronage are lost forever.

The distribution of parish churches in each town was different and reflected patterns of secular occupation as well as diverse historical factors, such as pre-urban influences and the location of the respective *burhs*. In Gloucester, the pattern was simple because the secular occupation pattern was simple: wealth and wealthy properties, population and traffic were concentrated on the four main streets – so too were the churches. In Worcester the secular geography was much more complex, and the one principal traffic street (the High Street) was dominated by a single ancient church that retarded the development of further church foundations along it.

The foundations of the friaries took place over more than a century, from the 1230s to the 1340s. Their siting was determined by the distribution of their patrons' landholdings and the availability of vacant land. As it happened, open land was still available within the twelfth- and thirteenth-century walls in Worcester, as it was within the walls of Gloucester, away from the four principal streets. As a consequence, most of the friaries – unusually – were able to find intramural sites.

Their precincts display a uniform pattern of enlargement through the acquisition of multiple land parcels within a century or so after their foundation, and a common pattern of planning in as much as although these precincts lay behind built-up frontages, the friars' churches were all easily accessible from the main streets via lanes and new access routes laid down in the event of precinct enlargement. Imposing gates were placed on main-street frontages to advertise the friaries' presence further back. A feature of some, and perhaps all, of these friaries was a more extensive cemetery than would be expected from the historical record such as that of wills. Slight as the evidence is, it points to these cemeteries as being the principal final resting place of the poorest from each town.

Hospitals and the nunnery of the Whiteladies in Worcester occupied classic peripheral or suburban locations. At any rate, the major institutions that had an independent existence and occupied purpose-built buildings did so; short-lived and doubtless poor hospitals, as well as those wholly owned by greater religious houses, evidently might occupy ordinary secular buildings, scarcely to be distinguished from the urban housing around them. Such was the tenement just inside the east gate of Gloucester in which St Peter's Abbey housed various paupers and invalids (*1455 Rental*, 94b).

Thus any determining influence these churches had on the overall shape and nature of the urban community can be sought only in the earliest centuries of their towns. The only substantial later initiative we have identified was the development of the northern suburb at Worcester, begun probably whilst the *burh* defences still stood, and so of quite early date, together with more limited involvement in the development of other suburban areas. The extent to which Lanthony Priory was wholly responsible for Gloucester's southern suburb – which archaeological evidence from one area suggests – or whether instead it took over a district where some suburban growth had already been initiated by the constables, must for the moment remain uncertain. Otherwise, in the post-Conquest centuries and particularly in the late middle ages the impact of the greater churches on the urban environment was confined to their own precincts and to their substantial holdings of houses and commercial premises. By contrast with the pre-Conquest period, when Gloucester's New Minster apparently planned its part of Hare Lane with marketing functions in mind, there is no evidence from later centuries that any of these churches planned their own land to secure any commercial advantage. There were no new suburban marketplaces, for instance, and no obvious attempts to develop new central areas to rival or supplement those established in the initial phases of town-planning in the decades around 900.

Some quantification of institutional involvement in the physical growth of the two towns, however schematic, has to be attempted. At Gloucester, the total late-medieval built-up area (including all ground covered by plots, but excluding the castle and religious precincts) may have covered an area of, very roughly, 137 acres (55.5 hectares). Of this, 86 acres (34.8 hectares), or 63 per cent of the total, seems to have originated in planned urban extensions. About 28 per cent of the total built-up area came into being as the result of town-planning by church institutions, and most of this activity took place before the Conquest. In Worcester, the total late-medieval built-up area (excluding all precincts, as above) probably covered about 129 acres (52.2 hectares). Of this, about 46 per cent may be identified as the result of planned urban extensions. The great majority of this figure, 39 per cent of the total built-up area, may be attributed to developments sponsored by successive bishops, the ecclesiastical lords of the city. The mainly post-Conquest west bank transpontine suburbs show few if any signs of organized origins, apart from the causeway approaching the

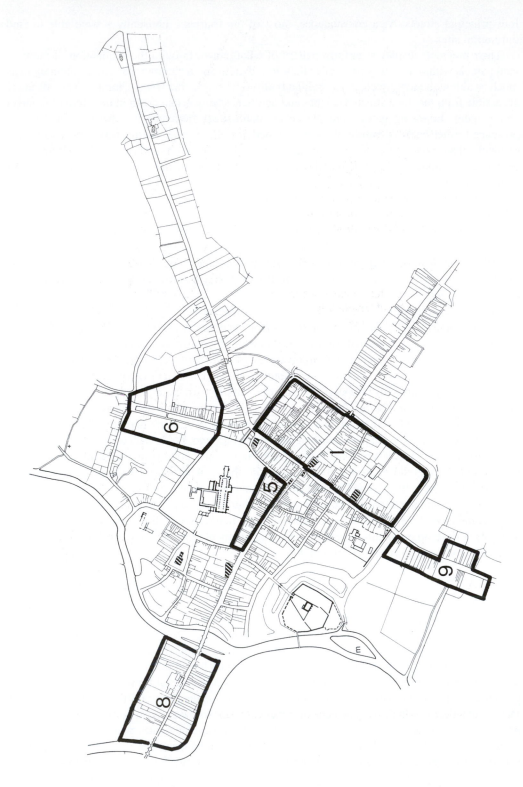

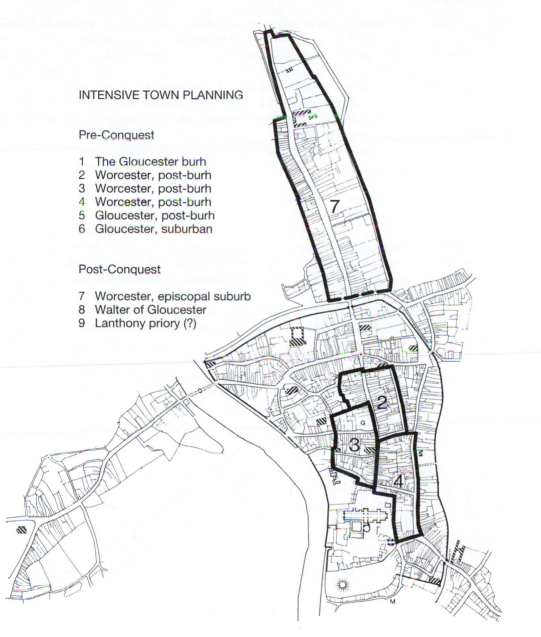

INTENSIVE TOWN PLANNING

Pre-Conquest

1 The Gloucester burh
2 Worcester, post-burh
3 Worcester, post-burh
4 Worcester, post-burh
5 Gloucester, post-burh
6 Gloucester, suburban

Post-Conquest

7 Worcester, episcopal suburb
8 Walter of Gloucester
9 Lanthony priory (?)

15.1   Institutional town-planning in medieval Gloucester (left) and Worcester (right).

bridge. On the east bank only, the percentage of the built-up area resulting from ecclesiastical town-planning rises to 46 per cent. This figure, however, almost certainly under-represents the degree of organization in the landscape. The 'unplanned' remainder is accounted for largely by intramural areas, some of which – like the western half of the *burh* – may well have been truly 'unplanned', and based upon centuries-old land parcels; but others – like Newport Street, and Sidbury – may, as we have seen, have been largely 'unplanned' in the conventional sense whilst yet perhaps concealing some attributes of organization in their landscape, whether in reclamation or the ordered apportionment of access to a natural resource.

In very broad terms: Gloucester, the royal foundation and capital, appears to have been spatially a more organized town than Worcester, though within some of the ordered frameworks – the new streets of the *burh*, for example – settlement at the level of the plot-series or individual plot was no more ordered than it was anywhere else. But despite this greater institutional involvement in urban growth, it was in Worcester, the episcopal city – as we might expect – that the Church had the higher profile. The role of the Church as a town-planner in the study towns was essentially determined by patterns of lordship established centuries before the foundation of the *burhs*.

'Town-planning' is less easily defined in the context of the growth of old towns than it is in the foundation of new ones. This is not just a function of the state of the evidence – the sharp divide between what might once have been termed 'organic' growth (Barley 1976) and deliberate, planned, urban extension begins to dissolve on closer inspection. Organized or planned urban landscapes could assume a range of forms. Was the Church's contribution in any way distinctive? Was there such a thing as ecclesiastical town-planning? Our conclusion is that there was not – that there was just town-planning by ecclesiastics. Town-planning ventures promoted by Church institutions seem no different, and depart from 'ideal' plans no more and no less than their secular equivalents. Precisely the same range of characteristics is apparent in all, regardless of lordship: there were no rules, styles or fashions, only recurrent features in varying combinations. As has been noted recently of the smaller urban foundations in the region: 'Benedictine town planning was without pretension' and, just like contemporary developments by secular lords, 'was directed primarily towards the effective development of urban estates' (Slater 1996).

No two planning episodes – whether street-systems, streets or suburbs – described here are identical; each appears to have incorporated attributes as appropriate to the site, and individually, these attributes – with one important exception – hardly varied from the beginning of the period (*c.* 900) to the end (*c.* 1200). The exception, the individual attribute that certainly did vary through time, was plot size, or more precisely, plot size in relation to location within the settlement. The large plots seen and documented in early Worcester must have been different in function and status from the strip-type plots or burgages that came later, though similarly large plots were of course to be found in marginal areas in all periods, or assembled in central areas in later periods. The only other variation through time that may, tentatively, be identified seems to be in the articulation or combination of individual attributes – seen most clearly in the relatively sophisticated provision for functional diversity inherent in the layout of the lanes and plot-types of the bishops' Foregate suburb in Worcester.

At the risk of stating the obvious, we would reiterate the generally accepted (and nonetheless true) point that medieval town life and culture were inseparable from the Church and churches. And although that theme – amply explored by other and abler historians and archaeologists – lay outside the intention and scope of this study, we are fully aware of how far the development of the varied pattern of urban churches was an aspect of the distinct identity developed by the emerging urban communities of the greater towns. If we have placed our emphasis on the range and scope of the

Church's direct contribution to the physical shape of the town, that is not to deny either the Church's essential contribution to urban culture, nor the impact that that culture itself had on the urban form. It was the impact of the Church as institution we set out to study, not the more subtle and even less measurable impact of Christian belief and practice on the town-planners. Only occasionally have we pointed to possible circumstances under which a Christian mentality influenced the planning process, as for instance in the almost ritual layout of the Northgate Street–Southgate Street axis in Gloucester, with its strategically placed churches in the centre and the gates at either end. Such observations can seldom go beyond speculation, and we have deliberately avoided extended discussion of such features, which included the cross-formation of Gloucester's main streets (not necessarily to be explained entirely in pragmatic terms, nor in terms of inherited Roman features), and the possible siting of particular churches for visual impact (see above, p. 232).

And finally: whilst we set out to assess the contribution played by the major churches in the early growth of both Worcester and Gloucester, and to inform our understanding of that early development through studies of the lesser churches and their parishes, we did not envisage that the role of the Church in urban growth could ever be quantified in any exact way. English medieval towns grew out of the diverse needs of a developing society and state for central places to fulfil a range of economic, administrative and strategic functions, and in that rapidly changing situation the institutions of the Church – themselves subject to far-reaching changes – played a succession of roles, and each of varying importance. That they did so in such a way as to make such a series of indelible marks on the urban form is not the least aspect of their enduring legacy.

Appendix

Cartographic methods and sources

The essential first step in the analysis of the medieval urban landscapes of Gloucester and Worcester has been the reconstruction, as far as possible, of their late-medieval town-plans: streets; ecclesiastical, political and property boundaries; defences; ecclesiastical buildings and precincts; and major public buildings. In the absence of pre-seventeenth-century maps, later maps that depict features that can be shown on documentary, archaeological or architectural grounds to have been present in the medieval period have been used.

Maps and plans presented in this study are therefore primarily based, unless otherwise stated, on the earliest available large-scale surveys. For both towns these are the first edition 1:500 Ordnance Survey town-plans published in the 1880s, though some use has also been made of the slightly earlier and larger-scale Board of Health plans of Gloucester. While the historicity or potential antiquity of much of the detail contained on nineteenth-century Ordnance Survey plans is widely recognized, the plans confront the reader with a dense mass of information that is difficult to sort visually. Potentially the most conservative townscape elements – streets and property boundaries – have therefore been extracted using a consistent formula throughout the cartography (outlined in Baker and Slater 1992, 46–9). The relationship or degree of correspondence between features extant in the medieval period and those surveyed in the eighteenth or nineteenth centuries is discussed in the text, particularly Chapters 3 and 6. The extent of settlement shown in the general plans is similarly based on the earliest reliable map available: for Gloucester, this is Hall and Pinnell's map of 1780, for Worcester, George Young's of 1779. It is recognized that the extent of the respective built-up areas at those dates cannot be assumed to reflect each town's final medieval extent (though the evidence of Speed's maps of the early seventeenth century, and other sources, suggests that they were not entirely dissimilar). The issue of changing settlement extent is also addressed further in the text. Marginal areas that may have reverted fully from urban to agricultural use in periods of decline, stagnation or civil war before the eighteenth century will not, of course, be represented in the cartography. Use was made of whatever reliable pre-Ordnance Survey cartography was available for each town to edit-out identifiable post-medieval changes in the town-plans and to reconstruct the preceding arrangements in those areas.

Source notes for Gloucester

The Cathedral Close (St Peter's Abbey) is based on the 1st edition O.S. plan, with corrections from the plan by Richard Bryant in Welander 1991, and details of the Abbot's Lodgings from plans by Waller in St John Hope 1897. The plan of the second royal castle is based on Hurst 1984; that of the first (Norman) castle (fig. 3.11) is derived from excavation and geophysics, from Atkin 1992a and pers. comm. The city wall is taken from the 1st edition O.S., with details added for demolished sections from archaeological sources, principally: Hurst 1986; Heighway 1983a; and Garrod and Heighway 1984. The course of the River Severn is derived from Hall and Pinnell's map of 1780, with archaeological evidence from Heighway and Garrod 1981 and Heighway and Bryant 1999; the former Foreign and Westgate Bridges are from Hurst 1974. The plan of the Dominican Friary is taken from Knowles 1932; that of the Franciscan Friary church is from Austin 1932 with amendments provided by J. Rhodes, and that of the Whitefriars from Heighway and Garrod 1981, p. 13. Details of Lanthony Priory are from the plan by J. Rhodes in *Glevum* 23, 1989, pp. 24–5. Streets and lanes altered in the late eighteenth and nineteenth centuries have generally been restored from the city maps by Hall and Pinnell (1780) and Arthur Causton (1844). Sheep Lane was restored from f. 32 of 'Plans of houses and lands owned by the City', 1826, by T. Commeline; details of St Mary Magdalene's Hospital from the Glos. Society for Industrial Archaeology, 1971, p. 41, derived from enclosure plans (GCRO Q/RI 70); and Bride Lane from a MS plan of 1743 (Gloucester Central Library NQ 30/36): the sources for these lanes were kindly provided by John Rhodes. The central street encroachments were reconstructed primarily from archaeological evidence in Atkin 1992b. Details of the Lower Westgate Street/Powke Lane area were supplemented from Heighway and Bryant 1999. The city's rural surroundings are derived principally from Hall and Pinnell's and Causton's maps.

Source notes for Worcester

The form of the Cathedral Close before the insertion of College Street, and the position/plan of St Michael's in Bedwardine, are based on Young's map of 1779 and on the 1794 'Plan of the intended road at Worcester' (College Street) in the 1824 Corporation Plan Book (HWRO BA 5268 f926.11). The Bishop's Palace ground-plan is derived from that in VCH Worcs., iv, 407. Details of the former castle are derived from Samuel Mainley's 1822 plan of Worcester Castle (reproduced in Carver (ed.) 1980). The City Wall is based on O.S. 1st edition, with additional information from Broad's map of 1768, Young's of 1779 and Doharty's of 1741, and archaeological data from Beardsmore and Bennett in Carver (ed.) 1980; the gates are depicted conventionally. The form of the medieval Severn Bridge is taken from Doharty's map of 1741 and Broad's of 1768, with additional information from Beardsmore 1980. The Dominican Friary: from Hughes 1986 (general plan) and archaeological evidence from Mundy 1986b and 1989. The Franciscan Friary: building outlines from Young's map of 1779, and an unidentified MS plan in Hughes and Molyneux 1984, 9. St Wulfstan's Hospital: plan derived from an unpublished survey by Molyneux (Worcester City Museum). Streets and minor lanes altered or added in the late eighteenth and nineteenth centuries are generally restored from Young's map of 1779 and the 1824 Corporation Plan Book; this includes Cornmarket, Silver Street, St Clement's Lane, Copenhagen Street/Warmstry Slip. Pre-railway property boundaries in Foregate Street have been taken from Worcester & Hereford Railway map (HWRO BA 438 f 209 161/166.1) of 1845. The city's rural surroundings (fields and lanes are generally taken from Young's map of 1779). Additional information for St John's was derived from Young's 1777 map of the Dean & Chapter properties in St John's and St Clement's (HWRO 971.2 BA 1691/43). Pitchcroft, and fields west of the Tything are based on an undated (eighteenth-century) MS estate map of holdings of St Oswald's Hospital (copy in files of Worcester City Museum).

Bibliography

Abbott, R. (1967), 'Excavations at the Shire Hall Site, Gloucester, 1965', *Transactions of the Bristol and Gloucestershire Archaeological Society*, 86, pp. 95–101

Allan, J., Henderson, C., Higham, R. (1984), 'Saxon Exeter', in Haslam, J. (ed.), *Anglo-Saxon Towns in Southern England*, Chichester, pp. 385–414

Allies, J. (1852), *On the Ancient British, Roman and Saxon Antiquities and Folk-lore of Worcestershire*, 2nd edn, London

Amphlett, J. (ed.) (1899), *Lay Subsidy Roll, AD 1332–3, and Nonarum Inquisitiones, 1340, for the County of Worcester*, Worcestershire Historical Society

Anon. (1880–81), 'Ancient charter relating to Woodchester', *Transactions of Bristol and Gloucestershire Archaeological Society*, 5, pp. 148–53

Arnold, T. (ed.) (1882–5), *Symeonis Monachi Opera Omnia*, 2 vols, Rolls Series, 75, London

Arnold-Forster, F. (1899), *Studies in Church Dedications*, 3 vols, London

Astle, T., Ayscough, S. and Caley, J. (eds.) (1802), *Taxatio Ecclesiastica Angliae et Walliae auctoritate P. Nicholai IV, circa AD 1291*, Record Commission

Atkin, M. (1987), 'Post-medieval archaeology in Gloucester: a review', *Post-Medieval Archaeology*, 21, pp. 1–24

— (1990), 'Southgate Gallery, Southgate Street site 3/89', in 'Excavations in Gloucester 1989 – an interim report', *Glevensis*, 24, pp. 3–7

— (1991a), 'Excavations in Gloucester 1990, site 20/90, MEB Works, Barbican Road', *Glevensis*, 25, pp. 6–10

— (1991b), 'Excavations in Gloucester 1990, site 3/89, Southgate Gallery, Southgate Street, *Glevensis*, 25, p. 15

— (1991c), 'Excavations in Gloucester 1990, site 8/89: Upper Quay Street/Westage Street', *Glevensis*, 25, pp. 16–18

— (1992a), 'Archaeological fieldwork in Gloucester in 1991', Blackfriars Assessment Project, *Glevensis*, 26, pp. 35–40

— (1992b), 'Archaeological fieldwork in Gloucester 1991: sewer renewals', *Glevensis*, 26, pp. 45–7

— (1992), 'Blackfriars assessment project: excavations on Ladybellegate Street Car Park', *Glevensis*, 26, p. 37

Atkins, I. (1937), 'The Church of Worcester from the 8th century to the 12th Century', *The Antiquaries Journal*, 17, pp. 371–91

— (1940), 'The Church of Worcester from the 8th century to the 12th Century', (I, II) *The Antiquaries Journal*, 20, pp. 1–38; 203–29

Austin, R. (1932), 'The Grey Friars, Gloucester', *Transactions of the Bristol and Gloucestershire Archaeological Society*, 54, pp. 117–27

Ayers, B. (1985), 'Excavations within the north-east bailey of Norwich castle, 1979', *East Anglian Archaeology*, 28, pp. 7–26, 63–5

Baker, N.J. (1980), 'Churches, parishes and early medieval topography' in Carver, M.O.H. (ed.), *Medieval Worcester, an Archaeological Framework: Transactions of the Worcestershire Archaeological Society*, 3rd series, 7, pp. 31–7

— (1980b), 'The urban churches of Worcester – a survey', in Carver, M.O.H. (ed.), *Medieval Worcester, an Archaeological Framework: Transactions of the Worcestershire Archaeological Society*, 3rd series, 7, pp. 115–24

— (1988), *The Archaeology of Walsall*, Birmingham University Field Archaeology Unit report

— (forthcoming), *Shrewsbury, an Archaeological Assessment*, English Heritage

— (ed.) (2002), 'Shrewsbury Abbey: studies in the archaeology and history of an urban monastery', *Shropshire Archaeological and Historical Society Monographs, no. 2*

— and Slater, T.R. (1992), 'Morphological Regions in English Medieval Towns', in Whitehand, J.W.R.

and Larkham, P. J. (eds.), *Urban Landscapes, international perspectives*, London, pp. 43–68

— Dalwood, H., Holt, R.A., Mundy, C.F., and Taylor, G. (1992), 'From Roman to medieval Worcester: development and planning in the Anglo-Saxon city', *Antiquity*, 66, pp. 65–74

— Lawson, J.B., Maxwell, R., and Smith, J.T. (1993), 'Further work on Pride Hill, Shrewsbury', *Transactions of the Shropshire Archaeological and Historical Society*, 68, pp. 27–8

— and Holt, R.A. (1996), 'The city of Worcester in the tenth century', in Brooks, N.P. and Cubitt, C. (eds.), *St Oswald of Worcester: Life and Influence*, Leicester, pp. 129–46

Ballard, A. (1904), *The Domesday Boroughs*, Oxford

Barker P.A. (ed.), (1969), *The Origins of Worcester: Transactions of the Worcestershire Archaeological Society*, 3rd series, 2

— (1994), *A short architectural history of Worcester Cathedral*, Worcester Cathedral Publications, 2, Worcester.

— (1996), 'The refectory undercroft', in Barker, P. A. and Guy, C. (eds.), *Archaeology at Worcester Cathedral: report of the sixth annual symposium, March 1996*, Worcester, pp. 4–11

— with Cubberley, A.L., Crowfoot, E. and Radford C.A.R. (1974), 'Two burials under the refectory of Worcester Cathedral', *Medieval Archaeology*, 18, pp. 46–151

Barley, M. W. (ed.) (1976), *The Plans and Topography of Medieval Towns in England and Wales*, Council for British Archaeology, Research Report 14, London

Barlow, F. (1963), *The English Church 1000–1066*, London

— (1970), *Edward the Confessor*, London

Barron, C. (1989), 'The fourteenth-century poll tax: returns for Worcester', *Midland History*, 14, pp. 1–29

Barrow, J. (1992a), 'How the twelfth-century monks of Worcester perceived their past', in Magdalino, P. (ed.), *The Perception of the Past in Twelfth-Century Europe*, London, pp. 53–74

— (1992b), 'Urban cemetery location in the high Middle Ages', in Bassett, S.R. (ed.) *Death in Towns*, Leicester, pp. 78–100

— (1996), 'The community of Worcester, 961–*c*. 1100', in Brooks, N.P. and Cubitt, C. (eds.), *St Oswald of Worcester: Life and Influence*, Leicester, pp. 84–99

Bassett, S.R. (1985), 'A probable Mercian royal mausoleum at Winchcombe, Gloucestershire', *The Antiquaries Journal*, 65, pp. 81–100

— (1989a), 'Churches in Worcester before and after the conversion of the Anglo-Saxons', *The Antiquaries' Journal*, 69, pp. 225–56

— (ed.) (1989b), *The Origins of Anglo-Saxon Kingdoms*, Leicester

— 1991), 'Anglo-Saxon Shrewsbury and its churches', *Midland History*, 16, pp. 1–23.

— (1992a), 'Church and diocese in the West Midlands: the transition from British to Anglo-Saxon control', in Blair, J. and Sharpe, R. (eds.), *Pastoral Care before the Parish*, Leicester, pp. 13–40

— (ed.) (1992b), *Death in Towns*, Leicester

Beardsmore, C. (1980), 'Documentary evidence for the history of Worcester city defences', in Carver, M.O.H. (ed.), *Medieval Worcester, an Archaeological Framework: Transactions of the Worcestershire Archaeological Society*, 3rd series, 7, pp. 53–64

Benedikz, B.S. and Brock, S. (1977), *Worcester Cathedral Library: Catalogue of Muniments, Class A*, Birmingham University Library, Birmingham

Bennett, J. (1980), 'Excavation and survey on the medieval city wall, 1973', in Carver, M.O.H. (ed.), *Medieval Worcester, an Archaeological Framework: Transactions of the Worcestershire Archaeological Society*, 3rd series, 7, pp. 65–71

Beresford, M. (1967), *New Towns of the Middle Ages: Town Plantation in England, Wales and Gascony*, London

Bevan, L. (ed.) (2001), *Indecent Exposure: Sexuality, Society, and the Archaeological Record*, Glasgow

Biddle, M. (ed.) (1976), *Winchester in the Early Middle Ages: Winchester Studies*, I, Oxford

— (1977), 'Alban and the Anglo-Saxon Church', in Runcie, R. (ed.), *Cathedral and City*, London

— (1983), 'The study of Winchester: archaeology and history in a British town, 1961–1983', *Proceedings of the British Academy*, 69, pp. 93–135

— and Hill, D. (1971), 'Late Saxon planned towns', *Antiquaries Journal* 51, pp. 70–85

Birch, W. de G. (1883–99), *Cartularium Saxonicum*, 3 vols and index, London

Blair, J. (1985), 'Secular minster churches in Domesday Book', in Sawyer, P.H. (ed.), *Domesday Book: A Reassessment*, London, pp. 104–42

— (1987), 'The 12th-century bishop's palace at Hereford', *Medieval Archaeology*, 31, pp. 59–72

— (1988), 'From minster to parish church', in Blair, J. (ed.) *Minsters and Parish Churches: The Local Church in Transition 950–1200*, Oxford University Committee for Archaeology, Monograph 17, pp. 1–19

— (1989), 'Thornbury, Binsey: a probable defensive enclosure associated with St Frideswide' *Oxoniensia*, 53, pp. 3–20

— and Sharpe, R. (eds.) (1992), *Pastoral Care Before the Parish*, Leicester

Bloom, J. Harvey (ed.) (1909), *Original Charters relating to the City of Worcester in Possession of the Dean and Chapter*, Worcestershire Historical Society

— (ed.) (1912), 'Charters from St Swithun's, Worcester', in Hamilton, S.G. (ed.), *Collectanea*, Worcestershire Historical Society, pp. 1–68

Bolland, J. (1695), *Acta Sanctorum, Junii I* , Antwerp. Reprinted 1969, Brussels

Bond, C.J. (1973), 'The estates of Evesham Abbey: a preliminary survey of their medieval topography', *Vale of Evesham Historical Society Research Papers*, 4, pp. 2–59

— (1975), 'The medieval topography of the Evesham Abbey estates: a supplement', *Vale of Evesham Historical Society Research Papers*, pp. 51–9

— (1988), 'Church and parish in Norman Worcestershire', in Blair, J. (ed.) *Minsters and Parish Churches: The Local Church in Transition 950–1200*, Oxford University Committee for Archaeology, Monograph 17, pp. 119–58

Bowen, J. A. (1992), 'Problems with the reconstruction of the monastic topography of Worcester Cathedral', in Barker, P. A., and Guy, C. (eds.), *Report of the second annual symposium on the precinct*, Worcester, pp. 18–20

Braudel, F. (1974), *Capitalism and Material Life 1400–1800*, London

Brewer, J.S., Dimock, J.F. and Warner, G.F. (eds.) (1861–91), *Giraldi Cambrensis Opera*, 8 vols., Rolls Series 21, London

Brock, S. (1981), *Worcester Cathedral Library: Catalogue of Muniments, Class B*, Birmingham University Library, Birmingham

Brooke, C.N.L. (1970), 'The church in the towns, 1000–1250', *Studies in Church History*, 6, Ecclesiastical History Society, Oxford, pp. 59–83

— and Keir, G. (1975), *London 800–1216: The Shaping of a City*, London

Brooks, E. St J. (1953), *The Irish Cartularies of Llanthony Prima and Secunda*, Coimisiun Laimscribhinni Na h'Eireann, Dublin

Brooks, N.P. (1971), 'The development of military obligations in eighth- and ninth-century England', in Clemoes, P., and Hughes, K. (eds.), *England before the Conquest: studies in primary sources presented to Dorothy Whitelock*, Cambridge, pp. 69–84

— (1979), 'England in the ninth century: the crucible of defeat', *Transactions of the Royal Historical Society*, 5th series, 29, pp. 1–20.

— (1984), *The Early History of the Church of Canterbury*, Leicester

— (1996), 'The administrative background to the Burghal Hidage', in Hinton, D., and Rumble, A., *The Defences of Wessex*, Manchester, pp. 128–150

— and Cubitt, C. (eds.) (1996), *St Oswald of Worcester: Life and Influence*, Leicester,

Brown, D. (1991a), 'Salvage recording at St Oswald's Almshouses, Worcester', *Hereford and Worcester County Council Archaeology Section*, Report 83

— (1991b), *Watching-brief at 3 College Precincts, Worcester*, typescript report, *Hereford and Worcester County Council Archaeology Service*

Bryant, R. (1980), 'Excavations at St Mary de Lode, Gloucester, 1978–1979', *Glevensis*, 14, pp. 4–12

Buchanan-Dunlop, W.R. (1936), 'All Saints church, Worcester', *Transactions of Worcestershire Archaeological Society*, new series 13, pp. 15–27

— (1937), 'St Andrew's church, Worcester', *Transactions of Worcestershire Archaeological Society*, new series 14, pp. 18–29

— (1939), 'St Helen's church, Worcester', *Transactions of Worcestershire Archaeological Society*, new series 16, pp.14–26

— (1942), 'Old St Michael's church and the College churchyard, Worcester', *Transactions of Worcestershire Archaeological Society*, new series 19, pp.19–24

— (1950), 'St Alban's church, Worcester', *Transactions of Worcestershire Archaeological Society*, new series 27, pp. 1–14

Buckland, P.C., Magilton, J.R. and Hayfield, C. (eds.) (1989), *The Archaeology of Doncaster, 2: the medieval and later town*, British Archaeological Reports, 202

Bullough, D.A. (1975), 'The continental background of the reform', in Parsons, D. (ed.), *Tenth-Century Studies*, London and Chichester, pp. 20–36

Bund, J.W. Willis (ed.) (1894), *The Inquisitiones Post Mortem for the County of Worcester*, Part I, Worcestershire Historical Society

— (ed.) (1902), *Register of Bishop Godfrey Giffard, 1268–1301*, Worcestershire Historical Society

— (ed.) (1909), *The Inquisitiones Post Mortem for the County of Worcester*, Part II, Worcestershire Historical Society

— and Amphlett, J. (eds.) (1893), *Lay Subsidy Roll for the County of Worcester, c. 1280*, Worcestershire Historical Society

Bunyard, B.M. (ed.) (1941), *The Brokage Book of Southampton 1439–40*, Southampton Records Society, 40

Burnham, B.C. (1987), 'The morphology of Romano-British "small towns"', *Archaeological Journal*, 144, pp. 156–90.

— and Wacher, J. (1990), *The 'small towns' of Roman Britain*, London

Butler, L.A.S. (1986), 'Church dedications and the cults of Anglo-Saxon saints in England', in Butler, L.A.S. and Morris, R.K. (eds.), *The Anglo-Saxon Church*, Council for British Archaeology, Research Report 60, London, pp. 44–50

Calendars of Charter Rolls, 6 vols. (1903–27), London

Calendars of Close Rolls (1902–), London

Calendars of Fine Rolls, 22 vols (1911–62), London

Calendars of Inquisitions Miscellaneous, 7 vols. (1916–69), London

Calendars of Liberate Rolls, 6 vols. (1917–64), London

Calendars of Papal Registers: Papal Letters, 14 vols. (1894–1961), London

Calendars of Patent Rolls (1891–), London

Caley, J. (ed.) (1810–34), *Valor Ecclesiasticus*, 6 vols., Record Commission, London

— Ellis, H., and Bandinel, B. (re-eds.) (1849) of Dugdale, Sir William (ed.), *Monasticon Anglicanum*, 6 vols. in 8, London

Cam, H. (1944), *Liberties and Communities of Medieval England*, Cambridge

Campbell, A. (ed.) (1962), *The Chronicle of Æthelweard*, London

Campbell, J. (1979), 'The Church in Anglo-Saxon towns', in *The Church in Town and Countryside*, Studies in Church History, 16, Oxford, pp. 119–35

— (1987), 'Some agents and agencies of the Anglo-Saxon state', in Holt, J.C. (ed.), *Domesday Studies*, Woodbridge, pp. 201–18

Carr, R.D. and Caruth, J. (1989), 'Archaeological excavations: Bury St Edmunds, the cathedral', *Proceedings of the Suffolk Institute of Archaeology and History*, 37, pp. 71–2

Carter, A. (1978), 'The Anglo-Saxon origins of Norwich: the problems and approaches', in Clemoes, P. (ed.), *Anglo-Saxon England* 7, pp. 175–204

Carver, M.O.H. (ed.) (1980a), 'Medieval Worcester, an archaeological framework', *Transactions of the Worcestershire Archaeological Society*, 3rd series, 7

— (1980b), 'The excavation of three medieval craftsmen's tenements in Sidbury, Worcester, 1976', in Carver, M.O.H. (ed.), 'Medieval Worcester, an archaeological framework', *Transactions of the Worcestershire Archaeological Society*, 3rd series, 7, pp. 154–219.

— (1987), *Underneath English Towns*, London

Cave, T. and Wilson, R.A. (eds.) (1924), *The Parliamentary Survey of the Lands and Possessions of the Dean and Chapter of Worcester, made in or about the year 1649*, Worcestershire Historical Society

Clanchy, M.T. (1979), *From Memory to Written Record*, London

Clark, A. (ed.) (1905), *The English Register of Godstow Nunnery*, Early English Text Society, Original Series 142, London

Clarke, H. (1980), 'Excavations at Worcester Cathedral 1970–1', in Carver, M.O.H. (ed.), 'Medieval Worcester, an archaeological framework', *Transactions of the Worcestershire Archaeological Society*, 3rd series, 7, pp. 127–37

Clarke, H.B. and Dyer, C.C. (1969), 'Anglo-Saxon and Early Norman Worcester: The Documentary Evidence', in Barker, P.A. (ed.), 'The Origins of Worcester', *Transactions of the Worcestershire*

Archaeological Society, 3rd series, 2, pp. 27–33

Cleary, A.S. Esmonde (1987), 'Extramural areas of Romano-British small towns', *British Archaeological Reports*, British series, 169

— (1989), *The Ending of Roman Britain*, London

Clemoes, P., and Hughes, K. (eds.) (1971), E*ngland before the Conquest: studies in primary sources presented to Dorothy Whitelock*, Cambridge

Coleman, O. (ed.) (1960), *The Brokage Book of Southampton 1443–44*, vol.1, Southampton Records Series

— (ed.) (1961), *The Brokage Book of Southampton 1443–44*, vol.2, Southampton Records Series

Colgrave, B. and Mynors, R.A.B. (eds.) (1969), *Bede's Ecclesiastical History of the English People*, Oxford

Conzen, M.R.G. (1968), 'The use of town plans in the study of urban history', in Dyos, H.J. (ed.), *The Study of Urban History*, Leicester, pp. 113–30

— (1969), 'Alnwick, Northumberland: a study in town-plan analysis', *Institute of British Geographers Publications*, 27 (revised edition of 1960 edition), London

— (1988), 'Morphogenesis, morphological regions and secular human agency in the historic townscape, as exemplified by Ludlow', in Denecke, D., and Shaw, G (eds.), *Urban Historical Geography, recent progress in Britain and Germany*, Cambridge, pp. 253–72

Cra'ster, M. D. (1961), 'St Michael's, Gloucester, 1956', *Transactions of the Bristol and Gloucestershire Archaeological Society*, 80, pp. 59–74

Crawford, S. (1998), 'Excavations at Worcester Cathedral chapterhouse lawn 1997', in Guy, C. (ed.), *Archaeology at Worcester Cathedral: report of the eighth annual symposium, March 1998*, Worcester, pp. 7–8

Cromarty, D. (1991), *Everyday life in Medieval Shrewsbury*, Shrewsbury

Crummy, P. (1979), 'The system of measurement used in town planning from the ninth to the thirteenth centuries', in Hawkes, S.C., Brown, D. and Campbell, J. (eds.), Anglo-Saxon Studies in Archaeology and History, I, *British Archaeological Reports*, British Series, 72, pp. 149–164

Curia Regis Rolls of the Reign of Henry III, 9 (1952), London

Currie, C. (1989a), *Birdport and its relationship to the topography of Worcester*, typescript, Deansway Archaeology Project Hereford and Worcester County Council Archaeology Section

— (1989b), *Deansway Archaeology Project Historical Synthesis*, typescript, Deansway Archaeology Project Hereford and Worcester County Council Archaeology Section

Dallas, V. M. (1932), 'The Grey Friars, Gloucester', *Transactions of the Bristol and Gloucestershire Archaeological Society*, 54, pp. 117–127

Dalwood, H., Mundy, C. and Taylor, G. (1989), 'HWCM 3899 – Deansway, Worcester', *West Midlands Archaeology*, 32

Dalwood, C. H., Buteux, V. A., and Jackson, R. A. (1992), 'Interim report on excavations at Deansway, Worcester, 1988–1989', *Transactions of the Worcestershire Archaeological Society*, 3rd series, 13, pp. 121–8

— Buteux, V. A., and Darlington, J. (1994), 'Excavations at Farrier Street and other sites north of the City Wall, Worcester, 1988–1992', *Transactions of the Worcestershire Archaeological Society*, 3rd series, 14, pp. 75–114

Dancey, C. H. (n.d.), History of St Michael's Church, Gloucester, MS, Gloucester City Library, Gloucestershire Collection 14259

— (1903), 'The Crypt Church, Gloucester, sometimes called St Mary of the South Gate', *Transactions of the Bristol and Gloucestershire Archaeological Society*, 26, pp. 293–307

Darlington, J., and Evans, J. (1992), 'Roman Sidbury, Worcester, excavations 1959–1989', *Transactions of the Worcestershire Archaeological Society*, 3rd series, 13, pp. 5–104

Darlington, R.R. (ed.) (1928), *The Vita Wulfstani of William of Malmesbury*, Camden 3rd series, 40, London

— (ed.) (1968), *The Cartulary of Worcester Cathedral Priory*, Pipe Roll Society new series, 38, London

— McGurk, P. and Bray, J. (eds.) (1995), *The Chronicle of John of Worcester*, vol. II: Annals 450–1066, Oxford

Darvill, T. (1988), 'Excavations on the site of the early Norman castle at Gloucester, 1983–84', Medieval Archaeology, 32, pp. 1–49

Davis, G.R.C. (1958), *Medieval Cartularies of Great Britain*, London

Davison, B.K. (1967), 'The late Saxon town of Thetford: an interim report on the 1964–1966 excavations', *Medieval Archaeology*, 11, pp. 189–208

Denton, J.H. (1970), *English Royal Free Chapels 1100–1300*, Manchester

Dobson, R.B. (ed.) (1983), *The Peasants' Revolt of 1381*, 2nd ed., London

— (1984), 'Mendicant ideal and practice in late medieval York', in Addyman, P. V. and Black, V. E. (eds.), *Archaeological papers from York presented to M. W. Barley*, York Archaeological Trust

Dolley, R.H.M. and Blunt, C.E. (1961), 'The chronology of the coins of Alfred the Great 871–99', in Dolley, R.H.M. (ed.), *Anglo-Saxon Coins: Studies Presented to F.M. Stenton*, London, pp. 77–94

'Dry as Dust Antiquary' (1895), 'The site of St Martin's Church', *Gloucester Journal*, Nov. 30th, 1895: cutting in Langston 1956–7

Durham, B. (1984), 'The Thames crossing at Oxford: archaeological studies 1979–82', *Oxoniensia*, 49

Dyer, A.D. (1973), *The City of Worcester in the Sixteenth Century*, Leicester

— (1991), *Decline and Growth in English Towns, 1400–1640*, Basingstoke

Dyer, C.C. (1969), 'The Saxon cathedrals of Worcester', in Barker, P.A. (ed.), 'The origins of Worcester', *Transactions of Worcestershire Archaeological Society*, 3rd series, 2, p. 34

— (1980), *Lords and Peasants in a Changing Society: The Estates of the Bishopric of Worcester 680–1540*, Cambridge

— (1985), 'Towns and cottages in eleventh-century England, in Mayr-Harting, H. and Moore, R.I. (eds.), *Studies in Medieval History Presented to R.H.C. Davis*, London, pp. 91–106

— (1996), '10,000 West Midland peasants', in Brooks, N.P. and Cubitt, C. (eds.), *St Oswald of Worcester: Life and Influence*, Leicester, pp. 174–193

Dyos, H.J. (ed.) (1968), *The Study of Urban History*, Leicester, pp. 113–30

Dyson, T. (1978), 'Two Saxon land grants for Queenhithe', in Bird, J., Chapman, H. and Clark, J. (eds.), *Collectanea Londiniensia*, London and Middlesex Archaeological Society, Special Paper 2, pp. 200–215

— and Schofield, J. (1984), 'Saxon London' in Haslam, J. (ed.) *Anglo-Saxon Towns in Southern England*, Chichester, pp. 285–313

Edwards, R. (1989), 'Evaluation at King's School, Worcester', *Hereford and Worcester County Council Archaeology Service*, report 33

— (1992), 'Trial excavation and salvage recording at St Oswald's Almshouses, Worcester', *Transactions of the Worcestershire Archaeological Society*, 3rd series, 13, pp. 181–91

Ekwall, E. (1960), *Concise Oxford Dictionary of Place Names*, Oxford

Eld, F.J. (ed.) (1895), *Lay Subsidy Roll for the County of Worcester, 1 Edward I* (*recte 1* Edward III), Worcestershire Historical Society

Eliasssen, F.E., and Ersland, G. A. (eds.) (1996), *Power, Profit and Urban Land: Landownership in medieval and early modern northern European towns*, Aldershot: Ashgate

Ellis, M.H. (1929), 'The bridges of Gloucester and the hospital between the bridges', *Transactions of Bristol and Gloucestershire Archaeological Society*, 51, pp. 169–210

Farley, A. (ed.) (1783), *Domesday Book*, 2 vols, London

Farmer, D.H. (1975), 'The progress of the monastic revival', in Parsons, D. (ed.), *Tenth-Century Studies*, London and Chichester, pp. 10–19

— (1978), *The Oxford Dictionary of Saints*, Oxford

Fendall, M. (1969), 'Sylloge of coins found in the city', in Barker, P.A. (ed.), 'The origins of Worcester', *Transactions of the Worcestershire Archaeological Society*, 3rd series, 2, pp.106–15

Finberg, H.P.R. (1954), 'An early reference to the Welsh cattle trade', *Agricultural History Review*, 2, pp. 12–14

— (1957), 'Some early Gloucestershire estates', in Finberg, H.P.R. (ed.), *Gloucestershire Studies*, Leicester, pp. 1–16

— (1961), 'The early history of Gloucester Abbey', in Finberg, H.P.R., *The Early Charters of the West Midlands*, Leicester, pp. 153–66

Finucane, R.C. (1977), *Miracles and Pilgrims: Popular Beliefs in Medieval England*, London

Fleming, R., (1993), 'Rural elites and urban communities in late-Saxon England', *Past and Present*, 141, pp. 3–37

Floyer, J.K. and Hamilton, S.G. (eds.) (1906), *Catalogue of Manuscripts Preserved in the Chapter Library of Worcester Cathedral*, Worcestershire Historical Society

Ford, D. A. (1995), 'Medieval pottery in Staffordshire, AD 800–1600: a review', *Staffordshire Archaeological Studies*, 7, Stoke-on-Trent

Fosbroke, T.D. (1819), *An Original History of the City of Gloucester*, London

Franklin, M.J. (1988), 'The secular college as a focus for Anglo–Norman piety: St Augustine's, Daventry, in Blair, J. (ed.), *Minsters and Parish Churches: The Local Church in Transition 950–1200*, Oxford University Committee for Archaeology, Monograph 17, Oxford, pp. 97–104

Fry, E.A. (ed.) (1910), *Inquisitiones Post Mortem for Gloucestershire 1302–58*, Index Library, 5, British Record Society, London

Fryde, E.B., Greenway, D.E., Porter, S. and Roy, I. (eds.) (1986), *Handbook of British Chronology*, 3rd edition, Royal Historical Society, London

Fullbrook-Leggatt, L.E.W.O. (1952), *Anglo-Saxon and Medieval Gloucester*, Gloucester

— (1964), 'The River Twyver and the Fullbrook', *Transactions of the Bristol and Gloucestershire Archaeological Society*, 83, pp. 78–84

— (1967), 'Glevum', *Transactions of the Bristol and Gloucestershire Archaeological Society*, 86, pp. 5–15

Fuller, E.A. (1884–5), 'Cirencester, the manor and the town', *Transactions of Bristol and Gloucestershire Archaeological Society*, 9, pp. 298–344

Galster, G. (1966), *Sylloge of Coins of the British Isles: Royal Collection of Coins and Medals, National Museum, Copenhagen. Part II: Anglo-Saxon Coins, Æthelred II*, London

Garrod, A. P. (1987), 'Deans Walk Inn (Site 21/85)', in 'Annual review of minor development sites in Gloucester', *Glevensis*, 21, p. 18

— (1989), '25–25A London Road (site 37/88)', in 'Annual review of minor development sites in Gloucester', *Glevensis*, 23, p. 15

— (1990a), 'St Catherine Street, Hare Lane (site 5/89)', in 'Annual review of minor development sites in Gloucester', *Glevensis*, 24, pp. 14–16

— (1990b), 'Inner Relief Road (Gouda Way) site 10/89', in 'Annual review of minor development sites in Gloucester', *Glevensis*, 24, pp. 17–19

— (1992), '47 Southgate Street (Site 10/1991)', in 'Archaeological fieldwork in Gloucester 1991', *Glevensis*, 26, p. 50

— and Heighway, C. (1984), *Garrod's Gloucester: archaeological observations 1974–81*, Western Archaeological Trust

Gelling, P. (1958), 'Excavations by Little Fish Street, Worcester', *Transactions of the Worcestershire Archaeological Society*, new series 35, pp. 67–70

Gem, R.D.H. (1978), 'Bishop Wulfstan II and the Romanesque cathedral church of Worcester', *Proceedings of the British Archaeological Association conference at Worcester, 1975*, pp. 15–47

Gilchrist, R. (1992), 'Christian bodies and souls: the archaeology of life and death in later medieval hospitals', in Bassett, S. (ed.), *Death in Towns*, Leicester, pp. 101–18

— (1993), *Gender and Material Culture: the Archaeology of Religious Women*, London

Goodrich, M. (1994), 'The White Ladies of Worcester: their place in contemporary medieval life', *Transactions of the Worcestershire Archaeological Society*, 3rd series, 14, pp. 129–47

Greatorex, P. (1991), 'Observations on the Eastgate Street sewer renewal scheme, Gloucester, 1990, (site 4/90)', *Glevensis*, 25, pp. 25–9

Greatrex, J. (1998), 'The layout of the monastic church, cloister, and precinct of Worcester: evidence in the written records', in Guy, C. (ed.), *Archaeology at Worcester Cathedral*, report of the eighth annual symposium, March 1998, Worcester, pp. 12–18

Green, A.S. (1894), *Town Life in the Fifteenth Century*, 2 vols, London

Green V. (1764), *A Survey of the City of Worcester*, London

— (1796), *The History and Antiquities of the City of Worcester*, 2 vols, London

Greene, K.T. (1975), 'The Romano-Celtic head from the Bon Marche site, Gloucester: a reappraisal', *Antiquaries Journal*, 55, pp. 338–45

Grierson P. (1967), 'The volume of the Anglo-Saxon currency', *Economic History Review*, 2nd series, 20, pp. 53–60

Grinsell L.V., Blunt, C.E. and Dolley, M. (1973), *Sylloge of Coins of the British Isles, 19: Bristol and*

Gloucester Museums, London

Guy, C. (1991), 'Worcester Castle', in Barker, P. A., and Guy, C. (eds.), *Worcester Cathedral, report of the first annual symposium on the precinct*, Worcester, pp. 3–4

— (1996), 'Archaeological work in 1995/6', in Barker, P. A., and Guy, C. (eds.) *Archaeology at Worcester Cathedral, report of the sixth annual symposium, March 1996*, Worcester, pp. 1–4

Hale, W.H. (ed.) (1865). *Registrum Prioratus Beatae Mariae Wigorniensis*, Camden Society 91, London

Hall, R. (1984), *The Viking Dig*, Bodley Head, London

Hamilton, N.E.S.A. (ed), (1870), *Willelmi Malmesbiriensis Monachi de Gestis Pontificum Anglorum*, Rolls Series, 52, London

Hamilton, S.G. (ed.) (1912), *Collectanea*, Worcestershire Historical Society

Hardy, T.D. (ed.) (1835), *Rotuli Litterarum Patentium, 1201–1216*, Record Commission, London

Hare, M. (1993), The chronicle of Gregory of Caerwent: a preliminary account', *Glevensis*, 27, pp. 42–4

Harmer, F.E. (ed.) (1914), *Select English Historical Documents of the 9th and 10th Centuries*, Cambridge

— (ed.) (1952), *Anglo-Saxon Writs*, Manchester

Hart, W.H. (ed.) (1863–7), *Historia et Cartularium Monasterii Sancti Petri Gloucestriae*, 3 vols, Rolls Series, 33, London

Haslam, J. (1983), 'The origins and plan of Bedford', *Bedfordshire Archaeology* 16, pp. 29–36

— (ed.) (1984), *Anglo-Saxon Towns in Southern England*, Chichester

— (1985), *Early Medieval Towns in Britain*, Shire Archaeology no.45, Aylesbury

— (1987), 'Market and fortress in England in the reign of Offa', *World Archaeology* 19, pp. 76–93

— (1988), 'Parishes, Churches, Wards and Gates in Eastern London', in Blair, J (ed.), *Minsters and Parish Churches: The Local Church in Transition 950–1200*, Oxford University Committee for Archaeology, Monograph 17, Oxford, pp. 35–43

Hassall, M., and Rhodes, J. (1974), 'Excavations at the new Market Hall, Gloucester, 1966–7', *Transactions of the Bristol and Gloucestershire Archaeological Society*, 93, pp. 15–100

Hearne, T. (ed.) (1723), *Hemingi Chartularium Ecclesiae Wigorniensis*, Oxford

Heighway, C. (1980), 'Excavations at Gloucester: fifth interim report: St Oswald's Priory 1977–8', *Antiquaries Journal* 60, pp. 207–26.

— (1983a), *The East and North Gates of Gloucester and associated sites, excavations 1974–1981*, Western Archaeological Trust Monograph no. 4

— (1983b), 'Tanners' Hall, Gloucester', *Transactions of the Bristol and Gloucestershire Archaeological Society*, 101, pp. 83–97

— (1984a), 'Saxon Gloucester', in Haslam, J. (ed.), *Anglo-Saxon Towns in Southern England*, Chichester, pp. 359–383

— (1984b), 'Anglo-Saxon Gloucester to A.D. 1000', in Faull, M (ed.), *Studies in late Anglo-Saxon Settlement*, Oxford, pp. 35–53

— (1985), *Gloucester, a History and Guide*, Gloucester

— (1986), 'A reconstruction of the 10th-century church of St Oswald, Gloucester', in Butler, L.A.S. and Morris, R.K. (eds.), *The Anglo-Saxon Church*, Council for British Archaeology, Reseach Report 60, London

— (1988a), 'Anglo-Saxon Gloucester', in *Victoria County History, Gloucestershire*, iv, pp. 5–12.

— (1988b), 'Archaeology in the Precinct of Gloucester Cathedral, 1983–5', *Glevensis*, 22, pp. 29–37

— and Bryant, R. (1999), *The Golden Minster: the Anglo-Saxon Minster and later Medieval Priory of St Oswald at Gloucester*, Council for British Archaeology, Research Report.117, York

— and Garrod, A.P. (1980), 'Excavations at Nos 1 and 30 Westgate Street, Gloucester: the Roman levels', *Britannia*, 11, pp. 73–97.

— and Garrod, A.P. (1981) 'Gloucester', in Milne, G., and Hobley, B. (eds.), *Waterfront Archaeology in Britain and Northern Europe*, Council for British Archaeology, Research Report 41, pp. 123–4

— Garrod, A.P., and Vince, A.G. (1979), 'Excavations at 1 Westgate Street, Gloucester, 1975', *Medieval Archaeology*, 23, pp. 159–213

— and Parker, A.J. (1982), 'The Roman tilery at St Oswald's Priory, Gloucester', *Britannia*, 13, pp. 25–77

Hemmeon, M. de W. (1914), *Burgage tenure in Medieval England*, Cambridge, Mass

Hereford and Worcester County Museum (1990), 'Analysis of "dark earth" from the Bull Entry site, Deansway Archaeology Project', *Deansway Interim Research Paper*, 1, Worcester

Hilton, R.H. (1966), *A Medieval Society*, London

— (1973), *Bond Men Made Free*, London

— (1985), 'Women traders in medieval England', in Hilton, R.H., *Class Conflict and the Crisis of Feudalism*, London, pp. 205–15

— (1990), 'Small town society in England before the Black Death', in Holt, R. and Rosser, G. (eds.), *The Medieval Town*, London, pp. 71–96

— (1992), *English and French Towns in Feudal Society*, Cambridge

Hollings, M. (ed.) (1934), *The Red Book of Worcester*, Worcestershire Historical Society

Holt, J.C. (ed.) (1987), *Domesday Studies*, Woodbridge

Holt, R.A. (1985), 'Thomas of Woodstock and events at Gloucester in 1381', *Bulletin of the Institute of Historical Research*, 58, pp. 237–42

— (1987), 'Gloucester: An English Provincial Town during the Later Middle Ages', Unpubl. PhD thesis, University of Birmingham

— (1990), 'Gloucester in the century after the Black Death', in Holt, R. and Rosser, G. (eds.), *The Medieval Town*, London, pp. 141–59

— (forthcoming), 'St Wulfstan's hospital and the hospital of St John of Jerusalem', in Mundy, C. (ed.)

— and Baker, N.J. (2001), 'Towards a geography of sexual encounter: prostitution in English medieval towns', in Bevan, L. (ed.) *Indecent Exposure: Sexuality, Society, and the Archaeological Record*, Glasgow, pp. 201–15

— and Rosser, G. (eds.) (1990), *The Medieval Town*, London

Hooke, D. (1980), 'The hinterland and routeways of late Saxon Worcester: the charter evidence', in Carver, M.O.H. (ed.) (1980), 'Medieval Worcester', *Transactions of the Worcestershire Archaeological Society*, 3rd series, 7, pp. 39–49

Hope, W.H.St.J. (1897), 'Notes on the Benedictine abbey of St Peter at Gloucester', *Archaeological Journal*, 54, pp. 77–119

Horsman, V., Milne, C. and Milne, G. (1988), 'Aspects of Saxo-Norman London: I, building and street development near Billingsgate and Cheapside', *London and Middlesex Archaeological Society*, Special Paper 11

Hoskins, W.G (1959), *Local History in England*, London

Household, H.G.W. (1946–8), 'The Fleece in Upper Westgate Street: a "Great Inn" of about 1500', *Transactions of Bristol and Gloucestershire Archaeological Society*, 67, pp. 37–57

Howitt, G. A. (1890) *Gloucester's ancient walls and gatehouses*, Gloucester

Hughes, P. (1980), 'Houses and property in post-Reformation Worcester', in Carver, M. O.H. (ed.), 'Medieval Worcester', *Transactions of the Worcestershire Archaeological Society*, 3rd series, 7, pp. 269–92

— (1986), *Worcester Streets: Blackfriars*, Worcester

— and Molyneux, N. (1980), 'Mapped and documented buildings of the 16th century and earlier', in Carver, M.O.H. (ed.) (1980), 'Medieval Worcester', *Transactions of the Worcestershire Archaeological Society*, 3rd series, 7, pp. 310–16

— and Molyneux, N. (1984), *Worcester Streets: Friar Street*, Worcester

Hunter, A. G. (1963), 'Excavations at the Bon Marche Site, Gloucester, 1958–59', *Transactions of the Bristol and Gloucestershire Archaeological Society*, 82, pp. 25–43

— (1980), 'Building excavations at the Cross, Gloucester, 1960', *Transactions of the Bristol and Gloucestershire Archaeological Society*, 98, pp. 105–7

Hunter, J. (ed.) (1840), *Ecclesiastical Documents*, Camden Society Original Series, 8, London

Hurst, H. (1969), 'Excavations at 11–15 and 22 Southgate Street', *Glevensis*, 3, pp. 5–12

— (1972), 'Excavations at Gloucester, 1968–1971: first interim report', *Antiquaries Journal*, 52, pp. 24–69.

— (1974), 'Excavations at Gloucester, 1971–1973: second interim report', *Antiquaries Journal*, 54, pp. 8–52

— (1975), 'Excavations at Gloucester: third interim report: Kingsholm 1966–75', *Antiquaries Journal*, 55, pp. 264–94

— (1976), 'Gloucester (Glevum): a colonia in the West Country', in Branigan, K., and Fowler, P. J. (eds.), *The Roman West Country*, Newton Abbott

— (1984), 'The archaeology of Gloucester castle: an introduction', *Transactions of the Bristol and Gloucestershire Archaeological Society*, 102, pp. 73–128

— (1985), 'Kingsholm, excavations at Kingsholm Close and other sites', *Gloucester Archaeological Reports*, 1, Cambridge
— (1986), Gloucester, the Roman and later defences', *Gloucester Archaeological Reports*, 2, Cambridge

Jack, R.I. (1970–73), 'An archival case history: the cartularies and registers of Llanthony Priory in Gloucestershire', *Journal of the Society of Archivists*, 4, pp. 370–83
John, E. (1966), 'St Oswald and the Church of Worcester', in John, E., *Orbis Britanniae and other Studies*, Leicester, pp. 234–48

Kealey, E.J. (1981), *Medieval Medicus: A Social History of Anglo-Norman Medicine*, Baltimore
Keene, D.J. (1985), *Survey of Medieval Winchester*, Winchester Studies 2, Oxford
— (1990a) 'Suburban growth', in Holt, R. and Rosser, G. (eds.), *The Medieval Town*, London, pp. 97–119
— (1990b), 'The character and development of the Cheapside area: an overview', in Schofield, J., Allen, P. and Taylor, C., 'Medieval buildings and property development in the area of Cheapside', *Transactions of the London and Middlesex Archaeological Society*, 41, pp. 178–93
Kelly, S. (1992), 'Trading privileges from eighth-century England', *Early Medieval Europe*, 1, pp. 3–28
Keynes, S. and Lapidge, M. (1983), *Alfred the Great*, Harmondsworth
Kingsford, C.L. (ed.) (1913), *English Historical Literature in the Fifteenth Century: Gloucester Annals 1449–1469*, Oxford, pp. 355–7
Kirby, I.M. (ed.) (1967), *Diocese of Gloucester: a Catalogue of the Records of the Dean and Chapter*, Gloucester
Kissan, B.W. (1940), 'The London Deanery of the Arches', *Transactions of the London and Middlesex Archaeological Society*, New Series, 8
Kjølbye-Biddle, B. (1992), 'Dispersal or concentration: the disposal of the Winchester dead over 2000 years', in Bassett, S.R. (ed.), *Death in Towns*, Leicester, pp. 210–47
Klein, P. and Roe, A. (1987), *The Carmelite Friary, Corve Street, Ludlow*, Birmingham University Field Archaeology Unit
Knowles, D., Brooke, C.N.L. and London, V.C.M. (1972), *The Heads of Religious Houses: England and Wales 940–1216*, Cambridge
Knowles, W. H. (1932), 'The Black Friars at Gloucester', *Transactions of the Bristol and Gloucestershire Archaeological Society*, 54, pp. 167–201
— and Fullbrook-Legatt, L. E. W. O. (1935), 'Gloucester Roman Research Committee: Report for 1934', *Transactions of the Bristol and Gloucestershire Archaeological Society*, 56, pp. 65–82

Laird, F.C. (1818), *The Beauties of England and Wales*, London
Langston, J.N. (1941), 'The priors of Lanthony by Gloucester', *Transactions of Bristol and Gloucestershire Archaeological Society*, 63, pp. 1–144
— (1956–57), *Old Gloucester Churches* (typescript), 2 vols, Gloucester City Library, MS 23423/4
Langton, J (1977), 'Late medieval Gloucester: some data from a rental of 1455', *Institute of British Geographers*, New Series, 2, pp. 259–77
Latta, C. (1977), *The Commandery*, Worcester
Lees, E. (1866), 'History of the convent of the "White Ladies", Worcester', *Associated Architectural Societies Reports and Papers*, 8, part 2, pp. 355–64
Letters and Papers, Foreign and Domestic, of the Reign of Henry VIII, 23 vols in 38, London (1862–1932)
Liebermann, F. (ed.) (1903–16), *Die Gesetze der Angelsachsen*, 3 vols, Halle
Lilley, K.D. (1994), 'Medieval Coventry: a study in town-plan analysis', Unpublished Ph.D. thesis, School of Geography, University of Birmingham
— (1998), 'Trading places: monastic initiative and the development of high-medieval Coventry', in Slater, T.R. and Rosser, G. (eds.), *The Church in the Medieval Town*, Aldershot: Ashgate, pp. 177–208
Lobel, M.D. (1935), *The Borough of Bury St Edmund's*, Oxford
— (ed.) (1975), *Historic Towns*, vol. 2, London
Loyn, H.R. (1961), 'Boroughs and mints, AD 900–1066', in Dolley, R.H.M. (ed.), *Anglo-Saxon Coins: studies presented to F.M. Stenton*, London

Luard, H.R. (ed.) (1864–9), *Annales Monastici*, 5 vols, Rolls Series, London (The Annals of Tewkesbury: Vol. I, 1864)

Luders, A., Tomlins, T.E., France, J., Taunton, W.E. and Rathby, J. (eds.) (1810–28), *Statutes of the Realm*, 11 vols in 12, Record Commission, London

MacCaffrey, W.T. (1958), *Exeter 1540–1640*, Cambridge, Mass

MacPhail, R. I. (1994), 'Soil micromorphology', in Dalwood, C. H., Buteux, V. A. and Darlington, J. (1994), 'Excavations at Farrier Street and other sites north of the City Wall, Worcester, 1988–1992', *Transactions of the Worcestershire Archaeological Society*, 3rd series, 14, pp. 83–5

Macray, W.D. (ed.) (1863), *Chronicon Abbatiae de Evesham*, Rolls Series, 29, London

Maddicott, J. R. (1992) 'Debate: Trade, industry, and the wealth of King Alfred: reply', *Past and Present*, 123, pp. 164–88

Magdalino, P. (ed.) (1992), *The Perception of the Past in Twelfth-Century Europe*, London

Mahany, C. and Roffe, D. (1982), 'Stamford: the development of an Anglo-Scandinavian borough', *Anglo-Norman Studies*, 5, pp. 196–219

Maitland, F.W. (ed.) (1884), *Pleas of the Crown in the County of Gloucester*, London

— (1897; 1960 edition), *Domesday Book and Beyond*, London

Mangin, W. P., and Turner, J. C. (1969), 'Benavides and the Barriada movement' in Oliver, P. (ed.), *Shelter and Society*, London, pp. 127–36

Marsh, F.T. (1890), *Annals of the Hospital of St Wulstan*, Worcester

Mason, E. (1990), *St Wulfstan of Worcester, c.1008–1095*, Oxford

Mawer, A. and Stenton, F.M. (1927), *The Place Names of Worcestershire*, English Place-Name Society, 4, Cambridge

Medland, M. H. (1894–5), 'An account of Roman and Medieval remains found on the site of the Tolsey at Gloucester in 1893–4', *Transactions of the Bristol and Gloucestershire Archaeological Society*, 19, pp. 142–58

— (1900), 'St Nicholas' Church, Gloucester', *Transactions of the Bristol and Gloucestershire Archaeological Society*, 23, pp. 109–28

Metcalf, D.M. (1976), 'Sceattas from the territory of the Hwicce', *Numismatic Chronicle*, 136, pp. 64–74

— (1965), 'How large was the Anglo-Saxon currency?', *Economic History Review*, 2nd series, 18, pp. 475–82

— report in Dalwood, H., *Excavations at Deansway, Worcester, 1988–89* (forthcoming)

Molyneux, N. (1978), Untitled typescript survey of the Commandery buildings (St Wulfstan's Hospital), Worcester City Council, SMR files.

— (1980), 'A late medieval stone building in Angel Street', in Carver, M.O.H. (1980), 'Medieval Worcester', *Transactions of the Worcestershire Archaeological Society*, 3rd series, 7, pp. 262–8

— (1981), 'The medieval hospitals of Worcester', *Worcestershire. Archaeology and Local History Newsletter*, 26, pp. 3–5

— (1992), 'The Edgar Tower, Worcester', in Barker, P. A., and Guy, C. (eds.), *Worcester Cathedral*, report of the second annual symposium on the precinct, Worcester, pp. 3–9

Moore, J.S. (ed.) (1982), *Domesday Book: Gloucestershire*, Chichester

Morgan, N. (1978), 'Psalter illustration for the diocese of Worcester in the thirteenth century' in *Medieval Art and Architecture at Worcester Cathedral*, British Archaeological Association Conference Transactions

Morris, R. (1989), *Churches in the Landscape*, London

Morton, A. (1992), 'Burial in middle Saxon Southampton', in Bassett, S.R. (ed.), *Death in Towns*, Leicester, pp. 68–77

Moss, P.A. and Spry, N.P. (1972), 'Southern's Stores – 3 Northgate Street, Gloucester', *Glevensis*, 6, pp. 2–5

Munby, J. (1984), 'Saxon Chichester and its predecessors' in Haslam, J. (ed.), *Anglo-Saxon Towns in Southern England*, Chichester, pp. 327–8

Mundy, C. (1985), *Trial Excavations in Worcester 1985*, Hereford and Worcester County Council Archaeology Section, typescript

— (1986a), *Worcester Archaeology Project 1985/6*, Hereford and Worcester County Council Archaeology Section, typescript

— (1986b), 'Worcester: Blackfriars', *West Midlands Archaeology*, 29, pp. 10–11

— (1989), *Deansway Archaeology Project Interim Excavation Report*, Hereford and Worcester County
   Council Archaeology Section
— and Dalwood, H. (forthcoming), *Excavations at Deansway, Worcester, 1988–89*

Nash, T. (1799), *Collections for the History of Worcestershire*, 2nd ed., London
Noake, J. (1849), *Worcester in Olden Times*, London
— (1866), *The Monastery and Cathedral of Worcester*, London

Ortenberg, V. (1992), *The English Church and the Continent in the Tenth and Eleventh Centuries*, Oxford

Palliser, D. (1988), 'Urban decay revisited', in Thomson, J.A.F. (ed.), *Towns and Townspeople in the
   Fifteenth Century*, Gloucester, pp. 1–21
Palmer, C.F.R. (1882), 'The Friar-Preachers , or Black Friars, of Gloucester', *Archaeological Journal*,
   39, pp. 296–309
Pannett, D. (1989), 'The River Severn at Wroxeter', *Transactions of the Shropshire Archaeological
   and Historical Society*, 66, pp. 48–55
Pantin, W. A. (1961), 'Medieval Inns', in Jope, E. M. (ed.), *Studies in Building History, essays in
   recognition of the work of B. H. St J. O' Neil*, London, pp. 166–91
— (1962–3), 'Medieval English Town-House Plans', *Medieval Archaeology*, 6–7, pp. 202–39
Parsons, D. (ed.) (1975), *Tenth-Century Studies*, London
Pearn, A.M. (1988), 'Origin and development of urban churches and parishes: a comparative study of
   Hereford, Shrewsbury and Chester', Unpublished PhD thesis, University of Cambridge
Peckham, W.D. (1933), 'The parishes of the city of Chichester', *Sussex Archaeological Collections*, 74,
   pp. 65–97
Pevsner, N. (1976), *The Buildings of England*, Gloucestershire, Harmondsworth
— and Metcalf, P. (1985), *The Cathedrals of England*, Harmondsworth
Phythian-Adams, C. (1979), *Desolation of a City: Coventry and the Urban Crisis of the Late Middle
   Ages*, Cambridge
Pipe Rolls, 5 Henry II – (Pipe Roll Society, 1, 1884–)
Platt, C. (1976), *The English Medieval Town*, London
Postan, M.M. (1966), 'England', in Postan, M.M. (ed.), *The Agrarian Life of the Middle Ages*, Cambridge
   Economic History of Europe, vol. 1, Cambridge, pp. 549–632
Pretty, K.B. (1989), 'Defining the Magonsaete', in Bassett, S.R. (ed.) (1989), *The Origins of Anglo-Saxon
   Kingdoms*, Leicester, pp. 171–83

Rackham, O., Blair, W. J., and Munby, J. T. (1978), 'The thirteenth-century roofs and floor of the
   Blackfriars Priory at Gloucester', *Medieval Archaeology*, 22, pp. 105–22
Reps, J. W. (1979), *Cities of the American West: a history of frontier urban planning*, Princeton
Richardson, L. (1956), 'The geology of Worcester', *Transactions of the Worcestershire Naturalists Club*,
   11, part 1 (for 1954–5), pp. 25–65
— and Ewance, P.F. (1963), 'City of Worcester College for Further Education: its geology and
   archaeology', *Transactions of the Worcestershire Naturalists Club*, 11, part 4 (for 1960–61),
   pp. 226–34
Robertson, A.J. (1956), *Anglo-Saxon Charters*, Cambridge
Robertson, A.S. (1961), *Sylloge of Coins of the British Isles: Hunterian and Coats Collections,
   University of Glasgow. Part I: Anglo-Saxon Coins*, London
Robinson, J.A. (1919), *St Oswald and the Church of Worcester*, British Academy Supplementary Paper,
   London
Rogers, A. (1972) 'Parish boundaries and urban history: two case studies', *Journal of the British
   Archaeological Association*, 3rd series, 35, pp. 46–64
Rollason, D.W. (1989), *Saints and Relics in Anglo-Saxon England*, Oxford
Romanos, A. G. (1969), 'Illegal settlements in Athens', in Oliver, P. (ed.), *Shelter and Society*, London,
   pp. 137–55
Ronchetti, B. (1991), 'The Old Palace', in Barker, P. A., and Guy, C. (eds.), *Worcester Cathedral,
   report of the first annual symposium on the precinct*, Worcester, pp. 9–13
Ross, C.D. (ed) (1964), *Cartulary of Cirencester Abbey*, London

Rosser, G. (1988), 'The Anglo-Saxon gilds', in Blair, J. (ed.), *Minsters and Parish Churches: The Local Church in Transition 950–1200*, Oxford University Committee for Archaeology, Monograph 17, pp. 31–4

— (1992), 'The cure of souls in English towns before 1000', in Blair, J. and Sharpe, R. (eds.), *Pastoral Care Before the Parish*, Leicester pp. 267–84

— (1998), 'Conflict and political community in the medieval town: disputes between clergy and laity in Hereford', in Slater, T.R. and Rosser, G. (eds.), *The Church in the Medieval Town*, Aldershot: Ashgate, pp. 20–42

Rossiaud, J. (1988), *Medieval Prostitution*, Oxford

Rotuli Parliamentorum, 6 vols, (1783), Record Commission, London

Rowbotham, F. W. (1978), 'The River Severn at Gloucester with particular reference to its Roman and medieval channels', *Glevensis*, 12, pp. 4–9

Roy, I. and Porter, S. (1980), 'The social and economic structure of an early modern suburb: the Tything at Worcester', *Bulletin of the Institute of Historical Research*, 53, pp. 203–17

Rudder, S. (1779), *A New History of Gloucestershire*, Cirencester

Rudge, T. (1815), *The History and Antiquities of Gloucester*, Gloucester

Runcie, R. (ed.) (1977), *Cathedral and City*, (London)

Russell, H.S. (1963), 'Evening News and Times extension, St Swithin's Street, Worcester', *Transactions of the Worcestershire Naturalists Club*, 11, part 4 (for 1960–61), p. 225

St. John Hope, W. H. (1897), 'Notes on the Benedictine Abbey of St Peter at Gloucester', *Archaeological Journal*, 54, pp. 77–119

Saunders, A. D. (1963), 'The Black Friars, Gloucester, interim report', *Transactions of the Bristol and Gloucestershire Archaeological Society*, 82, pp. 168–76

Sawyer, P.H. (1968), *Anglo-Saxon Charters: An Annotated List and Bibliography*, Royal Historical Society, London

— (1975), 'Charters of the reform movement – the Worcester archive', in Parsons, D. (ed.), *Tenth-Century Studies*, London, pp. 84–93

— (ed.) (1985), *Domesday Book: A Reassessment*, London

Sayles, G.O. (ed.) (1936–9), *Select Cases in the Court of King's Bench under Edward I*, 3 vols, Selden Society, London

Schofield, J. (1984), *The Building of London*, British Museum

— and Vince, A. (1994), *Medieval Towns*, London

Scrase, A.J. (1989), 'Development and change in burgage plots: the example of Wells', *Journal of Historical Geography*, 15, pp. 349–65

Sheppard, L. (1910), 'The Saxon wall and monastic ruins near the south-west corner of Worcester Cathedral', *Associated Architectural Societies, Reports and Papers*, 30, pp. 589–96

Shoesmith, R. (1982), *Hereford City Excavations, vol. 2: excavations on and close to the defences'*, Council for British Archaeology, Research Report 46, London

Sims-Williams, P. (1988), 'St Wilfrid and two charters dated AD 676 and 680', *Journal of Ecclesiastical History*, 39, pp. 163–83

— (1990), *Religion and Literature in Western England 600–800*, Cambridge

Slater, T. R. (1980), 'The analysis of burgages in medieval towns: three case studies from the West Midlands', *West Midlands Archaeology*, 23, pp. 53–65

— (1981), 'The analysis of burgage patterns in medieval towns', *Area*, 13, pp. 211–16

— (1987), 'Ideal and reality in English episcopal medieval town planning', *Transactions of the Institute of British Geographers*, new series, 12, pp. 191–203

— (1988), 'Medieval composite towns in England: evidence from Bridgnorth, Shropshire', *School of Geography, University of Birmingham, Working Paper Series*, 41

— (1989), 'Doncaster's town plan: an analysis' in Buckland, P.C., Magilton, J.R. and Hayfield, C. (eds.), *The Archaeology of Doncaster, 2: the medieval and later town*, British Archaeological Reports, 202, pp. 43–61

— (1990), 'English medieval new towns with composite plans: evidence from the Midlands', in Slater, T.R. (ed.), *The built form of Western Cities*, Leicester, pp. 60–82

— (1996), 'Medieval town-founding on the estates of the Benedictine order in England', in Eliasssen, F.E., and Ersland, G. A. (eds.) *Power, Profit and Urban Land: landownership in medieval and early modern northern European towns*, Aldershot: Ashgate, pp. 70–92

— (1998), 'Benedictine town planning in medieval England: evidence from St Albans', in Slater, T.R. and Rosser, G. (eds.), *The Church in the Medieval Town*, Aldershot: Ashgate, pp. 155–76

— and Rosser, G. (eds.) (1998), *The Church in the Medieval Town*, Aldershot: Ashgate

Smith, A.H. (1964), *The Place-Names of Gloucestershire, Part 2: The North and West Cotswolds*, English Place-Names Society, 39, Cambridge

Smith, J.Toulmin (ed.) (1870), *English Gilds*, Early English Text Society, Original Series 40, London

Smith, L.Toulmin (ed.) (1907–10), *The Itinerary of John Leland in or about the Years 1535–1543*, 5 vols, London

Smith, R. (1993), '5a College Yard', in Barker, P. A., and Guy, C. (eds.), *Worcester Cathedral*, report of the third annual symposium, Worcester, pp. 2–3

Spry, N. (1974), '14–24 St Mary's Street', in Hurst, H., 'Excavations at Gloucester, 1971–1973: second interim report', *Antiquaries Journal*, 54, p. 41

Stenton, D.M. (ed.) (1934), *Rolls of the Justices in Eyre for Lincolnshire 1218–19 and Worcestershire 1221*, Selden Society, London

Stenton, F.M. (1924), 'The City of Worcester', in *Victoria County History, Worcestershire*, iv, pp. 376–420

— (1971), *Anglo-Saxon England*, 3rd ed., Oxford

Stevenson, W.H. (ed.) (1890), *Rental of all the Houses in Gloucester AD 1455*, Gloucester

— (ed.) (1891), *The Records of the Corporation of Gloucester*, Historical Manuscripts Commission, Report 12, Appendix 9, London, pp. 400–529

— (ed.) (1893), *Calendar of the Records of the Corporation of Gloucester*, Gloucester

Stewart, I. (1978), 'Anglo-Saxon gold coins', in Carson, R.A.G. and Kraay, C.M. (eds.), *Scripta Nummaria Romana: essays presented to Humphrey Sutherland*, London, pp. 143–72

Stokes, E. (ed.) (1914), *Abstracts of Inquisitiones Post Mortem for Gloucestershire: vol. 6, 1359–1413*, The Index Library, British Record Society, London

Street, F. (1915–17), 'The relations of the bishops and citizens of Salisbury (New Sarum) between 1225 and 1612', *Wiltshire Archaeological and Natural History Society*, 39, pp. 158–257, 319–67

Stubbs, W. (ed.) (1874), *Memorials of St Dunstan*, Rolls Series, 63, London

— (ed.) (1880), *The Historical Works of Gervase of Canterbury: ii, Mappa Mundi*, Rolls Series, 73, London

— (ed.) (1887–9), *Willelmi Malmesbiriensis Monachi de Gestis Regum Anglorum*, 2 vols, Rolls Series, 90, London

Symons, T. (1975), '*Regularis Concordia*: history and derivation', in Parsons, D. (ed.), *Tenth-Century Studies*, London, pp. 37–59

Tait, J. (1897), review of Maitland (1897), *English Historical Review*, 12, pp. 768–77

— (1924), 'A new fragment of the Inquest of Sheriffs, 1170', *English Historical Review*, 39, pp. 80–83

— (1936), *The Medieval English Borough*, Manchester

Tanner, N.P. (1984), *The Church in Late Medieval Norwich, 1370–1532*, Toronto

Tatton-Brown, T. (1986), 'The topography of Anglo-Saxon London', *Antiquity*, 60, pp. 21–30

Taylor, C.S. (1957), 'The origin of the Mercian shires' in Finberg, H.P.R. (ed.), *Gloucestershire Studies*, Leicester, pp. 17–51

Taylor, H.M. (1971), 'Repton reconsidered', in *England before the Conquest*, Clemoes, P. and Hughes, K. (eds.), Cambridge, pp. 351–89

— (1978), *Anglo-Saxon Architecture*, 3 vols, Cambridge

Thacker, A. (1982), 'Chester and Gloucester: early ecclesiastical organization in two Mercian burhs', *Northern History*, 18, pp. 199–211

— (1985), 'Kings, saints and monasteries in pre-Viking Mercia', *Midland History*, 10, pp. 1–25

Thompson, A.H. (1921), 'The jurisdiction of the archbishops of York in Gloucestershire, with some notes on the history of the priory of St Oswald at Gloucester', *Transactions of the Bristol and Gloucestershire Archaeological Society*, 43, pp. 85–180

Thomson, J.A.F. (ed.) (1988), *Towns and Townspeople in the Fifteenth Century*, Gloucester

Thorpe, B. (ed.) (1848–9), *Florentii Wigorniensis Monachi Chronicon ex Chronicis*, 2 vols, London

Thorpe, L. (ed.) (1966), *Geoffrey of Monmouth's History of the Kings of Britain*, London

— (ed.) (1978), *Gerald of Wales: The Journey through Wales, and The Description of Wales* (London)

Toynbee, J.M.C. (1962), *Art in Roman Britain*, London
Turner, C.H. (1916), *Early Worcester Manuscripts*, Oxford

Urry, W. (1967), *Canterbury under the Angevin Kings*, University of London Historical Studies, 19, London

Victoria County History, Gloucestershire, ii (1907), London
Victoria County History, Gloucestershire, iv (1988), London
Victoria County History, Herefordshire, i (1908), London
Victoria County History, Shropshire, i (1908), London
Victoria County History, Shropshire, ii (1973), London
Victoria County History, Surrey, i (1902), London
Victoria County History, Worcestershire, i (1901), London
Victoria County History, Worcestershire, ii (1906), London
Victoria County History, Worcestershire, iii (1913), London
Victoria County History, Worcestershire, iv (1924), London
Vince, A. G. (1988), 'Report on the sub-Roman pottery from phase IVA', in Darvill, T., 'Excavations on the site of the early Norman castle at Gloucester, 1983–84', *Medieval Archaeology*, 32, pp. 21–2
— (1990), *Saxon London, an archaeological investigation*, London

Walker, D. (1958), 'Miles of Gloucester, Earl of Hereford', *Transactions of the Bristol and Gloucestershire Archaeological Society*, 77, pp. 66–84
— (1960), 'Ralph son of Pichard', *Bulletin of the Institute of Historical Research* 33, pp. 195–202
— (ed.) (1964), *Charters of the Earldom of Hereford 1095–1201*, Camden Miscellany 22, Camden 4th series, 1, London, pp. 1–75
— (ed.) (1976), 'A register of the churches of the monastery of St Peter's, Gloucester', *An Ecclesiastical Miscellany*, Bristol and Gloucestershire Archaeological Society, Records Section, 11, pp. 3–58
Walker, J.S. (1858), 'The churches of Worcester: their architectural history, antiquities, and arrangement', *Associated Architectural Societies Reports and Papers*, 4, part 2, pp. 323–49
Walters, M., and Atkin, M., (1991), 'Site 27/90: St Margaret's chapel, London Road', *Glevensis*, 25, pp. 11–13
— and Garrod, A. G. (1992), 'Upper Quay Street/Westgate Street sewer renewal scheme (site 2/91)', *Glevensis*, 26, pp. 45–7
Welander, D. C. St.V. (1991), *The History, Art, and Architecture of Gloucester Cathedral*, Stroud
White, R., and Baker, N.J. (2000), *The Star Hotel, Worcester, an archaeological assessment*, Birmingham University Field Archaeology Unit
— and Barker, P.A. (1998), *Wroxeter: Life and Death of a Roman City*, Stroud
Whitehand, J.W.R. (1987), 'M.R.G. Conzen and the intellectual parentage of urban morphology', *Planning History Bulletin*, 9, pp. 35–41
Whitehead, D. (1976), *The Book of Worcester*, Chesham
— (1979), 'Medieval trans-riparian defences in Worcester?', *Worcestershire Archaeological Newsletter*, 23, pp. 2–3
— (1982), 'John Gwynn R.A. and the building of Worcester Bridge, 1769–86', *Transactions of the Worcestershire Archaeological Society*, 3rd series, 8, pp. 31–46
Whitelock, D. (ed.) (1961), *The Anglo-Saxon Chronicle*, London
— (ed.) (1979), *English Historical Documents, I, c.500–1042*, 2nd edition, London
Whybra, J. (1990), *A Lost English County: Winchcombeshire in the Tenth and Eleventh Centuries*, Woodbridge
Wickham, C.J. (1981), *Early Medieval Italy*, London
Williams, A. (1989), 'A vice-comital family in pre-Conquest Warwickshire', in Brown, R.A. (ed.), *Anglo-Norman Studies*, 12, Woodbridge, pp. 279–95
Wilson, J.M. (ed.) (1919), *The Liber Albus of the Priory of Worcester*, Worcestershire Historical Society
Woods, H. (1987), 'Excavations at Wenlock Priory, 1981–6', *Journal of the British Archaeological Association*, 140, pp. 36–75

Young, J., and Vince, A. (1992), 'Mapping the Saxon city', *Current Archaeology*, 129, pp. 385–8

Index